Trav … ipanion
to
South-east Asia

edited by

Alastair Dingwall

Traveller's Literary Companions

Read your way around the world

In Print

Titles in the Traveller's Literary Companion series:
Africa (1994)
The Caribbean (1996)
Eastern and Central Europe (1995)
France (1996)
The Indian Subcontinent (1995)
Japan (1994)
South and Central America (1993)
South-east Asia (1994)

British Library Cataloguing in Publication Data: a catalogue record for this book is available from the British Library.

Paperback ISBN 1 873 047 25 8
Hardback ISBN 1 873 047 30 4

Cover design by Russell Townsend
Front cover photograph of Indonesian girls by Heather Swabey
Back cover photograph of Raffles Hotel courtesy of Raffles Hotel
Maps drawn by Andy Prigmore
Additional artwork by Zana Juppenlatz
Typeset by MC Typeset Ltd
Printed by Utopia Press

First published in 1994 by
In Print Publishing, 9 Beaufort Terrace, Brighton BN2 2SU, UK. Tel: (0273) 682836. Fax: (0273) 620958.

Series Foreword

This series of *Traveller's Literary Companions* is the series I have been looking for all my travelling life. Discovering new writers and new countries is one of the greatest pleasures we know, and these books will greatly increase the enjoyment of all who consult them. Each volume is packed with scholarly and entertaining historical, geographical, political and above all literary information. A country lives through its literature, and we have here an illustrated survey not only of a country's own writers, but also of the views of foreigners, explorers, tourists and exiles. The only problem I foresee is that each volume will bring about a compulsive desire to book a ticket on the next flight out.

The writers take us back in the past to each country's cultural origins, and bring us right up to the present with extracts from novels, poems and travel writings published in the 1980s and 1990s. The chapter introductions and the biographical information about the writers are invaluable, and will give any traveller an easy and immediate access to the past and present state of each nation. Conversation with hosts, colleagues or strangers on trains will be greatly assisted. An enormous amount of work has gone into the compiling and annotating of each volume, and the balance of fact and comment seems to me to be expertly judged.

Margaret Drabble

Using the Companion

Each country has its own chapter and each chapter is divided into four distinct sections: (1) an introduction to the geography and cultural and political background; (2) a booklist giving full publishing details of all the books mentioned in the introduction and extracted; (3) a selection of extracts; (4) biographical details and other 'literary notes'.

Extracts are ordered alphabetically by place and each is assigned a number to make it easy to locate from elsewhere in the chapter. A quick list of all the published works extracted in a chapter can be obtained from the **Booklist** where extract numbers are highlighted in bold type. Full source references for the extracts are included under 'Acknowledgements and Citations' at the end of the book.

The **symbol** ◊ after an author's name indicates that there is a biographical entry in the chapter. If there is a biographical entry in another chapter, the author's name is followed by the symbol and the relevant chapter in parentheses – eg W. Somerset Maugham (◊ Malaysia).

Bold type is used to highlight references to places.

There is an **index of authors** at the end of the book.

Translators are usually given in the booklist. Where an extract has been translated here for the first time, the translator's name appears in the headnote above the extract.

Accents have been omitted and **footnotes** kept to a minimum.

Contents

List of Maps

Introduction

This literary guide to South-east Asia is structured geographically. It begins and ends at the borders of the two great civilizations that have done so much to shape South-east Asia's history and literature; from Burma on the eastern flank of India, the *Companion* takes an anti-clockwise crescent-shaped route through mainland and archipelagic South-east Asia, ending in Hong Kong at the southern tip of China. Within each chapter extracts from literature are arranged according to location, allowing each country to be seen through the eyes of writers. As well as providing a fresh perspective on famous physical and man-made sites, the *Companion* also provides an insight into the cultural and physical milieux that shaped some of the region's great works of literature, and which influenced many of the Western writers who have visited South-east Asia.

Two examples illustrate the point. Singapore's Chinatown district is now all but destroyed, yet faint echoes of its full and turbulent history can still be felt in the streets around Telok Ayer. Catherine Lim's description of the old women caught between the old Chinatown and the new Singapore captures poignantly the loser's lot in the development process: 'And so she sat, tired and forlorn, waiting all day . . . There would be no one to offer prayers for her after her death' (p 277). Her stark portrayal of the sweat and blood of the district seems to me an essential guide to the few rather sanitized streets that have been left for tourists. On the other hand, the *Companion* contains numerous short but telling phrases which capture more clearly than any snapshot the essence of a place. In this category, Ophelia Alcantra Dimalanta's description of the misty hill town of Baguio in the northern Philippines can hardly be bettered: 'City of vaguely fashioned needs…' (p 386).

Language

The *Traveller's Literary Companion to South-east Asia* is intended primarily for English-speaking readers who do not read any of the South-east Asian languages. Thus the accent is on works which are available in English translation (although where these are thin on the ground, as in the case of Laos, some translations appear here for the first time). The translators (whose names appear in the Booklists) are the unsung heroes of such a collection. The importance of Harry Aveling, for example, in bringing much Malaysian and Indonesian literature to the attention of English-speaking readers cannot be overestimated.

Some modern South-east Asian literature (including that by Lim and Dimalanta already referred to) is written in English. This is particularly true in Singapore, Malaysia and Hong Kong, although South-east Asian writing in English can also be found in the Philippines and Thailand. As in other parts of the world, debates about the authenticity of South-east Asian writing in a European language are lively, especially in Malaysia.

The *Companion* includes a great deal of writing by 'outsiders' who have used South-east Asia as a setting for their work. Most of these works were written in English, but others are translated from French, Dutch, Spanish, Japanese and Chinese.

Common themes

The geographical structure of the *Companion* is not intended as a straitjacket and numerous common themes surface on the journey from Burma to Hong Kong.

The timelessness of love and loss appears and reappears; from the breathless excitement of the young Cambodians in 'The Tryst' (pp 167–168) to the chaste lovers of the Vietnamese 'Tale of Kieu' (p 194) and the infatuation of the Hong Kong plutocrat (pp 427–429). The darker side of male-female relations can be seen in the complaints of a Vietnamese second wife (p 195), the world of Bangkok sex shows (pp 87–89) and the enforced remarriage of an Indonesian divorcee (pp 340–341).

War is a theme in almost every chapter and its subplots of death and separation are as evident in the 18th century Burmese 'A Soldier's Letter' (pp 35–36) as they are in the graphic no-holds-barred writing of the contemporary Vietnamese writer Bao Ninh (p 186). Yet if all wars are the same they are also different, as can be seen in the conflicts of loyalty in second world war Indonesia brilliantly portrayed in Y. B. Mangunwijaya's *The Weaverbirds* (p 349–350) and Emily Hahn's comments on the blinkered attitude of the Hong Kong establishment towards the rise of Japanese militarism (p 416).

Until very recently, poverty has been a constant of South-east Asian history and literature. The portrayal of hunger in the classrooms of Thailand (pp 103–104) and Indonesia (pp 333–334), recalls the writing of García Márquez and other South American writers, yet again this universal issue is often given a distinctively South-east Asian twist, as in the novels of Pramoedya Ananta Toer, perhaps Indonesia's most well-known contemporary writer (pp 324–325 and 327–328) or those of the Malaysian, Shahnon Ahmad (pp 228–229).

Many of the contributors to this guide point out that for long periods the only literature written in South-east Asia was religious. The influence of Islam and Hinduism on Indonesian literature is clearly described by E. Ulrich Kratz (pp 294–295 and 300). Further north, Buddhism was as powerful an influence on the literature as it was on the building of temples in Thailand, stupas in Burma and the massive edifice of Angkor (although the latter also contains temples dedicated to the Hindu gods).

Liberation struggles have often spawned significant literatures and writers played a particularly prominent role in the uprising against the Spaniards in the Philippines at the end of the 19th century. A major world writer emerged from this period, Jose Rizal, whose two remarkable novels, *Noli me Tangere* and *El Filibusterismo*, deserve to be far better known outside South-east Asia (pp 395–396). On their side, South-east Asia's colonisers included a number of gifted writers, in particular Maurice Collis in Burma (pp 40–43) and Sir Hugh Clifford and Frank Swettenham in Malaysia (pp 230–232, 240–241).

Finally, long before mankind covered South-east Asia, the region contained a thriving wildlife, and animals feature throughout the literature, from the gods riding elephants, geese and rhinoceroses in the bas reliefs at Angkor (p 164) to the Indonesian forest wildlife in Mochtar Lubis's *Tiger!* (p 344). Dramatic and thrilling accounts of the largest of all South-east Asian jungle creatures can be found in two early 20th century British memoirs; *Elephant Bill* (p 45) and *Teak Wallah* (pp 93–95).

Common sources

The pre-modern literature of South-east Asia draws on numerous sources, and I touch on only a few here.

One of the most enduring influences has been the Indian epic the *Ramayana*, localized versions of which can be found in Thailand (pp 115–116), Cambodia (pp 156–157) and Laos (p 123). The *Ramayana* and *Mahabarata* stories also form the basis for Indonesian shadow-plays or *wayang* (p 300).

Even more influential were the *Paññа-jataka* tales which form the cornerstone of Theravada Buddhism. From the great pagodas of Pagan in Burma through Thailand, Laos, Cambodia and Vietnam, this collection of tales of the former lives of the Buddha has not only influenced religious writing, but also theatre, painting and architecture, and continues to do so today.

For reasons of language and religion, the two most closely linked literatures of the region are those of Malaysia and Indonesia. Among their common literary sources are the thrilling *Hikayat* (Arabic for 'story') tales which still provide inspiration for writers, as a recent play by the Malaysian Usman Awang shows (pp 235–236). To prevent repetition, therefore, traditional Malay language and literature is dealt with in greater depth in the Indonesia chapter, while that for Malaysia concentrates more on contemporary writers and literature written in English.

Finally, as South-east Asia has become more and more integrated into the world economy, so, despite the wishes of some of its leaders, it has become more open to ideas from outside the region. This is particularly true of 20th century poets, many of whom operate within worldwide literary movements as diverse as existentialism, 'new realism' and imagism. This *Companion* tries to represent the best of this new wave of writing, gathering together such diverse figures as the Malaysian poet Muhammad Haji Salleh (pp 226–227), the Hong Kong short story writer David Wong (pp 427–429) and the Singaporean Boey Kim Cheng (p 276).

Visitors

The *Traveller's Literary Companion* series aims to blend indigenous literature with that from outside. One reason for this is that outsiders are more likely to comment on physical and other features that local writers take for granted. No one reading Laurens van der Post or Eliza Scidmore's description of the Preanger region of Java could fail to be moved by a desire to see, in Scidmore's words, 'the most beautiful landscape in all Java, which should be world famous and whose charm it is almost as impossible to exaggerate as to describe' (pp 341–343).

Second, for the Western visitor to South-east Asia, the perceptive comments of observers such as Isabella Bird, Anton Chekhov and Marguerite Duras often help to articulate feelings that we feel but cannot always express.

Finally, a number of major 20th century writers have lived in and written about South-east Asia. Foremost of these is Joseph Conrad. Conrad appears throughout this *Companion*, in the Gulf of Thailand (pp 92–93), with Lord Jim in the jungles of Borneo (pp 239–240) and striding across the Singapore Padang with Captain Walley (pp 281–282). In the jungles of Borneo (and later in those of the Congo and South America) Conrad found a physical setting that perfectly complemented the psychological terrain that his characters inhabit, as Jim's description of his journey upriver to the village that was to become his home demonstrates (pp 239–240).

However, it is W. Somerset Maugham above all other writers who has done most to evoke South-east Asia's physical landscape and people for a Western readership. Maugham is identified most closely with what is modern-day Malaysia (pp 229–230 and 245–246), yet he travelled widely and set travel writing, short stories and novels in Thailand (p 92) and Hong Kong (pp 429–430), among others. His collected Malaysian stories will no doubt feature near the top of the reading list of many visitors to South-east Asia and rightly so, for, although his work often expresses views that seem dated and occasionally prejudiced, his tightly structured short stories provide numerous memorable vignettes of colonial life.

Important though Maugham's work was to the formation of a particular view of South-east Asia, it is only a fraction of the literature from and about South-east Asia. The well is almost bottomless and, although this *Companion* makes no claims to being comprehensive, I hope that it will lead readers to many exciting literary discoveries and new perspectives on familiar writers.

Alastair Dingwall

Contributors

Anna J. Allott is Senior Research Fellow at the School of Oriental and African Studies, University of London, where she has taught Burmese since 1953. She is Honorary Secretary of the Britain–Burma Society. She is co-editor of the *Burmese–English Dictionary*, compiled by J.A. Stewart and C.W. Dunn. She has published many articles on Burmese literature and has recently written *Inked Over, Ripped Out: Burmese Storytellers and the Censors*, 1993.

Mimi Chan is Reader in the Department of English, the University of Hong Kong. She has published papers on Chaucer, Shakespeare, translation and bilingualism and co-edited a collection of papers on *Asian Voices in English* (1990). In 1989 she published *Through Western eyes: Images of Chinese Women in Anglo-American Literature*.

Isagani R. Cruz is a Philippine playwright and critic writing in Filipino and English. He is a winner of the Southeast Asia Writers Award (SEAWRITE), 1991. His best plays are collected in *Josephine at iba pang Dula* (Josephine and Other Plays). His other books include *Beyond Futility: The Filipino as Critic* (1984).

Dudley de Souza teaches in the Language and Literature Department of the National Institute of Education in Singapore. His doctorate was on 'Identity in South-east Asian literature'. He is a poet and has worked as a journalist.

Alastair Dingwall is a Director of In Print Publishing. He was formerly Managing Editor of the *Malayan Law Journal* and of Butterworth & Co (Asia). He specializes in publishing related to South-east Asia and Japan.

Dana Healy lectures in Vietnamese at the School of Oriental and African Studies, University of London.

Thomas John Hudak is an Associate Professor of Linguistics and Thai Language at Arizona State University. His publications include *The Tale of Prince Samuttakote: A Buddhist Epic from Thailand*; *William J. Gedney's The Saek Language: Glossary, Texts, and Translations*; and *The Indigenization of Pali Metres in Thai Poetry*.

Judith Jacob was a lecturer in Cambodian language and literature from 1948–88 at the School of Oriental and African Studies, University of

London. Her publications include the first translation of the *Reamker*, the Cambodian epic based on the *Ramayana* and numerous articles on Cambodian literature. Her most recent book is *The Traditional Literature of Cambodia* (forthcoming).

Peter Koret is currently undertaking research in Laos and Thailand. He has a doctorate in Lao literature from the School of Oriental and African Studies, University of London. His publications include the chapter on Lao literature in the forthcoming *Literatures of Theravada Buddism*.

E. Ulrich Kratz is a Reader in Indonesian and Malay at the School of Oriental and African Studies, University of London. He has published a *Bibliography of Indonesian Literature in Journals* (1988), has co-edited an anthology of Indonesian poetry, *Walking Westward in the Morning* and has written several articles on traditional Malay philology and Indonesian literature.

K.S. Maniam is Associate Professor of English at the University of Malaya. A poet, novelist, playwright and short story writer, his short stories have been published in numerous journals and have been collected in *Plot, The Aborting, Parablames and Other Stories*. His first novel, *The Return*, was republished in 1993 and his latest novel, *In a Far Country* was published in the same year.

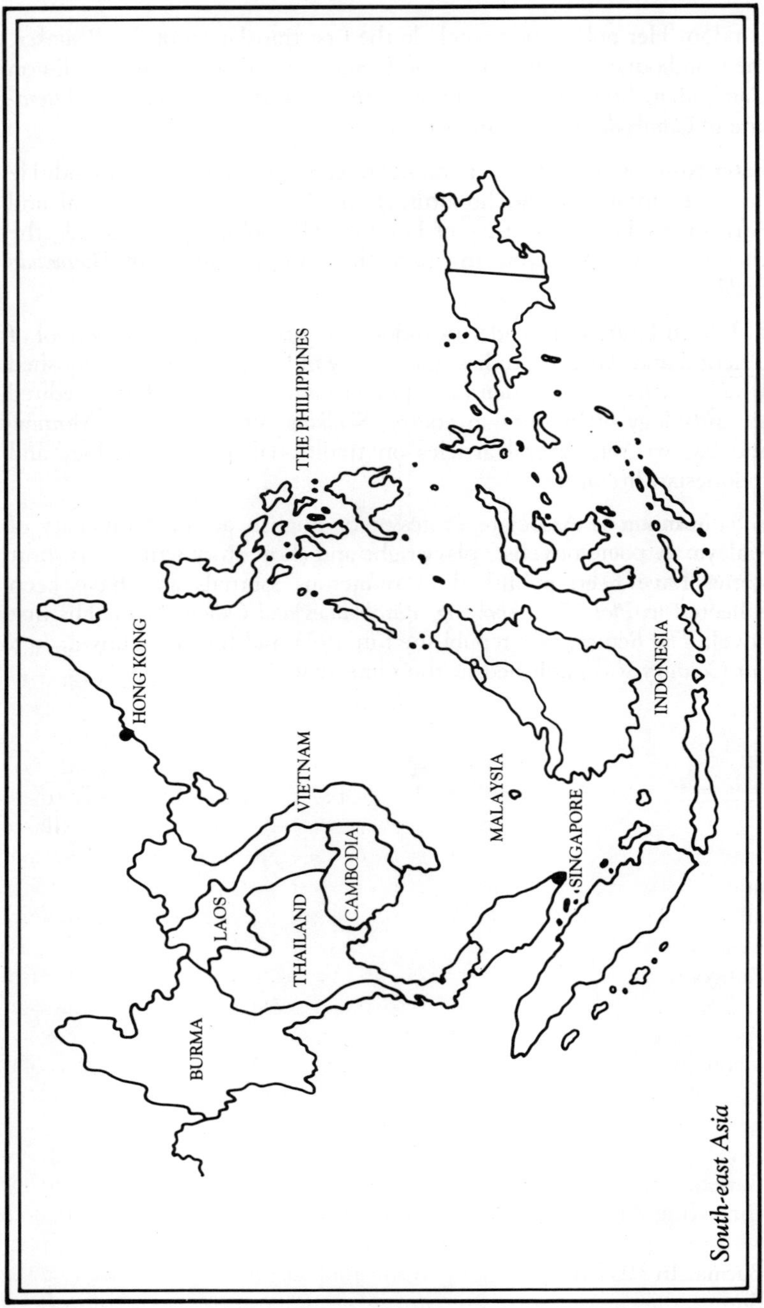

South-east Asia

Burma

Anna J. Allott

> 'By the old Moulmein Pagoda, lookin' lazy at the sea, / There's a Burma girl a-settin', and I know she thinks o' me; / For the wind is in the palm-trees, and the temple-bells they say: / "Come you back, you British soldier; come you back to Mandalay!"'
> *Rudyard Kipling, 'The Road to Mandalay'*

Burma (called Myanmar by the ruling military regime since 1989) is a small agricultural country rich in natural resources and relatively underpopulated, lying between two large and populous neighbours, India and China. Ethnically it is linked with China as its people are of Mongoloid stock and must have come originally from Central Asia, migrating slowly southwards down the great river valleys of the Chindwin and the Irrawaddy. Linguistically too it belongs with China, as Burmese is a tonal, basically monosyllabic language belonging to the great Sino-Tibetan family, with grammar and word order which are quite different from the languages of India and Europe. Its land frontiers are mountainous and it has been the long western coastline, stretching from Akyab (21°N) in the north past Rangoon and Moulmein to Mergui and the southern end of Tenasserim (10°N), which has left it open to successive waves of outside influence. As a result, the country has been dominated culturally throughout its recorded history by influences from the west, and above all from India, even though some of these actually reached it through its eastern neighbour Thailand, formerly known as Siam.

By the 11th century many Indian cults had found their way to Burma, but the only one which took firm root was Buddhism. At that time King Anawrahta established the first powerful Burmese kingdom with its capital at **Pagan** (pronounced to rhyme with 'a gun') in Upper Burma. In 1057 he had captured the ancient town of **Thaton** in Lower Burma, the capital city of an ethnically different people, the Mon (who are related to the Khmer of Cambodia). At the court there he found, so the legend goes, a complete set of the Pali *Tripitaka* the sacred writings or canon of Buddhism, which he took back with him to Pagan. From this time onwards the kings of Burma gave their official patronage to Hinayana Buddhism, the Buddhism of the southern school, usually called by its adherents 'Theravada – the teaching of the elders'. This remained the dominant religious and cultural influence in the life of Burma until it was challenged by Christian missionaries and by the British colonial power in the early 19th century, and by Western political ideas in the 20th. The Burmese language was extended and enriched by numerous words borrowed from Pali, an Indo-European language very close in form to Sanskrit – words which were necessary to express the religious and philosophical concepts of Buddhism.

Just as their language was enriched by words borrowed from an Indian language, so the Burmans' literary and artistic world was from now on inspired by the *Jatakas* ◊, the popular stories of former lives of the Buddha (himself an Indian), that are preserved in all Buddhist countries. These stories are scattered in various parts of the Pali canon, in particular in one large collection (called the *Jatakatthakatha*) of 547 tales. There is much humour in the stories, many moving episodes and delicate touches that have made them the delight of the Buddhist world to this day. In Burma they may form the basis of a popular all-night dance-drama entertainment, they may provide the underlying theme of a modern short story (just as Romeo and Juliet underlies West Side Story); or the name of the villainous Brahmin, Jujaka, in the last and most revered of the great ten Jatakas, the story of King Vissantara, may be chosen by the Burmese government to label its campaign against corruption. In fact, although these tales have a religious frame that attempts to present them as Buddha's ethical teachings, their actual concern is generally with secular behaviour and practical wisdom. Whereas much of the Buddhist canon was concerned with life hereafter, for the ordinary Burman the sky and earth were peopled with a multitude of spirits (*nat*), witches, ghosts and other good and evil supernatural beings ever-present in his imagination; the *Jataka* tales fitted well into this world and helped him to order his life so as to come to terms with them.

The Kingdom of Pagan

The first great Burmese capital city was established at **Pagan** on the east bank of the Irrawaddy river about 400 miles inland from the sea. Here in 1044, Anawrahta, a monarch of outstanding qualities, came to the throne. He founded a dynasty that lasted through eleven more reigns till 1287; during the course of his 33-year reign he managed for the first time to unite almost the whole of Burma under his control. He brought Theravada Buddhism to Pagan and with the construction of the great **Ananda Temple** he initiated a tradition of pagoda building which continued during the next 200 years until the plain around Pagan became filled with great temples and pagodas so that to this day it remains one of the unforgettable sights of the world.

The first written records in Burmese that have survived and the first manifestations of a literature date from after 1057. The captive Mon scholars and courtiers who had been taken back to Pagan by King Anawrahta taught the Burmans how to adapt the south Indian script that they themselves used and in this way Burmese was first reduced to writing. These written records are stone inscriptions – the most famous of which is the Mya-ze-di ◊ of 1333 – which were set up to record the building of the numerous pagodas, monasteries, and ordination halls, all dedicated to glorifying the Buddha and his teaching.

Towards the end of the 13th century the Tartars under Kublai Khan had annexed Yunnan to the north and were exerting pressure on Pagan. As the unity of the Burmese empire began to weaken, the Shan, Tai people from the east ('Shan' is the same word as 'Siam') attacked and seized the fertile rice-producing area of Kyauk-seh. The dynasty founded by Anawrahta collapsed and the first Burmese empire was no more. In the recently republished *She Was a Queen*, a historical novel set during the reigns of the last two monrchs of the dynasty, Maurice Collis ◊ creates a memorable portrait of the village girl, Ma Saw, rising to the position of chief queen (Extract 12).

The Kingdom of Ava

The two and a half centuries from 1287 – the collapse of Pagan – to around 1550 were a chaotic period in Burmese history characterized by protracted warfare between the Burmans, the Shan, and the Mon from the south. By 1364 the Shan had established a capital city at **Ava** (not far from modern **Mandalay**) and founded a dynasty which ruled until 1555. Here in spite of the Shan origin of the rulers, the influence of Burmese and of Buddhism prevailed, and it was during the last hundred years of the Ava period (around 1450–1550) that the first great flowering of Burmese imaginative literature took place. As the times were so unsettled it is perhaps not surprising that nearly all the outstanding works that have come down to us are by monk-poets, as only they could find the necessary peace and quiet to compose and copy poems. Literature was accessible only to a restricted circle of courtiers and clergy.

We must assume that by this time writing was no longer being done only on stone, but also on strips of specially treated palm-leaf; the writing was done with a metal stylus and the letters were wiped over with oil to make the incisions stand out more clearly. It was the need to avoid digging too deeply into the fibres of the palm-leaf that led the scribes to alter the straight-sided letters used in the stone inscriptions into the curves and circles of the present-day Burmese alphabet.

Written literature at this time, and indeed up to the end of the 19th century, consisted overwhelmingly of poetry; it was only in verse that the author brought his imagination into play and displayed his verbal skill. The climbing rhymes of verse forms in classical Burmese literature ◊ are described in 'Biographies and literary notes'. Prose was not considered an artistic medium and was used for works of a practical or technical nature such as texts dealing with law, kingship, astrology, medicine, grammar, and particularly those concerned with the interpretation of the Pali scriptures.

Taung-ngu Period

The indecisive wars of the Ava period were suddenly ended in about 1540 by the rise of the independent Burmese kingdom of **Taung-ngu**, a city situated between Ava in central Burma and the Mon capital of Pegu towards the sea coast. Within a few years the rulers of the Taung-ngu dynasty overcame first the Mon, then the Shan rulers of Ava and the neighbouring princedoms. After the death of King Tabin-shwe-hti, his brother-in-law, King Bayin-naung, made one conquest after another and built up an empire that included almost the whole of modern Burma, Manipur, parts of Yunnan as well as Laos and Thailand.

The courtiers and soldiers who served these successful monarchs wrote not only about the glories of their king but also more and more about their own personal emotions. They still used the classical four-syllable verse but in a different type of poem more suited to the active life of a soldier, a short poem of just three stanzas called a *yadu* ◊. Poets such as the soldier Nawade the Elder ◊ and Prince Nat-shin-naung ◊, when in distant parts of the country, would reach for a palm-leaf to write a *yadu* poem; now on the rainy season (a time when the Burman feels especially homesick), now on flowers, now on a pagoda, now on a dream of the loved one, now on the horrors of the battlefield (see Extract 8). Many hundreds of these poems were written, so much so that this period has been called 'the age of the *yadu*'.

The final hundred years of the Taung-ngu dynasty (1650–1752) were a time of weakness and insecurity; various parts of the Burmese empire revolted, the capital was moved back up north to **Ava** for greater safety, and then fell to a Mon attack from the south in 1751. The great days of the dynasty were past and, as D.G.E. Hall says in his *History of Burma*:

> the atmosphere of the court had become closer and its outlook more restricted. Kings rarely left the capital, they became palace prisoners, surrounded by all the jealousies and intrigues of harem life. Tradition prescribed that the chief queen must be the king's half-sister. Their children, together with those of the lesser queens, were numbered in scores, and all lived in frightful apprehension of the fact that when their father died, a mad scramble for the throne was likely to break out resulting in a blood-bath of all considered dangerous to the successful candidate.

This fatal weakness in the Burmese way of changing rulers persisted until the fall of the monarchy to the British in 1888, and may even be considered to be persisting until today, with the former ruler, U Ne Win, now isolated from the realities of life in Myanmar in his fortress house on the banks of **Inya Lake** in Rangoon.

By far the most important poet of the late 18th century was Pade-tha-ya-za (1633?–1754) ◊. As a court poet he wrote verses in praise of the royal family, but he also broke with tradition and introduced new genres, probably under Thai influence. He wrote the first Burmese court drama, about a magic horse with a ruby eye; the first classical songs and above all the first lyrical poems about ordinary village life. His attitude is neither sentimental nor patronizing; he rejoices in the health and vigour, in the happiness and sense of purpose of the common folk as he describes a raggedly dressed peasant family working in the fields (Extract 15). Pade-tha-ya-za formed a link between the new more personal court literature and the folk poetry of the common people.

Another new development in this period was the compilation around 1724 of the *Maha ya-zawin-gyi* (Great Chronicle) by U Kala ◊, the first person to attempt to write a continuous history of Burma by consulting local records, pagoda histories and other contemporary sources. Previous chronicles had merely presented lists of kings and their lineages.

The Kon-Baung Period at Ava and Mandalay

The Burmese did not remain long under Mon rule. By 1752 a rebel leader from the small town of **Shwe-bo** just north of the capital had rallied sufficient support to drive the Mon out of Ava. Assuming the title Alaung-hpaya ('Buddha-to-be') he founded the Kon-baung dynasty which ruled until the Burmese kingdom was conquered by the British in 1886. During the second half of the 18th century the Burmese Empire once again grew powerful, expanding eastwards into Thailand and westwards into Manipur and Arakan where it aroused anxiety among the British in India. **Ayuthaya**, the Siamese capital, was completely destroyed by the Burmese in 1767. In the same period the British empire was also expanding. Gradually, in three stages, Burma was attacked and annexed: the two coastal strips, Arakan to the north, Tennasserim to the south in 1826; Lower Burma including Rangoon in 1852; and Upper Burma including the seat of the court at Mandalay in 1886. The last king, Thibaw, together with his queen, Su-paya-lat, was sent into exile in India (for a description of the fate of one of Thibaw's descendants, see Extract 13). Not until the monarchy was ended, and the British administration established over the whole country, did a purely popular literature emerge, bringing with it, after the turn of the century, newspapers, magazines, novels and short stories.

With their morale restored and a new dynasty on the throne, literature received a new impetus. The classical verse forms such as *yadu* were composed with new vigour, especially by Sein-dakyaw-thu ◊, a court poet who introduced a new note of realism with his account of mud and mosquitoes on the battlefield (Extract 8). Other poets chronicled the triumphant conquests of King Bodaw-hpaya's reign (1782–1819) in vivid *mawgun* (poems to commemorate important public events).

By the beginning of the 19th century there was a move towards more secular themes and a certain liberalization, with the appearance of humour and satire, first in a kind of long narrative poem called *yagan*, which was very popular at court, and, from the 1840s, in dramas called *pya-zat* (literally 'shown-story') ◊. A *yagan* usually retold a *jataka* or well-known story or Hindu legend in verse (for example the story of Princess Manohari or of Rama and Sita), together with comic asides and satirical attacks on fellow writers and ladies of the court. Styles of writing also became freer, and many works were composed in a mixed style which had the varied phrase-lengths and cadences of prose together with the rhymes of verse. Such were the romances of court life or *nan-dwin-zat-daw-gyi wut-hut* ('within-the palace-play narrative'), by Minister U Sa and later those by the Princess of Hlaing ◊; the literary epistles called *myit-taza* (literally 'letters of loving kindness'), especially those of the famous playwright, U Pon-nya ◊; and finally and most important for the emergence of modern prose fiction in Burma, the popular plays, or *pya-zat*. The earlier plays were intended for performance at court, but by the 1870s these were succeeded by plays for a wider, less sophisticated audiences. The texts of these plays could now be printed cheaply and in large numbers as a result of the establishment of vernacular printing presses, so we have, dated 1875, the first printed version, complete with additional songs, of a new type of stage-play (still in verse), clearly intended for popular consumption.

We learn from accounts of visiting English envoys that drama, whether presented by puppets or human actors, was a very popular form of entertainment throughout Burma in the 19th century. The owners of the newly established vernacular presses (after 1870) soon realized that there was a good market for printed playlets; and a reading public, which could recognize itself in the partly real, partly fantasy world of these plays, was born. The plays, which continued to appear until well into the 20th century, mark the beginning of popular literature in Burma, and were only slowly replaced in the years after 1904 by novels and short stories. An excellent recent book by Noel F. Singer on Burmese puppets is included in the booklist and is recommended to all visitors. However, prose, which one might have expected to have developed sooner as a popular literary medium, remained through the 19th century largely at the service of government – both royal court and colonial power – and religious authorities, both Buddhist and Christian.

Colonial Period (1886-1948)

In Lower Burma, under British rule from 1852, a new type of literature was needed for a rapidly changing society. The development from verse literature for the royal court to popular prose fiction that would have naturally followed soon after the establishment of Burmese-owned printing presses in the 1870s was delayed by the arrival of English as the language of government (and thus of educational and social advancement). However, access to Western education enabled a number of talented Burmese to choose the right English works to be adapted into a natural Burmese setting in such a way that their fellow countrymen would enjoy reading them. James Hla Gyaw, a 40 year-old government translator, was inspired by the episode of the escape of young Edmond Dantes in *The Count of Monte Cristo* by A. Dumas to write the first Burmese novel. It appeared in 1904, handsomely published in hardback with charming photographic illustrations of contemporary Burmese scenes; entitled *Maung Yin Maung Ma Meh Ma wut-htu (The Story of Master Yin Maung and Miss Meh Mah)* it tells a straightforward story of love and adventure set in Upper Burma during the time of the monarchy. The work was immediately popular and set a new fashion. Newspaper editors asked their staff to produce more stories of the same kind. The more conservative sections of Burmese society (among them many monks) opposed the new stories, arguing that writers should restrict themselves to stories taken from the teachings of the Buddha (such as the *jataka* or the *Dhammapada*), rather than modern, invented stories. They sensed a danger to the moral integrity of society in this new type of writing, but their objections were not heeded and the modern 'novel of the day' (*ka-la-paw wut-htu*), as distinct from the 'narrative preached by Buddha' (*Hpaya-haw wut-htu*), became firmly established with the reading public – in the same way as did the wireless, the cinema and television in their turn.

Other novels soon followed but these, still combining features of the popular verse dramas together with the didactic aims of Burmese prose writing, tended to have a plot full of mystery and magic, and to include liberal quantities of useful knowledge, recipes for correct behaviour, and even short sermons as well as poetic passages and songs to illustrate the author's mastery of the languages. The most famous early novel, *Shwei-pyi-zo* (*Ruler of the Golden Land*) by U Lat ◊ has all these features together with the earliest portrayal in literature of disillusion with the West caused by a young man returning home from his studies at the English Bar and rejecting traditional Burmese Buddhist values and behaviour (Extract 11).

The development of the true modern novel, together with the short story, is closely linked to the emergence of weekly literary magazines, from 1915 onwards. Among regular contributors to these were two writers who were largely responsible for the abandonment of traditional palace tales and the introduction to the reading public of realistic stories about contemporary individuals: P. Monin ◊ and Shwei U-daung. The former was a journalist and novelist who encouraged Burmans to think for themselves and to break with tradition; he adapted Western books on sociology and psychology and his fiction is primarily concerned with the individual making his way in society; the latter, through a great number of masterly adaptations and translations, familiarized the Burmese reader with many of the best-known works of Western literature. Shwei U-daung's autobiography *Bawa tathet-ta-hnin atwe-ahkaw-mya* (*Notes and Thoughts of a Lifetime, 1962*) is a major document in the history of Burmese literature.

During the 1920s, at the same time that short stories and novels, often inspired by Victorian fiction (Rider Haggard, Conan Doyle, Mrs Henry Wood, Reynolds, Marie Corelli, Charlies Garvice) were introducing new attitudes towards personal and family relationships, a new feeling of national consciousness, of pride in traditional Buddhist culture, arose. This feeling was strengthened by the first historical novels about two great Burmese warriors – Prince *Nat-shin-naung* ◊ and King *Tabin-shwe-hti*, 1925 by U Maung Gyi (1879–1949), and more especially by the brilliant satirical verses of the great patriot, Thahkin Ko-daw Hmaing. No less a patriot in her own way was Burma's first important woman writer, Dagon Khin Khin Lay ◊ granddaughter of a minister from the Mandalay court. Today she would be called Burma's first feminist writer. Visitors to the platform of the **Shwedagon pagoda** can see the striking pagoda richly decorated with scenes from the Buddha's life which she had built as her own personal work of merit.

The 1920s and 1930s brought demands for independence from Britain, increasing concern for the status of the Burmese language, and a new interest in the style and content of literature. U Sein Tin ◊ perhaps better known by his pen-name Theikpan Maung Wa (1899–1942) wrote of small town and village life exactly as he experienced it working as a district officer. These short pieces (*Experimental Tales, Tales to Test the Age*), full of wry humour and gentle satire, were the model for a type of sketch-cum-essay much copied by other writers.

Little could be published between 1942 and 1946 but several later works deal with the Japanese occupation and the destruction of Rangoon (Extracts 9 and 14). Soon after the war was over and independence achieved in 1948, writing and publishing burst forth again in many forms, finding new sources of inspiration in Soviet as well as in English and American literature. A new, very influential literary magazine was started by the left-wing writer Dagon Ta-ya; he named it 'Star' (*Ta-ya Magazine*) after the red star of communism. In 1947 the government set up the Burma Translation Society – later known by its Burmese name *Sarpay Beikman* (the House of Literature) – to encourage worthwhile writing by subsidies and prizes. Numerous magazines started up – vital channels for the country's literary lifeblood as they carried all first printings of short stories and novels (which usually appear first in serial form). Since the 1920s these magazines have played an important role because they publish general articles, poems, cartoons, and several short stories every month, as well as a considerable number of novels, memoirs and autobiographies in serial form. Publication in one of the leading monthly magazines is the only way for a young author to enter upon the literary scene. Naturally in the 1950s and 1960s many authors wrote of their war-time experiences, and a dominant theme now became Burma's age-long struggle for independent nationhood, from the Mongol hordes threatening the capital Pagan in the 13th century to resistance to the British colonizer. In contrast to the earlier historical novels, the hero is now a peasant or a common soldier, not a king.

An important change in serious fiction after the war was the increase in closely observed, realistic portrayals of all aspects of life and of all classes of people. A model of this genre was Maung Htin's novel *Ng Ba* (*The Peasant*) (Extract 9), a moving account of the appalling sufferings of an ordinary peasant during the Japanese occupation.

Many writers felt that having been at the forefront of the fight for independence, they should now lead the struggle to establish a new, more equitable socialist society in independent Burma. For many younger writers this manifested itself in an impatience with pre-war literary trends, a tendency to look to the USSR for inspiration rather than to Britain, the former colonial power. Among leading left-wing writers at this time were Thein Pe Myint ◊, already well known before the war for his controversial novel *Tet Hpongyi* (*Modern Monk*) published in 1938, *Dagon Ta-ya* and *Bamaw Tin Aung*. *Modern Monk* created a sensation because of its portrayal of certain Buddhist monks as corrupt and sexually immoral. Thein Pe Myint is one of the most widely read and influential of Burmese writers.

After the military coup of March 1962, when the country's new rulers had enunciated their 'Burmese Way to Socialism' policy, writers came under great pressure to produce works of 'socialist realism', preferably showing workers and peasants faced with and then overcoming great hardships and difficulties. Maung Tha-ya (b 1931), a popular author of many sophisticated novels about the urban elite, showed that he was versatile enough to respond to this new challenge by writing a perceptive novel about a Rangoon taxi driver *Mat-tat-yat-lo lan-hma-ngo* (*Stand in the Road and Weep*, 1969) to do this he learnt to drive a taxi and then worked at the job for six months.

Not until this type of detailed, often critical observation is combined with successful character drawing, as for example in the prize-winning novel *Not Out of Hate* (*Mon-ywei mahu*, 1955) by an outstanding woman writer Ma Ma Lay (1917–1982) ◊, do we see modern Burmese fiction at its best (Extract 4). This is the story of the suffering of an intelligent young woman of traditional upbringing who falls in love with and marries a Westernized Burman who has lost all sympathy and understanding for the things she cherishes.

Although theatrical shows are immensely popular – all Burmans love a *pwe* (see Orwell's description in Extract 7) – written drama does not flourish; poetry, on the other hand, is everyone's pastime and pleasure. The greatest names are Zawgyi ◊ and Minthu-wun, already well-loved before the war; after the war there are too many names to list.

By far the most widely written and widely read genre today is the short story. The 1980s have seen a great increase in the number of monthly literary magazines on the market, and as they all carry several short stories there will normally be about 90–100 stories published each month! One of the main reasons for the short story being preferred to the full-length novel is the strict, and very often unpredictable, censorship exercised by the government Press Scrutiny Committee over everything that is published. It is a much smaller blow for an author to have a short story rejected than a long novel. This censorship has been in force since 1964, and has led in the 1970s and 1980s to a marked decline in the quality of major original works, and to a proliferation of adapted thrillers, romances and comic books. In the field of the short story it was the humorous, mocking, fearlessly honest Thaw-da Swe ◊ who more than any other was in tune with his fellow citizens in the

1950s and 1960s. Thaw-da Swe's full and riotous life-style provided rich material for his many-sided talent as a story-teller. In a country in which the writer's role is by tradition and by present government policy, a didactic one, he is unusual in refusing to offer himself as a model. On the contrary, many of his most popular stories are honest accounts of his own sins, written with such self-mockery and humour that all criticism is disarmed.

More recently several younger women writers have established major reputations for perceptive, realistic writing, full of critical observation and wry social comment (to the extent that it has been allowed past the censors) – among them MoMo In-ya, Ma Sanda and NuNu Yee. Their writings could well be characterized as 'anti-romantic', their heroines are short of money and tied down by small children, fed up with being pregnant for the fourth and fifth time, wishing that their husbands would take on more of the burden of looking after the children and elderly parents, wondering why they bothered to take a university degree.

Two further Burmese novelists writing in English should be mentioned: Maung Thiha, whose *The Chindits and the Stars* (published in England in 1956) takes as its subject matter the struggle begun by the Burmese Army in 1944 to liberate Burma from the Japanese regime, followed by the breakdown of understanding by the various races of the Union and the spread of civil war. At the end of the book, the hero Maung Tin lies dead, blown up in a train by his former comrades who are now insurgents. Wendy Law-Yone's *The Coffin Tree* was published in the USA in 1983 and in the UK soon afterwards. The action of the novel falls into two parts; the first quite short part, set in **Mandalay**, is given over to the politics of Burma. Stirringly evocative for anyone who spent their childhood in Mandalay, this section, full of myth, fantasy, symbolism and brilliant description, explodes with violence when the protagonist – a young Burmese woman of a rich, powerful and demented family – is cast out of Burma by a savage political coup that destroys her father. The second and longer part of the novel reveals her sufferings in America.

The book above all others that the visitor to Burma should try to read is *Burmese Family* (1946) by MiMi Khaing ▷. Written in English in Delhi early in 1945 when Burma was still occupied by the Japanese, this enchanting short book captures better than any other work the spirit which animates Burmese society and which captivates so many visitors to the country. It is an account of the author's own childhood, family and friends, inspired by nostalgia and happy memories, yet at the same time vividly detailed, informative and entertaining. The line drawings by E.G.N. Kinch are unforgettable (Extracts 2 and 6).

Western Literature Set in Burma

Perhaps this section should start with a denial – Kipling never visited Mandalay! The famous barrack-room ballad about the 'Road to Mandalay' and its well-known verse 'By the old Moulmein Pagoda, looking lazy at the sea, there's a Burma girl a settin', and I know she thinks of me', were composed on the strength of one short visit in 1889, when Kipling's liner called at **Rangoon** and **Moulmein** for a few days. 'The scene-painting of this song', he says (*Something of Myself*) is 'a sort of mix up . . . of the singer's memories against a background of the Bay of Bengal as seen at dawn from a troopship'. The subject is the nostalgia that the returned soldier in London feels for the warm and sensuous East.

Of the very large number of novels, personal memoirs, travellers' tales and wartime adventures that have been written about Burma, only a few can be described here. A search in a London library catalogue for novels about Burma yielded a list of 60 titles; even this lengthy list did not include many that are most important for helping the visitor to make that imaginative leap from interested observer to sympathetic participant. It may be helpful to a would-be reader to group the best works into four main categories – the adventure-romance, the fiction of mysticism and religion, the domestic novel, and the historical or political novel.

Adventures

One of the earliest in the first category is G.A. Henty's *On the Irrawaddy* (1896), an adventure story of the first Anglo-Burmese war (1824–26) for the juvenile reader, written from the point of view of the imperial power. Far more gripping however is the real-life *Personal Narrative of Two Years' Imprisonment in Burmah* (1860) by the merchant, Henry Gouger, who was unlucky enough to find himself chained and thrown into prison in the Burmese capital, Ava, at the outbreak of the war.

Set in the north-east of the country, Edward Thompson's *Burmese Silver* (1937) ◊ is the only adventure novel set in Burma which approaches the complexities of Joseph Conrad's *Heart of Darkness*, to which it owes a debt. In his preface to the 1943 Penguin edition, Thompson wrote: 'It is, I believe, the only novel whose scene is the glorious Chindwin valley and the still unexplored fastnesses to the north-eastward – regions which have moved into the foreground of our minds and are likely to remain there. Further, its details, grim or lovely, of the marches where China and Burma meet, and of their treasuries of gems and precious metal, in a few years will be known to be truth'. Readers should follow up this clue by reading Bertil Lintner's enthralling *Land of Jade* (1989) – see below.

Religious and mystical works

The second category is fiction which takes the reader to a greater or lesser extent into the spiritual world of the Burmese Buddhist. One of the earliest such novels is by Sir George Scott (writing in the Burmese fashion under a pen-name, Shwe Dinga) – *The Repentance of Destiny* (1913) which centres on a young Burman, Tun Min, who refuses his father's behest to become a monk, and who thereafter becomes involved in political intrigue involving British, Indian and Burmese officials. The tragic death of his sweetheart turns him back towards the religious life. The author's delineations of Burma and her people in this novel are excellent, which is only to be expected of the writer whose classic 600 page work, *The Burman, His Life and Notions* (1882) – under the pen-name Shway Yoe – remains to this day unequalled as a description of a people and its way of life.

Nevil Shute's post-war novel, *The Chequer Board* (1947) ◊ is set partly in Burma and partly in England; it tackles the theme of mixed marriages and incidentally shows how an Englishman has come to terms with Buddhism. However, the English novel which shows the most sensitive understanding of Buddhism is Ethel Mannin's *The Living Lotus* (1956). Here Burmese society in **Upper Burma** is described in loving detail, and Burmese Buddhism, with its attendant rituals including propitiation of local *nats*, is described with care and insight. People are shown realistically, with warmth, jealousy and treachery as much part of their lives as in any other culture.

A late work by Christopher Isherwood, *A Meeting by the River* (1967) is a novel in epistolary form which examines self-denial and religious conversion. Isherwood is one of a number of Western writers who have observed Buddhism in its Burmese setting and have tried to understand and to convey its importance in the lives of the people.

It is, however, to the Japanese writer Michio Takeyama that must go the highest praise for his portrayal of Buddhism and for his inspired story of a company of Japanese soldiers stranded in Burma at the end of the war. *Harp of Burma* (1964) ◊, is an unforgettable book. It was written by a man who had never visited nor, before he wrote the novel, studied Burma; but driven by concern for the youth of Japan and his awareness of the tragic futilities of war he sought in Burmese Buddhism the meaning of Japan's defeat and a way to reconstruct Japanese society. Takeyama's achievement is to convey Burma's impact upon the Japanese who went there as soldiers and who stayed long enough to be deeply affected by their contact with Burmese culture. He shows us rural Burma and its people through Japanese eyes, without sentimentality but in such a way as to set his readers thinking. In his farewell letter to his fellow soldiers the hero writes:

> Furthermore I never cease to marvel that the people of Burma, though certainly indolent, pleasure seeking, and careless, are all cheerful, modest and happy. They are always smiling. Free from greed, they are at peace with themselves. While living among them I have come to believe that these are precious human qualities. Our country has waged a war, lost it, and is now suffering. That is because we were greedy, because we were so arrogant that we forgot human values. Of course we cannot be as languid as the people of this country, and dream our lives away as they often do. But can we not remain energetic and yet be less avaricious? Is that not essential – for the Japanese and for all humanity?

Readers who are curious to learn more about the theory and the actual practice of Buddhist meditation in Burma should read *An Experiment in Mindfulness* (1958) by E.H. Shattock – a very practical, down-to-earth book by a former naval captain who tells of his search for peace of mind.

Domestic novels

In almost every novel in this category we meet the theme of racially mixed marriages and the problems of the children of such unions. The same theme occurs frequently in Anglo-Indian fiction written after the Indian Mutiny of 1857.

A Marriage in Burma (1905) by Mabel Cosgrove (Mrs Chan Toon) realistically documents the cultural and social gulf that yawns for a young Englishwoman, deeply in love with her Burmese husband, when the couple take up residence in his country. The 'novel' was autobiographical and sadly this marriage did not last, but on a happier note Mabel Cosgrove's friendship with Oscar Wilde and his family led to Wilde meeting her husband, Chan Toon, a barrister of the Middle Temple. The result of this meeting was Wilde's Burmese Masque, entitled *For Love of the King* (c 1894), which he said was the: 'outcome of long and luminous talks with your distinguished husband in the Temple and on the river, in the days when I was meditating writing a novel as beautiful and as intricate as a Persian praying-rug'.

During and after the second world war there came a significant and kindly softening of attitudes to mixed marriages and the children of such unions. The marriage of a Burmese princess to a European was movingly described in 1938 by Maurice Collis in his *Trials in Burma* (Extract 13). A mere ten years later, following the social upheavals of wartime, H.E. Bates's *The Purple Plain* (1947) was one of a number of second world novels that attacked the prejudices that existed on both sides. Squadron Leader Forrester, a Royal Air Force pilot, falls in love with Anna, an Anglo-Burmese girl. The action of the novel is Forrester's fight to survive after his plane crashes in the hot arid 'purple plain' of central Burma, but his will to survive is due entirely to his deep love for Anna whom he eventually marries.

Similarly, Bates's *The Jacaranda Tree* (1949) features an Englishman, Patterson, in love with a Burmese girl with the unlikely name of Nadia. Nadia lives with Patterson, and her young brother is a general odd-job man around the house. As the Japanese invaders draw nearer, Patterson is forced to lead a party of Englishmen and women out of Burma to safety. The jacaranda tree symbolises the unspoilt beauty of Burma, while the club in the novel, of course, is the emblem of the artificiality and petty-mindedness of British officialdom, as in Orwell's *Burmese Days*.

The Golden Stairs (1968) ◊ is one of the best, yet one of the least well-known stories of the war in Burma. Again the theme is the British flight from Burma to escape the invading Japanese but the main characters are three young children, one of whom is Anglo-Burman.

Political novels

Perhaps the best known work on Burma and a true political novel is George Orwell's *Burmese Days*, written in England, published first in America in 1934 and then in England by Gollancz in 1935, and apparently describing colonial Burma of the early 1920s (Extract 7). In fact it tells us much more how strongly Orwell felt about his fellow Europeans and their role as foreign masters in a fascinating country with a civilisation and culture to which they appeared largely indifferent if not hostile. Many British administrators and engineers who have spent their lives working in Burma consider that the picture Orwell paints is a cruel travesty. On the other hand, through the savage dialogue in the novel Orwell presents powerful arguments against the imperialist policies of any country, whether capitalist or communist. It must also be said that Orwell paints an unfavourable picture of Burmans and of Buddhism (see 'Orwell in Burma', pp 24–25).

A post-war political novel by Patrick Cruttwell, a former English teacher at **Rangoon University,** *A Kind of Fighting* (1959), is a *roman à clef*, depicting Burmese nationalism which exulted in the British exodus in 1942 and then faced the severe test of the Japanese occupation and the turmoil that followed Japan's defeat. The action is set in the fictitious nation of 'Sagha', quite obviously Burma, whose national hero, Dinzaw, is patently General Aung San. Although the novel met with official disapproval because of the too human weaknesses in the character of the hero who at the end of the novel falls victim to a

George Orwell (third from left, back row) at the Police Mess in Mandalay 1923

political assassin, as did General Aung San, it does represent an original effort to create a truly Burman hero who, although the product of Western education, never really loses his national identity.

The dividing line between political and historical novels moves with the passage of time. *Thibaw's Queen* (1900) by Fielding-Hall was written when Queen Supaya-lat was still in exile in British India, whilst F. Tennyson Jesse's *The Laquer Lady* (1929) was written long after her death. Both writers, particularly the former, were friends of Burma, but Fielding-Hall's account reads rather journalistically whilst Jesse's re-creation of the intrigues of a jealous and demanding chief queen as she manoeuvres and dominates her husband, Thibaw, has the stamp of real life. Her sources were documents and interviews with Burmese and Europeans who either had first-hand knowledge of the events or had received their information from participants or observers at the Burmese court. The pages of the novel are filled with detailed descriptions of the court and the palace, the city of **Mandalay** and its European and Burmese inhabitants. The bridge between East and West is an Anglo-Burman girl called Fanny who was educated in England and became a lady-in-waiting at the Burmese court. Fielding-Hall's writings on Burma are still much loved by Burmans (see, for example, Extract 3).

For the reader comparing the court in the 19th century with that of earlier centuries, Jesse's novel should be read alongside a later historical novel written about an earlier period – *She was a Queen* (1937) by Maurice Collis (Extract 12). This work is set against the reigns of the two last monarchs of the Pagan dynasty (c 1270), and the author tells us that: 'with a few minor exceptions, the characters, the structure and the story generally come straight from the [Great Glass Palace] chronicle ◊, while twenty years' experience of Burma has given me the blood and spirit with which to animate them'. This is the story of Queen Saw, one of the many remarkable women who have ruled eastern kingdoms. Daughter of a small Burmese farmer, she became the concubine and then the queen of Usana, King of Burma. After his death she married his second son and secured the throne for her husband. Following the horrors of a Tartar invasion, and her husband's death in her arms, she returned to her native village, to live her own life with a lover who was her equal.

In *Stranger in the Land* (1967) ◊ by Michael Pereira (Assistant Military Attache at the British Embassy in Rangoon in the early 1960s) the old theme of East-West ties is set in the midst of modern Burmese political divisions, in a way that uncannily foretells the course of events in Burma in the late 1980s.

Travel Literature Set in Burma

Westerners have been travelling to Burma for many centuries, and for a great variety of reasons – priests, missionaries, merchants, explorers, empire builders, colonial administrators (and their wives), soldiers, writers and journalists. Many of these visitors have left us written accounts of the time they spent in Burma, of the country and its peoples. Almost more valuable than their words are the superb illustrations to be found in many of these books, especially the sketches and original watercolour paintings of places, buildings, fashions no longer to be seen.

At the end of the 18th century the British Governor-General of India sent Captain Michael Symes on a mission to the Burmese court, in search among other things of a commercial treaty to permit trade in teak. The envoy proved to be a keen observer and he recorded his valuable observations and comments on all aspects of Burmese life in *An Account of the Embassy to the Kingdom of Ava sent by the Governor-General of India in 1795*. He was then sent on another mission, again recorded for us in his *Journal of a Second Embassy to the Court of Ava in 1802*. This book is important enough to have been reprinted in 1955.

In 1855 another British mission made its way up to the Burmese capital at Ava led by Colonel Arthur Phayre; travelling with him as secretary was Henry Yule, enlisted in the Bengal Engineers. Yule's 380 page report, *A Narrative of the Mission sent by the Governor-General of India to the Court of Ava in 1855* (1858) both records the voyage of the mission up the Irrawaddy to the court of King Mindon (this was before the capital was moved to Mandalay) and also provides a great deal of fascinating sociological information. The many beautiful illustrations include drawings and watercolours by the mission's official artist, Colesworthy Grant, as well as by the author, and helpful maps and photographs by Linnaeus Tripe. A facsimile edition was produced by Oxford University Press in 1968.

After the annexation of Upper Burma more administrators went out to Burma, among whom the most distinguished was surely Sir J.G. Scott, who became Superintendent for the Northern and later the southern **Shan States**. By 1882 he had published, under the pen-name Shway Yoe, a major work, *The Burman: His Life and Notions* which is still unsurpassed as a source of social and cultural information about Burma. to this day writers and novelists continue to plunder its pages for the local colour and authentic details that they need; compare, for example, the description of a *pwe* in Michael Pereira's *Stranger in the Land* ◊ with that by Shway Yoe.

Scott's books have comparatively few illustrations, though his writing is so vivid and packed with detail that one feels no need for pictures; but by the 1910s several magnificently illustrated travel books had been published. *The Silken East* (1905) by V.C. Scott O'Connor is a 'record of life and travel in Burma' which takes one all over the country, (to the great envy of the modern tourist). In his preface to a second edition the author describes travelling up the Irrawaddy:

> In those relatively early days there was not much railway communication. There were few roads. One rode on ponies or travelled by water; and travelling by water was inexhaustible in its pleasure and its variety. The Irrawaddy was navigable for nine hundred miles by the splendid craft of the Irrawaddy Flotilla Company; there were sea-going ships along the coast to Arakan and Tenasserim; steamers of the Royal Indian Marine, and Government launches; rafts and country boats . . . but perhaps the most enticing of all were the country boats. It was the custom to travel by night. The boats were long and narrow with a roof at one end, and under its shelter a bed was laid for the traveller. The great river did most of the work. As the night grew the boatmen fell asleep, the steersman nodded; the embers in the hearth fire faded, the stars or the moon came out, and the sky was bright and

Maurice Collis

> clear overhead. Slowly the boat drifted, making no sound, finding its way down the unresisting stream; the mighty Irrawaddy, whose shores were often invisible beyond the vast expanse of waters. These were incomparable experiences.

By 1907 this energetic author had published a second book, more magnificent than the first – *Mandalay and other Cities of the Past in Burma* with four more fascinating paintings by the Burmese artist, Saya Chone, depicting a royal audience, the ceremony of the royal ploughing, the surrendering of King Thibaw (in 1886) to British officials in a summer house in the Palace gardens, and the departure of King Thibaw and Queen Supayalat from Mandalay. Together with

Norman Lewis

numerous photographs this book gives us town-plans and a carefully drawn and labelled plan of the **royal palace at Mandalay** as it was in 1870. There were nine chambers and eight throne rooms; the palace had to be big enough to receive all visitors and to accommodate the king's 64 wives. Tragically the all-wooden palace burnt to the ground in 1945 and until recently only a model of it could be seen. Since 1991 the military commander of Mandalay district has set afoot a project to rebuild the palace in all its splendour.

At the end of the 19th century the ship on which Rudyard Kipling was travelling stopped briefly at Rangoon and then at Moulmein; this short visit, recorded in *From Sea to Sea* (1900) seems to have left a strong impression on him, sufficient to inspire his much-quoted verses about Mandalay and Moulmein. Another well-known writer who passed through Burma on his way elsewhere was Somerset Maugham, who describes his voyage up the Irrawaddy in *The Gentleman in the Parlour* (1930) – the book is subtitled 'A Record of a Journey from Rangoon to Haiphong'. Somerset Maugham also set a number of short stories in Burma.

Burma was lucky in receiving among the officials sent out to work as administrators and magistrates several very talented writers. One such was Maurice Collis. *Trials in Burma* (1938) is remarkable not only for the dramatic way that the author recounts the cases that came before him, but for its humanity, its humour and the delightful pictures it gives of Burmese life (Extract 13). All the books that Maurice Collis wrote about Burma are to be recommended, whether biography such as *Siamese White*, history such as *The Land of the Great Image*, or fiction such as *She was a Queen* (Extract 12). Of particular interest are his autobiographical writings of his time in Burma; following *Trials in Burma* were *The Journey Outward* and *Into Hidden Burma* (1953).

Having the experience to write with as much authority as Maurice Collis but on a very different subject, namely elephants, was Lt Col J.H. Williams, author of *Elephant Bill* (Extract 16). This was the name by which he was known throughout Burma, where he spent over 20 years in the jungle, living with elephants and their riders, working with them in the vast teak forests. He has stories to tell of elephants in every aspect of their lives: of the wild herds and the lonely tuskers, of mother elephants and their calves, of rogue elephants, and working elephants hauling great teak-trunks down from the mountains to the rivers. The thrilling stories are the most impressive for the quiet modesty of the writing, which is full of the author's humour and of the gentleness and charm which won him the confidence of the remarkable animals under his care. During the war, Elephant Bill became 'Elephant adviser' to the XIVth army, and during the big Japanese advance on India he brought out as many animals as possible by a new route over precipitous mountain-tracks and through pathless jungle. This feat, reminiscent of Hannibal's crossing of the Alps, is the climax of this exciting book. Williams wrote another book about elephants in Burma, *Bandoola* – the story of an exceptional working elephant and his *oozie* (rider).

Since the second world war several 'literary sightseers' have written lively and entertaining accounts of their visits to Burma, though it must be recognized that these have been based upon comparatively limited personal experience of a quite different kind to that of the books just described above. First into the field was Norman Lewis who arrived in the country at the beginning of 1951. He explains his reasons for going to Burma in the foreword to his book *Golden Earth – Travels in Burma* (1952) as follows:

> In 1949, with the creation of the People's Republic of China, that country became as remote and as inaccessible as Tibet had been of old. I believed that this policy of self-isolation might spread to neighbouring countries and, having determined to see before I died something of the Far East, I went in 1950 to Indo-China . . . In that year there was no slackening in the rate at which the Far Eastern lands were passing beyond the reach of the literary sightseer. Korea was scorched off the map, and if we were embroiled with China, said the observers, the flames of this conflagration might spread to Burma where Communist guerrillas were already firmly entrenched. Traditional Burma, with its archaic and charming way of life was in danger of vanishing.

This is a book to read for its brilliant writing, for its wit, for its unsentimental and merciless observation of the Burmese scene, and to remind one of exactly what was happening in the country at that moment of its troubled post-war history. The traveller interested in understanding Burmese politics is particularly recommended to read the chapter called 'Rival Parties' and to note the section on the language of political censure to find out how little has changed in the last 40 years. The original edition of the book has a map at the end showing how far Norman Lewis was able to travel – from **Rangoon** to **Moulmein**, **Tavoy** and **Mergui** by boat; then back by air to **Rangoon** and on to **Mandalay**, from there by land to **Katha**, **Myitkyina**, **Bhamo** and **Lashio**, and back by train to **Rangoon**. He tells us much of the now little-visited northern areas, including the Shan States, nothing of the tourist-weary places such as Pagan and Inlay lake.

Three years later at the beginning of February 1954 another experienced travel writer arrived in Rangoon. Ethel Mannin, author of well over 50 works, came in search of a subject for a novel but left after a busy, tightly organized two-month stay determined to write a book about Burma as well as a novel set in the country. Her *Land of the Crested Lion – A Journey through Modern Burma* (1954) is to some extent complementary to *Golden Earth*, in that it visited many of the same places just a few years later, meets different types of people and pays more attention to aspects of Buddhism in Burma. It is a gentler book, more concerned with personal relationships, but at the same time well observed and full of interesting information.

Several more recent visitors have included small vignettes of life in Burma in their books or have contributed a chapter to a larger book. Paul Theroux relates a hair-raising train journey in **Upper Burma** in one chapter of his *The Great Railway Bazaar* (1975), and Pico Iyer includes an amusing description of immigration procedures at **Rangoon airport** in his *Video Night in Kathmandu* (1990). For an affectionately humorous and very perceptive short introduction to Burma, via the **Strand Hotel, to Prome**, by river boat up the Irrawaddy to **Mandalay**, the visitor should turn to Miles Kington's section of *Great Journeys* (1989), a coffee-table book illustrated with superb colour photos. This journey was made in 1987, just before the country exploded violently with anger and frustration in the middle of the following year. Another recent work, *Great Rivers of the World* has an excellent section by Alexander Frater describing his journey up the Irrawaddy river a few years earlier.

Present-day visitors to Burma have no chance to reach the peripheral areas where the many other races live who altogether make up the extraordinarily varied racial and linguistic mix of the Union of Burma. These areas are not open to tourists because for most of the four decades since Burma regained independence from Britain they have been a battle zone where rebel armies of several ethnic minorities have been fighting a civil war against the central Burmese government. Almost no reports came from these areas until in 1990 Bertil Lintner published *Land of Jade* (1990), an enthralling account of a dangerous and difficult journey made by him and his wife through the rebel-controlled wilds of northern Burma from late 1985 until April 1987 – the first foreign journalist to travel this route since the 1940s. Travelling on foot, by boat, jeep, bicycle and elephant, the author, his wife and soon after the start of the journey, their new baby daughter are given safe conduct by successive groups of insurgents, all eager that their story should be told to the outside world. He lived long enough amongst tribes-people such as the head-hunting Nagas, the Kachins and the Wa to be able to observe their daily life and customs; he interviewed their leaders, and was even caught up in several jungle battles. This real-life adventure, brilliantly narrated, is more exciting than any fictitious spy story. A picture of life with the other main group of rebels in Burma is given in *True Love and Bartholomew – Rebels on the Burmese Border* by Jonathan Falla (1991). The author spent a year living illegally with the Karen rebels on the Thai-Burma border; his very personal account of life in the jungle, a 'behind-the-lines view of the Karen Free State', creates a moving portrait of a people fighting to preserve their way of life.

Acknowledgement. The author is pleased to acknowledge the assistance of 'Burma: fact or fiction' by Dr D.M. Burjorjee (presented at the Britain-Burma Society, London, 6 June 1984) in preparing the section on Western writers on Burma.

Orwell in Burma

Eric Blair spent almost five years in Burma. Upon arrival in November 1922, aged 19, he went straight up to **Mandalay** (the journey by mail train took 16 hours from Rangoon; present day travellers will find it still taking 13–14 hours by 'express' train) to the Burma Provincial Police Training School. This stood on the outskirts of the city near to the Police Mess where he was to live during the 16 months of training: 'The Mess was a long, low-lying brick building, with six bedrooms on the upper floor, approached by a semi-circular drive through a compound ablaze with acacia trees and canna lilies' (see photograph on p 16). Blair was fascinated by Mandalay and he delighted in exploring the city and countryside. In the early 1920s it was still essentially two cities, the British fort inside the mile-square, former palace walls, which was like a small outpost of England, and the other city with its bustling life and mud roads leading out into the country villages. His response to Burma can be seen in the descriptive passages of *Burmese Days* which as Richard Rees has pointed out in the 'Afterword' to the Signet edition 'are the most elaborate and probably the best he ever did. [Nothing else is] so vivid and striking as his descriptions of the climate, landscape, trees, flowers and smells of Upper Burma'.

Training finished, Blair was posted to **Myaungmya** in Lower Burma and then successively to **Twante, Syriam, Insein, Moulmein** and only briefly from April to July 1927 to **Katha**, north of Mandalay in Upper Burma. Sadly, tourists cannot visit any of these places. The town of 'Kyauktada' where the action of *Burmese Days* takes place is based on Katha but the key to its characters is surely to be found in all the stations Blair served in earlier.

Two other important Burma pieces by Orwell are the essay 'A Hanging' set in the prison at Insein, at that time the second largest in Burma and since 1988 notorious for housing not only criminals but a great number of political prisoners and his essay set in Moulmein, 'Shooting an Elephant', which has been described as: 'one of the masterpieces of the genre in this century – that may well stand as Orwell's finest single achievement in prose'.

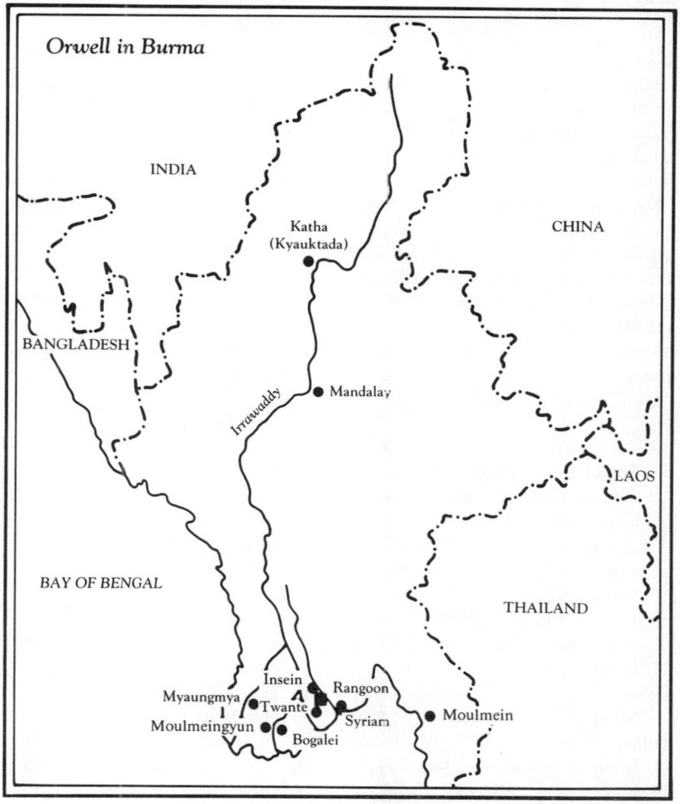

George Orwell's stations in Burma between 1922 and 1927 were as follows: **Rangoon**, *arrived November 1922;* **Mandalay**, *November 1922 to March 1924 (training);* **Myaungmya**, *March 1924 to May 1924;* **Twante**, *May 1924 to December 1924;* **Syriam**, *December 1924 to September 1925;* **Insein**, *September 1925 to September 1926;* **Moulmein**, *September 1926 to April 1927;* **Katha**, *April 1927 to July 1927;* **Rangoon**, *departed in July 1927. Source: Robert E. Vore in MaMa Lay,* Not Out of Hate, *Ohio University Press, 1991. There is an excellent, detailed account of Orwell in Burma in* The Unknown Orwell, *by P. Stansky and W. Abrahams, Constable, 1972, from which some of the text opposite derives.*

BOOKLIST

What follows is intended as a representative rather than comprehensive list of books about Burma. All the books included in the Extracts section or mentioned in the text are included. Where several editions exist, in general the latest and most readily available edition has been listed. Information on the original English language publisher can in many cases be found in the 'Acknowledgements' section at the end of the volume. Readers interested in pursuing a study of literature from and about Burma will find Patricia Herber's book (details below) absolutely essential.

Allott, Anna J., ed, *Inked Over, Ripped Out: Burmese Storytellers and the Censors*, Pen American Center, New York, 1993.

Aung San Suu Kyi, *Aung San*, University of Queensland Press, St Lucia, 1984.

Aung San Suu Kyi (Michael Aris, ed), *Freedom from Fear*, Viking/Penguin, 1991.

Bates, H.E., *The Jacaranda Tree*, Michael Joseph, London, 1949.

Bates, H.E., *The Purple Plain*, Michael Joseph, London, 1947.

Bosley, Keith, ed, *Elek Book of Oriental Verse*. Paul Elek, London, 1979. **Extracts 1, 8 and 16**. Extracts trans K Bosley and J. Okell.

Collis, Maurice, *Into Hidden Burma*, Faber and Faber, London, 1953.

Collis, Maurice, *The Journey Outward: An Autobiography*, Faber and Faber, London, 1952.

Collis, Maurice, *She Was a Queen*. New Directions, New York, 1992 (Reprint) (**Extract 12**).

Collis, Maurice, *Siamese White*, D D Books, Bangkok, 1982.

Collis, Maurice, *Trials in Burma*, Faber and Faber, London, 1938. **Extract 13**.

Cosgrove, Mabel (Mrs Chan Toon), *A Marriage in Burmah*, Greening, London, 1905.

Cruttwell, Patrick, *A Kind of Fighting*, J.M. Dent, London, 1959.

Falla, Jonathan, *True Love and Bartholomew: Rebels on the Burmese Border*, Cambridge University Press, 1991.

Fielding-Hall, H. *The Soul of A People*, Macmillan London, 1898. **Extract 3**.

Fielding-Hall, H., *Thibaw's Queen*, Harper and Brothers, London & New York, 1899.

Gouger, Henry, *Personal Narrative of Two Years' Imprisonment in Burmah*. John Murray, London, *1862*, 2 ed.

Hall, D.G.E., *Burma*, Hutchinson's University Library, London, 1960, 3 ed/New York Arms Press, 1974.

Henty, G.A., *On the Irrawaddy: A Story of the First Burmese War*, Blackie and Son, London, 1897.

Herbert, Patricia, *Burma*, World Bibliographical Series Vol 132, Clio Press, Oxford, UK, 1991.

Hla, U, *The Caged Ones*, White Lotus, Bangkok, 1986.

Htin Aung, *Burmese Drama: A Study, with Translations of Burmese Plays*, OUP, Calcutta, 1937 / Greenwood, Westport, Connecticut, 1978.

Htin Aung, *Burmese Monks' Tales*, Columbia University Press, New York, 1966.

Isherwood, Christopher, *A Meeting by the River*, 1967.

Iyer, Pico, *Video Night in Kathmandu*, Black Swann, London, 1990.

Jesse, F. Tennyson, *The Lacquer Lady*, (with a new introduction by Joanna Colenbranden) Virago Modern Classics, London, 1979.

Kelly, R. Talbot, *Burma: Painted and*

Described, Adams and Charles Black, London, 1905.

Kipling, Rudyard, *From Sea to Sea: Letters of Travel*, Doubleday & McClure, New York, 1899.

Kipling, Rudyard, *Something of Myself*.

Law-Yone, Wendy, *The Coffin Tree*, Alfred A. Knopf, New York, 1983.

Lintner, Bertil, *Land of Jade: A Journey through Insurgent Burma*. Kiscadale, Edinburgh, 1990, also White Lotus, Bangkok.

Lewis, Norman, *Golden Earth: Travels in Burma*, Jonathan Cape, London, 1952 / Eland Books, 1984.

MaMa Lay (Margaret Aung Thwin, trans), *Not Out of Hate*. Ohio University Press, 1991. **Extract 4**.

Mannin, Ethel, *Land of the Crested Lion: A Journey Through Modern Burma*, Jarrold, London, UK, 1954.

Mannin, Ethel, *The Living Lotus*. Jarrold, London, 1956.

Maugham, W. Somerset, *The Gentleman in the Parlour*, Doubleday, New York, 1930.

MiMi Khaing, *Burmese Family*, Longman, India, 1946. **Extracts 2 and 6**.

Myint Thein, *Burmese Folk Songs*, The Asoka Society, Oxford, UK, 1970.

Myint Thein, *When at Nights I Strive to Sleep: A Book of Verses*, The Asoka Society, Oxford, 1971.

O'Brien, Harriet, *Forgotten Land*, Michael Joseph, London, 1992.

O'Connor, V.C. Scott, *Mandalay and Other Cities of the Past in Burma*, Hutchinson, 1907.

O'Connor, V.C. Scott, *The Silken East*. Hutchinson, 1905.

Orwell, George, *Burmese Days*, Penguin, Harmondsworth, UK/ Harcourt, Brace, Jovanovich, New York. **Extract 7**.

Pereira, Michael, *Stranger in the Land*. G. Bles, London, 1967.

Singer, Noel F., *Burmese Puppets*, OUP, Oxford, 1992.

Scott, Sir George, *The Repentance of Destiny*, 1913.

Scott, Sir George, *The Burman, His Life and Notions*, Kiscadale Publications, Edinburgh, 1989 / W.W. Norton, New York, 1963.

Sein, Kenneth and Joseph A. Withey, *The Great Po Sein: A Chronicle of the Burmese Theatre*, Indiana University Press, Bloomington, USA, 1965.

Shattock, E.H., *An Experiment in Mindfulness*, Rider, London, 2 ed, 1970.

Shute, Nevil, *The Chequer Board*, William Morrow, New York, 1947.

Stansky, P. and W. Abrahams, *The Unknown Orwell*, Paladin, London, 1974.

Strachan, Paul, *Pagan: Art and Architecture of Old Burma*, Kiscadale, Edinburgh, 1989.

Symes, Michael, *An Account of the Embassy to the Kingdom of Ava sent by the Governor-General of India in the year 1795*, W. Bulmer, London 1800 / Gregg, Farnborough, England, 1969.

Symes, Michael, *Journal of a Second Embassy*, Allen and Unwin, 1955.

Takeyama, Michio (Howard Hibbett, trans from Japanese), *Harp of Burma*. Tuttle, Tokyo, 1966/ Tuttle, Vermont, USA.

Thein Pe Myint (P. Milne, trans), *Selected Short Stories of Thein Pe Myint*, Cornell University Press, Ithaca, New York, 1973 / reprint edition, Rangoon 1975.

Theroux, Paul, *The Great Railway Bazaar*, Hamish Hamilton, London, 1975 / Random House, New York, 1975.

Thiha, Maung, *The Chindits and the Stars*, Regency, London, 1971.

Thompson, Edward, *Burmese Silver*. Faber & Faber, London, 1937 / Pan, 1948.

Wadley, Monica, *The Golden Stairs*, Doubleday, Garden City, New York, 1968.

Williams, J.H., *Elephant Bill*, Rupert Hart-Davis, London, 1965. **Extract 16.**

Yule, Sir Henry (introduction by Hugh Tinker), *A Narrative of the Mission Sent by the Governor General of India to the Court of Ava in 1855*, OUP (Oxford in Asia Historical Reprints) 1968.

Yule, Sir Henry, ed, *The Book of Sir Marco Polo*, John Murray, 1929.

Zawgyi (various, trans), *Modern Burmese Short Stories*, Rangoon, 1981.

Extracts

(1) Burma: Buddhism

Nu Yin, '*Two Strings of Beads*'

A poem on the oft-treated theme of youth and age by one of Burma's leading 20th century woman poets, set here in a Buddhist context. A Burmese rosary has 108 beads, representing the 108 signs possessed by the Buddha. This version is from Keith Bosley, ed, The Elek Book of Oriental Verse.

With skill, with care
striving to be   fair, her two cheeks
she tinges rose,   serene, smiling
her arching brows   she touches black,
serene, content
her forehead fringe   she dabs with scent
her scarlet lips   she decorates
with lipstick both   to make them fair
her glossy black   sweet-smelling hair
she knots on top   and trails it down
and in that hair
all fragrant kinds   of flowers she binds:
thus anointed   and thus adorned
striving, scheming   to be more fair

around her neck she hangs a string
of splendid pearls and is serene –
such is the way of young girls.

Meditating
meanwhile on the momentary
chance conjunction which is the self,
considering
and finding peace in this doctrine,
the old lady lowers her head
and lifts off one hundred and eight
beads on a string
which ceaselessly she tells, within
she is filled with quiet joy.

(2) Burma: Longyis

MiMi Khaing, *Burmese Family*

The ubiquitous longyi continues to set Burma apart from the trouser-wearing majority. In this extract from one of the best books on Burma and the Burmese, MiMi Khaing shows that this colourful garment has hidden uses.

Our picnics [at the Taik Wun's] always began with a lot of water-fun. We never used bathing dresses, but adapted our longyis for swimming. This longyi is shaped and wrapped, like the more famous sarong, at the waist normally, but women and girls take it above the bosom when they discard their jackets. This enables all our poorer women to bathe with perfect decorum at public wells and streams. After the bath a dry longyi is slipped on over the wet one which is then washed clean straight away. The poorest, who do not always possess a spare longyi, sometimes let themselves into a stream gradually, lifting the longyi higher as they go in, and when the water is bosom-high they keep the garment on their head, letting it down again as they emerge. Our use for the adaptability of the longyi was to stand on a diving platform with it opened wide at the bottom, jump feet first and let the air rush in, nicking the longyi in at the ankles as we struck the water. This makes you land with a balloon which floats you for a minute or two like those swollen celluloid ducks in babies' tubs. My friend Tin Tin Thoung was just like a swan on these occasions; she was not pretty normally, being very thin and angular, but she had a long and graceful neck, and when she floated on the water, gliding along with her neck rising out of her big round longyi, she looked like a beautiful swan to me.

(3) Burma: Love Songs

H. Fielding-Hall, *The Soul of a People*

Fielding-Hall's writings about Burma are much loved by the Burmese. His own introduction to this section makes an excellent headnote: 'In Burmese the love-songs are in a short, sweet rhythm, full of quaint conceits and word-music. I cannot put them into English verse, or give the flow of the originals in a translation. It always seems to me that Don Quixote was right when he said that a translation was like the wrong side of an embroidered cloth, giving the design without the beauty. But even in the plain, rough outline of a translation there is beauty here, I think'.

The moon wooed the lotus in the night, the lotus was wooed by the moon, and my sweetheart is their child. The blossom opened in the night, and she came forth; the petals moved, and she was born.

She is more beautiful than any blossom; her face is as delicate as the dusk; her hair is as night falling over the hills; her skin is as bright as the diamond. She is very full of health, no sickness can come near her.

When the wind blows I am afraid, when the breezes move I fear. I fear lest the south wind take her, I tremble lest the breath of evening woo her from me – so light is she, so graceful.

Her dress is of gold, even of silk and gold, and her bracelets are of fine gold. She hath precious stones in her ears, but her eyes, what jewels can compare unto them?

She is proud, my mistress; she is very proud, and all men are afraid of her. She is so beautiful and so proud that all men fear her.

In the whole world there is none anywhere that can compare unto her.

(4) Burma: Love Below a Mango Tree

MaMa Lay, *Not Out of Hate*

This novel depicts the clash between Burmese tradition and Western attitudes through the medium of a moving love story, the more powerful for being delicately sketched rather than explicitly described. This extract is part of a scene in which the elder sister realises that her younger sister has fallen in love with the older, westernised man. A translation was published in 1991.

Hta Hta awoke at night and looked around her. She did not know when they had dropped off to sleep, what time it was, nor when Way

Way (her young sister) had got up from the bed. The mosquito net was not down, the window not closed, and the light was still on. She could see the moon shining dimly outside. Apart from Aunt Thet's loud snoring, the house was silent. Far off in the distance, she heard the barking of dogs; she couldn't tell if it was just one dog barking or different dogs barking one after another. She closed her eyes, felt she was dozing off but did not let herself sleep; she must tell Way Way to close the window at the foot of the bed so that it wouldn't rain on the clothes. Hta Hta waited for Way Way to return from the lavatory and wondered what was taking her so long. Reluctantly she got up to close it herself and staggered sleepily to the window. As she got there she halted suddenly shocked by what she saw. Her whole body froze except for her hands which trembled violently as she held on to the window.

Hidden from the main road by the big mango tree, but revealed to her by the faint dappled moonlight shining through its branches, she saw Way Way and U Saw Han standing face to face, his arms around her neck embracing her. At first glance in the dark they were not recognisable, but when she saw their silhouettes there was no mistaking that it was her sister with U Saw Han. He was wearing a dark jacket and trousers, and Way Way was dressed as she had been earlier in the evening. The couple could not see Hta Hta from where they were, but she could see them well. She didn't want to see any more. She rushed back to the bed and threw herself down on it. Her heart pounded fearfully; she had to force herself to take slow breaths to calm down. Her thoughts were in confusion, how was she to even start to think about this problem? She couldn't drive from her mind U Saw Han's figure bent in embrace and Way Way's upturned face.

(5) Burma: Monks

U Pon-nya

A translation of an extract from a myit-taza, a sort of epistle in verse (1850). The writer had received a message from a friend and benefactor telling him about certain rumours that were circulating in the town. In this letter to his friend U Pon-nya asks him not to believe all he hears and explains the circumstances which gave rise to the gossip. He begins by explaining that he had visited the house of a layman in search of medicine. Translated by A.J. Allott.

A certain fellow from your district, it seems, an ox, an oaf with his arse where his mouth should be, took this event and going from house to house like some paid henchman, spread it around that I was going courting, no longer mindful of my monk's habit. He spread slander unchecked, most offensive to the ears of all who heard it and managed to create quite a scandal. On account of this, my lord, it seems you were mightily distressed, as if a buffalo had gored your heart, at the way everyone, but everyone in the town was blackening my name. You took it upon yourself to send me word of what was being said, not as a reprimand but just that I should know.

And so when I try to think how much I am indebted to you, I feel that you are like my true elder brother. This fellow's slanderous accusations that I run after women, that I am so fond of the girls that all are disgusted, are utterly unjust. Even though the whole town maliciously names me as a fornicator, please use your own judgement and believe only what you think should be believed.

And if I *were* interested in the sort of thing that creature suggested (I can tell you this because you are my true friend), there are girls – pretty and slender, not too small or too tall, just well proportioned, slim and slender, tender buds not too full nor too tight, could we say like creamy coconut, soft to the spoon's caress, or if not soft then firm but yielding to the knife's thrust, just the sort for princes and monks and quite unsuited for the young lads of the town; girls who come, far too many of them, to visit my monastery; young things with their hair still trimmed short, or just tossing their raven locks. I even have to take a cane to them to drive them away.

(6) Burma: Monks

MiMi Khaing, *Burmese Family*

This extract from Burmese Family describes the background to the Shinbyu ceremony when a Burmese boy leaves home to join the order. Travellers to modern Burma may well encounter such a ceremony on the road or at a pagoda.

It is the Buddhist belief that the attainment of a perfect life is as a man, as shown in Gautama Buddha's life as Prince Siddhartha. Prince Siddhartha was the son of King Suddhodana, who surrounded his son with all the luxury and splendour that his kingdom on the slopes of the Himalayas could offer. To prevent his son from renouncing his princely life for one of poverty and meditation he kept all sights of sorrow, sickness and decay hidden from him. He found him a perfect wife, beautiful, meek and affectionate, who bore him a son; but the prince in his excursions to a park in the city came across a decrepit old man, a sick old man and a corpse, which sights made him sad at the thought of human misery in this world. The next time, however, he saw a hermit which suggested that peace of mind was achievable by renunciation of the vanities of the world. On the night that his son was born, Prince Siddhartha made the Great Renunciation and left everything to go into solitude and find out the cause of misery, and the means of its removal. The Dhammapada says of the world:

> Come! behold this world which is like a decked royal chariot, wherein the foolish immerse themselves; but for the wise there is no attachment.

It is this renunciation which we symbolize in the shinbyu ceremony when a boy leaves his home and lives in the order. A parent who fails to hold the ceremony or get his son initiated in some other way fails in his first duty towards his son, and those who hold a shinbyu for orphans or the sons of the poor achieve great merit.

To provide a background symbolic of Prince Siddhartha's circumstances, parents spend as much as they can afford; a flagged pavilion is put up before the house, a multitude of people are invited for feasting, the boy is dressed in princely garments and jewels, and rides around the town on a white horse, with a procession following. For him to return and wash the powder off his face, to doff the turban and show the newly shaven head, to change the glittering clothes of silk for a plain yellow robe showing golden on the bare brown skin, – this is moving indeed. And when he comes back the next day in procession with other monks, his eyes cast down and his bowl before him, his mother makes obeisance to him for the first time, not as her son now but as one of the priestly order, a hpongyi, a "great glory". That must be a moment of spiritual plenitude in a mother's life.

I do not remember much about my brother's shinbyu, but I remember the beauty of his face as he came back in procession on that first day. A good face has its nobility enhanced by the complete absence of such adornment, even as is provided by the frame of hair or the line of neck clothing; it has to stand alone. I am often struck with the beautiful calm faces of some older monks. There is a look of repose which they wear easily after years of daily meditation and freedom from petty irritations and personal relationships, and a glow to the brown skin which is the result of years spent in clean and open surroundings, with sufficient to eat, and regularity of hours; the strongly marked eyebrows giving a nobility to the face when the head has been shorn. The unconscious reflection of this look on the face of a small boy touches us profoundly; there is a sweet solemnity on the young shaven face; the most mischievous boys become awed and chastened without any prompting.

(7) Burma: A Pwe

George Orwell, *Burmese Days*

This vivid extract from Burmese Days shows the liberal Flory's unsuccessful attempts to interest Elizabeth in Burmese culture. They visit a pwe or historical drama but Elizbeth is unimpressed, as she is later when he takes her to a Burmese market.

As he heard the drums Flory remembered that a *pwe* was being acted a little further down the road, opposite U Po Kyin's house; in fact, it was U Po Kyin who had made arrangements for the *pwe*, though someone else had paid for it. A daring thought occurred to Flory. He would take Elizabeth to the *pwe!* She would love it – she must; no one with eyes in his head could resist a *pwe*-dance. Probably there would be a scandal when they came back to the Club together after a long absence; but damn it! what did it matter? She was different from that herd of fools at the Club. And it would be such fun to go to the *pwe* together! At this moment the music burst out with a fearful pandemonium – a strident squeal of pipes, a rattle like castanets and the hoarse thump of drums, above which a man's voice was brassily squalling.

'Whatever is that noise?' said Elizabeth, stopping. 'It sounds just like a jazz band!'

'Native music. They're having a *pwe* – that's a kind of Burmese play; a cross between a historical drama and a revue, if you can imagine that. It'll interest you, I think. Just round the bend of the road here.'

'Oh,' she said rather doubtfully . . .

'He's telling them to bring on their best dancer in our honour,' Flory said. 'Look, here she comes.'

A girl who had been squatting at the back of the stage, smoking, stepped forward into the lamplight. She was very young, slim-shouldered, breastless, dressed in a pale blue satin *longyi* that hid her feet. The skirts of her *ingyi* curved outwards above her hips in little panniers, according to the ancient Burmese fashion. They were like the petals of a downward-pointing flower. She threw her cigar languidly to one of the men in the orchestra, and then, holding out one slender arm, writhed it as though to shake the muscles loose.

The orchestra burst into a sudden loud squalling. There were pipes like bagpipes, a strange instrument consisting of plaques of bamboo which a man struck with a little hammer, and in the middle there was a man surrounded by twelve tall drums of different sizes. He reached rapidly from one to another, thumping them with the heel of his hand. In a moment the girl began to dance. But at first it was not a dance, it was a rhythmic nodding, posturing and twisting of the elbows, like the movements of one of those jointed wooden figures on an old-fashioned roundabout. The way her neck and elbows rotated was precisely like a jointed doll, and yet incredibly sinuous. Her hands, twisting like snakeheads with the fingers close together, could lie back until they were almost along her forearms. By degrees her movements quickened. She began to leap from side to side, flinging herself down in a kind of curtsy and springing up again with extraordinary agility, in spite of the long *longyi* that imprisoned her feet. Then she danced in a grotesque posture as though sitting down, knees bent, body leaned forward, with her arms extended and writhing, her head also moving to the beat of the drums. The music quickened to a climax. The girl rose upright and whirled round as swiftly as a top, the panniers of her *ingyi* flying out about her like the petals of a snowdrop. Then the music stopped as abruptly as it had begun, and the girl sank again into a curtsy, amid raucous shouting from the audience.

Elizabeth watched the dance with a mixture of amazement, boredom and something approaching horror. She had sipped her drink and found that it tasted like hair oil. On a mat by her feet three Burmese girls lay fast asleep with their heads on the same pillow, their small oval faces side by side like the faces of kittens. Under cover of the music Flory was speaking in a low voice into Elizabeth's ear, commenting on the dance.

'I knew this would interest you; that's why I brought you here. . . .

(8) Danu-byu

Sein-dakyaw-thu, '*A Soldier's Letter*'

Danu-byu is a town on the Irrawaddy north of Rangoon. This poem from the mid 18th century is to the soldier's wife at home, written in the three-stanza yadu ◊ form, describing all too clearly the real-life sufferings of a soldier from Upper Burma when fighting in the wet, stormy and mosquito-infested delta region of Lower Burma. The poem is taken from Keith Bosley, ed, The Elek Book of Oriental Verse.

In Danubyu
when our shining sceptred lord pitched
his pavilion,
southward, northward still overcast
we tried to moor jammed together
but found nowhere.
Squalls whipped the waves into whirlpools:
to left, to right no oar could steer
no pole could punt nor paddle shift.

The water rose, boat with boat locked
prow pushed, stern pulled, hooks slipped, we thrashed
in the water, sank, choked, got soaked
tugged at ropes' ends, jumped, grabbed reed, rush
to reach the bank all sterns awash:
in wretched state we made our camp –
the night gloomy, dark and dim . . .
Of present woe
you – who before you bound your breasts
and loosed your hair
loved only me held me captive
my demure one my faultless one –
you know nothing:
'He is having good times abroad
in the army' – do you think that?
I fear you do. But no: at dusk
at dawn we strive in vain to scare
gadflies, midges which bite, suck blood.
Swarming facefuls –
mosquito nets do not stop them.
Troubles pile up –
thickets, bushes, rushes, reeds thick
on the ground, night wind, rain strike, slap:
homesick, I grieve –
they warned us it would be grim.

(9) Delta region

Maung Htin, *NgaBa* (*The Peasant*)

The opening paragraphs of a novel about the experiences of a Burmese peasant farmer during the Japanese occupation; a tale of hardship, poverty, forced labour, and rape, presented as seen through the eyes of a good-hearted but politically naive peasant, concerned less with anti-colonialism and independence than with his relations with fellow citizens – Karen, Chinese, Indian – of different races, and with his masters, the Japanese. The action takes place in Labutta, the nearest big town being Bassein. Translated by A.D. Allott

NgaBa worked as a tenant farmer, renting some 25 acres of land from landowner U Tha Gaung at a land-rent of 250 baskets of rice a year. This way of working the land, this tenant farmer's existence, had been inherited from his parents, who in their turn had worked for the parents of U Tha Gaung who, as a landowner, adopted the policy of only evei spending what needed to be spent. When fixing the contract he never used to write in the date on the form, which cost a mere 50 pyas, but would just get NgaBa's left thumbprint on it so that the government officials would recognise that the agreement was firmly concluded, and then would use the form again the following year. 'What do you expect? Otherwise it would mean spending 50 pyas *every* year and that would be a waste' he used to say.

NgaBa's whole world consisted of the large area of paddy fields called Nauk-pyan-to where he and his fellow peasants lived and the nearby village of Hseit-kyi-gon, where U Tha Gaung lived. He had never even once visited any other town or village – and what need would he have to do so? Having once been to Hseit-kyi-gon village to buy provisions and having made friends there with the Chinese trader Hton-Ar at his general store, he had no need to go elsewhere.

At the times when he wanted a little extra money to make a special offering of food to the monks, it was a matter of pride that he was on good enough terms with the Indian money lender, Anapaleh, to be able to get some cash from him on credit (against the security of the coming rice crop) without letting U Tha Gaung know. As for Mandalay, Rangoon and other big towns like that, he sometimes dreamt about them at night when he had indigestion but that was all. And he remembered that the year he and his wife Mi Paw got married, when he had gone to U Tha Gaung's house to conclude his tenancy agreement, he had met a well-to-do city gentleman there. This person had said that in Rangoon the great Shwei-dagon pagoda was like a towering mountain of gold and that it shone so brilliantly that it filled one with awe. This had made a great impression on him. And, people said, there were rickshaws, motorcars, trams, great houses and buildings like heavenly palaces. He had returned to his paddy-fields at Nauk-pyan-to with all this ringing in his ears, and that night he had dreamt about the great city of Rangoon.

(10) Mandalay

Maung Maung, *To a Soldier Son*

This extract is taken from an account of Dr Maung Maung's childhood, early education and service in the Burma Defence Army. He also describes the history and background of the members of the Burma Army which has ruled the country since September 1988. In August 1988 Dr Maung Maung served briefly as prime minister.

Times were tranquil then. I could ride out on my bicycle way out of town, to fish, to hunt or roam. Yankin Hill to the east, Patheingyi village at its foot, and the Mandalay Hill northwards, were familiar haunts. And, of course, the palace, whose pillars and halls and rooms still remain vivid in my memory even though they are now gone. Friends and I would swim in the ponds where princes and princesses once played. But we were not awed by history; we swam there because there was nowhere else. . . .

There was a tamarind tree at the back of our home. The tree was my refuge. I would climb up and sit in its branches for hours, imagining myself a Tarzan. All I lacked was Jane. From the height of the tree I could observe the compound of the Convent behind our home; girls at play or at their daily chores, nuns in white moving about, always busy at something. . . .

Sometimes I would sit in the lower branches of the tamarind tree, proclaim myself the guardian *nat* and call upon my younger sisters to bring their offerings. They did, with great respect, and I would invoke the choicest blessings for them.

The tree provided food and fuel too. Sometimes mother found herself short of firewood and the money to buy it. I would go up with a chopping knife and cut down some dead and dry branches. Tender tamarind leaves in April provided tasty dishes and soup. Tender fruits were used for curry; ripe fruits could be stored, or made into sweets with jaggery and sugar.

The tree is no more. It was felled by bomb splinters during the war. Walls and the roof of our home were torn up too. One old Indian who had lived with us for many years was killed in the insurgent activities that swept Mandalay not long after independence [ie 1948–49]. Whenever I go home on all too brief visits I remember the tree and old Jathu.

(11) Mandalay: Arakan Pagoda

U Lat, *Shwe-pyi-so*

A scene from an early Burmese novel of great charm. The title means Ruler of the Golden City, the name of the hero. The young hero, Shwe-pyi-zo, sees the heroine, Khin Hta at the great Arakan Pagoda (known as 'Maha-myat-muni' in Burmese). They get separated in the crowd before he manages to talk to her. He discovers where she lives and visits the house on the pretext of returning a string of beads which he says she left on the pagoda platform. This ruse alarms young Khin Hta who has never talked with a resourceful bachelor before. Partly from fright she exchanges her beads with his. When he leaves Khin Hta questions her maid, Ma Gun. Translated by A.J. Allott.

K. *Hta*: What did he take my beads away for?
G*un*: Why, you gave them to him, my dear. Of course he would take them.
K. *Hta*: But I didn't *give* them to him.
G*un*: How could he take them if you didn't give them to him?
K. *Hta*: He just put them in his pocket, I couldn't stop him.
G*un*: Yes, but you took them off your wrist for him, didn't you, my dear?
K. *Hta*: How could I not take them off? He . . . He said 'Shall I take them off for you?' So of course I had to take them off quickly myself.
G*un*: You should have just refused to take off the beads.
K. *Hta*: But then *he* would have held my hand and taken them off.
G*un*: And what would have happened if he had held your hand, then?
K. *Hta*: Just you try having your hand held, Gun.
G*un*: Oh, if only that would happen to me, and as soon as possible, my dear.
K. *Hta*: You really are keen to have your hand held, aren't you?
G*un*: Yes, that's true. We poor women folk have to take a thing when it comes. Make hay while the sun shines, as they say. If you don't seize a chance like this, but just sit around and wait, then for sure we'll all end up old maids.
[The effect of Gun's advice is that from now on Khin Hta sadly neglects her lessons and Gun has to sing love-songs to her and repeat over and over again every word that the young man ever said.]

(12) Pagan

Maurice Collis, *She was a Queen*

Ma Saw, the innocent village girl in this extract, eventually goes on to become chief queen, in this novel set in the last two reigns of the Kingdom of Pagan.

Half an hour later the old woman approached and said:

'A message has come that His Majesty will see you this evening.'

Now Ma Saw was only an adolescent of sixteen. She had had no experience of life outside a country village, but she possessed the secret of an intense femininity. Very close to the earth, she had something of its power. At this intelligence that she was to go shortly into the presence, she was not as abashed as she might have been. She had seen the King in public and had some clue of how to conduct herself with him in private. Moreover, she was very intelligent and had plenty of aplomb. Accordingly she replied to the old woman with a little pout: 'When the King calls, I am ready.'

It was not very much after this that the call came. The old woman bustled onto her feet. Ma Saw rose gracefully and followed her. They passed down corridors open on one side to the night and were admitted into the King's chamber by a side door.

Usana half reclined on a low couch. He was dressed negligently in loose silk and though fatigued and anxious wore his habitual expression of good nature. To one side knelt a couple of ladies-in-waiting. Otherwise the lofty room, carved and lacquered in low relief, was empty. The old woman retired, leaving Ma Saw just inside the door.

'Come and sit here,' said Usana, pointing to a rug beside him.

With a fluttering movement, bent double, her palms together, she approached and like a little bird lit on the mat. She smiled.

The King was pleased. He did not care for shy women, more particularly that night, when he was upset. And she was very graceful, almost like that flying spirit on the temple wall. He had sent for her because he wished to distract himself from gloomy thoughts. . . . Ma Saw had now joined the King on the couch. She knelt beside him and had taken up a yak-tail whisk. There were a few mosquitoes about and these she dusted away, swinging the whisk in time with the music. Then dropping it, she pretended that one of the insects had bitten him on the arm. With playful concern she leant forward and rubbed the place with her tiny palm. As she did so, he breathed in her ear, 'Those hands, I knew they were lively,' in a tone which showed that the influence which Yazathingyan had seen approaching at Kanbyu was clasping him now. The ladies-in-waiting, happy that the master was more himself again, began singing a popular song of the day:

Our Father rowed to the Island,
Where grows the rose-apple tree:
The roses and apples were mingled,
A marvel to see.

O roses and apples, he chanted,
For ever that cluster and swing,
How is it I think of a finger
That enters a ring?

They sang this humorously, with its variations, sometimes pressing the innuendo, sometimes pretending to disguise it, as if startled.

Usana complained at this stage of irritation on his back. With quite an anxious look Ma Saw slipped off her jacket, to have her arms free, we must suppose, and leant over him. Putting her hand under the loose neck of his shirt, she peeped in.

'I have the place,' she exclaimed.

'How did you know without my telling you?' He laughed.

'The King has the softest skin,' she replied luxuriously. 'I saw a red streak and knew the irritation must be there. Let me massage it.' And taking a little ointment from a gold box by the bed, she began rubbing gently, letting her hand wander by degrees over his whole body.

The ladies-in-waiting, who for all the licence of their song had been watching the course of events with care, now decided that they had done their part. They could withdraw without risk of disturbing the close understanding clearly established between their master and the new lady. Indeed, looking again they saw that it was imperative for them to withdraw at once. So harping a vigorous finale they danced into the shadows.

(13) Rangoon

Maurice Collis, *Trials in Burma*

Whether writing fiction, autobiography or history, Collis was one of the most perceptive Western observers of Burma. This extract from his memoirs of his time as a colonial official describes the marriage of a descendant of Burmese royal family.

On another occasion chance allowed me a peep behind the scenes of Burmese life. One morning towards the end of 1928 I was sitting at home in my study when a car drove up to the door and a Burmese woman got out. I went into the hall to receive her.

'I am Ma Lat', she said in English, a perfect English without trace of an accent.

Ma Lat – I had not seen her before, but I knew of her, of course. She was the Princess Teik Tin Ma Lat of Limbin, the Middle Princess or second daughter of the Limbin Prince, who had been King Thibaw's brother. When the British took Mandalay in 1885, King Thibaw was exiled to a remote spot in the Bombay Presidency and, later, the Limbin Prince to Allahabad. Ma Lat was in her 'teens when the Crown Prince of Germany visited India before the war. It is related that he was introduced to her at a party in the Allahabad club of which her father was a member, and that afterwards he used to say that she was the most striking woman he had met on his eastern tour. She became engaged to be married about that time to the heir-apparent of Nepal – a love match it was said – but the story goes that the Brahmin hierarchy of Nepal set their faces against the marriage because Ma Lat was a Buddhist. The heir-apparent died, it was alleged, by poison.

After the war the Prince of Limbin was allowed to return to Burma. Besides Ma Lat, he had two other daughters and a son. They found the place much changed. The dynasty, Mandalay, the court were nearly forgotten. The Burmese took no interest in the remnant of the royal family. The aspirations of the upper class were now for a modern form of government, the talk being all of what sort of a constitution Parliament could be induced to grant. The country people, whose approach to such matters was astrological, believed that the mandate of the old dynasty was exhausted and that the new king – for that was the way they translated the constitutional change which was pending – would be of a different stock.

So it was that the princesses, charming, accomplished and accustomed to the best society in Allahabad, found themselves nonentities in their own country. English officials were too cautious to encourage them and the poor girls fitted in nowhere. They lived with their father in a house called Radana Theinga – the classical name of the former capital Shwebo – and made friends as best they could.

That was as much as I knew of Ma Lat. I took her into the drawing-room, wondering what it was that had brought her to see me.

She sat down on the sofa, a beautiful woman, in a blue silk skirt and a jacket of white lawn, her complexion corn-coloured, her eyes large and brilliant, and with exquisite hands. As she seemed a little diffident in beginning, I offered her some refreshment. At last she said:

'I have come to see you in your capacity as registrar.'

One of my minor offices was that of Registrar of Births, Deaths, and Marriages. I should have guessed her errand then, but I was slow.

'As registrar', I repeated. 'Yes?'

'I'm going to get married, and I want you to perform the ceremony'.

'Certainly', I replied. 'May I ask, are you marrying a – ?'

'No', she said, 'I'm marrying an Englishman'.

'If you will give me the particulars – '

'Herbert Bellamy'.

Mr. Bellamy was a bookmaker.

The marriage of the Princess Ma Lat of Limbin to Mr. Bellamy aroused little interest in Rangoon. The day was fixed, 19 October. Normally civil marriages were performed in my office, but on this occasion I arranged to go to the Prince's house.

There were not many guests and Mr. Merrikin, the Commissioner of Police, was the only high official present. Mr. and Mrs. Manook were doing the honours, Manook, the Armenian, whom King Thibaw had employed, and whose wife is known to the readers of *The Lacquer Lady* as Selah. Hardly a Burman of any position was to be seen. I took my seat at a table at the end of an upper room. The guests were arranged on chairs in front of me, leaving a passage to a door on the verandah. At 4.48 p.m. – the moment selected by the astrologers – the princess was seen approaching through the door, accompanied by her younger sister and the Prince of Limbin. She was dressed reminiscently of the court of Mandalay in a royal *htamein* of oyster-coloured silk set with silver diamanté; her hair, in the loose tail-style, was charged with orchids and there were pearls winding on her throat and breast. She came forward slowly, waving a white fan, with a look of dignity and emotion on her face. Mr. Bellamy followed in a morning coat.

The ceremony of civil marriage is exceedingly bald, for it consists of hardly more than the taking of oaths. When some documents are signed it is all over. On that occasion its abruptness seemed almost rude. I declared them married and took Ma Lat's hand. The occasion seemed to me strange and disturbing. Had the rape of Mandalay ended in this?

(14) Rangoon

U Sein Tin, War Diary

Despite the fears expressed in this extract, the destruction of Rangoon was not as bad as originally feared (he was writing in Mandalay in March 1942). Translated by Colleen Beresford.

Burma has met with a fate no one could have imagined possible. Rangoon is in ashes. Rangoon, the capital city, that has been such a pleasant seat of government for so long; a city we could be proud of, with its large buildings and gardens, its impressive riverfront and its strand, the paramount town in all the land, the fount of its literature, renowned for its newspapers; Rangoon is in ruins.

Tonight, a broadcast by Major Coates announced that all important buildings and installations in Rangoon have been destroyed. Last Saturday (5.3.42) at two in the afternoon, the Electricity Generating Station, all buildings and warehouses along the waterfront, all government buildings, and the installations of the Burmah Oil Company refinery at Syriam were blow up. [Translator's note: by the British as part of the denial or scorched-earth policy.] Fires which started that day are still raging. [They say that the] smoke and flames of the blazing city can be seen as far away as Tharrawaddy. Just to hear the description of flames leaping high into the sky makes my hair stand on end. Can any Burman hear all this without getting the shivers? For Rangoon to be destroyed in this way must mean that Burma's *karma* is bad, indeed.

(15) Syriam: Kyaik-hkauk Pagoda

Minister Pade-tha-ya-za, '*The Farmer's Family*'

A poem by one of the earliest writers to choose to write verse about humble peasant folk. The poet's grave still stands in Syriam, in the grounds of the Kyaik-hkauk Pagoda. The influence of song forms, probably from Thailand, is shown by the end-rhymes of the four stanzas (present in the English), which are additional to the usual internal rhymes of classical verse (not attainable in the English translation!). From Keith Bosley, ed, The Elek Book of Oriental Verse.

In the monsoon   when the rain falls
goodman and wife   merrily go
hand tugging hand   their bodies clad
in shirt, sarong   tattered and torn
with red cotton turbans on their heads.

Drenched by the rain   their bodies bare
sons and daughters   are borne along:
while the man ploughs   he grips his pipe
drawing furrows   across the field
and water brims over the rice-beds.

In their baskets   long-legged frogs
water-snails, jute   in a jumble
tender-stew-leaves   sweet potatoes
rot-thorn, pumpkin: they lug the lot –
a mass of legs, shells, leaves, flowers and buds.

Tasty? Oh yes –   oceans of juice:

moonflower, mouse-ear   mixed together.
When they get home   they rush to cook:
the rice is hot   the stew is hot
with (phew! phew!) chillies cut into shreads.

Crammed on all sides   the sturdy brood
gobble and gulp   fistfuls of food.

(16) Upper Taungdwin River

Lt Col J.H. Williams, *Elephant Bill*

Williams's memoirs of over 20 years spent working with elephants in the Burmese jungle are full of gripping stories. Here a female elephant, Ma Shwe, and her three-month-old calf are caught in a river in spate.

There was a sudden rise in the water, as if a two-foot bore had come down, and the calf was washed clean over the mother's hindquarters and was gone. She turned to chase it, like an otter after a fish, but she had travelled about fifty yards downstream and, plunging and sometimes afloat, had crossed to my side of the river, before she had caught up with it and got it back. For what seemed minutes, she pinned the calf with her head and trunk against the rocky bank. Then, with a really gigantic effort, she picked it up in her trunk and reared up until she was half standing on her hind legs, so as to be able to place it on a narrow shelf of rock, five feet above the flood level.

Having accomplished this, she fell back into the raging torrent, and she herself went away like a cork. She well knew that she would now have a fight to save her own life, as less than 300 yards below where she had stowed her calf in safety there was a gorge. If she were carried down, it would be certain death. I knew, as well as she did, that there was one spot between her and the gorge where she could get up the bank, but it was on the other side from where she had put her calf. By that time, my chief interest was in the calf. It stood, tucked up, shivering and terrified, on a ledge just wide enough to hold its feet. Its little, fat, protruding belly was tightly pressed against the bank.

While I was peering over at it from about eight feet above, wondering what I could do next, I heard the grandest sounds of a mother's love I can remember. Ma Shwe had crossed the river and got up the bank, and was making her way back as fast as she could, calling the whole time – a defiant roar, but to her calf it was music. The two little ears, like little maps of India, were cocked forward, listening to the only sound that mattered, the call of her mother. . . .

Biographies and literary notes

Burmese Silver (1937). This adventure novel by Edward Thompson involves a quest in which a retired Indian Civil Service official, Clive Powell, journeys to the Burma of the 1880s to look up a friend, Gabriel Travers. Like a Rajah Brooke of Sarawak, Travers has managed to set himself up as the prince of a tribe of Northern Burmese headhunters, where he becomes a sinister character in the same mould as Kurtz in *Heart of Darkness*. Thompson also works in the theme of the Eurasian: Travers's daughter, Princess Pradita, is half Shan, and Powell's travelling companion and guide, 'Gussie' is also half Burmese. These two characters, one a princess and the other a commoner, balance well in this indictment of race prejudice.

Chequer Board, The. This novel by Nevil Shute concerns a rough diamond, Captain John Turner, who had served in the second world war, survived an air crash on his way home to be demobbed in England, and is slowly dying of his head injuries. Like Powell in Edward Thompson's *Burmese Silver* ◊ Captain Turner sets out on a quest to find three of his war time comrades.

COLLIS, Maurice (1889–1973). British administrator and writer. Born and brought up in Ireland, he joined the Indian Civil Service in 1912 and was posted to Burma. His books set in Burma include *Trials in Burma* (1938, Extract 13) and *She was a Queen* (1937, Extract 12). His many other books on South-east Asia include *Siamese White* (1936) and a biography, *Raffles* (1966).

Glass Palace Chronicle, The (1829–32). A history of Burma in prose compiled at the command of King Ba-gyi-daw by a committee of scholars working in a chamber of the palace (decorated with coloured glass mosaic inlay – hence the name). The *hmannan ya-zawin-daw-gyi*, largely based on the previous chronicle of U Kala ◊ was written in 38 sections covering Burmese history up to 1821; the committee covered the accession to the throne of the reigning monarch and then halted. There is an English translation of the first section concerning Pagan. *She was a Queen* (Extract 12) by Maurice Collis is based on *The Glass Palace Chronicle*.

Golden Stairs, The (1968). Novel about the flight of a group of children from the invading Japanese in the second world war. One of them, Kyi Myint, or Ken, is the son of the Scot, Tom McNeil and Ma Hla Galay, Tom's Burmese wife. The children are left in the charge of Monica Wadley who is to lead them through various places in Burma and then out via the dreadful **Hukong Valley** trek (of 1941) to India. Ultimately, in order to survive, the children abandon Miss Wadley.

Harp of Burma (1964). This superb novel by the Japanese novelist Michio Takeyama concerns a company of Japanese soldiers stranded in Burma at the end of the second world war. The hero of the story is a corporal, Mizushima, who taught himself to play the Burmese harp and to lead his fellow soldiers in song to give them courage to face the enemy as they try to escape from Burma after the end of the war. The magic of this singing, especially of the tune 'Home Sweet Home', enables his company to surrender to the British army without bloodshed. Mizushima is separated from his fellows who, in the months that follow, search for him, longing to see him again, until in the end they learn to their amazement that he has decided to become a Buddhist monk and to spend the rest of his life in Burma.

HLA, U (Ludu U Hla) (1910–83). Prolific political journalist, publisher and writer. Founded a monthly magazine *Kyi-pwa-ye* (*Success*) in 1933, and the Ludu Daily newspaper (*The People*) in 1946 in Mandalay. During 1953–57 he was jailed in Rangoon for his communist sympathies; from this time he has left a record (translated as *The Caged Ones*) of the life stories of his fellow prisoners, the petty criminals, thieves and prostitutes, alerting his readers to the social conditions which drove so many young people to a life of crime. Perhaps his greatest debt to posterity is his life-long interest in the folk tales of the many races of the Union; these he collected tirelessly throughout his life, publishing some 40–50 books in all.

Jatakas. Some of these famous Pali tales are quite brief, while others are as long as novelettes. Those which relate the Buddha's experiences in a previous incarnation as an animal, (for example elephant, monkey, hare or quail) resemble the Greek fables of Aesop and are used to point a moral; in the longer tales (especially the last ten of the collection, in Burmese known as the *Zat-kyi hseh-ba*, 'the ten great stories') the Buddha usually appears as a royal personage exhibiting some virtue worthy to be emulated. Each tale begins by noting the occasion which gave rise to its telling and ends with the Buddha disclosing which of the characters in the story he was himself in a previous incarnation.

JUDSON, Adoniram (1788–1850). American Baptist missionary and linguist who compiled the first comprehensive Burmese-English dictionary, standard tool for 100 years and only just about to be replaced by modern dictionaries. During the first Anglo-Burmese war (1824–6) he was imprisoned; his wife's account of this dreadful period, of her struggle to feed him in prison, and of the death of her new-born baby, is almost too harrowing to read. There is a memorial stone to him at **Ava**; his first wife, who died in 1826 shortly after his release, is buried near **Moulmein**.

KALA, U (Maung) (1678–1738). Author of the first full-scale historical work in Burmese, the *Maha Ya-zawin-gyi* (*Great Chronicle*), covering the period from the beginning of the world to 1711 AD. The work is based on various sources (poems, legends, inscriptions), is written in an excellent prose style and was accepted as a standard reference. It was incorporated almost verbatim into later chronicles such as *The Glass Palace Chronicle* ◊. Little is known about U Kala except that he was a private scholar who apparently wrote for his own interest rather than for a royal master; his work shows a considerable concern for factual accuracy.

KHIN KHIN LAY (Dagon) (1904–83). The first important Burmese woman writer, she was the granddaughter of a minister from the court at Mandalay. During the 1920s and 1930s she wrote short stories, mostly published in *Dagon* Magazine (hence her pen-name), many of which depicted, often rather sentimentally, the hardships of peasant women's life, and the growing dissatisfaction in the country with colonial rule. Later, in tune with the rising spirit of nationalism, came stirring historical novels such as *Sa-hso-daw* (*Royal Bard*, 1935) set in Mandalay during the reign of the last Burmese king.

KIN-WUN, Mingyi (1822–1908). A remarkable man who served as a minister under the last two kings of Burma and later headed a consultative body of ministers under the British. He was sent as an envoy by King Mindon in 1871 and 1873 to Italy, France and Great Britain, and he wrote two detailed journals of these missions known as *The London Diary* and *The Paris Diary*. His intelligent interest in everything he saw and his careful accounts of the negotiations he undertook are a model of official reporting. He had never before seen a railway train or read by the light of gas-lamps; and the text of his diaries circulated in the palace at Mandalay in palm leaf copies, only seeing print after 1900.

LAT, U (1866–1921). The first important Burmese novelist (see Extract 11). Son of a Rangoon jeweller, he had an English education together with a true Burmese upbringing; he became a senior police officer and travelled widely. He knew his country well and felt great love and respect for the traditional Burmese Buddhist way of life and its moral values; he was concerned that these should not be swept aside by the advancing tide of Westernisation and English education. His two major novels were *Sabeh-bin* (*Jasmine*), 1911, and *Shwe-pyi-zo* (*Ruler of the Golden Land*, 1914). In both the main, somewhat idealized love story with a happy ending brought about by unlikely, virtually magic coincidences is interwoven with a true-to-life sub-plot set in Rangoon. In style his works are a mixture of old and new; songs as in the earlier *pya-zat* plays, quotations from classic poems, short sermons, proverbs galore, passages of poetic description together with exciting narrative and natural, often very comic dialogue.

MAMA LAY (Gya-neh-gyaw MaMa Lay) (1917–82). Modern Burma's foremost woman author as well as tireless journalist with a vigorous, independent intellect. Later in her life a determined advocate of traditional medicine. With her first husband, U Chit Maung she ran and wrote political articles for the *Gya-neh-gyaw* (*Weekly Thunderer*) from 1939. After the war she also wrote short stories and novels, not in large quantity but on serious social and cultural themes. A fearless and outspoken critic, she often depicts gifted independent-minded women at odds with their position in society. Her novel *Mon-ywei mahu* (*Not Out of Hate*, 1955) – Extract 4 – offers the reader a series of fascinating insights into the social history of the late colonial period and into the conflict between Western and Burmese culture. It is also a moving account of a young girl's struggle against misunderstanding and the suffocating love of her Westernized husband.

MIMI KHAING. Born into a Burmese Civil Service family, MiMi Khaing grew up in the town of Ye in the district of Tavoy. She went to Rangoon University and in 1937 won a scholarship to study domestic science in the UK. She spent the war years in New Delhi; from 1951–63 she was Principal of a school in Taung-gyi. As well as bringing up three children she was on her own for the six years (1962–68) that her husband was imprisoned by the then military government. In addition to *The Burmese Family* (Extracts 2 and 6) she has written *Cook and Entertain the Burmese Way* and *The World of Burmese Women*, a valuable sociological work.

MIN-THU-WUN (U Wun) (1909–). Poet, literary historian, translator, lexicographer. Studied at Rangoon, Oxford, London and Yale universities. One of the exponents of the modern *Khit*-san (Experiment for a New Age) movement, he brought new themes and attitudes into short stories and poetry in the 1930s, and demonstrated that great poetry could be written in simple language.

MONIN, P. (1883–1940). Burmese writer, of humble origin, he was educated in English and Latin at Catholic missionary schools in preparation for taking holy orders. At 19, realizing that if he became a priest he would have to remain celibate, he abandoned his training and plunged back into ordinary Burmese life. Always a rebel, he led an unsettled, impecunious life as a teacher, labourer, translator, journalist (from 1914 on the *Thuriya* (*Sun*) newspaper), novelist and film-producer. Opposed to the tyranny of tradition and superstition, his writings show a constant preoccupation with the individual.

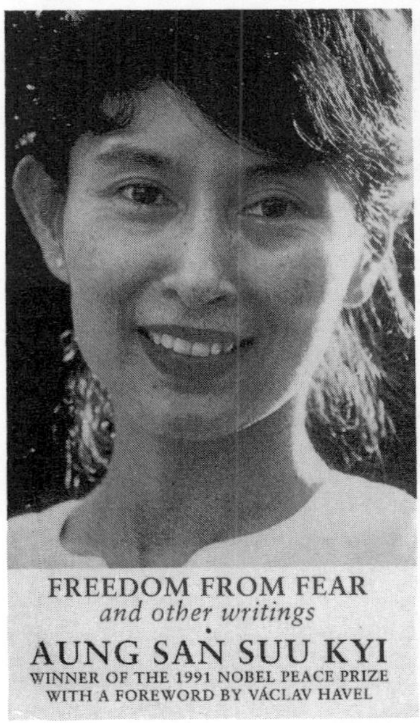

Mya-zedi inscription. A stone inscription set up in Pagan by Prince Rajakumar in 1113 to record the dedication of a temple, the Gu-byauk-gyi ('great decorated temple') that he had built in the hope of earning merit for his ailing father, the great King Kyan-zit-tha. The inscription, a four-sided pillar which stands now in the enclosure of the nearby Mya-ze-di pagoda where it was discovered in 1911, is famous for two reasons: first, because it has four different languages, Pali, Mon, Burmese and Pyu, on its four sides; secondly because it is the earliest dated inscription in Burmese, and thus could be said to mark the beginning of written Burmese literature. As the text is the same on all four sides, it also gives us clues to the Pyu language which is no longer understood today; hence it has earned the name of the Rosetta Stone of Burma.

Myit-taza. An epistle or highly stylized versified letter (lit 'letter of loving-kindness'), originally a letter written by a monk on behalf of a layman who did not know how to write, to convey an important message. The letter, on palm-leaf, would be passed round the village and read aloud and admired. In the 19th century, the writers of such epistles (the monk Kyi-gan Shin-gyi, U Pon-nya ◊) began to use the genre more and more to show off their own wit and literary prowess.

ORWELL, George (Eric Blair) (1903–50). See 'Orwell in Burma', pp 24–25.

PADE-THA-YA-ZA (1683?–1754). A court minister and poet of the Taung-ngu period, a brilliant innovator in genre and subject matter. He wrote a court drama about a magic horse with a ruby eye (*Maniket*), an entirely new form for Burmese literature; his best known *pyo* (*Thu-za pyo*) is not on a religious subject but is based on the Hindu legend of the fairy Manohari, which was well known in Thailand at the time. Most importantly, he left us four short songs, *tya-bweh*, which for the first time in Burmese literature tell about the pleasures of ordinary village life and describe simple peasants, farmers and boatmen at work.

PON-NYA, U (1812–67). Born in Sale, Upper Burma, much-travelled poet, dramatist, essayist and letter-writer. Today we should call him a 'man-about-town'; in his day he was a 'monk-about-court', learned and devout, brilliant and witty, eloquent and charming (see Extract 5). Women flocked to his monastery to hear his sermons, he was in constant demand as a composer of *myit-taza* (epistles) ◊ for other people, and he was one of the first writers of stage plays (*pya-zat* ◊, literally 'shown-story'). When Mindon came to the throne (1853), Pon-nya became the court poet of Crown Prince Kanaung, and was not afraid in his dramas to satirize various aspects of life at court, by apt choice of subjects from the *jataka*. He excelled in writing brilliant, flowing dialogue, which although rhymed, came nearer to the spoken language than the literary prose of his day. Never good at keeping out of trouble, he met his death at the hands of his 'gaoler' while detained on the king's orders under suspicion of conspiracy; it seems that the latter was jealous of U Pon-nya's intrigue with his wife.

Pya-zat. Burmese drama (lit 'shown story'; *zat* derives from Pali *jataka*).

Originally a stage presentation of a jataka story; by 19th century a play, in heavily rhymed prose, written, first for performance at court, later for a wider, more popular audience. *Pyazat* began to be printed, complete with additional songs, in the 1870s and sold widely throughout Burma. They are the precursors of the modern novel.

Pyo. A long Burmese poem (anything from 20–200 pages) in classical verse form, mostly on religious themes derived from *jataka* stories or episodes in the life of the Buddha. Earlier 15–16th century *pyo*, written by monks (Rat-hta-tha-ra), are more admired than later ones which have been written as recently as the early 20th century.

RAT-HTA-THA-RA (Shin) (1468–1530). A monk-poet, the greatest writer of the Ava period, famous for five long religious poems (*pyo*), the first written during his teens, as well as numerous lyrics and a detailed and lively *mawgun* describing the building of a pagoda at Tada-u in Upper Burma. His masterpiece, the *Kogan Pyo* (1523), literally '*pyo* in nine sections' is based on the *Hatthi-pala jataka* and presents in a striking way the conflicting claims of the celibate and the wordly life. In his youth he had composed a poem to his betrothed, 'a smiling princess with her golden breasts half-covered, half-exposed', and in the early days of his monkhood he was frank enough to admit in his verse that he was tempted to leave the Order and return to married life. His understanding of human emotions and his poetic skill have made him one of Burma's most cherished and admired poets.

SEIN-DAKAW-THU (U Aw) (1736–1771). Soldier-poet who began composing at a young age. He became court poet to King Alaunghpaya (1752–60), the founder of the last Burmese dynasty, for whom he wrote traditional eulogies and panegyrics. He is most admired today for his early *yadu* poems, into which he introduced new topics such as mud on the battlefield and mosquitoes in Lower Burma (Extract 8) and simple, vivid language.

SEIN TIN, U (1899–1942), widely known under his pen-name Theikpan Maung Wa. Essayist, literary critic, short story writer, the first graduate in Burmese literature from Rangoon University (1927). He spent a year at Oxford, about which he wrote an amusing work called *Oxford Diary*. Joined the ICS and served as a civil servant in many parts of Burma, until shot by bandits at the beginning of the Japanese occupation. He was the leading exponent of a new style of prose-writing known as *Khit-san* (Experiment for a New Age) together with leading poets Zaw-gyi and Min-thu-wun ◊. He is best known for his short sketches, part fiction, part documentary, of Burmese provincial and village life, whose hero, Maung Lu Aye, is largely a self-portrait. He gives a realistic and sympathetically critical picture of Burmese life between 1929 and 1936, pointing out its backwardness and follies with dry, unsentimental humour.

THAKIN Ko-daw Hmaing (U Lun) (1876–1964). Poet, playwright, political commentator and satirist, historian, staunch nationalist, the single most important literary personality in modern Burma before the second world war. Born in the village of

Waleh in Lower Burma, he was a great scholar in his own tongue and never learned English well. Under the name Maung Lun, by about 1910 he had reached a wide popular audience through his 80 or more plays (*pya-zat* ◊) on themes drawn from Burmese history and legend. Only four or five survive as he preferred not to attach his name to such 'frivolous' works. Around 1911 he became interested in politics through working with Burmese politicians on the *Thuriya* (*Sun*) newspaper; from then on he wrote regular pieces on current political events, brilliantly presented as literary poems with an accompanying satirical 'learned' commentary (called in Pali *tika*. An acknowledged master of his chosen poetic form (called *le-gyo-gyi*), he was also an inspiration to the growing generation of nationalists, urging them to decisive action (such as strikes) while at the same time chiding them for futile squabbling and political opportunism.

THAW-DA Swe (1919–). Born in Lower Burma, he was the eldest son of a well-to-do paddy farmer. He did not go to university and when war broke out, he found work as a pony-cart driver, then tried trading, lost money, lived an irregular life, and finally began writing with a very funny story (1947) in the newly established magazine, *Shu-mawa*. In his earliest work Thaw-da Swe was rarely able to resist a laugh, a pun, or a vulgar joke; but later he turned to satire, presenting sometimes quite unflattering portraits of his fellow writers, more often powerful condemnations of stupidity, greed and cruelty. Thus in the collection *Bawa hto hto*, (*Many Lives*, 1961) based on his war-time experience of running a tea-shop, he shocks the reader with the life-story of a young prostitute whom he had befriended. This story, 'Man preys on man', describes without a trace of sentimentality how local men look forward heartlessly to the death of the exhausted young prostitute, as her funeral will be the excuse for seven days of gambling and feasting.

THEIN Pe Myint (1914–78). Son of a minor government official from Upper Burma, Thein Pe Myint began writing fiction while a student at the University of Rangoon. He took up journalism while studying law in Calcutta, where he came in touch with Bengali communists and made a life-long commitment both to writing with a social purpose and to left-wing politics. His first novel *Tet hpon-gyi*, (*Modern Monk*; 1937) created a sensation because of its portrayal of certain Buddhist monks as corrupt and sexually immoral. Angry monks demanded that the work be banned. His pre-war experiences as a student, with the nationalist movement, his extensive travels inside and outside Burma, during the war, his expulsion from the Burmese Communist Party, and his involvement in political and social matters have all found their reflection in several major novels and thirty or so short stories; he has also chronicled his career as a writer in *yun-daw-i ahcit-u*, (*My First Love – Literature*, 1974). *Thabeik-hmauk kyaung-tha* (*Student Boycotter*, 1937) gives a picture of the 1936 students' strike at Rangoon University *Lan-za paw-bi* (*The Way Out*, 1949), covers the confused period of 1945–47; *Ashei-ga nei-wun Htwet-thi-pama* (*As Sure as the Sun Rising in the East*, 1958) captures the excitement of the growing anti-British nationalist movement between 1936 and 1942. All are based on events in the author's own life. *The Selected Short Stories of Thein Pe*

Myint (trans Patricia M. Milne) were published in 1975.

THI-LAWUN-THA (Shin) (1453–1520?). A monk from **Taung-dwin-gyi**, a town in central Burma, who came to the royal city of **Ava** soon after writing his first work at the age of 38, a *pyo* on the ten essential perfections of the Buddha, called *Parami-daw-gan Pyo*. He was famous for his erudition and for his profound (and often difficult) exposition of the tenets of Buddhism, in which the younger poet Rat-hta-tha-ra ◊ sought to rival him.

Verse forms in classical Burmese literature. Until the 18th century almost all the major genres of Burmese poetry were composed in a rather rigid verse form consisting of short lines of four syllables linked by climbing rhymes. As Burmese is a tonal language in which each syllable, broadly speaking, has its own 'meaning' and can be used as a word, what counts in verse is the rhyme (including a 'rhyming' tone) and the number of syllables in a line; rhythm, that is vowel length and stress, play almost no part. 'Classical' Burmese verse is composed of lines of four syllables, grouped into long stanzas of 30 or 40 such lines, the end of each stanza being marked by a longer irregular line of five, seven or nine syllables. The rhyme 'climbs' from the fourth syllable in the first line to the third syllable in the second line to the second in the next line, where a new rhyme appears in the fourth syllable. This climbing principle, with slight variations, runs through all Burmese poetry, modern as well as classical and seems to have originated in Burma. Sometimes in particularly dramatic passages the rhymes climb rapidly from fourth to second syllable with a new rhyme appearing at the end of the second line. It is impossible to copy this in English but the following stanza describing the Buddhist picture of the miseries of *samsara* – of the round of countless reincarnations – gives an idea of the denseness of this type of verse.

> Birth after birth, over and over, with dirt and besmirching, oppression and evil, fading and withering, longing and craving, crying and groaning, clutching and clinging, panting and gasping, sobbing and weeping, toil and weariness, all pervading, round and round like a spinning reel.

The repetitions of vowel sounds and the alliterations in English produce somewhat the same effect as the interlinked rhymes in Burmese. The extract, dating from 1523, is from the *Ko-gan pyo*; a *pyo* ◊ is a long religious poem which narrates an episode from the life of the Buddha or retells one of the *jataka* stories (ie a previous incarnation of the Buddha), together with a great expansion and embellishment of the religious and moral precepts embodied in the chosen tale. These long 'sermons in verse' (about 200–300 of the stanzas quoted above) are the closest Burmese equivalent to an epic poem; they were written during the Ava period mainly by monk poets such as Shin Maha Ra-tha-ra, the author of the above stanza and Shin Thi-lawun-tha.

Yadu. Short Burmese poem with a fixed form of three stanzas written in the classical climbing rhyme. They were written on a wide variety of subjects, sometimes in praise of the king, but mostly to express the poet's emotions, usually feelings of sadness at being separated from loved ones, or longing aroused by the beauty of nature seen while journeying by river or through the forest. The greatest *yadu*, written in the 16–18th centuries, are among the finest love poems in the language (Extract 8).

ZAW-GYI (U Thein Han) (1907–1991). Burmese poet, writer, leading literary critic and historian, he studied English, Burmese literature and history at Rangoon University, and then librarianship at London and Dublin. His first poems written in 1929 were the beginning of the new *Khit-san* (Experiment for a new age) movement, born out of the conflict between the old literary traditions and the new attitudes coming in with increasing western influence.

Thailand

Thomas John Hudak

> 'Hitherto all the views I had seen in Siam had been limited in extent, but here the beauty of the country is exhibited in all its splendour. Beneath my feet was a rich and velvety carpet of brilliant and varied colours; an immense tract of forest, amidst which the fields of rice and the unwooded spots appeared like little streaks of green'.
> *Henri Mouhot,*
> *Travels in Indo-China*

Slightly smaller than France, Thailand divides into four geographical regions: the central plains, Chao Phraya River basin and the capital **Bangkok** form the heart of the country; the north with **Chiang Mai** as its centre forms a second region; the north-east with the major urban centre **Khon Kaen** makes up the third; and the perinsular south with **Hatyai** and **Nakhon Si Thammarat** comprises the last. The estimated population of Thailand in 1990 was 54 890 000. While over 95% of the population is considered to be Buddhist, there are also smaller communities of Muslims, particularly in the south near the Malaysian border, and Christians. Traditionally, the king is the protector of all religions.

A member of the linguistic and cultural group referred to as Tai, the Thai or Siamese probably moved into northern Thailand from southern China at a very slow rate, encountering other ethnic groups, notably the Khmer, already established there. By the 13th and 14th centuries, however, the Thai had developed new and powerful states. One of these kingdoms, **Sukhothai**, founded in 1238, has come to be regarded by the Thai people as the first true Thai kingdom and the forerunner of the modern nation state. At the height of its power under King Ramkhamhaeng (c1279–98), the kingdom extended to **Luang Prabang** and **Vientiane** in modern Laos to the north, to Burma in the west, and to the Malay peninsula in the south. In his famous inscription (◊

Ramkhamhaeng inscription) Ramkhamhaeng characterizes himself as a benevolent and just monarch, accessible to the people to solve and mediate any dispute. Aside from its political accomplishments, Sukhothai is also remembered for its notable accomplishments in art and architecture, in particular, numerous monuments and a distinctive style of Buddhas, a walking Buddha characterized by flowing lines. After the death of Ramkhamhaeng in 1298, Sukhothai rapidly lost its power and disintegrated into groups of small principalities.

In 1351, U Thong created a new capital at **Ayutthaya** by reuniting the scattered principalities and incorporating areas from the remains of the Khmer empire in the region. Under the title of King Ramathibodi I (1351–69), he once again extended the kingdom through the central plains and into the peninsula. Then, during the 15th century, King Borommatrailokanat (1448–88) strengthened the kingdom with a series of legal and administrative reforms that ensured the proper functioning of the political and social order. His reign also produced significant religious and literary achievements. With the growth of power in the 16th century, Burma became a major threat to Ayutthaya, finally invading and conquering the kingdom in 1569. After several major battles, King Naresuan (1590–1605) defeated the Burmese and reestablished Ayutthaya as a kingdom.

In the 17th century under the rule of King Narai (1656–88) ◊, Ayutthaya grew into a major political, social, and cultural capital. Narai and his court gave patronage to writers, poets, and artists, producing some of the finest artistic and literary achievements in the

---

[a] *Many temples, including Wat Phra Sing, with murals depicting the Song of Prince Sang Thong.* [b] *Capital of the first true Thai kingdom; many temples, among the most famous being Wat Sri Chun with engravings of jataka tales.* [c] *Scene of the novel The Teachers of Mad Dog Swamp (Extract 19).* [d] *Contains King Narai's summer palace, a major literary landmark.* [e] *Buddha is said to have left his footprints here; Phra Phuttabaat temple is described in Extract 13.* [f] *Capital from 1351 to 1767 and major literary centre especially under King Narai (1656–88).* [g] *Site of numerous literary landmarks, including: National Museum, which contains the Ramkhamhaeng Inscription and puppets used for performances of the Ramakian; scenes from the Ramakian portrayed in the Royal Ordination Pavilion at Wat Benjamabophit; Wat Po, the 'university of stone' which contains bas relief panels depicting the Ramakian; Thammasat University, scene of the 1973 suppresion of students (Extract 6); Temple of Dawn, described in Yukio Mishima's novel of the same name (Extract 7); Wat Buddhaisawan, which has exceptional murals of the Buddha's life; Wat Phra Keo which contains the most detailed and complete rendition of the Ramakian.* [h] *Contains numerous Wats, many containing scenes from jataka tales.* [i] *Statue of Sunthorn Phu, probably Thailand's greatest poet.* [j] *Joseph Conrad's novel The Secret Sharer is set in the Gulf of Thailand.*

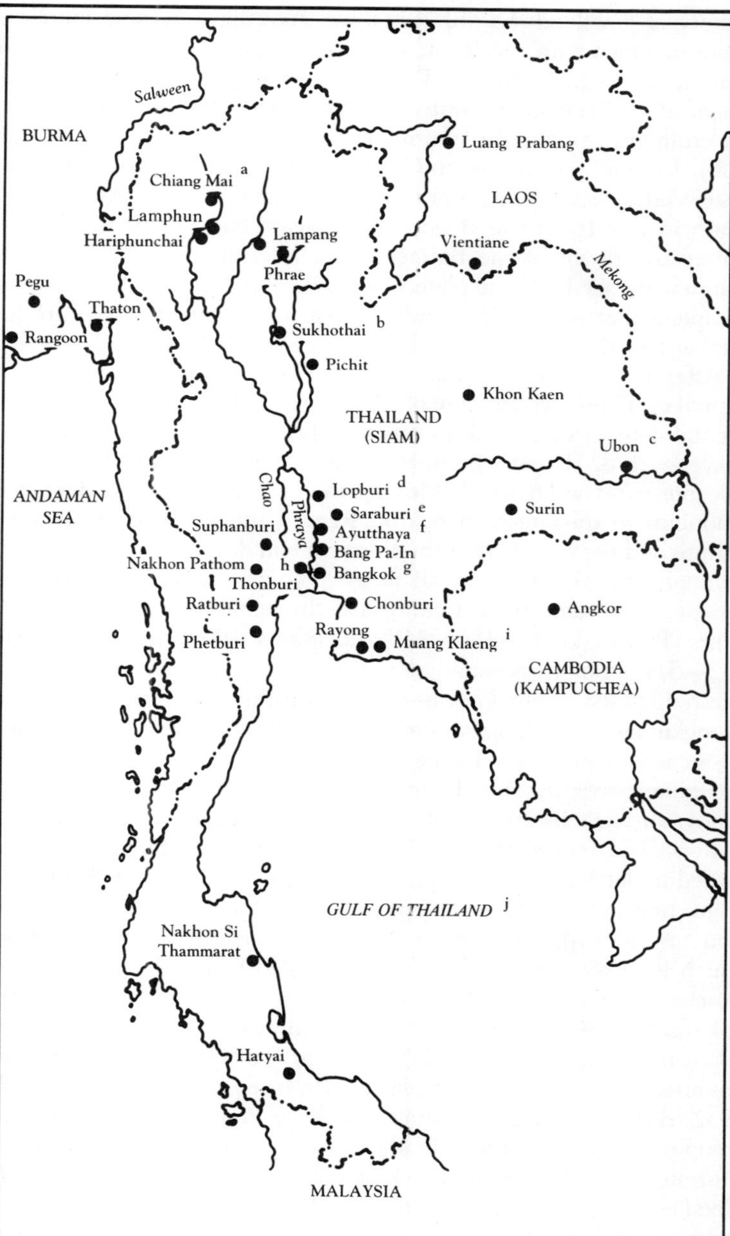

Literary Thailand

history of Thailand. During this time, Ayutthaya became more and more involved with the West. Commercial ties were sought with the Dutch, the English, and the French. During the latter part of Narai's reign, the Greek Constantine Phaulkon gained prominence in the government, rising to the position of Minister of Civil Affairs (Mahatthai). In time, his policies and his favouritism toward France inflamed anti-Western sentiment, and he was executed in 1688. After Narai's death in July 1688, the kingdom once again had to face the growing power and threat of the Burmese. Finally, after several attacks, the Burmese invaded and completely destroyed Ayutthaya, a destruction so complete that nearly all records, bureaucratic and literary, were lost forever (for the attack from a Burmese perspective, see p 6).

After the Burmese invasion, King Taksin (1767–82) moved the capital to **Thonburi**. Because of the severity of his rule and his growing mental deterioration, Taksin was overthrown by Rama I (Phra Phutthayotfa, 1782–1809), the first of the Chakri kings who continue to rule present-day Thailand. Moving the capital across the river from Thonburi to the site of **Bangkok**, Rama I sought to reconstruct the culture and the capital that the Burmese had destroyed. He attempted to duplicate Ayutthaya in all areas: political, religious, social, and artistic. This same revival continued through the reigns of Rama II (Phra Phutthaloetla, 1809–24) and Rama III (Phra Nang Klao, 1824–51). Prior to becoming King, Rama IV (King Mongkut to the West, 1851–68) spent 27 years as a Buddhist monk. In the monkhood, Mongkut pursued scholarly interests, studying and researching in nearly all areas of knowledge. He became proficient in numerous languages including Sanskrit, Pali, Latin, and English. As a ruler, he was an innovator, establishing major diplomatic relations with the European powers. The transformation of Thailand into a modern nation continued under Rama V (King Chulalongkorn, 1868–1910). During his reign, railways were built, the civil service established, the administration restructured, and slavery abolished. Through skillful diplomacy which involved the lose of some territory to French Laos and British Burma, King Chulalongkorn managed to keep Thailand free from colonization. While compulsory education was introduced under Rama VI (King Vajiravudh, 1910–25), his reign was characterized by numerous artistic and literary accomplishments, many by the king himself. In 1932, during the reign of Rama VII (King Prajadhipok, 1925–35), a group of military officers and radical students who had studied abroad, frustrated with the apparent lack of democratic progress, engineered a bloodless coup d'étât against the absolute monarchy. Since then, a constitutional monarchy has been the chief form of government with various military and civilian groups in power. The present king, Rama IX (Bhumibol Adulyadej) ascended the throne on 9 June 1946.

King Chulalongkorn

Pibul Songkhram, one of the leaders of the 1932 coup, held power in the new constitutional monarchy from 1938 until the end of the second world war. During the war, he sided with the Japanese, allowing Japanese troops to occupy Thailand. In 1942, he declared war on both the USA and the UK, although the Thai ambassador residing in Washington, Seni Pramoj, never delivered the declaration. Pibul was forced to resign in 1944, and Seni became premier. During the 1950s, General Sarit Thanarat established a repressive military dictatorship that abolished the constitution and imposed strict censorship. Following Sarit's death in 1963, the army officers, Thanom Kittikachorn and Praphat Charusathien, ruled Thailand, a time during which Thailand made significant economic progress through massive US aid programmes and by allowing the US military to use bases in the country to support the involvement in the Vietnam War. Growing political repression, outrage at corruption, and criticism of the government's policies and programmes led to demands for changes in the government by a coalition of students and workers in June 1973. Then in October, another demonstration was brutally suppressed by the military. When further bloodshed was prevented by the king and General Kit Sivara, Thanom and Praphat were forced to leave the country. Until 1976, an elected constitutional government ruled the country. However, mass demonstrations erupted again in 1976 when Thanom entered the country as a monk. The brutal backlash at Thammasat University in October (Extract 6) compelled numerous intellectuals, students, and left-wing sympathizers to disappear into the forest. These political events have become major topics and themes of contemporary literature. In 1981, a general amnesty was proclaimed and many intellectuals returned to active participation in Thai society. Since that time, Thailand has experienced a major economic boom, although the political scene remains fluid, with a military coup as recently as 1991.

The Thai Language

The Thai language belongs to the Tai language family, which extends from Assam and Burma in the west to northern Vietnam and south-eastern China in the east to the Malaysian border in the south. In the north, Tai languages are found in Yunnan, in the Sip Song Pan Na autonomous region, and throughout Laos. The languages cover Thailand, with Thai or Siamese being the most well-known, all the way into the southern peninsula toward the Malaysian border. The wider affiliation of Tai remains in dispute. One school considers Tai unique and unrelated to Chinese even though the two languages share a variety of typological features. A more recent school claims that Tai and Austronesian (a family that includes Malay, Indonesian, and Tagalog) belong to the same family.

Thai is a tonal language with each syllable receiving one of five tones. Three tones have a definite pitch level: high, mid, and low; the two remaining have pitch contours: falling and rising. Traditionally, Thai has been regarded as a monosyllabic language; however, the language does have a large number of polysyllabic words borrowed from Sanskrit and Pali. Other sources of borrowing include Khmer, Mon, Swatow, Chinese, and English. Grammatical patterns are fairly simple with subject-verb-object word order predominating. There are no inflections for case, gender, tense, or number.

King Ramkhamhaeng is credited with creating the Thai writing system sometime prior to 1292, the date of the earliest extant inscription in that script. Tradition holds that he adapted an Indic alphabet that was designed to represent the sounds of Sanskrit. He encountered the alphabet as it was being used by the Khmers. Utilizing that system, he retained the symbols for the Sanskrit sounds not found in Thai to reflect the pronunciation of the Indic loanwords. For the Thai sounds and tones which the alphabet could not represent, he created new symbols.

In Thailand, the dialect spoken in Bangkok and the central plains is viewed as the standard language; it is used in schools, in the media, and in all government affairs. Other dialects include Southern Thai spoken in the peninsula; Northeastern Thai or Isan spoken in the northeast; and Northern Thai or Kammuang in the north. Tonal variations and some vocabulary items account for the major differences between the representative dialects.

Verse Types and Prose

It has only been in the 20th century that prose has come to be accepted as a viable form for literature. Prior to this change all literature was written in poetry; in fact, literature was equated with poetry. With the exception of a few experimental forms, all of Thai poetry can be divided into five different types, four of which have been used since the earliest times: *rai* ◊, *khlong* ◊, *kap* ◊, *chan* ◊ and *klon* ◊.

While there has been some experimentation with blank and free verse in contemporary poetry, most modern poets continue to use the classical verse forms, favouring *khlong* and *klon*.

A Thai axiom states that without rhyme, poetry cannot exist. In fact, a literary anecdote relates that Prince Bidyalankarana inserted a few stanzas of blank verse into a speech to determine the importance of rhyme. He discovered that the audience remained unaware of the poetry because of the lack of rhyme. The two types of rhyme in Thai poetry are described under Rhyme ◊ in the 'Biographies and literary notes section'.

William J. Gedney, the pre-eminent scholar of Thai language and literature, suggests that much classical Thai poetry can be compared to that of Spenser. Emphasis is upon heroes and villains, and court pageantry, not on character and plot development.[1] In another commentary, he also states that the emphasis upon finding new and more elegant ways to express the same themes is suggestive of the music of Haydn and Mozart.[2] He also argues that the **old city of Bangkok** during the first two reigns was probably much like Elizabethan London.[3] As in London, the upper class lived in a close world where everyone knew one another and there was a supportive atmosphere for writers, poets, and artists. In both London and Bangkok, 'there was a pervasive atmosphere of creativity, of joy in poetry and the other arts, of appreciation and enthusiasm for the beautiful use of language'.[4]

Sukhothai Period

Most Thai people look to the Sukhothai kingdom as the first capital of the modern Thai nation. Extant literary pieces are rare; however, those that do remain indicate genres that have remained in the Thai literary corpus until the present day. While rarely thought of as examples of literature, most remaining inscriptions, regardless of their topic, are classified as literature. The most famous of these is the one attributed to King Ramkhamhaeng, often referred to as the Ramkhamhaeng Inscription or Inscription 1 ◊. Discovered in 1833 by King Mongkut and now housed at the **National Museum** in **Bangkok**, this four-sided stone stele is inscribed in a script said to have been devised by the king himself as the forerunner of the modern Thai alphabet.

Religious didacticism found expression in the description of the Buddhist cosmology, *Tray Phum Phra Ruang* (*The Three Worlds According to King Ruang*) composed by the heir apparent Phya Lithai in 1345 ◊. Basing his composition upon Theravada Buddhist scriptures and treatises, Phya Lithai describes in minute detail the three worlds that constitute the Buddhist cosmology: the world of desire, the world of form and the world without form. With its graphic descriptions of punishments and rewards, the *Tray Phum* has had great influence upon the literary and artistic heritage of Thailand. While not dating from the Sukhothai period, colorful murals depicting the *Tray Phum* can be seen at **Wat Suwannaram**, **Thonburi**, and **Wat Yai Intharam, Chonburi**. In the section describing the heavens, a depiction of Mt Meru, the home of the gods, is included. Two temples in Bangkok are said to be representations of this mountain, **Wat Arun** or the Temple of the Dawn and **Wat Saket** or the Temple of the Golden Mount. The composition is also said to have political overtones, with its description of the ideal Buddhist king. Only three copies of the manuscript are said to have survived the destruction of Ayutthaya by the Burmese in 1767.

Ayutthaya Period

The **Ayutthaya** period saw the development of many of the verse forms that have come to be associated with classical Thai poetry. Concomitant with this proliferation was the evolution of a number of genres that have been primary to the concept of literature and poetry until prose began to dominate in the 19th and 20th centuries. Thai historians traditionally divide the Ayutthaya period into three periods.

Much like the Sukhothai period, the first (1351–1628) has only a few extant works. An early work within the ceremonial genre is *Ongkan Chaeng Nam* (*The Water Oath*), one of the few compositions to have survived the reign of King Ramathibodi I. Written in one of the subvarieties of *khlong* ◊, the text is filled with arcane words and allusions to Hindu deities and was used by royal officials to swear their allegiance to the king.

Religious didactic works continued to dominate the literary scene. Sometime during the development of the Thai nation, the Indic *jataka* tales ◊, the stories of the Buddha's former births, entered South-east Asia (see also pp 47 in the Burma chapter and pp 150–151 in the Laos chapter). No real study has determined which of the 547 tales have been the most favoured, but they appear in numerous temple murals and engravings. Some of the most famous are those in **Sukhothai** at **Wat Sri Chum** where they are engraved in the walls and ceiling in the building that surrounds the enormous Buddha at the temple. More popular in Thailand have been the last ten lives of the Buddha before his last incarnation. These ten tales can be found in a variety of different formats and translations. An excellent collection of translations, along with colour photographs of murals depicting the stories can be found in *Ten Lives of the Buddha* by Wray et al. The ten tales and representative sites of murals include: Temiya, the Mute Prince (**Wat Yai Intharam, Chonburi** and **Wat Suwannaram, Thonburi**); Mahajanaka, the Lost Prince (**Wat Bang Yi Khan, Thonburi**; **Wat No, Suphanburi**; **Wat Phuthaisawan, Ayutthaya**; and **Wat Suwannaram, Thonburi**); Sama, the Devoted Son (**Wat Yai Intharam, Chonburi**; **Wat Bang Yi Khan, Thonburi**; **Wat No, Suphanburi**; **Wat Suwannaram, Thonburi**); Nimi, the Noble King (**Wat Yai Intharam, Chonburi**; **Wat Suwannaram, Thonburi**); Mahosadha (**Wat Bang Yi Khan, Thonburi**; **Wat Suwannaram, Thonburi**); Bhuridatta, the Naga Prince (**Wat Bang Yi Khan, Thonburi**; **Wat No, Suphanburi**; **Wat Yai Intharam, Chonburi**; **Wat Suwannaram, Thonburi**); Canda-Kumara, the Honorable Prince (**Wat Chang Yai, Ayutthaya**; **Wat Choeng Tha, Ayutthaya**; and **Wat Suwannaram, Thonburi**); Narada, the Great Brahman (**Wat Yai Intharam, Chonburi** and **Wat Suwannaram, Thonburi**); Vidhura-Pandita, the Eloquent Sage (**Wat Choeng Tha, Ayutthaya**; **Wat Suwannaram, Thonburi** and **Wat Yai Intharam, Chonburi**); and Vessantara, the Charitable Prince (**Wat Rachasitharam, Thonburi** and **Wat Suwannaram, Thonburi**). Of these ten tales, the last with its theme of great charity and generosity holds the most revered position in Thailand. Depictions of this tale can be found in most temples, on book covers, in television specials, and even on calendars. In Thai, this version is known as *Mahachat* (*The Great Birth*) and it appears in several poetic versions.

King Borommatrailokanat commissioned a royal version of this poem, the *Mahachat Kham Luang* (*The Royal Version of the Great Birth*). To duplicate the Pali version upon which it was based, the 1000 Pali verses (*gatha*) divided into 13 chapters (*kanda*) were kept intact but followed by translations into Thai in one of the following verse forms: *rai* ◊, *khlong* ◊, *kap* ◊, or *chan* ◊. Another version, the *Kap Mahachat* (*The Great Birth*), was completed in *rai* during the reign of King Songtham (1602–28). At the end of Buddhist Lent in October, many temples hold ceremonies that involve the recitation of the story in Pali as well as Thai. Tradition maintains that whoever hears the complete story will accrue great merit. Normally, 13 monks chant the story, one especially trained for each of the 13 chapters. Over time, some monks have become famous for their performance skills. Recent scholarship has suggested that King Borommatrailokanat commissioned the work not only to accrue merit but also to legitimize his reign.

Significant depictions of the life of the Buddha can also be found in numerous temples (**Wat Suwannaram, Thonburi**; **Wat Suwandararam, Ayutthaya** and **Wat Thong Thammachat, Thonburi**). **Wat Buddhaisawan** in **Bangkok** has exceptional murals of the Buddha's life from his marriage to his cremation. An interesting series of religious and secular representations done in lacquer can be found in the lacquer pavilion at **Suan Pakkard Palace** in **Bangkok**. Originally used as a library, the pavilion is a fine example of Siamese decorative art dating from the Ayutthaya period.

Perhaps even more influential than the *jataka* tales are the 50 extra-canonical tales known as the *Pañña-jataka* (*The Fifty Birth Tales*), said to have been composed in Pali by **Chiang Mai** monks between 1457 and 1657 (although a recent study dates them to 1265 in **Hariphunchai** in the present day province of **Lamphun**). Supposedly based upon indigenous folk tales, these stories have exerted an enormous influence upon the classical literature of Thailand. One source lists at least 61 poems based on 21 of the tales. Outside Thailand, these same stories can be found in Burma, Laos, and Cambodia.

Within this early period, one poem combines the historical and panegyrist genres, *Lilit Yuan Phai* (*The Defeat of the Yuan*), a depiction of the struggles between Ayutthaya and the northern kingdom of Lan Na over the provinces in the area of Sukhothai. The poem celebrates King Borommatrailokanat's battles and victories which led to the solidification of Ayutthaya as a major kingdom in South-east Asia. Scholars generally date the poem to Borommatrailokanat's reign or to his son's, Ramathibodi II (1491–1529) – see Griswold and Prasert na Nagara's 1976 essay (◊ Booklist).

King Narai's ◊ reign dominates the second part of the Ayutthaya period (1656–88). During this period, Thailand came into contact with the West through trading contracts and the influx of missionaries. Under Narai's patronage, writers, poets, and artists rose to prominence. Poetry and poetry composition became such an important activity in the court that it was said those who were poets were highly favoured by the king. Narai's **summer palace** in **Lopburi**, where so much of this activity took place, can still be seen today. Over time the era has come to be known as the Golden Age of Thai Poetry. New verse forms, elaborate imagery and vocabulary flourished. As in the earlier perods, the court poets found their themes in religion, historical events, and court ceremonies. In most cases, the court poets were anonymous, although one name does stand out, Maharatchakhru ◊. Utilizing the *Pañña-jataka* tales, he created the poetic version *Sya Kho Kham Chan* (*The Tiger and the Cow*), a tale of the strange friendship between a cow and a tiger that illustrates the importance of virtues and percepts found in Buddhism. He also turned to the extra-canonical tales to create *Samutthakhot Kham Chan* (*The Story of Prince Samutthakhot*), a depiction of the adventures of Prince Samutthakhot, the Buddha in a former life, as he travels through the heavenly realms. Transforming the original tale, Maharatchakhru added sections that elaborately describe elephants and the elephant hunt. Most Thai critics regard the elephant hunt and capture as indicative of Narai's prowess in the hunt. Elephant kraals as depicted in the poem can still be seen in **Lopburi** and elephant hunts or round-ups are staged for tourists every November in the north-east province of **Surin**. After Maharatchakhru's death Narai himself completed a section of the poem, but he too left it unfinished. It was not until the mid-19th century that the patriarch Prince Paramanuchit Chinorot completed the poem, following the story as outlined in the *Pañña-jataka* tale. Scenes from the story can be seen at **Wat Suthat** in **Bangkok**. Maharatchakhru wrote his poem in the form popular during the Ayutthaya period, *kham chan*, a combination of two types of verse forms, *chan* ◊ and *kap* ◊.

Under Narai's patronage another poetic form reached perfection. These poems, the *nirat*, frequently appear in the *khlong* ◊ verse form. They relate the poet's journey from either a loved one or a favourite place. With puns and word play, the poet demonstrates how various physical aspects of the journey remind him of his melancholy and sorrow at leaving. Over time, the *nirat* genre came to be used simply for the description of a trip abroad. Noteworthy examples include *Khlong Nirat Hariphunchai* (*The Journey to Hariphunchai*) by Si Thep which describes his journey from **Chiang Mai** to **Hariphunchai** in **Lamphun**. An even more influential work is Si Prat's ◊ *Khlong Kamsuan* (*A Mournful Journey*) which depicts the poet's journey of exile from **Ayutthaya** to **Nakhon Si Thammarat**.

Probably the most famous example of the romantic genre is *Phra Law* (*The Story of Prince Law*) which depicts the love triangle between the northern Prince Law and the two princesses of a neighbouring province ◊. An English prose version of the poem entitled *The Magic Lotus* was completed by Prince Prem Chaya during the 20th century.

Three types of stage performance also developed during this time, and references to the different types are frequently found in the literature of the period. The *nang* was the shadow puppet show which used large leather puppets. The Thai version of the *Ramayana*, the *Ramakian* ◊, generally provided the story lines for the performances. Puppets used for the performances can be seen at the **National Museum** in **Bangkok** as well as at temples in **Petburi** and **Ratburi** provinces. Maharatchakhru writes in *Samutthakhot Kham Chan* that it was composed for a puppet show for King Narai, although no evidence in the form of leather puppets remains. Shadow puppet shows are also mentioned in *Bunnowat Kham Chan* (*Discourse by Bun*, Extract 13). The *khon* was the masked drama danced by men; stories from the *Ramakian*, particularly the battle scenes, provided the subject matter. A battle scene from the *Ramakian* as presented in an outdoor *khon* performance can be seen in a mural in the **Royal Ordination Pavilion** at **Wat Benjamabophit** (The Marble Temple) in **Bangkok**.

With the end of Narai's reign, the Thai kingdom entered another period of war and its last period of literary production. Literary production declined with only a few significant works remaining. One of the most important, although very short, is *Bunnowat Kham Chan* (*Discourse by Bun*, Extract 13). Written by Phra Mahanak sometime between 1732 and 1758 in Ayutthaya, the poem combines the ceremonial with the religious genres. Rather than telling a story about the Buddha or one of his past lives, the poem describes the king's journey to the site in **Saraburi** where it is said that the Buddha left his footprints on a mountain top. Since Ayutthayan times, a temple, **Phra Phutthabaat**, has existed at that spot. The poem combines the legend of the footprints, a description of the temple, and a description of the ceremonies and temple fair that occurs at the temple when the king arrives. While the temple has been remodelled and refurbished many times since the poem's composition, the temple described is strikingly similar to the one that exists today. The *Nirat Phrabat* (*Journey to Phrabat*), composed by Prince Thammathibet (Chaofaa Kung) also describes a journey to this temple. In 1807, Sunthorn Phu, the great 19th century poet, completed his *nirat*, also entitled *Nirat Phrabat* (*Journey to Phrabat*), that relates a similar journey.

In 1767, the Burmese once again attacked **Ayutthaya**, completely destroying the capital and along with it most of the literature that had been produced during the previous centuries. After the destruction of

Ayutthaya, Taksin reestablished the capital at Thonburi and attempted to reproduce the lost *Ramakian* by writing four episodes of the poem in *klon*, although most critics feel that the poetry in these episodes is inferior to that found in the compositions produced by Rama I and Rama II. In a relatively short period of time, Taksin's reign grew very unstable, and he was overthrown. The new king, Rama I, moved the capital across the river, to the site of modern day **Bangkok**, and there began a major renaissance in all aspects of Thai culture and life.

Bangkok Period

Rama I ◊, whose home before he became king can be seen at **Wat Rakang** in **Thonburi**, attempted to construct Bangkok in the image of Ayutthaya, surely as an attempt to recapture the glory the capital once had. He established committees and institutions to research, describe, and implement the ancient customs and ceremonies of Ayutthaya. He planned his own coronation and cremation based on the ceremonies that were held in Ayutthaya. In the religious realm he had a new rendition of the *Tripitika*, the Buddhist scriptures, compiled. Bound in gold, the completed work was deposited in a special library on the grounds of the Temple of the Emerald Buddha. He also sponsored the compilation of two editions of the *Tray Phum*. The second was completed in 1802 and is probably the most comprehensive. Known as the *Tray Phum Winitchay*, this edition is far more comprehensive than any of the earlier compositions, containing numerous legends and stories that do not appear in the one composed by Lithai during the Sukhothai period. In its published form, the composition runs for 1 532 pages whereas the one composed by Lithai is only 373. The work is also significant because it emphasizes the importance of the government and the king, suggesting the legitimization of Rama I's new government. Continuing to stress this theme, Rama I ordered a new and complete recession of the laws of the kingdom, which was completed in 1804. In 1793 and 1850 revised versions of the chronicles of Ayutthaya were also produced.

Literary production was also revived under Rama I, who created and formalized the royal composition groups known as the *phraratchaniphon*. Thai literary historians maintain that within the royal composition groups different committees were established to write different parts of a poem, one to write battle scenes, another to write love scenes, and so on. At the end of the day, the newly composed parts were read and discussed by the entire composition group until a final version was determined. Rama I is reputed to have been skilled at writing battle scenes. Thus most lengthy poems were composed by a group of anonymous authors even though the king received the credit for the composition. Probably the most impressive literary composition attributed to Rama I is the only complete version of the *Ramakian* (Extract 17). Written in the new *klon* ◊ verse form, the complete poem runs for over 24 000 stanzas. The completion of this version produced the definitive Thai version with its incorporation of a variety of Thai traditions and customs. In many temples throughout Bangkok and the rest of Thailand, single murals exist depicting one or two episodes from the poem. However, the most detailed and complete rendition of the poem can be found in the galleries of **Wat Phra Keo** or the Temple of the Emerald Buddha in **Bangkok**. There, all the characters and subplots are outlined in 178 large panels. These paintings were begun during Rama I's reign, but extensive restoration has continued on a regular basis. Another depiction of the story can be found in the 152 bas-relief panels that surround the bot in **Wat Po**. Cadet's book *The Ramakian* reproduces these reliefs with a short plot summary. Other scenes are depicted on the doors in mother-of-pearl inlay. Murals of the story can also be found at **Wat Suthat** in **Bangkok**. Other depictions of the poem are usually confined to the dance drama, with performances held at the **National Theatre** or in hotels and restaurants for tourists. In almost all schools, students are trained in dance, and they present one or more of the episodes on various ceremonial occasions. These formal presentations aside, the characters and their exploits have long been part of the popular culture of Thailand with references and pictures of the poem found on calendars, advertisements, and TV shows. Other important poems from this period include two versions of the Javanese Panji cycle *Dalang* (*The Puppet Master*) and *Inao* (*The Prince Inao*). Both poems chronicle the adventures and loves of the Prince Inao (Panji) in 18th century Java.

Prose fiction first made its appearance during this period with *Sam Kok*, Chao Phraya Phra Khlang's translation of the Chinese classic *Romance of the Three Kingdoms*. Scenes from the tale can be found in the **Chinese pavilion at Wat Po** and in the vihara behind the main building at **Wat Boworniwet** in **Bangkok**.

The literary renaissance continued to flourish during the reign of Rama II ◊, Rama I's son. Rama II began his literary work as a member of the *phraratchaniphon* and continued when he became king. A daily schedule for Rama II shows that at noon he retired to his own quarters to work on his own literary and artistic projects. Later in the afternoon he would meet with the other court poets. Literary production became so intense and the quality so high that poets became highly esteemed during the period, receiving great patronage and attention. Rama II is credited with rewriting a lengthy section of the *Ramakian* so that it could be better performed in the *lakhon nai*, the dance drama for the inner court. Rama II also wrote a series of dramas based on local legends and the indigenous *jataka* tales for the *lakhon nok*, the dance drama performed by men outside the royal court. A literary anecdote maintains that the king composed these dramas at the challenge of the great *klon* poet Sunthorn Phu, who claimed that kings could not write as commoners did. Of these dramas, the most famous is probably *Sang Thong* (*The Story of Prince Sang Thong*), the story of the prince from the golden snail. Murals depicting the story can be found in **Wat Phra Sing** in **Chiang Mai**.

Probably Thailand's greatest poet, Sunthorn Phu (1786–1855) ◊, began his career during the reign of Rama II. An accomplished poet famous for his use of internal rhyme ◊, Phu completed five narrative poems including his masterpiece, *Phra Aphaimani* (*The Story of Phra Aphaimani*), numerous collections of proverbs, and nine *nirat* poems. The monumental *Phra Aphaimani* recounts the loves of the Prince Aphaimani for a sea giantess, a mermaid, and two princesses. Statues of the characters and the poet himself can be seen in a park at **Muang Klaeng** in **Rayong province**, Phu's birthplace. Paintings (c 1900) of scenes from the poem can be seen at **Varophatphiman Hall** at **Bang Pa-in**. His *nirat* poems frequently depict actually journeys and are filled with descriptions, eg *Nirat Muang Klaeng* (*Journey to Muang Klaeng*) which relates his journey to **Rayong** to see his father. The monk's cell where he did much of his writing can still be seen at **Wat Thepthidaram** in Bangkok.

Unlike Rama I and Rama II, Rama III devoted most of his energies to political, diplomatic, and religious concerns. He is famous for reconstructing **Wat Po**, creating a 'university of stone' where he had inscribed throughout the temple all the known medical formulae, historical information, and verse forms current to his reign. By doing this, he intended to make all the known knowledge available to as many people as possible. While much of the verse inscribed there is considered to be more academic than artistic, the inscriptions nevertheless present a picture of the knowledge current during this reign. Probably the most significant classical poetry composed was that done by Prince Paramanuchit Chinorot (1790–1853) ◊. A noted Indian classicist, Paramanuchit was responsible for completing the final portion of the poem *Samutthakhot Kham Chan*. He also composed *Talaeng Phai* (*The Defeat of the Mons*), a glorification of King Naresuan (1590–1605) and his battles with the Burmese.

During the reign of King Mongkut, Thailand once again established extensive relations with the West. Significant for the history of literature was the introduction of printing by the American missionary D.B. Bradley, who began to print Thai literature as well as government announcements and publications. Among the works published are the prose works *Sam Kok* (1865) and *Rachathirat* (1880); the text on writing poetry, *Cindamani* (1861); and the compilation of laws, *Kotmai Tra Sam Duang* (1863). In 1865, another missionary by the name of Smith also began publishing literary works such as the multi-authored *Khun Chang Khun Phaen* and Sunthorn Phu's *Phra Aphaimani*. At **Wat Boworniwet** in **Bangkok**, Mongkut commissioned a series of paintings that allegorically depicted the Dharma. Reflecting the 19th century world, these paintings include scenes of horse racing, an eye surgeon removing a cataract, Western-style brick houses, and Westerners contemplating a giant lotus.

Emphasis upon the production of prose continued into the reign of King Chulalongkorn, who contributed two significant prose compositions with *Klai Ban* (*Far from Home*), a collection of letters describing his 1907 journey to England, and *Phra Ratchaphithi Sipsong Duan* (*The Royal Ceremonies of the Twelve Months of the Year*), a description and historical discussion of the Buddhist, Hindu, and Brahmaic ceremonies that occur throughout the year. At **Wat Benjamabophit** (*The Marble Temple*) in **Bangkok**, Chulalongkorn's residence when he was a monk has been reconstructed. Inside are paintings of the king's trips to Europe and Asia.

Rama VI ◊ devoted much of his life to literary works, and it is said that during the day he would frequently retire to his inner quarters to work on his projects. His desk in the **Grand Palace** can be seen today. Many of his works were innovative with the reworking of Sanskrit legends he discovered while in England. He is famous for reworking parts of the Rama epic, composing the long poem *Phra Non Kham Luang* (*The Royal Version of the Legend of Nala*) based on the Nala legend, and translating several of Shakespeare's plays including *As You Like It*, *The Merchant of Venice*, and *Romeo and Juliet*. Always interested in literature and preserving the quality of the language, Rama VI began a literary club and established a committee to choose the best works produced in the different genres. Even though prose was flourishing at this time, an active interest in classical poetry remained.

The true flourishing of prose fiction probably began during the reign of King Chulalongkorn. His vast reforms in all areas of the Thai social and political scene helped to create a period of growth and excitement. In 1874, Prince Kasem Sophak began to publish the first Thai literary journal, *Darunowat* (*Advice to Young Men*). There new writers began to publish their short stories that reflected the tensions between the old elite, who resisted the new reforms, and the new elite, who actively supported them. The appearance of the short story and its variety of forms from satire to mystery to romance developed for many reasons. With more and more Thais going abroad for education, they increasingly encountered new literary forms. In addition, the growth of journalism and at the same time the reading public provided an outlet for experimentation with these new literary devices. Under both Rama V and Rama VI there was an atmosphere for artistic creation and social change. Stories by Conan Doyle, H. Rider Haggard, and Guy de Maupassant gained great popularity and the public's literary tastes began to change. The stories and adventures of princes and princesses declined in popularity to be replaced with the new mysteries and romances. A creative force in this new trend, Rama VI adapted the Sherlock Holmes stories in a collection known as *Nithan Nai Thong In* (*The Stories of Thong In*).

In 1901 a translation of the English Victorian novel *Vendetta* by Marie Corelli appeared and thereby introduced the novel to Thai literature. During the 1920s and 1930s three major authors dominated the literary scene with novels that dealt with new themes and concerns. Coming from an aristocratic background, Dokmai Sot (1905–63) ◊ produced stories that criticized the rapidly changing society of Bangkok. With more and more Thais returning from abroad with Western educations and the increasing influence of the West in Thailand, particularly in Bangkok, the old social mores and traditions of the society began to decline and disappear. Recreating this background, Dokmai Sot introduced novels of manners that criticized the disintegration of the old order and the uncritical imitation of Western ways. Among her notable works are *Khwamphit Khrang Raek* (*The First Mistake*) in 1930, *Sam Chai* (*Three Gentlemen*) in 1933 and *Phu Di* (*The Genteel*) in 1937. In an early work, *Kam Kao* (*Old Karma*, translated as *A Secret Past*) in 1932, she examines problems of honesty and family honour faced by a young Thai woman raised in England who returns to Thailand as an adult to discover long-hidden family secrets.

Approaching the rapid social changes in a different manner, Siburapha (1905–74) ◊ criticized the aristocracy and the new reforms for exploiting and denigrating the poor. As a major influence in socially concerned literature, Siburapha sought justice and democratic equality for the poor.

The third major influence in the development of the novel is Prince Akatdamkoeng Raphiphat (1905–32) ◊ who concentrated upon the interaction between Thais and Westerners. In *Lakhon Haeng Chiwit* (*The Circus of Life*) in 1929, he introduced an entirely new concept into Thai novels, the international novel. Rather than Thailand, the setting is England where the protagonist has gone for education. There he has a love affair, but never marries because of the problems that he anticipates between the East and the West. He returns to Thailand physically ill and broke.

With the change to a constitutional monarchy, the year 1932 marks a political and social watershed in Thai history. While interest in prose literature had been increasing and developing since the late 19th century, this change in government is also seen as representing a major change in the literary scene, for the centre of interest and production no longer lay with the court but had now shifted to the middle class. Like much of the prose literature, poetry began to be concerned with social criticism and social justice. An early proponent of these new themes was the journalist-poet Caw Phraya Thammasak Montri (1876–1943), also known as Khru Thep, who depicted the effects of capitalism upon the Thai farmer.

After the 1932 coup, the emerging literature of social criticism was interrupted, and literature developed into a series of superficial romances and mysteries. In the early 1950s, works by such writers as the Marxist Chit Phumisak (1932–65) ◊ began to attack whole political systems. In his 1956 manifesto, *Sinlapa Phua Chiwit Sinlapa Phua Prachachon* (*Art for Life, Art for People*), Chit attacked classical poetry for not meeting the concerns of the people; he maintained that the proper topics for poetry were social, political, and economic concerns. The topics of the aristocracy and their love affairs only further suppressed the lower classes. Realism and social criticism appeared in the novels of Seni Saowaphong, Isra Amnatakun, and Suwat Woradilok. However, once again the development of literature was stifled. The years 1958–63, the era of Field Marshall Sarit, have come to be known as the Dark Ages. In 1957, the proclamation of Article 17, the Act of Communism Suppression, forced intellectuals and social critics into hiding. Literature once again became a series of romantic stories with little or no substance; political criticism, implied or straightforward, was no longer tolerated. Probably the most significant writer to emerge during this time was Khamsing Srinawk (Lao Khamhom) who wrote sensitive and insightful stories of the farmers in northeast Thailand. His collection of stories *Fa Bo Kan* (Heaven has no Horizon, translated as *The Politician and Other Stories*) details the life of the northeast farmer, his poverty, and his encounters with the government bureaucracy (Extract 11).

In the superb collection of stories *In the Mirror*, Benedict R.O.'G. Anderson and Ruchira Mendiones have compiled and translated a group of stories that reflect the literature from 1967 to 1979 (Extracts 4, 14, 16, 18). Anderson describes the period from 1963 to 1973 as the American Era, that period of the great transformation of Thai society with massive US-sponsored development projects, the influx of the US military to support the Vietnam War, the expansion of the education system, and the rapid change of traditional values on all levels. This great change or transformation of the society and its values became the dominant theme of the writers of this generation.

Toward the end of the 1960s, the rapid transformation of the society generated criticism and concern upon the part of the educated and

Siburapha

intellectuals. The government and its activities increasingly came under the attack of the students and other groups aligning themselves until on 14 October 1973, the Thanom government was overthrown by a coalition of students, intellectuals, workers, and everyday citizens. Censorship was abolished and social criticism and leftist literature were once again rediscovered. Within two years, a right wing backlash developed and the democratic government was overthrown in a brutal coup with an attack upon the students and leaders at **Thammasat University** (Extract 6). Censorship followed and large numbers of intellectuals and students were underground. Many of the stories found in *In the Mirror* were written after the 1976 coup and document the increasingly dark view of Thai society. Si Dao Ruang in 'Mother of Waters, Thaokae, and a Dog', as in many of her other short stories, delineates the startling changes that have come to the village and the old traditions (Extract 14). Other areas of change are seen with Kon Krailat's depiction of sex shows in the notorious red light district on **Patpong Road** in Bangkok (Extract 4). Both Manop Thanomsi and Niwet Kanthairat depict how those who have succeeded in Thai society exploit the weak and the poor. Samruan Sing is another author in this collection, a more extensive collection of his writings can be found in *Voices from the Thai Countryside*. These stories are miniature pictures of

Sujit Wongthet

ordinary villagers faced with the rapidly changing social and economic conditions of modern Thailand.

Concern for minorities and the poor also dominated the novels of this period. Three representative examples examine the life of rural north-east Thailand. *Khru Ban Nok* (*The Teachers of Mad Dog Swamp*) by Khammaan Khonkhai ◊ depicts the difficulties a rural teacher encounters as he tries to institute change in the primary educational system in the rural areas around **Ubon** (Extract 19). In *Kha Ratchakan Khru* (*Teacher Marisa*) Khammaan concentrates on the problems found in a secondary school in a district town. *Luk Isan* (*A Child of the Northeast*) by Kampoon Boontawee follows the plight of the north-east peasant as drought strikes. All three novels are significant in that they not only tell a story but in many respects serve as source books on the north-east with lengthy descriptions of the foods, traditions, and customs of the people of the area. Writing in English in *Siamese Drama*, *People of Esarn*, and *Monsoon Country*, Pira Sudham ◊ also describes the world of the north-east and the north-eastern peasants in Bangkok. Chart Kobjitti's 1981 *Kham Phi Phaksa* (*The Judgement*) presents a scathing picture of the life and mores of a rural village and the effects gossip and public opinion have on the individual. Another account written in 1968 by Botan ◊ delineates the life of the immigrant Chinese; *Jotmai Jak Muangthai* (*Letters from Thailand*) offers a detailed view of life in **Sampeng**, the Chinese section of **Bangkok**, as well as perceptive comments upon the Thai and their way of life (Extract 2). The teak logging camps around the **Yom River** in central Thailand are the setting for Nikom Rayawa's *Taling Suung, Sung Nak* (*High Banks, Heavy Logs*) a novel that recounts the life of a woodcarver and the disappearing traditions of his community.

Kukrit Pramoj's popular 1981 *Si Phaendin* (*Four Reigns*) on the other hand, explores the past (Extract 3). Following the life of his protagonist, Ploi, from childhood to womanhood, he presents the world in and outside the royal court. Spanning the reigns of Chulalongkorn, Vajiravudh, Prajadhipok, and Ananda Mahidol, his novel offers a unique view of Thai life and tradition. In a famous earlier work *Phai Daeng* (*Red Bamboo*) in 1961, Kukrit borrows the format of the Italian Don Camillo stories to satirize Communism and government policies.

Probably the most important contemporary poet is Angkarn Kalayaanaphong, who is also one of the most important contemporary artists. Experimenting with short stories such as 'Grandma', a variety of verse forms and symbols, Angkarn examines the relationship between the natural and social, the material and the spiritual (Extract 15). Among his most influential works are *Lamnam Phu Kradung* (*The Song of Mt Phu Kradung*) and *Suan Kaew* (*The Crystal Garden*). Other important poets, using the October revolution as themes, include Sujit Wongthet and Naowarat Pongpaiboon in *Mere Movement* (Extract 6), 'The day that killed the dove', and 'From Sunday to Monday: October, 14, 1973'. Other examples of Angkarn and Naowarat's poetry, along with pieces by Wittayakon Chiangkun, can be found in *Three Thai Poets*. Poetry remains a vital part of the literary scene with numerous poets writing on a variety of themes that include the environment, political criticism, social injustice, and alienation. A totally different type of contemporary poetry is the lengthy *A Village Ordination* by the monk Phra Maha Thongyoy Worakawinto. The poem deals with the customs of a rural monastery and the ordination of a monk. Accompanying the poem is a series of photographs of the ordination. A mural of a monk's ordination in Bangkok can be found in the bot of **Wat Boworniwet**. While much contemporary poetry remains untranslated, the volume *A Premier Book of Contemporary Thai Verse* edited by Montri Umarijani and Robert and Deborah Cumming offers in English a representative example of current themes and styles. Other examples of contemporary poetry, along with short stories, essays, and songs can be found in Phillips's comprehensive *Modern Thai Literature*. Two small collections of short stories include the anonymously edited *Thai Short Stories* and Jennifer Draskan, ed and trans, *Taw and Other Thai Stories*.

Foreign Writers

An extensive travel literature on Thailand, mainly 19th century travellers' accounts, also exists. A famous early account is Loubere's *A New Historical Relation of the Kingdom of Siam*. Another early description, recorded by Guy Tachard in 1685, is found in *A Relation of the Voyage to Siam*. In *Travels in Indo-China*, Henri Mouhot ◊, the discoverer of the **Angkor temples** in **Cambodia**, records a visit to the **Phra Phutthabat temple** at **Saraburi**, as well as other sights in Indochina, during the mid-19th century (Extract 12). A week-long visit to Bangkok appears in *A Week in Siam: January 1867* by the Marquis of Beauvoir. A much more comprehensive record, based on a month's stay, is Sir John Bowring's, *The Kingdom and People of Siam*. Readable and lively travel accounts of Thailand and its neighbouring countries can be found in Frank Vincent's *The Land of the White Elephant* and Carl Bock's *Temples and Elephants*, which describes the trip from Bangkok to that area known today as **the Golden Triangle**. A famous account of a trip through northern Thailand, Bangkok, and other parts of Southeast Asia is Somerset Maugham's ◊ *The Gentleman in the Parlour: A Record of a Journey from Rangoon to Haiphong* (Extract 8).

Descriptions of the country, its people, and its traditions have also been recorded by long-time residents: Ernest Young's *The Kingdom of the Yellow Robe*; and the anonymous journals, *An Englishman's Siamese Journals: 1890–1893*. First published in 1920, *A Physician at the Court of Siam* by Malcolm Smith, official physician to the Royal Court, chronicles the activities of the Court during the reign of King Chulalongkorn (Extract 1). With easy access to the royal family for over five years, Smith obtained much of his information from the Queen Mother, Queen Saowapa, daughter of King Mongkut. A totally different view of life in Thailand is offered by Reginald Campbell in *Teak-Wallah*, a description of daily life in teak logging camps in the 1920s (Extract 10). An amusing retelling of a housewife's life in Bangkok in the 1950s can be found in Carol Hollinger's *Mai Pen Rai*. A more recent account of life in Thailand comes from an American professor at a Thai university, Stephen A. Garrett's *Bangkok Journal: A Fulbright Year in Thailand*. A still different view of Thailand emerges in *Hello My Big Big Honey*, David Walker and Richard S. Erlich's collection of love letters to Bangkok bar girls.

In both serious and popular fiction Thailand remains a popular setting. Conrad ◊ uses the **Gulf of Thailand** for *The Secret Sharer* (Extract 9) and the **Chao Phraya River** for *Falk: A Reminiscence*. Yukio Mishima ◊ depicts pre-second world war Bangkok and post-second-world-war Japan in *The Temple of the Dawn* (Extract 7) for his meditations upon youth, age, reincarnation, and nationalism. The building of the famous Death Railroad in **Kanchanaburi** province during the second world war is the subject of Pierre Boulle's *The Bridge over the River Kwai*. Both the bridge and cemeteries containing the labourers who died there can be seen in Kanchanaburi.

The world of 17th century Ayutthaya and the reign of Narai are favoured settings for historical fiction. In *Siamese White*, Maurice Collis relates a account of piracy and Phaulkon at Narai's court. A more imaginative rendering of Phaulkon's rise to power and prominence comprises the plot of Axel Aylwen's *The Falcon of Siam*. J.C. Shaw's *The Seal of Tammarati* recounts a love affair between a Thai princess and an English assistant to Phaulkon. Fantasy, witchcraft, and the creation of automata in 17th century Europe, China, and Ayutthaya provide the backdrop for *The Enchantress* by Han Suyin.

Anna Leonowens's *The English Governess at the Siamese Court*, probably the most famous novel about Thailand, is a romanticized depiction of Anna Leonowens's role as governess to the children of King Mongut; the book was later transformed into the movie *The King and I*. A retelling of the story is Margaret Landon's *Anna and the King of Siam*. A sequel, *Fanny and the Regent of Siam* by R.J. Minney, narrates the relationship between Fanny Knox, the eldest daughter of the British Consul-General, and Louis Leonowens, Anna's son, and their eventual defiance of the Regent of Thailand, Sri Suriwong. Other views of 19th century Thailand by Leonowens are found in *Siamese Harem Life*. A typical building of the late-19th century, with its graceful architecture, is the **Ministry of the Interior** in Bangkok.

Prostitution, the drug world, and the Thai underworld form the plots and settings for an increasing number of contemporary novels and mysteries. In *A Woman of Bangkok*, Jack Reynolds treats an Englishman's obsession for a Thai prostitute in 1950s Bangkok. Christopher G. Moore in *Spirit House* graphically depicts Bangkok's underworld from the redlight districts of **Patpong Road** and **Soi Cowboy** to the slums of **Klong Toey**. Similar plots and themes make up Moore's *A Killing Smile* and its sequel *A Bewitching Smile*, set in northern Thailand among the Lahu. John Ralston Saul describes the duplicitous world of drug dealing and murder in north-eastern Thailand and Laos in *The Paradise Eater*. A different twist is added in *The Next Best Thing*, an adventure story that combines drugs, murder, and an attempt to steal twenty 11th century Buddhas from Pagan in Burma. Anthony Grey creates a journalist's search to find her father's murderer and the secret to the assassination of Rama VIII in the controversial *The Bangkok Secret*. *Thai Horse* by William Diehl chronicles the drug world in Thailand and Vietnam and its extension into the USA. Different from all of these novels and mysteries is Jason Schoonover's *Thai Gold* (Extract 5).

Moving across Asia from Tibet to the Golden Triangle to Bangkok, the adventure relates the attempts of an amateur anthropologist to find the lost skull of the Buddha and to evade the CIA, the KGB, and the Nazis.

[1]William J. Gedney, 'Patrons and practitioners: Chakri monarchs and literature', *Crossroads*, Vol 2, No 2, 1985, p 8.
[2]William J. Gedney, 'Siamese verse forms in historical perspective', in Robert J. Bickner, John Hartmann, Thomas John Hudak, and Patcharin Peyasantiwong, eds, *Selected Papers on Comparative Tai Studies*, Michigan Papers on South and Southeast Asia No 29, Center for South and Southwest Asia, The University of Michigan, Ann Arbor, 1989, p 489.
[3]Gedney, *op cit*, Ref 1, p 9.
[4]*Ibid*, p 9.

BOOKLIST

What follows is intended as a representative rather than comprehensive list of books about Thailand. All the books available in English included in the Extracts section or mentioned in the text are included. Where several editions exist, in general the latest and most readily available edition has been listed. Information on the original English language publisher can in many cases be found in the 'Acknowledgements' section at the end of the volume, as can the exact location of the extracts and the editions from which they are taken. Extract numbers are highlighted in bold.

Anderson, Benedict R. O'G. and Ruchira Mendiones, *In the Mirror: Literature and Politics in the American Era*, Editions Duang Kamol, Bangkok, 1985. **Extracts 4, 14, 16, 18**.

Anon (introduced by Witt Siwasariyanon), *Thai Short Stories*, 2 ed, PEN Thailand-Centre, Bangkok, 1971.

Anon, *An Englishman's Journals: 1890–1893*, Siam Media International Books, Bangkok, no date.

Angkarn Kalayaanaphong, 'Grandma', in Herbert P. Phillips, ed, *Modern Thai Literature: With an Ethnographic Interpretation*, University of Hawaii Press, Honolulu, 1987. **Extract 15**.

Angkarn Kalayaanaphong, Nawarat Pongpaiboon, and Witayakorn Chiengkul, *Three Thai Poets*, The Siam Society, Bangkok, 1979.

Aylwen, Axel, *The Falcon of Siam*, Methuen-Mandarin, London, 1989.

Beauvoir, Marquis of, *A Week in Siam: January 1867*, a reprint of an extract from the French *Voyage autour du Monde* in its original English translation, first published in 1870, with the illustrations from the French edition of the same year, The Siam Society, Bangkok, 1986.

Bock, Carl, *Temples and Elephants*. London, 1884 / White Orchid Press, Bangkok, 1985.

Bofman, Theodora Helene, *The Poetics of the Ramakian*, Monograph Series on Southeast Asia Special Report Number 21, Northern

Illinois University, Center for Southeast Asian Studies DeKalb, IL, 1984. **Extract 17**.

Botan (Susan Fulop, trans), *Letters from Thailand*, Editions Duang Kamol, Bangkok, 1982. **Extract 2**.

Boulle, Pierre, *The Bridge over the River Kwai*, Bantam, New York, 1990.

Bowie, Katherine A., ed and trans, *Voices from the Thai Countryside: The Short Stories of Samruan Singh*, Center for Southeast Asian Studies Monograph 6, University of Wisconsin, Madison, WI, 1991.

Bowring, Sir John, *The Kingdom and People of Siam*, London, 1857, 2 vols, Oxford University Press, Kuala Lumpur, 1969.

Brun, Viggo, *Sug, the Trickster who Fooled the Monk*, Scandinavian Institute of Asian Studies Monograph Series No 27, Curzon Press, London, 1976.

Cadet, J.M., *The Ramakian: The Stone Rubbings of the Thai Epic*, Central Department Store, Bangkok, 1982.

Campbell, Reginald, *Teak-Wallah: Adventures of a Young Englishman in Thailand in the 1920s*, Oxford University Press, Singapore, 1986. **Extract 10**.

Chart Kobjitti (Laurie Maund, trans), *The Judgement*, Laurie Maund, Bangkok, 1983.

Chaudhuri, P.C. Roy, *Folk Tales of Thailand*, Sterling Publishers, New Delhi, 1976.

Chit Phumisak, 'Art for Life's Sake' in Robert Cumming, Deborah Cumming and Pornpan Sodsie, trans, *A Premier Book of Contemporary Thai Verse*, Amarin Press, Bangkok, 1985.

Chula Chakrabongse, Prince (Alvin Redman, ed), *Lords of Life: A History of the Kings of Thailand*, London, 1967.

Collis, Maurice, *Siamese White*, DD Books, Bangkok, 1982.

Conrad, Joseph, *Falk: A Reminiscence* in Morton Dauwen Zabel, ed, *Tales of the East and West*, Hanover House, Garden City, NY, 1958.

Joseph Conrad, *The Secret Sharer*, in *Twixt Land and Sea: Tales, Joseph Conrad Complete Works*, Vol XIX, Canterbury Edition, Doubleday, Page, & Com, Garden City, NY, 1924 / Penguin, Harmondsworth, UK, 1990. **Extract 9**.

Dhanit Yupho, *The Khon and Lakon*, The Department of Fine Arts, Bangkok, 1963.

Diehl, William, *Thai Horse*, Ballantine Books, New York, 1989.

Dokmaisot (Ted Strehlow, trans), *A Secret Past*, Southeast Asia Program, Cornell University, Ithaca, NY, 1992.

Draskau, Jennifer, ed and trans, *Taw & Other Tai Stories*, Heinemann Educational Books, Hong Kong, 1975.

Duangtip Somnapan Surintatip, *On Thai Proverbs and Sayings*, The National Identity Board, Bangkok, 1985.

Feinstein, Alan S., *Folk Tales from Siam*, A.S. Barnes, South Brunswick, NJ, 1969.

Garrett, Stephen A., *Bangkok Journal: A Fulbright Year in Thailand*, Southern Illinois University Press, Carbondale, IL, 1986.

Grey, Anthony, *The Bangkok Secret*, Pan Books, London, 1990.

Griswold, A.B. and Prasert na Nagara, 'Epigraphic and historical studies No 9: the inscription of Ramkhamhaeng of Sukhothai (1292 AD)', *Journal of the Siam Society*, Vol 59, No 2, 1971, pp 179–228.

Griswold, A.B. and Prasert na Nagara, 'A fifteenth-century Siamese historical poem' in C.D.

Cowan and O.W. Walters, eds, *Southeast Asian History and Historiography: Essays Presented to D.G.E. Hall*, Cornell University Press, Ithaca, NY, 1976.

Han Suyin, *The Enchantress*, Bantam Books, New York, 1986.

Hollinger, Carol, *Mai Pen Rai*, Houghton Mifflin, New York, 1965.

Hudak, Thomas John, trans, *The Tale of Prince Samuttakhote*, Monographs in International Studies, Southeast Asia Series, No 90, Ohio University, Athens, OH, 1993.

Hudak, Thomas John, *The Indigenization of Pali Meters in Thai Poetry*, Monographs in International Studies. Southeast Asia Series Number 87, Ohio University, Athens, OH, 1990. **Extract 13**.

Kampoon Boontawee (Susan Fulop Kepner, trans), *A Child of the Northeast*, Editions Duang Kamol, Bangkok, 1988.

Keyes, Charles F., *Thailand: Buddhist Kingdom as Modern Nation-State*, Westview, Boulder, CO, 1987 / Duang Kamol, Bangkok.

Khammaan Khonkhai (Gehan Wijeyewardene, trans), *The Teachers of Mad Dog Swamp*, University of Queensland Press, St Lucia, Queensland, Australia, 1982. **Extract 19**.

Khammaan Khonkhai (Gehan Wijeyewardene, trans), *Teacher Marisa*, Pandora, Bangkok, 1984.

Khamsing Srinawk (Domnern Garden, trans), *The Politician and Other Stories*, Oxford in Asia Modern Authors, Oxford University Press, Kuala Lumpur, 1975. **Extract 11**.

Kon Krailat, 'In the mirror', in Benedict R. O'G. Anderson and Ruchira Mendiones, eds, *In the Mirror: Literature and Politics in Siam in the American Era*, Editions Duang Kamol, Bangkok, 1985. **Extract 4**.

Krueger, Kermit, *The Serpent Prince: Folk Tales from Northeastern Thailand*, World Publishing, New York, 1969.

Krull, G., and D. Melchers, *Tales from Siam*, Hale, London, 1966.

Kukrit Pramoj, *Red Bamboo*, Progress Publishing, Bangkok, 1961.

Kukrit Pramoj (Tulachandra, trans), *Si Phaendin (Four Reigns)* 2 vols, Editions Duang Kamol, Bangkok, 1981. **Extract 3**.

Landon, Margaret, *Anna and the King of Siam*, The John Day Company, New York, 1944.

Leonowens, Anna, *The English Governess at the Siamese Court*. Boston, 1870 / Oxford University Press, Singapore, 1988.

Leonowens, Anna, *Siamese Harem Life*, E.P. Dutton, New York, 1953.

de la Loubère, Simon, *A New Historical Relation of the Kingdom of Siam*, Thomas Horne, London, 1693 / Oxford University Press, Kuala Lumpur, 1969.

Manas Chitakasem, 'The development of political and social consciousness in Thai short stories' in J.H.C.S. Davidson and H. Cordell, eds, *The Short Story in Southeast Asia*, School of Oriental and African Studies, London, 1982.

Mattani Rutnin, *Modern Thai Literature: The Process of Modernization and the Transformation of Values*, Thammasat University Press, Bangkok, 1988.

Mattani Rutnin, ed, *The Siamese Theater: A Collection of Reprints from the Journal of the Siam Society*, The Siam Society, Bangkok, 1975.

Maugham, W. Somerset, *The Gentleman in the Parlour: A Record of a Journey from Rangoon to Haiphong,*

Paragon, New York, 1989. **Extract 8.**

Minney, R.J., *Fanny and the Regent of Siam*, The World Publishing Company, Cleveland and New York, 1962.

Mishima, Yukio (E. Dale Saunders and Cecilia Segawa Seigle, trans), *The Temple of the Dawn*. Pocket Books, New York, 1975 / Tutlle, Tokyo and Vermont, **Extract 7.**

Moffat, Abbot Low, *Mongkut, the King of Siam*, Cornell University Press, Ithaca, NY, 1961.

Montri Umavijani, Robert and Deborah Cumming, eds, *A Premier Book of Contemporary Thai Verse*, Amarin Press, Bangkok, 1985.

Montri Umavijani, *Sunthorn Phu: An Anthology*, The Office of National Culture Commission, Bangkok, 1990.

Moore, Christopher G., *A Bewitching Smile*, White Lotus, Bangkok, 1992.

Moore, Christopher G., *A Killing Smile*, White Lotus, Bangkok, 1991.

Moore, Christopher G., *Spirit House*, White Lotus, Bangkok, 1991.

Mouhot, M. Henri, *Travels in Indo-China. (Travels in the Central Parts of Indo-China (Siam), Cambodia, and Laos)*, London, 1864 / White Lotus, Bangkok, 1986. **Extract 12.**

Naowarat Pongpaiboon, 'The day that killed the dove', in Naowarat Pongpaiboon, Robert Cumming, Deborah Cumming, Michael Wright, and Pornpan Sodsie, trans, *Mere Movement*, Kao Kai Publishing, Bangkok, 1984. **Extract 6.**

Naowarat Pongpaiboon, Robert Cumming, Deborah Cumming, Michael Wright, and Pornpan Sodsie, trans, *Mere Movement*, Kao Kai Publishing, Bangkok, 1984. **Extract 6.**

Nikom Rayawa (Richard C. Lair, trans) *High Banks, Heavy Logs*, Penguin Books, Ringwood, Australia, 1991.

Niwet Kanthairat, '12:00 Noon', in Benedict R. O'G. Anderson and Ruchira Mendiones, eds, *In the Mirror: Literature and Politics in Siam in the American Era*, Editions Duang Kamol, Bangkok, 1985. **Extract 18.**

Olsson, Ray A., *The Ramakian*, Praepittaya Co, Bangkok, 1968.

Phayaphrom (Soren Egerod, trans), *The Poem in Four Songs*, Scandinavian Institute of Asian Studies monograph Series No 7, Studentlitteratur, Lund, Sweden, 1971.

Phillips, Herbert P., *Modern Thai Literature: With an Ethnographic Interpretation*, University of Hawaii Press, Honolulu, 1987.

Pira Sudham, *Monsoon Country*, Shire Books, Bangkok, 1988.

Pira Sudham, *People of Esarn*, Shire Books, Bangkok, 1987.

Pira Sudham, *Siamese Drama*, Shire Books, Bangkok, 1983.

Prem Chaya (HH Prince Prem Purachatra), *Magic Lotus: A Romantic Fantasy*, Chatra Books, Bangkok, 1946 (a rewritten prose version).

Prem Chaya (HH Prince Prem Purachatra), *The Story of Khun Chang Khun Phan*, Book I, Chatra Books, Bangkok, 1955.

Rama II, King (trans into prose by Prem Chaya – HH Prince Prem Purachatra), *Krait'ong (The Crocodile Killer Kraithong)*. Thammasat University Press, Bangkok, 1981.

Rama II, King (Pensak Chagsuchinda, trans), *Nang Loi: The Floating Maiden*, Scandinavian Institute of Asian Studies Monograph Series No 18, Lund, Sweden, 1973.

Rama II, King (Fern S. Ingersoll,

trans), *Sang Thong: A Dance-drama from Thailand*. Charles E. Tuttle Co, Tokyo and Vermont, 1973.

Ramkhamhaeng, King, *Maxims of King Ruang*, Abha Bhamorabutr, Bangkok, 1985.

Reynolds, Frank E. and Mani B. Reynolds, trans, *Three Worlds According to King Ruang*, Berkeley Buddhist Studies 4, Berkeley, CA, 1982.

Reynolds, Jack, *A Woman of Bangkok*, Editions Duang Kamol, Bangkok, 1985.

Saul, John Ralston, *The Next Best Thing*, Grafton, London, 1986.

Saul, John Ralston, *The Paradise Eater*, Fawcett Crest, New York, 1988.

Schoonover, Jason, *Thai Gold*, Bantam Books, New York, 1989. **Extract 5**.

Shaw, J.C., *The Seal of Tammatari*, Duangphorn Kemasingki, Bangkok, 1985.

Si Dao Ruang, 'Mother of Waters, Thaokae, and a Dog' in Benedict R. O'G Anderson and Ruchira Mendiones, eds, *In the Mirror: Literature and Politics in Siam in the American Era*, Editions Duang Kamol, Bangkok, 1985. **Extract 14**.

Siburapha, 'The awakening', in David Smyth, trans, *Behind the Painting and Other Stories*, Oxford University Press, Singapore, 1990.

Siburapha, 'Behind the painting', in David Smyth, trans, *Behind the Painting and Other Stories*, Oxford University Press, Singapore, 1990.

Siburapha, 'Lend us a hand', in David Smyth, trans, *Behind the Painting and Other Stories*, Oxford University Press, Singapore, 1990.

Siburapha, 'Those kind of people', in David Smyth, trans, *Behind the Painting and Other Stories*, Oxford University Press, Singapore, 1990.

Silcock, Thomas, *A Village Ordination*, Scandinavian Institute of Asian Studies Monograph Series No 25, Curzon Press, London, 1976.

Smith, Malcolm, *A Physician at the Court of Siam*. Country Life Ltd, 1957 / Oxford in Asia Paperbacks, Oxford University Press, Singapore: 1982. **Extract 1**.

Sujit Wongthet, 'Second nature', in Benedict R. O'G. Anderson and Ruchira Mendiones, eds, *In the Mirror: Literature and Politics in Siam in the American Era*, Bangkok, Editions Duang Kamol, 1985. **Extract 16**.

Sunthorn Phu (HH Prince Prem Purachatra, trans), *Nirat Muang Klaeng (Journey to Muang Klaeng)*, The National Identity Board, Bangkok, 1984.

Sunthorn Phu, (Montri Umavijani, trans), *Nirat Phra Prathom (Journey to Phra Pathom)*, Amarin Press, Bangkok, 1986.

Sunthorn Phu, *Nirat Phu Khao Thong (Journey to Phu Khao Thong)*, in Montri Umavijani, *Sunthorn Phu: An Anthology*, The Office of National Culture Commission, Bangkok, 1990.

Sunthorn Phu (Prem Chaya – HH Prince Prem Purachatra, trans), *The Story of Phra Abhai Mani*, 3 ed, The National Identity Board, Bangkok, 1986.

Sunthorn Phu, *Swasdi Raksa (Safeguarding One's Welfare)*, in Montri Umavijani, *Sunthorn Phu: An Anthology*, The Office of National Culture Commission, Bangkok, 1990.

Tachard, Guy, *A Relation of the Voyage to Siam*, London, 1688 / White Orchid Press, Bangkok, 1981.

Vella, Walter F., *Chaiyo!*, The

University Press of Hawaii, Honolulu, 1978.

Vella, Walter F., *Siam Under Rama III*, Locust Valley, J.J. Augustin, NY, 1957.

Vincent, Frank, *The Land of the White Elephant*, London, 1873; New York, 1884 / White Lotus, Bangkok, 1988.

Wajuppa Tossa, *Phadaeng Nang Ai: Translation of a Thai-Isan Folk Epic in Verse*. Bucknell University Press, Lewisburg, 1990.

Wanich Jarunggidanan (Jarungkitanan), *The Capital*, Chulalongkorn Translation Center, Bangkok, 1985.

Walker, David, and Richard S. Erlich, *Hello My Big Big Honey*, White Lotus Co, Bangkok, 1992.

Wyatt, David K., *Thailand*, Yale University Press, New Haven, CT, 1982.

Wray, Elizabeth, Clare Rosenfeld, and Dorothy Bailey, *Ten Lives of the Buddha*, Weatherhill, New York and Tokyo, 1972.

Young, Ernest, *The Kingdom of the Yellow Robe*, Archibald Constable & Co, London, 1898 / Oxford University Press, Singapore, 1986.

Extracts

(1) Bangkok in 1851

Malcolm Smith, *A Physician at the Court of Siam*

Smith's memoirs provide an intimate picture of court life 80 years ago by the Physician, a European, to the Royal Family.

They called it 'Krung Tep', the 'City of the Angels', a shortened form of its full title 'Krung Tep Maha Nakon Amara Ratana Kosin', the Angelic City of the Precious Jewel of Indra. The name Bangkok, from Bang, a village, and Kok, a species of wild plum, by which it is known to Europeans, has never been much used by the Siamese. It originated with the Portuguese who came to the country early in the 16th century.

The new city grew rapidly. By 1851 it had a mixed population of some quarter of a million inhabitants. The number of Chinese living there was greater than the number of Siamese, a somewhat surprising state of affairs until one considers the structure of the community which formed the city. The Chinese were the shopkeepers and merchants, and nearly all the trade of the City was in their hands. The Siamese, on the other hand, were the administrators, men drawn from every rank, whose whole existence centred round the Court, each one dependent for his living upon the man above him. Princes, nobles, lesser officials, underlings, servants, to name them in a descending scale, formed together a gigantic pyramid, on the summit of which sat the King . . .

Communication in and around the city was mainly by water. 'Tout le monde', wrote Mgr Pallegoix, 'va en barque'. There were tracks on land leading in various directions, but it was only in the interior of the City, in the neighbourhood of the markets, that one found roads. They were paved with large bricks. There was not a single carriage in the whole capital. At the end of the rainy season, when the surrounding country was flooded, the greater part of the city was also liable to be under water. A few years later the first roads were constructed. One extended round the city just inside the walls, and two or three more went a short distance from the palace. The New Road went as far as Ban Mor; it was not completed until 1864. The long narrow street fringing the river and known as Sampeng was in existence, at any rate in parts; it survived in almost its original form until the beginning of the present century. At the southern end of the City was the great market or bazaar, the daily rendezvous of thousands of people. It was the chief centre of distribution for fruit, vegetables, eggs, pork, fish and all those perishable articles of food upon which the people depended for their existence. The fish were sold alive, being brought to the market in tanks and then kept in ponds. The Marquis de Beauvoir who visited the market in 1867 saw 'in stalls placed side by side, pools full of young sharks, soles, eels, sunfish, a kind of fish which fastens on to the hulls of ships and makes a sort of deep cooing noise, and finally boa-constrictors'. His boa-constrictors were of course pythons, many specimens of which were caught annually in the city and its vicinity. The Marquis adds that 'Pere Larnaudie, who has tasted this dish, declares it to be delicious' . . .

That was one side of the picture, but there was another and less pleasant side. Like all crowded cities in the tropics in those days, without sanitation or proper supply of drinking water, without any form of modern medical control, disease was rampant. The fly-borne plagues of dysentery and the diarrhoeas took heavy toll of the children. The mortality in the first three or four years of life was between 70 and 75 per cent. Smallpox was a constant scourge. Vaccination had been introduced by the American missionaries as far back as 1840 by means of dried scabs sent from Boston, a voyage in those days of five or six months. They did it first of all for the protection of their own children, and having succeeded, tried to introduce it to the country. The King believed them and sent his physicians to learn the art of inoculation, and for a short time it was practised. But the supply of scabs was not always forthcoming for we read that in 1842 'the missionaries were again so surrounded by smallpox, without any hope from vaccination, that they inoculated their children and others with the smallpox, but not without loss of life'. It was not until the beginning of the present century, when vaccination was enforced, that the disease was really controlled.

(2) Bangkok: Chinatown

Botan, *Letters from Thailand*

This extract is taken from a novel that depicts the life of the immigrant Chinese in Bangkok. It is noted for its frequently critical views of Thais and Thai society. This is the opening of the third 'letter' in the collection, entitled 'Third day of the waning moon, seventh lunar month, year of the cock', ie 25 August 1945.

I know you are anxious to hear all about my new surroundings, so I shall attend to describing the household of Nguan Tong and the neighborhood called Sampaeng Lane before writing of anything else.

Nguan Tong, his wife and their two daughters live in a store. That is, except for the kitchen and their bedrooms upstairs, every inch of the house is devoted to the storage of incoming merchandise. Their store stands in the center of a row of wooden houses; in every one, a family shares space with a business of one kind or another. The front of each store is open to the street, so that during the day all the neighborhood opens onto the busy life of Sampaeng Lane and is absorbed by it. Then, there is little sense of the separateness of families one feels in the evenings, when the great wooden doors are pulled shut all along the row and across the street too.

Many of the families on Sampaeng Lane are Chinese, but there are a few Thai families; in fact, there is one directly next door. Klong Ong Ang is a canal which runs behind the row of houses, a different kind of avenue and one not less busy than the lane itself. Across the street from us the houses are identical, but they are less fortunate than we, for the klong behind their row has been filled in, and another row of shops stands where it once flowed.

All day long, men and women paddle small boats back and forth on Klong Ong Ang selling sweets, fruit, clothing, pots and pans; some sell gui tiow, noodles they ladle from great charcoal-heated drums. I saw many people taking their own bowls down to the water's edge at noon to wait for a gui tiow boat. When one does come in sight, the waiting customers cluster together and wave to it from one of the rickety piers that line the bank. The vendor paddles to shore and, after tossing a heap of steaming noodles into each bowl, garnishes them with peanuts, sugar, vinegar, and pickled vegetables, according to the taste of his chattering, gesturing customers. Then he hands up the bowls in exchange for a few coins, and paddles on to the next pier.

I noticed that the Thai boat vendors may be distinguished from the Chinese (of whom there are surprisingly many) by their hats – the Thai straw hat is not pointed like ours, but has a flat top and is raised off the head by some kind of band. It is surely cooler than the Chinese hat, more suited to this tropical land.

There are a few trees along the klong behind the houses in Sampaeng Lane, but most of them, and the grass too, must have been destroyed when the building went up. It is too bad. The other side of Klong Ong Ang isn't built up yet, and many graceful coconut and banana palms still grow there.

(3) Bangkok: Klongs

Kukrit Pramoj, *Four Reigns*

This extract describes Klong Bang Luang, a canal along the Chao Phraya River near Bangkok, and the vibrant life along the waterways of the city. The novel examines life inside and outside the royal court spanning the reign of four kings.

Their ferryboat was turning into the river Chao Phraya when Ploi's mother said to her: 'Pay attention to what I'm saying, Ploi. When the time comes for you to take a husband, make sure you find one with a single heart. Keep away from the great lover who must have many wives about him, or you will suffer like your mother'. A short pause followed before the advice was concluded: 'And you must never become any man's minor wife. Never. Do you hear?'

Ploi heard and, duty done, peered out from under the awning at life on the Chao Phraya. There were boats, floats, houses and people – and sky and flowing water, as on their klong – the Klong Bang Luang they had left behind only moments ago. And yet how different. So much more of everything out here on the river – boats, houses, people, water, everything. More, larger, merrier, moving brightly along in every direction, looking, sounding, smelling altogether new. A born-and-bred klong child having her first taste of the open river, Ploi took it all in and was more excited than she could say. And, stealing a glance at Mother, she said nothing. This was the first time Ploi had travelled so far from home. Her mother had told her they were never going back there, never to set foot on the old landing again, that they had left it for ever, unto death.

Their home on Klong Bang Luang had a brick-and-iron fence running the length of the grounds on the klong side. A pavilion at the landing place, then a spacious courtyard to cross to the big house where resided Ploi's father, His Excellency the Chao Khun. This brick mansion was considered highly stylish by Bangkok's fashionable citizens of these years of the mid 1880's–90's, during the long reign of Rama V, His Majesty King Chulalongkorn Phra Buddha Chao Luang the Great. From the courtyard one climbed either of the twin staircases that merged into a platform, whence rose another flight of steps up to the veranda with its green ceramic balusters. Set back off the veranda, which shielded them on all sides from direct contact with the heat and glare of the sun, were the three large rooms of His Excellency's suite, and that smaller one where the urns containing the ashes of his ancestors stood on symmetrically arranged tiers of mother-of-pearl inlaid altars. Ploi was particularly afraid of this room and, given a choice, would rather not go too near it. Not that she had to very often; she did not live in the big house, but in one of the several wooden houses to be found among the trees and footpaths farther back in the compound. Nevertheless now and again she had to make her way past its closed, silent door, and had never been able to do this without feeling shivery and her heart beating faster. Over the last few years, there had been those few times she was summoned inside by Chao Khun Father to pay homage to Chao Khun Great-grandfather and other forbears, to light candles and incense sticks and prostrate herself before the altars. This experience – the fact that she had been face to face, so to speak, with the contents of the room – had not served to temper her fear of it in any way, except to give that fear a more definite shape and flavour.

(4) Bangkok: Patpong

Kon Krailat, *'In the Mirror'*

This extract is from the title story of an excellent collection of short stories from the 1960s and 1970s, edited by Benedict R. O'G. Anderson and Ruchira Mendiones. It vividly depicts the degradation and victimization of the employees of the bar.

Many of the people up front move closer and closer. Some of them even poke their faces in, right close up – as though this were the single most extraordinary thing in life, something they'd never seen from the day they were born. Some of the customers who have girls sitting with them begin to grope them obscenely. His gaze meets their eyes and in a flash he senses in that some things men may not understand other men at all. In their eyes glitter a thousand and one things – pleasure and desire. Some of the men pretend to be unaffected by the scene, though in fact their souls are seething through every vein.

'What have I become?' Chiwin asks himself. He feels like a male animal in the rutting season, brutishly copulating with a female animal, right before the eyes of a group of studmasters. The more powerfully he performs, and the more varied the couplings, the more they're satisfied.

He glances down at Wanphen for a moment. He is now fully astride her body. She is sighing and groaning, twisting and writhing her body as if she's being aroused to the limit, even though actually she experiences nothing from what she's doing. This is the first time that Chiwin understands her life clearly, and he feels a heart-rending pity for her. He wants to ask her just one question: how much does she suffer from living this way? Having intercourse with a man she doesn't love in front of a crowd. Pretending to experience so much pleasure to arouse all these people . . . in exchange for no more than a hundred baht a night. Do her children back home know what's going on? Isn't there a night when she goes back home, lies down and cries? After all, she still has feelings, doesn't she?

Chiwin lifts his head and stares once again at the audience, as if searching for even one person with some understanding of the things that go on in the stories of the people working here. But he sees nothing but faces burning more hotly than ever with satisfaction and excitement. In fact, it looks like some of them have even reached a climax.

Chiwin begins to see the truth . . .

All of us here are simply victims . . . Latda . . . Wanphen . . . me . . . Even those people sitting there watching with such satisfied expressions. All of them feel the pressure of the society outside. So they come here for emotional compensation, to build up a superiority complex. They come to eat and drink. They come to sit and watch others expose their genitals and perform every variety of sexual intercourse. This allows them to feel contempt for people they can then regard as lower than themselves. Man has a deep abiding instinct to shove his way up over his fellow men. The truth is that we're all animals of the city, who live lives of pain and suffering in the midst of a demented society. The only difference between us is that those who have greater advantages stand on top of those who have less, and so on down the line.

(5) Bangkok: Patpong Road

Jason Schoonover, *Thai Gold*

This extract shows Patpong from the other side of the bar and is taken from an adventure story that recounts an amateur anthropologist's efforts to find the skull of the Buddha.

Ah. Patpong. Home. Finally.

And it was the evening of Loy Krathong, the most magical festival in Thailand, held on the twelfth full moon of the year. Many of the bars had set up elaborate ponds before their establishments and smiling Thai girls were strolling around them, holding the pretty floats they would later launch in propitiation to the Goddess of Water.

Powdered, pampered and perfumed, I was already floating on a soft cumulus on which winged nymphs sang seraphic tunes, as I drifted down the neoned strip, past the deaf vendors flogging their watercolors and wares, past touts flashing cards advertising 'pussy Smoke Ckga Lett show' and 'pussy pingy-pong show' and 'Resbien show with dildow', past sexy, bikini-clad girls trying to lure me into the throbbing hearts of bears with names like the Pussy A-Go-Go, Erotica, Flashtastic. I ignored them all – there was only one bar I was interested in tonight. My favorite bar on my favorite street in my favorite city in my favorite country in the world.

Crazy Horse.

I skipped up the steps and bounced in, breathing deeply of the scented air that felt crisp and cool as a mountain morning, while the beat of the best of *Billboard* boomed out of the speakers. I surveyed the bright neon interior: the glistening white rectangular island bar, the high-tech room which center it dominated, the showcased a-go-go stage raised to high-heeled ankles at eye level. Above the bikinied dancing girls admiring themselves in the mirrored walls orbited a Star Wars satellite system of flashing, twirling lights. The place was doing wall-to-wall business as usual, and sexy, semiclad Thai girls were resting on the arms and laps of *farangs* – foreigners – all over the sparkling room. The energy level was high, hot and horny.

(6) Bangkok: Outside Thammasat University

Naowarat Pongpaiboon, *'The Day that Killed the Dove'*

Democracy demonstrations were brutally suppressed outside Thammasat University on 6 October 1976. The poem is from the collection Mere Movement.

See the hand, the drooped cigarette,
the eye set asquint on the gun,
and the uniforms, crouched, looking on.
One by one the students each slouch.

See the blood exchanged for a face.
Fists replace a jaw, boots a haunch.
Billy-clubs bounce like the beats of a march.
Torsos twitch, relax, and are still.

They are necklaced with ropes, they are piled
in a field. Bare backs ooze and swell
and stain. Shiny billy-clubs dull
with the swill of blood and stray hair.

See the tongue emerge, the neck stretch,
the trunk pirouette, dance in air.
See it curtsey when smashed with a chair.
Then a boot shares its mouth with its teeth.

A wisp of smoke, a match fire
licks the tire that crowns the limp heap
of bodies beginning to steam.
Each one shrinks like a stump in the flames.

See a chest caved in by a stick
now too weak to beg, too ashamed.
See helmets, machine guns that gleam.
See a quick saffron glint, a shaved head.

This photo, that photo . . . who shot.
This bullet, that bullet . . . who bled,
yesterday, today . . . still less blurred.
Every day more clear cut in my heart.

(7) Bangkok: Temple of the Dawn

Yukio Mishima, *The Temple of the Dawn*

This description of the Temple of Dawn is taken from Yukio Mishima's novel of the same name. It is a metaphysical work that examines Mishima's meditations on youth, age, nationalism and reincarnation.

Honda had crossed over to the other bank on a hired boat early the previous morning and visited the Temple of Dawn.

He had done this precisely at sunrise, a most fitting time. It was still darkish, and only the very tip of the pagoda caught the first rays of the rising sun. The Thon Buri jungle beyond was filled with the piercing cries of birds.

As he approached, he realized that the pagoda was all inlaid with countless fragments of Chinese porcelain of either red or blue glaze. Each tier was marked by a balustrade; the one on the first story was brown, on the second green, and on the third a purplish blue. Countless porcelain dishes that had been placed there formed flowers: yellow ones represented the cores from which extended petals of plates. Some had a core of inverted lavender wine cups and here colorful golden dishes formed the petals. Chains of such flowers ascended to the summit. The leaves were all tile; and from the top, four white elephant trunks hung down at the four cardinal points.

The repetitiveness and the sumptuousness of the pagoda were almost suffocating. The tower with its color and brilliance, adorned in many layers and graduated toward the peak, gave one the impression of so many strata of dream sequences hovering overhead. The plinths of the extremely steep stairs were also heavily festooned and each tier was supported by a bas-relief of birds with human faces. They formed a multicolored pagoda whose every level was crushed with layers of dreams, expectations, prayers, each being further weighted down with still other stories, pyramid-like, progressing skyward.

With the first rays of dawn over the Menam River, the tens of thousands of porcelain fragments turned into so many tiny mirrors that captured the light. A great structure of mother-of-pearl sparkling riotously.

The pagoda had long served as a morning bell tolled by its rich hues, resonant colors responding to the dawn. They were created so as to evoke a beauty, a power, an explosiveness like the dawn itself.

In the eerie, yellowish brown morning light reflecting ruddily in the Menam River, the pagoda cast its shining reflection, presaging the coming of still another sweltering day.

(8) Bangkok: Temples

Somerset Maugham, *The Gentleman in the Parlour*

Although Maugham is more well-known for his short stories set in peninsular Malaysia and Borneo, he travelled widely throughout South-east Asia. This travel book is subtitled 'A Record of a Journey from Rangoon to Haiphong' and includes descriptions of Bangkok and northern Thailand.

. . . these incredible buildings [are] unlike anything in the world, so that you are taken aback, and you cannot fit them into the scheme of the things you know. It makes you laugh with delight to think that anything so fantastic could exist on this sombre earth. They are gorgeous; they glitter with gold and whitewash, yet are not garish; against that vivid sky, in that dazzling sunlight, they hold their own, defying the brilliancy of nature and supplementing it with the ingenuity and the playful boldness of man. The artists who developed them step by step from the buildings of the ancient Khmers had the courage to pursue their fantasy to the limit; I fancy that art meant little to them, they desired to express a symbol; they knew no reticence, they cared nothing for good taste; and if they achieved art it is as men achieve happiness, not by pursuing it, but by doing with all their heart whatever in the day's work needs doing. I do not know that in fact they achieved art; I do not know that these Siamese wats have beauty, which they say is reserved and aloof and very refined; all I know is that they are strange and gay and odd, their lines are infinitely distinguished, like the lines of a proposition in a schoolboy's Euclid, their colours are flaunting and crude, like the colours of vegetables in the greengrocer's stall at an open-air market, and, like a place where seven ways meet, they open roads down which the imagination can make many a careless and unexpected journey.

(9) Mouth of the Chao Phraya River in the Gulf of Thailand

Joseph Conrad, *The Secret Sharer*

The Secret Sharer is a novella that explores the question of personal identity when a mysterious stranger appears on board a ship. Conrad (who was then merchant seaman Korzeniowski) received his first command at Bangkok.

On my right hand there were lines of fishing-stakes resembling a mysterious system of half-submerged bamboo fences, incomprehensible in its division of the domain of tropical fishes, and crazy of aspect as if abandoned for ever by some nomad tribe of fishermen now gone to the other end of the ocean; for there was no sign of human habitation as far as the eye could reach. To the left a group of barren islets, suggesting ruins of stone walls, towers, and blockhouses, had its foundations set in a blue sea that itself looked solid, so still and stable did it lie below my feet; even the track of light from the westering sun shone smoothly, without that animated glitter which tells of an imperceptible ripple. And when I turned my head to take a parting glance at the tug which had just left us anchored outside the bar, I saw the straight line of the flat shore joined to the stable sea, edge to edge, with a perfect and unmarked closeness, in one levelled floor half brown, half blue under the enormous dome of the sky. Corresponding in their insignificance to the islets of the sea, two small clumps of trees, one on each side of the only fault in the impeccable joint, marked the mouth of the river Meinam we had just left on the first preparatory stage of our homeward journey; and, far back on the inland level, a larger and loftier mass, the grove surrounding the great Paknam pagoda, was the only thing on which the eye could rest from the vain task of exploring the monotonous sweep of the horizon. Here and there gleams as of a few scattered pieces of silver marked the windings of the great river; and on the nearest of them, just within the bar, the tug steaming right into the land became lost to my sight, hull and funnel and masts, as though the impassive earth had swallowed her up without an effort, without a tremor. My eye followed the light cloud of her smoke, now here, now there, above the plain, according to the devious curves of the stream, but always fainter and farther away, till I lost it at last behind the mitre-shaped hill of the great pagoda. And then I was left alone with my ship, anchored at the head of the Gulf of Siam.

(10) North-east Thailand

Reginald Campbell, *Teak Wallah*

Siam at the beginning of the 20th century had considerably fewer European residents than neighbouring Burma or Malaysia, but some Europeans worked up country as teak inspectors. Reginald Campbell's account of his years in Thailand in the 1920s has a breathless 'Boys Own' quality, but, as the extract below shows, the dangers he faced were real enough and his infectious enthusiasm makes his account memorable and enjoyable. In this extract one of Campbell's fellow inspectors sets a trap for a killer elephant.

Dawn. Orwell goes to the office, summons the village headman, his own chief headman, and some of his coolies and mahouts. He points to a strip of harvested paddyland opposite the company compound on the other side of the river.

'Dig a pit', he tells them, 'there, in the centre of that field. Let it be nine feet deep and six feet wide, and let every man available get on with the work. When the pit is finished, conceal it with a covering of leaves and bamboo, then place a plank across the middle so that a man may get over in safety and an elephant may not.'

'So', murmurs the brown audience, puzzled but vastly interested.

'When everything is ready', Orwell continues, 'the mahouts shall drive two cow elephants into the field in the hopes of luring Poo Kam Sen after them'.

'But the pit', objects the village headman. 'Of what use is it, master? For it will only be by the merest chance that Poo Kam Sen will go near enough to fall into it'.

'It will not be by the merest chance', returns Orwell, 'because a man will go into the middle of the field, and the elephant, seeing him, will charge. The man will then make for the pit and run across the plank, leaving Poo Kam Sen to . . . surely it is clear?'

'Meh', exclamations of awe rise from a dozen dusky throats. 'And who . . . who will be the man, master?'

'I will be', says Orwell, and grins.

Thus it came about that the pit was dug, the females driven into position, and Poo Kam Sen lured out after them into the middle of the field. Behind the pit, armed with bamboo spears and ropes, stood numerous mahouts and coolies. And with them was Orwell.

'I'm going', said he, after a final glance round at the preparations. Then, perhaps a little white of face, he walked half-way down one side of the field, after which he swung boldly out into the open.

Poo Kam Sen, dallying with his cows, saw him, let out one great bellow of wrath, surged his whole colossal bulk forward to blot out this impudent pigmy. Orwell, turning, fled for his life towards the pit.

He had worked it all out beforehand; he was a good sprinter, and knew that in *open* ground a man, provided he has a reasonable start, can keep ahead of a charging elephant for, at any rate, a short distance; and he had, he thought, judged time and distance to a nicety.

But had he? Would the pit *never* be reached? On and on he ran, with the great death swinging along behind him. He made to turn his head, but in so doing tripped over a tuft of stubble and nearly fell, at which his heart started hammering perilously. One fall – and all would be over for him.

Poo Kam Sen was gaining on him, gaining, gaining; though he dared not turn round, he was *sure* of it. Ah, there was the concealed pit – at least, and there the plank leading to safety. One, two, three, four – and he was over.

Crash! With a thud that literally shook the earth the vast body smashed down into the pit.

'Quick! The ropes!' pants Orwell.

The coolies and mahouts leap forward, their object being to secure Poo Kam Sen's legs and thus render him helpless against the company elephants that will shortly arrive to drag him to a tree; but the awesome spectacle of the huge leviathan, bellowing and trumpeting and rumbling and bubbling, smashing and heaving and goring at the sides of his prison, causes their hands to tremble and the ropes to get confused.

'Out. He's getting out!' suddenly shrieks one of the men.

A pause, in which, to their horror, they see that Poo Kam Sen, thanks to his stupendous might, has actually managed to tear down part of one side of the pit and is beginning to heave himself up over the falling earth. Up he comes, up, up . . . then the coolies and mahouts wait for no more. Dropping their ropes, they flee in terror across the Mae Ngow river. Orwell, finding himself alone and helpless, has no course left him but to follow them.

The party gain the further bank of the river and run up into the company compound. There they see Poo Kam Sen sullenly rolling off into the jungle beyond the paddy-fields. But the fall has evidently shaken him, for he walks with a limp.

That evening news comes that he has killed another man.

(11) North-east Thailand

Khamsing Srinawk, *'Breeding stock'*

This short story satirizes the misunderstandings that occur between villagers and officials of aid programmes. Taken from The Politician and Other Stories.

The previous year the authorities from the District Office came to their house and praised her and her husband so much that while she forgot some things they said she did remember that they said her husband was one of the hardest workers of the district and that he should go to the District Office to receive an award the government was going to give him. Early the following morning her husband had left and returned just before dark carrying a little shiny cup and a young chicken. He boasted to his wife that it was a prize cup made of silver sent from Bangkok. Bewildered, she studied it for she couldn't understand how the little whitish thing could be a cup. She questioned her husband but he assured her it really was and even insisted she take good care of it because the District Officer told him it was very valuable and he should keep it safely. But still she didn't understand. Often wondering what it was for, she speculated that maybe the people of Bangkok had a different kind of shrimp paste and chilli sauce that needed this funny kind of cup but even so why didn't the District Officer give her husband a real cup she could use for the sauce? She would secretly show it to the neighbours but none of them could tell her what it was really for. Some of them thought that from the shape of it, it was probably meant to be used for water for the chickens and she tended to agree because on the day her husband brought it, he also brought a young chicken telling her it was a breeding chicken given by America. He went on to say that they would have to become up-to-date because the country was advancing, for proof of which he pointed to the chicken that he said had to be ordered from America.

He exaggerated a bit, 'When this chicken is full grown it will be only a little smaller than a vulture. What do you think of that! The authorities said our Thai chickens are out of date; too small and the price is no good so we have to get roosters from America.'

She listened with some anxiety, thinking that her chickens were going to be the size of vultures. She closed her eyes trying unsuccessfully to imagine what her house on stilts would be like when a flock of enormous fowl ran under around underneath it. She would miss the pretty sight in the mornings and evenings, of her nice mottled and multicoloured chickens. Still, she didn't feel she should say she objected and she marvelled to herself at the progress and changes going on. As time passed, her husband's frequent accounts of the oddities of progress finally brought her around to enjoying tales of what she never thought could be in this world.

(12) Patawi

M. Henri Mouhot, *Travels in Indo-China*

The intrepid Mouhot travelled throughout Thailand, Cambodia and Laos in the late 1850s. This section describes his reaction to a view from a temple in eastern Thailand.

The priests were much surprised to see a 'farang' (foreigner) in their pagoda, but some trifling gifts soon established me in their good graces. The superior was particularly charmed with a magnet which I gave him, and amused himself with it for a long time, uttering cries of delighted admiration as he saw it attract and pick up all the little pieces of metal which he placed near it.

I went to the extreme north of the mount, where some generous being has kindly had constructed, for the shelter of travellers, a hall, such as is found in many places near pagodas. The view here is indescribably splendid, and I cannot pretend to do justice either with pen or pencil to the grand scenes which here and elsewhere were displayed before my eyes. I can but seize the general effect and some of the details; all I can promise to do is to introduce nothing which I have not seen. Hitherto all the views I had seen in Siam had been limited in extent, but here the beauty of the country is exhibited in all its splendour. Beneath my feet was a rich and velvety carpet of brilliant and varied colours; an immense tract of forest, amidst which the fields of rice and the unwooded spots appeared like little streaks of green; beyond, the ground, rising gradually, swells into hills of different elevations; farther still to the north and east, in the form of a semicircle, is the mountain-chain of Phrabat and that of the kingdom of Muang-Lom; and in the extreme distance those of Korat, fully sixty miles distant. All these join one another, and are, in fact, but a single range. But how to describe the varieties of form among all these peaks! In one place they seem to melt into the vapoury rose-tints of the horizon, while nearer at hand the peculiar structure and colour of the rocks bring out more strongly the richness of the vegetation; there, again, are deep shadows vying with the deep blue of the heaven above; everywhere those brilliant sunny lights, those delicate hues, those warm tones, which make the *tout ensemble* perfectly enchanting. The spectacle is one which the eye of a painter can seize and revel in, but which his brush, however skilful, can transfer most imperfectly to his canvas.

(13) Saraburi: The Temple Phra Phutthabat (or Prabat)

Phra Mahanak, *Bunnowat Kham Chan*

A poem that describes the king's pilgrimage to the Phra Phutthabat temple in Saraburi and contains a complete picture of one of Thailand's most famous temples. Translated by Thomas John Hudak, see Booklist.

On levelled ground stands the mondop,
Magnificent with the most superior jewels,
Equal to Indra's palace, Witchayan,
Equal to the palaces of the gods.
Encased within that mondop lie the footprints
Of the Great Sage of Highest Teachings.
At the mountain's summit, this glorious enclosure shines.
Five peaks pierce the clouds, lustrous gems shimmering
With colors blazing in the brilliant sun.

Branching sheaths, with layered gold and precious stones,
Cover the supports in spirals and coils.
At the top, radiantly renewed,
Rest gracefully curved finials.
From four similar sides spring gables
Arrayed in arabesques of tendrils,
Interlaced with luxuriant vines,
Trimmed in borders of crystal and gold.
Entwined nagas encircle the ascending eaves;
Prominent, flashing, arching upward,
They blend into scores of multi-hued animal heads.
Flower petals in bands of gold, sparkling in splendor,
Follow limpid jewels in bands of leaves.
Golden leaves dangle from the Bho tree,
Loose pendants in orderly rows
Which the breeze blows, creating sounds
That ring melodiously and delightfully,
That echo stringed orchestras plucking preludes
And dancing deities singing softly.
Raised on the base's surface stands a garuda;
Swaggering, chest swelling, seizing a naga,
He lifts slightly, seeming to fly.
Elsewhere, lions mouthe luminous sapphires;
Angels implore with palms pressed together;
Kinnarees gracefully sway in rows, their arms entreating.
Giants with arms raised, shoulder gnarled clubs.
Tall, strong, flashing fangs bared, they seem to live.
Mirrored walls blaze, reflecting images
That ripple, blur, and travel through the crystal.
Over the four entrances, gilded archways
Gleam in patterns of Brahma's bow,
Covering and tying together the door posts.
Above the sheaths, jewelled flowers shine in rows,
Splendid lotus petals become patterns of nagas.
In the door's peaked gable, Indra sits
Astride Ayyaraa, his three-headed elephant,
Its tusks curved gracefully, its trunk curled
Raising a conch across noble breast chains
Glittering with jewels and gold.
Mother-of-pearl doors gleam in brilliant colors
As if, Viswa-karma, the celestial architect,
Created and erected them all.
On the doors, intricate vines entwine;
Carved glimmering leaf clusters reflect light;

Twisted sprays and coiled tendrils
Change to animals swirling about;
A trunked lion, and the king of beasts;
Peacocks, golden swans;
Brave Ongkot, the monkey warrior;
Hanuman, the aspiring, the ambitious;
Sugriva, the monkey king, cavorts,
Flourishing a large, flashing knife above his head;
And still another monkey king, the supreme Phali.
Carved in perfect patterns like wooden trays,
Eight equal entries, all colorful clusters,
Glittering, gleaming, and blurring the eyes.
Within, immaculate, pure, paved gold
Embellishes the surface that surrounds the footprints
Of the Unsullied One who possessed the ten powers.
Within that new mondop, assorted jewels
And fragrant flower garlands hang resplendent.
Auspicious stars from lanterns glisten and gleam
Above the storeyed umbrella all nature praises.
Tiered flowers lie before the lotus-like footprints
Formed from gold and nine auspicious gems.
The garlands disperse delicious perfumes
As in the divine palace of heavenly lotuses.
Torches on walls flicker, the interior becomes day
From rays of moon-bright light.

(14) Thailand: After a Buddhist Fair

Si Dao Ruang, *'Mother of Waters, Thaokae Bak, and a Dog'*

This is a short story that emphasizes the changes in traditional village ways brought about by development. The action takes place in a temple compound after a Buddhist fair to ask forgiveness of the Mother of Waters. It is taken from In the Mirror edited by Benedict R. O'G. Anderson and Ruchira Mendiones.

It was not quite dawn when the cry of the coel bird became faintly audible from the ricefields behind the houses. Adults and children who normally rose at that hour got up out of the worn, musty-smelling mosquito-nets under which they all slept together. Thong Muan's mother, who'd stayed home all night to guard the house, didn't go off anywhere. She stepped down from the porch to gather firewood, and made a bonfire in the middle of the yard, just to take the edge off the cold. And any family that had at least a bunch of green bananas to spare would sit around the fire, roasting them and keeping warm. By the time it was light enough to go off to work, they probably wouldn't need to eat again – even having roasted bananas for their breakfast was considered quite a piece of luck.

The village children, including Thong Muan, were still admiringly discussing the bravery of the *like* hero. As for the old folks, they were breathing sighs of relief that the day for asking forgiveness of the Mother of Waters had now passed, and that they'd had the chance to make their wishes in silent prayer. If these prayers were granted, the rice-stalks in the fields would grow up tall and strong. The Mother of Waters would not make the waters overflow their banks and flood the fields as in previous years. Furthermore, in the coming hot season they'd be able to measure out enough rice to pay off their debts to Thaokae Bak, and so relieve their poverty for another year. Until the next Floating Basket Day came round.

The morning of that same day, after the monks and novices had finished breakfast, they all joined in a big sweep-up of the temple compound, picking up fragments of baskets, paper, and banana leaves, and stacking them at one side of the temple – until they became a huge new heap of garbage piled on top of the old. When the sweeping was done, the abbot turned back towards the temple, mumbling out loud: 'Even the temple dogs don't starve to death. Let alone we human beings . . . don't you agree?' He seemed to be reflecting on the miserable fate of a mangy dog that was lying, shivering with cold, beside the pile of garbage.

Once the monks and novices were all safely inside the temple, the mangy, shivering dog got up and walked disconsolately towards the mount of garbage. Its head bobbing up and down, it snuffled irritably – for it found nothing there to ease its cruelly famished belly. It poked its head up and down, twisted its body this way and that, for a little while, before doing all it found to do – lower its rump to drop some turds on the heap of baskets, scratch with its paws two or three times, and then run out of the temple compound with an indifferent air.

(15) THAILAND: MAN AND NATURE

Angkarn Kalayaanaphong, *'Grandma'*

This extract is taken from a short story that interprets the traditional Thai view of the close link between man and nature.

She has regained consciousness, but her fever has not abated. Poor dear, she is delirious. She is confused and goes down to pick some watercress. The watercress cries out in warning, 'Grandma, don't come down here. There are dangerous snakes near the edge of the pond. They are mating'. However, she does not hear the entreating voice and walks on down, straight ahead.

So it happens, in a moment of fate, she steps on the tip of the tail of a vicious cobra. The cobra is startled. It swings around and bites her fully. The fangs are buried into her. She feels a sudden pain at the back of her foot, so she moves to soothe it with her hand. The cobra strikes again, this time at her hand, and she begins to realize that she has been bitten by a snake. Panic-stricken, she loses consciousness, and falls at the edge of the pond. Before long, the deadly poison of the cobra works its way against the current of her bloodstream. In old age, the woman has little resistance. The poison forces itself through the blood into the depth of her heart, bringing her pulse to an end. The old woman breathes her last. But her eyes are still open wide, as if to express her concern for the vegetables, trees, and flowers who are her companions. Their friendship has no comparison.

A portion of the waning moon still shows faintly and then disappears behind the trees. The day is beginning to dawn. The rain has abated some time ago. The air is calm and chilly, creating an atmosphere of solitude and silence, except for the reverberations of nature. Exploding dewdrops crackle on leaves. Only one lingering star still glitters in the immaculate womb of heaven.

For anyone having the power to hear beyond the range of the human ear the sobbing of the trees and flowers in that field would be very clear. The watercress, the papayas, the tamarinds, and the *tamlyng* shoots are all lamenting and weeping.

A tiny flower with a trembling voice said, 'Older brothers and sisters, I am so unhappy because I was hoping this morning to bloom into a bright violet flower. If Grandma could have seen my brilliant color it would have helped to relieve her pain. It is so sad'.

The *tamlyng* said, 'Look at that! An army of fire ants is eating away at the pupils of Grandma's eyes. They are chewing away at her eyes in swarms. In a few days her corpse will rot and swell. The vultures and crows will peck at her body and feed from her flesh. Her bones will be scattered over the soil and sand. It is so pitiful'.

After its lamentations, the *tamlyng* again begins to sob until tears come forth from the center of its pure white blossoms. The tears blend with the dew and overflow the petals, as if they are a stream of remorse mourning the death of this old woman who has said farewell to the world and has disappeared forever.

(16) Thailand: Modern Clothing

Sujit Wongthet, *'Second nature'*

This short story from Benedict R. O'G Anderson and Ruchira Mendiones's collection shows the disillusionment a village boy experiences on returning home after becoming a successful teacher in the city.

'The girls in Bangkok wear such gorgeous stretch-pants! Deputy Phichit brought me two pair from Bangkok, and I bought one myself in the provincial capital. All three have such marvellous colors! And they all fit so snugly! Didn't you bring any clothes from Bangkok, Thian? Why are you wearing your father's old things? Aren't you afraid the villagers'll say how out of it you are, even though you've come from Bangkok?'

'Don't you realize, Bun Lam, that the way you're dressed tonight is even more "out of it"?' answered Thian sarcastically, with a feeling of great irritation. But no matter how much exasperation he felt, he didn't express it too openly. He wanted to tell to her that stretch-pants were repulsive; but he held back, reflecting that he still had a few days left to explain to her that Bangkok boys with education and good taste regarded all girls who wore stretch-pants as low-grade whores; for any girl who clothed her body with such provocative tightness must be basically hard and far too forward. The young men were all agreed that a real Siamese beauty would never be brazen enough to display her bag of sexual tricks like that before the public.

(17) Thailand: a Royal Bath

Rama I, *Ramakian*

This episode from the Thai version of the Indian Ramayana describes the ceremonies and regalia involved in a royal bath (taken from Bofman's translation).

Then
The Giant Totsasian of the royal family of the giants
Made his royal progress

And entered the bathing place.
samee

He had them open a jewelled pipe
Fragrant with the odor of pollen.
He bathed in water with a fragrance that diffused through the air.
His trunks and epaulettes were jewelled.
Then he put on a lower garment
Interwoven with golden designs.
He put on a jewelled cloth,
A scarf bright with jewels.
He put rings on his fingers.
He put on three necklaces.
He lay two ruby bands across his chest.
On his arms were ornaments of gold in the shape of dragons.
He had on an ornamented yellow diamond ring.
Each finger of his hand was shining.
He wore a jewelled crown with flowers tucked in it.
Earrings shone on his ears.
A garland of heavenly flowers hung down.
In his right hand he grasped an arrow.
He was beautiful, like Brahma himself.
He ascended the royal carriage.
baat sakunii

(18) Thailand: Rural Schoolroom

Niwet Kanthairat, *'12:00 Noon'*

This short story set in the early 1960s describes the plight of the poor in their encounters with the arrogant middle class (taken from In the Mirror by Benedict R. O'G. Anderson and Ruchira Mendiones).

The morning sunlight pouring into the classroom gradually withdraws and vanishes through the window. By the time the sun has reached dead-center above the roof, the moment everyone is waiting for is only minutes away.

The teacher, still attractive, though single and a bit long in the tooth, stretches her body and leans comfortably against the backrest of her chair. The weather today is burning hot, with not the least breath of a breeze. Were it not for the gentle, steady fanning coming from the notebook in Mali's little hands, the teacher would be on the point of screaming.

But right now she's beginning to feel hungry . . . hungry . . . hungry . . . like the little girl fanning her, and like the forty or more children, boys and girls, sitting there in class in expectation of the moment so important to them all.

Some of the children are so hungry that it shows on their faces. Unable to stand it any longer, they turn and whisper to their friends sitting close by:

'I'm so hungry . . . aren't you?'

Their friends nod in agreement, since by now everyone has exactly the same feeling.

'I didn't eat a thing this morning. It was already late, and I was afraid I wouldn't be on time'.

Such is the reasoning of many of her friends – and of some of the teachers, too. For arriving at school even the slightest bit late means a big fuss and does one a lot of harm.

But Mali's reasons are quite different. She didn't eat this morning because there was nothing for her to eat. The few minutes left before the noon break seem immensely important to her friends. But for Mali they really don't mean a thing, for, when the moment arrives, she'll have to go hungry again, as she has no money to buy lunch . . .

Her mother is dirt poor. Even the plot of land on which her shack is built is rented. And she has no idea at all when the landlord will expand the housing development that far. But when that day comes, Mali and her mother will have to move somewhere else, and keep on moving. No one can possibly tell where they will have to flee to in the end. The land of the Thai is broad and wide, to be sure, but today every inch of it is someone's property.

Mali's mother hires herself out locally to do odd domestic jobs. Rich people, who live in beautiful houses, never seem to have time for housework. So there's usually plenty of work for her mother. And for several other poor people like her. As for the beautiful, brightly-colored clothes those people wear, it's her mother who washes and irons them all. And if the open spaces in the front of those houses have well-kept lawns, that's also the result of her mother's careful cutting.

But recently her mother's earnings have been getting smaller, because those houses have been hiring live-in servants to do everything instead. Not just that: people have been coming in to compete with her mother in cutting the grass too. And Mother really can't hold her own, for they've been coming with power-mowers, really handy machines. One just starts up the motor, pushes the machine along, and the job's done – and the lawn looks much nicer than when her mother uses her two hands and that sharp old knife of hers.

(19) THAILAND: WEDDING CEREMONY

Khammaan Khonkhai,
The Teachers of Mad Dog Swamp

Teachers of Mad Dog Swamp examines the problems found in rural primary schools and the often futile attempts to solve them. The novel introduces the reader to the lives and traditions of the north-eastern villagers. This extract gives an excellent picture of a traditional wedding.

The *thaw cam*, the officiant who would perform the *khwan* ceremony, usually called a Brahmin in the towns, was an old man wearing a white cloth round his waist and another wrapped around the upper part of his body. He came and sat by the tray with the ritual equipment. The bridegroom sat in front of him and the guests, friends and relatives sat in a circle around them, all with their palms together in front of them, in the attitude of devotion. The *thaw cam* chanted the sacred formulae. The headmaster came up and joined the circle, while Piya backed off and sat against the wall, with his hands together like everybody else.

The words the *thaw cam* chanted were in the local rural dialect. He began by announcing to all the gods and goddesses that this couple loved each other and were now married, their bodies devoted to building a family which would be prosperous, tranquil and happy. Then came the 'calling of the *khwan*', that is, the infusion of inner strength into both of them. They were then blessed, and prosperity and happiness invoked on their behalf. The chanting was done from a set of old palm leaf manuscripts handed down through many generations. The important and powerful quality of this ritual lies in the officiant having a voice that is cold and heavy and a manner dignified and deliberate.

Until the officiant reached the part of the chant in which the *khwan* is called, a couple outside kept calling 'Come! *der! khwan! err-ii!*' dragging out the two syllables *der err-ii*. When the correct point was reached, the entire company began to repeat this refrain: 'Come! *der! khwan! err-ii!*', all together, as loud as possible, till the sound became a concerted yell. The microphone picked up the sound and it boomed through the village and far out into the fields: 'Come! *der! khwan! err-ii!*'

Piya too was swept up in the excitement and helped swell the sound of calling the *khwan*. His mind went back to his childhood – when he was about seven or eight he had nearly drowned, and his mother had had the ritual performed for his benefit.

'Come! *der! khwan! err-ii!*' Piya joined in the second time round and thought to himself, 'They are calling for their own *khwan* rather than for that of anyone else'.

The *thaw cam* then took one of the eggs from the tray and cut it in two. He gave the egg to the groom who fed the bride with it, with all guests looking on. Then came the 'tying of wrists'. In former times the wrists of bride and groom were tied with the thread itself and with nothing else. Now, however, banknotes, ten, twenty, or one hundred-baht notes according to the station of the guest, are tied onto the arms of the couple. This money is a gift to the newlyweds. The parents can't take any part of it as their share or as a contribution towards expenses. The headmaster turned towards Piya and said, 'Come here a moment. Come, tie the wrists of the bride and groom'.

Piya picked up a piece of thread, about a span in length which the headmaster passed to him. The crowd was pushing back and forth, making their way to the couple, tying their wrists and moving away. Some tied the wrists of one, some the other, some both. The method of tying was to loop the thread below the right wrist and then twist the ends together so that they wouldn't come undone or the thread fall off the wrist. While doing this the guest or relative uttered any words of blessing or congratulations he or she thought appropriate. Those nearby would hold the hand or elbow of the person actually doing the tying, giving expression to their sense of community and sense of togetherness. Piya moved up to the bride. She was sweating profusely, moisture pouring down her forehead, and someone had to mop it up for her. He looped the thread around her left wrist and twisted the ends together, saying softly, 'May you have happiness and prosperity, may you have ever-increasing good fortune'.

'Thank you,' she said, avoiding his gaze, embarrassed. Both of them were quite unaware that the groom was glaring at them suspiciously.

Biographies and literary notes

AKATDAMKOENG Raphiphat, Prince (1905–32). Born in **Bangkok**, he studied English, French and history in the UK. He returned to Bangkok in 1928 via the USA and Japan. In 1932, he died from malaria in Hong Kong. He is noted for developing what is termed the international novel, an exploration of relationships between Thais and foreigners in countries outside Thailand. The most famous is *Lakhorn Haeng Chiwit (The Circus of Life)* published in 1929, which is said to be a fictionalized account of his experiences in the UK. Other major works include *Phiu Luang Phiu Khao (Yellow Skin, White Skin)* published in 1930 and *Wiman Thalai (Paradise Crumbled)* published in 1931.

ANGKARN Kalayaanaphong (1926–). The most respected contemporary Thai poet and a noted artist, Angkarn was born in southern Thailand in **Nakhorn Si Thammarat**. As part of his education, he participated in restoring and conserving traditional Thai paintings in **Ayutthaya** and **Petburi**. This experience is reflected in his own artistic work that frequently accompanies his poetry. His poetry began to appear in 1963 and is noted for its traditional allusions to Buddhism and Hinduism and for the juxtaposing of these allusions with contemporary scenes and problems. Probably his most famous poem, *Scoop Up the Sea* (1967), a description of the chaos of contemporary society, caused a sensation with its depiction of the pantheon of Buddhist gods and deities descending to the earth and eating dung. His best known collections include *Lamnan Phu Kradung (The Song of Mount Kradung)* and *Suan Kaew (The Crystal Garden)*. Angkarn has also written short stories (Extract 15).

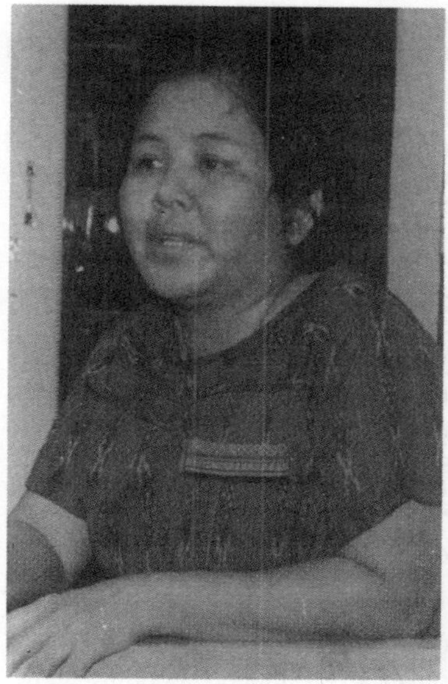

Botan

BOTAN (Supa Luesiri). A contemporary woman novelist noted for novels dealing with social problems. She is most famous for her novel *Jotmai Jak Muangthai (Letters from Thailand)* ◊, a view of Thai society by a Chinese immigrant (Extract 2).

Bunnowat Kham Chan (Discourse by Bun). A poem written in the *kham chan* verse form probably by the monk Phra Mahanak of the temple **Wat Tha Say** in **Ayutthaya** during the latter part of the Ayutthaya period. The poem is significant for its depiction of the merit making activities of the king at the **Phra Phutthabat** temple in **Saraburi** (Extract 13). A partial translation can be found in Hudak, *The Indigenization of Pali Meters in Thai Poetry* (see Booklist).

Chan. The *chan* metres had their origin in Sanskrit and Pali counterparts. The probable source of the metres first borrowed is the Pali treatise on metrics, the *Vuttodaya*. With the Pali metres, the line is determined not only by the number of syllables but also by the type of syllable, light or heavy, syllables which bear resemblance to the short and long distinction in English prosody. Because of the restrictions on syllable type and arrangement, the *chan* metres were a very erudite metre composed and appreciated by educated court audiences. Poetry composed in *chan* is filled with loanwords from Sanskrit, Pali, and Khmer, included to help fulfil the syllabic requirements. In addition, a special set of conventions is often applied to the reading of the metres so that they scan correctly. During the Ayutthaya period, and even during the *chan* revival in the late 19th and early 20th century, compositions in *chan* also included the *kap* verse forms in a style of poetry known as *kham chan*.

CHART Kobjitti. A contemporary novelist born in 1954 to a merchant family in central Thailand. In 1982 his novel *Kham Phi Phaksa (The Judgement)*, a realistic study of the effects of gossip and public opinion on the individual, was voted the Book of the Year by the National Literary Council of Thailand.

Child of the Northeast, A (1976). A novel by Kampoon Boontawee depicting a year in the life of a poverty-stricken north-eastern family. It is more of an encyclopedia of north-east culture than a novel, and the author calls upon his childhood memories to describe the food, occupations, customs, traditions, villages, and way of life of the north-east region during the 1930s. Made into a successful movie, A *Child of the Northeast* was translated into English by Susan Fulop Kepner in 1988.

CHIT Phumisak (1932–65). Marxist poet, critic, and philologist noted for his analyses and attacks upon classical Thai literature. In a 1956 polemic, *Sinlapa Phua Chiwit Sinlapa Phua Prachacon (Art for Life, Art for People)*, he called for the rejection of all classical literature because it failed to meet the needs of the people and for the creation of a new and meaningful literature.

CHULALONGKORN, King (1868–1910). The fifth king of the Chakri Dynasty and a noted reformer and administrator. He is also a noted prose stylist with his study of the royal ceremonies, *Phra Ratchaphithi Sipson Doen (The Royal Ceremonies of the Twelve Months)*, and his letters home from abroad, *Klai Ban (Far from Home)*. He also composed the play *Ngo Pa* which relates a Romeo and Juliet style romance among the pygmy negroids of **Yala province** in southern Thailand.

CONRAD, Joseph (1857–1924). Born Konrad Korzeniowski in Russian Poland. Spent 15 years at sea (of which the years 1883–88 were spent in South-east Asia), which provided the raw material for much of his fiction. 'Falk' and 'The secret sharer' (Extract 9) are based on Conrad's experiences in Bangkok. Despite the **Oriental Hotel**'s claim to a Conrad connection, he probably stayed at the now defunct Universal, or more probably, onboard ('In Bangkok . . . I hardly ever left the ship except to go to my charterers').

DOKMAI SOT (M.L. Buppha Kunjara Nimmanhemin) (1905–63). One of the first Thai novelists. Born into an aristocratic family in **Bangkok**, she lived for a time in the compound of the **Royal Palace**. While majoring in French in secondary school, she discovered Western literature and began her own attempts at short stories. From about 1929, she produced almost a novel a year. Her novels are sensitive portraits of the conflict between traditional Thai values and the rapid changes occurring in the aristocratic society. Her most famous works include *Khwamphit Khrang Raek (The First Mistake)*, published in 1930, *Sam Chai (Three Gentlemen)*, published in 1933, and *Phu Di (The Genteel)*, published in 1937.

Four Reigns, The, (1950). A historical novel by M.R. Kukrit Pramoj. In minute detail, the novel chronicles the life of the protagonist Ploi from the reign of King Chulalongkorn through the reign of Rama VIII (1892–1946). The story begins when Ploi is placed in the care of a royal benefactress in the Inner Court of the **Grand Palace**. It then traces Ploi's life in the court, her marriage in the aristocracy, her motherhood, and finally her death. The novel is famous for its realistic picture of the monarchy (Extract 3).

High Banks, Heavy Logs. A novel by Nikom Rayawa published in 1991 and set in the teak logging camps around the Yom River that depicts a woodcutter's life and the changes brought to his community by social and economic change.

In the Mirror. An important collection of short stories by a group of young writers who grew up during the tremendous political, economic, and social change that characterized the period 1963–69. The stories depict a realistic picture of the lower classes, the elderly, the minorities, and the dispossessed. The delineated picture of Thai society contrasts sharply with the one presented by tourist promotion schemes. The collection was compiled and translated by R. O'G. Anderson and Ruchira Mendiones (Extracts 4, 14, 16, 18).

Jataka Tales. A collection of 547 stories that describe the previous births of the Buddha. Of these tales, the last ten are the most popular and influential in Thailand with their themes of renunciation, courage, loving kindness, resolution, wisdom, perseverance, forbearance, equanimity, truthfulness, and charity. The last of the ten tales, the *Vessantara Jataka*, known in Thailand as the *Mahachat (The Great Birth)*, is the most important in Thailand. An excellent retelling of all ten tales can be found in *Ten Lives of the Buddha* by Elizabeth Wray, Clare Rosenfield, and Dorothy Bailey. The volume includes excellent colour photographs of temple murals that illustrate the stories. References to the Jataka Tales are found in many of the literatures of South-east Asia (see for example p 47 and pp 150–151).

KAMPOON Boontawee. A contemporary novelist who grew up in north-east Thailand. He uses many of his childhood experiences in his most famous novel, *A Child of the North-east*.

Kap. Probably sometime during the Ayutthaya period, the *kap* verse forms began to be used. Thai literary scholars contend that these meters originated in Indic forms; however, William J. Gedney, basing his claims upon comparative literary and linguistic studies, suggests that these forms were probably borrowed from Cambodian. Three main types of *kap* appear in the compositions of the Ayutthaya period. Although no study has actually been done, a close examination of some early works may reveal a number of other types.

KHAMMAAN Khonkhai (Sompong Palasoon). A contemporary author who grew up in **north-east Thailand**

Khammaan Khongkhai

and was a rural school teacher there, an experience that provided much of the detail for his novels and short stories. He is probably most noted for *Khru Ban Nok* (translated as *The Teachers of Mad Dog Swamp*, Extract 19), a vivid account of problems encountered by a young school teacher in a rural primary school.

KHAMSING Srinawk (pseud Lao Khamhawm) (1930–). Probably the most important short story writer in Thailand. Born to a farming family in **Khorat** in north-east Thailand, left university because of an illness and then worked as a forest ranger in the north for three years. He began publishing short stories in 1957. In 1958, the publication of *Fa Bo Kan (The Sky is No Barrier)* made him famous, but he stopped writing during the persecution of writers and intellectuals by Field Marshal Sarit Thannarat. After the 1973 coup, he became head of the Socialist Party of Thailand, but fled into the jungle because of the repression and violence following the coup on 6 October 1976. In 1977 he went into exile in Sweden but returned to Thailand a few years later. Expanded editions of *Fa Bo Kan* appeared in 1974 and 1979. A translation of the 1958 edition was published as *The Politician and Other Stories* by OUP (Extract 11).

Khlong. This is a very old and sophisticated verse form that is heavily dependent upon specific tonal placement. Two main types of *khlong* exist, their difference dependent upon the number and arrangement of syllables in the last line of each stanza and the placement of tones. As with the other types of Thai verse, numerous subtypes exist. Sometime during the Ayutthaya period, the original three tone system split into the present day five tone one. Because of these splits, *khlong* composition has become a highly intellectual activity. When *khlong* and *rai* alternate, the form is known as *lilit*; in these compositions, the *khlong* is generally used for commentary and dialogue while *rai* is reserved for describing action.

Khun Chang Khun Phaen. A *klon* ◊ poem probably written during the reign of Rama II by several authors, the most famous being Sunthorn Phu and Rama II. The poem relates the love story between the woman Wan Thong and two men, Khun Chang and Khun Phaen. During their youth, the three protagonists were playmates and best of friends. After growing up, a complex love triangle develops, with Wan Thong marrying both men at different times. Because she loved both, she could never decide which one she wanted. In the end, she was condemned to death because of her inability to choose.

Klon. Literary examples written in *klon* start to appear only in the Thonburi period, with the proliferation of *klon* beginning in the reign of Rama I. Since that time, *klon* has become the favoured verse form with compositions totalling thousands and thousands of stanzas. Two main *klon* types are used, one with six syllables per line in a four-line stanza and one with eight syllables per line in a four-line stanza.

Kraithong (The Crocodile Killer Kraithong). A dance drama written in *klon* ◊ by Rama II. The story is based upon the northern legend of the miraculous crocodile Chalawan, but it departs from the legend and treats the fate of the crocodile's wife and her affair with the crocodile killer Kraithong. The plot details the marital problems Kraithong encounters when he brings the crocodile's wife to meet his other two wives. The play is noted for its close examination of marital relationships.

KUKRIT Pramoj, M(om) R(ajawongse) (1911–). Born in Bangkok and educated at Suan Kulap School, Trent College in the UK, and at Queen's College, Oxford University, where he read Philosophy, Politics, and Economics. A noted politician and political analyst, he has served as the Speaker of the National Assembly (1974) and the Prime Minister (1975). He is also a noted author – his most famous novels include *Phai Daeng (Red Bamboo)*, *Lai Chiwit (Many Lives)*, and *Si Phaendin (Four Reigns)* – Extract 3.

LAO KHAMHAWN, see Khamsring Srinawk.

Lend Us A Hand, a short story by Siburapha that depicts the exploitation of the rich by the poor. The story then dramatically shifts and places the rich in the same position as the poor.

Letters from Thailand. An epistolary novel by Botan ◊ that offers a penetrating and insightful look at the attempts of Chinese immigrants to establish a life in Thailand. The plot follows the life of Sang U, from his departure from China to his marriage and his establishment of a successful business. The novel is noted for its often critical view of Thais, Thai society and Thai culture (Extract 2).

Mahachat Kham Luang (The Royal Version of the Great Birth). The story of the Buddha's penultimate life on earth. Known as the *Vessantara Jataka*, the story is enormously popular and influential in Thailand, existing in several different forms. Exemplifying the virtue of charity, the story follows the fortunes of the Prince Vessantara (Wesandorn in Thai) after he gives away the kingdom's revered and auspicious white elephants to a neighbouring kingdom. When the prince is banished for this act, he and his family give away all their possessions and become ascetics. Following this act of charity, the prince then presents his children to the Brahmin Jujaka, who is seeking servants. Fearing that the prince's charity would extend to giving away his wife, Indra disguises himself and asks for the prince's wife to protect her. When the gods see the great generosity of the prince, they rejoice and return

Manop Thanomsi

the prince's wife and his children. Afterwards, they all return to rule the kingdom.

MAHANAK, Phra. A monk at Wat Tha Say in **Ayutthaya**. Sometime during the latter part of the Ayutthaya period, he is said to have composed *Bunnowat Kham Chan (Discourse by Bun*, Extract 13) and *Nirat Phrabat (Journey to Phrabat)*.

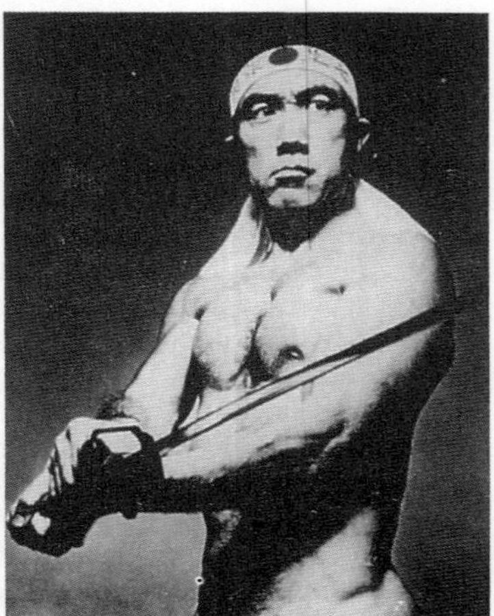

Yuko Mishima

MAHARATCHAKHRU. An important poet during the reign of Narai, although little is known about his life. It is assumed that he served as a teacher to Narai (the name translates as 'great royal teacher'). He is recognized as the author of the poems *Sya Kho Kham Chan (The Tiger and the Cow)* and *Samutthakhot Kham Chan (The Story of Prince Samutthakhot)* and the poetic textbook *Cindamani*.

MANOP Thanomsi. Contemporary novelist and short story writer born in 1948 outside Bangkok. Besides writing several collections of short stories, he is also well-known for his novels: *Dek Chay Thong Opchoey (The Boy Thong Opchoey)* published in 1982; a story of a bargirl, *Kinnari Luy Flo (The Kinnari Wades along the Floor)* published in 1983; and a story of a poor north-eastern girl working in an illegal factory, *Bo Hak Bo Tong Songsan (If You Don't Love, No Need to Pity)* published in 1984.

MAUGHAM, William Somerset (1874–1965). Born in Paris and trained in London as a doctor. His travels in the East won him few friends among the planters and other expatriates whose lives he mercilessly exposed in his famous short stories. Nevertheless, the short stories and novels dealing with South-east Asia have proved enormously popular, then and now. Despite his own realistic judgement of himself as 'being in the very front row of the second raters', Maugham was one of the best chroniclers of the end of British colonialism in South-east Asia. *The Gentleman in the Parlour: A Record of a Journey from Rangoon to Haiphong* is a travel book which includes an account of Maugham's travels in Bangkok and northern Thailand (Extract 8). See ◊ Malaysia and Hong Kong.

MISHIMA, Yukio (1825–1970). Japanese novelist, playwright and short story writer. *The Temple of the Dawn* is the third volume of *The Sea of Fertility* tetralogy that was to be his final work (Extract 7). On 25 November 1970 he delivered to his publisher the manuscript for the final novel in the cycle, *The Decay of the Angel*, staged a doomed 'coup' and committed *hara-kiri*.

Monsoon Country (1988). A novel written in English by the north-eastern writer Pira Sudham. The novel recounts the author's life and his studies abroad, pointing out the contradictions between the traditional and contemporary ways of life in Thailand. The author describes the farmers of **north-eastern Thailand**, depicting their strengths as well as their weaknesses.

MOUHOT, M. Henri (1826–1861). Born in Montbeliard, France. Philologist, teacher, scientist, traveller and writer. Was the first Westerner to discover the ruins at Angkor Wat. Spent the last four years of his life travelling throughout Siam, Laos and Cambodia, before dying of jungle fever. Mouhot's experiences are vividly described in *Travels in Indo-China* (Extract 12).

NAOWARAT Pongpaiboon (1940–). A contemporary poet born in Kanchanaburi. While a student, he helped to establish the **Center for Literary Arts** at **Thammasat**. An interest in folk forms and themes have long influenced his poetry. Romantic and religious themes dominate many of his poems, but some of his most famous poems deal with the contemporary condition of society and the problems faced by the farmers. His well-known collection of poems, *Mere Movement*, depicts in graphic detail the events and consequences of the mass political movements and demonstrations of 1973 and 1976 (Extract 6).

NARAI, King (1656–88). King in the Ayutthaya period noted for his interest in literature and his cosmopolitan court. Narai is reputed to have composed the second part of *Samutthakhot Kham Chan (The Story of Samutthakhot)* and the didactic poems *Khlong Phali Son Nong (Phali Teaches the Young)*, *Khlong Thotsarot Son Phra Ram (Thotsarot Teaches Phra Ram)*, and *Khlong Ratchasawat (The Ideal King)*.

NIKOM, Rayawa (1944–). Contemporary novelist born in Sukhothai and educated at Thammasat University in Bangkok. His books include *Takuad Khap Khophu (A Monitor*

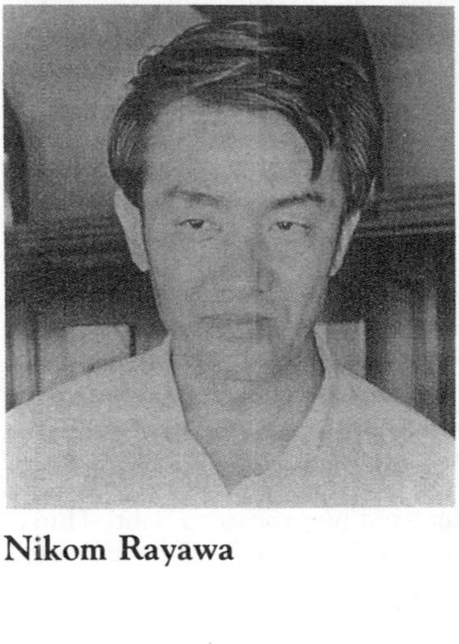

Nikom Rayawa

Lizard and a Decayed Branch), *Khon Bon Tonmai (Man on a Tree)* and *Taling Sung, Sung Nak (High Banks, Heavy Logs)*.

NIWET Kanthairat (1945–). Contemporary short story writer born in **Bangkok** (Extract 18). After teaching for several years, he became an editor and professional writer. In addition to short stories, he has written the novels *Thanon Nok Muang (The Road out of Town)* published in 1981 and *Phan Pai Muan Say Lom (Passing like the Wind)* published in 1982.

Pañña-jataka Tales. A collection of 50 extra-canonical stories of the Buddha's former lives reputedly based upon local legends. Very influential in Thailand, these stories have been used as the subject of sermons, dramas, and poetry.

PARAMANUCHIT Chinorot, Prince (1790–1853). A noted Indic scholar and poet. He is famous for *Talaeng Phai (The Defeat of the Mon)*, for two studies on the *chan* ◊ verse forms, and completing the poem *Samutthakhot Kham Chan (The Story of Prince Samutthakhot)*.

Phra Aphaimani (The Story of Phra Aphaimani). A lengthy poem written in *klon* ◊ by Thailand's most famous poet, Sunthorn Phu ◊. Originally written in instalments to secure an income, the poem follows the adventures and loves of the two brothers, Phra Aphaimani and Phra Suwan. When the two brothers are sent out by their father to attain an education, Phra Aphaimani learns to play the flute and his brother to fight. Thinking the two brothers have wasted their time, their father banishes them. In their exile, they meet a sea ogress, a mermaid, and several different princesses. An epic of romance and wonderment, the poem is noted for its descriptions of cultural change and the influence of the West as it was occurring in Thailand at the time of the poem's composition.

Phra Law (The Story of Prince Law). The Thai classic of the romantic genre written in *lilit*. The date of composition has been placed during the reign of Narai (ie 17th century), but it has also been placed much earlier, perhaps as early as the reign of Borommatrailokkanat (1448–88). This classic romance depicts the love triangle between the prince Phra Law and two princesses of a neighbouring kingdom. Because the prince's father has killed the princess's father, the marriage between the children can never occur. Secretly, the lovers meet but they are discovered and in the ensuing battle, the prince and princesses are all killed. Only after this tragedy and elaborate funeral ceremonies are the two kingdoms united. The poem is celebrated not only for its exceptional poetry but also for its depiction of ancient Thai customs and traditions. The plot was rendered into English in 1936 by Prem Chaya under the title *Magic Lotus*. Various stanzas appear in Bickner (see Booklist).

PIRA Sudham (1942–). Contemporary novelist and short story writer born in a north-eastern province bordering Cambodia. Writing in English, Pira portrays the poverty-stricken life of the north-easterners. His work includes *Siamese Drama* (1983), *People of Esarn* (1987) and *Monsoon Country* (1988) ◊.

Politician and Other Stories, The. An important collection of short stories by Khamsing Srinawk. These stories sensitively portray the farmers of the north-eastern part of Thailand as they attempt to deal with new government bureaucracies, development programmes, and clashes between traditional and modern ways of living (Extract 11).

Rai. The earliest type of verse form is *rai*, a type of rhymed prose. Stanzas of *rai* usually consist of five-syllable lines linked together by rhyme between the last syllable of the line with one of the first three in the next. Any number of lines may complete a stanza. Probably the oldest of the verse forms, *rai* is frequently used for chronicles, religous tracts, and laws.

King Rama I

RAMA I (1782–1809). First king of the Chakri dynasty. He moved the capital from **Thonburi** to the present-day site of **Bangkok** and attempted to re-establish the capital in imitation of the old capital of **Ayutthaya**. He is credited with a major literary revival and the composition of a group of classic *klon* ◊ poems: a complete version of the *Ramakian* ◊ which incorporated numerous Thai legends, customs, and traditions; *Dalang (The Puppet Master)* and a portion of *Inao (The Prince Inao)*, both reworkings of the Javanese Panji cycle.

RAMA II (1809–24). The son and successor to Rama I. He is noted for being an excellent poet and for continuing the literary revival begun under his father. Filled with a variety of rhyming patterns, his *klon* verse is considered to be sweet and melodious. Writing for the dance-drama, he completed versions of the *Ramakian* ◊ and *Inao (The Prince Inao)* as well as a group of dramas that could be performed outside the court, including *Sang Thong (The Story of Prince Sang Thong)* and *Kraithong (The Crocodile Killer Kraithong)*.

RAMA VI (1910–25). The sixth king of the Chakri dynasty, noted for his intense interest in literature and the arts. Besides his own poetic compositions, he translated several of Shakespeare's plays.

Ramakian. The Thai version of the Indic *Ramayana*. Enormously influential in all aspects of Thai culture and the arts, the epic exists in a number of different versions. The only complete one is attributed to Rama I ◊ and his court poets; the *klon* poetry in this composition is noted for its vigour and for its direct use of the language. A more melodious and shorter version for use in the dance-drama was completed by Rama II. Other poets who composed various scenes from the epic include King Taksin, King Mongkut, and Rama VI. In its barest outline, the story depicts the abduction of Rama's wife Sita by Ravanna to Lanka, the ensuing pursuit by Rama and the monkey armies, the destruction of Lanka, and the return of Sita to Rama. For comparison, see the other South-east Asian versions of the Ramayana, eg, pp 164–165. A partial translation can be found in Bofman (Extract 17) and a prose translation can be found in Olsson (see Booklist).

Ramkhamhaeng Inscription. Dated 1292, this famous stele can be divided into three separate sections: the first describing Ramkhamhaeng's life from birth until the start of his reign; the second outlining the physical development and customs of the Sukhothai kingdom; and the third consisting of praise for Ramkhamhaeng. Most Thais regard the inscription as one of the earliest examples of a clear and harmonious style that reflects the poetic nature of the Thai people. In point of fact, the inscription does include numerous lyrical phrases and rhyming patterns that have come to characterize Thai poetry. In recent years, a significant debate has arisen over the authenticity of the inscription, with one group claiming that the entire inscription was fabricated by Mongkut in the 19th century for his own political ends and the other maintaining its authenticity. Ramkhamhaeng is also credited with a collection of ethical maxims and proverbs known as *Suphasit Phra Ruang (Maxims of king Ruang)*. Written in the rhymed prose known as *rai* ◊ and said to be based upon a Pali collection *Lokaniti*, these didactic maxims represent a genre that runs through the history of Thai literature. Topics include friendship, ambition, and respect for teachers and elders. Numerous collections exist, but the Ramkhamhaeng version is said to be the 160 verses inscribed during the 19th century on marble slabs at **Wat Po** (Wat Chetuphon, The Temple of the Sleeping Buddha) in **Bangkok**. Various translations exist, but the most complete study and translation can be found in Griswold and Prasert na Nagara (see Booklist).

King Rama VI

Rhyme. Two types of rhyme exist in Thai poetry, external and internal. External rhyme, considered compulsory for poetry, occurs between the last syllables of lines; it also includes a pattern between the last syllable of the line with one of the first three syllables of the following line. In older forms of poetry, rhyme also included the same tones. Besides producing pleasing aesthetic affects, external rhyme helps to establish the stanza and to maintain the demarcative rhythm characteristic of the syllabic stanzas. Internal rhyme involves the rhyme between syllables within a line. This rhyme may be either consonantal (alliteration) or vocalic, both occurring in a wide variety of patterns. While it is never stated that internal rhyme is compulsory, it seems fairly certain that no poem exists without it. In fact, the more internal rhyme, Thais claim, the better the poem. In some of the *klon* compositions of the 19th century, every syllable rhymes with the surrounding ones.

Sam Kok. The Thai version of the Chinese epic romance *Romance of the Three Kingdoms*. The story takes place during the period 168–280 AD, and relates how China was split into three separate kingdoms because of corruption and jealousy. Translated into Thai by Chao Phraya Phra Khlang, the composition is noted for its elegant Thai prose. It is said to have been influential in the early development of the Thai novel.

SAMRUAN Sing (Surasingsamruan Chimpanao). Contemporary short story writer born in 1949 in **Thonburi**. His short stories generally deal with minority cultures and social problems in the north.

Samutthakhot Kham Chan (The Story of Prince Samutthakhot). An expanded version of one of the *Panna-jataka* tales. Written over a period of 150 years by three different authors – Maharatchakru, King Narai, and Prince Paramanuchit Chinorot – the poem has a cohesive style and beauty. It is considered to be a classic of the *chan* ◊ verse form. The story follows the adventures of Prince Samutthakhot and his wife as they tour the heavenly realms with the aid of a miraculous sword. Throughout the story, various adventures provide the impetus for explaining the precepts of Buddhism. Translated as *The Tale of Prince Samutta Khote* by Hudak – see Booklist.

Sang Thong (The Story of Prince Sang Thong). Dance-drama composed in *klon* ◊ by Rama II for outside the inner court. Based on one of the *Paññajataka* tales, the story tells of a queen who bears a child in a conch shell and then is banished to the forest. Out of the conch shell, the child disguises himself as an ugly, kinky-haired man. In a series of contests, he distinguishes his skills and abilities, and a king's daughter chooses him as her husband, much to the dismay of her father. After the intervention of the god Indra, the child reveals his identity and is placed on the throne.

Secret Past, A. A 1932 novel by Dokmai Sot ◊ that explores the questions of integrity and honor when a young Thai woman raised in England returns home and discovers a long-hidden family secret.

SIBURAPHA (Kulap Saipradit) (1905–74). After writing a critical history of the 1932 revolution and opposing Thailand's entry into the second world war on the Japanese side, he was imprisoned, which ended only with the change in government in 1944. He was again imprisoned in 1952 because of his leftist views and his opposition to Thailand's entry into the Korean War. Released under a general amnesty in 1957, he spent the rest of his life in the USSR and China. In his first novel, *Luk Phuchai (A Real Man)* published in 1928, he tells the story of a self-made man, the model of a Thai gentleman, who attains his success through virtue and hard work. In his later works he becomes far more concerned with the plight of the poor; and in *Songkhram Chiwit (The War of Life)* in 1932, he criticizes class discrimination as he does in the short story '*Khon Phuak Nan*' ('Those Kind of People'), which details the clash between the rich and the poor in three separate instances. In *Kho Raeng Noi Thoe (Lend Us a Hand)*, he directs his attacks against the entrepreneurs who exploit the poor. The gradual awakening of a political consciousness among the destitute forms the theme of '*Khao Toen*' ('The Awakening'), a story depicting pedicab drivers and their attempts to improve their lives. Temporarily abandoning his overt political ideology in *Khang Lang Phap (Behind the Painting)* in 1937, he recounts a story of frustrated love between a young man and an older woman imprisoned by her class and age. Highly regarded by critics, the novel is one of the first from Thailand to deal honestly and realistically with characters and their emotions.

SI DAO RUANG (Wanna Thappananon) (1943–). Contemporary short story writer born to a poor family in 1943 in **Phitsanulok** in central Thailand. She went to **Bangkok** when she was 12 and worked as a maid, factory worker, and a labourer in various other jobs. She has produced a large number of short stories dealing with the poor as well as a short novel, *Chao Kawao Oey (Oh, Mr. Kawao)* in 1981 and a pair of novellas, *Dek Bin Dai (Kids Can Fly)*, in 1984. A number of her stories have been translated.

SI PRAT. Considered to be one of the best poets in the court of Narai. He is said to have been a royal page, and at the age of nine demonstrated his poetic abilities by completing lines of poetry for the king. Tradition holds that he was exiled to the southern city of **Nakhon Si Thammarat** because of his sharp wit and biting sarcasm. There, he again flirted with ladies of the court and offended the governor, who subequently ordered his execution on the beach. When Narai discovered the execution, he had the governor put to death. His most noted poem is *Nirat Khlong Kamsuan (A Mournful Journey)*, which describes his journey into exile from Ayutthaya to Nakhon Si Thammarat.

SUJIT Wongthet (1945–). Contemporary writer born in 1945 in the central province of **Prachinburi**. His early work emphasized a Thai nationalism, but he later moved to more liberal views. His two part novel with an English title *Made in the USA* (Part I, 1971; Part II, 1975) depicts Thai students in the anti-war movement. A prolific author, he continues to write short stories, poetry and critical essays on Thai archeology and history.

SUNTHORN PHU (1786–1856). Unquestionably Thailand's greatest poet. Noted for his melodious verse and simple direct speech, he is referred to as the 'Poet of the People'. Sunthorn Phu was born in the southern province of **Rayong**, but was raised in and around the palace when his mother became a wet nurse for the palace. Educated in the near-by temples, he eventually entered government service. A love affair with a lady of the palace named Chan led to his imprisonment. Upon release, he left to visit his divorced father in Muang Klaeng in Rayong. His journey produced the famous *Nirat Muang Klaeng (Journey to Muang Klaeng)* in which he addressed many lines to the lady Chan. Excerpts from his *Nirat Phrabat (Journey to Phrabat)* can be found in Montri Umavijani's anthology (see Booklist). After an illness, he returned to **Bangkok** and married his love, although the marriage was to end in separation because of his drinking. Under Rama II, he was given a position at court and made part of the royal composition group where he is said to have offered consultation to Rama II on his *Ramakian* ◊. After a fight with his mother, he was again imprisoned. While in prison, he composed and sold parts of *Phra Aphaimani (The Story of Phra Aphaimani)*. Freed from prison to help with *Khun Chang Khun Phaen*, he made an enemy of the king's oldest son, Prince Jesdabodindra, by criticizing some of his extemporaneous poetry. When the prince ascended to the throne as Rama III, Sunthorn Phu became a monk at **Wat Thepthidaram**. A son of Rama III took him under his patronage, but when the prince died, he was once again without a patron. Finally, after several years of wandering, he was restored to his position by King Mongkut.

Sya Kho Kham Chan (The Tiger and the Cow). A composition in *chan* ◊ by Maharatchakhru and based on one of the *Panna-jataka* tales, the story relates the strange friendship between a cow and a tiger who are later turned into two princes who experience a series of adventures with a magic sword.

Teachers of Mad Dog Swamp, The. A socially realistic novel that depicts the problems a young school teacher encounters in a rural primary school. Also noted for its vivid detail of life in the north-east (Extract 19).

Ten Lives of the Buddha, The. Prose summary of the last ten lives of the Buddha before his final reincarnation. An excellent collection, it was compiled by Elizabeth Wray, Clare Rosenfield, and Dorothy Bailey. The volume includes colour photographs of old murals depicting the stories; the photography was by Joe D. Wray.

Trai Phum Phra Ruang (The Three Worlds According to Phra Ruang). A lengthy and detailed description of the three worlds of the Buddhist cosmology. The prose work is attributed to King Lithay when he was the heir apparent in 1345.

Laos

Peter Koret

> 'Luang Prabang town is in many ways what idealists picture the cities of Utopia to be, whatever insurance companies may think of the fire-risks involved in more thatch than tile roofs'.
> *Harry A. Franck,*
> *East of Siam*

Laos is a small landlocked country bordered by Thailand, Burma, PR China, Vietnam, and Cambodia. Its population is approximately four million. Although there is a great diversity of ethnic groups and languages, the people of Laos are commonly categorized into three major divisions according to the altitude at which they live.

The Lao Lum, or Lowland Lao, is the most prominent group socially, politically, and economically within the country. Members of this group constitute slightly under half of the country's population. The Lao Lum are Buddhist and speak Lao, a member of the Tai linguistic family. They live in valleys of the **Mekong river** and its many tributaries. The major towns in Laos are also largely composed of Lao Lum. Besides the Lao Lum, there are approximately one million speakers of related Tai languages, including the Tai Daeng, Tai Dam, and other groups.

The Lao Theung, or Mountainside Lao, are composed of a wide variety of ethnic groups, including the Kammu, So, and Kuy. They inhabit altitudes between 500 and 1 000 metres above sea level. Believed to be earlier inhabitants than the Lao Lum, they speak languages within the Mon-Khmer family. There are approximately 600 000 Lao Theung within Laos. Recently a series of books has been printed, *Folk Tales From Kammu*, with translations and commentary on Kammu oral tales (see Booklist).

The Lao Sung, or Mountain-Top Lao, live at altitudes exceeding 1 000 metres. They are the most recent of the three groups to enter Laos, some having arrived from China and Burma within the past century. The Lao Sung are divided into several groups, including the Hmong and Yao. The Lao Sung speak languages within the Hmong-Yao family, and number approximately 300 000. There are also several ethnic groups, including the Akha and Lahu, that are commonly grouped together with the Lao Sung. They differ, however, in that they speak languages within the Tibeto-Burman family and live at slightly lower altitudes.

History

Very little is known about the early history of Laos. The **Plain of Jars**, in the province of Xiang Khouang, is named for what appear to be giant stone jars that are spread over the landscape. According to legend, they are jars of whisky that once belonged to the soldiers of an ancient King, Thao Cheuang. Archaeologists believe that these jars were in fact funeral urns, belonging to a civilization, possibly Mon-Khmer in origin, that dates back several thousand years. At the beginning of the Christian era, Indian-influenced civilizations existed in Laos, leaving behind inscriptions that are scattered throughout the country. During the 10th to 12th centuries, Laos came under the power of the Khmer empire. Sites such as **Vat Phu**, in Champhasak, show the influence of the ancient Khmer.

The Lao became dominant in the region in the 14th century when King Fa Ngum, with Khmer backing, succeeded in uniting Laos and much of present-day north-eastern Thailand into Lan Xang, The Kingdom of a Million Elephants. He brought Therevadan Buddhist monks and scriptures from Cambodia and strengthened the role of Buddhism in Laos. Like many Lao Kings that succeeded him, Fa Ngum attempted with limited success to eradicate animist beliefs. During the two centuries that followed, the Kingdom of Lan Xang developed an impressive Buddhist culture. In the 16th century it shared close political and cultural ties with the neighbouring Kingdom of Lanna which occupied what is now Chiang Mai and northern Thailand.

Due to inner rivalries, Lan Xang split into three separate kingdoms at the end of the 17th century: Luang Prabang, Vientiane, and Champhasak. Lao fortunes fluctuated with the power of its two neighbours, Siam to the west and Vietnam to the east. By the 19th century much of Laos was either a vassal of Siam or Vietnam, or both at the same time. When Chao Anu of Vientiane fought for independence in the early 19th century, the Thai army razed the city of Vientiane. Many of the Lao were driven out of Laos and settled throughout Thailand.

In 1883 the French took control of Laos. In the treaty they signed with the Thai, the Thai recognized French sovereignity over the east bank of the Mekong river but kept control of present-day north-east

Thailand. The Lao thus gained a new colonizer and at the same time lost a large part of their country and most of their population. There are now over five times as many Lao Lum, or Lowland Lao, within Thailand as there are in Laos. Laos remained a French protectorate until 1953. Because of the difficult terrain and relative lack of valuable resources, it remained less developed under French rule than did France's other colonies in Indochina.

The Lao independence movement, known as the Free Lao (*Lao Issara*) began during the second world war. It started as an effort to drive out the Japanese invaders, and when this was accomplished, its objective changed to driving out the French. Following independence from the French in 1954, Laos was faced by the larger and more powerful North Vietnamese and was drawn into the Vietnam war. For the Soviet-backed North Vietnamese, control of Lao territory was essential in their war with the USA. The **Ho Chi Minh** trail, located in eastern Laos, was an important route for transporting troops and supplies. For the Americans, it was equally vital to stop the flow of troops and supplies. Without the consent of the American people or congress, US governments under Presidents Johnson and Nixon conducted a secret war in the Lao countryside: 2 093 000 tons of bombs were dropped on Laos, making it per head the most heavily bombed nation in the world. Despite the destruction of the Lao countryside (and the people who lived there), the massive bombardment did not stop the flow of men and ammunitions along the Ho Chi Minh trail. In April 1975, approximately two years after the ceasefire between the Vietnamese and the Americans, the communists took complete control of Laos.

With the communist victory came the biggest exodus of Lao from their own country since they were driven out by the Thai in the past century. Over 300 000 Lao fled to Thailand. Many of the refugees were either businessmen or people with ties to the past regime. They filled large refugee camps in Thailand, the lucky ones accepted to resettle in foreign countries, such as the USA, Australia and Japan. At present, there is a repatriation programme for the refugees who have been lingering in the border camps for over 15 years.

With communist rule in Laos, the monarchy was abolished and the last Lao King died in a re-education camp in northern Laos. Tens of thousands of Lao people who had worked for the previous government were sent to re-education camps, which involved more labour than learning. In the mid-1980s, the majority of the detainees were released. The economic policy pursued by the communists made a country that was already poor much poorer, and in 1986, it slowly began to be liberalized. For the first time in more than a decade small privately-owned stands sold goods in Vientiane. With the fall of communism in the USSR, and the end of foreign aid in Laos, the Lao government has been forced to re-establish friendships with its former enemies. Laos has strengthened its relationships with the USA, Japan, and particularly with its neighbour, Thailand.

Lao Literature and Religion

Lao literature is a branch of a larger literary tradition that is shared by several Tai speaking groups of mainland South-east Asia, including the Yuan, Kheun, and Leu. Literature within this tradition can be found throughout Laos, north and north eastern Thailand, north-eastern Burma, and parts of southern China. Lao literature, like other literatures within the tradition, is closely linked to the Buddhist religion. In traditional Lao society, the centre of education and culture has been the temple. Most Lao men spent part of their lives as monks or novices and it was in the temple that they acquired literacy. The majority of Lao literary works, whatever their origin or contents, are presented as if they were religious tales.

The major inspiration of Lao literature is a collection of stories known as the *Pañña-jataka* (◊ Bodhisattva, Tales of) that originated either among the Yuan (the people of present-day Chiang Mai and Northern Thailand) or the Mon. The *Pañña-jataka* was composed in imitation of the Indian Canonical *Jataka* Tales (◊ Bodhisattva, Tales of), accounts of the various lives of the Bodhisattva that form a part of the Tripitaka, the Pali Buddhist scriptures. The Bodhisattva, or the one who will become the Buddha, must perfect himself through the course of many life times before he will achieve enlightenment. Lao composers, influenced by the *Pañña-jataka*, wrote the majority of Lao literary works in the form of Indian canonical Jataka tales (see also p 47 and p 109).

A visitor to a Lao temple cannot fail to see the close relationship between literature and religion. One of the most beautiful parts of a Buddhist temple is the artwork depicting life-stories of the Bodhisattva. The most frequent illustrations show the last 10 lives of the Bodhisattva before his enlightenment. By far the most popular is the last of the 10, the *Vesantara Jataka*, where the Bodhisattva gives up all his earthly possessions, including his wife and children (see also the Burma chapter, pp 2 and 47). In **Vientiane**, there are many temples that show scenes from the life of Vesantara, including **Vat Naxai**. In **Luang Prabang**, **Vat Mai**, a temple near the palace museum, has a beautiful bas-relief depicting scenes from the same story.

Phra Lak Phra Lam, the Lao version of the Indian *Ramayana*, is another popular inspiration for temple art. It is interesting to see a Lao adaptation of a Hindu story decorating the walls of a Buddhist temple.

Perhaps the most impressive example of these illustrations is to be seen as **Vat Upmong**, a temple on Luang Prabang road in Vientiane, about a kilometre's distance from the National Library. For anyone familiar with the Indian (or Thai) version of the story, the illustrations that cover the walls of this temple will demonstrate just how different the Lao version actually is. In Luang Prabang, the doors and windows of Vat That, near Phusi hotel, are covered with golden carvings that also illustrate scenes from *Phra Lak Phra Lam*.

In the past many people have confused the South-east Asian *Pañña-jataka* tales with Jataka tales that originated in India. Many travellers who visit Lao temples are similarly not aware that many of the stories depicted in temple art are actually Lao or South-east Asian folklore in the guise of religious tales. One prominent example is *Khatthanam* (Extract 5), a popular Lao story derived from *Sihananad Jataka* within the *Pañña* collection. Inside **Vat Xiang Thaung**, Luang Prabang's most famous temple, there are some very old paintings depicting scenes from this work. Khatthanam has two companions who travel with him, Mr One Hundred Trees and Mr One Hundred Carts. In one scene, Khatthanam orders them to borrow charcoal from an evil *Yaksa* giant disguised as an old woman. One painting on the temple wall shows Khatthanam's two companions shortly after they have asked for the charcoal, trapped in a cage by the giant as she prepares to eat them. The next picture shows Khatthanam grabbing the *Yaksa* by its neck and brandishing a knife, demanding the return of his men. If you have the chance to visit the inside of the **royal palace** in **Luang Prabang**, which has been converted to a museum since the revolution, illustrations from the same story can be seen on the walls of the throne room.

Other Lao stories are also represented on Lao temple walls. Inside **Vat Xiang Thaung** in Luang Prabang are paintings of *Suvanna Hoi Sang*. Although not one of the more well-known works of Lao literature, a famous Thai poem, *Sang Thaung*, was adapted from the original version of this story in the *Pañña-jataka*. In this painting, the hero saves his father-in-law's kingdom by meeting the Lord Indra's challenge to defeat him at a game known as *Khi* that is similar to polo. As the paintings on the walls of Vat Xiang Thaung are quite old and the writing that accompanies them is frequently faint to the point of illegibility, it is a challenge to guess which pictures come from which scenes in what stories.

The influence of Lao literature can also be seen in many Lao temples where people have their fortunes told in a game known as *Siamsi*. Destiny is believed to have a hand at deciding which stick will be the first to fall. For a small donation towards the upkeep of the temple, visitors are given a sheet of paper with the same number as their fallen stick. On it, their future is presented in poetic form. The fortunes, sometimes good and often quite bad, compare the subject's future with that of major Lao literary characters. An example of a bad fortune is to have one's fate compared with that of Sumuntha, a character in the well-known Lao story, *Sinxai* ⇨ (Extract 7). Sumuntha was abducted by an evil giant who kept her as hostage for so many years that by the time her relatives came around to rescuing her, she no longer wanted to be rescued.

MANUSCRIPTS

There are several methods of recording Lao texts. The majority of Lao writing is recorded on the leaves of a species of palm tree. The leaves are cut into long strips that serve as pages. A metal stylus is then used to inscribe the words on the leaves and rubber oil is applied to darken the

Inscribing a Lao manuscript with metal stylus

grooves made by the stylus. Once inscribed, the leaves are tied together into bundles, each bundle consisting of roughly 20 leaves. An average story consists of four of five bundles but long stories such as *Phralak Phralam* can consist of as many as 40. When a manuscript is completed, the bundles are held together inside two long strips of wood that serve as covers and then commonly wrapped in silk and precious cloth. Under good conditions palm leaf manuscripts can last over 100 years. Lao literature is continually re-copied, both for purposes of circulation and to preserve the texts as the leaves they are written on begin to deteriorate.

Lao literature is also occasionally written on folding books made of white mulberry paper, a practice more common among the Kheun and Leu.

Temple libraries are known as *Hau Tai*, literally, Buildings of the Tripitaka, the Buddhist Scriptures. Libraries traditionally make up one building within a temple compound. They are frequently quite beautiful, roofed with pagoda-style tiers, and sculpted with elaborate carvings. They are raised above the ground by tall wooden pillars to protect the fragile manuscripts from dangers of the elements, such as flooding, rats and termites. Unfortunately, rats and termites are ingenious, and a nibbled manuscript is an all too common sight within a temple library.

Perhaps the most beautiful temple library in **Vientiane** is one that is

Temple library

no longer in use. The **Hau Tai** of **Vat Si Saket**, facing Lan Xang road, is the oldest library left standing in the capital. Vat Si Saket, at present a museum, is the only temple that the Thai spared when they razed the city in the early 19th century. Although the manuscripts have long since been removed, the respect that the Lao have for a library of religious books can be seen in the fact that people still regularly make offerings of flowers, incense, and candles. If one wishes to have a look at temple libraries that are still in use, the libraries at **Vat Meexai** and **Vat Naxai** are among the largest in Vientiane.

Temple libraries are often worth seeing from the outside. To see the inside of one is more difficult. Unfortunately but understandably, most temples are reluctant to open their libraries for visitors' inspection. One reason is that they are afraid of the theft of manuscripts. Another reason is simply the difficulty of the task. Often the libraries must be opened with several sets of keys. Once unlocked, all of the doors and windows must be opened to drive out several decades' worth of dust. A ladder is often necessary to climb up the different layers within the building where the manuscripts are kept. Finally there is the problem of actually opening the manuscript itself. Manuscripts are wrapped carefully in cloth, and bound tightly with string. Having to untie a manuscript which has often not been untied for years, and then retie it in the same carefully symmetrical way that it was originally bound, is a daunting task most monks would rather not face. The easiest way for a visitor to see palm leaf manuscripts is not at a temple library, but rather at the **National Library** on Sethathirat Road, not far from the Lan Xang hotel. With the help of Australian funds, the library has built an air-conditioned room housing over two thousand bundles of palm leaf manuscripts.

The actual process of transcribing manuscripts is a dying art in Laos. Many works of Lao literature, however, have been preserved in book form both in Thailand and in Laos. There is also a religious firm that has issued a dozen works of Lao literature, mass-produced, printed in Thai script onto palm leaves at a factory in Bangkok.

History of Lao Literature

The themes of Lao literature have their origins both in regional oral folk stories and the Indian *Jataka* tales. An examination of the stories, both written and oral, of other Tai and non-Tai speaking groups within the region, such as the Tai Dam, Tai Daeng, Kheun, Yuan, and Kammu, show similar stories with similar motifs. At the same time, there is evidence to suggest that Kaun An, the most prevalent poetic form of Lao literature, has its origins in orally composed Lao poetry, known as *Phanya*.

Traditionally, the Lao language and its literature have been written in two scripts, Lao and Tham. The Lao script is believed to have originated from the script of King Ramkhamhaeng of Sukhothai in Thailand. Lao inscriptions on monuments in Laos and North-eastern Thailand date from as early as the mid-14th century and are particularly common from the 16th century onwards. The Tham script is derived from the Lanna script (of present-day **Chiang Mai** and northern Thailand), which in turn originates from ancient Mon. The earliest known Tham inscription in Laos dates from the end of the 15th century.

The exact origin of Lao literature is a matter of speculation. When King Fa Ngum united Laos in the 14th century, he brought both Buddhist monks and scriptures from Cambodia. For the next two centuries Laos, or the Kingdom of Lan Xang as it was called, developed a thriving culture. Many of its kings were ardent supporters of Buddhism. It is not known, however, what if any manuscripts or literature existed.

In the 16th century, the Kingdoms of Lan Xang and Lanna enjoyed a very close relationship. At the time **Chiang Mai** was renowned for its high level of culture, in particular Buddhist scholarship. Historical chronicles of both the kingdoms of Lanna and Lan Xang record several times during this period that religious scriptures were brought into Laos from Chiang Mai. The *Pañña-jataka* tales, a major source of inspiration for Lao literature, probably entered Laos at this time. Outside this collection, there were over 200 additional stories in Lanna that were composed in imitation of the Indian Canonical *Jataka* tales. These stories also formed an important influence on Lao literature. Whereas the great majority of tales written in imitation of the Canonical *Jataka* in Lanna were composed either in prose or a poetic form known as *Hay*, the Lao transformed the majority into a verse known as *Kaun An* ◊. At the same time Lao poets adapted the stories' context using Lao settings and Lao cultural symbolism to make them relevant to a Lao audience. The evolution of specific works between Lanna and Lan Xang is not certain however, and some tales may have been borrowed by the people of Lanna from the Lao. According to Lao historical chronicles, Lao literature reached its highest stage of development during the reign of King Suriyavongsa from 1633 to 1690.

The Lao language and its literature suffered with the deterioration of the Kingdom of Lan Xang. When the Thai army razed Vientiane in the early 19th century, they destroyed the Buddhist temples and took with them thousands of manuscripts from temple libraries. Later in the century, when the French annexed Laos, they established French as the official language of the country. In high schools and colleges in the major towns, French was the sole language of instruction, and French history and culture was taught in place of Lao. The Lao elite often came to look down on their own culture and language in which they were largely uneducated. Indeed much of the Lao literature that was written by the Lao elite during the colonial period was composed in French in imitation of French literary styles. The ethnic Lao who inhabited what is present-day north-eastern Thailand were similarly taught to disregard their own culture. The Thai established schools in the mid-19th century that taught exclusively Thai history, literature, and language in an attempt to integrate the people as members of the Thai state. However, despite the lack of official sponsorship, the rural Lao continued to preserve the tradition of composing, performing, and preserving the literature. A large percentage of Lao poetic works were composed after the decline of the kingdom of Lan Xang, as can be seen by the great number of stories which have an extremely limited geographical distribution (often near religious centres) far from the traditional cultural centres of Lan Xang.

In the past half-century, traditional Lao literature has begun to be forgotten. This is particularly the case in the larger towns. Fewer and fewer Lao men enter the monkhood and learn the traditional scripts that are the necessary key to reading the texts. The art of transcribing manuscripts is known by few. Monks rely on printed texts for their sermons, and radio, films, and television are starting to replace ancient Lao epics as sources of entertainment. However, in much of rural Laos the performance of Lao literature is very much alive, and *Mau Lam*, musical performances based on Lao literature, still remain popular both in Laos and North-eastern Thailand (see below under 'Performance').

Lao Tales of the Bodhisattva

In terms of their origins, Lao tales of the Bodhisattva can be divided into the following categories, all of which are described in the 'Biographies and literary notes' section under '*Bodhisattva, Lives of*': *Canonical Jataka Tales, Paññа-jataka Tales, Apocryphal Jataka Tales outside the Paññа Collection with similarities to Yuan literature* and *Lao Apocryphal Jataka tales*.

The majority of Lao tales of the Bodhisattva (and Lao literature in general) can be divided according to plot into four basic types. These types are not peculiar to Lao literature but also exist in other literatures of mainland South-east Asia. They include:

1) The story of a prince who departs from his home, encounters great hardship and acquires supernatural powers, often gained through studies with a hermit in the forest or by his victories with various mostly non-human enemies, such as ghosts, mythical serpents

known as *nagas* or mythical giants known as *yaksa*. The hero is watched over and continuously aided by the god Indra. In the course of his journeys the hero meets and courts various princesses. In the end he brings the princesses back to his own kingdom and inherits the throne. Stories of this type are often very long and cover the adventures of two or three generations within the same family. Such stories include *Sinxai* (Extract 7), *Khatthanam* (Extract 5), *Kalaket*, *Suriwong*, *Thao Sowat* and *Champha Si Don*.

2) The story of a man born in a poor family with a grotesque outward appearance. The hero, for example, is born as a lizard, a leper, or even a human head unattached to a body. As a young man, the hero is shunned but at the same time amazes people through his performance of various miraculous acts. In the course of the story he successfully courts the princess and inherits her father's throne. During the courtship, the hero's body is revealed to be merely a superficial shell from which he emerges as a beautiful prince. Stories of this type are often humorous. They include *Thao Kam Ka Dam* (Extract 6), *Thao Bae*, *Suranna Hoi Sang*, *Thao Kapaum Kham*, and *Thao Hua*.
3) The story of a hero born as a poor orphan who receives a beautiful wife through the help of the god Indra. The orphan suffers various injustices at the hands of an evil king who desires the orphan's wife. The king loses his legitimacy in the eyes of his subjects as they watch him bully the poor orphan. The king is eventually defeated and the orphan is presented the throne. In some stories such as *Kampha Phi Noi*, *Suphom Mokka*, and *Thao Padaek Pasamau*, the King challenges the orphan to various competitions or assigns him impossible tasks under threat of death. The orphan is usually victorious through the help of the god Indra, but in some stories he defeats the king through his superior wit.
4) The tragic story of a love affair ends in the suicide of the two lovers. Such stories include *Khunlu Nang Ua* and *Phadaeng Nang Ai* (see Booklist for English translation), in which the leading male character is not the Bodhisattva. In *Khunlu Nang Ua*, the heroine's suicide is brought about by her mother's insistence that she marry a Lao Theung man rather than the Lao Lum man with whom she is in love. There are fewer examples of this type of story than there are of the previous types.

Lao Tales in Which the Hero is not the Bodhisattva

A relatively small amount of Lao Literature falls into this category. The majority of such works include Buddhist teachings and cannot be considered less religious than their counterparts in the previous category. One type of work, didactic literature, teaches behaviour and morals, often framing such teaching within the context of a story or the counsel of a father to his child.

Thao Hung Thao Cheuang is an epic tale, considered to be one of the greatest works of Lao literature. It relates the life and battles of a historical figure, King Cheuang. Several other stories such as *Thao Ba Cheuang* and *King Cheuang Han* also describe the exploits of this king. The character of King Cheuang can refer both to a historical figure and a mythical figure revered by many Tai and non-Tai ethnic groups in Laos.

Siaw Sawat is a collection of short stories, parables, and riddles taken from a variety of sources. It is intended to teach the proper behaviour for different groups within Lao society, emphasizing the proper roles and responsibilities of the monarch.

Xiang Miang is similar to many other trickster tales throughout South-east Asia. It describes the humorous episodes of a clever man who continuously outwits the king.

Phralak Phralam is the Lao version of the Indian *Ramayana*. It varies greatly from the original Indian text. It is very lengthy and in great detail places the Indian epic in Lao geographical context.

Phuan Lom (Extract 11) is unique to Luang Prabang province. It is particularly interesting for the humorous way that it plays around with Lao literary conventions.

Prose and Poetry

There are two basic types of Lao literature which fill overlapping roles within Lao society. Stories written in a prose form known as *Nitsay* ◊ are recorded exclusively in the Tham script and read as religious sermons. In contrast, tales composed in the poetic form of *Kaun An* ◊ can be written either in the Tham or Lao script, and depending upon the script can either be chanted by monks for religious purposes or performed by laymen as a form of entertainment. The poetic form, with its greater flexibility, is the more popular of the two types among the Lao.

Performance

Lao stories were traditionally meant to be read aloud to an audience. The stories were chanted, the type of chant varying with the region. Good readers were particularly valued and considered to breath life into the stories. The type of chants used to read the texts were later developed into various forms of Lao folk music.

The *Nitsay* ◊ or religious prose versions of Lao literature are meant to be chanted during sermons. In the course of a Buddhist festival, an entire story is often read. During Khao Phansa, the Buddhist Lent, a long story or sometimes several short stories may be paced to be completed within its three-month period. The Lao poetic versions have traditionally been read whenever people have an occasion to gather together. It was common in the past during funerals for people to congregate for three nights at the house of the deceased and read sections from Lao stories. Another popular occasion for reading Lao poetic works was after a woman had given birth to a child as she spent up to a month's time recuperating by a fire.

If you are in Laos during Khao Phansa (three months starting approximately June/July) you can easily attend a performance. Most temples will have daily readings, although the times and length of readings vary. It would be worthwhile to enquire in advance, because in some temples readings may go on for over an hour a day while others may last a mere 10 minutes to allow the novices to hurry off to their morning classes. The monk who chants the text will frequently sit on a tall chair with elaborate carvings high above his audience. Often the chanting is quite beautiful. This will be as close as you will come to hearing a Buddhist monk sing a song. During the festival known as Boon Phawet, which occurs in or around the month of May, there will be an all-day reading of the *Vesantara Jataka*, where monks or novices will take turns chanting from the manuscript. If you are in Laos at this time, the festival is well worth attending to see the colourful procession, the ornate temple decorations, and to hear the varying style of chants of the different performers.

Mau Lam, the secular musical rendition of Lao literature, is still commonly performed throughout Laos and north-eastern Thailand. Usually there will be performances at festival times, where *Mau Lam* is one of the many nighttime attractions. At present, performances are strongly influenced by the contemporary Thai pop scene. Scenes from ancient stories will continuously be interrupted by troupes of girls wearing skimpy clothes dancing to modern songs played on electric guitar. You can also buy recordings of *Mau Lam*. The Lao recording industry is still at a very basic level, so the best tape recordings (and video) of *Mau Lam* are recorded in north-eastern Thailand. The best collection of tapes is available at **Ratchabutr Stereo in Ubon**, where many performances are recorded. They can, however, be purchased all over north-eastern Thailand as well as Bangkok, which is home (if a temporary one) to several million Lao-speaking north-eastern Thai labourers. *Mau Lam* has a variety of styles and content. If you are interested in performances of Lao literature, look for tapes sold in sets with pictures of men and women dressed in gaudy costumes on the cover. Many of the major Lao works have been transformed into *Mau Lam*, for example, *Sinxai* (Extract 7), *Thao Kam Ka Dam* (Extract 6), *Khun Theung*, *Kalaket*, *Phadaeng Nang Ai*, and many others. Besides traditional Lao works, there are quite a few new stories being written and performed.

General Characteristics of Lao Literature

Lao literature shares much in common with tales throughout the world that are intended for a listening audience. It makes use of formulaic phrases, stock scenes and repetition in building up story line.

An important device that Lao poets and transcribers use to give dimension and character to a story is the insertion of what is known as *Phanya*. *Phanya* is a type of oral poetry that was traditionally an important part of Lao speech, used to comment on all aspects of Lao society. Young men and women would exchange *Phanya* during courting, testing each other's adeptness at fitting these witty sayings appropriately to a given situation. *Phanya* often have several levels of meaning and commonly include sexual connotations.

Another important and intriguing aspect of Lao literature is the use of parallelism. Parallelism, which is found in narrative traditions throughout the world, consists of the pairing of lines, sections, or scenes that are similar to one another both in their meaning and use of language. In Lao literature, the progression of plot is generally structured around a pattern consisting of three parts, in which two parallel sections are followed by a third concluding section. Patterns of this type vary in size. For example, the weariness of the hero might be described twice in two consecutive lines, followed by a third line in which the hero falls asleep. At a more general level, a story might consist of three journeys. In the first two, the hero travels to two different kingdoms. Both of the journeys parallel one another in the adventures that the hero faces and in the language that the narrator uses in describing the adventures. In the third and final journey, which forms the story's conclusion, the hero returns to his kingdom and fulfils his wishes, becoming the king. Many layers of overlapping patterns complement one another in the building of plot within Lao literature.

Another interesting aspect of the literature is the fact that there are no two identical manuscripts of the same story. Each time that a tale is transcribed from an old palm leaf onto a newer one, there is invariably a certain amount of change that is made. Whereas the changes are frequently relatively minor, at times the story is expanded by hundreds of leaves or entirely retold. Therefore, rather than considering a story to be the work of a single composer, the Lao often state that the tales are the collective works of many generations.

Contemporary Lao Literature

Contemporary Lao literature originated in the revolutionary struggle of the *Neo Lao Hak Sat*, or Communist Party of Laos. Its writers include those who were actively involved in the struggle, those who came of age after the revolution, and writers from the old regime who adapted their writing to fit the revolutionary aims.

Lao literature includes novels, short stories and poetry. A major theme has been historical attempts on the part of the Lao to free themselves from foreign occupiers. A book-length poem by the writer Somsi Desakomphu, *Pheui San Leup Bau Sun*, interprets an ancient Lao poem as a thinly-coded plea for the Lao to rise up against Thai invaders. The novel, *Love* by Khamliang Phonsena, tells of a valiant soldier in the war of liberation against the French. The hero leaves his lover to fight for his country and returns many years later, after the French defeat at **Dienbienphu**. In the meantime his lover, having heard false news of his death, has married another man. The hero of the story is a symbol of Lao youth willing to sacrifice personal aspirations for the sake of freeing their country.

Many works tell of the success of the revolutionary struggle of the *Neo Lao Hak Xat.* The novel, *Escape From Prison*, by Tongsia Kotwongsa, is an account of how the leaders of the Lao Communist Party escaped from a heavily guarded prison where they were kept by the right-wing forces in Vientiane. Their escape was due to the popular support they held among the people of **Vientiane**. *The Second Battalion*, by Suwanton Buphawong, relates the difficulties faced by the second battalion of the Lao revolutionary army, their braveness in the face of it, and their ultimate victory. In *Two Sisters*, by the same author, twins from the province of **Xiang Khouang** are separated at an early age as the result of the war. The older sister grew up comfortably in Vientiane while her younger sibling faced great hardships in the countryside and joined the Lao revolutionary army.

Stories often tell of the suffering caused by the war. There are many stories portraying the damage caused by American bombing. The short story, *What Remains*, by Saisuwan Paengpong, tells of a group of American soldiers who come to look for remains of American pilots who were shot down over Laos. A Lao villager explains to the soldiers the destruction and death caused by American bombs (Extract 3).

A theme of many stories is the injustice perpetrated by the old regime and how it was rectified as a result of the revolution. *The Sun Rises on Nang Island*, a short story by Uthine Bounyavong, portrays the life of a prostitute in **Vientiane**. She is forced into prostitution because of poverty. After the revolution, she is sent with other prostitutes to

Nang island to be reformed. She is grateful to the revolution for helping her regain her dignity.

Lao literature also deals with many concerns of present day Lao society. There are stories, for example, that tell of the problem of deforestation and the damage caused by American fragment bombs that were left over from the war. Many stories provide role-models, portraying Lao people with exemplary behaviour. In the short story, *The Dawn Of A New Day*, an irrigation worker is lazy and self-indulgent, but after joining the communist Youth Association he becomes a motivated worker and leader. In *Value And Price* (Extract 8), a short story by Duang Champa, a government worker, despite low wages, resists a bribe. He feels pride in being an honest civil servant.

Recent Lao collections of short stories show a tendency to be less overtly political than in the past.

Western Writers on Laos

Several books on Indochina were written by European explorers and adventurers in the late 19th and early 20th centuries. Many expeditions were made – and diaries kept and published – by French explorers.

Travels in Indo-China And The Chinese Empire by Louis De Carne (Extract 12), describes a Frenchman's journey in Indochina in 1867, two decades before the French colonized the region. He introduces Laos with the ominous words:

> It had been predicted that we should have to pass some months in Laos – a region of evil name, protected by the rocks with which its river bristles, and still more by the miasma exhaled by the sun's heat, from the curiousity or ambition of its neighbours.

The author does, however, begrudgingly pay a compliment to its inhabitants:

> We fancied, moreover, that we had nothing to fear from the Laotians; for their extreme gentleness left us without anxiety, so far as they were concerned.

Early accounts of Laos describe the beauty of the royal capital Luang Prabang, which appears to have changed little. The most famous early traveller to Laos was Henri Mouhot, a French naturalist who is renowned as the first European to visit the Khmer ruins of **Angkor Vat**. His account of his journey, *Travels in Indo-China*, has recently been reprinted (Extract 10). He travelled through north-eastern Thailand and Laos in 1859–60, where he died of malaria in the province of **Luang Prabang**. His burial spot can still be seen, a few kilometres from town, between the village of **Ban Phanom** and the **Khan** river. Eighty years later in 1926, in *East of Siam*, the American Harry A. Franck also wrote in glowing terms of **Luang Prabang** (Extract 9).

Luang Prabang may have changed little within the past century, but Vientiane presents a different story. Louis De Carne in his account of his travels during the 1860s describes **Vientiane** 40 years after the Thai invasion. The author arrived there by canoe and found the town overgrown with jungle (Extract 12).

BOOKLIST

What follows is intended as a representative rather than comprehensive list of books about Laos. Where several editions exist, in general the latest and most readily available edition has been listed. For most of the extracted works, information on the original English language publisher can be found in the 'Acknowledgements and Citations' at the end of the volume, as can the exact location of the extracts and the editions from which they are taken. Extract numbers are highlighted in bold. Extracts not included in Booklist translated specially for this volume.

Compton, Carol, *Courting Poetry in Laos: A Textual And Linguistic Analysis*, Center of Southeast Asian Studies, Northern Illinois University, Dekalb, IL, 1979.

De Carne, Louis, *Travels in Indochina And The Chinese Empire*, Chapman Hall, London, 1872. **Extract 12.**

Finot, Louis, *Recherches Sur La Litterature Laotienne*, Bulletin de L'Ecole Extreme Orient, Tome XVII Paris, 1917.

Franck, Harry A., *East Of Siam*, T. Fisher Unwin, London, 1926. **Extract 9.**

Ingersoll, Fern S., *Sang Thong: A Dance Drama From Thailand*, Charles E. Tuttle, Tokyo and Rutland, Vermont, 1973.

Krueger, Kermit, *The Serpent Prince: Folk Tales From Northeastern Thailand*, Cambridge University Press, Cambridge, UK, 1970.

Miller, Terry, *Traditional Music Of The Laos*, Greenwood Press, Westport, CN, 1985.

Mouhot, Henri, *Travels in Indochina*, White Lotus, Bangkok, 1986; Oxford University Press, Kuala Lumpur, 1992. **Extract 10.**

Peltier, Anatole, *Le Roman Classique Lao*, L'Ecole Francaise D'Extreme Orient, Paris, 1988.

Sahai, Sachchidanand, *The Krsna Saga in Laos (A Study In The Brahkutd Brahpan)*, P.K. Publishing, Delhi, 1978.

Sahai, Sachchidanand, *The Ramayana in Laos (A Study In The Gvay Dvorahbi)*, P.K. Publishing, Delhi, 1976.

Tambiah, S.J., *Buddhism and Spirit Cults in Northeast Thailand*, Cambridge University Press, Cambridge, UK, 1970.

Tossa, Wajuppa, *Phadaeng Nang Ai*, Bucknell University Press, Lewisburg, 1990.

Extracts

(1) Laos: Beside the Logging Road

Outhine Bounyavong, *Just a Pair of Birds*

The changes to the rural ecology wrought by large-scale logging. Translated by Outhine Bounyavong.

In the front yard, near the ladder to their house, was a sandy heap with some empty beer cans and Pepsi cans on it. With their flashy bright colours, they were a novelty in the village. Her son had picked them up from the road and kept them to play with, but neither he nor his mother had ever tasted their contents. Scattered along the entrance to their yard were also crushed Benson and 555 cigarette packets, tossed out by the drivers of the logging trucks and pick-up trucks as they roared past.

The men at the wheels of these vehicles were at first referred to by the villagers as 'traders'. These gentlemen from the town apparently disliked being called that, however, and said that they were 'businessmen'. But since the villagers thought of all businessmen as traders, they ended up calling these men 'log-trading businessmen'. Why these businessmen often carried long-barreled guns remained a mystery.

Today, as Nang Un sat on the veranda, the flocks of birds had all but disappeared from the sky over the ricefields. Only a few were seen heading for their nests. But Nang Un and her son did not see the pair of hornbills. Could they have suddenly changed their route? But she had seen them only yesterday. Perhaps somebody had discovered their nest in the forest and stolen their eggs, so that they had moved to another spot. She frowned. She did not like to think of the majestic hornbills interfered with like that. 'Soon', she reassured herself silently, 'they will be flying over the fields, straight over the palmyra tree just like every other day'. In her mind, she could imagine the pair of them gliding by, their great wings flapping overhead. She looked hopefully at the palmyra tree, but could see no sign of them. Her son, too, remained silent by her side.

A convoy of logging trucks drove past, churning up clouds of dust on the dirt road. Recently so many trucks had passed down their road, hauling huge teak logs out of the nearby forest, that even the flame of the forest blossoms were coated a dirty brown now.

As the dust was settling, her husband Tit Tan arrived home.

He told her that he had just seen a pair of hornbills dangling from the back of the last logging truck. One of the 'businessmen' must have shot them dead, he said.

Nang Un stood there, speechless. She felt her heart clutching tightly, as if it were turning into a hard rock. The sun had slipped behind the mountain ridge. Darkness was setting in, melting with the shadows. Only the empty tin cans in the front yard glinted in the fading light. More cans, less birds, she thought vaguely.

A dry breeze sprung up, and rustled the fronds of the palmyra tree. Nang Un looked at the top of the fronds in the twilight, but there was nothing there.

She never saw the pair of hornbills again.

(2) Laos: Courting Scene

Phuan Lom

The Prince of Phulom travels to a foreign kingdom where he has heard that the princess is a great beauty. This is his first meeting with the princess. After this scene, the princess's father refuses to marry the two. The Prince, angered, gathers together his troops and attacks and defeats the kingdom, stealing the princess to take her as his bride. Translated by Peter Koret.

The prince was engrossed with thoughts of the young woman. He dressed in his best clothes and headed towards her palace. When he arrived, he stopped to rest on her jewelled throne.

Yotika Kaew saw him and was surprised.

'Why does the prince come here alone? Why do you abandon your precious wife? Why is she far from your chest? How is it that you lost your way in the forest and have come to reach me here?'

'Younger sister, I have come from the far-off land of Phulom. I have come because I wish for you, my summit of love, my golden heart, my younger sister. If you do not show compassion for your older brother, I shall be delighted. I shall be as happy as if I had ten thousand billion pieces of gold to put in my bag. If you are willing to set down your heart and tie it together with mine, I shall feel as happy as if I were caged. I ask for us to bind together a strong friendship comparable to the leaves of the caladium and taro plants.[1] As long as I do not have you to return with me, younger sister, I am not willing'.

The young woman answered:

'My lovely necklace, listen to your younger sister's words. Since I was born, I have never had a lover, only men who sleep by my side, one thousand five hundred each night. If you still truly desire me, quickly flee and return home. If you are fed up with me, twist around me and do not unroll'.

They spoke together and understood one another perfectly. Each knew the other's words of love. Each knew sexual desire of the world that circles back and forth. It is comparable to powder, fluff and fine strands of thread. Can they stay near the fire without burning? Then the two knew each other's hearts and did not speak. They each raised an eyebrow and entered the bedroom. The two braided their bodies together, embraced, entwined and shared their warmth. The hour grew later and later, the stars moved across the sky, the chickens crowed. The two embraced tighter. Never did they grow tired of their love.

[1]The leaves of these plants are brittle and break very easily, thus they are not appropriate as a simile for strong friendship.

(3) Laos: Death of a Loved One

Saisuwan Paengpong, *What Remains*

In this story, three American soldiers visit a village in Laos to try to find the remains of an American pilot who had been shot down during the Vietnam war. A villager explains how his lover was killed by a bomb. Translated by Peter Koret.

There was silence for a moment. The speaker clenched his teeth together as if in great pain and continued speaking.

'My love disappeared with that bomb. I wiped blood off the top of my left arm. I ran, crying, in search of her. I turned over the corpses of many women, but none of them were her. A friend, just before she died, told me that my lover had run to seek refuge along a small path, and for what reason she did not know, had fallen at the same time as the dropping of the bomb. I searched in the area that she spoke of, turning over dirt displaced by the bomb, and sorting through rice straw and rice debris. From the centre of the ditch, I searched as far as the bushes at the edge of the field. She had left us – gone – without a day when she will come back to sit and enjoy the waterfall – without a day when she will come and listen to the birds and the insects by my side – there is nothing that remains of her. Nothing of her is left, not even a bone the size of a finger joint. Not even a piece of skin the size of my small finger. Not even a shred of her hair . . .'.

The middle-aged man slowly lifted his head up from the bomb crater that had not been transformed into a fish pond. He looked at the faces of the American soldiers, one at a time. He tugged my arm tightly.

'Friend', he said, 'please translate so that they will understand. Ask them to go and tell this story for the friends and family of the pilot to hear. Tell them that they have lost a friend, a beloved son or grandson, but they still have pictures, they still have mementos, still have some bones that are left. But as for me, I have nothing. No pictures, no mementos. The only thing that remains in the heart of a young man toughened by his experience is the feeling of being fed-up and disgusted with war'.

(4) Laos: A Drink of Water

Kai Kaew

It is a popular belief among the Lao that one continually meets and marries one's true mate during one's various lifetimes. In this story, the hero is born a poor orphan. His wife from a previous lifetime has been born as the princess of the Nagas, a race of mythical serpents that live in the underworld. In this scene the orphan meets the Naga princess. As a result of his courtship, she brings him a pitcher of miraculous water. She bathes him in it and he is transformed into a beautiful prince. Translated by Peter Koret.

He saw the young woman weaving. Sida[1] was small and beautiful. The sound of her inserting the shuttle into her loom was pleasant and melodious. Truly amazing was the loud resounding noise of the loom's reed. His heart quivered, overwhelmed. He looked at the woman, beautiful as if cast. Her cheeks were so lovely it seemed that they would drip down. The royal woman's figure were as if it had been drawn and her body shined as if it had been turned on a lathe. As for her breasts, they rose as if golden lotus flowers. She wore ornamental chains, a golden band wrapped about her forehead and jewelled royal rings that shined on her fingers. Her fragrant smell was enough to tear apart one's chest, to make one's heart quiver and slip out of one's breast.

He saw the bowl of water in which she soaked her threading spools. He wished to drink from it and searched for a coconut shell ladle from which to scoop. Then he crept up close to the small young woman and asked if he could drink her water.

'Young woman, I ask to drink water from your golden bowl. Please give as charity the water that you use to soak your spools. I have travelled here through dense forest. I am exhausted and thirsty'. Then he lifted up his ladle and asked her to pour water inside. 'I cannot do without water. Please be charitable'.

The small young woman stepped down from her loom.

'This water cannot be drunk, older brother. I use it to wash my hands. From which country do you come from, travelling to me in my land?'

He answered the young woman, telling her everything truthfully.

'It is my Kam'[2] that has driven me here. I am impoverished, an orphan, and the king bullies me. He has forced me to come, descending through a chicken's hole. I have thus abandoned my mother alone in her small house.

The woman of royalty heard him speak. She understood everything.

Then he continued to plead with the young woman.

'I wish to have some water. Younger sister, please be compassionate. Please lift up your bowl and pour it into my scooper. If you do not give me this charity I shall truly die. Even if the water is used to wash your hands or even feet, I shall take it. Please show compassion on this poor man'.

The beautiful young woman felt pity on him. She asked him to tell her about the path on which he had travelled. But before she could finish speaking, he interrupted her, pleading. His throat was dry and he begged her for water. The young woman pitied him greatly. She poured the water from her bowl onto the ground and told him to wait.

'Wait here, older brother, be patient. Do not be in a hurry to leave. Restrain yourself, sit down and wait for me. I shall bring back beautiful, clear water for you to drink. The water that I have here is for soaking spools for thread. Please do not drink it. I am fearful that it shall be a sin that shall be quick to come back for retribution.[3]

[1]Sida is the name of the heroine of the Ramayana. There are several scenes in this story that show the influence of the Indian epic. [2]*Kam* is misfortune that comes about as a result of sins committed in the past. [3]The water is considered unclean and a sin to partake of as is love before marriage.

(5) Laos: A Fight in the Forest

Thao Khatthanam

Khatthanam meets the 'Man of One Hundred Trees' in his search for his father. Translated by Peter Koret.

At that time there was a man whose power was equal to seven elephants. He was carrying trees to make a fence to surround his field. As for his name, he was called, 'The Man of One Hundred Trees.' Everyone called him by that name. He was pulling trees to collect in his field. In the course of a single trip he transported four hundred trees. The sound of his pulling the trees was as loud as the wind or the rain and reached up to the sky with never a moment of silence.

At that time the child Khatthanam, the Bodhisattva, heard the commotion and went to search for its source. He saw the man pulling trees, moving as fast as a normal man runs. The Bodhisattva jumped up and grabbed a branch of one of the man's trees. The man of one hundred trees could no longer move. He stood still. His strong rope, as thick as a leg, broke into pieces. Losing his balance, he was thrown for a distance of two hundred metres. The man was furious. He leaped over a tree and saw the Bodhisattva. He descended again and ran towards the child, intending to beat him to death. He grabbed the Bodhisattva's arm in order to wrestle with him, but it were as if he were grabbing Meru mountain.[1] It were as if he were an ant climbing up the leg of an elephant. The child Khatthanam, the Bodhisattva, pressed down his shoulders. The man of one hundred trees sank into the earth down to the level of his shoulders and cried out, 'Oi Oi.' He shook in fear of his life, and said, 'I ask to be your slave.' When Khatthanam, the Bodhisattva, heard the words of the man asking to be his slave, he asked the truth of those words. Then he allowed the man of one hundred trees to rise up from the earth and to bathe. He had the man eat food as he desired. He then prepared for his oncoming journey.

For what reason did the man of one hundred trees possess 'Bun Somphan'[2] and power equal to seven elephants? In his previous life-time, he had given an offering of seven packets of rice and other food. He gave his offering to seven monks who had gone out collecting alms. He had also given flowers and wooden toothbrushes in worship of the Buddha. He gave seven bundles, in each bundle seven hundred wooden brushes. He had given this offering to seven monks. The merit from his offering came back to repay the man of one hundred trees.

[1]Mount Meru, a great mountain in Indian mythology. The second level of heaven, ruled by the god Indra, is located on its summit. [2]Power one achieves as the result of good deeds performed in past lives.

(6) Laos: Looking for Food

Thao Kam Ka Dam

Little Black Crow is born ugly and monkey-like. His mother despises him and sets him adrift on a raft. With the help of the God Indra, he lands in a garden of fruit. He manages to cut down the sugarcane belonging to the youngest princess and exclaims, 'I will take what belongs to her and make it mine'. First he takes her virginity, then her hand in marriage and finally her father's kingdom. Translated by Peter Koret.

'I shall eat my fill', said Little Black Crow. 'I shall eat my fill from now until midnight'. After he mumbled these words, he climbed up a banana tree, fell down and climbed up again. He climbed up once and then twice. He was exhausted. He rested to collect his strength, then climbed up for a third time and fell down, rolling about. He struck his head against the hard earth and was dazed. He was truly furious, grumbling over and over. His head hurt as if he had drunk three jars of whisky. 'If I had a sword I would slash down the entire garden to make me feel better. It is too late to eat anyway', he muttered. The he moved on . . .

He saw many beautiful ripe jackfruit. 'Phutho Phuthai'[1] – these jackfruit are as ripe as can be, about to fall. Phutho – the fruit hangs from the branches down to the earth'. The beautiful boy walked on, hungry. 'I shall eat to fill my stomach and then continue onwards. I cannot be deprived. Desire has come to me'. He plunged at the tree and yanked at the fruit. He tugged with all his might and fell over, his rear end striking against the earth. He sat crouched on his knees. He climbed up and fell down again. He climbed up twice and then three times and grew exhausted. The jackfruit did not move the slightest bit and gave the appearance of being firm and immovable. Little Black Crow had a heart filled with great anger. 'This ugly jackfruit will not move'. He lifted up his foot, kicking the fruit with all the strength he could muster, and in the process fell over backwards. This time the pain was greater than last time. The beautiful figured man rubbed his swelling forehead. The swelling on his forehead seemed to balance the swelling on the back of his head. Then the beautiful-faced Black Crow rubbed his head continuously with his hand. 'If I had a knife or an axe of the greatest sharpness, I would slash down the entire garden until it disintegrated into dust'.

After he grumbled, he continued onwards, his eyes scanning the distance. He saw, scattered about, stalks of beautiful sugarcane. He wished to eat them. 'Now I shall eat just enough sugarcane to fill myself'. Using both hands, he tugged at the sugarcane with all his strength. He fell over, his behind striking against the ground. He wanted the sugarcane but could not have it. All he could do was look. Mischievous-looking Black Crow was troubled at heart because his *Bun*[2] was not great enough to get what he desired.

He turned his head and saw a garden of sugarcane belonging to the king's youngest daughter. There were six clumps arranged in beautiful rows. As he passed by, he glanced at them. He wanted to cut them down but was sobered by his previous lessons. Using both hands, he grabbed them with all his might. The sugarcane broke, collapsed and fell to the ground and he did as well. 'I shall break what belongs to my younger sister[3] and take it as my own', he murmured. If I fail, I shall be greatly distraught'. This field of sugarcane belonged to the youngest daughter of the king whose *Boon* was equal to his. He could therefore break it as he wished.

[1]An exclamation expressing amazement. Phutho refers to the Buddha. [2]Fortune and power that one achieves as a result of good deeds performed in past lives. [3]Affectionate term for women of similar or younger age.

(7) Laos: Search for a Lover

Sinxai

The story of Sinxai is known to most Lao. It begins with an account of the great power and wealth of Kusarat, King of the Land of Bengchan. Kusarat has a beautiful younger sister named Sumuntha of Great Beauty. In the extract, a Yaksa, or giant, known as Kumphan learns from a deity that Sumuntha is his pre-determined lover. Despite warnings he vows to kidnap her and take her as his wife, no matter what the consequences. Following this scene, the giant swoops down from the sky and steals Sumuntha while she is travelling with her entourage in a flower garden. The story of Sinxai is the tale of how Kusarat retrieves her from her kidnapper. Translated by Peter Koret.

He headed towards the golden stairway of the king of celestial beings. He passed through the clouds, hurrying towards his destination. He prostrated himself before the golden king and queen.

The king was pleased and said:

'I am glad to see you, Kumphan, great yaksa of wordly-reknown. How is your family? Are they still in good health?'

Kumphan, the great noble, understood, and answered his words:

'My family is well. There is neither worry nor sorrow in any of my lands. The only one who despairs is myself, the king, with a heart that is tied up and obsessed. I despair because I am separated from my queen. She has gone from me and is far far away. Please, my king, consider carefully what I have told you. Be compassionate to me and tell me the truth. Point out the mate that has been matched for me from the ancient past. I shall then go to court her and take her as my lover'.

The celestial being understood the reason that Kumphan was disturbed. He thought very carefully. If he did not give an answer, the Yaksa would surely suffer and die. The king therefore gave the following counsel:

"The woman you speak of was born in a great city in the land of humans. She is the younger sister of the king of Bengchan.[1] She is known as Sumuntha with figure as beautiful as if drawn. With the highest of Bun,[2] she is of the royalty of a great country. Her figure is so lovely it seems that it might drip down. Her looks are reknowned in ten thousand lands. There is no one of equal dignity to be by her side. She has ten thousand young women to serve her. Day and night, she lives as if in Dawadeungsa, heaven, one of the three worlds.[3] She is entertained by the great sound of music, played harmoniously for her in her palace. Her older brother rules over a vast kingdom. They are of the most revered of lineage. Their troops are as many as minerals piled up in the middle of a large body of water. They are reputed far and wide, every earthly land fearing their might and offering tribute. But I am afraid that if you take her it shall be a sin that shall come back to oppress you. You should listen to me and refrain yourself. I am fearful that it shall look bad in the future'.

Then Kumphan answered, his words arrogant but manner respectful:

'I am not fearful to anyone. If it was my Bun to have her in past life-times, is it possible then that I abandon her in this one?'

[1]Bengchan was a great kingdom in Lao literature and is now a village in present-day Naung Khai Kai province in north-eastern Thailand on the Lao border. [2]Bun is power or rank acquired as a result of acts of merit performed during previous lifetimes. [3]Dawadeungsa is the second of six levels of heaven. It is ruled by the God Indra. The three worlds include heaven, earth and hell.

(8) Laos: The Virtuous Government Worker

Duang Champa, *The Value and the Price*

This idealistic story shows the poverty of government workers in the 1970s and early 1980s. Government workers still make meagre salaries, about $5–10 per month. However, the story is dated and it is no longer an uncommon sight to see Lao civil servants drinking bowls of noodle soup and/or drinking Lao beer, which is incredibly cheap. Translated by Peter Koret.

'A bowl of noodle soup, with small noodles', he spoke in a voice he forced to sound as relaxed as possible. The way in which he sat down – slowly, with manners, without resting the weight of his back on the chair – was the way of one familiar with such shops. No one else but him was aware that this was only a pretense to fool other people. A noodle shop was not a place that he stopped at every day – especially when the price of a bowl of noodles had risen up to two hundred keep[1] as was the case . . .

[After he sat down, a young woman whom he had never met asked him to sign his name on a document. It is implied that through his position, the young woman can make a profit if she obtains his signature illegally. In exchange, she offers to pay for his soup and a can of beer.]

What did this woman want? He was just sitting and minding his own business when she came up and offered to pay for his soup and a can of expensive beer as well – something which he would never have been able to afford out of the money he had in his pocket. A chill went down his spine.

He felt startled. 'That woman wants . . .'

His hands froze. If he drank that can of beer, the six hundred keep he had remaining would not be enough to pay for it, because a can of beer certainly cost much more than that.

His responsibility at work was to sign documents correctly. But what if he was to sign them improperly? Was his signature to be traded for a bowl of soup and a can of beer?

'How much is the noodle soup? Two hundred keep? Take that beer to another table'.

He walked away from the noodle shop, not forgetting to take a good look at the face of the fat young girl with the loud mouth. He watched her with the eyes of one who had dignity, proud that he was a government worker who performed his duty with honesty. He did not need to drink anyone's beer in exchange for his signature.

He lifted up his head with greater pride than before, admiring his own thoughts.

[1]US$1 is approximately 700 keep.

(9) Luang Prabang

Harry A. Franck, *East of Siam*

The American Harry A. Franck found in Luang Prabang in 1926 a heaven on earth.

Luang Prabang, venerable capital of the ancient kingdom of the same name, is a spacious town of a few wide French streets, softly paved, if at all, with narrow Laotian streets like lovers' lanes between them. It is well wooded, with roomy yards usually whispering with palm trees. In other words it is not a city at all, in the crowded, noisy, Western sense, but a leisurely congregation of separate dwellings of simple lines, each in its ample garden-park, or at least with sufficient ground so that its opinions or doings need not intefere with its neighbors. In short, Luang Prabang town is in many ways what idealists picture the cities of Utopia to be, whatever insurance companies may think of the fire-risks involved in more thatch than tile roofs.

(10) Luang Prabang

Henri Mouhot, *Travels in Indo-China*

Henri Mouhot's travels in Thailand and Indo-China in 1859/60 are graphically recorded in Travels in Indo-China. Here he describes Luang Prabang, near which he was to die of malaria. Like Franck 80 years later, Mouhot compared it to paradise.

On the twenty fifth of July I reached Luang Prabang, a delightful little town, covering a square mile of ground . . . The situation is very pleasant. The mountains which, above and below this town, enclose the Mekong – form here a kind of circular valley or amphitheatre, nine miles in diameter, and which, there can be no doubt, was anciently a lake. It was a charming picture, reminding one of the beautiful lakes of Como and Geneva. Were it not for the constant blaze of a tropical sun, or if the mid-day heat were tempered by a gentle breeze, the place would be a little paradise.

(11) Luang Prabang

Phuan Lom

The text of Phuan Lom, a story from Luang Prabang province, consists of three separate stories. This is the last and shortest of the three, 'The story of the sinful Kuan fish'. It serves as an amusing Buddhist allegory for people whose suffering is caused by the blind following of desire that never knows satisfaction. Translated by Peter Koret.

Now I shall relate to you a story. I shall tell you a riddle. Whoever has the intelligence, keep this story in mind. There was once a great pool, one hundred thousand *yot*[1] in width. It overflowed with fish and crabs. The pool was located near the great City of Phulom. It was filled with beautiful lotus flowers, bright and blossoming. Once there was an evil sinful fish of great size and width. It was immense beyond expectation. Its name was sinful Kuan[2] and it had existed from the beginning of time. It fed on toads and frogs, together with butterfly larvae and crabs. These animals became scarce, and thus it chased after fish. The fish, frightened, scattered. At that time there was a large tree trunk in the depths of the great pool. It had sunk to the pool's base. It was hollow on its inside from top to bottom. The fish took shelter in the trunk, hiding inside. 'Doom Doom,' – Listen to the sound of the great Kuan fish moving about. It had already eaten all of its own children and continued to eat all the small fish in the pool. The fish that remained floated into the hollow trunk. Throughout the great pool there was not a single fish travelling about. The Kuan fish had driven them all away.

The Kuan fish suffered greatly. It had no food to eat. Its flesh grew thin. It was lonesome and as if in fever. Then it discovered the tree trunk and saw its hollow aperture. It saw that it was filled with fish. 'My luck', it thought, 'has come at last'. It opened up its mouth to receive the fish at one end of the trunk. It inserted its tail into the other end and thrashed it continuously, driving the fish towards the end where it placed its mouth. The fish were frightened of the tail of the great Kuan fish. They scattered, attempting hurriedly to flee. The great and sinful Kuan fish opened its mouth to receive them and devoured them all. Every fish that lived in the great pool died at that time. There were none that managed to escape. The Kuan fish diligently guarded the trunk opening and ate the fish, morning and night. In many days, the fish were finished. There were none that remained.

At that time Wera[3] approached the large and evil Kuan fish. Its tail, inserted at one end of the hollow trunk, now reached up to the other. It reached up to its own head. The Kuan fish did not understand that this in fact was its own tail but thought that it was a tail belonging to another fish. It bit and chewed, eating away at its own tail. Biting and chewing for many days, it reached its stomach. It bit its belly and then reached its stomach, and then reached up to its gills. Biting its gills, it reached up to its own head. Because it was starving and suffering greatly, it was biting and eating without being aware of its own body. All that was left was its big pointy head and that was swallowed in one single gulp. What an amazing thing – eating one's own head without even being aware of it!

Listen, people living in this world. Whoever reflects on this story and understands it shall laugh.

[1]A measurement equal to about 16 kilometres. [2]A large fish, similar to snake-head mullet, believed to eat its own children. [3]Bad fortune that serves as retribution for bad deeds.

(12) Vientiane

Louis de Carne, *Travels in Indo-China and the Chinese Empire*

Vientiane was razed by the Thai army at the beginning of the 19th century and when the Frenchman Louis de Carne visited in 1867 much of the city was still in ruins. Vat Pha Kaew, which the author describes as the finest of the ruined temples, is now a museum.

Our rowers at once stopped, telling us we had got to Vien-Chan; and we landed, no little astonished, for we could see nothing on the banks but dense forests . . . Scaling the steep bank by the help of a bamboo ladder, we found ourselves among the prickly bushes, which always grow thickly among ruins, as if they were a veil drawn by nature over the weakness of man and the vanity of his works . . . Heaps of bricks, lying here and there, were probably bastions. After long and anxious search we found that the town had no other monuments remaining but the king's palace, some pagodas, and the libraries for the sacred books; but there were even so many of these, that we gave up the attempt to count them. The pagoda of Pha Keo was one of the largest and finest. The trees which half hid it, and the creepers which bound its pillars together, and spread a mysterious shadow over the ruins, made one feel something of that awe which filled men of old at the threshold of a sacred wood. The enclosure of the pagoda was of sun-dried brick. Grand staircases led up to its platform. A contorted dragon stretched along the balusters, lifting its head threateningly from its thrown-back neck . . . innumerable pyramids are hidden in the forest, which, after first half throwing them down, keeps them from falling farther by the trees . . . Thousands of kilogrammes of copper and bronze run into figures of Buddha, heaps of brick, no end of pagodas, and, amidst all this, the traces of only one secular human habitation – the palace of the king – was the sum of what I saw in a ramble of some hours in the ruins of Vien-Chan.

Biographies and literary notes

Bodhisattva, Tales Of. In terms of their origins, Lao tales of the Bodhisattva fall into four main categories.

(1) Canonical *Jataka* Tales. Canonical *Jataka* tales are a collection of over 500 stories that describe the Bodhisattva in his various incarnations. The Bodhisattva, or the one who will become the Buddha, must perfect himself through the course of many lifetimes before he will achieve enlightenment. *Jataka* tales form a part of the Buddhist religious canon, known as the Tripitaka. Tales from the *Jataka* collection, particularly accounts of the last 10 lives of the Bodhisattva, are popular throughout Buddhist South-east Asia. The *Vesantara Jataka*, the last of the ten, is considered to be one of the finest examples of both Lao and *Lanna* poetry. Each year it is read in its entirety at a major religious festival known in Laos as Bun Phawet. It is believed that a person who listens to the entire story within a day's time will gain great merit and be born again in time to see Phra Maitreya, the future Buddha.

(2) *Pañña-jataka* Tales. This collection of approximately 50 stories was written in imitation of the Canonical *Jataka* tales. Modern scholars believe it to be the work of either Buddhist monks from the kingdom of Lanna or Mon monks from the Kingdom of **Hariphunchai**. It draws as its sources both regional South-east Asian oral folk tales and Buddhist works. Varying versions can be found among many peoples of mainland South-east Asia, including the Burmese, Kheun Yuan, Lao, and Khmer. The stories are written in *Nitsay* ◊ prose. They are composed both in Pali (the language of the Buddhist Scriptures), and in the language of the society in which they occur. The Lao borrowed this collection from the Kingdom of **Lanna** during the 16th century. Stories within the collection have served as the inspiration for important Lao prose works such as *Khatthanam* ◊ (Extract 5) and *Thao Hua* and poetic works such as *Nok Kajauk*, *Nang Auraphim*, and *Thao Sithon*. Although there is a complete Lao version known as *Ha Sip Sat* (50 Lives), it is rare to find it in its entirety.

(3) Apocryphal *Jataka* Tales from Lanna Outside the *Pañña* Collection. The traditional literature of the kingdom of Lanna largely consisted of independent Apocryphal *Jataka* tales written in imitation of the *Pañña-jataka*. These stories differ from stories within the collection in their lessened use of the Pali language. Out of over 200 independent *Apocryphal* Jataka tales in Lanna, approximately 30 are shared by the Lao. Lao prose works influenced by these stories include *Suphom Mokkha*. Poetic works include *Thao Kam Ka Dam* (Extract 6), *Thao Sowat*, *Phanya Khankhak*, and *Bua Haung Bua Hiaw*.

(4) Lao Apocryphal *Jataka* Tales. Many of the Lao stories of the Bodhisattva appear to have originated in written form inside Laos. The themes and motifs in the majority of these stories are similar to those that occur in the literature of the Yuan, Leu, and Kheun. This similarity is not necessarily the result of one society's literary influence upon another but rather the fact that the stories originate from a common source: the oral folk tradition of story-telling that has been shared between the different but

closely related cultures. Important Lao prose works within this category include *Thao Padaek Pasamau*, and *Khun Theung*. Poetic works include *Kalaket*, *Kai Kaew*, *Khunlu Nang Ua*, and *Phadaeng Nang Ai* (see Booklist).

Kai Kaew. The Bodhisattva was a poor boy who set traps for wild chickens to support himself and his mother. The princess of the *nagas* had been his wife in previous lifetimes. One day she rose from her underground kingdom disguised as a white chicken and left one of her feathers in his trap before disappearing into a chicken hole. The fragrance of the feather reached the king, who sent his servants in search of its source. Of all the people in the kingdom, only the poor boy was able to go down the chicken hole in search of the white chicken. He was lowered down for seven days and nights by a ship attached to a long rope. Once in the underworld, he met and married the *naga* princess. They lived together in her kingdom. Missing his mother, he invited his wife to return to his homeland. The boy's ship was prepared so that pressure on its seat would cause it to automatically return to the boy's home. The princess ignored her husband's warning to wait for him before entering the ship. She was therefore catapulted alone up to his kingdom, leaving her husband stranded in the underworld. Upon arrival, the king attempted to make her his wife. The god Indra, however, protected her by making her body unbearably hot. The Bodhisattva continued to travel through the underworld. He met and courted the beautiful daughter of a *yaksa*, or giant. Escaping from her father, they went to a land where the Bodhisattva obtained a magic tongue. Speaking with the magic tongue, everything he said became true. He revived a princess who had died of a snake bite and was given her hand in marriage. With his two new wives at his side, he returned to his mother's home. When the king refused to return his first wife, he fought and defeated the king's forces. He was then given the throne. After he became king, he visited the kingdoms of his three different wives (Extract 4).

Khatthanam. Once there was a poor woman who lived alone. One day the rice in her field was trampled by an elephant, which was strange as none of her neighbours' fields had been damaged. Thirsty, she drank the water that filled one of the elephant's footprints and afterwards gave birth to Khatthanam. He grew up to be a man of great strength and the pride of his country. However, one day he decided to go in search of his father and, after measuring the footprint, he went in search of an elephant with a similar size foot. Khatthanam met two followers 'The Man of One Hundred Trees' (see Extract 5) and 'The Man of One Hundred Carts' and eventually reached his father who turned out to be the god Indra, disguised as an elephant.

Kaun An. The most popular form of Lao poetry. The tonal nature of the Lao language encourages more different forms of poetic expression than does the English language. Whereas the rhyming of vowels and final consonants is a prominent characteristic of Western poetry, in *Kaun An* and other forms of Lao poetry the most important feature is the placement of words of certain tones in specific positions within the poetic line. See *Nitsay* ◊ for a description of the prose form of Lao literature.

Henri Mouhot

MOUHOT, Henri (see under Thailand).

Nitsay. The prose form of Lao literature is known as *Nitsay*. Although considered prose, it includes many poetic characteristics such as alliteration, assonance, and a high level of parallelism. Stories written in *Nitsay* generally imitate the style of Canonical *Jataka* tales. Phrases of Pali are included in the text with varying frequency, followed by explanations in Lao, giving the story the appearance of being a translation from the Buddhist scriptures. For the most popular form of Lao poetry, see *Kaun An* ◊.

Sinxai. The younger sister of King Kusarat of the Kingdom of **Bengchan** was stolen by the giant, or *yaksa*, Kumphan. King Kusurat left his wife and kingdom and, disguised as a monk, went in search of his sister. While travelling he met seven daughters of a wealthy man of Champa. He returned home, gave up his monk's robes and took the daughters as his queens. His first wife gave birth to a lion named Siho. The youngest of the seven sisters from Champa gave birth to the child Sinxai, the Bodhisattva, who was born with a shell and magic weapon. The six older sisters gave birth to sons. The astrologer, bribed by the jealous older sisters, told King Kusurat that Sinxai would cause bad luck to befall their kingdom. The king therefore exiled him from the city. His mother joined him and raised him in the forest. When the six sons of the older sisters were grown, they told their father that they would leave their kingdom to study with a hermit in the forest. They met Sinxai, who was greatly skilled in magic, and then returned home, deceiving their father, telling him that they had completed their studies. King Kusarat told his six sons to go in search of Sumunta, his sister, and to retrieve her from the giant. The brothers then went to Sinxai, and told him that his father wished for his help in retrieving their aunt. The seven brothers travelled together. Before they reached the land of the giants, Sinxai left his brothers in the care of Siho and continued on alone. He defeated the giant, and brought back Sumuntha and her daughter, who was married to the King of a mythical race of serpents called *naga* that lived in the underworld. During his journey home, Sinxai was pushed off a cliff by his brothers, who hoped to claim the honor of having saved their aunt. The God Indra rescued Sinxai and brought him home. When King Kusurat discovered the truth, he banished the astrologer and the six deceitful queens and their sons, and invited Sinxai and his mother back into the kingdom (Extract 7).

Thao Kam Ka Dam. The Bodhisattva was born dark and monkey-like in appearance. Hated by his mother, he was abandoned on a raft. Through the help of the god Indra, he reached the land of Inthapatha where he was raised by an old woman who cared for the royal garden. He enjoyed teasing her, particularly by making comments that he would find her an old, bald and toothless man to be her lover. When he grew up, he fell in love with the king's seventh daughter. At night he went to play in the city, at first shunned by the village women for his ugly appearance. However when he played the *Khaen*, a Lao wind instrument, he enchanted people all over the kingdom, including the king, who sent his servants to find out who played with such skill. After playing the *Khaen*, he went unseen to the princess's palace and stepped out of his ugly costume. Emerging as a beautiful prince, he courted and made love to the princess. In the morning, he put on his monkey costume and returned home. He convinced the old woman who raised him to ask the king for his daughter's hand in marriage. The bridal price was to build a bridge of gold and silver from the old woman's home to the king's palace. He was aided in his effort by the god Indra. Triumphant, he dressed in his best clothes and was paraded to the palace. His appearance however was that of a well-dressed monkey and upon seeing him, the princess refused to take part in the wedding. After he abandoned his ugly costume, she agreed to marry him and he was given the throne. He then brought the old garden-keeper to his palace. He had servants travel to his old home and bring back his father. He magically gave them back their youth and provided them each with a palace to live in. Extract 6 contains a scene in the royal garden.

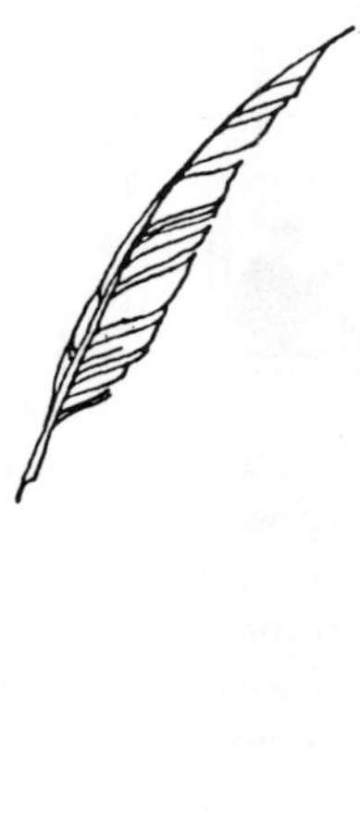

Cambodia (Kampuchea)

Judith M. Jacob

> 'Then he went through the air directly over the splendid, bejewelled palace, decorated with gold, lofty and pointed / It burst into flames which leaped angrily to the top, high aloft, with a loud crackling, blotting out everything with / thick black smoke fusing, rising up. The fire blazed up obliterating all. With loud crashes the palace fell down, bit by bit.
> *The Reamker*

Cambodia (Kampuchea) is situated in Indochina. The rich flat basin of the Mekong contains the majority of the population, although there are forested mountains to the north and west. The famous monuments of **Angkor**, dating from the 9th to the 13th centuries, remain as witness to the splendid and prestigious civilization which the country once enjoyed. From the 14th to the 19th centuries the country was reduced in power and was constantly attacked by its two neighbours, the Siamese (Thais) and the Vietnamese. From 1863 until 1953 Cambodia was a Protectorate of France, but it remained a kingdom until 1953, when Norodom Sihanouk abdicated to become Head of State. After the deposition of Sihanouk and a civil war, the communist Khmer Rouge exerted their oppressive authority over the country from 1975–8, causing over a million deaths. Since the Vietnamese liberated the country from the Khmer Rouge at the beginning of 1979, a government sympathetic to Vietnamese communism has been in power. In late May 1993 a UN-sponsored election (boycotted by the Khmer Rouge) produced a majority for the pro-royalist Funcinpec party.

The majority of the people of Cambodia are farmers, living in wooden houses on stilts on the Mekong plain. Right up to this century they have used farming tools which were shown on the bas-reliefs at Angkor. Rice, vegetables and fruit are grown, while the numerous

Freize at Angkor

rivers provide a super-abundance of fish. It is a landscape of bright green ricefields, dotted with palm-trees. Water is everywhere, in rivers, canals, dykes and ponds. Once a year the Mekong floods and the force of water changes the direction of the river which normally flows south to Phnom Penh from the Great Lake (the Tonle Sap). A Water Festival, with boat races, has been held yearly in Phnom Penh at that time.

Cambodia is a Buddhist country, where monks in their saffron robes used to be seen everywhere. The Cambodians, as Buddhists, are patient, non-violent and long-suffering. If they go to the monastery on holy days and observe the Precepts, the next life will be a better one, even socially better. Buddhism permeates every area of Cambodian life, especially the literature. The hero of the Indian *Ramayana* was turned into the Buddha in the Cambodian *Reamker*. The *cbap* poems (see below) form a practical guide to Buddhism and in the *Satra Lbaeng* the effect of *karma*, 'retribution', is constantly endured by the heroes and heroines.

As a nation the Cambodians are artistic in every way. They sit by the wayside playing a haunting air on a one-stringed fiddle. When they make a utensil it is a thing of beauty. For fun, they engage in spontaneous repartee, rhyming and playing with words most cleverly. At the same time they have a tendency towards melancholy and this is reflected in their literature, where sad songs and sad endings to stories are almost *de rigueur* (see, for example, *Phka Srapon* ◊).

Writers have been associated with the king's court which moved from one place to another during the unrest of the 14th to 19th centuries. Until the 20th century they have belonged either to royalty or to the priesthood but in this century civil servants, including palace officials, as well as monks have become writers. They have almost without exception originated from **Phnom Penh** or its environs.

There is a very small scattered community of ethnic Chams, who are Muslim. Cambodian (Khmer) is the language of the country although dialects have been spoken by tribes in the mountainous regions.

Classical Literature

The most spontaneous literature of the Khmers is to be found in the orally transmitted songs and folktales, neither of which concerns us here. The literature proper was written in verse; prose was reserved for everyday information. It was incised with an iron stylus on manuscripts made of palm-leaf. These either succumbed to the local conditions, (being eaten by insects or becoming mouldy through damp), or were copied over and over again with inevitable mistakes and 'corrections'. The recorded literature was from its beginning heavily influenced by Sanskrit and the Indian epics, since Indians began to trade and settle in Cambodia from the second century AD onwards. The first literary works written during the Angkor period were entirely in Sanskrit, as we know from the inscriptions on which they are mentioned. From the 11th century, Buddhism became the religion of Cambodia. Inscriptions of the 16th to 19th centuries are written in a Cambodian literary prose style, expressing fervent Buddhist belief. Pali loanwords occur increasingly beside Sanskrit and the *jatakas* or birth-stories of the Buddha became a favourite subject.

Versification

Khmer versification demands that the poet should have the full range of poetic vocabulary always at the ready. While supplying the correct number of syllables for each verse, as required by the metre, and conforming to an exacting rhyme scheme, he must also satisfy the taste of Cambodians (as of Thai and other South-east Asian peoples) for what seems to the Western ear an excess of alliterating and chiming syllables. The metres ◊ used in Khmer poetry over the centuries are outlined in the 'Biographies and literary notes' section.

Epic

The best-known and almost certainly the earliest work written in Khmer and still extant, is the *Reamker* (Cambodian *Ramayana*) ◊ of which there is one partial manuscript in the British Museum and many complete ones at the **Bibliothèque Nationale** in Paris (Extracts 3 and

4). The Rama story has pervaded all art forms: the scenes on **the bas-reliefs at Angkor**, the shadow theatre, *Nang Sbaek*, for which it was the only subject and the frescoes – those at the **Silver Pagoda, Phnom Penh**, are fine examples – on temple walls throughout Cambodia. The popular dance-drama, the *Ikhaon*, continued to play scenes from the story until and including this century. The recreated Royal Ballet or dance-drama still enacts scenes from the *Reamker*. The Khmer version of the Ramayana is very much a Cambodian (or Cambodian–Thai) concern. One significant fact is that Rama is presented as the Buddha and several incidents are different from the Indian (Valmiki) version. The favourite scenes are the stealing of the heroine, Sita, by Ravana, the King of the devils, and the burning of Ravana's city of Lanka by Hanuman, the powerful white monkey who helps Rama in his search for Sita. The *Reamker* may be based on a version dating back to Angkor times, although the work as we have it has been shown by Saveros Pou from linguistic considerations to be partly from the 16th/17th and partly from the 17th/18th centuries. The earliest dated work, *Lpoek Angar Vat*, 'The story of Angkor Vat', was written in 1620 AD and designed to be used for showing people round the monument. The Rama story is told in the poem by describing the bas-reliefs in order as they appear in the galleries of Angkor Vat (Extract 2).

The style of these, the earliest extant literary works in Khmer, is learned. Sanskrit and Pali loanwords or 'doublets' of Sanskrit and Khmer abound. Another feature which has survived up to the 20th century is the Khmer love of alliteration and of rhyming, chiming or repetitive couplets. The language does not need to have subjects or objects or time indicators repeated so the action moves quickly, with a minimum of words and those mostly either monosyllables or disyllables. The descriptions of battles are vigorous and concise.

Cbap or 'Codes of Conduct'

These were poems, written from the 17th century onwards, at first chiefly by monks, who encouraged a good social behaviour consistent with the observance of Buddhist morality. The early *Cbap* were used as texts for reading in monastery schools. The *Cbap Kram* reminds the pupils that the teacher is *in loco parentis* as he trains them in the way of the Dharma. The subject sounds dull but in fact the simply-expressed advice to peasant farmers and the comparisons with birds or animals well known to the readers is quite charming. The householder must not sleep until broad daylight, the *Cbap Ker Kal* tells us. He must be up to collect his slaves together and go off to work the ricefields and look for creepers to construct good pens. He must keep a tidy house with raked ground outside. The *Cbap Kon Cau* warns against imitating the parasite plant which takes its nourishment from the host tree and ruins it. This *Cbap* contains the well-known passage about the light of the Dharma (Extract 7). In the *Cbap Pros* the householder is urged to take care in preparation for the night. He must check that all goods are safe and the bowls filled with water. He must place offerings to the gods and make sure that the fire outside the house will last the night, as a source of light, which may be required. The *Rajaneti* tells of the kite which needs the wind to fly, the officer who needs his protective soldiers in order to be admired and the household which needs a good, economical wife.

A political comment comes into the *Trineti* which discusses the state dignitaries who oppress the people. They are like water and the people are like fish. When the water becomes too hot the fish do not know where to turn. The officials are like tigers or snakes which turn into *yaksas* (ogres) when the people ask for help.

Satra Lbaeng, 'Works for pleasure'

These are verse-novels and are usually very long. They tell almost exclusively the extremely involved tales of the *jatakas* or birth-stories of

Part of Bayon monument, Angkor

the Buddha. The most popular ones come from the extra-canonical '50' *jatakas* which were written originally in Pali by a monk or monks, probably in Laos, many centuries ago. Typically the Bodhisattva (future Buddha) is born as a prince with some defect, which may eventually prove to be magic and a help to him. Through the jealousy of one of the queens, who makes an astrologer foretell doom if he stays, he is expelled from the kingdom to wander in the forest. There he finds a hermitage, is educated by the hermit in the martial arts, overcomes a *yaksa*, meets a princess from whom he is separated in a storm, for example. It is *karma*, 'a bad fate', due to a wrong committed possibly in a previous life, which separates them. In the end all the threads are drawn together and the Bodhisattva is acknowledged and is crowned king.

One *Satra Lbaeng* which has given rise to a dance drama, performed in villages until the early part of this century, is the *Khyang Sang*. The Bodhisattva is born with a shell, banished and brought up by a *yaksa*, who eats humans. Discovering this, he escapes, stealing a *Ngos* (an outfit, including an ugly mask and sandals with which he can fly). He arrives in a kingdom where he is accepted as husband by the youngest princess, who is in disgrace for rejecting all suitors. She can see through the disguise. He has to pass certain hunting tests, together with the other six sons-in-law. He does this with great credit, and helps the others too, but it is only when he is seen in all his glory, defeating an enemy which surrounds the city, that the king accepts him and hands the kingdom over to him. The literary version was written in 1729.

Tum Teav ◊ is written in the form of a verse-novel but its content is quite different from the *jataka* stories. It is a true love-story from the 15th century and it is very dear to Cambodian hearts. It was written by Mok ◊ at the turn of the 19th century but the manuscript became tattered. Som is said to have re-written it, with the torn manuscript of Mok before him. The text of Mok was printed, nevertheless, by four people in 1961. Som's verse is very much influenced by a style said to be Thai in origin. The story was written again in verse by Nou Kan in 1942.

In the *Satra Lbaeng*, the story is interrupted, during the narration of the journeys made by the hero, to give 'descriptions' of the natural scenery. These are little more than lists of trees or animals or fish, which the poet puts into verse, choosing alliterative or chiming words to place next to each other and supplying here and there a few words of actual description. The resources of the poet in knowing unusual words for natural plants and creatures and in combining them into verses are tested to the utmost. The poets are of course aware of the 'purple passages' of previous poets which they strive to outdo. Other favourite subjects for a long digression are the king's army or his palace. Passages like these are characteristic of Thai verse-novels too. Although the nobility tend to address each other formally and to have expected reactions to situations, when 'ordinary' people are involved, Khmer poets are very clever at putting colloquial conversation and robust reactions into verse.

Lyrics

The collection of lyrics published in the journal *Kambujasuriya*, 1939–1942, by HRH Princess Peang Poh and published again during the 1960s, include the works of several royal persons, beginning with King Sri Dhammaraja, who wrote at the beginning of the 18th century. Themes such as regret at separation from the loved one, reminiscences about the time they were together contrasted with pairs of birds settling on a branch together at sunset are tenderly treated. They seem closest of all written literary works to the songs, expressing spontaneously the sadness which Khmer people feel so readily.

20TH CENTURY LITERATURE

The Modern Novel

During the early part of the 20th century Khmers felt that inspiration was stifled by the colonial presence. Madame Seth wrote *Bimbabilap* in 1900 (to be published in 1942). Som produced his version of *Tum Teav* in 1915. In 1921 In wrote *Gatilok*, a collection of short stories chiefly from Indian and Buddhist sources. However, with the establishment of a printing press in 1926 and the launching of the journal, *Kambujasuriya*, in that year, the possibilities for publication improved.

The first modern novel, *Sophat* (*Name of the Hero*), was published in 1938, followed by *Tik Tonle Sap* (*The Waters of the Tonle Sap*) in 1939. Then came 14 others in the 1940s; *Phka Srapon* (*The Faded Flower*) ◊ is one of the best. The novels formed a total break from traditional literature. Not only were they written about ordinary people but they were written in prose, not poetry, and contained natural conversation. There were Western-style detective novels, mysteries, adventure stories, historical novels about the Angkor period or later, autobiographies and, last but never least, love stories. At first they contained passages of poetry because it seemed inconceivable to leave verse out entirely. Gradually they conformed to the Western pattern. Plays were also written in the Western style. A thousand novels were printed, usually in short runs of 500, between 1938 and 1972.

From 1972 until the Vietnamese drove out the Khmer Rouge, almost all literary activity ceased. In the West, the most well-known memoir of the Khmer Rouge years is Dith Pran's, made into the popular film,

Margaret Drabble

The Killing Fields. The sufferings endured by the Cambodian people during the last 20 years are vividly brought out in Molyda Szymusiak's *The Stones Cry Out: A Cambodian Childhood* (Extract 10).

Cambodia's troubles of the last 20 years have produced some literature in English concerning refugees and the stories they have to tell. The situation in Cambodia during the 1980s, when the Khmer Rouge were still active, despite the efforts of the Vietnamese-backed government, is treated in the trilogy by Margaret Drabble, (*The Radiant Way*, *A Natural Curiosity* and *The Gates of Ivory*), particularly in the last volume (Extract 1).

BOOKLIST

What follows is intended as a representative rather than comprehensive list of books about Cambodia. Where several editions exist, in general the latest and most readily available edition has been listed. For most of the extracted works, information on the original English language publisher can be found in 'Acknowledgements and Citations' at the end of the volume, as can the exact location of the extracts and the editions from which they are taken.

Dhammaraja, Sri, 'Last poem to a loved one', Kambujasuriya, 1939. **Extract 5.**

Dhingra, Baldoon, *Asia Through Asian Eyes. Parables, Poetry, Proverbs, Stories and Epigrams of the Asian Peoples*, Thames and Hudson, London, 1959. **Extract 6.**

Drabble, Margaret, *The Gates of Ivory*, Penguin, London, 1992. **Extract 1.**

Han Suyin, *The Four Faces*, Panther, London.

Jacob, Judith M. and Kuoch Haksrea, trans, *Reamker (Ramakerti). The Cambodian Version of the Ramayana*, Royal Asiatic Society, London, 1986. **Extract 4.**

Jacob, Judith M. and Edwin Morgan, trans, 'Extracts from Reamker', in Keith Bosley, ed, *The Elek Book of Oriental Verse*, Paul Elek, London, 1979. **Extract 3.**

Jacob, Judith M. and Edwin Morgan, trans, 'The code of behaviour for the young', in Keith Bosley, ed, *The Elek Book of Oriental Verse*, Paul Elek, London, 1979. **Extract 7.**

Keng Vannsak (Judith Jacob, trans), *Guk Kam Kiles (Prison de la Passion)*, Phnom Penh, 1956. **Extract 9.**

Mathers, E. Powys, *The Eastern Anthology*, Vol IV, *Eastern Love. Love Tales of Cambodia and Songs of the Love Nights of Lao*, Vol 10, John Rodker, London, 1929. **Extract 8.**

Pang, 'Lpoek Angar Vat (The Story of Angkor Vat)' in E. Aymonier (Judith Jacob, trans), *Textes Khmers*, Saigon, Vietnam, 1878. **Extract 2.**

Szymusiak, Molyda (Linda Coverdale, trans from the French), *The Stones Cry Out: A Cambodian Childhood*, Jonathan Cape, London, 1986. **Extract 10.**

Extracts

(1) Angkor

Margaret Drabble, *The Gates of Ivory*

The third volume in Margaret Drabble's trilogy is set in the late 1980s. Three intrepid travellers have set out from Phnom Penh with the intention of meeting the Khmer Rouge and have now reached the environs of Angkor.

[They] put up for the night at the Hotel de la Paix. Gutted by war and apparently deserted, it still stands by the verge of Highway Six. Once it had received tourists on their way to the ruins. Now it is empty, its door ajar, its windows broken, its veranda invaded by creepers. They knock on the open door, and call. Nobody answers, so they penetrate to find a reception desk, a few old ledgers, a dusty glass jug, a cracked vase and the remnants of a bar and a restaurant. In the courtyard a fig-tree breaks the paving stones. There is, of course, no electricity to operate the 1930s wall brackets, the large ceiling fan. A 1950s advertisement for Pernod is still attached to a flaking wall next to a photograph of the Bayon and a faded list of Prices for Tours and Guides. . . .

An old man and a small boy . . . inform them that they are the only remaining staff of the Hotel de la Paix, and would the guests like some dinner? The meal is very simple. A bowl of rice, bamboo shoots, a salad, a watery soup, a plate of bananas. The old man cooks over a fire in the derelict courtyard, in a cooking pot resting on three stones. They eat outdoors. The old man is wrinkled, very dark of skin, wizened, bent. His gestures have a timeless gentleness. The small child watches, open-eyed, open-mouthed, as the old man stirs and scoops with a ladle made from a coconut shell. . . . He tells them his story, softly, with many pauses. . . . Most of his family are dead in the wars and troubles. . . . How does he live? He lives off the forest. This child is his great-grandson. For me, he says, the night is near, but for him, the day begins. The child will be a monk. He will be a holy man of the forest.

(2) Angkor

Pang, *The Story of Angkor Vat*

This extract is from the 17th century guidebook to Angkor Vat, which was designed to be read while looking at the bas reliefs. Pang describes the bas-reliefs, which depict the story of Rama. The two here tell the story of the contest of the bow.

The King of Mithila is depicted, inviting the gods to raise his bow of a thousand strings. Twelve gods come flying down, mounted on various beasts – an elephant, a horse, a royal goose, a strutting peacock, a swift goat-antelope, a rhinoceros, a lion, a tiger, a *yaksa*, a *naga*, a *gandharb* – to strive in contest with each other. They cannot raise the bow!

Then Rama of mighty deeds is shown. He raises the bow! And Sita is his, as he desires.

(3) Angkor

The Reamker (Cambodian Ramayana)

The exiled Rama, with his wife and brother, passes through a forest, destroyed by fire. The forest returns to life as he approaches. Although this extract has been placed under Angkor because of its bas reliefs, the evocative description of the forest's rebirth would be just as appropriate to the jungles north and west of Phnom Penh. This extract from Jacob and Morgan, trans (see Booklist).

It was the season of heat and sun,
the sun-rays focused on
the broken wood that strewed their track.

The earth was dried up into cracks;
the light was a blinding flash.
Flames ran sizzling through the air,

melting the forest everywhere.
Death to fruit and flower:
leaf and blossom dropped, shrivelled.

Some leaves were charred, and some were red.
The forest fire spread
till straw and grass and reed were blighted.

Rama, meditation-strengthened,
one of the Enlightened,
guided his wife along the way.

And the great forest canopy
of branches began to play
gentle and fresh on either side.

Flowers sprang up far and wide
suddenly, richly displayed,
as if by an arranger's art.

Huge, bone-dry trees stood dead and silent,
coiled with leaves that bent
shaking and waving into the wind.

The flowers fluttered out their fund
of perfume, which unwound
sweetness pervading all the scene.

Buzzing, honey-bearing bees
murmured as they breathed
the nectar; busy were their wings.

Their hum strummed out like plucked strings
into the silence, stirring
the royal wanderers in the wood.

The sunlight, bright as it was, glowed
in the sky as glad and bland
as brilliance sent from a full moon,

and could not burn one royal person
in that trio – the sign
of Rama's virtue in that journey.

(4) Angkor

The Reamker (Cambodian Ramayana)

Hanuman, the powerful monkey prince who helps Rama in his fight against the devils, has told them to set light to him – the only way to kill him! This translation from Jacob and Haksrea (see Booklist).

The mighty Hanuman went higher and higher, swaying about, fire and all, as he went up into the sky. / He called out a warning. 'Hey there! King Rab(n)! Watch out for Lanka! This fire will spread in all directions'. / Then he went through the air directly over the splendid, bejewelled palace, decorated with gold, lofty and pointed. / It burst into flames which leaped angrily to the top, high aloft, with a loud crackling, blotting out everything with thick, black smoke fusing, rising up. The fire blazed up, obliterating all. With loud crashes the palace fell down, bit by bit. / There were explosive bursts as sparks shot off and were scattered to shower in all directions and to flit, redly glowing across the sky. / The fire rose and spread, hotly raging. Every ogre house was in turmoil, as it flared up with great heat. / The fire glared, throwing light to a great distance, to the heavens beyond. Far up above, it blazed brightly. / It spread to the apartments of the demon Rab(n), who sprang up and ran out, hot and terrified. / The bejewelled royal couch caught fire. The sleeping quarters of Mandogiri[1] caught fire / and the women, faint from shock – being women – and fearful, their minds a blank, went here, there and everywhere in a state of consternation. / Amid the bangs and cracks and the tremors, they ran, falling over one another, heaped up over each other. / Some ran for their belongings, to take them along. Others carried their children on their hips, their muslin shawls falling off, torn and not covering them. / The point came when the various thoroughfares of the city were wiped out and all the valuables in it were destroyed utterly. / The ordinary ladies of the court beat their breasts and wailed loudly, shaking. / Even the evil Dasamukh[2] supported himself from falling, shamefaced and downcast, deep in thought, saying not a word to anyone.

[1]Wife of the King of the devils, Rab(n) (Ravana). [2]A name for Rab(n).

(5) Cambodia: Last Poem to a Loved One

King Sri Dhammaraja

Pursued by enemy soldiers, Sri Dhammaraja climbed a sugar palm and wrote this poem to his loved one, Yuor Vadey, before his capture and death.

I, Preah Reach Samphear, at the top of a sugar-palm, am surrounded and shot at by the wretched Portuguese, who have no respect for my authority. They hem me in – there's no escape! . . . Passion has led me to the brink of extinction. I prefer to die and adhere to the Dhamma. May all the gods help me in their divine wisdom! . . . Alas for the king, highest of all! His heart yearns for his lady. At the end of his life he pens this note for his best of sweethearts for her to read afterwards.

(6) Cambodia: Love under the Cinnamon-apples

'The Tryst'

The breathless excitement of the lovers in this beautiful love poem has a universal quality. Taken from Baldoon Dhingra (see Booklist).

In thy presence my arms, my hands, my lips, all my being,
  Tremble as tremble the leaves
Of the cinnamon-apples shaken by the wind.

The leaves of the cinnamon-apple do not tremble, O my love,
They shiver under the caress of the wind.
Which drinks deep of their perfumed kisses.

Come with me tonight under the cinnamon-apples
And like their leaves you will shiver under my caress,
And like the wind I will drink deep of your perfumed kisses.

I will come. But what will you give me for my kisses?
For your kisses I offer you my kisses.
What will you give me for my heart?
For your heart I offer you my heart.
What will you give me for my love?
For your love I offer you my life.

I accept your kisses and your heart and your life;
And I give in exchange myself to be all yours.
And all trembling this night I will come to offer you my kisses
Under the cinnamon-apples caressed by the wind
And in the wind that drinks deep of their perfumed kisses.

(7) Cambodia: The Path of Virtue

'The Code of Behaviour for the Young'

The Cbap *or 'codes of conduct' were moral poems, written mainly by monks, exhorting readers to follow Buddhist morality. This passage is from the* Cbap Kon Cau. *Translated by Judith M. Jacob and Edwin Morgan (see Booklist).*

It is said that the fire is bright,
but surely the sun is brighter.
It is said that the brilliance of the sun
(so bright, so clear in the sky)
is surely not as bright
as the divine Dharma
of the Buddha.

The bright fire loses desire,
the bright fire ends its time,
it is lost, extinguished, extinct.
The brilliant sun sails high
in its sky and as surely sinks
and as it sets grows dull,
its rays pale.

But consider the precious Dharma:
bright and more than bright
in this world and no less bright
in the next world it goes through to:
it shines into huge distance, its
virtue is exemplary, inextinguishable
its glory.

(8) Cambodia: A Surprise Visit

Anon, *Sang Sel Chey*

This passage is from a verse-novel. Prince Sang Sel Chey, a future Buddha, arrives at the palace of his aunt, Neang Montea, after a hazardous journey, intending to rescue her from the yaksa (ogre) who carried her off long ago. Contained in E. Powys Mathers (see Booklist).

Neang Montea was indeed astonished to see an elegant Prince thus brave the snares which had been sown about her pavilion, and she was even more so when she learned his name. Her happiness at listening to her delightful nephew as he spoke of the land which she had left was great enough, but she regretted that her husband King Kompon was not there to welcome him. He was again conducting his daughter to her marriage with the King of the Nagas.

As she spoke with him, she looked at him carefully, and was forced to say to herself in vexation: 'Alas, why did this honest and distinguished nephew of mine not visit my country sooner? He would most certainly have pleased my dear Sampor, and now she has gone in a sad consternation to the Naga king.'

Sanselkey[1] still believed that his aunt saw in him a liberator before all else: at length, pained and surprised that she did not seem to understand what had brought him, he said:

'O deeply respected aunt, make no mistake. I have not come here on a visit. The King your brother, my father Kotorash, has sent me to rescue you from the monster Kompon and to kill him!'

Seeing her nephew so charming in everything and yet hearing him say such terrible words, Neang Montea answered with a laugh: 'Dear child of my brother, you must be careful of your language here. In a very short time my king will return, and I should be very much grieved if you, who have so pleased me, should anger him'. The eyes of the young man became injected with blood and shot forth lightenings; his aunt suddenly realised their misunderstanding, and saw disaster wheeling down upon her life. To avert it, she said again: 'If my brother loves me, he ought to forget what happened so long ago. I am very happy, and not for the world would I leave the tranquil pleasures I enjoy with Kompon'.

Sanselkey as he stepped from the room, cried out: 'You shall follow me back! If necessary I will kill all your servants to make you do so. Behold my power!' Taking his bow, he let fly a steel-tipped arrow, whose long and shrieking passage was so terrible that all the palace trembled to its foundations. It struck a giant tree, which was set on fire and fell apart in ruins.

Returning to his aunt, he found her upon her knees. 'Have you decided to flee with me?' he asked.

'Oh, my dear nephew,' she answered, 'I see in you all the power of Pra En. Ah, be as pitiful! I would rather die than leave this place before hearing news of my daughter Sampor; for she is unhappy. I will soon have these tidings, since Kompon is even now approaching; I will hide you when he comes, and while he is asleep we will speak again'.

At this moment the loud trumpeting of twenty elephants announced the return of the Yack[2] King, and Sanselkey, seeing the grief and terror of his aunt, said grudgingly: 'Very well, hide me'.

[1]Sang Sel Chey. [2]*Yaksa* or ogre.

(9) Phnom Penh

Keng Vannsak, *'Prison de la Passion'*

This poem was written when the author was a political prisoner, under Prince Sihanouk.

Iron bars, a small screen, four huge walls,
A super lock. Above, the roof,
Below, slabs of stone. If you turn to look at something,
The guard looks too.

My dearest darling, when I held you close
Asking for your love, you cried out 'No'.
You slipped away saying, 'Wait' – until
Now I'm looking at the walls!

My dearest darling, I really am looking at them.
But there's nothing to prevent us thinking of each other.
We can leap over the walls. Prison doesn't incarcerate
Hearts which love each other.

(10) Vat Thmey

Molyda Szymusiak, *The Stones Cry Out: A Cambodian Childhood*

This is a passage from the description of life under the Khmer Rouge, written in Paris by a Khmer girl who was 12 in 1975.

I met our Mekong,[1] Met Yai, at our door; armed with a big notebook, she was counting and registering the chickens being raised by villagers near their huts. We happened to have a chicken, brought by Sy Neang one evening the previous week when he had come to stay overnight. Met Yai wrote down: 'One chicken at the Man-Vi house'.

Two days later the chicken laid an egg. It's difficult to share one egg. 'Let's keep it', said Mi Vi,[2] 'we'll have chicks'. And in fact, one month later, we had eight or nine chicks. Mi Vi announced at that point that we were going to kill the chicken. 'Watch out, Mi Vi, the Mekong will cut your head off'. She yielded to reason and abandoned the idea. The chicks grew bigger; Srei Peu had tamed them, they came when she called. But no joy lasts for long: the Mekong came to requisition the chicks for the community. . . .

Mi Vi was busy plucking the chicken. We watched her work, following her every move. Before the morning was over, the chicken was cooked, and Mi Vi settled down to eat it by herself. I'd have liked at least to have drunk the bouillon, but she didn't offer us anything. Finally, satisfied, she couldn't finish the whole bird and offered us what was left. . . .

Mi Vi went out to bury the bones and feathers, then hurriedly planted some manioc over the spot. And it was a good thing she did, because Met Yai soon came to get the chicken registered in her list for the communal kitchen (which probably meant just for the Mekongs). 'Where's your chicken?' I saw Mi Vi press her white lips together to keep them from quivering. 'I don't know', she whispered. The Mekong went around the hut looking for telltale traces. She dug here and there in the ground – there must be feathers someplace. In the grass? Nothing. Over here, perhaps? It was the place where Mi Vi had buried the incriminating remains. Met Yai leaned over and noticed tiny manioc shoots. She wouldn't disturb this area, which promised food as much for herself as for those who lived in the hut. We were relieved when she went away, muttering to herself. It had been a close call.

[1]Khmer Rouge overseer. [2]The moderately friendly woman with whom the children share a hut.

Biographies and literary notes

ANG DUONG, King (1799–1860, reigned 1841–1860). Educated in Siam, Ang Duong became a renowned scholar and poet. He was a good king who made education compulsory for boys and encouraged scholars to write. *Neang Kakey* is his best known work, with *Cbap Srey* a close second. King Ang Duong also wrote plays and at least one lyric poem.

DRABBLE, Margaret (1939–). British novelist and critic. Born in Sheffield. Her novels include *A Summer Birdcage* (1963), *Jerusalem the Golden* (1967), *The Radiant Way* (1987) and *A Natural Curiosity* (1989). *Gates of Ivory* was first published in 1991 and is set in Cambodia in the late 1980s (Extract 1). Margaret Drabble received the CBE for services to English literature in 1980.

KENG VANNSAK (1925–). Studied in Paris as a young man and spent two years in London. Returning to Cambodia he became a member of parliament. He opposed Sihanouk and was imprisoned as a political prisoner (Extract 9). He was a Professor of Khmer Literature at the **University** in **Phnom Penh**. He now lives in France.

Metres. The following metres have been used in Khmer poetry for several centuries. They have two characteristics in common: (1) that the last syllable of the stanza rhymes with the end syllable of the second and/or third verse of the next stanza and (2) that there are internal rhymes either between the second, third or fourth syllable of a verse and the last syllable of the previous verse or between the second and fourth syllables of the same verse. In *Pad Bol*, 'Metre for speaking', a metre used in the early poetry, the stanzas have four verses which are very free in composition, having any number of syllables between four and nine. The *Pad Bamnol*, 'Metre for Speech', has a verse of six syllables, a verse of four and a verse of six (6:4:6) in the stanza. It is used when fights, quarrels, storms or threats are being described. It is used a great deal in the older part of the *Reamker* as a narrative metre. The next two metres, *Pad Kakagati*, 'Crow's Gait Metre', and *Pad Brahmagiti*, 'Brahma's Song Metre', occur here and there in the *Reamker* but are used constantly in the *Cbap*, 'Codes of Conduct', which is the next oldest, or may possibly be as old as the early *Reamker*. *Pad kakagati* has seven verses of four syllables in the stanza (4:4:4:4:4:4:4). It has been used for reporting news or information. The *Pad Brahmagiti* has stanzas of four alternating verses with five and six syllables (5:6:5:6). It is used to express sadness, separation or lamentation. The *Lpoek Angar Vat*, which is dated 1620 AD uses the three metres, *Bamnol*, *Kakagati* and *Brahmagiti*. The metres used in the poem on the inscription No 38 of the Inscriptions Modernes d'Angkor, dated 1701 AD are again *Pad Kakagati* and *Pad Brahmagiti* but it also uses the *Pad Bhujunglila*, 'Serpent's Gait Metre'. This has a verse of six followed by two verses of four syllables to the stanza (6:4:4). It is used to describe pleasant situations or activities, such as the king going to refresh himself in a pool of water. The *Pad Pandol Kak* or *Mandukgati*, 'Frog's Leap Metre', has alternating verses of four and six syllables to the stanza (4:6:4:6). It is used for amusing passages, for repartee, often between animals. Then there are metres in which the stanzas have the same number of syllables in each of four verses: four, six, seven, eight, nine, and more rarely ten, eleven, twelve and fourteen. They are said to have been borrowed from the Thai *klong*. They are called according to the number of syllables, *Pad Baky 7*, 'Seven-syllable Metre' for example, with the syllable scheme (7:7:7:7). The whole of the second part of the *Reamker* (17th–18th centuries) is written in the Six-syllable Metre. The Seven-syllable Metre became popular during the late 19th and early 20th centuries. Each of the metres is recited with an individual air.

MOK (1834–1908). After the Vietnamese arrested his father, a palace official, and his mother, Mok was brought up in the cultural atmosphere of the royal monastery at **Udong**. He was very poor, however, and wrote with charcoal on bits of brick or tile. Leaving the priesthood he became an official in the service of King Ang Duong's ◊ mother, at whose request he translated from Pali into verse two extra-canonical *jatakas*, *Devand* and *Sinhanad*. After the death of King Ang Duong's mother he went to King Norodom's court in **Phnom Penh** and was in charge first of the Library of the Royal Secretariat, then of the Law Department and finally of the Ministry of Finance. Mok was often taken on outings by the king because he had a gift for producing amusing verses on the spur of the moment about any incident which occurred. His more serious works include, apart from those mentioned above, *Tum Teav* ◊ and *Vimand Cand*.

NGOY, or Ou Ngoy, Kram Ngoy, Phirom Pheasa Ngoy (1865–1936). Educated and ordained in a monastery not far from Phnom Penh, where he studied and translated the *Tripitaka*, Ngoy was well known for his verbal skill and was still invited to preach at ceremonies. He was a gifted singer and player of the guitar and with a partner he performed a very amusing act. He had a serious aim, apart from entertaining people; he wanted to persuade them to use their wits and their gifts and not to be lazy. King Munivong heard of him and summoned him. Monsieur Georges Cœdès took Ngoy to **Bangkok** where he sang for the Siamese king. All Ngoy's works were in the form of Cbap.

NONG (19th century, exact dates unknown). A monk, and later abbot, at the Cathedis monastery, **Udong**. He was the most illustrious poet during the reigns of Kings Ang Eng and Ang Chand. He was tutor to the four sons of King Ang Eng. When one of the sons, Ang Duong ◊ became king, he asked him to re-write and up-date the Chronicles. He was put in charge of both lay and religous education. He wrote a *Cbap*, the Chronicles and many verse-novels, of which Bhogakulakumar is one. His dates are not known and it has been argued that there may have been two or even three Nongs.

Phka Srapon. In this novel by Nou Hach, it is understood that, when he has finished his studies in Phnom Penh, Bun Thoeun will marry

Vitheavi. However, when Bun Thoeun's father suffers a financial loss, Vitheavi's mother, Yeay Nuon, is ready to ignore the arrangement and, encouraged by her friend, Yeay Chan, to engage Vitheavi to Neay Sot, a businessman's son. Vitheavi writes to tell Bun Thoeun, now back in Phnom Penh, and he replies that he will be poor and she must do as her mother says. Vitheavi is too well brought up to tell her mother that she dislikes and distrusts Neay Sot. Through unhappiness she becomes ill. She goes with her mother to stay with friends in Siem Reap. Visiting Angkor, they see Neay Sot. Vitheavi refuses to go for a trip round in his mother's car. Instead she and her companions are soaked when it rains and she becomes feverish. Vitheavi has consumption. Back at home, Yeay Nuon calls a French doctor who advises rest but Neay Sot's mother interferes. First she brings a *guru* who sprinkles cold water on her and lets people crowd round her. Then she brings a spirit medium. Bun Thoeun, on vacation, goes with a party of men to the forest for honey, fish and wood. When he returns he hears funeral music. He goes to the monastery and sees Vitheavi's photograph on a coffin.

SRI DHAMMARAJA, King or Preah Reach Samphear, known in his youth as Preah Ponhea To (c 1600–1630 or 1631, reigned 1625–30 or 31). He was in the priesthood for several years before acceding to the throne. Sri Dhammaraja did not enjoy administration. He left much of the work to his Uncle Utey, while he wrote poetry and history at some distance from the capital, **Udong** (about 20 miles north-west of Phnom Penh, there are some remains of this site). He was betrothed to his step-sister, Puppha Vadey, later called Ang Vadey or Yuor Vadey, but his uncle married her while he continued to be a priest. During a stay with his uncle, who was ill, Sri Dhammaraja saw Yuor Vadey daily; and they met secretly at Angkor when they were each staying there separately. Yuor Vadey left her husband 'for a few days' and went to live with Sri Dhammaraja. The uncle set off after him with a military force. When they were gaining on him, he climbed a sugar palm and sat there writing a poem about the plight in which he found himself (Extract 5). He was shot and later Yuor Vadey was condemned to death. His surviving works are poems which are almost all love lyrics written to or about Yuor Vadey.

Tum Teav. This tale has been told in the form of verse-novels by Mok, Som and Nou Kan. The novices, Tum and Pech, have permission to travel about, selling decorative stands for use in monasteries, which they make themselves. They also sing, recite and play the guitar. In **Tboung Khmum** they sing at the house of Teav, a beautiful young girl. Tum and Teav fall in love. They return to the monastery and ask to leave the priesthood. The Master refuses Tum, having looked at his horoscope and seen that he will die within the year. Tum leaves the religious life without the Master's permission. Returning to Tboung Khmum, they find that the Governor's son is accepted as Teav's fiancé. Teav tells Tum to go away but her mother asks him to stay. Tum and Teav become lovers.

The King hears of Tum and Pech and sends for them, to hear them perform. They please the King and have no option but to stay with him.

The King decides to look for a chief concubine. Teav is chosen and is brought with her mother to the palace. Tum is summoned to sing. He sings the story of their love. The King is angry with Teav but decides not to punish her. Instead he organizes their marriage.

Teav's mother goes home and tells Arjun to prepare for the wedding. She tricks Teav into coming home by sending a message that she is ill. Teav sends a letter to Tum who tells the King. Tum, with an order from the King to Arjun to stop the wedding, goes with Pech to Tboung Khmum. They circulate among the guests. Tum speaks to Teav. Arjun and his son attack him, take him away and kill him. Teav and her companion go and see Tum's body and kill themselves. Pech returns to tell the King who goes himself with his men to punish the miscreants. The chief offenders are boiled in water; the rest are buried alive in a pit.

Vietnam

Dana Healy

> 'By 7.30 it was beyond beserk with bikes, the air was like LA on short plumbing, the subtle city war inside the war had renewed itself for another day, relatively light on actual violence but intense with bad feeling: despair, impacted rage, impotent gnawing resentment . . .'
> *Michael Herr, Dispatches*

Vietnam (the Vietnamese Socialist Republic, Cong Hoa Xa Hoi Chu Nghia Viet Nam) lies on the eastern side of the Indochinese Peninsula. In terms of land area, it is not one of the largest countries in Asia, but its strategic geographical position affording access to the whole of South-east Asia has long attracted invaders and adventurers. The territory of Vietnam is long and narrow, the distance as the crow flies from north to south being 1 650 kilometres. The country includes about 1 000 islands, two of the best known being Phu Quoc on the border with Cambodia and Con Dao to the south of Ho Chi Minh City, the latter having earned infamy under its French name Poulo Condor as one of the largest prisons for political prisoners. Also well known are Hoang Sa (the Paracel Islands) and Truong Sa (the Spratly Islands), which are subject to a dispute with China and other regional powers.

About three-quarters of Vietnam is made up of mountains. In the north, the Hoang Lien mountain range encroaches into Vietnam from China and along the western border with Laos and Cambodia stretches the Truong Son range. Vietnam also has large lowland areas; in the north is the lowland of the **Red River** which joins the coastal plain and in the south there is the fertile lowland of the **Mekong River**. The complex geological formation of the country means Vietnam has a wide variety of mineral deposits, the most important being black coal, bauxite, tin and, in smaller quantities, lead, zinc, copper, brown coal and others. Extensive drilling for oil and natural gas is presently being carried out.

The climate varies greatly between the subtropical north of the country and the tropical south. Because of the monsoon, there are periods of continual rain followed by periods of dry heat.

Vietnam has over 66 million inhabitants and the population is growing quickly. It is distributed unevenly over the country, with the heaviest population density being in the lowlands and along the coast and the sparsest in the mountain regions. Vietnam has an ethnically diverse population; Vietnamese make up nearly 90% of the population, but there are also about 60 ethnic minorities. The most significant of these are the Tay, the Thai, the Muong, the Hoa, the Kho Me, the Meo, the E De and the Gia Rai.

The earliest known forms of religion in the area of present-day Vietnam were animism and totemism. Confucianism, Taoism, Buddhism and Christianity have all had an impact on the Vietnamese people.

The influence of Confucianism was very strong and throughout many centuries it was a major support of the feudal monarchy in Vietnam. The **Van Mieu** (or The Temple of Confucius) in **Hanoi** is still one of the most popular sights in the city.

Buddhism was introduced into Vietnam in about the second century AD and has planted its roots deeply in Vietnamese culture. Today the majority of the population (about 55%) are Buddhists. Buddhism was brought to Vietnam from China (Mahayana Buddhism) and also by sea from India. Mahayana Buddhism is predominant in Vietnam. Many Buddhist temples and pagodas (*chua* in Vietnamese) were built, for example, the **Ambassador's Pagoda**, which was the official centre of Buddhism in **Hanoi**. In 1963 Vietnamese Buddhists shocked the whole world when they decided to take action against the persecution of their religion by the Catholic president Ngo Dinh Diem. Self-immolation by Vietnamese Buddhist monks was the strongest possible form of protest. Photographs of burning monks were seen all over the world and drew international attention to the plight of Buddhists in Vietnam.

In the 16th and especially in the 17th centuries European missionaries began to arrive in Vietnam and spread Catholicism (see for example, Alexandre de Rhodes ◊, Extract 2). There were periods when Catholic missionaries were viewed with hostility and Christianity was seen as a threat to the monarchy. Many missionaries were persecuted and expelled from the country. Today, about 8% of the population is Catholic.

The 20th century saw the emergence of several new religions, for example Cao Dai and Hoa Hao. Cao Daism is a synthetic belief combining elements of Confucianism, Taoism, Buddhism, Chrisianity,

Graham Greene

Islam and the cult of some famous historical figures (among its many Saints are, for example, Victor Hugo, Winston Churchill and Shakespeare). The organization of the sect is along military lines. In the past, the Cao Dai sect was very strong and well-organized. The centre of the Cao Dai sect – The Holy See – is situated at **Tay Ninh**. *The Quiet American* by Graham Greene has a vivid description of this unique sect and its annual festival (Extract 8).

History

The history of Vietnam is dominated by its struggle for independence. From earliest times it attracted the attention of enemies eager to gain control of its strategically important position. Mainly Vietnam has had to defend itself against its neighbour to the north, China. In 111 BC China conquered Vietnam, which remained for the next thousand years a Chinese province. After many uprisings of varying strength and success, a victory by Vietnamese forces over the Chinese in 939 AD in a famous battle at the **Bach Dang** river gave Vietnam its independence again. In the following centuries, especially during the rule of the Ly (1009–1225) and Tran (1225–1400) dynasties, Vietnam became a strong centralized state. In the 13th century, the Vietnamese fought off the Mongols and gained another famous victory over the Chinese Ming dynasty in the early 15th century. The first signs of crisis in the feudal state of Vietnam appeared in the 16th century and deepened in the following centuries. It was a time of confusion, division, extreme political swings and struggle for power. Peasant uprisings in various parts of the country culminated in the Tay Son revolt (1771–1802). The revolt was a reaction to feudal persecution and the presence of the Chinese army, which had come to the aid of the Vietnamese king. This revolt was successful and its leader, Nguyen Hue, became a king and took the name of Quang Trung. During his reign many political, administrative, economic and cultural reforms were carried out (for example, he replaced classical Chinese with *nom* script to be used in official documents and education). The Tay Son era did not last long; conflicts arose on the death of Quang Trung weakening the country and in 1802 the Nguyen dynasty overthrew the government and seized power.

In 1858 the French invaded Vietnam and gradually gained control of most of the country. In 1884 the Vietnamese ruler was forced to sign an agreement making Vietnam a French protectorate. A similar fate befell Laos and Cambodia and in 1887 these three countries were united to form French Indochina. From the outset, opposition to French rule was manifested by numerous movements, all of which shared a common aim – the overthrow of colonial rule. In 1930 the Communist Party of Vietnam (later the Communist Party of Indo China), was founded under the leadership of Ho Chi Minh. The Viet Minh Front (Viet Nam Doc Lap Dong Minh) was established in May 1941 and assumed a leading role in the struggle against the French. After the defeat of the Japanese at the end of the second world war, a conference in August 1945 called for a national uprising; within a week the people had taken power throughout Vietnam and on 2 September 1945 the Vietnamese Democratic Republic was declared. Peace had still not been achieved, however, and in 1946 the resistance war began and lasted until the defeat of the French at the battle of Dien Bien Phu in 1954. The war ended with the signing of the Geneva Agreements which temporarily divided the country along the seventeenth parallel. The demarcation line established in Geneva was intended to allow the forces of both sides to regroup and was supposed to end after the withdrawal of the French and the holding of an election. In the north there was the Vietnamese Democratic Republic with a communist government and in the south the Republic of Vietnam with a pro-American government. Vietnam remained divided for the next 20 years. The 1950s in Vietnam are vividly portrayed by Graham Greene in *The Quiet American* (Extract 8).

During this period the USA increased its involvement in Vietnam, hoping to preserve the independence of pro-Western South Vietnam from the communist north. The struggle for dominance in Vietnam was eventually to lead to one of the major conflicts of modern times. With US support, Ngo Dinh Diem became president of South Vietnam. The Americans provided him with extensive material and financial help and many American advisers were dispatched to Vietnam. Diem established firm rule, important posts in the government were occupied by members of his family and all opposition was suppressed. In 1960, The National Liberation Front was founded, joining different opposition groups against Diem's pro-American regime. Under the Kennedy administration American material and financial aid to the South Vietnamese army was stepped up and mass bombings and the spraying of toxic chemicals became part of the fight against the resistance. Diem's unpopularity culminated in the events of 1963, when Vietnamese Buddhists protested against his regime by setting fire to themselves. As Diem was beginning to be an embarrassment and indeed a threat to US interests, the USA encouraged the military coup in 1963 which resulted in his death.

During 1964 there was an escalation of the fighting, the bombing of North Vietnam began and in the USA public opposition to the war increased. When Richard Nixon came to the White House in 1969, the policy of 'Vietnamization' of the war was born, designed to support the South Vietnamese army and make it the main fighting force while preserving American influence in South Vietnam. The policy failed and it took another three years of intensive fighting, bombing and spraying of chemicals before the conflict approached its end and peace negotiations started. In January 1973 the 'Agreement on the Cessation of the War and the Restoration of Peace in Vietnam' was signed in Paris, obliging the Americans to withdraw all their forces from South Vietnam. Fighting between the Vietnamese, however, continued until April 1975 when Saigon was taken by the liberation forces (without, however, the much feared bloodbath). Vietnam was formally re-unified as the Vietnamese Socialist Republic under communist control in 1976.

Since unification, Vietnam has pursued an at times isolated path, shunned by its pro-American South-east Asian neighbours and facing an openly hostile People's Republic of China to the north. Vietnam and China fought a short war in 1978/79 and have an on-going territorial dispute over ownership of the Spratly Islands. Internally, Vietnam has implemented a Communist economic policy, backed up by an authoritarian political regime. Since the late 1980s, Vietnam has pursued its own version of *Perestroika*, known as *Doi Moi*, in which economic liberalization has been accompanied by greater social and cultural freedoms.

Language and Script

Vietnamese is the official language of Vietnam. It is the mother tongue of the Viet (or Kinh) people and at the same time the common language of more than 60 ethnic minorities living in Vietnam. Each ethnic minority has its own native language, thus making the linguistic map of Vietnam very varied. It is not completely clear to what language group Vietnamese itself belongs, although it shares many similarities with languages related to Thai and some of its vocabulary is related to the languages of the Mon-Khmer group.

Vietnamese is a tonal language, which means that words are pronounced with different pitch levels and the tones have a distinctive function. Standard Vietnamese (defined as the language spoken by an educated person from the Hanoi area) has six tones. There are several other dialects, the most important being the central and southern dialects. These differ mainly in phonetics (for example, they have fewer tones than standard Vietnamese) and lexicology, but not as regards grammar.

Traditionally, Chinese was used as the official and literary language in Vietnam. Later there developed a special script for recording Vietnamese based on Chinese called *chu nom*. When *nom* first appeared is not known exactly but the oldest surviving documents are from the 14th century. In the 17th century a romanized script *quoc ngu* was devised. Its origin is closely connected with the Roman Catholic missions in South-east Asia. The early missionaries, Portuguese, French, Italian and Spanish, needed a simple way of transcribing the Vietnamese language. Outstanding among the many missionaries was Alexandre de Rhodes ◊, a French Jesuit, who made a great contribution to the study of Vietnamese (Extract 1). He published the first dictionary of Vietnamese – *Dictionarum Annamiticum, Lusitanum et Latinum* (Annamese–Portuguese–Latin Dictionary) and the first Vietnamese grammar. Initially, *quoc ngu* was used only in Catholic circles but, with the arrival of the French and the onset of French colonial rule, it became the official script. Early opposition to *quoc ngu*, which was perceived to be an instrument of colonial rule, gradually faded. Its undoubted advantages as a writing system, and especially the fact that it was relatively easy to learn won over its critics.

Literature

As in countries in the Far East, literature written in Chinese was for a long time dominant in Vietnam. The oldest extant literary works date back to the 11th century and are connected with Buddhism. They are the poems of Buddhist monks explaining the fundamental principles of Buddhism, commenting on historical events or drawing their themes from the wider world, for example, by praising the beauty of nature. In the 13th century numerous historical, geographical and encyclopaedic works appear.

Of far greater significance for the history of Vietnamese literature are works written in the Vietnamese language. It was not until after the 1 000-year yoke of Chinese domination had been thrown off in the 10th century that conditions for the independent development of Vietnamese literature were created.

Chinese was the language of the educated classes, a language which was well suited to philosophical, historical, religious and political texts, but which could scarcely be an appropriate medium for the Vietnamese national consciousness. The *chu nom* system of writing down the Vietnamese language was developed over a long period; the oldest preserved documents date from the 14th century. Gradually, a large number of works written in *nom* appeared and existing classics were translated from Chinese. As the feudal system in Vietnam moved into crisis, so the importance of literature in the national language increased. Literature written in classical Chinese did not, however, disappear and the following centuries saw the development of literature in both Chinese and *nom*. Chinese remained in use until the beginning of the 20th century when the system of official mandarin examinations was abolished.

Among the earliest works in *nom* to come down to us are the poems of Nguyen Trai ◊. This scholar, poet, politician and humanist played an important role on the historical scene of the 15th century when Vietnam had to face the Ming dynasty. His extensive literary works include a collection of 254 poems written in *nom*, *Quoc Am Thi Tap*. An important source of information about literature in *nom* is *Hong Duc Quoc Am Thi Tap* (*Collected Poems of the Hong Duc Period*), one of the earliest anthologies of Vietnamese *nom* poetry. It contains about 300 poems and has great historical and literary significance.

In the 16th century the Vietnamese feudal monarchy entered a crisis and with it Confucianism, which was the support and foundation of the monarchy. The moral and ideological crisis of Confucianism had one positive influence on literature – it gave writers a new outlook on the world around them and the literary language became richer and more colourful. Classical Vietnamese literature reached its golden age in the second half of the 18th and the early 19th centuries. It was a period abundant in literary works. Especially popular were long narrative poems in verse (called *truyen* in Vietnamese). For the first time personal feelings, dreams and desires entered literature. Women also made their first appearance, portrayed not merely as some abstract ideal but as real women defending their rights to love and to be happy.

Among the best known narrative poems is *Chinh phu ngam* (*Lament of a Warrior's Wife*) originally written in classical Chinese but made famous by Doan Thi Diem's ◊ translation of it in *nom* (Extract 13). Another is *Cung oan ngam khuc* (*Lament of a Royal Concubine*) by Nguyen Gia Thieu ◊. This was also the time when a famous Vietnamese poetess, Ho Xuan Huong ◊ started publishing her poetry. Her strongest weapon was satire which she used to make vehement attacks on feudal society and Confucianism. Her poems are full of double meaning and are a sharp criticism of all that was bad and decaying in Vietnamese society (Extract 11).

Special mention should be made of Nguyen Du and his novel in verse *Truyen Kieu* ◊, also known as *Kim Van Kieu* ◊ (*The Tale of Kieu*). Nguyen Du is without doubt the most popular Vietnamese poet. He succeeded in transforming a quite common Chinese story into a poetic masterpiece highly regarded for its beautiful language and style (Extract 10).

Modern Vietnamese literature has its roots in the beginning of the 20th century. Inevitably, the far-reaching changes in Vietnamese society in the colonial period influenced cultural and literary life. Vietnamese authors gradually broke free from Chinese tradition and all the rules by which the classical literature was restricted. The romanized script *quoc ngu* pushed out the old ideograms. The introduction of printing methods facilitated access to books and for the first time in Vietnam's history journalism began to flourish. The first newspapers and magazines were published and first publishing houses opened. Vietnamese literature came into contact with European works and new genres developed. For the first time prose emerged in a literature previously dominated by poetry. Not only did the authors change but also the reading public as literature lost its elitist image, in part because of increasing literacy.

Important changes came about as the result of the New Poetry movement which started in the 1930s. This was a movement against the strict rules of classical Chinese poetry. A new generation of poets demanded freedom both in form and content. They yearned to express their emotions and feelings, with the poet becoming the most important subject of the poem, avoiding the symbolism of the old poetry. The New Poetry advocated complete freedom in prosodic rules.

Various directions and streams asserted themselves in prose of the 20th century. There appeared works which were influenced by Romanticism and yet, at the same time, the realistic novel developed. Revolutionary literature flourished. Particularly during the war of resistance shorter literary forms prevailed. Following the division of Vietnam, Vietnamese literature developed along two separate paths. In the north it was mainly socialist realism and resistance literature; in the south, there was a variety of directions with writers addressing the problems of society under US influence and many facing the dilemma of, on the one hand, hatred of communism and, on the other hand, dismay at atrocities carried out by US soldiers. *The Sorrow of War* by Bao Ninh (Extract 1) is a recent and graphic account of a North Vietnamese soldier's problems in coming to terms with the horror of his wartime experience. Perhaps unsurprisingly, the suffering of the main protagonist Kien bears a striking resemblance to the trauma of the US 'vets' as portrayed in numerous books and films.

In 1986 the Sixth Congress of the Communist Part of Vietnam approved the programme of renovation (*Doi Moi*) of Vietnamese society. The exact meaning of this programme as regards literature was defined in Resolution 5 of the Politbureau of the Central Committee of the Vietnamese Communist Party on 'Renovating and enhancing the leadership and management of literature, arts and culture to a higher step of development' passed on the 28 November 1987. While writers in Vietnam have more freedom than before, it would be naive to think that they have complete freedom of speech. They are encouraged to criticize corruption, prostitution, favouritism and drug addiction but they must never question the current political situation in Vietnam. New publishing houses were established and new magazines and journals provided new space for literary polemics. Cultural life was also inevitably affected by economic changes. Publishing houses under pressure to be profitable are forced to publish romances, thrillers, biographies of pop stars and even pornography.

Despite all the limitations, Vietnamese literature after 1986 has been much more exciting and colourful than before the introduction of *Doi Moi*. Writers are trying to experiment, to question established views and there is a strong tendency to stress the role of the individual rather than to concentrate on society as a whole. Among the most famous writers to have emerged in Vietnamese literature since 1986 are Duong Thu Huong, Pham Thi Hoai, Nguyen Huy Thiep ◊, and Bao Ninh ◊.

BOOKLIST

What follows is intended as a representative rather than comprehensive list of books about Vietnam. Where several editions exist, in general the latest and most readily available edition has been listed. For most of the extracted works, information on the original English language publisher can be found in 'Acknowledgements and Citations' at the end of the volume, as can the exact location of the extracts and the editions from which they are taken. Extract numbers are highlighted in bold.

Ba Huyen Thanh Quan, *Reminiscences of the Old Thang Long City*. Vietnamese Studies, Hanoi, 1977. **Extract 3**.

Bao Ninh (Frank Palmos, Vo Bang Thanh, Phan Thanh Hao, Katerina Pierce, trans) *The Sorrow of War*, Secker and Warburg, London, 1993. **Extract 1**.

Doan Thi Diem, 'The Lament of a Warrior's Wife', in *A Thousand Years of Vietnamese Poetry*, New York, 1975. **Extract 13**.

Duras, Marguerite (Barbara Bray, trans), *The Lover*, Flamingo, London, 1986. **Extract 7**.

Greene, Graham, *The Quiet American*, Heinemann, London, 1979. **Extract 8**.

Halberstam, David, *One Very Hot Day*, The Bodley Head, London, 1964. **Extract 16**.

Herr, Michael, *Dispatches*, Picador, London, 1977. **Extract 6**.

Ho Chi Minh, *Prison Diary*, Foreign Languages Publishing House, Hanoi. **Extract 12**.

Ho Xuan Huong, 'Complaint of the No.2 Wife', in *All She Wants*, Tuba Press, London, 1987. **Extract 11**.

Larteguy, Jean, *Yellow Fever*, London, 1965. **Extract 4**.

Nguyen Cong Hoan, 'The Carrion Eaters', in *Vietnamese Literature*, Foreign Languages Publishing House, Hanoi, 1982. **Extract 9**.

Nguyen Du, 'The Tale of Kieu', in *Vietnamese Literature*. Foreign Languages Publishing House, Hanoi, 1982. **Extract 10**.

Nguyen Huy Thiep (Greg Lockhart, trans), *The General Retires and Other Stories*, OUP, Singapore, 1992. **Extract 15**.

Rhodes of Vietnam, *The Travels and Missions of Father Alexandre de Rhodes in China and other Kingdoms of the Orient*. Newman Press, Westminster, MD, USA, 1966. **Extract 2**.

Truong Vinh Ky (Honey, trans), *Voyage to Tonking in the Year AT-HOI*, SOAS, London, 1982. **Extract 5**.

Vassal, Gabrielle M., *On and Off Duty in Annam*, Heinemann, 1910. **Extract 14**.

Extracts

(1) Central Highlands

Bao Ninh, *The Sorrow of War*

Bao Ninh served with the Glorious 27th Brigade of the North Vietnamese Army and his heavily autobiographical novel draws extensively from his wartime experiences. Here, the main protagonist, Kien, is working in a 'body-collecting team' after the end of the war. He is working in what came to be known as the Jungle of Screaming Souls where he saw action during the war.

Kien knows the area well. It was here, at the end of the dry season of 1969, that his battalion 27 was surrounded and almost totally wiped out. Ten men survived from the Unlucky Battalion, after fierce, horrible, barbarous fighting.

That was the dry season when the sun burned harshly, the wind blew fiercely, and the enemy sent napalm spraying through the jungle and a sea of fire enveloped them, spreading like the fires of hell. Troops in the fragmented companies tried to regroup, only to be blown out of their shelters again as they went mad, became disoriented and threw themselves into nets of bullets, dying in the flaming inferno. Above them the helicopters flew at tree top height and shot them almost one by one, the blood spreading out, spraying from their backs, flowing like red mud.

The diamond-shaped grass clearing was piled high with bodies killed by the helicopter gunships. Broken bodies, bodies blown apart, bodies vaporized.

No jungle grew again in this clearing. No grass. No plants.

'Better to die than surrender my brothers! Better to die!' the Battalion Commander yelled insanely; waving his pistol in front of Kien he blew his brains out through his ear. Kien screamed soundlessly in his throat at the sight, as the Americans attacked with sub-machine-guns, sending bullets buzzing like deadly bees around him. Then Kien lowered his machine-gun, grasped his side and fell, rolling slowly down the bank of a shallow stream, hot blood trailing down the slope after him.

(2) Hanoi

Alexandre de Rhodes, *Rhodes of Viet Nam*

Alexandre de Rhodes was a French missionary who came to Vietnam in the early 17th century. One of his most important contributions to Vietnamese studies was the first dictionary of the Vietnamese language. Here are some of his impressions of Vietnam and his missionary work there.

As soon as we arrived in the capital of Tonkin, called Checho [Ke-cho, Hanoi], which is a very large, very beautiful city where the streets are broad, the people numberless, the circumference of the walls at least six leagues around, the king had a house and a lovely church built for me. News of it spread throughout the kingdom, and such crowds gathered that I was forced to preach at least four and more often six times a day.

The fruit was so great I could hardly believe it. A sister of the king and seventeen of his close relatives were baptized. Several famous captains did likewise, and many more soldiers. Those baptized the first year numbered 1,200; the following year there were 2,000; and the third year 3,500.

Nothing so astonished me as the ease with which I was able to convert the idolatrous priests, who are usually the most obstinate. I found them marvelously open to reason. I baptized 200 of them, who will be of unbelievable help to us in converting the others. One of them alone brought me 500 of those he had disabused of error by teaching them the truths of the faith, and they have since become our most fervent catechists.

(3) Hanoi

Ba Huyen Thanh Quan (Nguyen Thi Hinh), *Reminiscences of Old Thang Long City*

Hanoi was formerly called Thang Long – City of the Soaring Dragon. This poem was written in the 19th century during the time when the Nguyen dynasty ruled in Vietnam. The Nguyens transferred the capital to Hue and tried to destroy most of the monuments in Hanoi. The poetess recollects the beauty of old Hanoi and shows her dislike of what the new dynasty did.

Why has the Creator paraded so many varied scenes
across the stage of life,
Since days of old, countless starry nights and dewy mornings
have passed.

The soul of autumn grass hovers over the tracks of carriages
and horses of bygone days,
A waning light from the setting sun catches the foundations
of former palaces.
The stones brave the inclement weather to preserve
the memories of past glories,
The lake waters grimace before the vicissitudes of fate.
In the mirror of the centuries, let us look at the past and
the present,
The painful spectacle tears my innards.

(4) Hanoi

Jean Larteguy, *Yellow Fever*

In 1858 France embarked on its colonial adventure in Vietnam. Along with other countries in Indochina, Vietnam became the target of France's 'mission civilisatrice'. After the defeat at Dien Bien Phu the French had to leave Vietnam. Before their departure from Hanoi they destroyed one of the most famous historical monuments in the city, One Pillar Pagoda. The pagoda was later rebuilt using the original plans.

At five o'clock that evening the Pagoda of the Single Pillar was blown up. The explosion shattered the windows of the Press Camp, and all the journalists leaped into the jeeps which the army had put at their disposal. Even the Squid dragged himself out of his armchair. The little pagoda stood on a stone base in the middle of a small lake. The plastic charge had gutted it completely and decapitated the gilt Buddha inside.

The guardian of the temple had seen nothing, heard nothing. At least that was what he told Julien, who was first on the scene.

'It's utterly idiotic', said Rovignon. 'What's the point of blowing up this old building? . . . Sheer vandalism!'

(5) Phat Diem

Truong Vinh Ky, *Voyage to Tonking in the Year AT-HOI*

Phat Diem in the Ninh Binh province is a famous centre of Catholicism in north Vietnam with a monastery used for the training of Vietnamese clergy and a cathedral. In 1876 Truong Vinh Ky visited Tongkin (he himself was from Cochinchina). Five years later he published his personal account of the trip. The reason for his journey remains something of a mystery; at that time it was unusual for people to travel merely for pleasure and it is perhaps not surprising that he was accused by many Vietnamese of being a spy for the French colonial authorities. Whatever the truth, the work is an eye-witness account of life in north Vietnam before the French took over. The author leads us through various provinces, acquaints us not only with mandarins but also with ordinary people and their customs.

I took my leave of Father Nghiem and we sailed down the river to the province of Ninh-binh. My primary object was, however, to go down to Phat-diem and visit Father Sau. At 6 o'clock on the morning of the 8th day we reached the post of Loc-bo and, at 1 o'clock, we turned off towards the post of Binh-hai, in the estuary of Hai-lieu. There we anchored to await high water so that we might enter the small river called the Gioi, or the Kim-giang, and so make our way to Phat-diem, the place where Father Sau lived.

It was already twilight when we reached the port and the boat anchored out in the stream. I sent somebody up to deliver my card to Father Sau, and he despatched a man to the port to fetch me. He had me escorted to his square house, into which he invited me for a drink of tea. After this he led me upstairs, where we chatted together until 11 o'clock before parting to retire to bed. In the morning he invited me to hear mass and afterwards we went to see the Sacred Heart chapel. The Church of the Blessed Virgin was small in size but very fine. The altar, the tabernacle, and the altar rail were all made from Thanh-hoa stone and all carved. Before the entrance to the church was an artificial hill set in the centre of a lake with a bridge leading out to it.

In front of the cathedral is a portico or elaborate entrance gateway. The altar in the cathedral is made from Thanh-hoa stone, beautifully carved and most attractive to look at. In a roofed workshop with open sides I saw the workmen carving objects from this Thanh-hoa stone. They were busily occupied in carving a crucifix from a single piece of stone which they would later place on the roof of the cathedral.

(6) Saigon (Ho Chi Minh City)

Michael Herr, *Dispatches*

Dispatches was first published in 1977. It is a picture of Viètnam as seen through the eyes of the narrotor – a journalist posted to South Vietnam during the war. It is widely considered to be one of the best accounts about the war. The following extract captures the special atmosphere of Saigon of the late 1960s, with its alluring mixture of danger and beauty.

Beautiful for once and only once, just past dawn flying towards the centre of the city in a Loach, view from a bubble floating at 800 feet. In that space, at that hour, you could see what people had seen forty years before, Paris of the East, Pearl of the Orient, long open avenues lined and bowered over by trees running into spacious parks, precisioned scale, all under the soft shell from a million breakfast fires, camphor smoke rising and diffusing, covering Saigon and the shining veins of the river with a warmth like the return of better times. Just a projection, that was the thing about choppers, you had to come down sometime, down to the moment, the street, if you found a pearl down there you got to keep it.

By 7.30 it was beyond berserk with bikes, the air was like LA on short plumbing, the subtle city war inside the war had renewed itself for another day, relatively light on actual violence but intense with bad feeling: despair, impacted rage, impotent gnawing resentment; thousands of Vietnamese in the service of a pyramid that wouldn't stand for five years, plugging the feed tube into their own hearts, grasping and gorging; young Americans in from the boonies on TDY, charged with hatred and grounded in fear of the Vietnamese; thousands of Americans sitting in their offices crying in bored chorus, 'You can't get these people to do a fucking thing, you can't get these people to do a fucking thing.' And all the others, theirs and ours, who just didn't want to play, it sickened them.

(7) Saigon (Ho Chi Minh City)

Marguerite Duras, *The Lover*

The schoolgirl protagonist and her wealthy Chinese lover live out their intense and defiant affair against the backdrop of 1930s Saigon. The novel is narrated by the girl grown old and remembering times and passions lost. Here, they step out into the city that so often is perceived in noise, heat and smells from behind the shutters of the room where they make love.

On the sidewalk the crowd, going in all directions, slow or fast, forcing its way, mangy as stray dogs, blind as beggars, a Chinese crowd, I can still see it now in pictures of present prosperity, in the way they go along together without any sign of impatience, in the way they are alone in a crowd, without happiness, it seems, without sadness, without curiosity, going along without seeming to, without meaning to, just going this way rather than that, alone and in the crowd, never alone even by themselves, always alone even in the crowd.

We go to one of those Chinese restaurants on several floors, they occupy whole buildings, they're as big as department stores, or barracks, they look out over the city from balconies and terraces. The noise that comes from these buildings is inconceivable in Europe, the noise of orders yelled out by the waiters, then taken up and yelled out by the kitchens. No one ever merely speaks. On the terraces there are Chinese orchestras. We go up to the quietest floor, the Europeans' floor, the menus are the same but there's less yelling. There are fans, and heavy draperies to deaden the noise.

I ask him to tell me about his father's money, how he got rich. He says it bores him to talk about money, but if I insist he'll tell me what he knows about his father's wealth. It all began in Cholon, with the housing estates for natives. He built three hundred of these 'compartments', cheap semi-detached dwellings, let out for rent. Owns several streets. Speaks French with a rather affected Paris accent, talks money with perfect ease. He used to own some apartment blocks, but sold them to buy building land south of Cholon. Some rice-fields in Sadec were sold too, the son thinks. I ask about epidemics. Say I've seen whole streets of native compartments closed off from one day to the next, the doors and windows nailed up, because of an epidemic of plague. He says there's not so much of it here, the rats are exterminated much more often than up-country.

(8) Tay Ninh

Graham Greene, *The Quiet American*

Probably the most famous novel about Vietnam written in the English language, The Quiet American is set in Saigon around 1952 against the background of the war between the French and the Viet Minh. The following extract takes us to Tay Ninh – the centre of the Cao Dai sect.

Along the route to Tanyin flowed a fast stream of staff and C.D. cars, and on the more exposed sections of the road Foreign Legionaries threw out cover across the rice-fields. It was always a day of some anxiety for the French High Command and perhaps a certain hope for the Caodaists, for what could more painlessly emphasize their own loyalty than to have a few important guests shot outside their territory?

Every kilometre a small mud watch tower stood up above the flat fields like an exclamation-mark, and every ten kilometres there was a larger fort manned by a platoon of Legionaries, Moroccans or Senegalese. Like the traffic into New York the cars kept one pace – and as with the traffic into New York you had a sense of controlled impatience, watching the next car ahead and in the mirror the car behind. Everybody wanted to reach Tanyin, see the show and get back as quickly as possible: curfew was at seven.

One passed out of the French-controlled rice-fields into the rice-fields of the Hoa-Haos and thence into the rice-fields of the Caodaists, who were usually at war with the Hoa-Haos: only the flags changed on the watch towers. Small naked boys sat on the buffaloes which waded genital-deep among the irrigated fields; when the gold harvest was ready the peasants in their hats like limpets winnowed the rice against little curved shelters of plaited bamboo. The cars drove rapidly by, belonging to another world.

Now the churches of the Caodaists would catch the attention of strangers in every village; pale blue and pink plasterwork and a big eye of God over the door. Flags increased: troops of peasants made their way along the road: we were approaching the Holy See. In the distance the sacred mountain stood like a green bowler hat above Tanyin – that was where General The held out, the dissident Chief of Staff who had recently declared his intention of fighting both the French and the Vietminh. The Caodaists made no attempt to capture him, although he had kidnapped a cardinal, but it was rumoured that he had done it with the Pope's connivance.

It always seemed hotter in Tanyin than anywhere else in the Southern Delta; perhaps it was the absence of water, perhaps it was the sense of interminable ceremonies which made one sweat vicariously, sweat for the troops standing to attention through the long speeches in a language they didn't understand, sweat for the Pope in his heavy chinoiserie robes. Only the female cardinals in their white silk trousers chatting to the priests in sun-helmets gave an impression of coolness under the glare; you couldn't believe it would ever be seven o'clock and cocktail-time on the roof of the Majestic, with a wind from Saigon river.

(9) Vietnam: Corruption

Nguyen Cong Hoan, *The Carrion Eaters*

Xich died on Sunday. In order to bury him, his family needs a document from a local mandarin. As the carrion eaters hover around the body, the mandarin delays signing the relevant certificate. He demands a bribe before he gives the permission for the body to be buried. In the same way as the carrion eaters, he also preys on the dead.

'Monsieur Mandarin I call to witness the soul of my poor son I would never dare to tell you a lie. If I am concealing anything I am ready to submit to any tortures . . . I entreat you, give me leave to bury my son. I shall show you my gratitude . . .'.

The Mandarin turned his face towards Cuu with a softened expression as though to show that he could allow his feelings to be affected as readily as the next man.

'And what will be the extent of your gratitude for my trouble?' he enquired mildly.

'Ten piastres, Monsieur Mandarin!'

'Oh come now' said the Mandarin, laughing; 'the petrol alone has already cost me ten piastres!'

The clerk came bustling up to put his word in.

'With the greatest respect . . . this is an affair of quite sizeable proportions, Monsieur Mandarin'.

Then turning towards Cuu he bitterly reproached him:

'Look here – with your fortune surely you can rise to a hundred piastres to show your gratitude and get your son a decent burial. That's your common folk for you, Mr Mandarin! . . . Fools! They want to have everything arranged for them but don't want to think about the price!'

Old Cuu scowled and whispered in the clerk's ear:

'I beg you to speak for me to Monsieur Mandarin. I can't give a hundred piastres, would he accept fifty?'

The bulging eyes of the clerk rolled in an expression of total rejection as though to prevent Cuu from adding anything even more ridiculous.

'You're incredible! . . .'

He leaned towards Cuu to continue in a lowered voice.

'As a friend I promise to do my best. But it'll be eighty for him you know and ten for me – right?

'But indeed I do not possess that sum'.

'No matter. Your word will be quite sufficient. You can pay later. I myself will stand surety for you – as a trifling service. Just think . . . how can you have the heart to leave your own child in such a state?'

Cuu heaved a sigh.

He turned round for a moment and caught sight of his wife. She was rolling on the ground in paroxysms of grief. He could no longer hold back his tears. He made an effort to continue the haggling but was finally obliged to consent to pay up twenty piastres.

Half an hour later flies, fish and crows found themselves suddenly bereft. How were they to know that it was district chief Mandarin Le Tri Huyen who had deprived them of their prey?

(10) Vietnam: Falling in Love

Nguyen Du, *The Tale of Kieu*

The most famous poem in Vietnamese literature. It tells a story of a talented and beautiful girl Kieu. The following passage is from the beginning of the poem. Kieu has met Kim, a young soldier, and they fall in love. One evening, she goes to see him and they swear an oath of eternal love.

The flowers grew richer, their perfume more insistent,
The ardour in their eyes lit in one flame,
Kim's passion surged within him, a strong flood
And now some licence pierced his tenderness.
She warned him . . . Let us not treat lightly this great love
Now let me speak to you one simple word.
Tender is the blossom of the peach and to the bluebird's coming
Never would I lock the garden gate,

But we have sworn to marry and for that
She who must wear the wife's plain smock her body must keep pure
If like wantons in the mulberry-groves I fail,
And all unworthy prove you I merit your contempt.
Should we the passing flower of a day thus seize
To stain henceforth the wholeness of our love?
Remember Thoi and Truong's love so beautiful,
Alas the rains and storms too quickly spoiled
Their treasured loves, the too fond willing flowers

Faded before the birds of Spring. Their pinions touched,
The feathers interlaced . . . already love was fading,
Contempt was whispering in their hearts, their vows undone
That they held sacred once. And so love died in shame.
The lovely Thoi her shuttle should have thrown
To bind, not loose her love. Why should we haste
To break the branch and snatch the flowers?
The day will come when love will answer love.

(11) Vietnam: Marriage

Ho Xuan Huong, *Complaint of the No 2 Wife*

A poem written by Ho Xuan Huong – a Vietnamese poetess sometimes considered to be the first feminist in Vietnam. Written in the early 19th century, the poem describes the difficult fate of a second wife (in Vietnam, polygamy was frequent, the first wife being the most important, the second one playing very often the role of a servant).

Being an extra wife isn't worth much,
Condemned to shiver while she shares the bed.
I see the man maybe twice a year
When I eat his sticky rice cake.
I work just like a servant
But even a servant gets paid.
If I'd stopped to think about it,
I would never have married.

(12) Vietnam: Prison

Ho Chi Minh, *Prison Diary*

In August 1942 Ho Chi Minh was arrested by the police on the Chinese side of the Sino-Vietnamese border and while in prison he wrote his collection of poems. He wrote the poems in Chinese hoping that his guards would not confiscate them since they could understand them. The collection forms a diary of his life in prison, his sufferings and anxieties, his recollections of his family, friends and homeland. Despite the hardness of prison life, little things give him pleasure – the moonlight, the sunshine, the birds – and strengthen his belief that he will be free again.

On the road

Although they have tightly bound my arms and legs,
All over the mountain I hear the songs of birds,

And the forest is filled with the perfume of spring-flowers.
Who can prevent me from freely enjoying these,
Which take from the long journey a little of its loneliness?

Gambling

Outside the jail, people who gamble are arrested,
But once inside the jail, they can gamble just as they like:
So, of course, in jail the prisoners are often heard to complain:
'Why on earth did I never think to come to this place before?'

(13) Vietnam: A Sense of Loss

Doan Thi Diem, *The Lament of a Warrior's Wife*

A long narrative poem describing the fate of a young woman whose husband had gone to war. In the following passage she ponders the cruelty of war and hard life of the soldiers.

Since your departure to the far southeast
I never know where you are.
After so long at war
Soldiers must value their lives like grass and leaves:
How long can they hope to live, brave men
Fighting to repay their emperor?
Above Ch'i mountain the moon hangs alone,
Winds along the Fei river blow over the deserted tombs,
Gusty winds howl over the souls of the dead
As the moon whitens their faces:
How many dead soldiers will leave relatives behind,
To call on their souls, to paint their ancestral portraits?
And when war is over all will be as it was,
Travellers will pass through with pity in their hearts.

(14) Vietnam: Tet

Gabrielle M. Vassal, *On and Off Duty in Annam*

Travel sketches written by a wife of a French official during the time when Vietnam was a French protectorate. The following passage describes the preparations for the biggest festival in Vietnam – the Tet (the New Year festival), which is celebrated according to the lunar calendar.

The Tet is the greatest fête in the calendar; it is the Annamese New Year. It takes place during the new moon in February, and extends over a period of ten days. There is not a single native in Annam who does not celebrate this event; however rich or however poor he may be, he will manage to break his daily routine and take part in some sort of merrymaking.

The preparations for this occasion are manifold, but chiefly of a religious character. All the graves must be tended, the dwellings thoroughly cleansed, especially around the altar, and the red papers with black characters which adorn the inside and outside of the house must be renewed. Money is imperatively necessary. At this season, therefore, the Annamese collect any outstanding debts, drive hard bargains, or even steal, if the offence can be committed without detection. Every sapek is of value. All the savings of the last few months, or maybe those stored up since the last Tet, are now expended – some on gifts for the altar, some on new tunics and turbans, a certain amount on squibs and crackers, and all that remains on gambling. On the last day of the Tet the whole family will be penniless. Indeed they will be fortunate if they have not to hand over the clothes on their backs, their newly purchased tunics, to pay their gambling debts. Gambling is the greatest defect of the Annamese character; they seldom drink, nor are they quarrelsome or violent, but their love of this vice is inherent in their natures. It is this which prevents thrift and results in a hand-to-mouth existence, even among the regular and skilled workers. The Tet festivities tempt those who do not habitually gamble to give themselves up to it.

(15) Vietnam: Town and Country

Nguyen Huy Thiep, *'Lessons from the Country'*

This short story is taken from the collection The General Retires and Other Stories. Hien is comparing life in the countryside to life in Hanoi.

'It's very lonely in the country,' murmured Hien. 'I've only been to Hanoi once. I wasn't married then. I had a terrific time, but it scared me too. Hanoi people all looked wicked to me. One day, at a bus-stop, there was a man with a wispy moustache wearing dark glasses. He was old enough to be my father. "Hey there, my dear," he leered, 'how about coming with me?" I was horrified: "Oh no!" I said, "How could you ask such a thing?" He just laughed and said: "Sorry, my dear, I mistook you for a tart." I didn't know what a tart was. But a few minutes later when Tan – that's my husband – came by the bus-stop, the other fellow had taken off. This was the first time I met Tan, and when I told him the story he looked dark and said "City louts, they're guttersnipes, the lot of them." I don't know if what he said was true, but city people are good talkers. They'll say "Sorry, my dear" for nothing.'

Hien went on: 'In the country, boredom is the worst thing. I don't mind the work. But I often get so bored that it shrivels me up. When Tan joined the army, I was so depressed that I contemplated suicide. I lay down in a corn field on a bull ants' nest. I was sure the bull ants would bite me to death. But they didn't. Did they fell sorry for me, do you think? They probably thought that I was too young to die, that it'd be a waste.' Hien laughed. I was numb. I thought of my father: he had a wispy moustache and wore dark glasses. And my mother: if she lay on an ants' nest, she would surely die; she is so restless that the bull ants could not ignore her.

Hien said: 'Of course, we also have our happy times in the country. It's good when the theatrical companies come around. I remember a performance of *Tran Si My's Neglect*. I brought along a pocketful of roasted grass hoppers. They were very tasty. I went with my friends Luoc and Thu, and the three of us ate them while we watched the play.

(16) Vietnam: War

David Halberstam, *One Very Hot Day*

The author was a reporter for The New York Times covering the American War in Vietnam. One Very Hot Day portrays the frustrations and emptiness of this war. The hero, Captain Beaupre, is an American adviser to the Vietnamese army.

'Beg your pardon, sir', Beaupre said, 'but the map did make a mistake, but it's not the other side of the canal. We've been working it for the last twenty minutes and they don't have it either'.

'But there must be a village there, must be people there. Why we even have reports saying the people are hostile, so that proves it. If they're hostile, they've got to be there', the Colonel insisted. 'Look around yourself, Captain Beaupre, what do you see?'

'Sir, Vietnamese, a lot of them, a lot of trees, some bushes'.

'What are the troops doing, Beaupre?'

'Sir, the troops are sitting down, and talking and some of them are already impurifying the canal, and a few of them are starting to break out the rice'.

'Just a minute', the Colonel said. 'You wait there a minute, Beaupre, and don't go anywhere. Don't leave the place you're at. Think of it as Ap Than Thoi'.

Then he sent a spotter plane over and it circled the area for a few minutes without finding the village or drawing fire. Finally the plane radioed back and the Colonel called Beaupre and said, 'Beaupre, cross Ap Than Thoi off your map. Forget about it. It's not your fault, Captain'.

Beaupre thanked him (he liked the Colonel) and made a note that someone should draw up some new maps, since these were twenty years old and not always accurate.

That night the Colonel said nothing, but apparently the entire advisory group knew what had happened and almost overnight Ap Than Thoi became a part of the vocabulary. One went away to Saigon but claimed he was going to Ap Than Thoi; someone violently ill for three days claimed he had contracted the bug at Ap Than Thoi; if an officer with a girl met a buddy in Saigon, he always introduced her as being from Ap Than Thoi; if something went wrong in the field, a terrible snafu, it always took place at Ap Than Thoi; if an operation were being planned and someone wanted to know the local political climate, he would be told it was no worse than Ap Than Thoi.

Biographies and literary notes

BAO Ninh (1952–). Served in the Glorious 27th Youth Brigade; of the 500 who went to war in 1969 he was one of only 10 to survive. His first novel, *The Sorrow of War* (Extract 1) was a bestseller in Vietnam and critically acclaimed in the West.

Chinh phu ngam (*Lament of a Warrior's Wife*). Doan Thi Diem's translation of a work in classical Chinese originally written by Dang Tran Con (Extract 13). A young woman is left behind while her husband has gone to war. She is alone with her worries and everything around her evokes memories of him. As time passes she falls into despair. Her only hope is that peace will be restored and she will be reunited with her husband. The 477 free verses from the Chinese original were transferred into 102 stanzas of

Marguerite Duras

four lines each using the 7,7,6-8 verse (*song that luc bat*). This enables more variations than the 6-8 verse (*luc bat*) frequently used in narrative poems of that period. The imagery and perfection of form make this work a classic of Vietnamese literature superior to the original.

DOAN Thi Diem (1705–1748). An educated woman, she wrote poems and a collection of legends in Chinese. Born in **Hien Pham**, she took care of her mother and married late at the age of 37. Her husband was sent on a mission to China and during this time she wrote her most important work *Chinh phu ngam* (*Lament of a Warrior's Wife*) ◊, a translation into Vietnamese of a poem in Chinese by Dang Tran Con (Extract 13). Her other work is a collection of legends in Chinese *Truyen ky Tan Pha*.

DURAS, Marguerite (1914–). Duras was born on 4 April 1914 in **Giadinh** in Indo-China. From 1935 to 1941, Duras was Secretary at the French Ministry for the Colonies. She published her first novel, *Les Impudents*, in 1943 and has since become a prolific and respected woman of letters. One of her most notable screen credits was for the screenplay of *Hiroshima mon Amour*, 1960. She has drawn on her experiences in Indo-China for some of her most important work. *The Lover* (Extract 7) is perhaps her most famous book, and vividly evokes the passion of a young girl for an older and wealthy Chinese man in the exotic setting of 1930s Saigon. The narrative, told by the girl grown older, is written with striking immediacy and economy, and deals impressively with erotic love, death, and the tragic tensions within a family. The skilful structure of the novel effectively conveys the psychology of a woman feeling and learning through memory. *The Lover* received the Prix Goncourt in 1984.

GREENE, Graham (1904–91). After his studies in Oxford, Greene worked for four years as an assistant director for the London *Times* and later was appointed film critic of the *Spectator*. After the second world war he was an independent journalist. Greene travelled a lot and used his experience from his travels in his literary work. He was a prolific author, whose works include novels (eg *The Heart of the Matter*, *The End of the Affair*, *The Quiet American* (Extract 8), *The Honorary Consul* and *Monsignore Quixote*), many short stories, plays, four travel books, two books of autobiography, books for children, many essays and reviews and screenplays for some of the films based on his novels. In 1954 he was the Vietnam correspondent for the *Sunday Times* and the character of Fowler in *The Quiet American* is believed to have been based on Greene himself.

HO Chi Minh (real name Nguyen Tat Thanh, also known as Nguyen Ai Quoc, 1890–1969). More famous for his military and political activity than his literary achievements, Ho was President of the Democratic Republic of Vietnam. His literary work includes speeches, essays, articles, letters and appeals, for example *Ban tuyen ngon doc lap* (*The Declaration of Independence of the DRV*, 1945), *Tu gui tu nuoc ngoai* (*A Letter from Abroad*, 1941), *Loi keu goi toan quoc khang chien* (*Appeal to Nation-wide Resistance*), *Ban Di chuc* (*Testament*). Ho also wrote poetry and his collection of poems written in classical Chinese *Nhat ky trong tu* (*Prison Diary*) was published in 1964 (Extract 12). It was written during Ho Chi Minh's detention by Chang Kai-Shek's police between autumn 1942 and autumn 1943. This is a collection of sketches from prison life, memories of friends, places and his thoughts.

HO Xuan Huong (end of 18th century–beginning of 19th century). Not much is known about this Vietnamese poetess. She was born in Hanoi, married twice, each time being the second wife (Extract 11). She was an educated woman, travelled a lot and knew many writers of the period. Her poems collected in *Xuang Huong thi tap* (*Poems of Xuan Huong*) are known for their daring and controversial style. Her poetry is simple, reminiscent in style of Vietnamese folk poetry. In a society ruled by Confucian principles she dares to criticize corrupted mandarins and monks, defends women and unmarried mothers and preaches free love. Her language is fresh, popular and vulgar at times and she makes use of plays on words and allusions giving her poetry several meanings. Although she did not write many poems she is one of the most admired of Vietnamese poets.

NGUYEN Cong Hoan (1903–1977). Novelist and a story-teller. Born into a family of scholars, Nguyen later became a teacher. His literary career started during French colonial rule in Vietnam. As a teacher, he was closely watched by the French and often transferred from one place to another. He became connected with the patriotic movement in Vietnam and after the August revolution held posts in the government and the army. From 1957 he was a chairman of the Writers' Union. Nguyen Cong Hoan chose satire as his main weapon to attack the upper classes of Vietnamese society – corrupt mandarins, landlords, all those who profited from collaboration with the French (Extract 9). His short stories and novels are full of sympathy and admiration for ordinary people – peasants, beggars, workers. Nguyen's chief works include the novels *Co giao Minh* (*Minh the Lady Teacher*), *La ngoc canh vang* (*Leaves of Jade and Branch of Gold*), *Buoc duong cung* (*Impasse*), short stories *Kep Tu Ben* (*The Actor Tu Ben*). He also wrote travel notes and memoirs.

NGUYEN Dinh Chieu (1822–1888). Known as 'the blind poet of Nam Bo', Nguyen was born in **Tan Khanh** and studied in **Hue**. His life was full of personal misfortunes. Upon learning that his mother died, he went straight back home but on his journey he became blind. He refused to collaborate with the French and supported popular resistance. His work includes

Luc Van Tien (a novel in verse drawing from his own life), *Van te nghia si Can Giuoc* (*Funeral Oration for the Heroes of Can Giuoc*), *Ngu tieu van dap* (*Dialogue between a Fisherman and a Woodcutter*).

NGUYEN Du (1765–1820). Considered to be the greatest Vietnamese poet, Nguyen Du was born into a family of scholars in **Tien Dien**. He successfully passed the provincial examinations at the age of 19 and served as a military mandarin under the Le kings. After the downfall of the Le dynasty, he refused to serve the Tay Son. He lived in a retreat in the countryside, getting to learn more about the lives of ordinary people and folk literature. Later he accepted public functions and in 1813 was sent on a diplomatic mission to China. He died in 1820 before leaving for another mission. He wrote both in classical Chinese and Vietnamese. His most famous work is *Truyen Kieu* (*The Tale of Kieu*, also known as *Kim Van Kieu* after the main characters) ◊ a long narrative poem in *nom* (Extract 10). Other works in Vietnamese include *Van te thap loai chung sinh* (*Call to Wandering Souls*) and *Thac loi trai phuong non* (*An Answer to the Boys of the Guild of Hat Makers*). His work in Vietnamese comprises *Thanh Hien thi tap* (*Poems of Thanh Hien*), *Bac hanh tap luc* (*Travels to the North*) and *Nam Trung tap ngam* (*Poems Written in the South*).

NGUYEN Gia Thieu (1741–1798). A Vietnamese poet from a noble family in **Lieu Ngan**, he held an important post as Captain of the Royal Guards from the age of 19. After the Tay Son revolt he left his career and spent the rest of his life in a retreat. He is best known for *Cung oan ngam khuc* (*Lament of a Royal Concubine*) written in *nom*. This narrative poem deals with a very topical theme of those times – the life of a young, beautiful and lonely woman in a harem. The author concentrates on the emotional rather than the social aspect of the life in harem and the poem becomes a criticism of the feudal monarchy. The poem is written in the *song that luc bat* (7,7,6-8) verse. Nguyen Gia Thieu also wrote poems in classical Chinese.

NGUYEN Huy Thiep (1950–). Born in **Hanoi**, Nguyen studied history at Teachers' College. After graduating, he taught history for 10 years. At the beginning of the 1980s he started publishing short stories. It was not until 1987, however, when several of his stories appeared in *Van Nghe* (the weekly of the Vietnamese Writer's Association), the he became the subject of passionate discussion. He loves to experiment, to question facts and pushes readers into thinking and reaching their own conclusions. (Extract 15).

NGUYEN Trai, pseudonym Uc Trai (1380–1442). Poet, writer, statesman and humanist. Born in **Nhi Khe** he was an important historical figure at the beginning of the 15th century. He joined the fight against the Ming and became an adviser to Le Loi – the leader of the resistance and the founder of the later Le dynasty. He was made a Minister of the Interior under the Le dynasty. After the fall of the Le dynasty his enemies fabricated a plot against him and in 1442 he was executed. He wrote both in Chinese and the national language. His collection of poems in *nom*, *Quoc am thi tap* (*Poems in the National Language*), is one of the earliest works in *nom* that has survived. His best known poem in Chinese is *Binh Ngo dai cao* (*Proclamation of the Victory over the Ngo*).

RHODES, Alexandre de (1591–1660). A French Jesuit and a missionary to Vietnam, Rhodes first arrived in Cochinchina in 1624. He made a great contribution to the study of Vietnamese by codifying and regularizing the romanized system of the Vietnamese language and published a trilingual dictionary of Vietnamese: *Dictionarum Annamiticum, Lusitanum et Latinum* (*Annamese–Portuguese–Latin Dictionary*) and the first Vietnamese grammar – *Linguae annamiticae seu tunchinensis brevis declaratio* (*Short Statement on the Annamese or Tonkinese Language*). In 1645 he was expelled from Vietnam and later published a book of sketches of his travels (Extract 2). He also worked to help establish the Society of Foreign Missions but died before it was founded in 1664.

Truyen Kieu also known as *Kim Van Kieu* (*The Tale of Kieu*). This is considered to be the greatest and the most loved poem in the Vietnamese language. It is a long narrative poem (*truyen*) written by Nguyen Du. The poem is an adaptation of a Chinese romance. It consists of 3 245 lines of the 6-8 verse (*luc-bat*). Nguyen Du succeeded in achieving a harmonious synthesis of the popular and classical language. The poet uses the story of a young girl to paint a picture of his own times. Careful composition, beautiful language and deep psychological insight into the souls of the main characters are the reasons why this poem is still enormously popular. (Extract 10).

Kieu is a beautiful and talented girl. She meets a young scholar Kim and they fall in love. They meet together and swear their eternal love. Kim has to leave to attend the funeral of his uncle. At the same time misfortune has descended on Kieu's family. Her father and brother are falsely accused of a crime and put in jail. The family needs money in order to save them. Kieu decides on a painful solution – to sell herself as a concubine to a merchant Ma Giam Sinh and to use the money to free her father and brother. She undergoes numerous hardships, and eventually takes refuge in a Buddhist temple.

Meanwhile, after returning from his uncle's funeral, Kim learns what has happened. In accordance with Kieu's wish he marries her younger sister Van but never stops looking for Kieu and hoping for their reunion. One day, chance brings him to the monastery where Kieu is living. Kim and Kieu meet again. Their love has remained unchanged. Kim wants to marry but on Kieu's insistence they agree to live as friends thus respecting their chaste love (Extract 10).

TRUONG Vinh Ky, also known as Petrus Ky (1837–98). A scholar, journalist, writer and translator. From the age of five he studied Chinese and later *quoc ngu*. When he was 11 he went to Cambodia and Penang to continue his studies. In 1858 he returned to Vietnam and became an interpreter for the French and spent some time in France. On his return he became a teacher and in 1869 was appointed editor of *Gia Dinh Bao*. Later he retired and devoted his time to writing. Truong Vinh Ky was a prolific author, he wrote many language courses and books on the history of Vietnam and China, on Vietnamese literature, dictionaries, poetry, translations and travel sketches (Extract 5).

Malaysia

K.S. Maniam

> 'Of course she had read novels about the Malay Archipelago and she had formed an impression of a sombre land with great ominous rivers and a silent, impenetrable jungle . . . In the distance stretched blue mountains, range after range, as far as the eye could see. She had no sense of confinement nor of gloom, but rather of openness and wide spaces where the exultant fancy could wander with delight'.
> *W. Somerset Maugham*
> *'The Force of Circumstance'*

Malaysia, known to ancient mariners as 'The Land Where the Winds Meet', comprises peninsular Malaysia and Sabah and Sarawak in Borneo and lies between latitudes 1° and 7° N. It covers a land area of around 330 433 square kilometres. Malaysia is further divided into 13 states, and has a population close to 18 million.

Malaysia has a long and varied history, some of it still to be discovered. Recent discoveries of stone-age implements in **Perak** suggest that the country was inhabited as far back as 35 000 years ago. The aboriginal *orang asli*, literally 'original people', can still be seen (notably in the **Cameron Highlands** and **Taman Negara** national park) but in the 20th century more and more of them have emerged from the jungles to embrace Islam or modern lifestyles. The Malays came from somewhere near Taiwan and settled along the rivers and sea coasts. A Hindu period (100BC–1400AD) ended when the Malays adopted Islam. Muslim **Malacca** in the 15th and 16th centuries enjoyed an unsurpassed reputation not only as a flourishing trading city but also as a centre of culture (Extracts 9 and 10). The Malay kingdom of Malacca fell to the Portuguese in 1511 and was subsequently wrested from them by the Dutch, whose mark can still be seen in the famous **Stadhaus** (Town

Hall). The British acquired Malacca through the Anglo-Dutch Treaty in 1824. By 1826, with the inclusion of Singapore and Penang, the Straits Settlements were formed. With the strategic ports in their hands, the British were able to push into the interior of peninsular Malaysia, in quest of tin. Tin also attracted Chinese immigrants and unrest ensued when members of rival secret societies warred against one another, notably in **Kuala Lumpur** in the 1860s and 1870s. To stem the unrest and create a more stable climate for trade, the British introduced the Residential System, under which the Malay Chiefs would have to accept advice on running the district from a British Resident, who would also help to keep the peace but would not interfere with Malay customs, law or religion. Between 1874 and 1895 four states, Perak, Selangor, Negri Sembilan and Pahang, were brought under this system. A treaty with Thailand brought Kedah, Kelantan and Trengganu under British rule. By 1919, when Johore agreed to accept a Resident, the whole of Malaysia – Brunei, now Sarawak and North Borneo, now Sabah, had already succumbed – was entirely under British administration. It was the isolated and lonely lives of these British Residents and planters that Somerset Maugham was to portray so mercilessly in his famous short stories.

Malaysia was occupied by the Japanese between 1942 and 1945 and when the British returned a more complicated political situation emerged. The United Malay National Organization (UMNO) was formed to create a truly Malaysian sense of nationalism. The Malayan Chinese Association (MCA) and the Malayan Indian Congress (MIC) were formed close on its heels. The stage was set for independence when these three associations formed the Alliance Party. In the first national election held in 1955, the Alliance Party won 80% of the votes.

In 1957 the Federation of Malaya became an independent country. Six years later, in 1963, Malaysia came into existence. Singapore withdrew in 1965 leaving peninsular Malaysia, Sabah and Sarawak in present day Malaysia.

This chapter attempts to give an impression of the country, its peoples, cultures and uniqueness of place by depending on works written in English and works translated into English from Bahasa Malaysia into English. As it is impossible to examine all the relevant works, only a selection will be considered, in order to convey the particular flavour of a writer or type of literature.

Pre-independence Literature in Malay

Before the colonial period the Malay Peninsula had a well-established administrative machinery, social structure and a developed language.

Though by the 19th century the political units were smaller, usually confined to each state, 'the concept of a political unit covering the whole of the Malay Peninsula dates back to the time of Malacca'.[1] **Malacca's** influence on the other states reached its peak in the pre-Portuguese period when it was already the centre for the study for Islam. With the 'spread of Islam to Malacca [came] the development of literature, for, with Islam also came the Jawi script'.[2] Islam not only exerted a strong influence on Malay literature (as witness the current resurgence of strictly Islamic novels, short stories and poetry) but also on Malay architecture. The most common expressions of this influence are to be found in the mosques throughout the country. The **Kuala Lumpur Mosque** opposite the railway station, the vast and elaborate new mosque at **Shah Alam** and that at **Alor Setar** testify to deep stirrings of thought and imagination. Malay became not only the language of the court but also of the *rakyat* (people). By the 19th century there was a rich and varied tradition of literature:

> On the one hand there is the written literature of the court, sophisticated and cosmopolitan, reflecting the international cultures that the Malay courts along the Straits of Malacca were constantly exposed to. On the other hand there is the literature of the *rakyat*, the folk literature, mostly an oral tradition.[3]

The *Sejarah Melayu* or *Malay Annals* (Extract 10) and the many *hikayats* (stories), outstanding among them *Hikayat Hang Tuah*, have been the sustaining and enriching supports of this tradition. The *Sejarah Malayu* contains genealogies, poems, historical traditions, moral insights, characterizations and legends. The *Hikayat Hang Tuah*, centred on the warrior, Hang Tuah, has continued to inspire present-day writers' concepts of the hero and the Malay peoples' approach to nationalism. The story has been retold many times; a recent version was 'Death of a warrior' by the poet and playwright Usman Awang (Extract 9) – see also Extract 8 in Indonesia.

The existing tradition of Malay literature was built upon and extended in the early 19th century and received a further impetus when the Jawi script was romanized in the 1870s. Its *pantun*, *syair*, *gurindam* and *seloka* have led to the development of the *sajak*, free verse, form in modern Malay poetry. These poetic forms have been an integral part of Malay cultural life and landscape and the *pantuns*, specifically, carry in them many images of the country (see the Indonesia chapter for descriptions of different verse forms and genres of Malay literature). A further impetus to the development of Malay literature came in the years between the two world wars. Malaysians – and, particularly, the Malays – became aware of their position within a global context, which is reflected in the works produced during this period. A further broadening and deepening of perceptions occurred after the second world war. Present day Malay literature has blended the traditional and the modern in invigorating and exciting ways, some of which are discussed below.

Pre-independence Literature in Tionghua and Tamil

Because they came from immigrant sections of Malaysian society, Tionghua and Tamil literatures have tended to align themselves with the literature produced in their respective countries of origin. Writers often sought publication outlets and acceptance in magazines and publishing firms in China and India. Although since 1949 Chinese writers have focused on literary approaches and concerns divorced from the influences from China, their works have not been substantially translated into English. The same can be said of the works of Tamil writers though some of them have been translated into Bahasa Malaysia.

Pre-independence Literature in English

Literature in English in Malaysia is closely related to the history and use of the English language in the country. Britain's initial contacts with Asia, and subsequently with South-east Asia, were through a trading body, the East India Company. The attitudes and policies of the Court of Directors of the East India Company had a substantial influence on the educational systems that emerged in Singapore and Malaysia between 1818 and 1900. A democratic attitude prevailed and Stamford Raffles was able, in 1823, to found the Singapore Institution, an Asian-centred centre of learning. When Raffles left Singapore in 1819 for Bencoolen he left William Farquar in charge as Resident (for a portrayal of the conflicts between Raffles and Farquar see Extract 6 in Singapore), who was in turn succeeded by John Crawfurd. Crawfurd scaled down Raffles's proposals for reading and writing in Malay and Chinese and recommended teaching, reading, writing and arithmetic in English. It became evident that education interested neither the new Resident nor the East India company and it was left to individual insight and private institutions to effect significant changes.

Though English education made a foothold in the country (mainly through missionary and private schools), it was mainly confined to the towns and small immigrant communities. There was resistance from the Malay community to education in English and from the 1870s a parallel system of education was adopted; that is, instruction in schools was offered in English and in the vernacular languages.

The increased demand for English education and, therefore, for the language itself was dependent, especially after the first world war, on the wider utilitarian use of English. Possessing a good qualification in English became a visa for entry into the professions. The English language became inevitably associated with practical functions in the lives of Malaysians, which accounts for its delayed emergence as a literary medium. Not until the late 1940s was it thought of in a cultural context and even then not in specifically literary terms.

In addition to its practical utility, until the forced absence of the British from the country between 1942–1945, Malaysians seemed to revere the English language in the same way as they did the British administrator and the Union Jack. Even when a Malaysian dared to use the language, with all the attendant implications that he was putting himself on par with his British ruler, as did G.W. de Silva in the 1930s, it was with a distinctly 'expatriate' distance. G.W. de Silva's books, *Suleiman Goes to London* (1930), *Princess of Malacca* (1938), *Only a Taxi Dancer* (1939) and *Lupe: A Historical Romance of Portuguese Malacca* (1939) all support, in subject matter and approach, the desire not to rock this reverent attitude towards the English language. In the 1940s, when Malaysians had witnessed the fall from power of the British at the hands of the Japanese, this entrenched attitude can be seen in the preface to Ooi Cheng Teik's *Red Sun Over Malaya: John Man's Ordeal*: 'This book commemorates also the return of the English language to Malaya, an event of great significance, like the return of someone highly admired and esteemed'.[4]

Modern Malaysian writers

No one is a better spokesman for a country than someone born in and nurtured by its climate, its physical and social landscapes, its politics and its dreams. The Malaysian writer, whether he uses Bahasa Malaysia (literally 'language of Malaysia') or English, is no different from his fellow writers in other parts of the world, except that where the use of English is concerned, he appeared rather late on the scene. Malaysian writers brought with them perceptions and outlooks inaccessible to the expatriate or international writer. While the many visitors and sojourners provide an external view of the country and its peoples, the indigenous writers look at Malaysian life, cultures and the country itself, from the inside.

The passionate nature of Malaysians' commitment to the country is seen in the fact that, immediately after independence, they chose to express this relationship through poetry. As has been generally accepted, poetry depends on the images emotional experiences create. The deepest and truest feelings about the country that first received expression through poetry in the 1950s have continued to be revealed in that form. What I propose to do here is to highlight some of the poets who have written from their particular ethnic standpoints about their experiences of Malaysia. It is hoped that this representative selection will present a balanced picture of the country.

Edwin Thumboo in his introduction to *The Second Tongue: An Anthology of Poetry from Malaysia & Singapore* has this to say: the poetry from this region falls into 'an imitative phase, in which poetry was a leisurely, respectable pastime, which then yielded to the compulsions of changes within society, usually nationalism, and, finally, a stage in which poets wrote as they pleased, discovering poems both in their surroundings and in themselves'.

Ee Tiang Hong ◊ was one of the Malaysian poets who pioneered for an indigenous tradition of poetry in English in the late 1950s and early 1960s. He makes this clear in a poem called 'Dead End' from the collection *I of the Many Faces*:

> No more the days I would compel
> My heart to make up words.
> Waste all my time at singing well
> Some mimicry of foreign words.

These lines declare his intention to shake off the rhythms of the language and the perceptions of life he inherited from his colonial masters. He would from then on devote his energies to discovering 'What power can drive Malaya's pulse/Or tap a rhythm for its song?'. Having set his sights on detaching himself from the British literary tradition, Ee Tiang Hong is able to listen to his own voice that issues, in his case, from the struggles of discovering his own cultural existence within a cross-cultural, ex-colonial ambience. He looks to history to provide a definition for his cultural background in such poems as 'Heeren Street, Malacca' (Extract 8), 'Portuguese Hamlet, Malacca' and 'Tranquerah, Malacca'. It is no coincidence that these poems are set in and around **Malacca**. Historically, it seems not only to have fascinated the colonisers but the settlers, the Chinese and Indians, as well.

Writing in the 1950s and 1960s and returning to poetry in the 1990s, after a lapse of almost 20 years, Wong Phui Nam extends the tradition Ee Tiang Hong initiated and developed (Extract 6). He seeks an identity with the cultural and historical past of the multiracial society in which he lives. To this complexity he brings his own cultural inheritance, namely, that of the Chinese tradition, that residue of memory originating in China and reaching him through the line of predecessors who formed the first few generations of settlers in Malaysia. *How the Hills are Distant* is a series of poems, closely interrelated, which comes from the landscape that represents simul-

Muhammad Haji Salleh

taneously the physical layout of the country, the social environment, and his interior consciousness. The landscape, recording the archetypal memory of man, evolves from a natural, rural environment, shaped by the elements to the urban, shaped by man.

While Wong Phui Nam struggles for an identity with the country,

Muhammad Haji Salleh writes, often in a celebratory vein, about the country and tradition of life from which he comes (Extract 1). Edwin Thumboo (◊ Singapore) says this of Muhammad Haji Salleh and his poetry: 'His poetry is rooted in Malay traditional culture, rural life and their concomitants. His themes are drawn from changes in this traditional society, from its confrontation with the forces of modernisation, especially their disruptive aspects'. In 'Keroncong', a poem that exhibits his lyrical strength, the poet bathes himself in the generative powers of his tradition:

> no, i shall never wade this river
> of music of the upper bank of dryness.
> the flute and the heart-stringed ukelele
> soak a slow rhythm into me.
> how can i ever dry myself
> from a keroncong,
> a sad song.
> the music and the singer
> they continue
> with another keroncong.

The broad spectrum of society does not always have to be put together by reading communally-centred poetry. There has been some crossing over from one cultural perspective to another; sometimes there is even a common Malaysian perspective as the poem by Usman Awang ◊, 'Chinese Neighbour's Child' demonstrates (Extract 15).

Usman Awang's humanist attitude has not a little coloured the perspectives of other Malaysian poets, short story writers and novelists. Such broad perspectives, in themes and approaches, are also found in poets such as Salleh ben Joned ◊ whose collection *Sajak Sajak Salleh: Poems Sacred and Profane* (1987) readily testifies; and Shirley Lim whose *Crossing the Peninsula and Other Poems* won the Commonwealth Prize for Poetry in 1980.

A much wider canvas is available in the prose works of Malaysian writers. Prose lends itself to a more leisurely entrance into character and landscape. Malaysian writers in Bahasa Malaysia and English have used semi-biographical and autobiographical writing and short and extended fiction to depict the communities they come from; the attempt to fit into a society that is rapidly modernizing; and the struggle with the elements and the search for a Malaysian identity.

Quite a number of works emerged in the late 1940s and early 1950s which dwelt on life in the country under the Japanese occupation between 1942 and 1945. This kind of writing, mainly semi-biographical and autobiographical, dealt with the extraordinary, with the disruptions caused by war, the suffering that followed and also the experience of self-definition. As the title ironically suggests, Tan Thoon Lip's *Kempeitai Kindness* (1946) records his imprisonment by the Japanese for two months. The outlook here is almost Anglicized with comparisons and images drawn from a British education and outlook. Gurchan's Singh's *Singa: The Lion of Malaya* (1949), more personal in content and less British in style, details the resistance he offered the Japanese, being himself a member of the former Malayan Police Force. Chin Kee Onn's *The Silent Army* (1952), reissued as *Ma-rai-ee* in 1981, perhaps represents the best of the works that used the Japanese Occupation as their subject. *Ma-rai-ee* is both literary and objective. In this category Han Suyin's ◊ *And the Rain My Drink* (1956), which deals with guerrillas of the Malaysian Communist Party could also be included, although she is of Chinese and Belgian parentage.

The Malaysian writer in English began to function as a genuine literary artist from the early 1960s onwards. Some of the earliest examples of fiction, in the form of the short story, were in the literary magazines and journals from the University of Malaya, then in Singapore, in the late 1950s. These are included in *Bunga Mas: An Anthology of Contemporary Malaysian Literature* (1964). These and other stories are found in another anthology, *Twenty-two Malaysian Stories* (1968), edited by Lloyd Fernando ◊. The stories in this anthology represent a period of rapid change, encompassing the immediate post-independence years down to the formation of modern Malaysia. These years, just about a decade, produced a disturbing process of national and self-questioning. Kassim Ahmad's 'A Common Story', for instance, questions where one's roots lie: in the *kampung* that was the cradle of Malay culture or in the inherited post-colonial culture? The answer, a temporary one, seems to be a return, personal and possessive, to the culture into which one was born.

The parameters in the other stories are drawn by communal consciousness or a chosen lifestyle, which may often be infused with Western values, customs and habits. It is this drawing of the communal and lifestyle boundaries that enables one to recognize the variety of approaches to life that confronts the Malaysian. Among the writers in this anthology, Lee Kok Liang's ◊ 'Return to Malaya' is not so much a story as series of vignettes of Malaysian scenes and landscapes in the late 1950s or early 1960s. The story constitutes the narrator's, and indirectly the writer's, reacquaintance with the country, its cultures and its peoples. We can detect in it an intensity and a love for detail that indicates the writer's desire to make real a landscape and a people from which he has been absent for some time.

The sequel to *Twenty-two Malaysian Stories* did not appear until 13 years later, in 1981. *Malaysian Short Stories*, also edited by Lloyd Fernando, includes some earlier writers but also introduces new writers to the Malaysian literary scene. In this anthology there does not seem to be the frenetic attempt at self and cultural definition as found in the earlier anthology. The stories in this later volume still retain recognizable and separate cultural territories, the Eurasian, Chinese and Tamil, but there is not the volatile cultural definition characteristic of the earlier anthology. Instead, there is a sense of reassurance that these separate cultures have survived in spite of the dangerous question of what constitutes a Malaysian culture. Cynthia Anthony's 'Nannan' is a poignant evocation of the life and struggles of a Eurasian grandmother, who, though dead, survives in the memories of her grandchildren: 'Part of the gold from her wings keeps floating down on us'. 'Ratnamuni' by K.S. Maniam ◊ gives an insight into the Tamil immigrant's rootlessness and the pain of being cut off from an older, more established cultural tradition. Both Shirley Lim and K.S. Maniam have their own collections, *Another Country* (1983) and *Plot, The Aborting, Parablames & Other Stories* (1989), respectively.

Of the many Malay writers in the last 30 years, Shahnon Ahmad ◊ is notable. His novel *Ranjau Sepanjang Jalan* (1966), translated into English with the title *No Harvest but a Thorn* (1972), has enjoyed great success and been made into a film (Extract 3). In Shahnon Ahmad's works one encounters the collision of the traditional Malay world with the modern world. A number of stories in *The Third Notch and Other Stories* (1980), deal with this theme in a variety of ways: comically, critically, satirically and ironically. His anger at the Westernizing influences that are brought into the country is often undisguised: 'My Proudfoot', in this collection, is a savage lampooning of the cultural imperialist. 'The Third Notch', on the other hand, shows Shahnon's presentation of a Malay world from well within the centre. The ritual that is to be followed on the mother's death, contained in a letter from the narrator to his sister, demonstrates, indirectly, the sense of consideration and strength entrenched in the Malay culture.

Malaysian writers using English as their writing medium have had to span cultures not always their own. The English language and its implied cultural landscape have often been the scaffolding for their works. This is not to imply that English and its attendant culture were or are seen as the unifying medium for the multiracial and multicultural Malaysian society. Rather, English is used often to run a parallel course in the search for a common citizenship. English is the language that Lloyd Fernando employs in his novel *Scorpion Orchid* (1976), but the synthesizing ground for Malaysianness is derived from other sources: from common myths, the sense of journeying/voyaging and the shaping of a common nation.

Flowers in the Sky (1981, Extract 17) is not prescriptive in the way *Scorpion Orchid* is; rather, the way it looks at Malaysian society is incisively ironic. Through the setting and ambience, Lee Kok Liang ◊ examines, almost as a counterpoint to Fernando's novel, the achieved realities of post-Independence Malaysia. To signal the collision between the old and the new, the traditional and the modern, the spiritual and the materialistic, Lee uses characters who are poles apart in their vocations and sensibilities. The paths of Venerable Hung, the Buddhist monk, and Mr K, the surgeon, do cross in a way as to suggest that the traditional cannot do without the modern: the monk, though spiritually independent, does need the surgeon's skills for the treatment of his hernia. The novel seems to ask: will such practicality prevail in other situations? Take, for instance, the linguistic situation: 'nurses were trained in the National Language while the surgeons were operating in the English Language'.

The Return (1981), K.S. Maniam's novel, grapples with the issue of spirituality from the periphery. This novel sees the true sense of belonging to a country in the individual's ability to put down his spiritual roots there. Written from within the psyche of the Indian community, the work presents Kannan, the protagonist Ravi's father, as the spiritual seeker attempting to localize his Hindu roots on Malaysian soil. Ravi only begins to understand the dilemma after his father's death. Only then does he realize how he has been led astray from the question of national identity by his colonial education and the acquisition of a Western outlook and sympathies (Extract 18).

Malaysia in Western Literature

Malaysia was first made known to the West by foreign writers. Claudius Ptolomy's second-century *Guide to Geography* refers to the region as 'Chrye Khersonese' ('Peninsula of Gold'), which Isabella Bird, a visitor to the country in the late nineteenth century, was to convert into the title of her book, *The Golden Chersonese* (Extract 11), Marco Polo on his return voyage home from China (1289–1292) was to pass through the Malay Archipelago and carry back tales of its wonders to Europe. The Portuguese conquest of **Malacca** invested the country with another image: that of the legendary Ophir, the site of King Solomon's mines mentioned in the Old Testament.

The first major group of foreign writers to write about Malaysia belonged to the British Civil Service in Malaysia. Their duties brought them into constant contact with their subjects, especially the Malays, and this gave them the opportunity to observe, at close quarters, their customs, cultural practices and behaviour. Of the highly placed officers, the Residents Frank Swettenham ◊ and Hugh Clifford ◊ wrote extensively about the country and its people. Frank Swettenham (1850–1946) produced works that stand somewhere between non-

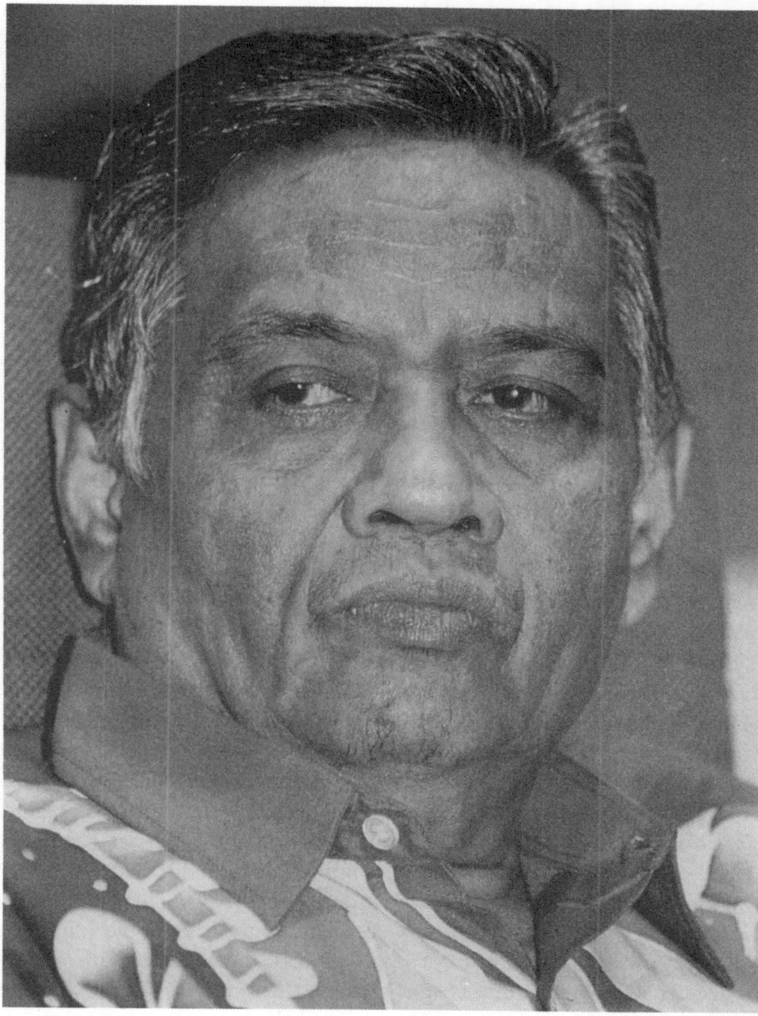

Shahnon Ahmad

fiction and fiction. His interest in and sympathy for the Malays, together with his knowledge of the Malay language, allowed him to enter, to some extent, Malay character and behaviour. Among his books, *Malay Sketches* (1895, Extract 13) and *The Real Malay Pen Pictures* (1899) stand out. The former is the more insightful and significant:

> *Malay Sketches* is a work by one who came to love the Malayan World from long experience. The delight, almost exhileration, Swettenham feels is evident in his description of sunset across a 'golden harvest' of ripened grain surrounding the nestled huts of the Malay kampung: 'A wide, flat plain covered by the golden harvest . . . One yellow sea of yellow ears . . . The sea is broken by islands of palms and fruit trees in which nestle the picturesque brown huts of cottagers, houses of wood, built on wooden piles with palm-thatched roofs and mat walls'.[5]

Hugh Clifford (1866–1941) ◊ was a more prolific writer. His collection of short stories, *East Coast Etchings* (1896), *In Court and Kampung* (1897), *In a Corner of Asia* (1899) and *Bushwacking and Other Sketches* (1898) provide detailed descriptions of the country and have a broader scope than Swettenham's in that they include Malay, Chinese, Indian and Orang Asli (aborigine) characters (Extract 5). In these and his novel, *A Prince of Malaya* (1904), Clifford viewed life in Malaysia as a kind of pastoral idyll, the people leading simple lives linked to the land, the rivers and the sea. Perhaps this had to do with the European, mythologized conception, in the late 19th century, of the 'noble savage' except that, in the case of Malaysia, he was the 'noble peasant'.

Since the last quarter of the 19th century, many writers have come to Malaysia, some as visitors, others seeking backdrops for their works. Many aspects of the country they described can still be seen in modern Malaysia, despite the country's recent economic progress. The jungle that Isabella Bird writes about in *The Golden Chersonese* 1883 (Extract 11), still retains its varied flora and fauna – as a visit to **Taman Negara** (National Park) in Pahang will demonstrate – suggesting that at least in these secluded regions time has not moved on.

The Malay Archipelago fascinated other writers, such as Joseph Conrad ◊ because it offered their works a landscape that could highlight their heroes' rejection of a corrupted European world for the uncorrupted existence in a remote and primeval world. Conrad crossed the **Straits of Malacca** and the Java Sea several times, as a second mate, on his voyages to Australia and the Orient. On the second voyage the coal in the hold of his ship, the *Palestine*, began to smoulder when it was deep into the Malay Archipelago. The ship sank and the crew had to row 13 hours to reach land. The island he touched on probably gave him his first intimate view of the East. When they were later taken to **Singapore**, Conrad stayed a month there and extended his experience of living in the East. This experience – shipwreck and forced search for sanctuary – he fictionalized in a long short story, *Youth* (1898), in which the narrator expresses his heightened sense of wonder with the East.

This marvellous pull of the East did not desert Conrad, for after he had written several early novels set in the region, he went on to complete *Lord Jim* (1900, Extract 12), which explores more fully his obsession with the Orient. *Lord Jim* may have been fashioned after the 'White Rajahs' found in a number of states in Peninsular Malaysia as well as in Sabah and Sarawak and it has been shown that Conrad borrowed quite liberally from actual people and incidents in order to fashion the personality in a work of fiction. Stamford Raffles, the founder of Singapore, Humphrey Berkeley, the District Officer of Grik in Perak and James Brooke (who after quelling a long-term rebellion was given Sarawak and made its Rajah by the Sultan of Brunei in 1841) may have served as his models. Sir Charles Brooke is commemorated in

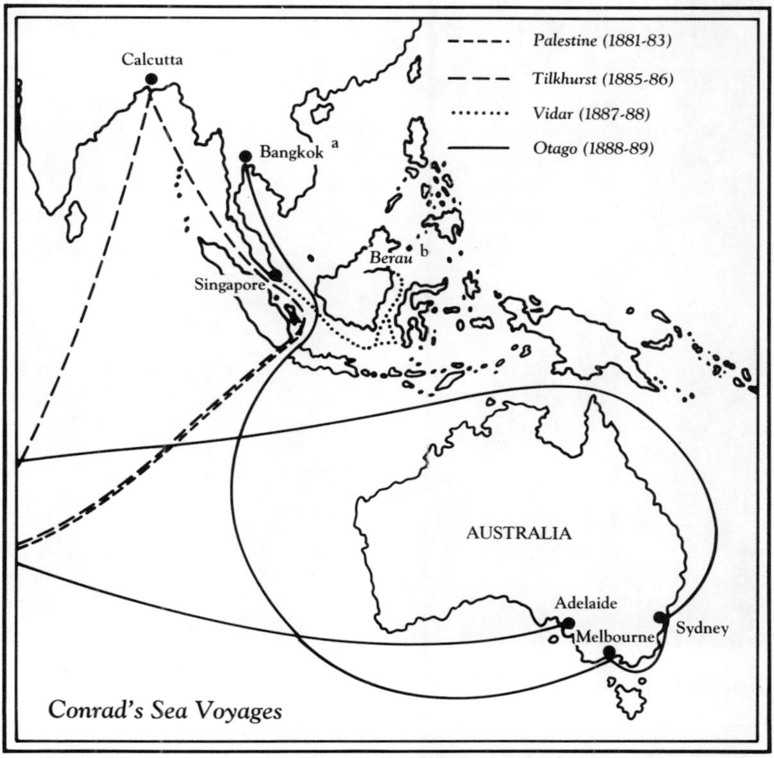

Conrad's Sea Voyages

[a] *Conrad received his first command from Bangkok, the Otago.* [b] *Berau in present day Indonesia is the 'Patusan' of Lord Jim (Extract 12) and formed the locale for several other stories and novellas (see Norman Sherry, Conrad's Eastern Seas). Map source: Gavin Young, In Search of Conrad, Hutchinson, London, 1991.*

Joseph Conrad

a **memorial** in front of **Kuching's Supreme Court**. The history of the Brooke 'dynasty' is recorded in the readable *The White Rajahs of Sarawak* by Robert Payne. Jim's behaviour as 'Tuan' in Patusan serves as commentary on Eurocentric values. It questions the imperialistic motives of the European powers and their belief that they brought benign guardianship to the so-called less civilized peoples of the East.

The writer who made the Malay archipelago most widely known to Western readers was Somerset Maugham ◊. In his lifetime he was often regarded as the most knowledgeable writer on the region. For him the Malay archipelago covered an extensive area: Dutch East Indies, Indonesia, Borneo and peninsular Malaysia. He was in the region between 1922 and 1923 and again in 1929. Maugham's Malaysian-based stories first appeared in collections such as *The Casuarina Tree* (1926) and *Ah King* (1933). They are currently available in a four volume *Collected Short Stories* (see booklist).

There is a fundamental difference between the way Conrad and Maugham used the region as a locale for their fiction. Conrad was obsessed with the workings of evil as his other, later, novels, particularly *The Heart of Darkness*, reveal. He had mapped out a special area of concern in his writing and was to pursue this preoccupation through different approaches and backdrops. Geography and location are incidental in his fiction and serve only to highlight the trauma of his characters and the painful isolation of being trapped in a moral dilemma. Maugham's stories work in a different way. They belong to the realistic tradition and locales, however vaguely named, advance his plots and themes. The setting, atmosphere and ambience impinge upon the thoughts, feelings and behaviour of his characters.

Maugham's stories record what he saw and heard in his travels through the Malay peninsula. He read, fairly accurately, the political situation in the region, observed the acceptable and the unacceptable in colonial society and put to fictional use his personal encounters with men and women he met in the ports, the European Club, the estate bungalows and the outstations (Extracts 4 and 19). Sometimes he had more access to the truth than did the law because he was a confidante to the parties involved, say, in a murder case. In fact, Maugham roused the anger and indignation of quite a number of people whose confidences he had thinly disguised as fiction. With such a focus, he was unable to do justice to the indigenous peoples, the Malaysians themselves, but given his European readership this is perhaps understandable.

Malaysia's seductive charm for the British, Dutch, French and Germans was not merely its economic wealth. While many of them desired to better their material lot, quite a few came to the country because of its exotic pull. It possessed all the requirements for an adventurous sojourn: a native population, an unfamiliar landscape, alien cultures and an aura of mystery surrounded by the possibilities of unexpected danger. Maugham made use of all these expectations. Quite a number of his stories are set in the jungle or at least on its edge. Here is the way Doris, a character in 'The Force of Circumstance' registers the country:

> Of course she had read novels about the Malay Archipelago and she had formed an impression of a sombre land with great ominous rivers and a silent, impenetrable jungle . . . In the distance stretched blue mountains, range after range, as far as the eye could see. She had no sense of confinement nor of gloom, but rather of openness and wide spaces where the exultant fancy could wander with delight.

Instead of the 'sombre land' and 'ominous rivers' she had expected she is overcome by the country's beauty and serenity. Other characters in Maugham's stories do not share the delight of Doris. Darya Munro in 'Neil McAdam' stays close to her civilized society. On the rare occasion that she accompanies her husband and McAdam she is repulsed by the fear she has for the jungle. Darya gets lost and the search party that goes out for her gets caught in the storm that destroys the beauty of the jungle:

> The storm broke suddenly. A great wind blew and then the lightning rent the darkness, like a scream of a woman in pain, and the tortured flashes, quick, quick, one on the heels of the other, like demon dancers in a frantic reel, wriggled down the night. The horror of the forest was revealed in an unearthly day.

Maugham also uses the European clubs as his setting in many stories. An example is the **Selangor Club of Kuala Lumpur**, restored and extended but still retaining its former appearance. Maugham, and by implication some of his narrators, picked up plots and characters from visits to these clubs. 'Footprints in the Jungle', for example, has its origins and development in such a club. Besides the Selangor Club there are still others remaining in other parts of the country: the **Idris Club** in **Kuala Kangsar**, Perak, and the **Sungei Ujong Club** in **Seremban**, Negri Sembilan. The **Coliseum Cafe** in Jalan Tungku Abdul Rahman, Kuala Lumpur, resembles and served as a sort of Club until the late 1930s and still does so for Malaysians.

Being a writer, Maugham was invited to the bungalows and residences in rubber plantations and outstations. He was able to capture the isolation and rather perverse psychology of the people he met there. The isolation in these isolated places often placed restrictions on natural human behaviour. Some of the wives of the planters conducted illicit affairs with men from adjacent estates; if the men were single they were compelled to take native 'wives' to satisfy their sexual and companionship needs. To retain their sanity some men in the outstations relied on the European ritual of dressing for dinner, a habit which they retained even when they had no guests. The clash between this very formal British attitude to the tropics and the relaxed style of the

W. Somerset Maugham

more modern breed of colonialist is beautifully portrayed in Maugham's story, 'The outstation'. The Resident, Mr Warburton, has invited his new assistant, Allen Cooper, to dinner on his first evening at the station.

> The only concession he made to the climate was to wear a white dinner jacket; but otherwise, in a boiled shirt and high collar, silk socks and patent-leather shoes, he dressed as formally as though he was dining at his club in Pall Mall. A careful host, he went into the dining-room to see that the table was properly laid. It was gay with orchids, and the silver shone brightly. The napkins were folded into elaborate shapes. Shaded candlesticks shed a soft light. Mr Warburton smiled his approval and returned to the sitting-room to await his guest. Presently, he appeared. Cooper was wearing the khaki shorts, the khaki shirt, and the ragged jacket in which he had landed. Mr Warburton's smile of greeting froze on his face.

Maugham's writing became a window into the South-east Asia – the stories take the readers from the seas that lap at its shores, through the ports, the outskirts of service-providing towns, the plantations, the edge of forests, to the jungles themselves.

Another writer who explored Malaysia but wanted to get to its soul was Henri Fauconnier. His novel was published in French as *Malaisie* (1930) and translated into English in 1931 as *The Soul of Malaya*. The novel focuses on people and landscapes that Maugham's stories kept at the fringe: the Tamil world of the labourers on the rubber estates. Plantation life is still to be found in the extensive rubber estates in Johore, Kedah and, to a certain extent, Perak.

Nearer to the present and, therefore, bringing different impressions was Anthony Burgess ◊. His stay in Malaysia from 1954 to 1957 was much more prolonged than those of Conrad, Maughan or Fauconnier. He moved about the country, from **Perak** on the west coast to **Kelantan**, on the east coast. The longer sojourn, his efficiency in the Malay language and his deliberate choice to mix with the local populace gave him more than glimpses into the peoples and the country. He also taught in **Brunei** for three years, from 1957 to 1960. His novels *Time for a Tiger* (1956, Extract 6), *The Enemy in the Blanket* (1958) and *Beds in the East* (1959) were reissued by Penguin in 1972 under the title *The Malayan Trilogy*, and subsequently in the United States in 1981 as *The Long Day Wanes: A Malayan Trilogy*.

It was not only Burgess's residence in the region – almost seven years – but also his attachment to the country, for he thought of becoming a Malaysian citizen, that brings a different perspective to his works. Unlike Conrad and Maugham, he did not write, as far as possible, from the outside. As his autobiography, *Little Wilson and Big God: Being the First Part of the Confessions of Anthony Burgess* reveals, he tried to get as deeply as possible into the psychologies of the various races and the soul of the country. What Conrad and Maugham treat peripherally, he places at the centre: the variety and diversity of the Malaysian peoples. His novels take us into what was, and still is, an exhilerating human landscape, as revealed by the following extract:

> Crisp, exquisite, the Chinese girls toddled in sororities, the cheongsams split to their thin thighs. A half-naked Tamil carried the corpse of a fish, Chettiars in dhotis waved money-loving arms, talking excitedly with frank smiles. Wrinkled Chinese patriachs raked their throats for residuary phlegm. A Sikh fortune-teller jabbed repeatedly at a client's palm. Sellers of *sateh* – pieces of tripe and liver on a skewer – breathed in the fumes of their fires. Soft-drink sellers brooded over blue and green and yellow bottles. In the barber shops the many customers lay back like the sheeted dead. Over all presided the fetid, exciting reek of durian, for this was the season of durians.

The scene is slightly changed these days; coloured bottles have been replaced by packet drinks and most barber-shops have been replaced by unisex hair saloons but the overall atmosphere with its smells and colours remains.

Burgess is concerned in these novels with a sort of unity in diversity and though this still remains unattainable in deeper psychological terms, outwardly one can witness the conjunctive flow of the various cultural streams in any town or city. Perhaps this comprehensive outlook has helped to restore to Burgess's Malaysia a vitality lacking in the fiction of other visiting/sojourning writers. His works arouse not only visual images but also other sensory responses – to the sounds of the many languages and dialects of Malaysia and to the varieties of English spoken.

Other international writers, too many to mention here, also produced fiction based on their experiences in Malaysia. These works either repeat what such masters of fiction as Conrad and Maugham did or present simplistic clichés. Of the many other books by Western writers describing Malaysian life, Agnes Keith's ◊ *Land Below the Wind* (1939) is worth mentioning, for it is perhaps the best-known book written on **Sabah**.

In the post second world war period, when Malaysia and other countries in South-east Asia had acquired distinct reputations, works of a commercial and sensational nature were published and one or two turned into television series. Most notable among these is Nevil Shute's *The Legacy*, which was later reissued as *A Town Like Alice*. Made into a film in 1956, it tells of the forced march of expatriate women in Malaya by the Japanese; still later it was made into a TV mini-series under the title, *Rape of Malaya*.

[1]Zainal Abidin bin Abdul Wahid, ed, *Glimpses of Malaysian History*, Dewan Bahasa dan Pustaka, 1970, p 23.
[2]*Ibid*, p 25.
[3]Ismail Hussein, *The Study of Traditional Malay Literature with a Selected Bibliography*, Dewan Bahasa dan Pustaka, Kuala Lumpur, 1974, p 10.
[4]Ooi Cheng Teik, *Red Sun over Malaya: John Man's Ordeal*, Ooi Cheng Teik, Kuala Lumpur, 1948, p x.
[5]Sharilyn D. Wood, *English Fiction of British Malaya, Singapore and Malaysia, 1890–1990*, PhD dissertation, University of Malaya, 1990, p 20.

BOOKLIST

What follows is intended as a representative rather than comprehensive list of books about Malaysia. All the books included in the Extracts section or mentioned in the text are included. Where several editions exist, in general the latest and most readily available edition has been listed. Information on the original English language publisher can in many cases be found in the 'Acknowledgements' section at the end of the volume, as can the exact location of the extracts and the editions from which they are taken. Extract numbers are highlighted in bold.

Abdullah, bin Abdul Kadir Munsyi (A.H. Hill, trans), *The Hikayat Abdullah*, Oxford University Press, Singapore, 1985.

Aveling, Harry, ed and trans, *Fables of Eve*, Dewan Bahasa dan Pustaka, Kuala Lumpur, 1991.

Aveling, Harry, ed, *Malaysian Poetry: 1975–1985*, Dewan Bahasa dan Pustaka, Kuala Lumpur, 1988.

Baha Zain, 'Toilet paper city', in Muhammad Haji Salleh, ed, *The Puppeteer's Wayang: A Selection of Modern Malaysian Poetry*, In Print, Brighton, UK, 1992. **Extract 14.**

Bird, Isabella, *The Golden Chersonese and the Way Thither*, Oxford University Press, Kuala Lumpur, 1967. **Extract 11.**

Brown, C.C., trans, *The Malay Annals*, OUP, Kuala Lumpur, 1970. **Extract 10.**

Burgess, Anthony, *Little Wilson and Big God: Being the First Part of the Confessions of Anthony Burgess*, Penguin, Harmondsworth, UK, 1987.

Burgess, Anthony, *The Long Day Wanes: A Malayan Trilogy* (comprising *Time for a Tiger, The Enemy in the Blanket* and *Beds in the East*), Penguin, Harmondsworth, UK, 1972. **Extract 7.**

Chin Kee Onn, *Ma-rai-ee*, Eastern Universities Press, Kuala Lumpur, 1981.

Clifford, Hugh, *A Prince of Malaya* Harper & Bros, New York, 1926.

Clifford, Hugh (William R. Rolf, ed), *Stories by Sir Hugh Clifford*, Oxford University Press, Kuala Lumpur, 1966. **Extract 5.**

Conrad, Joseph, *Lord Jim*, Penguin, Harmondsworth, UK, 1964. **Extract 13.**

Dewan Bahasa dan Pustaka, *Modern Malaysian Stories II*, Dewan Bahasa dan Pustaka, Kuala Lumpur, 1983.

Dewan Bahasa dan Pustaka, *Shahnon Ahmad*, Dewan Bahasa dan Pustaka, Kuala Lumpur, 1976.

Ee Tiang Hong, *I of the Many Faces*, Ee Tiang Hong, Malacca, 1960.

Ee Tiang Hong, *Myths for a Wilderness*, Heinemann, Singapore, 1976.

Ee Tiang Hong, 'Heeren Street' in Edwin Thumboo, ed, *The Second Tongue: An Anthology of Poetry from Malaysia and Singapore*, Heinemann, Singapore, 1976. **Extract 8.**

Fauconnier, Henri, *The Soul of Malaya*, Oxford University Press, 1990. **Extract 16.**

Fernando, Lloyd, ed, *Malaysian Short Stories*, Heinemann Asia, Kuala Lumpur, 1981.

Fernando, Lloyd, *Scorpion Orchid*, Heinemann Asia, Kuala Lumpur, 1976.

Fernando, Lloyd, ed, *Twenty-two Malaysian Stories*, Heinemann Asia, Kuala Lumpur, 1968.

Han Suyin, *And the Rain my Drink*, Panther, London, 1973.

Ismail Hussein, *The Study of Tradi-*

tional Malay Literature with a Selected Bibliography, Dewan Bahasa dan Pustaka, Kuala Lumpur, 1974, p 10.

Keith, Agnes, *Land Below the Wind*, Ulverscroft, Leicester, UK, 1969.

Keri Mas, *Jungle of Hope*, Dewan Bahasa dan Pustaka, Kuala Lumpur, 1990.

Lee Kok Liang, *Flowers in the Sky*, Heinemann, Singapore, 1981. **Extract 16.**

Lim, Shirley, *Another Country*, Times Books International, Singapore, 1982.

Lim, Shirley, *Crossing the Peninsula and Other Poems*, Heinemann Asia, Kuala Lumpur, 1980.

Maniam, K.S. and M. Shanmughalingam, *An Anthology of Malaysian Poetry*, Dewan Bahasa dan Pustaka Brunei, Bandar Seri Bagawan, Brunei, 1988.

Maniam, K.S., *Plot, The Aborting, Parablames & Other Stories*, AMK Interaksi, Kuala Lumpur, 1989.

Maniam, K.S., *The Return*, Heinemann, Singapore, 1981; Skoob Books, London, 1993. **Extract 18.**

Maugham, W. Somerset, 'A casual affair', *Maugham's Malaysian Stories*, Heinemann, London and Singapore, 1969. **Extract 4.**

Maugham, W. Somerset, 'The yellow streak', *Maugham's Malaysian Stories*, Heinemann, London and Singapore, 1969. **Extract 19.**

Maugham W. Somerset, *Short Stories*, 4 Vols, Mandarin, London, 1990.

Muhammad Haji Salleh, 'Three Beserah fishermen', *Time and its People*, Heinemann, Singapore, 1978. **Extract 1.**

Muhammad Haji Salleh, ed, *The Puppeteer's Wayang: A Selection of Modern Malaysian Poetry*, In Print, Brighton, UK, 1992.

Newman, Barclay M., trans, *Modern Malaysian Poetry*, Dewan Bahasa dan Pustaka, 1982.

Ooi Cheng Teik, *Red Sun over Malaya: John Man's Ordeal*, Ooi Cheng Teik, Kuala Lumpur, 1948.

Salleh ben Joned, *Sajak Sajak Salleh: Poems Sacred and Profane*, Teks Publishing, Kuala Lumpur, 1987.

Samad Said, A., *The Morning Post*, Dewan Bahasa dan Pustaka, Kuala Lumpur, 1990.

Shahnon Ahmad (Abidah Amin, trans), *No Harvest But a Thorn*, Oxford University Press, Kuala Lumpur, 1972. **Extract 3.**

Shahnon Ahmad, *The Third Notch and Other Stories*, Heinemann Asia, Singapore, 1980.

Swettenham, Frank, *Malay Sketches*, Graham Brash, Singapore, 1984. **Extract 13.**

Theroux, Paul, 'Reggie Woo' in *The Consul's File*, Penguin, 1979. **Extract 2.**

Thumboo, Edwin, *The Second Tongue: An Anthology of Poetry from Malaysia and Singapore*, Heinemann, Singapore, 1976.

Usman Awang, 'Chinese neighbour's child', in Usman Awang, *Salam Benua: Greetings to the New Continent*, Dewan Bahasa dan Pustaka, Kuala Lumpur, 1982. **Extract 15.**

Usman Awang, *Death of a Warrior (Jebat)*. Dewan Bahasa dan Pustaka, Kuala Lumpur, 1992. **Extract 9.**

Winstedt, R.O., *A History of Malaya*, Marican, Kuala Lumpur, 1982.

Wong Phui Nam, 'Poem for a birthday' in Edwin Thumboo, ed, *The Second Tongue: An Anthology of Poetry from Malaysia and Singapore*, Heinemann, Singapore, 1976. **Extract 6.**

Wood, Sharilyn D., *English Fiction of British Malaya, Singapore and Malaysia, 1890–1990*, PhD dissertation, University of Malaya, 1990.

Zainal Abidin bin Abdul Wahid, ed, *Glimpses of Malaysian History*, Dewan Bahasa dan Pustaka, Kuala Lumpur, 1970.

Extracts

(1) East Coast

Muhammad Haji Salleh, *'Three Beserah Fishermen'*

The east coast of Peninsular Malaysia is scenic with palm trees and beaches, fishermen, boats and fishing nets. These point to a tradition, on the surface at least, of graceful, leisurely living. The poem goes beneath the surface to capture the hard business of survival within this tradition.

three small souls in a frail old sampan
in the bowl of the sea.
between the teeth of the waves,
between the sea and the home
there was no choice
against the big winds
and the capricious sea.

the wind has no heart –
nor the sky nor the sea,
and the heart was for words of prayer;
time between the stretches of a red imagination
was a promise of hope,
for the heart knows its logic
and the pains of the whipping winds.

what of the wives, sons and daughters,
the tomorrow, the eye of the day,
the rice and the fish, the school fees?
on land how heavy the soul is loaded;
to survive was as hard as to die.
to go down into the bottom of the sea-dish,

the bare dish;
to jump and swim into time and hope?

the early morning nets, the boats,
the friends, the gregariousness,
and the sea-saw
on the fulcrum of the shore.
harsh land pushed them
into the uncertain sea
deep into eclipsing death.

do not make this wind our hangman
and the sea where our souls are soaked.

(2) Johore

Paul Theroux, *'Reggie Woo'*

Although Ayer Hitam is a common Malay placename, the town of that name in Paul Theroux's collection of stories The Consul's File is an imaginary one. That characters that inhabit the stories are common enough though, such as the returned scholarship student described here. *See also pp 269–270 in the Singapore chapter.*

His father, Woo Boh Swee, had chased after the English in that shy, breathless Chinese way, hating the necessity of it and making his embarrassment into haste. He had gone from Canton to Hong Kong to work on an English ship and later come to Ayer Hitam to supply the rubber estates with provisions. But the rubber price had fallen, many English and American families left the town, and the Chinese who replaced them imported or grew their own food; so he started the City Bar.

It was the biggest coffee shop in town, the meeting place for a secret society – but the gang was only dangerous to other Chinese and did not affect Woo's regular trade, the remaining English planters and the Tamil rubber tappers. Woo – or 'City Bar' as he was known – was thoroughly Chinese; he was a chain smoker, he played mah-jongg on a back table of the shop, he observed all the Chinese festivals with *ang pows*. The shop smelled of dusty bottles and beancurd, and dark greasy ducks and glazed pork strips hung on hooks in the front window. He and his wife were great gamblers, and they had two children.

The children went to different schools. It was as if, this once, the Woos, were hedging, making an each-way bet. The girl, Jin Bee, was at the Chinese primary school; the boy Reggie, had been to the Anglo-Chinese school, then to Raffles Institution and the University of Singapore. He was the English child; he played cricket and tennis and was a member of the Ayer Hitam Club. He had distinguished himself by appearing in the Footlighters' production of Maugham's play *The Letter*. It was the first play to attract a local audience. It ran for a week and Reggie's picture was in the *Johore Mail*. That picture, bright yellow with age, was taped to the wall of City Bar. Everyone had hopes for Reggie. He was that odd figure you sometimes see in the east, the person who leaves his race behind, who goes to school and returns home English. Ayer Hitam was not an easy place to be English but Reggie, an actor, had certain advantages. He was right for the part. And though drinks at the Club were more expensive than at City Bar, Reggie was at the Club, drinking nearly every evening.

(3) Kedah

Shahnon Ahmad, *No Harvest but a Thorn*

Kedah is called the Rice Bowl of Malaysia because the state produces most of the country's rice. This passage outlines the daily routine of a padi-planting family and the quiet violence with which the members guard the source of their livelihood.

He went on sharpening his *parang*.[1] His children had disappeared in different directions. Two or three of them had gone in to help Jeha in the kitchen. The rest were at the chicken-house, shooing in the fowls for the night. Lahuma went on with his job of sharpening the *parang*. Tomorrow the *belukar*[2] would be cleared. And tomorrow would begin his days of rice-growing. After the *belukar* had been cleared, the earth would be loosened and levelled. The rice would be sown. And while waiting for the seedlings to reach a certain age, Lahuma and his family would work in the rice-field. *Tajaks*[3] would have to be wielded to uproot the thick weeds and *menerong*.[4] Lahuma thought of the huge leeches that would be swimming nimbly in search of his legs. This year at least one *chupak*[5] of his blood would go into the leeches' bellies. Lahuma thought of the tiny crabs that had nibbled at the stems of his tender young rice-plants last year. There were thousands and tens of thousands of those white crabs. He remembered how in the beginning they had collected those crabs and stepped on them with their heels. But after some time their heels were bruised and the crabs had to be pounded with a heavy pestle. This crushed the bellies of those little creatures that were such a big pest. What would their attack be like this year? Lahuma did not know yet, but judging by the weather signs in the sky it was certain that the pest would come again. This time Lahuma would be ready with a cauldron to boil those accursed crabs.

Twilight enveloped the village of Banggul Derdap, a village rich in poverty. Kerosene lamps were lit. The houses perched on the edges of the rice-fields grew hazy and gradually faded from view. Tomorrow the people would come out to clear the land for sowing. The jungle, rising straight and formidable beyond the village, grew dark. The tall green trees slowly merged into the darkness. In the sky a few scattered stars appeared.

Lahuma brushed the edge of his *parang* with his rough calloused palm. Then he tested its keenness against the back of a finger-nail. The finger-nail was torn a little as the edge sliced into it. Lahuma was satisfied. The smaller trees would certainly fall prostrate at the touch of that *parang* edge.

Slowly he went up into his house. And slowly he leaned the *parang* in a corner of his bedroom. Early tomorrow he would rise. And the *parang* would rise with him.

[1]Parang – a cleaver or chopper. [2]Belukar – secondary jungle. [3]Tajak – a planter's weed-cutter. [4]Menerong – a kind of sedge. [5]Chupak – about half a coconut shell full.

(4) On the Kelang River

W. Somerset Maugham, *'A Casual Affair'*

Though the extract below may not refer to a specific town along the Kelang River, it is a typical picture of riverine towns. Many such towns have succumbed to modernization but there are still some left, in Perak or Johore, for instance, which retain the old picturesque flavour of isolated Chinese existence.

I was D.O. in Selangor and one day they came and told me that a white man was dead in a small town a couple of hours up the river. I didn't know there was a white man living there. I thought I'd better go and see about it, so I got in the launch and went up. I made inquiries when I got there. The police didn't know anything about him except that he'd been living there for a couple of years with a Chinese woman in the bazaar. It was rather a picturesque bazaar, tall houses on each side, with a board walk in between, built on piles on the river-bank, and there were awnings above to keep out the sun. I took a couple of policemen with me and they led me to the house. They sold brass-ware in the shop below and the rooms above were let out. The master of the shop took me up two flights of dark, rickety stairs, foul with every kind of Chinese stench, and called out when we got to the top. The door was opened by a middle-aged Chinese woman and I saw that her face was all bloated with weeping. She didn't say anything, but made way for us to pass. It wasn't much more than a cubby-hole under the roof; there was a small window that looked on the street, but the awning that stretched across it dimmed the light. There wasn't any furniture except a deal table and a kitchen chair with a broken back. On a mat against the wall a dead man was lying. The first thing I did was to have the window opened. The room was so frowsty that I retched, and the strongest smell was the smell of opium. There was a small oil-lamp on the table and a long needle, and of course I knew what they were there for. The pipe had been hidden. The dead man lay on his back with nothing on but a sarong and a dirty singlet. He had long brown hair, going grey, and a short beard. He was a white man all right. I examined him as best I could. I had to judge whether death was due to natural causes. There were no signs of violence. He was nothing but skin and bone. It looked to me as though he might very likely have died of starvation. I asked the man of the shop and the woman a number of questions. The policeman corroborated their statements. It appeared that the man coughed a great deal and brought up blood now and then, and his appearance suggested that he might very well have had T.B. The Chinaman said he'd been a confirmed opium smoker. It all seemed pretty obvious. Fortunately cases of that sort are rare, but they're not unheard of – the white man who goes under and gradually sinks to the last stage of degradation. It appeared that the Chinese woman had been fond of him. She'd kept him on her own miserable earnings for the last two years. I gave the necessary instructions. Of course I wanted to know who he was. I supposed he'd been a clerk in some English firm or an assistant in an English store at Singapore or Kuala Lumpur. I asked the Chinese woman if he'd left any effects. Considering the destitution in which they'd lived it seemed a rather absurd question, but she went to a shabby suit-case that lay in a corner, opened it and showed me a square parcel about the size of two novels put together wrapped in an old newspaper.

(5) Kelantan

Sir Hugh Clifford, *Stories by Sir Hugh Clifford*

Clifford provides a glimpse into the character of the Malay, his attachment to the land and the sea and his versatile personality.

If you run up the East Coast of the Peninsula, past the smiling shores of Pahang and Trengganu, you at last reach the spot where the bulk of the Kelantan river-water formerly made its way into the China Sea. The better entrance is now a mile or two farther up the Coast, but the groves of palm-trees show that the people have been less fickle than the river, and that the villages at the old mouth are still tenanted as of yore. It is here that Umat was born and bred, the son of a family of Fisher Folk, countless generations of whom have dwelt at Kuala Kelantan ever since the beginning of things.

If you look at Umat's round face, and observe it carefully, you may read therein much that bears upon the history of his people. The prevailing expression is one of profoundly calm patience – not that look of waiting we understand by the term, the patience which, with restless Europeans, presupposes some measure of anticipation, and of the pain of hope long deferred – but the contented endurance of one who is satisfied to be as he is; of one whose lot is unchanging, and whose desires are few. It is a negative expression, without sadness, without pain, or the fever of longing, and yet sufficiently far removed from dullness or stupidity. It speaks of long years during which Umat's forebears have laboured stolidly, have been as driven cattle before prince and chief, and yet, since the curse of knowledge that better things existed had not fallen upon them, have accepted their lot as they found it, unresisting and uncomplaining.

This is what one reads in Umat's face when it is in repose, but when emotion changes it, other things may be seen as clearly. Suddenly, his features break up into a thousand creases, the brown skin puckering in numberless spreading lines, like the surface of a muddy puddle into which a stone has fallen. A laugh like the crowing of a cock, combined with the roaring of a bull, accompanied this phenomenon, and you may then know that Umat's keen sense of humour has been tickled. It does not take much to amuse him, for, like most Malays, he is very light-hearted, and anything which has a trace of fun in it delights him hugely. Almost every Kelantan fishing boat that puts to sea carries its *alanalan*, or *jester* along with it, for toil is lightened if men be merry, and in days gone by, Umat was the most popular man in his village. A quaint phrase; a happy repartee, not always in the most refined language; the rude mimicry of some personal eccentricity; word or two of rough chaff; or a good story; such things are his stock in trade and, this is why Umat is so well beloved by his fellows.

But he can be grave, too. As my raft whirls down a rapid, a clumsy punt sends it reeling to what looks like certain destruction. Umat's face sets hard. His teeth are clenched, his lips compressed tightly. His bare feet grapple the slippery bamboos with clinging grip, and his twenty-foot punting-pole describes a circle above his head. The point alights, with marvellous rapidity, and unerring aim, upon the only projecting ridge of rock within immediate reach, and all Umat's weight is put into the push, while his imprisoned breath breaks loose in an excited howl. The raft cants violently, and wallows knee-deep but the danger of instant destruction is averted, and we tear through the fifty yards of foaming, boiling, rock-beset water, which divides us from the rapid's foot, without further mishap. Then, Umat's face relaxes, and his queer laugh resounds, as he chaffs the man, whose clumsiness had nearly been our ruin, with unmerciful disregard for his feelings.

(6) Kuala Lumpur

Wong Phui Nam, *'Poem for a Birthday'*

This poem offers the experience of the struggle to enter the Malaysian landscape, especially by the migrant communities, and the pain of being unable to do so.

To be most myself is to be
this darkness that pervades the land;
to be, in this foul weather, a climbing up
the turning wooden backstairs
to a rainless sleep; and in the morning,
in the small hours of the soul,
the cold that comes, making large
the doorways – the body in its spell
is a scatter of small stones beneath the porch.

This then is a country where one cannot wish
to be. The spirit not given its features
festers in the flesh, incites the year
to come upon it like the tiger. The city's parks,
odd street corners and the public buildings
bear the stench, the torn fur
of trivial remembrances. Thus in the flesh
am I hunted out, creature of my days,
vocal perhaps to seem some kind of Job

tending my sores to an emptiness,
the hoarse throat my psaltery to make such sounds
as may breed some hint for the soul's endurance.
Who would be comforters, do not begin to dress
or even touch these scabs –
their peeling leaves
a spreading terrain
where all conclusions, all arguments are broken down
to miles of striations, the soft mud-flats.

(7) Lanchap (a fictitious name for Perak)

Anthony Burgess, *Time for a Tiger*

Malaysian states have had colourful historical backgrounds: Indian, Dutch, Portuguese, British and Thai. While states may be associated with a single influence, British, for instance, it cannot be denied that there has been interpenetration and, sometimes, integration of these influences. The passage below captures this sense of interpenetration and integration.

Victor Crabbe slept soundly, drawn into that dark world where history melts into myth.

The history of the state differs little from that of its great neighbours, Johore and Pahang. A prince of Malacca settled on its river at the time of the Portuguese invasions. He had known the old days of quiet and leisure, the silken girls bringing sherbet, the long, subtle theological debates with visiting Islamic philosophers. The Portuguese, sweating in trunk-hose, brought a niggling concern with commerce and the salvation of pagan souls. Francis Xavier preached about the love of an alien God, tried to fracture the indivisible numen and establish a crude triune structure, set up schools where dreary hymns were sung, and finally condoned the rack and the thumbscrew. Now the royal house of Malacca began to substantiate its old hypothetical claim to over-lordship of the entire peninsula. Bendahara Yusuf set up a meagre palace on the swampy shore of the Lanchap and tried to divert the outrageous revenues collected by the chiefs into his own coffers. He bequeathed to his successors an arduous task, made no easier by the bullying of the Achinese and the ubiquitous Bugis, exacerbated by the ruthless greed of the trumpeting Dutch. The rulers themselves lived unedifying lives. Yahya never moved out of an opium-trance; Ahmad died of a surfeit of Persian sweetmeats; Mohammed lashed at least one slave to death every day; Aziz had syphilis and died at the age of eighteen; Hussain had a hundred wives.

(8) Malacca

Ee Tiang Hong, *'Heeren Street, Malacca'*

Malacca is often associated with the founding of the first Islamic sultanate. With the coming of the Chinese and Indians to the country from the early nineteenth century onwards, it also became the seat of the Nyonya-Baba culture. Tiang Hong's poem, however, explores the decline of that culture.

I
Gharry and palanquin are silent.
The narrow street describes
Decades of ash and earth.

Here in the good old days
The *Babas* paved
A legend on the landscape,

And sang their part–
God Save The King–
In trembling voices.

Till the Great Wars came,
And the glory went, and the memories
Grave as a museum.

Ah, if only our children
On the prestige of their pedigree
Would emulate their fathers

Blazing another myth
Mediating in every wilderness
Of this golden peninsula.

II
Newcomer urchin strides the gutter,
Reeking cockroach, rat and faeces.
On *charpoy jaga* fast asleep.

Beneath antique lanterns,
The *Babas*, comfortable on old benches,
Gaze at Fords and Mercedes

While swallows shrill
Shriek in the twilight
Stealing over the obscurity of eaves.

(9) Malacca

Usman Awang, *Death of a Warrior (Jebat)*

The kris (dagger) has always fascinated Malay society and figures prominently in its classic literature. Its variety and potency can be gauged by the many legends inspired by its power and history. Usman Awang's play is based on the Hikayat Hang Tuah (Story of Hang Tuah) (◊ Indonesia). In the final scene Hang Tuah has stolen Jebat's magic kris, Taming Sari. See also Extract 8 in Indonesia.

Hang Jebat: This is your day, Tuah
for in truth you have understood
that Taming Sari was mine.
Now you can surely wound me.
Observe how you shall shout in joy
Blood! Blood! The Blood of Jebat is spilt.
Honour! Honour! The King's honour is
forth coming.

(*JEBAT dashes forward thrusting his kris and both of them fight again.*)

Background voice: (*The stage is pitch-black*)
The blade of the kris dances in the air,
shivers, flies, thrusts forward and sideways,
Oh, who is he that temporarily trembles,
how the steely blade of Taming Sari
disappears in the soft flesh and veins
to let flow blood! Red blood clots.

How coolly Taming Sari
cuts asunder those entwined flesh
too easily, soft in the stricken hours
yet releasing pain so deep
that rends and stretches veins and heart,
ah, Jebat staggers!
A pair of eyes still sharp in its fading sight,
shining the light of wonder
mixed with a gleam of sadness
but nowhere is there humiliation,
as they pierced his friend,
Hang Tuah bows his head, avoiding
the look that touches his heart,
the pair of eyes that once looked in love's friendship
in those last seconds were splashed with red blood,

its whiteness disappears
under the King's throne
that separates them!

In slow movements, Hang Tuah leaves the hall
a warrior lost and forelorn!

Hang Jebat grabs a sultan's ceremonial scarf
wraps it around his wound, the throbbing pain
pierces
the palace in shadow darkness
his heart thumping wildly,
dimly he hears shouts of joy
'Hang Jebat has fallen! Hang Jebat's fallen!'

Even as he bandages his wounds
in his heart vengeance blooms!

(*The stage is lighted. JEBAT is in the process of finishing to dress his wounds. With all his last strength, JEBAT shouts*).

Hang Jebat: Citizens of Malacca,
I have fought tyranny with blood,
my own blood.
Uphold the belief that
to do good do it measure for measure,
to do bad do it all out.
The blood that has flowed, and spilt for justice
and for the justice I give this blood.

(*So saying he jumps, like a hungry lion*
to run amok among the crowd
milling around the palace
and blood! Blood! The blood of the people of Malacca
swiftly flows in the welcoming echoes of death!)

(10) MALAYSIA: HALL OF AUDIENCE

The Malay Annals

Reception or audience halls are to be found in palaces, balai besars and in some large penghulu's houses. These have been the settings for exciting verbal and physical encounters and were filled with pomp and ceremony on important occasions. Taken from Brown's translation (see Booklist).

Now there was a minister of Sultan Mahmud Shah, Tun Perpateh Hitam. He was a descendant of Tun Jana Buga Dendang and he had a son named Tun Husain, who was an extremely well-built man. And Tun Husain said, 'If ever the conduct of my father is called in question, I shall fight!' Now it happened by the evil will of God that Tun Perpateh Hitam had a dispute with a foreigner, and he was called upon to appear before the Bendahara with the foreigner. The Laksamana was present at the time, for it was the custom of the Bendaharas of Malaka that if the Bendahara was inquiring into disputes the Temenggong and the Laksamana should always be with him. If anyone shewed disrespect to the Bendahara, it was the Laksamana who put him to death; and in cases where it was proper to arrest anyone and put him in fetters, it was the Temenggong who made the arrest. Such was the custom in the days of Malaka. When Tun Perpateh Hitam had been summoned to appear before the Bendahara, Tun Husain came to join his father. And when Tun Perpateh Hitam beheld Tun Husain coming armed with his long creese, he thought to himself, 'It looks as though Tun Husain's going to be as good as his word!': and he rose to his feet and kicked up the mat, saying, 'A fine sort of minister this is, to call my conduct in question like this!' Thereupon the Laksamana drew his sword, saying, 'How dare you show disrespect, kicking up the mat in the presence of the Bendahara?' And he slashed at Tun Perpateh Hitam with his sword while at the same time others drew their weapons and stabbed at him. In vain did the Bendahara try to restrain them, they heeded him not and Tun Perpateh Hitam was killed. When Tun Husain saw this, he drew his creese to fight. But the Laksamana said, 'You're going to be disloyal, are you, Tun Husain, that we may treat you as we've treated your father?' And Tun Husain was struck down there and then. The Laksamana went forthwith to Sultan Mahmud Shah and related to him all that had happened. And the king said, 'If you had not killed them then, Laksamana, assuredly we would have killed them later, for we consider disrespect in the presence of the Bendahara to be as though it were done in our own presence, no less'. And Sultan Mahmud Shah rewarded the Laksamana with robes of honour.

God knoweth the truth.

(11) Malaysia: Jungle

Isabella L. Bird,
The Golden Chersonese and the Way Thither

The Malaysian jungle, while serving as the background for writers, is in itself a landscape teeming with a variety of flora and fauna. Isabella Bird, with a keen observer's eyes, captures these in her literary snapshot.

The Linggi above Permatang Pasir, with its sharp turns and muddy hurry, is, I should say, from thirty to sixty feet wide, a mere pathway through the jungle. Do not think of a jungle, as I used to think of it, as an entanglement or thicket of profuse and matted scrub, for it is in these regions at least a noble forest of majestic trees, many of them supported at their roots by three buttresses, behind which thirty men could find shelter. On many of the top branches of these other trees have taken root from seeds deposited by birds, and have attained considerable size; and all send down, as it *appears*, extraordinary cylindrical strands from two to six inches in diameter, and often one hundred and fifty feet in length, smooth, and straight until they root themselves, looking like the guys of a mast. Under these giants stand the lesser trees grouped in glorious confusion, – coco, sago, areca, and *gomuti* palms, *nipah* and *nibong* palms, tree ferns fifteen and twenty feet high, the bread-fruit, the ebony, the damar, the indiarubber, the gutta-percha, the cajeput, the banyan, the upas, the bombax or cotton tree, and hosts of others, many of which bear brilliant flowers, but have not yet been botanised; and I can only give such barbarous names as *chumpaka*, *Kamooning, marbow, seum, dadap*; and loveliest of all the *waringhan*, a species of ficus, graceful as a birch; and underneath these again great ferns, ground orchids, and flowering shrubs of heavy, delicious odour, are interlocked and interwoven. Oh that you could see it all! It is wonderful; no words could describe it, far less mine. Mr. Darwin says so truly that a visit to the tropics (and such tropics) is like a visit to a new planet. This new wonder-world, so enchanting, tantalising, intoxicating, makes me despair, for I cannot make you see what I am seeing! Amidst all this wealth of nature and in this perennial summer heat I quite fail to realise that it is January, and that with you the withered plants are shrivelling in the frost-bound earth, and that leafless twigs and the needles of half-starved pines are shivering under the stars in the aurora-lighted winter nights.

(12) Malaysia: Jungle

Joseph Conrad, *Lord Jim*

Conrad depicts here the blend of an interior landscape within the individual and the exterior of the immovable forests of Borneo, which he used to landscape the psychology of the morally displaced individual. Here Lord Jim travels up river to the village that is to become his home.

'He sat in it, as I've told you, on his tin box, nursing the unloaded revolver on his lap. He sat with precaution – than which there is nothing more fatiguing – and thus entered the land he was destined to fill with the fame of his virtues, from the blue peaks inland to the white ribbon of surf on the coast. At the first bend he lost sight of the sea with its labouring waves for ever rising, sinking, and vanishing to rise again – the very image of struggling mankind – and faced the immovable forests rooted deep in the soil, soaring towards the sunshine, everlasting in the shadowy might of their tradition, like life itself. And his opportunity sat veiled by his side like an Eastern bride waiting to be uncovered by the hand of the master. He, too, was the heir of a shadowy and mighty tradition! He told me, however, that he had never in his life felt so depressed and tired as in that canoe. All the movement he dared to allow himself was to reach, as it were by stealth, after the shell of half a coco-nut floating between his shoes, and bale some of the water out with a carefully restrained action. He discovered how hard the lid of a block-tin case was to sit upon. He had heroic health; but several times during that journey he experienced fits of giddiness, and between whiles he speculated hazily as to the size of the blister the sun was raising on his back. For amusement he tried by looking ahead to decide whether the muddy object he saw lying on the water's edge was a log of wood or an alligator. Only very soon he had to give that up. No fun in it. Always alligator. One of them flopped into the river and all but capsized the canoe. But this excitement was over directly. Then in a long empty reach he was very grateful to a troop of monkeys who came right down on the bank and made an insulting hullabaloo on his passage. Such was the way in which he was approaching greatness as genuine as any man ever achieved. Principally, he longed for sunset; and meantime his three paddlers were preparing to put into execution their plan of delivering him up to the Rajah.

' "I suppose I must have been stupid with fatigue, or perhaps I did doze off for a time," he said. The first thing he knew was his canoe coming to the bank. He became instantaneously aware of the forest having been left behind, of the first houses being visible higher up, of a stockade on his left, and of his boatmen leaping out together upon a low point of land and taking to their heels. Instinctively he leaped out after them. At first he thought himself deserted for some inconceivable reason, but he heard excited shouts, a gate swung open, and a lot of people poured out, making towards him. At the same time a boat full of armed men appeared on the river and came alongside his empty canoe, thus shutting off his retreat.

(13) Malaysia: The Kampung

Frank Swettenham, *Malay Sketches*

Malaysia's multicultural population makes the observation of the various races in their own environments a colourful experience. In the extract below, Frank Swettenham offers his own views and impressions of the Malays in the closing decade of the 19th century.

To begin to understand the Malay you must live in his country, speak his language, respect his faith, be interested in his interests, humour his prejudices, sympathise with and help him in trouble, and share his pleasures and possibly his risks. Only thus can you hope to win his confidence. Only through that confidence can you hope to understand the inner man, and this knowledge can therefore only come to those who have the opportunity and use it. . . .

The real Malay is a short, thick-set, well-built man, with straight black hair, a dark brown complexion, thick nose and lips, and bright intelligent eyes. His disposition is generally kindly, his manners are polite and easy. Never cringing, he is reserved with strangers and suspicious, though he does not show it. He is courageous and trustworthy in the discharge of an undertaking; but he is extravagant, fond of borrowing money, and very slow in repaying it. He is a good talker, speaks in parables, quotes proverbs and wise saws, has a strong sense of humour, and is very fond of a good joke. He takes an interest in the affairs of his neighbours and is consequently a gossip. He is a Muhammadan and a fatalist, but he is also very superstitious. He never drinks intoxicants, he is rarely an opium-smoker. But he is fond of gambling, cock-fighting, and kindred sports. He is by nature a sportsman, catches and tames elephants, is a skilful fisherman, and thoroughly at home in a boat. Above all things, he is conservative to a degree, is proud and fond of his country and his people, venerates his ancient customs and traditions, fears his Rajas, and has a proper respect for constituted authority – while he looks askance on all innovations, and will resist their sudden introduction. But if he has time to examine them carefully, and they are not thrust upon him, he is willing to be convinced of their advantage. At the same time he is a good imitative learner, and, when he has energy and ambition enough for the task, makes a good mechanic. He is, however, lazy to a degree, is without method or order of any kind, knows no regularity even in the hours of his meals, and considers time as of no importance. His house is untidy, even dirty, but he bathes twice a day, and is very fond of personal adornment in the shape of smart clothes.

(14) Malaysia: The Modern City

Baha Zain, *'Toilet Paper City'*

The Malaysian city has its traditional way of expressing itself: through the streets, shophouses, high-rise buildings and embellishments. A more telling code of significance, often ignored, can be found in the bric-a-brac in and around its massing places, as this extract from Baha Zain's poem shows.

the city is hard rocks
transforming into a region of conflict
the meeting of trouble shooters
student leaders, labourers, administrators and academicians
bricks to the city's rise
however hopeless the situation
we may not escape from ourselves
that together carry the burden and hate this filthy city
that emerges as cancer to environment's greenness

we cannot avoid boredom
because it gives us breath for another day
so what then must I do?
collect the tissue paper discarded by nose-wipers
manufactured from a hundred-year-old trees
or write poems on them
as the last notes
that may be reached by rubbish collectors:
this is paper from toilets
from a tissue-paper civilization
I seek for an answer
perhaps it's best that I resign tomorrow
and not report to the employment office
apply for a job at a big hotel
because the best and lucrative profession
is prostitution

(15) Malaysia: Multiracial Society

Usman Awang, *'Chinese Neighbour's Child'*

Usman Awang's poem is a good example of a humanist, cross-cultural perspective on Malaysia's complex racial make-up.

Tiny he stands near the fence
the shine of his eyes beckons Iskandar
whoever passes looks on with a smile
to see them laughing at play.

A Chinese child born here
on this green earth amidst rubber and rice fields
he can tell whoever asks
this is his land and his mother's forever.

Look, they are struggling over the toy pistol
hei, do not fight
ah, children in their innocent ways
fight only to play together again.

Look, they are laughing merrily
Ah Chew has a gap in his teeth
Iskandar wipes his nose on his shirt
now they wait for the ice-cream man.

Beloved earth, absorb your inspiration
their hearts are your skies
their blood your rivers
their breath your air.

(16) Pahang

Henri Fauconnier, *The Soul of Malaya*

Malaysia impresses writers in different ways. For Henri Fauconnier it embodies the soul of a dreamland awakened in the early consciousness of adventurous childhood. His description here of a trip by river through Pahang shapes that dream into reality.

That dream of all childhood, the impossible dream that a child tries to realise in his games at least, here it is in my very life. We are on a boat, gliding down the river at the foot of the mountains. I don't want to know its name. As a boy I used to say: Orinoco, Irrawaddy; but now the marvellous cadences of those names seem artificial. I want a nameless river in a limitless land. We shall twist and turn along that winding river – shall we ever reach the sea? I never grow tired of gazing, in a sort of blissful torpor, at the racing currents, the stir and ripple of the surface, the fascinating little whirlpools.

Our boat moves among much strange wreckage of the jungle in a broad uniform motion of the stream. The sun revolves around us. The banks slide past, new and yet unchanging. We keep close in at the bends to take advantage of the swifter current. Then the sky is darkened by a vault of virgin forest, above a tangle of lianas hung with great red fruit. Astonished monkeys, motionless, watch us pass, until a sudden thrill of terror scatters them among the branches. An azure king-fisher skims the shadowy shore.

Eight bronze men take turns at the oar and the boat-hook. Their task is easy; it is merely to keep us in the current, and to avoid projecting rocks and great trees floating downwards like ourselves, tangles of roots and branches torn up by floods or landslides. Islets of verdure, thickets of palms and creepers, when we try to pass them, suddenly swing round across our course and are swept against the bank. Sometimes a strong current surges out of deep backwaters and tips the boat sideways into the centre of the stream. Our Malays love these anxious moments. Lethargic where endurance is needed, they are stimulated by sudden peril. Then follow shouts and laughter, and sometimes a dive into the water after a lost pole and a sharp turn while the spluttering swimmer comes up to the surface. When the moment is past they doze again in the bottom of the boat, and roll their clove-scented tobacco in twists of pandanus leaves.

I watch them. They are placid, but easily excited. They look melancholy, especially the younger ones, and will laugh at a trifle. Aloof at first, they are now growing tamer. They understand that they are understood. Malays are polite because they are proud. Never give displeasure if you would never to be displeased. Shame is the only emotion that they cannot bear. Already I know them well enough to realise that the distrust of the first few days was not dislike. But I have yet to learn that a true Malay will sooner die than live with the memory of even an imagined affront.

(17) Penang

Lee Kok Liang, *Flowers in the Sky*

Leekok Liang evokes the stresses of life in Georgetown's congested Chinese district.

There was Ah Chong, the tiny hunched reporter from a Chinese newspaper, who, when drunk with beer, moved his Adam's apple vigorously and who had once called on Inspector Hashim to do him a favour. Ah Chong lived in a cubicle on the third floor in Campbell Street above a Chinese herbalist, and the landlady had accused him of indecent behaviour.

The landlady was a middle-aged widow, squat and talkative, and was one night squatting over the toilet when Ah Chong came home drunk and without bothering to find out if anyone was inside unbuttoned himself and opened the door with a quick pull. The plastic string which held the door close snapped. The landlady gave a scream and stood up quickly and abused him. Other tenants arrived and crowded round. Ah Chong stood there in the middle of the crowd dazed and unable to defend himself.

A little boy suddenly shouted, 'Ah Chong. Ah Chong. Your trousers'.

Everyone laughed and the women giggled and the landlady was furious. On the following day she asked a lawyer to send Ah Chong an eviction notice and made a police report. Inspector Hashim did Ah Chong a favour. He threatened the landlady, telling her that if she did not stop harassing poor Ah Chong, he, Inspector Hashim, would send her son away under a Restriction Order. That made some sense to the landlady. Her son was mixed up in some Secret Society. Everything returned to normal; that is, Ah Chong could now go back to drinking with his visibly moving Adam's apple. The door to the toilet now had a wire string: the landlady was still mean enough not to provide it with a proper latch. Some thought she had other motives. There were many younger and more masculine tenants in the building.

(18) Kedah: Bedong

K.S. Maniam, *The Return*

The extract below captures the mood and landscape of the rubber plantation and, faintly, the determination of the Indians in Malaysia.

My grandmother's life and her death, in 1958, made a vivid impression on me. She came, as the stories and anecdotes about her say, suddenly out of the horizon, like a camel, with nothing except some baggage and three boys in tow. And like that animal which survives the most barren of lands, she brooded, humped over her tin trunks, mats, silver lamps and pots, at the junction of the main road and the laterite trail. Later she went up the red, dusty path, into the trees and bushes, the most undeveloped part of Bedong. The people of this small town didn't know how she managed, but they saw her before a week passed, a settled look on her face, a firm gait to her walk.

A bit of land had been cleared beside the infrequently trodden path to the Hindu cemetery. From salvaged planks, no one knew from where, she nailed the first shelter among the many she was to design. Her three sons cowered in there most of the time.

'They were like chickens afraid of slaughter', a man who had known my grandmother when she first got to Malaysia, said, laughing.

'She was a great walker in those days. She trudged to the estates, sometimes ten miles away, a load of saris she had brought from India on her shoulders. They were soon gone.'

(19) Sarawak

W. Somerset Maugham, *'The Yellow Streak'*

Many parts of Sarawak remain accessible only by boat through its rivers. Here Maugham provides a description of typical Dayak hospitality in the long-house.

The two prahus were dropping easily down stream, one a few yards ahead of the other, and in the first sat the two white men. After seven weeks on the rivers they were glad to know that they would lodge that night in a civilised house. To Izzart, who had been in Borneo since the war, the Dyak houses and their feasts were of course an old story; but Campion, though new to the country and at first amused by the strangeness, hankered too now for chairs to sit on and a bed to sleep in. The Dyaks were hospitable, but no one could say that there was much comfort to be found in their houses, and there was a monotony in the entertainment they offered a guest which presently grew somewhat wearisome. Every evening, as the travellers reached the landing-place, the headman, bearing a flag, and the more important members of the household, came down to the river to fetch them. They were led up to the long-house – a village really under one roof, built on piles, to which access was obtained by climbing up the trunk of a tree rudely notched into steps – and to the beating of drums and gongs walked up and down the whole length of it in long procession. On both sides serried throngs of brown people sat on their haunches and stared silently as the white men passed. Clean mats were unrolled and the guests seated themselves. The headman brought a live chicken and, holding it by the legs, waved it three times over their heads, called the spirits loudly to witness and uttered an invocation. Then various persons brought eggs. Arak was drunk. A girl, a very small shy thing with the grace of a flower but with something hieratic in her immobile face, held a cup to the white man's lips till it was empty and then a great shout arose. The men began to dance, one after the other, each treading his little measure, with his shield and his parang, to the accompaniment of drum and gong. After this had gone on for some time the visitors were taken into one of the rooms that led off the long platform on which was led the common life of the household and found their supper prepared for them. The girls fed them with Chinese spoons. Then everyone grew a little drunk and they all talked till the early hours of the morning.

Biographies and literary notes

BAHA ZAIN (1939–). Pen name of Baharuddin Zainal. Born in **Perak**, he received his education at the University of Malaya and the University of Indonesia. Baha Zain was formerly Head of the Literature Department and Deputy Director General of Dewan Bahasa dan pustaka. Baha Zain received the SEA Write Award in Bangkok in 1980. His published poetry includes *Perempuan dan Bayang-Bayang* (1974), *Dari Kertas Catatan Tengah Malam* (1978) and *Tiga Catatan Perjalanan*, which has been translated into English as *Three Sketches from a Journey* (1980). He is first and foremost a social critic in his poems (Extract 14).

BIRD, Isabella (1831–1904). After a spinal operation at the age of 24, Isabella Bird was advised to recuperate abroad. This led to a lifetime of often unconventional travel. Her most famous book is probably *Unbeaten Tracks in Japan* (1880), an unsentimental picture of the poverty of Meiji Japan. *The Golden Chersonese* (1883, Extract 11) is her account of a journey through Malaysia.

BURGESS, Anthony (1917–94). Born in Manchester, UK. After serving in the army, Burgess was an education officer in the Colonial Service, stationed in Malaya and Borneo, from 1954 till 1960. His *Malayan Trilogy* established him firmly in the literary world. This trilogy, consisting of *Time for a Tiger*, *The Enemy in the Blanket* and *Beds in the East*, explores a crucial period, the pre-Independence years (1954–1957), in the history of Malaysia. In these novels, Burgess, who made it a point to mix with all the races of the country, sees the possibility of the Malaysian people living in a truly Malaysian nation. This possibility he expressed through the image of a musical symphony in which all the elements of the various cultures come to form strands but work harmoniously to shape a common tradition of life (Extract 7).

Baha Zain

CHIN Kee Onn (1909–). Chin's professional life was a varied and colourful one and included spells as a teacher, a Data Collector, State Information Officer, Press Attache with the Malaysian High Commission, Australia, Bank Manager and Head of Proof-Reading at New Straits Times Press. His works began with the Japanese Occupation (1942–45) and include *Malaya Upside Down* (1946), *Ma-rai-ee* (1952) and *The Grand Illusion* (1961). He has also given attention to the Baba-Nyonya culture in his *Twilight of the Nyonyas* (1984).

CLIFFORD, Hugh (1866–1941). Clifford began his career in what is now Malaysia as secretary to the Resident in **Perak** and eventually became the Resident of **Pahang**, serving in Malaysia for 20 years (1883–1901, 1927–29). In his last years in the country he wrote numerous short stories which reflect his sympathy and understanding for the peoples of the country and portray almost all the races, Malays, Chinese, Indians, Orang Asli (Extract 5). Clifford had a romantic view of Malaysia, and he often saw the Malay as a 'noble peasant'. His short stories are collected in *East Coast Etchings* (1896), *In Court and Kampung* (1897), *Studies in Brown Humanity* (1898), *In a Corner of Asia* (1899) and *Bushwacking and Other Sketches* (1901); his novels include *Since the Beginning* (1898), *A Freelance of Today* (1903) and *A Prince of Malaya* (1904).

CONRAD, Joseph (1857–1924). Born in Russian Poland, at the age of 17 Conrad became an apprentice in the merchant marine, which allowed him later to visit the East and use his experiences there as material for his short stories and early novels. He is, of course, well known for his exploration of evil in such novels as *The*

Heart of Darkness and *Lord Jim* (Extract 12). His early novels set in and around the Malay Archipelago, broadly mapped out, include *Almayer's Folly* and *An Outcast of the Islands*. See ◊ Thailand and ◊ Singapore.

EE Tiang Hong (1933–1989). Born in **Malacca** Ee was a teacher and lecturer, who emigrated to Australia in 1975. He wrote poetry from the 1950s and pioneered the Malaysian tradition of poetry in English. Most of his poems examine the plight of an individual who is denied his place in the country of his domicile, his cultural displacement by a technological society and his sense of exile (Extract 8). Ee's poetry is to be found in *I of the Many Faces* (1960), *Lines Written in Hawaii* (1973), *Myths for a Wilderness* (1977) and *Tranquerah* (1985).

FAUCONNIER, Henri. A Frenchman who worked as a planter in Malaysia in the 1920s. He fictionalized his experience in his novel, *Malaisie*, later translated into English as *The Soul of Malaya* (1931, Extract 16). This novel centres on the life of the planter who comes in constant contact with the Indian labourers, the rubber tappers and weeders; it also explores the mystical effect of the country on a man's psyche.

Lee Kok Liang

FERNANDO, Lloyd. A prominent critic and academic, Fernando also encouraged young authors and has edited *Twenty-two Malaysian Stories* (1968) and *Malaysian Short Stories* (1981). His novel *Scorpion Orchid* (1976) explores the theme of individuals from different cultural and racial backgrounds trying to understand each other and form lasting relationships.

HAN Suyin (1917–). Han Suyin comes from a mixed Chinese and Belgian parentage and lived in Malaysia from 1952 to 1965. Her novel *And the Rain My Drink* (1956) deals with the guerrilla terrorism of the Malayan Emergency in the 1950s. See ◊ Hong Kong.

KEITH, Agnes. After going to **Borneo** with her husband in 1934, Agnes Keith wrote *Land Below the Wind* (1939), a work that broadens out from being a personal narrative to include the history and lore of the region.

LEE Kok Liang (1927–92). Born in **Alor Setar**, Kedah, but was raised and educated in Penang. A lawyer trained in London, his short stories look at the Chinese community and often they focus on the individual who is alienated and prevented from realizing his own potential. This canvas is broadened in his later works to include characters from other racial groups such as the Malays and Indians. His stories are found in *Mutes in the Sun* (1964) and *Twenty-two Malaysian Stories* (1968); his novel *Flowers in the Sky* was published in 1981 (Extract 17).

LIM, Shirley. Educated in Malacca and the USA, she is currently Professor of Asian–American Studies at the University of California, Santa Barbara, USA. With her American experience she is able to view her Asian characters in *Another Country* (1982) with a sense of contrast. These stories together with her poems in *Crossing the Peninsula & Other Poems* (1980) offer enlightened views about the immigrant Chinese culture in Malaysia.

K.S. Maniam

MANIAM, K.S. (1942–). Educated in **Kedah** and the UK, he teaches in the English Department of the University of Malaya. His stories, novel and plays, focus primarily on the Indian community, exploring the rootlessness of its individuals and their search for a national identity (Extract 18). His stories are found in *Malaysian Short Stories* (1981) and *Plot, The Aborting, Parablames & Other Stories* (1989); his novel, *The Return*, was published in 1981.

MAUGHAM, W(illiam) Somerset (1874–1965). Maugham travelled widely throughout his life and passed through the Malay Archipelago in 1922–23 and again in 1929. His experiences in this part of the world provided the material for a substantial number of his stories. He has earned a reputation for being the one writer who made known widely to Western readers the attractions and fascinations of the Malay Archipelago. His knowledge of this region served as a backdrop to his study of the European character in new and unpredictable settings. In his stories he explored the effects loneliness and separation from their homeland had on British planters, administrators, professionals and businessmen. Through his stories one catches glimpses of a world beyond the European awareness, a world as menacing as it is mysterious. Most of his Malaysian stories are available in the four-volume *Collected Short Stories* (1976). See Extracts 4 and 19. See ◊ Thailand and ◊ Hong Kong.

MUHAMMAD HAJI SALLEH (1942–). Born in Taiping, Perak, and educated in the Kuala Kangsar, the UK, Singapore and the USA. He began writing in the UK (1963–64) and has continued despite academic and administrative duties in the National University of Malaysia, where he is the head of the Centre for Malay Literature. He has written ex-

Usman Awang

tensively on Malay Literature and was awarded the National Library Award for his creative and critical works in 1991. His poems in English are all collected in *Time and its People* (1978) and offer insights into the Malay world, its culture and traditions (Extract 1).

SALLEH BEN JONED (1941–). Born in **Malacca**, Salleh has worked in Australia, in the English Department, University of Malaya, and the drama section of a television station. His poems in *Sajak Sajak Saleh: Poems Sacred and Profane* (1987) are unconventional and invigorating and explore with arresting sensuality subjects often confined to the philosophical and personal.

SHAHNON AHMAD (1933–). Born in **Banggul Derdap**, Sik, Kedah, he is currently Professor and Director of the Islamic Centre at Science University of Malaysia. He has written numerous novels in Malay for which he was awarded the National Literary Award and one of these, *Ranjau Sepanjang Jalan*, has been translated into English as *Not a Harvest but a Thorn* (1972, Extract 3). Some of his short stories are collected in *The Third Notch and Other Stories* (1980). Shahnon looks at the Malay world and its culture from various angles and examines the confrontations of this world with the West; he is often satirical and ironic about these encounters and clearly recreates for his readers the centre of the Malay world and its strengths.

SWETTENHAM, Frank (1850–1946). The first Resident of **Perak**, he subsequently became Governor of the Straits Settlements, 1901–1904. His *Malay Sketches* (1895, Extract 12) and *The Real Malay Pen Pictures* (1899) contain descriptive and semi-narrative pieces which originate from the writer's long stay in and love for the country and is accompanied by a sense of delight in the discoveries about the land and the people.

THEROUX, Paul. See under Singapore.

USMAN AWANG (1929–). From humble beginnings, Usman Awang rose to become head of the Literary Development Division of Dewan Bahasa dan Pustaka (National Language and Literary Agency). He was awarded the National Literary Award for his contribution to Malay Literature. His poetry treads a humanist ground and is not sectionalist in its outlook and perceptions (see, for example Extract 15). Such an all-embracing world, in terms of cultures and races, can be found in *Salam Benua: Greetings to the Continent*

(1982). Usman has also written a number of plays (Extract 9).

WONG Phui Nam (1933–). After an education in **Kuala Lumpur** and **Singapore** Wong has worked mainly in development finance and banking. His poems, collected in *Remembering Grandma and Other Rumours* (1989), portray a world in which men are incapacitated and suppressed to the point of becoming non-human; through his poems the reader enters the surreal experience of the Malaysian world (Extract 6).

Singapore

Dudley de Souza

> 'an unusual house this is / dreams are here before you sleep / tread softly into the three-storeyed gloom / sit gently / on the straits-born furniture / imported from china / speak quietly to the contemporary occupants'
> *Arthur Yap,*
> *'Old house at Ang Siang Hill'*

Singapore is at the southern tip of the Malaysian Peninsula in the middle of South-east Asia. It is an island state of 625 square kilometres. In 1819 Sir Stamford Raffles planted the British flag and it was not till 1965 that it became a separate independent republic. Before that date Malaysia and Singapore were treated as one political entity first under British jurisdiction and then in the short-lived Federation of Malaysia (1963–65). Consequently, as a literary entity, in the pre-independence era, Singapore was treated as one with Malaysia and it was not till the late 1960s that a distinctly Singaporean literary voice began to be audible.

Geographically, Singapore is 1°N in the centre of what is known as the Association of Southeast Asian Nations (ASEAN). To the north are Malaysia and Thailand, to the south is Indonesia, to the north-east are Brunei and the Philippines. It is thus at the confluence of major trading routes and a variety of vastly different cultural influences.

Singapore Literature

Physically, Singapore is linked to Malaysia by a short causeway and, because of its political and historical ties with its immediate neighbour, the early stages of the development of the literatures in both countries shared a great deal in common. This is especially true of the literature in English.

In the first phase of the growth of an indigenous literature in English in the region, Singapore and Malaysia were then under one political administration bearing the name 'Federation of Malaya'; consequently the intellectuals of that era spoke of a Malayan literature in English rather than separate Singapore or Malaysian literatures.

In Singapore, the Malays form 14.9% of the population while the Chinese form the vast majority, 76.4%. Minorities such as Indians form 6.4% of Singapore's population, while Eurasians and other ethnic groups comprise the remaining 2.3%. Thus, one might assume that there is a fairly diverse mix of cultures and, consequently, a multiplicity of literatures. This, however, is not so, largely because of the fundamentally British education system – underpinned by the Cambridge Examination Syndicate – which Singapore inherited from the colonial government and which has since evolved into the Singapore Education System: a system which relies almost solely on English as the medium of teaching and learning despite the pursuit of a bilingual education policy.

The sense of nationhood essential to the creation of a national literature was, as Edwin Thumboo ◊ notes, not apparent until after the second world war: 'It was the growing political consciousness, the pressure of rising nationalism that furnished the incentive and the occasion for a more vital poetry'.

There were two main ways in which writers tried to integrate an education that was largely British-oriented into the Malayan context in order to establish a Malayan literature in English. First, some writers reverted to a more intense consciousness of their ethnic identities. These writers wrote in their mother tongues, even when they had been educated away from their communities (through English-medium schooling) and even when their concerns no longer showed a high degree of congruence with those of their communities. Second, other writers used the English language with a high degree of sophistication; they had been formed in the mould of liberal Western learning and as a consequence their training enabled them to communicate only with a select minority – the English-educated elite.

One obvious form which the new literature took in the minds of the local literati was the importation of Malay and Chinese lexical items in works written primarily in English. Attempts like the one by Wang Gungwu (writing under the pseudonym 'Awang') in a university publication, *New Cauldron*, entitled 'Ahmad' mixes Malay with English to good effect. It is perhaps the earliest convincing attempt at localizing Singapore poetry in English. The Malay phrases are used to underline the humour behind the lightweight content: 'Can get lagi satu wife, lah! (will be able to get another wife)'. Other early attempts to localize Singapore literature were less successful, employing clichéd symbols culled from the local environment. Images like the coconut tree, the kampong, Malay and Chinese nouns were relied upon as an easy means of introducing what was often mistaken for 'authenticity'. However, one must regard works using 'local colour' as the initial stage in the evolution of an authentic Malayan literature in English.

Singapore Fiction in English

The late 1960s to the early 1980s saw a rapid growth of fiction in English in Singapore. This was not always for the better but it meant that there was greater interest in both reading and writing fiction. Development can be seen in the way the Singapore context begins to be presented with a greater degree of authenticity of detail; in addition, the way character is created and the kind of issues focused on seem a lot more Singaporean than in the fiction of the older writers.

Edwin Thumboo

Claire Tham's ◊ portrayal of character and setting in *Homecoming*, for example, rings with a Singapore cadence:

> The man said, 'Really, ah? I didn't know he had a son. In fact, didn't even know he was married. He was so quiet, you know —'.
>
> 'Yes, I know', the son said softly, and closed the window panes, but so gently that it hardly seemed like a snub. There was a tentative tap at the window again: he ignored it and the tap was repeated. Far below he could hear someone's radio blaring out the American Top 40 while a piano was being thumped in the flat above. He could even hear the raised voice of a mother furiously and nasally scolding her child in Hokkien. He had forgotten about the noise all those years away . . .

There is no longer any groping for the features of the Singapore context but a confident presentation of items of the local environment; the life of the Housing Development Board (HDB) apartments unfolding through carefully selected details. The mingling of Chinese dialect with the sounds of the American Top 40 and piano practice meant that a whole new world of fiction had began to surface. The unmistakable atmosphere of the HDB estate had, at last, been captured in print.

This feeling for the real world – the world of the major portion of Singapore's population is seldom stronger than in the work of Michael Soh. In his novel *Son of a Mother* we share the life of a Chinese grocer who is threatened with eviction. The response to hardship, the sense of filial duty, the self-control and so forth are attitudes which one would perhaps hope to find enshrined, at some future date, in the nation's cluster of core values.

The dilemma of traditional practices coming to terms with modernization or the pressures of daily life seems to be a particularly relevant aspect of Soh's fiction. His characters face problems that are not uncommon among members of the Chinese community in Singapore, as in this quotation from *Son of a Mother*:

> Sis, she's already twenty-two and nearly twenty-three. How can I continue to hope that she'll not marry out of the family until I find myself a wife to take her place in the nursery?

The close relationship between family, occupation and marriage, the need for the girl to move out with the husband – the almost stifling sense of familial linkage – is an aspect of the Singapore context which Soh explores with authority.

This intimacy with typically Singaporean dilemmas or contexts points to the emergence of a kind of Singaporean consciousness and is very much apparent in the work of the younger writers. The work of Philip Jeyaretnam ◊ published in the late 1980s, for instance, is replete with awareness of the contradictions that inhabit the texture of Singapore society: the contradictions between 'material success' and individual satisfaction, the need to find personal fulfilment while maintaining one's sanity in the rat race of *Raffles Place Ragtime*.

In one of Jeyaretnam's short stories, 'Evening Under Frangi-pani', Prakash, the central character, observes that:

> Personal worth seemed to be measured by the size of one's wage packet, because that is how much society is willing to pay for one's services. So Prakash without a job felt like a man without a contribution to make, shadowy, ephemeral and drifting.

Philip Jeyaretnam's view of the Singapore social context is generally studded with social criticism. There is a kind of knowing, half-cynical attitude to society at large which informs the perspective of the protagonist in the story:

> Prakash knew what he should say: a few easy words about commitment to nation, family and job, a glib remark about being eager to learn and anxious to get on! His interviewer did not require much: just a token submission to the game.

While social criticism comes through the incidentals in the tale, it is notable that the central concern of the story is the love relationship between a Straits born Chinese girl and an Indian boy. What is notable is that far from being an inter-racial relationship it is actually treated as an intra-racial one; the barriers between the two are not so much race as idiosyncracies of character and circumstance. Even the objection of the prospective mother-in-law to Prakash is not couched in terms of ethnic differences:

> She had always considered Prakash slow and stupid and imagined him as physically aggressive, worrying that he would bully Elaine out of her depth.

Singapore fiction has begun to reflect the degree of fusion between

---

[a] *Ronald Alcantra's play An Eclipse Leaves No Traces contains scenes in Government House in Fort Canning Park.* [b] *Raffles Hotel, one of the world's leading literary landmarks (see page 263).* [c] *Site of the Substation, performing arts centre.* [d] *The Padang appears in numerous tourist snapshots and novels based in Singapore, among them J. G. Farrell's Singapore Grip (Extract 10) and Patrick Anderson's Snakewine. In The End of Tether, Conrad's hero Captain Whalley walks to the Padang from what is now the Central Business District (Extract 9).* [e] *Ang Siang Hill near Chinatown is described in Extract 1.* [f] *There are two mosques in the Kampong Bahru area – hence the opening lines of Wong May's poem (Extract 7).*

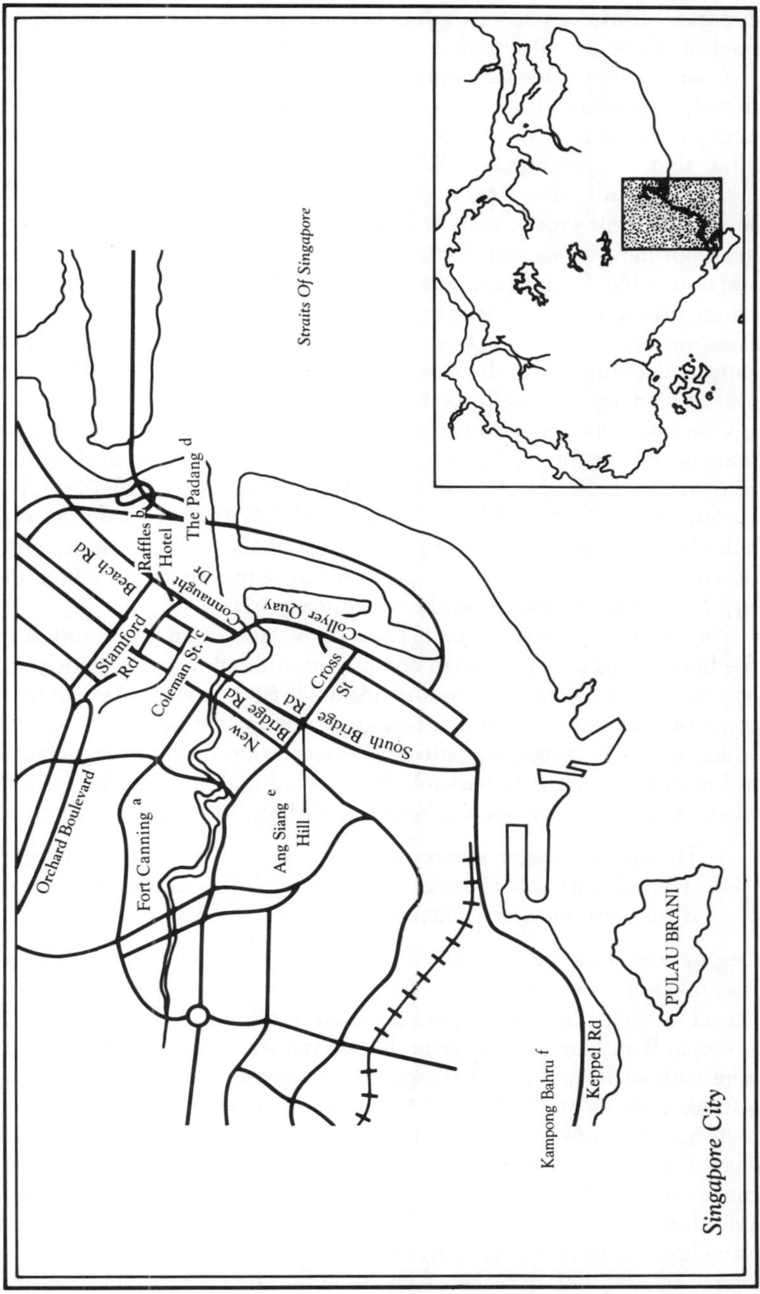

Singapore City

disparate ethnic groups that has been achieved through the use of English in the school system and in the daily affairs of society at large.

A writer who made her mark in 1978 with the publication of *Little Ironies*, Catherine Lim ◊ (a Malaysian who became a Singapore citizen), produces fiction which appears to have just the opposite tone from that of Jeyaretnam. While the latter seems to favour the underdog, Catherine Lim's stories seem to favour the 'overdog'. Minority ethnic groups such as Indians and Eurasians generally appear in a poor light in her stories; they are either comic and ugly or slothful and unreliable. Despite a tendency to depend on stereotyped characterization and some lack of insight, she is able to spin yarns with topically arresting story-lines. Her ghost story collection *They Do Return* and her early collections, *Little Ironies* (1978) and *Or Else the Lightning God* (1982) were commercially very successful (Extract 5).

One phenomenon which the current Singapore writing scene presents us with is the emergence of new fiction from a cluster of writers who are past 50. Such writers as Rex Shelley (b 1930) ◊, Gopal Baratham (b 1935), and Lim Thean Soo (b 1924) are beginning to be household names in Singapore now. Rex Shelley, for instance, published his award-winning first novel on Singapore's Eurasian community, *The Shrimp People*, when he was already 61!

The Shrimp People (Extract 11) is a fairly substantial presentation of the life of Singapore's Eurasian community through the turbulent years of the 1950s when Communist-inspired riots and strikes were a common occurence in the city state. Shelley's prose has a vitality which is rare in Singapore writing; his recreation of the idiosyncracies of Eurasian speech is remarkable for its bold authenticity. In a scene where a bus company riot was being quelled one of the characters says:

> He hit the bugger square in the face . . . Barp! . . . Blerd . . . Then the other bars drivers moved in . . . You see, it was a sort of a bars terminus, not like dose dese days . . .

Despite the lack of a tightly-knit plot, the novel is successful in transmitting a slice of the life of the Eurasian community in a specific period of Singapore's social and political development.

Gopal Baratham's *A Candle or the Sun* is a serious attempt to come to grips with social and political aspects of Singapore society. The book is a frank assessment of what, to some extent, is wrong with Singapore society. The book is an account of how Hernie Perera's life takes a change when he loses his job, his father is found to have terminal cancer and his lover joins an obscure Christian sect with political ambitions. Hernie, who dabbles in story writing, has to decide between providing the government with information on the sect – which could lead to official literary success – and maintaining his personal integrity.

Around this plot Baratham weaves a serious study of private and public dilemmas, often broaching areas where angels fear to tread.

Lim Thean Soo has written about Singapore and the second world war in *Destination Singapore* (1976) and about the makings of a particularly Singaporean personality in *Ricky Star (1978)* but has shown a great deal more energy in the area of short fiction. His *Fourteen Short Stories* (1979), *Bits of Paper and Other Stories* (1980) and *Blues and Carnations* (1985) provide an uneven rendering of different aspects of Singapore society with a strong underlying refrain on the inroads materialism has made in modern Singapore society.

Ho Min Fong is a very talented Singaporean writer whose novels *Sing to the Dawn* (1975) and *Rice Without Rain* (1986) are set in other South-east Asian countries. Although *Sing to the Dawn* is set in Thailand, the writer is Singaporean in perspective and reveals outstanding descriptive skills:

> . . . shimmer of raindrops on smooth banana leaves . . . the mud oozed through her toes as she ran, and sometimes cool puddle-water splashed up and streaked her bare legs.

Contemporary Singapore Poetry

The poetry scene today in Singapore is flavoured by a mix of what might be considered as the 'old pioneers' and fresh talent. The 'old pioneers' established themselves during the 1950s when the only university in Singapore – the University of Malaya in Singapore – saw a bubbling forth of campus poets, helped by the presence of writers like Patrick Anderson ◊ in the early years, and D.J. Enright ◊ who established the longest running English language literary journal in Singapore, *Focus*.

It was, to some extent, to Enright's credit that Wong May (now an American writer) ◊, Lee Tzu Pheng ◊, Arthur Yap ◊, the Malaysian writer Mohammad Haji Salleh, who studied for his BA in Singapore (Malaysia ◊), Robert Yeo, Dudley de Souza, Chandran Nair and a host of others found a ready platform for poems and short stories in *Focus*. Here, I shall focus on the poetry of the 1970s until the present: a period that saw the continued evolution of the 'old pioneers' and the emergence of fresh talent.

The 1960s had seen the rise of two important Singapore poets: Arthur Yap (Extract 1) and Lee Tzu Pheng (Extract 3). Both were English literature honours students during D.J. Enright's chairmanship of the English Department in the Bukit Timah campus. The 1970s, 1980s and 1990s, have to some extent, produced more of the same, since many of the figures from previous generations have continued to attract most attention (eg Thumboo or Yeo) despite the emergence of a sprinkling of new writers like the initially promising Geraldine Heng, Angeline Yap, Simon Tay, Koh Buck Song, Heng Siok Tian and the articulate Kirpal Singh. Out of this rash of verse-writing one or two truly significant poets could emerge and such a person has, indeed, emerged here; perhaps Singapore's best bet for a Commonwealth poetry prize, Boey Kim Cheng ◊ author of *Somewhere-bound* (1989) and *Another Place* (1992, Extract 4). A protege of Lee Tzu Pheng, he displays a rare mastery of form coupled with a maturity of vision that sets him apart from the general run of local poets.

Singapore Drama

Before the second world war Singapore theatre was in four water-tight compartments:

(1) The Chinese *Wayang* or street theatre based on Chinese legends and history – subdivided along dialect lines (eg Cantonese or Mandarin opera). The *Wayang* still lives sporadically in side streets off **Serangoon Road** and the **Jalan Besar** area – a stone's throw from Thieves' Market.
(2) Tamil Dance Drama like the Bharatha-natyam or Karthakali based on folk traditions. Performances are now seen only in formal settings like the **Victoria Theatre.**
(3) Malay drama based on what was known as the Bangsawan tradition which was similar in inspiration to the Chinese street theatre. The Malay village or *kampung* was the traditional setting for such performances but again, one has to wait for a performance at the Victoria Theatre for a resurrection of the past.
(4) Meanwhile the English medium schools were producing a generation of anglicized civil servants and professionals familiar with the cultural offerings of the colonials. The plays of Oscar Wilde, George Bernard Shaw and Henrik Ibsen were staged by the expatriate community.

In the post-war period local playwrights, imbued with a sense of cultural nationalism, began to forge a link between their Asian cultural experience and their response to Western theatre.

Lim Chor Pee's plays *Mimi Fan* (1962) and *A White Rose at Midnight* (1964) were among the first to appear, followed by Goh Poh Seng's *The Moon is Less Bright* (1963), *The Room with Paper Flowers* and *The Elder Brother* (1966). Dr Goh's first play was significant both for dealing with an aspect of local history (the Japanese occupation) and for bringing to the fore political preoccupations.

In general, however, the 1950s, 1960s and 1970s were not productive decades for Singapore drama. The plays of Robert Yeo were an exception. *Are You there Singapore?* was staged in 1974 by the Experimental Theatre Club. Its focus on local politics and the use of local forms of expression helped to gain local attention. Its sequel, *One Year Back Home* (Extract 16) was staged in 1977.

Historical themes continued to interest local playwrights. A competition in 1977 was won by Ronald Alcantra's *An Eclipse Leaves No Shadows* (Extract 6), which was based on the early years of Singapore. A slightly different twist was provided by Robert Yeo in 1992, with *The Eye of History*, which featured a friendly confrontation between Sir Stamford Raffles, founder of Singapore, and Lee Kuan Yew, the former Prime Minister.

The 1980s saw a major change. According to Ong Keng Seng who headed TheatreWorks, one of Singapore's leading stage companies:

> In the late 'eighties, Singaporean English language theatre exploded. This was evident from the number of theatre productions, a mushrooming of theatre companies, an increase in practitioners including an increase in people willing to 'invest' in training abroad, the setting up of training programmes and the beginnings of corporate sponsorship in theatre. Most importantly, the audience expanded.

A handful of dedicated Singapore producers and directors such as Kuo Pao Kun, Max LeBlond, Chandralingam, Ong Keng Sen and others have helped local theatre come to the fore. There began to be an increasing awareness of the need for a culture unique to the place and time. This manifested itself in a self-conscious pride in things Singaporean and plays were seen as more relevant and rivettingly interesting – especially when the characters spoke in Singapore English or Singlish. Among the names that became increasingly familiar to the regular stage goer in the 1980s were Stella Kon, Kuo Pao Kun, Eleanor Wong, Ovidia Yu and Tan Tarn How.

Stella Kon is best known for her monodrama entitled *Emily of Emerald Hill* which was the first Singapore play performed overseas – at the Edinburgh Festival. Her play focuses on the heritage of Peranakan culture – the life-style of the Straits-born Chinese – from the viewpoint of a reminiscing Peranakan woman. The play was a sell-out as it seemed to satisfy the local audience's desire for things Singaporean.

The 'Substation' is a new performing arts project, blessed by the Singapore government. It is housed in an old building in historic **Coleman Street** – a stone's throw from the National Library – converted to enable local theatre and performance groups to hold shows for audiences of about a hundred or so at a time. The building in Coleman Street – across the road from one of the oldest and largest bookstores in Singapore, **MPH**, became synonymous with the local avant-garde including occasional performances from visiting foreign talent – especially during the Singapore Arts Festival season. A local playwright who had the first performance of her work at the Substation was Chin Woon Ping, a Chinese-American author who was born in Malaysia. *Details Body Cannot Wants* was a monodrama which electrified the audiences with its boldness. Staged in 1992, the play was subsequently attacked by a local journalist and defended (by a resident writer at the National University of Singapore) in the pages of the local press. The author herself played the central figure in her monodrama.

Although by and large theatre in Singapore has stayed with the proscenium arch – ie the 'through the window' view of the setting – the 1980s brought on a few attempts to break with tradition. This culminated in 1991 with performances in radically different settings – abandoning the artifice of the stage entirely. The TheatreWorks version of *Trojan Women*, for example, was set in an abandoned granite quarry and audiences were thrilled to be transported to the site in coaches. Yet another play was performed in a disused warehouse while another had the audience being moved indoors and outdoors at **Fort Canning Hill.**

These 'performance art' attempts were aimed at breaking the rigidity of theatre performances in Singapore and enabling theatre to reach the people in the streets. Ironically, there might come a time when – like the traditional Chinese *wayang* – English language drama in Singapore may be a happening in the streets.

Western Writers

Singapore has been written about by a number of expatriate writers. Perhaps the most distinguished is Joseph Conrad ◊. Conrad appears to have had a deliberate policy of concealing the names of cities in his novels based in South-east Asia, but there is no doubt that the 'eastern port' of *Lord Jim* is Singapore. Like many sailors of the time, Conrad spent quite a lot of time in Singapore between voyages and in 1887 was hospitalized there with an injury to his leg caused by a falling spar (an experience that he worked into his fiction in 'The mirror of the sea' and *Lord Jim*). The Malabar Hotel in *Lord Jim* is the now demolished Hotel de l'Europe which stood on the **Padang**.

The work by Conrad which deals most directly with Singapore is *The End of the Tether*, a short novel which details Singapore landmarks very precisely. In his substantial book on Conrad's time in South-east Asia, *Conrad's Eastern Seas*, Professor Norman Sherry shows how the walk taken by Captain Whalley in the novel passes many landmarks which can still be seen today (Extract 9). Conrad's description captures the

Raffles Hotel is one of the world's leading literary landmarks and Singapore's main tourist attraction. Re-opened after extensive refurbishment in 1991, the hotel now includes a museum dedicated to reproducing the 'Golden Age of Travel' (1880–1939).

Although the hotel claims Joseph Conrad was one of its earliest guests the year after the hotel opened in 1887, this is disputed (see Conrad ⇨). Nevertheless, he almost certainly visited Raffles, as did Rudyard Kipling in 1888, who was on a round the world trip.

In 1921, six years after barman Ngiam Tong Boon had created the first Singapore Sling, W. Somerset Maugham ⇨ made the first of his trips to Raffles Hotel. He was to return in 1926 and 1959; legend has it that he wrote in the morning under a frangipani tree in the Palm Court.

The 1920s were in many ways the heyday of Raffles as a stop for the rich and famous, and visitors during that decade included Charlie Chaplin, Maurice Chevalier and Jean Harlow, with Noel Coward (⇨ Hong Kong) staying in 1930.

Raffles Hotel, 11 Beach Road, Singapore 0718. Tel: +65 337 8041.

Raffles Hotel 1907 postcard series

atmosphere of Singapore at that time: a crossroads and intercultural melting pot poised on the verge of technological revolution as steam ships replaced sail; hot, vibrant, exotic.

More recent writers who have taken inspiration from the Singapore setting include Patrick Anderson, originally British, who went on to become a well-known Canadian writer, D.J. Enright, the British poet, novelist and critic, and, undoubtedly the best-known, Paul Theroux, the transatlantic novelist and travel-writer. All three spent time as academics, in the same campus, though at somewhat different times, in Singapore.

Patrick Anderson ◊ was earliest. He was at the **Bukit Timah campus** of the University of Malaya in Singapore in the 1950s and produced a semi-autobiographical work called *Snakewine*, commemorating the colourful, if turbulent, time he had at the Singapore campus. The book became a kind of cult work for the Singapore literary crowd of the 1950s and 1960s since many of the people mentioned in it were clearly recognizable to generations of academics and even students who came after Anderson. Replete with vivid and poetic writing – Anderson also made a mark as a minor poet in a style reminiscent of Louis Macniece and Cecil Day-Lewis – *Snakewine* is an autobiographical, picaresque novel which deals with perhaps the most politically turbulent time in Singapore's history (Extract 2). This was the time of the Communist insurgency and racial riots. Bombs were let off in various parts of the city; strikes were generated by Communist activists; and this was the decade that saw the worst racial riots in Singapore history, the Maria Hertogh Riots when the Malays rose against Singapore's white colonial rulers as a consequence of a court ruling affecting the adopted daughter of Muslim guardians reclaimed by her Dutch Christian mother.

However, it would be a mistake to assume that Anderson's work attempts to focus on the political turbulence of the times: for him this serves as a colourful backdrop for a narrative of the kind of life an expatriate academic lived while working in Singapore. And life for Anderson revolved around pub-crawling, the life of the streets, boring campus parties, nature jaunts with a department chairman who was an inveterate butterfly collector, dalliances with precocious, literarily-inclined undergraduates, discussions with local intellectual young men, adjusting to life on campus and having a Chinese servant like Ah Ting, revelling in the kind of lush tropical landscape surrounding the Bukit Timah campus. Although many of the places Anderson describes are no longer there or quite the same, one gets an idea of the flavour of the place through his vivid, evocative powers. His accounts of the life in Singapore bars are especially dramatic:

> I went into the Savoy for a drink. It's almost empty at this time of

> day, except for a stray or two from the congregation of servicemen at the Singapore Bar; one can watch Terence and the girls preparing for the night and talk to them more freely than later when the crowds come begin. Sadie comes swinging in through the Shangai doors in one of her extraordinary costumes: red, velvet bodice, orange sarong and a sort of cummerbund in green, pats her hair in front of the looking-glass behind the bottles, tilts her head, makes sure of an earring and then, with that characteristic pose and humour which is common to all of them, sweeps around, all magnificent haughtiness, bursts into laughter and says something to Terence in unrepeatable Malay. They dance, fight, hiss curses at each other but always, in the midst of the teasing, assume those consciously theatrical gestures which fill me with exhaustion and wonder.

But low-life, although it accounts for a fair portion of the book, is not what Anderson is primarily concerned with. His perspective encompasses Singapore's natural landscape, which he describes with great authenticity as Extract 2 shows. The urban landscape is also memorably depicted in *Snakewine*. Chinatown which is rapidly dwindling in terms of size and losing its traditional character, is pithily depicted through one of its major features:

> After a little you take it all for granted: walking in Chinatown below the crossed flags of laundry hung on poles from the upper windows, but the pastel blurred colours of the buildings themselves and the damp heat suggest that you are wading through the washing itself . . .

The city centre, which has changed somewhat since Anderson's time, is seen in this light:

> How handsome the city looked in its characteristically limpid fashion! – butter-yellow churches and cupolas, a Cathedral of icing-sugar, the broad meadow called the *padang*, with the Cricket Club arm in arm with the Supreme Court Building, and an oleander reaching up towards Sir Stamford Raffles' bronze buttonhole.

Despite the changes, however, the significant sights – **St Andrew's Cathedral**, **the Padang**, and the **statue of Sir Stamford Raffles** – are all still standing in the city centre although St Andrew's has now been painted a pale ash and is no longer 'butter-yellow'. Undoubtedly, the continuing charm of Anderson's book is that it enables the reader to savour the flavour of the Singapore of the 1950s with its sense of danger and excitement, which contrasts with present-day Singapore with its rather faceless modernity.

D.J. Enright arrived in 1959 to head the English Department in the University of Malaya in Singapore – as it was then called. Two of his prose works and a number of poems partly drew inspiration from the decade or so he spent in Singapore. Unlike Anderson, Enright does not give us much in the way of the visual surface – the physical context of the country – however, in both prose and poetry, with wit, warmth and, occasionally, sharp sarcasm, he provides us with an insight into the character of Singapore society.

Figures of Speech (1961) is an undeservedly neglected novel, set largely in Bangkok and Tokyo. It focuses on the relationship between the English-educated Singapore secretary Mattie Neo – engagingly forward as well as spontaneous – and the Chinese-educated Chung Lu from Hong Kong – steeped in old world Confucianism, withheld and conservative. The mix of the Western and the Oriental makes for a delightful comedy, especially since the two are in the company of George Lester, an English Professor – perhaps modelled upon the author himself.

Intrinsic to the comedy is the typical Enright satirical bite. Here is Singaporean Mattie Neo describing the function of Singapore's Ministry of Culture:

> 'In my country we have a Ministry of Culture but not very much culture.' . . .
>
> 'The chief purpose of the Ministry', she continued, 'is to put down any sort of culture which might offend some other sort of culture. Quite gently, of course, – ours is a civilized state – but gentleness is usually enough. Chinese dancing comes from some part of China. Unlike Indian dancing, which comes from some part of India. Our Indians find Chinese music incomprehensible, our Chinese find Indian music boring. And I must say' – her voice rose slightly – 'that to be bored is a perfectly legitimate reaction . . .'.

The book deserves to be better known – especially among Singaporeans.

Enright's other prose work, *The Memoirs of a Mendicant Professor* (1969) is autobiographical. Part of it focuses on the furore created in Singapore when an aside made during his inaugural lecture was blown up into a major controversy involving the government guardians of culture. The book is topical and highly readable – especially for those readers who are familiar with the social context and the events depicted.

However, the sharp wit and humane sense of humour that characterizes Enright's tone is more permanently exemplified in the poetry he wrote during his period in Singapore (see, for example, Extracts 14 and

D.J. Enright

15). The poem 'The Board of Selection' provides an amusing insight into the Singapore mentality:

> The dean of the faculty is an
> Economist of repute and utility.
> But what is the difference, he asks,
> Between prose and poetry?
> The candidate proposes adroitly that
> Poetry is more economical than prose,
> Viz., it says as much in half the space.
>
> The economist is not satisfied.
> In half the space, he muses . . . but

It takes him four times as long to understand
A piece of poetry as a piece of prose –
Which means . . .

The board make hasty calculations . . .
Which means that poetry is a false economy,
More haste, less speed.
The chairman remembers he has to build a nation
By the end of the month.

Today, undoubtedly the best-known Western writer to have used Singapore in his novels is Paul Theroux, who spent some time at the Bukit Timah campus during the time that Enright was Chairman of the English Department. His novel *Saint Jack* (1973) is set in Singapore – off-shore Singapore that is, since a large part of the action takes place in a junk off Singapore waters (Extract 13). The central character is Jack Flowers who starts a new kind of brothel service for sailors anchored off Singapore. His success with a boatload of bargirls initiates 14 years of enterprise during which he establishes Dunroamin, a massage-parlour with fringe attractions, and Paradise Gardens, a hotel where the American marines spent their bouts of Rest and Recreation after action in Vietnam. Paradise Gardens is most probably based on **Serene House**, now a cheap-looking condominium block located on the fringe of the Bukit Timah campus of what was, in Theroux's time, the University of Singapore. It used to house American GIs during R&R at the time of the Vietnam War.

Although the book focuses largely on expatriate life, a fair proportion of the cast, nevertheless, appears to have been mustered from the Singapore social context and some readers are inclined to believe that there are parallels with the academics Theroux knew during his stint in Singapore – a gang-leader here and a waiter there – albeit in thick disguise.

One valuable aspect of the book, however, is the vivid account of the aura of low-life in Singapore – something which cannot be found with authenticity even in the writings of Singaporeans themselves:

> The completely Chinese flavour of vice in Singapore made it attractive to a curious outsider, at the same time releasing him from guilt and doubt, for its queer differences (Joyce Li-ho had the tattoo of a panther leaping up her inner thigh) made it a respectable diversion, like the erotic art anthropologists solemnly photograph, maharani and maharajah depicted as fellatrix and bugger on the Indian temple. The sequence of activities in a Chinese brothel parodied oriental hospitality: the warm welcome – the host bowing from the waist – the smoke, the chat, the cold

Paul Theroux

> towel, then the girl – usually the feller chose from one in a parade: money changed hands in the bedroom when the feller was naked and excited; then the stunt itself, and afterwards a hot towel and a glass of cold tea on the verandah while some old amahs ironed bedsheets and yapped beyond the rail.

Nonetheless, *Saint Jack* is, by and large, a frothy tale; a more sober attempt at depicting the underlying ethos of the region is the cluster of short stories entitled *The Consul's File* (1977) which, although ostensibly based on the Malaysian town of Ayer Hitam, focuses to a some extent on Singaporean characters (Extract 2 in Malaysia). The character sketch entitled 'Reggie Woo' focuses on a potential scholarship winner – ostensibly Western-educated and articulate – who ends up in a cultural cul-de-sac, swearing in a Chinese dialect, gambling behind his father's shop, a failure in his own eyes, trying to camouflage his sense of defeat by a process of cultural retrogression. The story provides a sad but psychologically convincing picture of the traumatic reaction of an English-educated young Chinese to non-success – a reaction which ends in a rejection of Western culture and all it stands for. The picture of Reggie gambling at the back of his father's shop is a vivid reminder of how culturally vulnerable the Western-educated philosophy graduate is, and encapsulates one of the major themes of the literature, whether by outsiders or by Singaporeans themselves, the relationship between Western education or cultural conditioning and 'Asian values':

> When I saw Reggie in the back, hunched over the mah-jongg table in the short-sleeved shirt that made him anonymous, his legs folded, kicking a rubber sandal up and down, I knew it would be an intrusion to go any further. I heard him abuse his opponent in sharp, unmistakably Hokkien barks as he banged down the mah-jongg tile. I left before he caught sight of me and went back to the Club, crossing the road with that sinking feeling you get at a national boundary or an unguarded frontier.

BOOKLIST

What follows is intended as a representative rather than comprehensive list of books about Singapore. Where several editions exist, in general the latest and most readily available edition has been listed. For most of the extracted works, information on the original English language publisher can in many cases be found in the 'Acknowledgements and Citations' at the end of the volume, as can the exact location of the extracts and the editions from which they are taken. Extract numbers are highlighted in bold.

Alcantra, Ronald, 'An Eclipse Leaves no Shadows' in Robert Yeo, ed, *Prize Winning Plays I*, Federal, Singapore, 1980. **Extract 6.**

Anderson, Patrick, *Snakewine: A Singapore Episode*, Chatto & Windus, London, 1955. **Extract 2.**

Baratham, Gopal, *Figments of Experience*, Times Books International, Singapore, 1981.

Baratham, Gopal, *Sayang*, Times Books International, Singapore, 1991.

Boey Kim Cheng, 'Jungle Trek' in *Somewhere Bound*, Times Books International, Singapore, 1989. **Extract 4.**

Boey Kim Cheng, *Another Place*, Times Books International, Singapore, 1992.

Chandran Nair, *Once the Horseman and Other Poems*, Woodrose, Singapore, 1972.

Chandran Nair, *After the Hard Hours This Rain*, Woodrose, Singapore, 1975.

Chandran Nair, 'Leta' in E. Thumboo, ed, *The Fiction of Singapore*, Vol IIA, ASEAN Committee on

Culture and Information, Singapore, 1990.

Chin Woon Ping, *The Naturalization of Camellia Song*, Times Books International, Singapore, 1993.

Conrad, Joseph, *Almayer's Folly*, World's Classics, OUP, 1992.

Conrad, Joseph, *Lord Jim*, Everyman Classics, Dent, 1988.

Conrad, Joseph, *An Outcast of the Islands*, World's Classics, OUP, 1992.

Conrad, Joseph, *The Rescue*, Penguin, 1989.

Conrad, Joseph, *The Secret Sharer* and other sea stories, Dover, 1993.

Conrad, Joseph, *The Shadow Line* World's Classics, OUP, 1985

Conrad, Joseph, *Typhoon* and other stories, Everyman's Library, 1991.

Conrad, Joseph, *Victory*, World's Classics, OUP, 1986.

Conrad, Joseph, *Youth, Heart of Darkness and The End of the Tether*, Everyman's Library, J.M. Dent, London, 1974. **Extract 9**.

Elangovan, K., *Thiraikku Pinnal*, Singapore, 1979

Enright, D.J., *Figures of Speech*, Heinemann, London, 1967.

Enright, D.J., 'Small Hotel' and 'The Mysterious Incident at the Admirals Party' in *Selected Poems 1990*, OUP, Oxford, 1990. **Extract 14**.

Enright, D.J., *Memoirs of a Mendicant Professor*, Carcanet, Manchester, 1990.

Farrell, J.G., *The Singapore Grip*, Fontana, London, 1979 **(Extract 10)**.

Goh Poh Seng, *If We Dream Too Long*, Island Press, Singapore, 1972.

Goh Poh Seng, *The Immolation*, Heinemann Asia, Singapore, 1977.

Goh Poh Seng, *Bird With One Wing*, Island Press, Singapore, 1982.

Greet, Annie and Syd Harrex, *Flinders University Jubilee Anthology*, CRNLE, Australia, 1991.

Harris, Stuart, *William Shakespeare Visits the Musical Fountain on Sentosa and Other Poems*, Hwa Chong Junior College, Singapore, 1983.

Harris, Stuart, *Themes and Images*, Heinemann Asia, Singapore, 1989.

Hicks, Bonnie, *Excuse Me, Are You A Model?*, Angsana Books, Singapore.

Ho Min Fong, *Rice Without Rain*, Heinemann, Singapore, 1986.

Ho Poh Fun, ed, *Focus 1983: 21st Commemorative Issue*, NUS Literary Society, Singapore, 1983.

Jeyaretnam, Philip, *First Loves*, Times Books International, Singapore, 1987.

Kandiah, Thiru, ed., *Prize Winning Plays*, Singapore, UniPress, Singapore, 1991.

Koh Buck Song, *A Brief History of Toa Payoh and Other Poems*, Imperial Publishing House, Singapore, 1992.

Kon, Stella, *Emily of Emerald Hill*, Macmillan, Singapore, 1989.

Kuo Pao Kun, *The Coffin is too Big for the Hole*, Times Books International, Singapore, 1990.

Lee Tzu Pheng, *Prospect of a Drowning*, Times Books International, Singapore, 1980.

Lee Tzu Pheng, *Against the Next Wave*, Times Books International, Singapore, 1988.

Lee Tzu Pheng, *The Brink of an Amen*, Times Books International, Singapore, 1991.

Lim, Catherine, 'The Chosen One' in *Little Ironies*, Heinemann Asia, Singapore, 1978. **Extract 5**.

Lim, Catherine, *Or Else, the Lightning God*, Heinemann Asia, Singapore, 1982.

Lim Suchen Christine, *Fistful of Colours*, EPB, Singapore, 1993.

Lim Thean Soo, *Destination Singapore*, Singapore, 1976.

Lim Thean Soo, *Blues and Carnations*, Singapore, 1985.

Pakir, Anne, *Voices of Singapore*, Faculty of Arts & Social Sciences, NUS, Singapore, 1990.

Sharma, G.N., ed, *Literature and Commitment*, CACLALS, Canada, 1988.

Shelley, Rex, *The Shrimp People*, Times Books International, Singapore, 1991. **Extract 11**.

Sherry, Norman, *Conrad's Eastern Seas*, Cambridge University Press, 1977.

Singh, Kirpal, *Palm Readings*, Graham Brash, Singapore, 1986.

Singh, Kirpal, *Critical Engagements*, Heinemann Asia, Singapore, 1986.

Singh, Kirpal, *Twenty Poems*, Singapore, 1987.

Soh, Michael, *Son of a Mother*, Oriental Press, Singapore, 1973.

Tay, Simon, '5', The Shell Literary Series, Singapore, 1985.

Tham, Claire, 'Homecoming' in E. Thumboo, ed, *The Fiction of Singapore*, Vol II, ASEAN Committee on Culture and Information, Singapore, 1990.

Theroux, Paul, *Saint Jack*, Penguin, Harmondsworth, UK, 1976. **Extract 13**.

Theroux, Paul, *The Consul's File*, Penguin, UK, 1979.

Thumboo, Edwin, ed, *The Flowering Tree*, EPB, Singapore, 1970.

Thumboo, Edwin, ed, *The Second Tongue*, Heinemann, 1976.

Thumboo, Edwin, ed, *The Fiction of Singapore*, ASEAN Committee on Culture & Information, Singapore, 1990.

Thumboo, Edwin, ed, *The Poetry of Singapore*, ASEAN Committee on Culture & Information, Singapore, 1988.

Thumboo, Edwin, *Gods Can Die*, Heinemann Asia, Singapore, 1977.

Thumboo, Edwin, *Ulysses by the Merlion*, Heinemann Asia, Singapore, 1979. **Extract 8**.

Wong May, *A Bad Girl's Book of Animals*, Harcourt Brace & World, New York, 1969.

Wong May, *Reports*, Harcourt Brace & World, New York, 1972.

Wong May, *Superstitions*, Harcourt Brace Jovanovich, New York, 1979.

Wong May, 'Kampong Bahru, 1975', in Edwin Thumboo, ed, The Poetry of Singapore, ASEAN Committee on Culture & Information, Singapore, 1988. **Extract 7**.

Wong Yoon Wah, *Beyond Symbols*, Singapore Association of Writers, Singapore, 1984. **Extract 12**.

Yap, Arthur, *Man Snake Apple and Other Poems*, Times Books International, Singapore, 1986.

Yap, Arthur, *Commonplace*, Heinemann Asia, Singapore, 1977.

Yap, Arthur, *Down the Line*, Heinemann Asia, Singapore, 1980.

Yap, Arthur, 'Old House at Ang Siang Hill', in Edwin Thumboo, ed, *The Poetry of Singapore*, ASEAN Committee on Culture and Information, Singapore 1988. **Extract 1**.

Yeo, Robert, *One Year Back Home*, Solidaridad, Manila, 1990. **Extract 16**.

Yeo, Robert, *A Part of Three*, Select Books, Singapore, 1989.

Yeo, Robert, ed, *Singapore Short Stories*, Heinemann Asia, Singapore, 1978.

Extracts

(1) Ang Siang Hill

Arthur Yap, *'Old House at Ang Siang Hill'*

The old Chinese family houses so evocatively described in this poem have all but disappeared. However on Emerald Hill Road (off Orchard Road) there are a number of renovated houses that retain something of the ghostly atmosphere of Yap's poem. Ang Siang Hill is near Chinatown.

an unusual house this is
dreams are here before you sleep
tread softly
into the three-storeyed gloom
sit gently
on the straits-born furniture
imported from china
speak quietly
to the contemporary occupants

they are not afraid of you
waiting for you to go
before they dislocate your intentions
so what if this is
your grandfather's house
his ghost doesn't live here anymore
your family past is
superannuated grime
which increases with time
otherwise nothing adds or subtracts
the bricks and tiles
until re-development
which will greatly change
this house-that-was
dozens like it along the street
the next and the next as well

nothing much will be missed
eyes not tradition tell you this

(2) Botanical Gardens

Patrick Anderson, *Snakewine*

A passage that reveals Patrick Anderson's skill at describing the natural surroundings of Singapore. The protagonist is entering the Botanical Gardens through the back entrance, which is still wooded and jungly – it belongs to the Sultan of Johore to this day.

The road was now dark, although sprinkled with patches of sun, and from the Gardens there came the smell of damp vegetation. I've often read in books that the jungle is 'sticky' and 'rotting' – read of 'fleshy' carnivorous flowers and strange moths and the sudden brilliance of a parrot against the gloom – and for a moment the Gardens did suggest all that, but with the disqualification that their effect would inevitably be to some extent contrived. But as I entered them, and subsequently walked right round them, without as yet exploring the actual forest, the adjectives that came to mind were not 'wild' or 'corrupt' but 'charming', 'lyrical', in fact Shakespearian. They belonged to the Forest of Arden, Prospero's island and *Twelfth Night*.

The path kept close to the trees, running in their shadow, but on its other side the grass shelved away, glistening with dew, and in this small valley there stood all sorts of palms which burst out of the grass in fountains, suspended themselves high in the air in floating showers like those that rockets trail, or maintained a delicate equilibrium between plumes gently pointed at the sky and plumes languidly bent towards the ground. Palms wrestled with themselves, fitted themselves with cogs and gears until they spun around in a sort of mad machinery, grew exhausted and buried themselves deep in moss. I looked at some of their names – I can remember one: *Borassodendron Machidonis*. There were trunks notched and bulbous, shaggy and slim, and about all palms there seems to hang an air of effort and decay; coconut palms have an eccentric elegance because they look so slim and spring from the earth at such odd angles, bearing aloft dead fronds as well as living, but many of the other species are so complicated that half of them seems dead all the time. It's surprising that more hasn't been written about them for they are certainly literary trees. As for this deadness, you find it everywhere in a land where there are no seasons. There is a touch of Autumn all through the year, stealing like a ghost amongst the foliage.

(3) Botanical Gardens

Lee Tzu Pheng, *'Bridal Party at the Botanics'*

Having your photograph taken in front of luxuriant flora at the Botanical Gardens is de rigueur for newly married Singaporeans, as any weekend visit will show.

Her two hundred dollar face
is melting in the sun,
her cool licked by the heat
she's a river of distress her
thousand dollar gown
cannot possibly redress,
and the roses are growing redder
by the minute. This surely is the last
(well of course it must be), though
the first time she will trip,
literally, under that pergola. Why
had she – no, they – given in
to the temptation of this garden?
And he, her super-man,
an accessory in this, now
how was it she had not noticed
how stupid he looked
black-stuffed, oil-slicked, fainting
in his finery, by the shrubbery?

'Look this way
(Please)
Smile (Please!)
Just one more . . .

Just one more?

(4) Bukit Timah

Boey Kim Cheng, *'Jungle Trek'*

Although Boey's poem refers to the experience of urban man or woman in the wilds of South-east Asia, rather than in the well-ordered Bukit Timah Reserve, this small natural park in the centre of Singapore is a reminder of the jungle that covered much of Singapore even into the early 20th century.

The steaming presences of decay
press upon us. Everywhere the eye
sinks into the heart of rot
and every step brings
a new crossroads. The compass
never fails to point away
from our heart and toes,
never fails to give a new reading
of our loss, and the thick tangle
is quick to cancel all our steps;
the tangle in the brains
shutting daylight and starry nights out.
We, who had every street mapped
and named, followed faithfully
each well-lit path to the end,
sink in now, and sob
like Jonahs in a green whale
in a green sea. When the mission is done
we will not be raised into prophecy
out of the Leviathan's belly. Nor will
we speak of persecution by monsters
dressed in green. Years laced with salt,
we will rather take pleasure in moments
that are like hour-long cigarettes,
and revolve with colours other than green,
and the vicious shades it hides.

(5) Chinatown

Catherine Lim, *'The Chosen One'*

The old Chinese women who, like old women in many cultures, did much to define the Chinatown district of Singapore, have now all but vanished along with the historic shophouses that were demolished in the 1970s and early 1980s. However, Catherine Lim's short stories provide a frank and occasionally brutal insight into the life of the crowded terraced houses of Chinatown. Something of old Chinatown can still be found around Telok Ayer Street.

I used to see many of them – now there do not appear to be many anymore – old women in their faded black long-sleeved cotton blouses and loose pants, sitting patiently behind little wooden trestles on which they had set up their wares – small bottles of sweets, packets of dried ginger and plums, cigarettes in loose sticks of five or six stuck in a little tin. And there was the inevitable lit joss-stick standing in a tin in front of the meagre wares, a reminder to the gods that they were to be kind to these old women and give them good business. Sitting behind their trestles by the side of the passageways in front of shops and houses, and largely ignored by the flow of people shopping and going about their business in the city, they became a separate, pathetic little world unto themselves. Only occasionally was their existence acknowledged – by a hurrying pedestrian in need of a quick smoke, by a child who wanted a sweet or some dried plums. But by and large, they were forgotten in the pitiless hustle of city life, for with the modern shops which sold everything, who would want to buy the pitiably inadequate wares of an old woman?

And so she sat, tired and forlorn, waiting all day, and the large pocket inside her blouse was without the little coins she had dreamed would fill it. In her old age she wept easily, and so she shed tears over the sweets and small biscuits going soft and sticky for want of anybody to buy them. She put a larger joss-stick in the tin, her lips moving desolately in prayer, imploring the great goddess Kuan Yin to have mercy on her, an old woman of sixty, alone in the world. She had never married and therefore had no children to take care of her in her old age. There would be no one to offer prayers for her after her death.

(6) Fort Canning Park

Ronald Alcantra, *An Eclipse Leaves No Shadows*

The 'Government House' referred to in the stage directions was in Fort Canning (now the site of a sports and restaurant complex). Alcantra's play is set in 1823, in the time of Raffles (who appears as one of the characters). Farquhar was Raffles's replacement in Singapore.

Office in Government House, a few days later. Lt Hull is seated at his desk. Farquhar enters. He is agitated but holds back and is seething under his attempt to keep control of his temper.

HULL. Good morning, Colonel

FARQUHAR. Good morning (*impatiently*). What is it this time?

HULL. Sir Stamford has again expressed his consternation.

FARQUHAR. His Excellency always seems unduly concerned.

HULL. He is perturbed over the occupation of land on the left bank. He asks how the squatters can be cleared.

FARQUHAR. I have already fully explained every point as far as the occupation of land in Singapore is concerned. Now I feel myself imperially called upon to debate the question once more.

HULL. The matter is far from being resolved. What do you intend to do about the property on the land?

FARQUHAR. There are letters still under consideration.

HULL. Are you going to withdraw the grants?

FARQUHAR. I issued no grants. I am ready to take the most solemn oath that I never issued any permanent grants of land to anyone.

HULL. Then, how did the buildings appear on the restricted areas?

FARQUHAR. The land by the Singapore River and the houses and property on it are on pledge – they would be returned if we required it.

HULL. I hope so. But Sir Stamford is also upset about the question of the issue of licences for opium, liquor and gambling.

FARQUHAR. Gad! Man! How does he expect the Settlement to function without revenue?

HULL. But there are funds.

FARQUHAR. Funds? What funds? Do you know what he left me with in 1819? Hardly anything. I had to raise funds to build up what you see. No complaints were made at the time!

HULL. But he left specific instructions. Especially with regard to the vices.

FARQUHAR. He and his specifics. He just does not understand. The vices are part and parcel of the life of the people.

HULL. Sir Stamford is against exploiting the weaknesses of the people.

FARQUHAR. You seem to echo Sir Stamford. It is a way of life here.

(7) Kampong Bahru

Wong May, *'Kampong Bahru 1975'*

Kampong Bahru is in the western part of the island, near Mount Faber and Telok Blangah. There are two mosques in the vicinity, Masjid Telok Blangah (State of Johor) and Radis Mas.

The expanse
of sadness inherent in the Muezzin's voice makes
distances
near: a motion really
that moves the immediate
the hair, the sleeves, the burnt grass
near the gravel. Dawn or Dusk, especially
in the dusk that lays waste
the skies; Immutable – from what
neighbouring planet year
after year
the same ray, half-serene, half-
terrible as over an ancient battle-field?

Calling from all corners
not a corner
not his minaret. The voice
looks in all nooks &
crevices
a scent really,
released
from the earth.

If as a child I've said
"one day I shall have no home"
nearing that hour of the
day, prompted by
that voice, & partly in
answer, now it is said
over & again
echoing everywhere, creeping like lizards
the lostness that 20 years later has
fetched me here.

(8) Merlion

Edwin Thumboo, *'Ulysses by the Merlion'*

One of Singapore's major poets wonders whether the Merlion Statue in Singapore harbour (symbol of east and west) reflects a people's yearning for something beyond the here and now.

I have sailed many waters,
Skirted islands of fire,
Contended with Circe
Who loved the squeal of pigs;
Passed Scylla and Charybdis
To seven years with Calypso,
Heaved in battle against the gods.
Beneath it all
I kept faith with Ithaca, travelled,
Travelled and travelled,
Suffering much, enjoying a little;
Met strange people singing
New myths; made myths myself.

But this lion of the sea
Salt-maned, scaly, wondrous of tail,
Touched with power, insistent
On this brief promontory . . .
                Puzzles.

Nothing, nothing in my days
Foreshadowed this
Half-beast, half-fish,
This powerful creature of land and sea.

Peoples settled here,
Brought to this island
The bounty of these seas,
Built towers topless as Illium's.

                They make, they serve,
                They buy, they sell.

Despite unequal ways,
Together they mutate,
Explore the edges of harmony,
Search for a centre;

Have changed their gods,
Kept some memory of their race
In prayer, laughter, the way
Their women dress and greet.
They hold the bright, the beautiful,
Good ancestral dreams
Within new visions,
So shining, urgent,
Full of what is now.

Perhaps having dealt in things,
Surfeited on them,
Their spirits yearn again for images,
Adding to the dragon, phoenix,
Garuda, naga, those horses of the sun,
This lion of the sea,
This image of themselves.

(9) Padang

Joseph Conrad, *The End of the Tether*

In this extract, the main protagonist, Captain Whalley, walks from the general post office to his hotel near St Andrew's Cathedral. The same walk can be done today, passing many of the major landmarks, although of course the 'slummy street of Chinese shops' has disappeared. Conrad's novella paints a vivid picture of Singapore at the turn of the century as steam ships replaced sail.

Captain Whalley pushed the paper into his waistcoat-pocket, took his stick from under his arm, and walked down the street.

It was a recently opened and untidy thoroughfare with rudimentary side-walks and a soft layer of dust cushioning the whole width of the road. One end touched the slummy street of Chinese shops near the harbour, the other drove straight on, without houses, for a couple of miles, through patches of jungle-like vegetation, to the yard gates of the new Consolidated Docks Company. The crude frontages of the new Government buildings alternated with the blank fencing of vacant plots, and the view of the sky seemed to give an added spaciousness to the broad vista. It was empty and shunned by natives after business hours, as though they had expected to see one of the tigers from the neighbourhood of the New Waterworks on the hill coming at a loping canter down the middle to get a Chinese shopkeeper for supper.

Captain Whalley was not dwarfed by the solitude of the grandly planned street. He had too fine a presence for that. He was only a lonely figure walking purposefully, with a great white beard like a pilgrim, and with a thick stick that resembled a weapon. On one side the new Courts of Justice had a low and unadorned portico of squat columns half concealed by a few old trees left in the approach. On the other the pavilion wings of the new Colonial Treasury came out to the line of the street. But Captain Whalley, who had now no ship and no home, remembered in passing that on that very site when he first came out from England there had stood a fishing village, a few mat huts erected on piles between a muddy tidal creek and a miry pathway that went writhing into a tangled wilderness without any docks or water-works.

(10) Padang

J.G. Farrell, *The Singapore Grip*

This scene takes place some 50 years or so after Captain Whalley's walk (Extract 9). Singapore is on the brink of occupation by the Japanese and Farrell vividly portrays a corrupt and superficial world of taxi girls at the 'Great World' dancehall, cocktail parties in Tanglin and idle expatriate liaisons.

At Monty's direction the taxi turned away from Raffles Hotel along the sea-front. On the right now was the starlit expanse of the *padang* and beyond it, just visible against the sky, the dignified silhouette of the former Grand Hôtel de l'Europe, the benefits of whose dance-floor Matthew had longed in retrospect to transfer to Geneva. The driver evidently knew what was expected of him without having to be told, for their progress had slowed to a crawl and he had half turned in his seat awaiting further instructions. Monty was peering intently at the shadowy figures of women sitting in rickshaws or standing idly in groups of two or three beneath the trees which lined the road. 'Stop!' he said, and the taxi drew in to the kerb.

Hardly had they come to a halt when there was a great stirring in the darkness; from what had seemed to be empty rickshaws shadowy figures emerged. Further shapes could be seen shifting in the obscurity beneath the trees; beyond, anchored at sea in the inner roads, were a great number of ships of which only the lights were visible. In a moment, to Matthew's surprise, the open windows of the taxi were entirely filled with women's faces, piled one on top of another like coconuts; shortly the windscreen, too, was blocked by the faces of yet more women leaning over the bonnet. A soft murmur filled the air from which an occasional word in English detached itself: 'OK John!' . . . 'Nice!' . . . 'Back all same flont!' 'Whisky soda!'

Meanwhile, the driver, an elderly Malay with a brown face and the white hair of a grandfather, had groped for an electric torch and shone its beam on one window after the other.

'Can these be real women?' wondered Matthew as the beam wandered unsteadily over the serried painted masks. Yet on many of these masks the wrinkles stood out despite the paint and powder; the angled light etched them all the more harshly, replacing sunken eyes with a blob of darkness. At the same time, here and there skeletal arms and stretched through the open windows to trail about in the interior of the cab, floating and flickering like sea-weed, plucking weakly at his shirt and trousers, palping his arm or thigh.

'Hags!' declared Monty. 'Drive on!'

(11) Rochore Canal

Rex Shelley, *The Shrimp People*

Rochore Canal is the biggest man-made waterway in Singapore. During the Japanese Occupation (1942–45) Javanese labourers were imported by the Japanese; many of them eventually gathered around the Rochore Canal to obtain food.

It was only when her father died suddenly of meningitis in 1949 that her mother told them what her father did during the war. It brought a rush of emotion and tears of pride to Sheelah. Rita said that he used to go out very early every morning just before dawn towards the end of the occupation. Between sobs Rita told them of the thousands of Javanese labourers the Japanese had brought to Singapore. When they got sick and too weak to work, the Japanese turned them out into the streets. They gathered along the Rochore canal with sticks and wires. Each man found a rusty old soup can, balanced it on three stones over a fire and cooked the dead rats and rotting vegetable matter he fished out of the canal. They were living skeletons with just a thin layer of skin stretched over their bones. Most of them had sores filled with maggots.

Edwin went to these wretched people every morning before it became bright enough for anyone to notice him because the Japanese might not have condoned it. With his limited stock of medicines, he tended to them, knowing that the man he was treating may die within the hour or, at most, last a week. But more than the medical attention, he brought to them hope. And perhaps a touch, some vestige of faith in their fellow men.

"He used to pound *jambu batu* leaves and make some kind of mixture because he said that was the only thing he had to try to stop the purging."

"He made me promise not to tell anyone while he was still alive . . . while he was still alive, he said . . . " Rita broke off weeping.

(12) Sentosa

Wong Yoon Wah, *'Fort Silosa'*

Fort Silosa on Sentosa island is a four hectare complex of tunnels and gun emplacements, complete with a waxwork depiction of the surrender of Singapore by the British in 1942.

The cannons, stubborn and rusty,
are still pointing wrongly at the south
and are aiming at the waves in the open sea.

Everyday,
the tourists, like the British artillery men of the past.
are restless and tired.
Through the barrel of the gun
They watch
the falling leaves in the wind
and the tide which is coming in and going out.

The children are always running around like fireflies,
Deep in the tunnel
the tourist-guide,
like the British officers of the past,
fell asleep in the underground chamber,
like a shell, cold and indifferent,
waiting for the night attack from the sea.

The wild orchids
unable to bear the smell of ammunition
are stretching out their bodies through the crack,
looking amazingly at
the surrender chamber on the hill top,
where the war is merely a series of pictures and wax men,
where the exhibition is free for everybody.

(13) Singapore: Bars

Paul Theroux, *Saint Jack*

Jack's Dunroamin is actually rather more than a bar and would certainly not be allowed to operate today. However, Theroux's exuberant novel is a celebration of the seedier side of Singapore's pre-Independence status as one of the world's great shoreleave ports.

Dunroamin worked smoothly, but it was older than my devising. The system of payment – the chit-pads in the bar, the shakedown in the bedroom – Ganapaty, the *jaga* at the front gate who said, 'I am a dog, only here to bark'; the thickly waxed oxblood-coloured floors in the graceful white house camouflaged by vast *angsana* trees that dripped tiny yellow blossoms and flanked by servants' quarters and a carriage shed, sloping rattan chairs with leg-rests on the top-floor verandah, the light knock on my back room and (though I insisted they call me Jack) the soft cry of '*Tuan*' with the morning tea, the skill of the Indian musicians and Weerakoon's habit of saying 'Blast' when he played a wrong note – it was all a colonial inheritance, and it had fallen to me. But if my whorehouse was a scale model of the imperial dream, I justified my exploitation by adding to it humour and generous charity, and by making everyone welcome.

What Chinese fellers visited us, mostly embarrassed businessmen with names like Elliot Ching and Larry Woo, did so for the same reason the rest of the Chinese stayed away – because my girls made love to red-heads. I watched from my corner of the long bar, near the telephone and Ganapaty's emergency buzzer, greeting arrivals with 'Glad you could make it – what can I do for you?' and later saw them go down the gravel drive, each one depleted, rumpled from having dressed hurriedly – their ties and sometimes their socks stuffed in their back pockets – and wearing the pink face people associate with outrage but which I knew to be the meekness that comes after spending energy in a harmless way. It was pleasant to see them leave with new faces and I was flattered and reassured by their promises of generosity: 'If there's ever anything I can do for you, Jack –'

But I was the host. 'Just settle your bar-bill at the end of the month, thank you, and a very good night to you all.'

(14) Singapore: Hotels

D.J. Enright, *'Small Hotel'*

The shady 'small hotels' prevalent in Enright's time have almost completely dwindled away. However, the 'backpacker hotels' on Bencoolen Street retain some of the atmosphere of the old hotels.

Not *Guest* –
The Chinese, those corrected souls, all know
A guest is never billed, whereas the
Essence of my aspect is, I pay –

But *Occupier*. Good words cost no more.
The Occupier is hereby kindly warned,
It is forbidden strictly by the Law
– In smudged ungainly letters on his door –
Not to introduce into this room
Prostitutes and gambling, and instruments of
Opium Smoking and spitting on the floor.

By Order, all the lot, *The Management*.
The Chinese have immense respect for Order,
They manage anything you name except

To keep their voices down. Outside my door
The Management all night obeys the Law,
Gambles and introduces prostitutes,
And spits upon the floor and kicks around
The instruments of opium smoking.

It is forbidden to the Occupier
To sleep or introduce into his room
Dreams, or the instruments of restoration.
He finds he has his work cut strictly out
To meet the mandates of the Law and Order.

Coffee, frying garlic and a sudden calm
Imply the onset of a working day.
Kings and queens and jacks have all departed,
Mosquitoes nurse their bloody hangovers.

So large a bill of fare, so small the bill!
A yawning boy bears off my lightweight bag,
Sins of omission make my heavier load.
Insulting gringo. Cultural-imperialist.

Maybe a liberal tip will mollify
The Law, the Order, and the Management? –
With what I leave behind on that hard bed:
Years off my life, a century of rage
And envy.

(15) Singapore: Language Problems

D.J. Enright, *'The Mysterious Incident at the Admiral's Party'*

Although nearly all Singaporeans speak excellent English, different cultural and linguistic backgrounds sometimes lead to misunderstandings.

Moored in his favourite Eastern port,
This jolly British Admiral
Must give a party on his ship,
With jolly guests, Malays, Chinese,
And Indians and English too.
Says he, 'I like the sarong well,
Trim gear, I wear it when I can.'
Good Jack, who likes Malay costume!
Approval flutters like the gulls,
Down go the drinks, up come the words.
'Although,' he says, 'it tends to slip,
It slips and slides below my hips,
It's hard to keep a sarong up.'
A Chinese lady speaks, sedate
And sweet. 'Then Admiral you need
A songkok.' Songkok as you know
Is headwear proper to sarong.
But Admiral and nearby guests,
They do not know what songkok is,
They think they hear some other words.
Some gape, some giggle and some gasp,
And jolly shaken Jack withdraws
Upon his bridge, and all disperse.
This Chinese lady at a loss,
She asks her spouse in Mandarin,
But what, but why? Who, unbeknown,
Now scouts about the huddled groups.
Then joins his wife. 'Ah me, my dear,'
He murmurs in their tongue, 'To keep

His sarong up – they thought you said –
The Admiral needs a strong –'
'For shame!' in spotless Mandarin
This well-bred lady cries, 'Oh filthy –
Minded foreign hounds! Oh deep disgrace!
What can they think of Chinese dames,
These British gentlemen? Away!'

(16) Singapore: Politics

Robert Yeo, *'One Year Back Home'*

This 1977 play focuses on the dilemma faced by two friends in opposing political camps.

POLICEMAN I. (*Produces a document from his shirt pocket, opens and reads.*) According to our reports, on the evening of 23 July at a by-election rally in Queenstown, you said that, and I quote, 'Singapore cannot continue to be governed in this way. There has to be a change and change is not always peaceful . . .' On 28 July, at another rally, you said, 'What is Papism but another ism that can be replaced by isms like Marxism, Liberalism . . .' On 1 August at –

FERNANDEZ. Okay, okay, you don't have to go on. I know what I said and I'll answer your questions.

CHYE. Who is in charge here? (*Policeman I turns to face him and recognizes him.*)

POLICEMAN I. Excuse me, are you Mr Ang Siew Chye, the new MP?

CHYE. Yes, I am.

POLICEMAN I. What are you doing in Mr Fernandez's house, Mr Ang?

CHYE. Mr Fernandez and I are friends. We have known each other since student days. If you are taking him away, I'll go off with Mr Fernandez and you both.

POLICEMAN I. Okay, Mr Ang. But I still cannot understand what you're doing here. Excuse me.

CHYE. I will explain to you later. But I know what I am doing.

POLICEMAN I. Okay, Mr Ang. But can we go off now, please?

CHYE. Yes, if Mr Fernandez is ready.

FERNANDEZ. I'm ready. (*Then points to Chye unexpectedly.*) But you're not coming with me, Chye.

CHYE. (*Aghast*) But, Reg, we've just agreed.

FERNANDEZ. I know we did. But I have just changed my mind. I can cope by myself.

CHYE. But, Reg, why?

FERNANDEZ. Being your friend didn't help.

CHYE. But I just told you, Reg.

FERNANDEZ. I know, but I'm not convinced.

CHYE. I told my Party chiefs you were forced to say some of the extreme things in your speeches –

FERNANDEZ. Then why are they here? (*Indicating the policemen*).

CHYE. They are here on their own. It's a security thing. The Party didn't send them here. They are here because of your speeches.

Biographies and literary notes

BOEY, Kim Cheng (1965–). A graduate in English from the National University of Singapore, Boey has published short stories in the local press but is better known for two collections of poetry which reveal a surprisingly mature grasp of the concerns that set the serious writer apart from the dilettante. His first volume, *Somewhere-bound* (1989), exhibits an inwardness and honesty that is quite distinct in Singapore poetry (Extract 4). Some of the poems deal with his experience in the army where he served as a national serviceman while others deal with religion and human relations. His second volume of verse, *Another Place* (1992) is more outward-looking.

CONRAD, Joseph (1857–1924). Born Josef Korzeniowski at Berdiczew in Poland. Conrad worked in the East as a merchant sailor from 1883 to 1888. His books which deal in some way with the Eastern Seas are listed in the Booklist. Conrad spent quite a lot of time in Singapore on and off during these years and the city appears in several of his books, notably *Lord Jim* and *The End of the Tether* (Extract 9), where Singapore harbour is described as having: 'muddy shores, a harbour without quays, the one solitary wooden pier . . . jutting out crookedly'. Although Raffles Hotel claims that Conrad stayed there in 1888, in *Conrad's Eastern Seas* Professor Norman Sherry argues that he probably stayed in the nearby 'Officers Sailors' Home'. However, it seems probable that Conrad would have visited Raffles on one of his trips to Singapore. See Malaysia (Extract 12), Thailand (Extract 9) and map on p 217.

ENRIGHT, D.J. (1920–). Born in Leamington, in 1959 Enright was appointed head of the English department at the University of Malaya in Singapore. Many of the works in his *Collected Poems* (1981) are based on his experiences overseas (Extracts 14 and 15). He is also the editor of *The Oxford Book of Contemporary Verse (1945–80)* (1980). His other works include the novels *Academic Year* (1955) and *Insufficient Poppy* (1960) and the semi-autobiographical *Memoirs of a Mendicent Professor*.

FARRELL, J.G. (1935–1979). British novelist whose works included *The Siege of Krishnapur*, which won the prestigious Booker Prize in 1973.

Singapore Grip is an evocative portrayal of pre-war Singapore with its potent mixture of tawdriness and genteel drinks parties (Extract 10). His other novels include *A Man from Elsewhere* (1963), *The Lung* (1965), *A Girl in the Head* (1967), *Troubles* (1970) and *The Hill Station: An Unfinished Novel and An Indian Diary*, ed J. Spurling (1981).

LEE, Tzu Pheng (1946–). Singaporean by birth, now a Senior Lecturer in the Department of English Language and Literature, National University of Singapore where she has been employed in since 1980. She was educated at Raffles Girls' School and the University of Singapore from which she graduated with first class honours in English Literature. Her first volume of poems, *Prospect of a Drowning* (1980) won the Singapore National Book Development Council Award for Poetry in 1982. Her next collection of poems was *Against the Next Wave* (1988) which showed a consolidation of her poetic powers and returned her to the front rank of Singapore poets. In 1989 she became a Roman Catholic – an event which affected her very deeply. She still shows concerned awareness of the Singapore landscape in poems like 'Singapore River' and 'Bridal Party at the Botanics' (Extract 3). Lee Tzu Pheng was awarded the Singapore Cultural Medallion in 1985 and the Southeast Asian WRITE award in 1993.

LIM, Catherine (1942–). Born in **Penang** but spent a great deal of her childhood in a small Malaysian town called **Kulim**. Catherine Lim had a convent education followed by tertiary education at the University of Malaya where she obtained an Arts degree. She eventually moved to Singapore where she obtained a doctoral degree in 1988. She has worked as a Project Director with the Curriculum Development Institute of Singapore and lectured at the SEAMEO Regional Language Centre. Her collections of short stories are listed in the booklist. In 1982 and 1988 she received Commendation Awards for two of her collections of short stories. Her fiction has been praised for its strong attention to the story line but generally, the characters tend to be drawn simplistically. She is more successful in her comic portraits; her serious portrayals seem to verge on melodrama (Extract 5).

SHELLEY, Rex (1930–). Shelley came to Singapore from Malaysia and set up a company importing engineering equipment. He graduated in engineering from Cambridge University and has been a public figure serving on the Public Services Commission for many years. He was not associated with writing until the publication of the novel *The Shrimp People* (1991) at the age of 61. However, the book was well received, and was described in the *Straits Times* as 'the furthest on the road towards being *the* Singapore novel' (Extract 11). It is a work of tremendous scope, focusing on the small Eurasian community in Singapore through the turbulent 1950s with its racial riots and political unrest to the 1980s and the substantial spate of migration to Australia. His novel impresses with its sense of authentically documenting the Eurasian lifestyle within a multi-racial setting and the author's inventive command of the colloquial Eurasian idiom.

THAM, Claire (1967–). After reading law at Oxford, Tham came to prominence in the Singapore literary scene after winning two prizes in the 1984 National Short Story Writing Competition organized by the Ministry of Community Development. Published a collection of stories entitled *Fascist Rock* in 1990. The collection entitled *Saving the Rain Forest and Other Stories* (1993) reveals more clearly Tham's penchant for incisive social commentary.

THEROUX, Paul (1941–). Born in Massachusetts, Theroux has travelled widely and used his travels to form the backdrop to his fiction and travel writing. He taught at the university in Singapore while Enright ⇨ was head of department. *Saint Jack* (1973) is a vigorous and often amusing story of the underbelly of Singapore. The 'hero', Jack Flowers, is a rootless expatriate who establishes a brothel in Singapore (Extract 13). *The Consul's File* (1977) is a collection of linked short stories, set in a small Malaysian town and containing many of the character types of modern Singapore and Malaysia society (Extract 2 in 'Malaysia'). His other works include *Waldo* (1968), *Girls at Play* (1969), *Jungle Lovers* (1971), *The Black House* (1974), *The Family Arsenal* (1976), *Picture Palace* (1978), *The Old Patagonian Express* (1979) and *The Mosquito Coast* (1981).

THUMBOO, Edwin N. (1933–). Born in Singapore; now Professor at the National University of Singapore, Head of the Department of English Language and Literature. One of the pioneering poets of Singapore literature in English. Has published four volumes of poetry. His first, *Rib of Earth* (1956) was influential as a pioneering collection of lyrical poems from a Singaporean. The collection included nostalgic lyrical pieces on love as well as a lengthy elegiac work on the death of a friend. It was while working as an academic that his next volumes *God Can Die* (1977) and *Ulysses by the Merlion* (1979) appeared. The former showed a different side of Thumboo; no longer the young romantic, he appeared to have turned somewhat cynical with age and experience – questioning the motives of the people around him and perceiving the loss of ideals in Singapore in an era of rapid modernization. To some extent, *Ulysses by the Merlion* seemed like an antidote for the earlier sense of obvious disenchantment. This collection focuses on the poet's optimistic perception of the evolution of a new Singapore – symbolised by the Merlion – where Western and Eastern influences are blended (Extract 8). His fourth volume, *A Third Map: New & Selected Poems*, appeared in 1993. He has also helped the development of a Singapore literature

Wong Yoon Wah

through editing anthologies of Singapore writing (see Booklist). His books of verse won him the National Book Development Council Award for Poetry in 1978 and in 1980; in addition, he received the Southeast Asian WRITE Award in 1979, the Cultural Medallion for Literature in 1980 and the ASEAN Cultural Award in 1987.

YAP, Arthur (1941–). Born in Singapore and educated at St Andrew's School. He continued his education in the University of Singapore which he entered as a State Scholar in 1968. He graduated with an Honours degree in English Literature and became a secondary school teacher before joining the Regional English Language Centre and later the English Language and Literature Department of the National University of Singapore. He was perhaps the first Singaporean to have a collection of verse reviewed favourably in the *Times Literary Supplement*. This review was based on his first published volume entitled *Only Lines* (1971). This was followed by *Commonplace* (1977), *Down the Line* (1980) and *Man Snake Apple & Other Poems* (1986). He received the Cultural Medallion in Singapore for his achievements and the Southeast Asian WRITE Award in Bangkok. He has also made a name for himself as a contemporary Singapore painter (Extract 1).

WONG, Yoon Wah (1941–). Poet and essayist born in Perak, Malaysia, he is now a citizen of Singapore. He uses Mandarin as the medium for writing and is an associate professor in the Chinese Studies Department of the National University of Singapore. Wong has published literary criticism in international and local books as well as journals but is better known as a poet among the Chinese writers. He has several collections of his poetry in Chinese and *Beyond Symbols* (1984) has been translated into English (Extract 12). His work also appears in serveral anthologies. He has also translated European fiction – the best-known of which is Joseph Conrad's *Heart of Darkness*.

Indonesia

E. Ulrich Kratz

> 'The great forest spread over the whole island, reaching from the sandy beaches, where ocean waves generated in the far Antarctic lashed the shore after their long journey, to the high mountain peaks perpetually blanketed in thick clouds. The face of the forest was ever changing'.
> *Mochtar Lubis, Tiger!*

Indonesia, whose approximately 13 000 islands form a 'bracelet of green emeralds' along the equator, is a country of many parts. It has a population of about 180 million people belonging to hundreds of ethnic groups, yet the 60% who are ethnically Javanese live on approximately 5% of the available landmass of Indonesia – the most fertile part of the archipelago – while the other ethnic groups (whose names are often identical with those of the islands they inhabit) are scattered over the rest. In terms of government and authority, there is a tradition of tribal leadership based on either matrilineal or patrilineal kinship as well as highly centralized feudal structures based on the concept of (godlike) absolute rulers, who, not unlike the Chinese 'Son of Heaven', symbolized and ensured the well-being of their countries. In terms of religion, tribal belief systems still stand side by side with Islam, Christianity, Hinduism and Buddhism, as well as those other expressions of faith which try to retain and encompass aspects of some or most of these beliefs in a syncretic fashion. About 90% of Indonesia's population acknowledge Islam as their religion.

Languages

At least 250 different languages and an equal number of dialects are spoken in Indonesia. They are part of the huge Austronesian family of languages, which stretches from Madagascar in the west to the Easter Islands in the east, from beyond the northern coast of Australia in the south to the Philippines in the north.

Modern Indonesia itself has lent its name to the western branch of the Austronesian language family, which extends, roughly speaking, as far as the Moluccas to the East and includes the Philippines, while the Eastern or Oceanic branch derives its name from an area which embraces the whole of the Pacific Ocean. This branch also includes some of the languages of the Eastern Moluccas and those of Irian Jaya, the Indonesian part of New Guinea, whose population, in ethnographic terms anyway, would appear more akin to that of the Pacific than to the Java Sea. Of the western Austronesian or Indonesian languages, Malay, although spoken as a first language by only about 5% of the peoples of the archipelago, has for centuries been the language of diplomacy and commerce, the *lingua franca* of the archipelago, before under the name of Indonesian (*Bahasa Indonesia*) it developed into the national language of the modern republic. Under the name of Malaysian (*Bahasa Malaysia*) Malay also became the national language of Malaysia, and only in Singapore and Brunei Darussalam does it retain its original name.

Religions

In the course of their history, the islands of present-day Indonesia have been exposed to a variety of influences from India, China, the Middle East and 'the West'. Tracing the distribution of world religions throughout the archipelago, certain patterns can be observed.

Christianity as the most recently arrived world religion did not begin to spread seriously until the 19th century, when systematic missionary efforts began in selected parts of the archipelago. Christianity would appear to have developed most strongly among those ethnic groups which for one reason or another had not adopted Islam and which in their culture were remote from the sea and a seafaring way of life. Foremost among these are the Toraja of Central Sulawesi (Celebes), the Batak of North Sumatra who settle around Lake Toba, the Dayak of Kalimantan (Borneo) and most of the ethnic groups from Nusa Tenggara (South-eastern Indonesia).

Although its presence in the archipelago has been documented from the 13th century, Islam spread only gradually and over several centuries from the northern part of Sumatra to most of the other islands. Java is said to have been converted to Islam in about the 16th century and South Sulawesi, whose inhabitants are known today for their religious fervour, did not accept the religion until early in the 17th century. However, there are still ethnic groups, even on Java, which so far have resisted the advances of both Islam and Christianity and have held on to indigenous belief systems which, in the western part of the archipelago, were deeply influenced by Buddhism and Hinduism and elsewhere still show strong autochtonous traits. Hidden Sumatran brick temples and the central Javanese monument of **Borobudur**, the world's largest Buddhist structure, together with the Hindu temple complex of **Prambanan** and many other impressive Hindu-Buddhist monuments and religious sites of central and Eastern Java and of Bali show the strength and sophistication of Hinduism and Buddhism in parts of the islands for many centuries prior to the arrival of Islam.

In contrast to those coming from a westerly direction, Chinese religion and philosophy have made little obvious impact on the people at large. The ancient Chinese temples of **Banten** and **Semarang**, both located on Java's northern coast, provide evidence however of the length of contact between the Chinese and the other inhabitants of the archipelago.

History

Politically and socially, the peoples of Indonesia show a wide range of systems and structures, as is reflected for example by the highly feudal, paternalistic structure of Javanese society, the matrilineal character of Minangkabau society in West Sumatra and the many other tribal systems displaying various kinds of political leadership from headmanship on kinship lines to simple forms of kingship.

Historically, the archipelago has known a succession of large and small kingdoms and empires whose centres of power can always be closely identified with particular ethnic groups and types of economic activity. The notion of the nation state with clearly defined boundaries is a recent concept and the boundaries which the newly emerging republic fought for against the Dutch between 1946 and 1949 and then again, when claiming West Irian, were those of the former Dutch East Indies and not those of any earlier Indonesian empire. By the same token, the Indonesian claim over East Timor (which had been left to the Portuguese by the Dutch in the 17th century) was based on the strategic concept of a global conflict of ideologies rather than on any specific historical link. It is clear however, that the peoples of Eastern Timor are ethnically, linguistically, socially, and even in terms of their Christian faith, closely akin to the peoples of Indonesian Western Timor and to the rest of Nusatenggara Timur or eastern South-east Indonesia.

Little is known about those early empires of the past, some of which we know only by name. In fact the very existence of one of the most important ones, the legendary Srivijaya, was long in doubt. What all seem to have had in common is a lack of clearly defined borders, and it would probably be better to look at them in terms of centres of power eradiating influence which decreased with distance from the centre. Thus when it was claimed that the Javanese empire of Majapahit had controlled a territory as large as that of today's republic this was correct in the sense that Majapahit's economic and perhaps even political links extended as far as present-day West Irian. It would be wrong however to argue that these territories were ruled directly by Majapahit which did not in fact even have total territorial control over the whole of the island of Java. Besides the larger centres of power there were also many smaller centres which operated in similar ways; many of these were connected to each other by marriage and were mutually linked by economic and political interests.

It may help towards a better understanding of those times if we distinguish between different kinds of empire in the archipelago rather than describe individual ones in detail. Basically, there were two types, epitomized by the two empires already mentioned: Srivijaya and Majapahit. Srivijaya, a seaborne empire with far-flung links and an international outlook dominated the archipelago between the 7th and the 13th centuries. The remains of its capital are now said to have been located in **Karanganyar** on the left bank of the river Musi, upstream of present day **Palembang** in **Southern Sumatra**. The Malay trading state *par excellence*, its power and wealth state were based on successful trading brought about by the creation of commercial conditions favourable to the safe conduct of international trade, with the *raja* who later also would call himself *sultan* frequently acting as the chief trader. Its capital base, usually the seat or palace of the ruler, was placed in a commanding position at the estuary of a navigable river which provided exclusive access to the interior.

In contrast to the seaborne Malay empire of Srivijaya is Majapahit, the land-based central Javanese state which dominated much of Western Indonesia between the late 13th and the 16th centuries. This Hindu state had developed a highly hierarchical feudal structure which centred on the (god-) king and, at its core, was tightly controlled. The roots and strength of Majapahit rested in the fertile ricefields of central and eastern Java where the archaeological remains of its former grandeur can still be witnessed. Majapahit boasted many sites many of which are said to have vanished under a rain of lava and a flood of mud from natural disasters. Most prominent of these is probably **Trowulan**, situated only one hour's drive south-west of **Surabaya**. Once the site of the ancient capital of Majapahit, it boasts the remnants of temples, graves and palaces. Examples of its arts which were unearthed in abundance are displayed in a new museum.

Another site worth mentioning here is **Penataran** close to the southern town of **Blitar** where the monumental mausoleum of former President Sukarno can also be found. Penataran is distinguished by the richness and grace of its architecture.

There were other states too. The 15th century Malay city-state of **Melaka (Malacca)** on the west coast of the Malay Peninsula was, until its conquest by the Portuguese in 1511, famed as the richest city in the world. Today Melaka still houses some fine Dutch public buildings of 17th century provenance, some more recent examples of British colonial architecture and the replica of what is thought to have been the palace of the 15th century Malay Sultan of Malacca. At the northern tip of Sumatra, 17th century **Aceh** which liked to see itself as the porch of Mecca and which offered fierce resistance to the Dutch in the second half of the 19th century was another state in the Srivijaya mould, while 16th and 17th century **Mataram** in eastern Java followed the pattern set earlier by Majapahit. The sultans of **Ternate** and **Tidore** together controlled much of 17th century eastern Indonesia, while the Makassarese and Buginese rulers of southern Sulawesi directly and indirectly exerted their influence in the western and central parts of the archipelago in the 18th and 19th centuries. Thus, for example, in West Kalimantan the impressive wooden mosque and palace of the sultans of **Pontianak** which were completed in 1771 remain eloquent witnesses of past grandeur. Brunei's influence was much greater and more far reaching than its present territorial base suggests, spreading along the coastline of Borneo/Kalimantan and into the Philippines and representing a permanent challenge to the authority of the post-Malaccan states of the Malay Peninsula. There were also the Hindu rulers of Bali who remained fiercely independent until their suicidal military and popular resistance against the Dutch in 1905 ended in their total destruction.

Colonial Rule

Indonesian nationalist ideology has it that the country was under colonial rule and oppression for more than 300 years. However, study of its history reveals a different picture. When European trading companies and states made their presence felt after the fall of Malacca in 1511, this did not alter the basic pattern of commerce, alliance and economic pragmatism for quite some time. Initially at least, the Europeans let themselves be merged into the economic and political system they found in operation in the archipelago. This can be seen for example in what is left today of the now remote port of **Banten** on the north coast of the island of Java situated close to the Sunda Straits where the seasonal fleets of junks from China used to call regularly prior to the arrival of the Dutch in 1596; and where Portuguese and British competed for trade until the United Dutch East India Company

(Vereenigde Oostindische Compagnie, VOC) gained a complete monopoly. Today there are still the remnants of a Portuguese fort, an ancient Chinese temple, an intriguing mosque whose unique minaret resembles a lighthouse, VOC buildings and traditional West Javanese huts.

Only after the financial collapse of the privately-owned VOC did the Dutch state take control and possession of the territories formally controlled by the VOC on 1 January 1800. This period is represented best in the architecture of **old Jakarta**, the colonial Batavia which, not to mention a **Portuguese church**, boasts the **old Dutch fort** near today's *Pasar Ikan* or Fish Market, godowns (a word which probably comes from the Malay *gudang* for warehouse), and quarters for the Company's employees and generous administrative offices (see Extract 3 for a view of life in colonial Batavia). Outside Batavia the period is remembered in, for example, the forts of **Ujung Pandang** (Macassar, South Sulawesi) and **Ternate** (Moluccas) both of which have matching indigenous counterparts in the fortifications of South Sulawesi and of Tidore; it can be seen as well in the splendid 'VOC architecture' of the remote island of **Banda** whose own governor's palace was a model for that of the Dutch Governor Generals of a later period in Batavia (now occupied by the President of the Republic of Indonesia). The 1824 Treaty of London adjusted the interests of Britain and the Netherlands in the region. The permanent division of the archipelago split the traditional heartlands of the Malays and gave Britain control over the Malay Peninsula and Singapore, while the whole of the archipelago was left to the Dutch.

While the economically most important parts of the archipelago had fallen under Dutch control one after the other in accordance with the changing needs of the Dutch and European markets of the time – first spices from the Moluccas, later plantation crops mainly from North Sumatra, and later still minerals from central Sulawesi, southern Sumatra, and New Guinea – it should not be forgotten that some parts of the archipelago did not formally come under Dutch rule until the 1920s. Even Bali, as was mentioned above, did not yield to Dutch rule until 1905.

The speedy Dutch surrender to the Japanese in March 1942 and the rule, albeit brief, of the Japanese until August 1945 were of tremendous importance for the further development of the Indonesian nation. The total Japanese victory had shown that the Dutch were not invincible and the harsh nature of the subsequent Japanese rule by force – which furthermore totally rejected all things European without being able to replace them with things Japanese – encouraged the feeling of the common identity of the Indonesian nation. Under Japanese rule Indonesians were given greater responsibilities than they had ever been allowed to enjoy under the Dutch and, since the use of European languages was banned and Japanese was still little known, the potential of Malay as a modern language of education, politics and communication developed to an extraordinary degree. Renamed 'Indonesian' by the nationalists in 1928, Malay became the unchallenged candidate for the status of national language when the country declared its independence on 17 August 1945. After a protracted war against The Netherlands, which seemed to want to continue where it had left off in 1942, Indonesia's independence was finally acknowledged by its former colonial masters in 1950.

Education and Culture

Among all the other fundamental changes revolution and independence brought to Indonesia, mention should be made here of the introduction of a compulsory general, secular, primary education which guarantees each young Indonesian at least a few years of formal education. In colonial days, Western style education was a privilege available only to the children of the small indigenous elite, the *priyayi*, who worked for and under the Dutch. This is not to say that the rest of the population was illiterate, as private religious (ie Islamic and Christian) education was open to those who wanted it. In fact Islamic education has been a feature of Indonesian cultural life for centuries and has always proved an alternative to the elitist nature of court culture which had retained the power of writing and reading in the hands of a few who worked under the patronage of a ruler who, it must be said, was not always able to read himself. Missionary schools played an important part in the Western-style education of the Indonesian elite particularly during this century.

Traditional Malay literature within and outside the courts had basically been an oral and aural literature: recited, listened to and consumed communally. This changed drastically with colonialism which during the 19th century brought about considerable social, economic, political and educational changes. Eventually, these changes led to the end of court culture as a creative power and the development of new forms of individual literary production and consumption outside the traditional courts.

The Arts

Indonesian arts very much reflect the nature of the archipelago as an international meeting-point of long standing and the encounter with a range of cultural traditions which the peoples of the archipelago were able to absorb. As a result we have today tribal arts of considerable sophistication, such as those of the Dayak in **Kalimantan** and the Asmat in **Irian Barat**, best known for their intricate woodcarvings, standing side by side with the monumental arts of the Hindu period most prominently displayed in the temples or shrines (*candi*) of central and East Java, **Candi Borobudur**, **Candi Prambanan**, **Candi Penataran**. Then there are the arts of Bali whichs traditionally exhibit elements of both kinds of art as seen in **Tampaksiring** or in the most sacred of sacred places of the Balinese: the temple complex of **Besakih** on the slopes of Mount Agung. Islamically influenced architecture and decorative arts which have become the most prominent feature of Indonesian arts over the last few centuries in all Islamic regions of Indonesia have not yet been able to find a distinct style of their own. Islam has managed to impose its puritan and censorious mark on existing developments without however contributing much new of its own. This is partly because of the specific nature of the type of Islam which came to the archipelago, which distinguishes itself both by its strong emphasis on strict obedience to the law – according to the Shafi'i school – and by its rejection of anything 'worldly'. Islamically influenced Indonesian art (which among other things is against the portrayal of the human being as being the image of god) for a long time laid great emphasis on the decorative arts. As the Hindu-Buddhist art of Java showed then the Balinese art shows today, the peoples of Indonesia are artistically gifted and creative. The rejection of the arts by Islamic scholars, the *ulama*, however meant that these talents were not developed further in those parts of the archipelago which had turned to Islam; and not even the spirit of an Islamic art as it can be found in say, Persia or Moghul India, was caught by the Indonesian artist. Neither calligraphy nor architecture, let alone painting or sculpture, seem to have found the approval of the *ulama*. It goes without saying that this puritan and austere attitude had its impact on literature as well and it explains the ambivalent attitude shown until today towards any Indonesian literature which is non-didactic and non-religious.

Of the performing arts, it is the shadow-play and the dance arts of the royal courts of Java (and Bali) which remain outstanding. The shadow-play or *wayang* which, interestingly, is said to have been brought to Java by one of the saints who introduced Islam to the island, thus explaining its survival in a changed world, bases its stories, just as court dance does, on the Indian epics the *Ramayana* and *Mahabharata*. The fascination *wayang* still exerts over modern Indonesians from Java can be seen by the fact that Satyagraha Hurip ◊, a contemporary writer and journalist, has adapted one of stories of the Mahabharata, the story of the warrior priest Bisma, for modern readers (Extract 10).

Regional Languages and Literatures

Indonesian literature of today, just like the Indonesian language, is a product of these developments yet, quite apart from any European influences, its literary origins cannot be linked to any single indigenous tradition. There were and still are several regional literatures, sacred and profane, ie literatures written in the various regional languages, such as Javanese, Balinese, Buginese, Sundanese, Acehnese, Batak, Malay and Minangkabau, which can look back on a long oral and written tradition and which exert some influence on the shape and nature of Indonesian language and literature. Of those, Malay is the most important for two reasons. Historically, Malay was the language of communication throughout the archipelago, the language through which Islam spread, and in the present century it was Malay on which Indonesian was built most immediately. Broadly speaking, the 'Malay element' in the work of a modern writer will be stronger if he comes from the Malay speaking areas of Sumatra or the Malay Peninsula than in the case of a writer whose mother tongue is not Malay, but some other Indonesian language.

Traditional Malay Language and Literature

It must be emphasized that the philological and literary study of Malay texts as well as that of other Indonesian literatures of the same kind has only just begun, and that much of our knowledge is still preliminary. We do not yet have a satisfactory conceptual framework which allows us to look at these non-Western literatures in other terms than those of the Western tradition.

Traditional Malay literature as it is known to us stretches over a period of approximately 500 years. It came to a close by the end of the 19th century despite internal changes and major efforts to adjust to the times. Generally speaking, traditional Malay literature was a court literature. Inherent in Malay literature were didactic qualities which manifest themselves in even the most entertaining texts and which are quite obvious in a text like the *Hikayat Hang Tuah* which sets a model of behaviour to Malay subjects in a narrative form (Extract 8) – see also Extract 9 in Malaysia.

Traditional Malay literature is a literature of manuscripts. Some of the texts found in those manuscripts have come to us in scores of copies, various traditions and different versions, others have survived in single unique manuscripts only. The manuscripts we know date from the 16th to the early 20th century and cover a wide range of subjects from theological treatises, legal digests and texts of a historical nature to religious fiction, popular mythology and folklore. The texts are written in poetry and prose.

The oldest manuscripts in existence today are those which were brought to Europe at a very early time. There exist hardly any 16th or 17th century Malay manuscripts in South-east Asia itself although the **National Library** in **Jakarta** which has the only public collection of any importance in Indonesia, and the **National Archives** and the **National Manuscript Centre** of **Malaysia** own some fairly old manuscripts. In Europe, the Library of the **University of Leiden**, Netherlands, The **Bibliothéque Nationale** in Paris, and the (former) **Royal Libraries of Berlin** and of **Copenhagen** hold important collections of manuscripts. In the UK the **British Library** (with the India Office Library), the Library of the **Royal Asiatic Society**, and the Library of the **School of Oriental and African Studies** must be mentioned together with the **Bodleian** in Oxford and the **John Rylands Library** in Manchester.

The majority of the manuscripts found today are 19th century copies from one particular area, **Riau**. This, unfortunately, has led to a strong emphasis on the importance of this particular area as a centre of Malay culture and literature to the disadvantage of other areas, such as Aceh, the Malay Peninsula, West and Southwest Kalimantan, Palembang (and perhaps even Java); areas which must have had active literatures too, but from which only a few Malay manuscripts have survived the trials of time and climate. It can be said without exaggeration that the existence and survival of certain texts, most of which are copies of copies of copies, are to be regarded as coincidental and fortuitous rather than by design.

As far as Malay philology and our knowledge of Malay literature in general are concerned, probably the greatest single known catastrophe which befell Malay manuscripts since the destruction of the palace of Malacca in 1511 was the fire in 1824 on the ship *Fame* on which Sir Stamford Raffles, the founder of Singapore, had commenced his return to Europe and which caught fire and sank off Bencoolen in West Sumatra. Raffles, his wife and the crew were rescued, but the fire destroyed all the hundreds of manuscripts, which according to the autobiography of Abdullah, Raffles's teacher and servant, had been collected on Raffles's instructions all over the Malay world during the period of his residence. Raffles's collection might well have included many 'unique' copies.

Today, 'new' old manuscripts are still to be found, both within and outside the Malay world. So far only about 30 texts out of the estimated 1 000 texts in existence (as opposed to manuscripts of which there are many more) have been studied in detail, and most of our manuscript catalogues, many of which were published nearly a century ago, are still rather tentative.

History

We know from inscriptions that a courtly language which can be called Old Malay existed in the 7th century, but epigraphic material in general is scarce. The so-called Trengganu inscription, named after the region on the Malay peninsula where it was found, and dating from the 4th century, is another important document for establishing the history of Malay. The Trengganu inscription is written in a language very similar to the Malay of the manuscripts and, just like the later manuscripts, uses *Jawi*, ie the Arabic script to which five letters which are specific to Malay have been added. It is generally assumed that a written literature existed during the times of the famous 15th century court of Malacca, yet our earliest existing manuscripts date from the 16th century. At that time Islam was firmly embedded in the Malay world and it has been argued that a written literature was only introduced by and with Islam. Still, from some of the surviving texts we gain the impression that their reference to and reverence for Islam are superimposed and that these texts actually have a tradition going back to pre-Islamic times and relating to a period of closer contact with Hinduism and Buddhism. Others argue that the protagonists of the new faith furthered the destruction of an earlier 'heathen' literature. This suspicion is strengthened by the evidence of some of the earliest 'Islamic' texts which call for the destruction of certain other texts and recommend their use as toilet paper. On the basis of our present knowledge it is impossible to come to a decisive answer on this sensitive issue.

Genres of Traditional Malay Literature

Generally speaking Malay literature falls into several categories which are distinguished either thematically or by literary genre. The most prominent literary genres are *hikayat* ◊ and *syair* ◊ which respectively represent prose and poetry.

Prose. Thematically a distinction is made between *kitab* (Arabic for book) ◊, ie religious or theological books, *adab* ◊ (Arabic for culture, civilisation), ie mirrors of conduct and books of moral value extolling the virtues of a proper life, and *undang-undang* (Malay for laws) ◊ or legal codes, while historical texts and all 'prose-fiction' fall under the genre label of *hikayat* ◊.

Poetry. Several poetic forms originating from Indian metres are known in traditional Malay, yet these forms are only of minor importance compared to the indigenous *pantun* ◊ and the *syair* ◊ which regard final rhyme, internal rhyme, alliteration, consonance, and assonance as their most prominent stylistic features.

The 19th Century

The 19th century saw a major change in Malay literature and the emergence of a different kind of literature. This change was as much in form as in content, and while in certain centres, as for example, the island **Penyengat** in the **Riau Archipelago**, men and women were copying manuscripts for European buyers, none of these texts found their way to Singapore, where lithograph printing had led to the blossoming of a different kind of literature. This new kind of literature was more topical and journalistic and was aimed at the very large number of people outside the court circles who due to their religious education, the only education available to the average Malay at that time, were able to read *Jawi* and were interested in all kinds of news and literary entertainment. This 'popular' literature was traditional in form yet contemporary in content. It was associated with the introduction of the printing press and the lithograph, both of which took surprisingly little notice of courtly literature. In contrast to traditional literature, popular literature is still flourishing today and it is no exaggeration to claim a direct link between its 19th century version and more modern forms.

Beginnings of Contemporary Literature

Different dates have been suggested to mark the origin of Indonesian literature. In chronological order they are: the early 19th century and the work of Abdullah Munsyi ◊, the author of the *Hikayat Abdullah*; the early years of the 20th century and the work of a socialist Javanese journalist, Mas Marco Kartodikromo ◊, who indulged in a kind of literary social criticism which is perhaps better seen in the context of 'popular' literature; 1921, when Balai Pustaka, the government publishing house published its first Malay novel; 1928 and the *Sumpah Pemuda* (*The Pledge of the Youth*) which gave official birth to the term *Bahasa Indonesia* – the Indonesian language; 1933 and the founding of the first purely literary journal, *Poedjangga Baroe* (*The New Poet*); 1942 and the Dutch defeat by the Japanese; and finally 1945, the year when the Republic of Indonesia declared its independence. It is probably more useful, rather than looking at any particular date or event, to concentrate on specific literary manifestations such as 'popular' or trivial literature and the *belles lettres* of the Dutch educated middle class elite.

Beginning with the sonnets of the 1920s and 1930s, from there to free rhyme and rhythmical prose, and on to what is called the concrete poetry of the late 1970s, poetry has been the most popular literary genre. Traditional forms are used less frequently, although it has to be said that some of the most accomplished examples of Indonesian poetry stylistically echo the *pantun* and *syair*. While the novel has experienced periods of varying popularity, at times it was greatly overshadowed by the short story, which itself saw a continuous development from its origins in the anecdotal stories of the 1920s to the surrealistic and absurd stories of present times. Both novel and short story are frequently marked by a semi-autobiographical realism. The first Indonesian drama was published in the 1920s; however its development was, and is, impeded by the fact that in general Indonesian plays are rarely published.

Though originally greatly indebted to foreign (Western) models, movements and trends, more recently writers have become increasingly aware of their own traditional and regional roots without, however, leading Indonesian literature back into provincial isolation.

Indonesian Literature Before Independence

Balai Pustaka – the Hall of Letters – was the name of the government publishing house set up in 1917 to produce good literature for the masses and to act as a counterweight to the popular literature and the so-called *bacaan liar* (unregulated reading) linked to the nationalist movement which threatened to 'contaminate' the reading public. Balai Pustaka was best known for its novels, the most famous of which were written by authors originating from Minangkabau in West Sumatra. Sentimental in nature, these still highly popular novels are best known for their themes such as forced marriage and individual choice of spouse.

The poetry of Balai Pustaka, although thematically in line with the new form of the novel or *roman* as it was called then, still retained the *syair* form, while away from Balai Pustaka the quest for new forms of poetic expression already had begun. Free verse and lyrical prose soon were to show themselves but the most expressive and accomplished achievements were the experiments of young poets with the sonnet form. This form has a more than superficial link with the traditional Malay *pantun* ◊ in that the sonnet too consists of two parts, comparable to *sampiran* and *isi* of the pantun, and that the final part is said to clinch the thought. A famous Italian or Petrarchan sonnet by Sanoesi Pane ◊ which was first published in 1927 makes this clear. This poem which is simply entitled *Sajak* (*Poem*) and despite its references to traditional rhyming schemes is thoroughly modern in content, rejecting all that is traditional (Extract 22).

It has been said, not without reason, that the people who wrote poetry of this kind were part of the Western educated intellectual elite and had been strongly influenced by Dutch literature and in particular by the Movement of the 1880s. It would be wrong however to think of the Indonesian literature of the 1920s and 1930s as a mere copy of Dutch literature of some 40 years earlier. As the relationship between the sonnet and the *pantun* ◊ shows, there are valid literary reasons from within Indonesian poetics to explain the Indonesian interest in the sonnet which earlier had found the favour of the Dutch Movement of the 1880s. Both movements fought against cherished conventions and saw themselves as fighters against rigid and fossilized poetic norms and forms which had stifled the creativity of the individual in their countries. Thus, far from seeing the one as a carbon copy of the other, they both might be seen as different facets of the ultimately global modernist movement which had its origins in late 19th century Europe; a movement which reflected the artists' attempt to come to terms with

Soetan Takdir Alisjahbana

their own experience of the universal social, political and economic upheavals of those times.

In due course the efforts of these intellectuals led in 1933 to the establishment of an independent literary periodical *Pujangga Baru* (*The New Poet*) which was to give its name to the period leading up to the end of Dutch rule. *Poedjangga Baroe*, as it was spelt then, never had many subscribers, a figure of 150 is usually mentioned, yet its influence was considerable. Its three founders were Soetan Takdir Alisjahbana (1908–) ◊, Armijn Pane (1908–1970) ◊, the younger brother of Sanusi, and Amir Hamzah (1911–1946) ◊ who each in his own way contributed significantly to the development of the new literature.

Soetan Takdir Alisjahbana remains until today the tireless champion for a total renewal of Indonesian cultural values on Western lines. His model is the Renaissance and he argues that only by following the path taken by Europe to come out of its own Dark Ages, will Indonesia be able to take its rightful place among the peoples of the world. After all, the attitude and philosophy of her own peoples had been unable to repel colonial rule.

While agreeing with the aims of Soetan Takdir Alisjahbana's campaign, writers such as Sanoesi Pane, who had visited India in the 1920s, did not favour his radical and relentless approach. They argued that only the contemplative attitude of the East could lead to a harmonious solution and that ultimately only a merging of the figures of Faust, who would sell his soul to the devil in the pursuit of knowledge, and of Arjuna, the one-time warrior who sought enlightenment through meditation, would provide the answer. Soetan Takdir Alisjahbana's reply to this question was why, if the Eastern approach was so much superior to that of the West, was it that Indonesia had been colonized by such a small country as Holland.

These cultural polemics, waged through fiction and critical essays by the adherents of both views and started more than 50 years ago, are still as lively today as they were then, while the issue itself has remained undecided. Not even the Japanese interregnum from 1942 to 1945 assisted a solution since the alleged meditative calm of Eastern philosophy clashed manifestly with the brashness of Japanese imperialism and its ideological terror.

A distinction now began to be made between so-called belles lettres, *susastra*, the 'real', high-brow literature, and the allegedly low-brow literature of the non-literary journals. It was argued that *susastra* used proper standard written Indonesian and was artistic and creative and original whereas that other literature lacked any of these features. However, it is a fact that despite many protestations to the contrary the same writers wrote for and published in both types of publications.

Not much was published or written during the Japanese period and under its strict censorship rules, and most of what was published bore the mark of Japanese propaganda. This is not to say that there was no other writing, but very little managed to pass the censor's desk. One poem that did escape, at least the first time around, was 'Diponegoro' by Chairil Anwar ◊, first published in a newspaper in 1943 (Extract 27). This poem in praise of a 19th century Javanese prince who, according to nationalist propaganda had challenged Dutch rule, was originally taken as a rallying call in support of the goals of the Japanese. When, after closer reading the possibility of its interpretation as a rallying call for Indonesian independence was seen, its intended re-publication was immediately stopped.

With the onset of the revolution and its liberal attitude to writing it was as if the floodgates had been opened. Only in 1961 was censorship to be reintroduced by Sukarno (it has still not been lifted) and a noticeable change in the volume and nature of publishing could be observed from there on.

Indonesian Literature After Independence

The writers of the period beginning with the declaration of independence on 17 August 1945 are often referred to as *Angkatan 45* (The Generation of 45) or even as *Angkatan Revolusi* (The Generation of the Revolution). From a historical and literary point of view the difference between the pre-war writers and the Generation of 45 is not as large as it was perceived to be at the time and a poem by Soetan Takdir Alisjahbana, *Menuju ke laut* (*To Sea, the New Generation*) bridges the gap to the time after independence well (Extract 11).

This spirit of awakening, of breaking away from all human and social order and the total belief in one's own self was expressed most drastically by Chairil Anwar who is still considered Indonesia's most famous poet. But it is not only his total rejection of all social norms which explains Chairil Anwar's notoriety. He was also most radical and successful in his use of the new colloquial Indonesian, not shying away from bending the rules and inventing new ones as they fitted his poetry. The poem *Semangat* (*Spirit*) which is also known under the title *Aku* (*I*) by Chairil Anwar is probably the poem known best by many Indonesians, partly perhaps for the reason that the spirit expressed is still considered outrageously alien to most of them. Not surprisingly this poem was not published until after the Japanese occupation (Extract 9).

The period of the Revolution with all its suffering and trauma was also the period of the introduction of what is generally called new realism into Indonesian prose writing, most closely associated with the name of Idrus. His impassioned sketches of the revolutionary struggle,

Pramoedya Ananta Toer

collected under the title *Surabaya* (1948), brought him the name of a traitor as he refused to apportion blame in a one-sided manner and dared to highlight some of the discrepancies between the fiction and fact of nationalist propaganda (Extract 26).

The flourishing of the new realism did not mean however the end of other kinds of literature; *Atheis* (*Atheist*, 1949) by Achdiat Karta Mihardja ◊ is a novel of ideas and the novel *Jalan tak ada ujung* (*Road with No End*, 1952) by Mochtar Lubis ◊ could not be imagined without the presence of French existentialist thought (Extract 3). It was in the late 1940s and early 1950s that Pramoedya Ananta Toer ◊ first published his short stories and novels which are all set in Java and which made him the unchallenged master – to this day – of Indonesian realist prose writing. Pramoedya Ananta Toer is a narrator par excellence whose early stories depict the suffering of the times and the inherent injustices of the feudal, social order of the Javanese to whom he belongs. Unlike many of his contemporaries, he succeeds in transcending matters of merely autobiographical interest to expressions of universal human relevance and concern. *Cerita Dari Blora* (*Stories from Blora*, 1952); his home town in **East Java,** *Keluarga Gerilya* (*The Guerilla Family*, 1950), *Bukan Pasar Malam* (*Not a Night Fair*, 1951) are works which remain an essential part of Indonesian literature and its history despite the continued ban on their publication and circulation first issued in 1965 by the New Order Government. Since the late 1950s Pramoedya Ananta Toer's work has found a more thematic focus and the late colonial period of late 19th and early 20th centuries has become his particular interest. The fictional biography (Extract 7) of his mother, *Gadis pantai* (*The Girl from the Coast*, 1962) and more recently his novel based on the life of the journalist R.M. Tirto Adhi Soerjo (1880–1918) who was active in the nationalist movement give further evidence of his skills and interests. This novel consists of four volumes *Bumi Manusia* (*This Earth of Mankind*, 1980), *Anak semua bangsa* (*A Child of All Nations*, 1980), *Jejak langkah* (*Footsteps*, 1985), and *Rumah kaca* (*Glasshouse*, 1988) which easily make them the largest work in Indonesian deserving literary recognition. Pramoedya Anata Toer however was not alone in his activities, and in many ways the first decade of independence can be seen as one of the most fruitful periods of Indonesian literature.

The mood of those times is said to have been captured best by the poet Sitor Situmorang ◊, whose treatment of the prodigal son, *Si Anak Hilang* (*The Lost Child*, 1953), a theme he was to work on twice again over the years, treating it differently each time, has come to be considered most representative of this particular attitude (Extract 16). Like Amir Hamzah and Chairil Anwar in their most successful poetry before him, he employs a 'pantunesque' style.

In 1950 the literary organization *Gelanggang* (Arena) published its literary creed, the *Surat Kepercayaan 'Gelanggang Seniman – Merdeka' Indonesia* (*The Testimony of the Arena of Free Artists of Indonesia*). Beginning 'We are the rightful heirs of world culture and we perpetuate this culture in our own way', no other document describes more clearly and succinctly the concerns of the liberal, humanist writers of those days.

The relationship between theologians, the *ulama*, and modern writers has had not always been an easy one since it has been hard to persuade Islamic scholars of the intrinsic merits of non-theological literature and of fiction. Some young *ulama* had first attempted to join in the literature heralded by Balai Pustaka and Pujangga Baru in the early 1930s, among them Haji Abdul Malik Karim Abdullah (1908–81) who is better known by his initials, Hamka ◊. Hamka, who later in life became Chairman of the Indonesian Council of Ulama, was at first accused by fellow Muslims of pornography when turning his hand to poetry and fiction. A major issue of concern to the more traditional *ulama* was that of the role and function of literature but it seems accepted today that literature has a part to play in any Islamic culture, provided it is used for *dakwah*, that is as a means of religious propagation. Poetry and prose with a religious spirit, some of it showing a mystical inclination, plays an ever increasing part in the national literary life. Poets such as Abdul Hadi WM ◊, Emha Ainun Nadjib ◊, Syahril Latif and Taufiq Ismail come immediately to mind. In prose, the short story rather more than the novel is important to writers with a stronger religious background such as Danarto ◊, Djamil Suherman ◊, Muhammad Ali, Muhammad Diponegoro who also distinguished himself as a poetic translator of the Quran, and Muhammad Fudoli to name but a few. Among 'Christian' writers, religion has been less of an issue in their literary work.

1965 to the Present

In late September and early October 1965 several army generals were abducted by rebel troops whose political loyalties and motives were never fully established, only to be murdered brutally with the participation of Communist activists. These events led to the end of the rule of Sukarno and the beginning of the so-called New Order regime of President Suharto which has remained violently opposed to the political left. The traumatic birth of the New Order brought with it fratricide on a catastrophic scale as different ethnic, social and ideological groups took the opportunity to settle old scores in a violent manner. The upheaval led to a complete change of the political landscape and the trauma of those days still overshadows today's political, social and intellectual life. On the literary side this meant that works of writers considered to have belonged to the political left were banned; even if they were written at a time when all writers saw themselves united in the struggle for a new and better Indonesia during the revolution and into the early 1950s. Furthermore, many of these writers were imprisoned, some of them for up to 13 years without proper legal proceedings, and they still find it difficult to publish new work or to find employment commensurate with their expertise and knowledge. Others live or have died in exile. Irrespective of their political views, the work of writers such as Pramoedya Ananta Toer ◊, Rivai Apin (a friend of Chairil Anwar), or of S. Rukiah ◊ (one of the Indonesia's few outstanding female writers), and Utuy Tatang Sontani ◊ (Indonesia's most distinguished playwright of the period) forms an integral part of Indonesian literary history without which its present shape cannot be imagined.

One of the constant accusations made against the New Order is that continued government censorship and, even worse, government imposed self-censorship of artists and publishers gradually stifled free expression again, and slowly strangled any overt expressions of the critical spirit found in Indonesian literature. In short, the self-imposed task of the Indonesian writer to educate his or her readers and to voice social and human concern is being made extremely difficult. This is quite apparent for example in the case of Rendra, an outspoken poet, a playwright, director and gifted actor who has played a part in Indonesian cultural life for the last 40 years. The charismatic Rendra, whose social commitment and political wit are famous, found it difficult at times to have his work published, he saw performances he directed banned, and even found himself in prison for several months during the late 1970s.

This is not to say however that little happened in a literary sense. In fact, the 1970s saw a process coming to fruition which will probably be more significant for the future shape of Indonesian literature than any earlier proclamations of generations and movements. The increasing regionalization of Indonesian literature may well indicate the beginning of a second major period in Indonesian literature. As a result of this regionalization, Indonesian literature began gradually to lose its uniform look, both linguistically and thematically.

One could argue that in the regionalization of literature in the 1970s, Indonesian writers followed a global trend which set greater store by the ethnic roots and local origins of a writer rather than in conforming to any pre-established aesthetic norms and perceived standards of proper use of language, imagery and expression. It must not be forgotten, however, that in the Indonesia of the 1970s politically too the situation was more favourable to any expression of regional pride and identity than it had ever been before; the relative peace under the New Order and the stability enjoyed by the government allowed a greater expression of regional identity than before while, at the same time, deflecting some attention from the fact that central power was falling increasingly under Javanese control. Ahmad Tohari ◊, Aspar, Gerson Poyk ◊, Korrie Layun Rampan, Linus Suryadi AGN, Umar Kayam ◊, Wildan Yatim are among the authors who consciously and successfully have made an Indonesian regional setting the focus of their prose fiction. Mention must be made too of those writers part of whose work is semi-autobiographical and gains some of its strength from its use of a clearly defined regional and local background. Here mention must go not just to Pramoedya Ananta Toer but also to other highly accomplished but internationally less well known authors such as the Sundanese Ajip Rosidi ◊ and the Central Javanese Nh. Dini ◊ whose memories of her childhood stand out particularly. The increase in the number of historical novels is another example of this aspect of Indonesian literature. Historical novels cover many aspects of Indonesian history from pre-colonial days, the first encounters with Europeans, colonialism, revolution and independence, to the traumas of contemporary history. Of the more recent writers mention again must go to Ajip Rosidi and Pramoedya Ananta Toer, to Yudhistira Ardhi Noegraha and to the prolific writer Y.B. Mangunwijaya ◊ a Roman Catholic priest and trained architect, whose novel *Burung-burung Manyar* (*The Weaverbirds*) caused considerable controversy, for its hero fought on the side of the Dutch during the revolution (Extract 28). Another important development was the growing importance of the so-called *sastra pop* or popular literature which, though scorned by some as trivial and kitsch, at its best defies this easy classification with its thematic and linguistic originality.

In poetry too there has been a movement towards a stronger emphasis on the indigenous element of the Indonesian language and literature. Although it is undeniable that much of the poetry considered good today displays many of the best features and linguistic devices innate to Indonesian languages, since the 1970s there has been a conscious effort to recall traditional, regional poetic forms. Sutardji Calzoum Bachri ◊ became a champion of the Malay *mantra*, and others such as Linus Suryadi AGN experimented with Javanese forms. Despite this assertion of self-confidence, however, it cannot be denied that Indonesian writers remain torn between two different worlds, the highly individualistic and frequently inhuman world of modern man and the pastoral idyll of the blue skies and blue seas of home.

Western Writing

Although writers such as Conrad and Maugham tended to ignore the artificiality of colonial boundaries, the then Dutch East Indies and present day Indonesia have never really stirred the imagination of writers of English, unlike Malay(si)a, let alone India and other parts of the former Empire. There never seems to have been more than a fleeting interest in the archipelago. Notwithstanding the (ill-fated) British interest in the **Spice Islands** in the 18th century which, in the

Y.B. Mangunwijaya

end, led to the exchange of a remote British island in the Banda Sea called Run for the Dutch island of Manhattan; despite the British West Sumatran Residency towards the end of the same century and despite the British Interregnum over the whole of the archipelago during the Napoleonic wars in Europe at the beginning of the 19th century, we are left with little literary evidence of these days in English. The early travelogues published by the venerable Haklyut Society refer to the Archipelago literally only in passing and we must turn to the translations of Dutch works, some of which have already been referred to.

The exception to the rule are the works of two outstanding 19th century administrators cum scholars, William Marsden and Sir Stamford Raffles who compiled, presumably with the assistance of local research assistants, full histories and descriptions of the islands of Sumatra (Marsden in 1811) and Java (Raffles in 1844). These works are still a pleasure to read today not least for their comprehensive nature. Marsden also compiled a Malay Dictionary and a Grammar and

Raffles, who distinguished himself as the founder of Singapore (not to mention his part in the foundation of London Zoo), is famous not just for the hotel named after him, but also as the man who gave his name to one of the world's rarest, largest, strangest and most oddly smelling plants (Rafflesia, R. Br.) which, in Indonesia, can be found only in **West Sumatra**. Its flowering is celebrated as a special event in the tourist calendar. In this same period as the works of Marsden and Raffles fall Thomas Horsfield's *Zoological Researchers in Java, and the Neighbouring Islands (1824)*.

The 1824 Treaty of London drew a clear demarcation line between British and Dutch interests in South-east Asia, leaving Singapore with the British and adding Malacca to the British Empire without further argument, while all of the archipelago was handed to the Dutch, with the exception of the backwater of Portuguese East Timor, which remained unaffected by all these goings on between the European powers of the day.

In the second half of the 19th century and quite in line with the general public interest of the era in a scientific conquest of the world combined with unprecedented ease of travel, we soon witness the publication of a number of travelogues in English by men and women alike. These are however small in number if we compare them with the large number of travel books about the Indies published in other European languages at that time. Foremost among these books ranks of course the work of Alfred Russel Wallace (Extract 17). Quite apart from the unacknowledged moral and academic debt Darwin seems to owe to Wallace for his contribution to the formulation of the theory of evolution, the general reader has to thank him for a splendid description of the fauna of *The Malay Archipelago* (1869), his classic book which also provides the first definition of the boundary line between Eurasian and Australian flora and fauna. Although revised repeatedly since, this boundary which runs through the Archipelago roughly from the northern tip of **Sulawesi** down to the islands of **Bali** and **Lombok** is still known by the name of its initial discoverer and analyst as the Wallace line. The *Rambles in Java and the Straits in 1852* (1853) by a 'Bengal Civilian', has a certain Empire flair while Albert S. Bickmore's *Travels in the East Indian Archipelago* (1869, Extract 18) which came out simultaneously with Wallace's book and E.R. Scidmore's description of *Java: The Garden of the East* (1899, Extract 21) offer a distinct American perspective in their appreciation of what their authors saw and experienced. Sydney J. Hickson, another scientist, tried desperately, as he confesses himself, to find a corner of the Archipelago not looked into by either Wallace or Bickmore. His travels were published under the title *A Naturalist in North Celebes* (1889). Anna Forbes, who had followed her husband, described the Spice Islands in *Insulinde.*

Experiences of a Naturalist's Wife in the Eastern Archipelago (1887, Extract 2).

A prominent feature of these books is of course the scholarly pretensions of their authors and it is interesting to trace how this learnedness permeates other travel writing right into the present. Mention could be made here for example of the little known book by Miss M. McMillan who had followed her brother and her sister-in-law on *A Journey to Java* (1914, Extract 5) travelling across the island from **Surabaya** in the East to **Batavia** in the West shortly before the First World War.

Only in the course of this century has Indonesia provided the background for or been the focus of some fictional writing. Still, a considerable part of 20th century writing in English on Indonesia, be it fiction or non-fiction, is autobiographical. In most cases it reflects its authors' individual response to an alien world to which previously they had little direct access, literary or otherwise. The 1930s in particular saw the publication of books, most of which are still available as reprints, which were probably triggered off by this century's first wave of mass tourism to the tropics which had been made possible by fast and huge ocean-liners. To the writers of those days, this of course spelt imminent doom for the peoples and cultures thus invaded. Reading their accounts today, in the age of mass tourism, it is all the more interesting to compare then and now, and to view with admiration the resilience of the peoples visited and their positive response to the challenges of the times. Violet Clifton sailed through the *Islands of Queen Wilhelmina* – now republished as *Islands of Indonesia* (1927). Hickman Powell of the USA found *The Last Paradise* (1930) in the five years he lived in Bali and G.E.P. Collins expressed his loves in two books on *Makassar Sailing* (1937) and *Twin Flower: A Story of Bali* (1934).

Looking for 20th century classics in English with an exclusive focus on Indonesia we have to turn to *The Island of Bali* by the Mexican artist Miguel Covarrubias and the historical novel by the German romancier Vicki Baum, *A Tale from Bali*. Both works were published in 1937 and reflect the highly intensive and personal encounters of these two artists with the world of **Bali** to which they had been introduced by a circle of permanently resident European artists who created a romantic image of Bali at which foreigners and Indonesians alike still would seem to worship. The musician Colin McPhee who also belonged to this circle, first published his own memoirs of *A House in Bali* in 1947 (Extract 1). The classic description of *Dance and Drama in Bali* (1938) was written by the group's two most prominent members, Beryl de Zoete and Walter Spies.

Well known in its day, *Tropic fever: The Adventures of a Planter in*

Sumatra by Ladislao Székely (1937) is one of the few books of that period not concerned with Bali. *Rubber* (1933, Extract 24) and *Coolie* (1936), two plantation novels originally written in Dutch by Madelon H. Lulofs were also extremely popular.

There has been very little autobiographical writing covering the period after the war. Given their literary nature and particular background, Laurens van der Post's ◊ semi-fictional stories published in 1963, *The Seed and the Sower* (which were filmed as *Merry Christmas Mr Lawrence*) as well as the highly personal and philosophical references to West Java in *The Night of the New Moon* (1970, Extract 20) hold a special place here. Van der Post had been captured behind Japanese lines and was held as a prisoner of war in a camp near **Bandung**. He relates the circumstances of his imprisonment, his inner attitude towards the Japan of the Second World War and some of his activities as a British intelligence officer in Indonesia after the Japanese surrender. But his is the exception and most works continue in the mould of the scientific/ethnographic travelogue.

After demobilization, H. Wilcox found his very own spiritual sanctuary during *Six Moons in Sulawesi*. This book was published originally in 1949 under the title *White Stranger: Six Months in Celebes*, whence he tried to find his inner peace again under the benevolent protection of the recently returned Dutch Resident and in the rural tranquillity of life among the Toraja in a place yet untouched by the nationalist struggle for independence.

By nature totally different are the impressions of the British couple who taught English in Yogyakarta in the early 1950s. *Flowering Lotus: A View of Java in the 1950s* by Harold Forster was published in 1958 at a time when, for various political reasons, it became increasingly difficult again for foreigners to travel, let alone settle in Indonesia. It provides the reader with historical, sociological and political observations and views of Java shortly after the full recognition of Indonesia's independence by the Dutch. More recently, the country had a visitation by V.S. Naipaul. However, *Among the Believers* (1981) tells us more about its author's attitude towards the country and the people he met rather briefly than about the peoples and cultures themselves.

Novels based in Indonesia include Eric Ambler's enigmatic *The Night-comers* (1956) and *The Year of Living Dangerously* (1978) by the New Zealander Christopher J. Koch which was made into a successful film. The title was taken of course from the oratory of the late President Sukarno, who had proclaimed 1964 as *tavip* or *tahun vivere pericoloso* ie 'the year of living dangerously' at his annual Independence Day Speech to a fully comprehending nation. Derwent May's *The Laughter in Jakarta* (1963) is set against that same historical background which, in 1965, saw a tremendous political upheaval with the banning of the Communist Party, the slaughter of innumerable people most of whom one must presume were innocent of the crimes they may have been accused of, and the birth of the present New Order Government under then General Suharto. This is the background to the more recent novel *Monkeys in the Dark* (1980) by the Australian Blanche d'Alpuget which is set in the Jakarta of the late 1960s.

Most recently, the distinguished British travel writer Norman Lewis has published an account of his travels in Sumatra, East Timor and Irian Jaya (*An Empire of the East: Travels in Indonesia*, 1993). While containing many acute descriptions of Indonesian life, Lewis's account is also highly critical of some current Indonesian government policies, among them the controversial transmigration policy, involving the transplanting of Javanese to less crowded regions of the archipelago.

This section cannot conclude without reference to the letters of Raden Adjeng Kartini, the Javanese aristocrat who died in childbirth leaving behind a collection of letters written in Dutch to Dutch friends at the turn of the century and published soon after with an English translation following in due course (1921, Extract 6). In these letters she tried to describe what it meant to be Javanese and above all a Javanese woman fighting for women's education and emancipation at a time when even in other 'more developed' parts of the world these ideals still looked healthier on paper than they were in actual life.

BOOKLIST

What follows is intended as a representative rather than comprehensive list of books about Indonesia. Where several editions exist, in general the latest and most readily available edition has been listed. For most of the extracted works, information on the original English language publisher can be found in the 'Acknowledgements and Citations' section at the end of the volume, as can the exact location of the extracts and the editions from which they are taken. Extract numbers are highlighted in bold.

Abdullah bin Abdul Kadir Munsyi (A.H. Hill, trans), *The Hikayat Abdullah*, OUP, Singapore, 1985.

Achdiat K. Mihardja (R.J. Maguire, trans), *Atheis*, University of Queensland Press, St Lucia, Queensland, 1972.

Amal Hamzah, 'Spyglass', in J. Echols, ed, *Indonesian Writing in Translation*, Cornell, Ithaca, NY, 1956. **Extract 14**.

Armijn Pane (John McGlynn, trans) *Shackles*, Lontar Foundation, Jakarta, 1988.

Aveling, Harry, ed and trans, *From Surabaya to Aramageddon*, Heinemann, Singapore, 1976. **Extract 26**.

Aveling, Harry, trans, *Sri Sumarah and Other Stories*, Heinemann Educational Books (Asia) Ltd, Kuala Lumpur, 1976.

Bickmore, Albert, *Travels in the East Indian Archipelago*, OUP, Singapore, 1991. **Extract 18.**

Bontekoe, Willem Ysbrandtszoon, 'Memorable Description of the East-Indian voyage 1618–1625', in Cornelia Niekus Moore, ed, *Insulinde: Selected Translations from Dutch Writers of Three Centuries on the Indonesian Archipelago*, University of Hawaii, Honolulu, HI, 1978. **Extract 25.**

Danarto (Harry Aveling, trans), *Abracadabra*, Heinemann, Singapore, 1978. **Extract 12.**

Djamil Suherman, 'Becoming a Santri', in Soenjono Dardjowidjojo and F. Lamoureux, eds, *In the Surau. Seven Islamic Short Stories from Indonesia*, South East Asian Papers, Honolulu, 1983.

Echols, J., ed, *Indonesian Writing in Translation*, Cornell, Ithaca, NY, 1956. **Extracts 4 and 11.**

Forbes, Anna, *Insulinde: Experiences of a Naturalist's Wife in the Eastern Archipelago*, William Blackwood and Sons, Edinburgh, UK, 1887. **Extract 2.**

Hamka, 'A deserted child' in Rufus S. Hendon, trans, *Six Indonesian Short Stories*, Yale University Southeast Asian Studies, Translation Series No 7, 1968. **Extract 19.**

Hasnah Haji Ibrahim, ed, 'Hikayat Hang Tuah', in *Malaysia: Indigenous Traditions*, Ministry of Education, Malaysia, Kuala Lumpur, 1985 (Anthology of ASEAN Literatures, Vol 1). **Extract 8.**

Hendon, Rufus S., trans, *Six Indonesian Short Stories*, Yale University Southeast Asian Studies, 1968.

Idrus, 'Surabaya', in Harry Aveling, ed and trans, *From Surabaya to Aramageddon*, Heinemann, Singapore, 1976. **Extract 26.**

Iwan Simatupang (Harry Aveling, trans), *Drought*, Heinemann, Singapore, 1978.

Lulofs, Madelon H., *Coolie*, OUP, Singapore, 1987.

Lulofs, Madelon, H., *Rubber*, OUP, Singapore, 1989. **Extract 24.**

Mangunwjiaya Y.B. (Thomas M. Hunter, trans), *The Weaverbirds*, Lontar Foundation, Jakarta, 1991. **Extract 28.**

McGlynn, John, ed, *Menagerie 1*, Lontar Foundation, Jakarta, 1992.

McMillan, M., *A Journey to Java*, Holden and Hardingham, London, 1914. **Extract 5.**

McPhee, C., *A House in Bali*, OUP, Kuala Lumpar, 1979. **Extract 1.**

Mochtar Lubis (A.H. Johns, trans), *A Road with No End*, Hutchinson, 1968. **Extract 13.**

Mochtar Lubis (Florence Lamoureux, trans), *Tiger!* Select Books, Singapore, 1991. **Extract 23.**

Moore, Cornelia Niekus, ed, *Insulinde: Selected Translations from Dutch Writers of Three Centuries on the Indonesian Archipelago*, University of Hawaii, Honolulu, 1978. **Extracts 3 and 25.**

Pramoedya Ananta Toer (Harry Aveling, trans), *The Girl from the Coast*, Select Books, Singapore, 1991. **Extract 7.**

Pramoedya Ananta Toer, 'Vanished childhood', in J. Echols, ed, *Indonesian Writing in Translation*, Cornell, Ithaca, NY, 1956. **Extract 4.**

Satyagraha Hurip (David Irvine, trans), *Bisma, Warrior priest of the Mahabharata*, Sinar Harapan, Jakarta, 1990. **Extract 10.**

Scidmore, Eliza Ruhamah, *Java: The Garden of the East*, OUP, 1984. **Extract 21.**

Sitor Situmorang, 'Mother Goes to Heaven', in Harry Aveling, ed and trans, *From Surabaya to Aramageddon*, Heinemann, Singapore, 1976. **Extract 16.**

Soetan Takdir Alisjahbana, 'With sails unfurled', in J. Echols, ed, *Indonesian Writing in Translation*, Cornell, Ithaca, NY, 1956. **Extract 11.**

Stavorinus, Johan Splinter, 'Voyages to the East Indies', in Cornelia Niekus Moore, ed, *Insulinde; Selected Translations from Dutch Writers of Three Centuries on the Indonesian Archipelago*, University of Hawaii, Honolulu, 1978. **Extract 3.**

Raden Adjeng Kartini, *Letters of a Javanese Princess*, Norton, New York, 1964. **Extract 6.**

N. Riantiarno (Barbara Hatley and John McGlynn, trans), *Time Bomb & Cockroach Opera*, Lontar Foundation, Jakarta, 1992.

Van der Post, *The Night of the New Moon*, Penguin, Harmondsworth, UK, 1977. **Extract 20.**

Van der Post, *The Seed and the Sower*, Penguin, Harmondsworth, UK, 1983.

Wallace, Alfred Russel, *The Malay Archipelago*, Graham Brash, Singapore, 1983. **Extract 17.**

Wilcox, Harry, *Six Months in Sulawesi*, OUP, Singapore, 1989.

Extracts

(1) Bali

Colin McPhee, *A House in Bali*

Balinese music given shape by the aficionado.

At first, as I listened from the house, the music was simply a delicious confusion, a strangely sensuous and quite unfathomable art, mysteriously aerial, aeolian, filled with joy and radiance. Each night as the music started up I experienced the same sensation of freedom and indescribable freshness. There was none of the perfume and sultriness of so much music in the East, for there is nothing purer than the bright, clean sound of metal, cool and ringing and dissolving in the air. Nor was it personal and romantic, in the manner of our own effusive music, but rather, sound broken up into beautiful patterns.

It was, however, more than this, as I was to find out. Already I began to have a feeling of form and elaborate architecture. Gradually, the music revealed itself as being composed, as it were, of different strata of sound. Over a slow and chantlike bass that hummed with curious penetration the melody moved in the middle register, fluid, free, appearing and vanishing in the incessant, shimmering arabesques that rang high in the treble as though beaten out on a thousand little anvils. Gongs of different sizes punctuated this stream of sound, divided and subdivided it into sections and inner sections, giving it metre and meaning. Through all this came the rapid and ever-changing beat of the drums, throbbing softly, or suddenly ringing out with sharp accents. They beat in perpetual cross-rhythm, negating the regular flow of the music, disturbing the balance, adding a tension and excitement which came to rest only with the cadence that marked the end of a section in the music. . . .

I sat watching the concentration of the players. Boys of fourteen, men of twenty or sixty – all gave themselves up to the serious business of rehearsal. The music was rapid, the rhythms intricate. Yet without effort, with eyes closed, or staring out into the night, as though each player were in an isolated world of his own, the men performed their isolated parts with mysterious unity, fell upon the syncopated accents with hair's-breadth precision. I wondered at their natural ease, the almost casual way in which they played. This, I thought, is the way music was meant to be, blithe, transparent, rejoicing the soul with its eager rhythm and lovely sound. As I listened to the musicians, watched them, I could think only of a flock of birds wheeling in the sky, turning with one accord, now this way, now that, and finally descending to the trees.

(2) Banda Islands

Anna Forbes, *Insulinde, Experiences of a Naturalist's Wife in the Eastern Archipelago*

A 19th century view of the little changed heart of the Spice Islands.

There had been much talk during the voyage of the islands of Banda, the chief nutmeg-garden of the world, and we were naturally curious to see them for ourselves.

Banda is the most lovely spot we have yet visited. Coming on deck early, we found ourselves approaching a dense and brilliant vegetation, in strong contrast to the bare spurs of Timor, which we had left a few days before. Steaming in through a narrow winding entrance, which seemed after giving us passage to glide together, we found ourselves in a deep-blue inland lake. But only apparently. The Banda group is composed of four small islands, three of which form this secure harbour. Three of the four are covered over almost their entire surface with nutmeg-trees. As though to form an offset to this luxuriance and fertility, towers the terrible fire-mountain Gunung Api, which reeks eternally from its shapely cone, like a fierce guardian of these gardens of Paradise. A sulphurous smoke ever rises from its bare and scarred summit, but its base and flanks are green with trees, amid whose shade a white dwelling here and there peeps out, heedless of the internal fires that blister the smouldering cone. How strange it was to lean on the ship's rail, and gaze down into the tranquil harbour, whose waters are so transparent that living corals, and even the minutest objects, are plainly seen on the volcanic sand at a depth of seven or eight fathoms; then to lift the eyes to the smoking mountain, and picture the terrible tumult in the fiery caverns within.

Passing from the shore, along which runs a row of clean-looking whitewashed houses, the steep shady path to the left leads to the gardens; keeping to the right, you ascend to the town. Following one street and then another, having on each side Arab, Chinese, and Malay shops, where all necessities, such as food, clothing, and coffins, are displayed for purchase, you emerge on a green level bordered by some good houses and a church. On the sward is the village well, where there seems always to be a group of busy washers; and in the centre is a large school, where every educational advantage may be enjoyed, so that European residents need not, as formerly, send their children to distant parts to be educated. On its left rises the battlemented fort built by the Portuguese, but now flying the Dutch ensign, from the top of which a magnificent view is to be had of the surrounding islands and out over the boundless sea. Sitting on the topmost of a long flight of steps, we looked down on the Banda isles, so small in their vast setting, – on the volcano, from whose crest the vapour-cloud had temporarily lifted, leaving the whole symmetrical outline clearly defined, – on the reposeful town, heedless of the terrible devastation which has overwhelmed, and at any moment may again overwhelm it from the overshadowing fire-mountain, – on the land-locked bay, bathed in sunlight and gently ruffled by the breeze, which floated out the flags on the shipping, – and down on the old fort, which tells how the spice-gardens of Insulinde were valued in other centuries.

(3) Batavia (Jakarta)

Johan Splinter Stavorinus, *Voyages to the East Indies*

A picture of life in colonial Batavia in the late 18th century, provided by a captain in the East Indies Company.

Europeans in Batavia all live in much the same way, whether they are Dutch or of other nations and regardless of their rank or station. In the morning they rise at daybreak, five o'clock or earlier. Most of them then go out and sit on their veranda for a time; others stay indoors, clad only in the *kebaja* or light gown in which they have slept. After drinking tea or coffee, they get dressed and leave for work. Everyone who is employed is supposed to be on the job by eight o'clock and to remain until eleven or eleven thirty. Dinner is at twelve. Then comes the afternoon nap, until four. From four to six they are either back at work or in a carriage making a tour of inspection outside the city. Around six the men gather in small groups to play games or chat until nine, when nearly everyone goes back home. Those who wish to stay are invited to do so. Eleven is the usual hour of retiring.

Conviviality seems to reign everywhere. This mood is, alas, accompanied by an indefinable circumspection which is the consequence of an arbitrary government. The slightest word inadvertently uttered can have disastrous effects if it reaches the ears of someone who is insulted by it or imagines himself insulted. I have often heard it said that in this country one cannot even trust his own brother.

Women folk do not take part in these get-togethers, but have gatherings of their own. In fact, husbands spend scant time with their wives, and do not show a great deal of respect for them. Most of them do not even take the trouble to instruct their wives in normal methods of housekeeping or in the ways of society. Hence, even after many years of marriage, women are often as ignorant as on their wedding day. It is not that they lack capacity, but the menfolk have little desire to develop them.

The men usually dress in Dutch fashion, and most wear black. As soon as a visitor steps into a house where he will remain for more than an hour, the host will invite him to make himself comfortable by taking off one or more articles of apparel. This is done by laying aside the musket and removing the outer coat and the wig (for most men wear wigs). The latter is replaced by a small cap usually carried around in the pocket for this purpose.

When anyone goes out on foot he is attended by a slave to hold a parasol, known as a *sambreel* or *pajung*, over his head. No one below the rank of junior merchant is allowed to do this, however; such a one must carry a small parasol himself.

(4) Blora: West Java

Pramoedya Ananta Toer, *Vanished Childhood*

Like most of Pramoedya's semi-autobiographical work, this story is set in the region of Blora in East Java where he was born and brought up.

The Lusi River flows in a semi-circle around the southern half of the small township of Blora. During the dry season, the river bed, which is covered with stones, gravel, mud and sand, bobs up through the water and is exposed to the sky. At that time there are parts of the river where the water is only a few feet deep. But with the arrival of the rainy season the greenish waters turn yellow, thick and muddy and the forest-covered mountains are shrouded in clouds and the sun does not appear for forty or fifty hours. The water levels rises in uncontrollable leaps, sometimes up to twenty yards, at times beyond that. And the otherwise calmly flowing river becomes turbulent and runs amuck. It carries away the bamboo bushes alongside its banks, just like young children pulling out grass. The river undermines its banks, and washes away parts of the arable land of the people.

The Lusi River is eroding its own banks.

In this life a swift current sometimes carries away man and human destiny and without his knowing loses part of his life.

From the front of our house the dark green tops of bamboo bushes were visible. When the wind blew they swayed gracefully. Sometimes their lowly whistling was audible in the rushing of the wind. When I was a child, seeing and hearing this frightened me. Then I would quickly run to my mother's lap and cry.

Even now I can still hear my mother asking me, 'And why are you crying?' And her hand which was no longer soft as it had been when she was a girl caressed my flat cheek. And in my baby-talk I answered between sobs:

'Mother, the bamboo is crying'.

Then mother lifted me up on her lap and ventured to say: 'It isn't crying, no, it's actually singing'.

And then she sang tender songs which always made my fear, sorrow and anger over something disappear. She sang a folksong from our area. Her soft sweet voice and her humming often put me to sleep. Sometimes when she was singing I would caress her wind-tousled hair and I would play with her ears which were adorned with diamond pendants. And then, after a while, I could hear her voice, ending the song by saying: 'You're drowsy, let me put you to bed'.

And I would open my eyes as wide as possible so as to enjoy my mother's singing longer. But I could not keep my eyelids open any more.

But all this has passed. It had disappeared, just like the steep banks and the bamboo bushes which have been carried away by the swollen waters of the Lusi. And I am powerless to stem this vast stream which nature has turned loose upon mankind. Only too well can I sense how easily man can be set aground and put adrift again by the waves of time from one place to another, from one sentiment to the next.

(5) Bogor: Java

M. McMillan, *A Journey to Java*

The Botanical Garden in Bogor as witnessed and experienced by Miss McMillan.

You enter the Gardens through a stone gate close to the Chinese market, and at once find yourself in a long avenue of magnificent kanari trees, planned and laid out over 80 years ago by the famous horticulturist Teysmann. Against these tall trees climbing plants are trained and the trunks are covered with staghorn ferns, ratans, and large orchids such as the Grammato-phyllum speciosum, which often bears three thousand blossoms at a time.

Right and left of the avenue are plots of ground devoted to the culture of various kinds of trees and plants, more than ten thousand species being represented. One is reminded of that once popular book 'The Swiss Family Robinson', and that gifted family's experiences in the desert island upon which they were wrecked, where they found trees to supply all their wants. What had seemed impossible in fiction was here in fact; sausage trees with fruit shaped like that tasty edible: soap trees whose fruit is used for washing purposes by the natives; candle trees with what looked like clusters of wax candles hanging on the branches; bread fruit trees; the various palms yielding sugar, sago, oil, dates, cocoanuts, etc., together with fragrant spice trees of clove and cinnamon; all had their place in this wonderful garden. In addition, the whole array of tropical fruits, pines, melons, mangosteen, mangoes, etc., also flourish and abound. Hanging from the trees are marvellous orchids which look like butterflies or moths fluttering on the branches, as you pass under them to the river which flows through the grounds. On its banks a large number of aquatic plants are cultivated, such as mangroves, giant plants from seaside marshes, and the Egyptian papyrus. Great thickets of frangipanni (Plumieria acutifolia), the Javanese flower of the dead, are planted, to afford the required shade to delicate shrubs and seedlings, while in beds and on banks are countless many-hued flowers, yellow, white, red, interspersed with beautiful foliage plants, such as crotons, etc., which have their home in this tropical paradise. There is a fine avenue of banyans, those curious trees whose branches hang down till they touch the earth, when they immediately take root and form other trees; near them was a fine specimen of the traveller's palm (Ravenala), whose stems contain the water so welcome to the thirsty wayfarer. . . .

A monument, in the form of a Greek temple, marks the last resting place of Lady Raffles, who died while Sir Stamford was Governor of Java. She was buried in this beautiful spot, which was then only a park, and was later made into a botanical garden. A special clause concerning the care and upkeep of this tomb was inserted in the treaty that restored Java to the Dutch.

(6) Japara: Java

Raden Adjeng Kartini, *Letters of a Javanese Princess*

Kartini introduces herself to her correspondent. Her letters are translated from the original Dutch and were written in the early years of the 20th century.

I am the eldest of the three unmarried daughters of the Regent of Japara, and have six brothers and sisters. What a world, eh? My grandfather, Pangeran Ario Tjondronegoro of Demak, was a great leader in the progressive movement of his day, and the first regent of middle Java to unlatch his door to that guest from over the sea – Western civilization. All of his children had European educations; all of them have, or had (several of them are now dead), a love of progress inherited from their father; and these gave to their children the same upbringing which they themselves had received. Many of my cousins and all my older brothers have gone through the Hooge-Burge School – the highest institution of learning that we have here in India; and the youngest of my three older brothers has been studying for three years in the Netherlands, and two others are in the service of that country. We girls, so far as education goes, fettered by our ancient traditions and conventions, have profited but little by these advantages. It was a great crime against the customs of our land that we should be taught at all, and especially that we should leave the house every day to go to school. For the custom of our country forbade girls in the strongest manner ever to go outside of the house. We were never allowed to go anywhere, however, save to the school, and the only place of instruction of which our city could boast, which was open to us, was a free grammar school for Europeans.

When I reached the age of twelve, I was kept at home – I must go into the 'box'. I was locked up, and cut off from all communication with the outside world, toward which I might never turn again save at the side of a bridegroom, a stranger, an unknown man whom my parents would choose for me, and to whom I should be betrothed without my own knowledge. European friends – this I heard later – had tried in every possible way to dissuade my parents from this cruel course toward me, a young and life-loving child; but they were able to do nothing. My parents were inexorable; I went into my prison. Four long years I spent between thick walls, without once seeing the outside world.

(7) East Java

Pramoedya Ananta Toer, *The Girl from the Coast*

The harshness and double standards of Javanese social norms are brought home movingly in this story of personal suffering set in East Java. The girl is returning home as the wife of the feudal lord.

'Sing another song', the coachman suggested.

The Girl did not hear him. She was still thinking of her father. Because of him, I'm alive today. Oh, bapak . . . She thought of her mother. What would she be doing?

Suli and Kardi were well in front of everyone else. All of a sudden, brands appeared in the distance, coming to meet them. Sparks flew from the dried coconut branches and scattered in the wind.

'Who are they, Mas Nganten?'

'My parents. My neighbours. My friends'.

The children rushed forwards, instantly, shouting: 'Here comes the Girl from the Coast! Here comes the Girl from the Coast!'

The brands and lamps multiplied in the dark, until the members of the procession could clearly see the sweating faces of those who were coming to meet them. 'The Girl from the Coast! The Girl from the Coast!'

'Hush, be quiet! Don't be so rude, children!' snapped a member of the welcoming party.

The Girl forgot about her melancholy, as the hairs on the back of her neck began to rise. No one had ever treated her like this before. She felt strange. In the distance she saw her father carrying a brand made from a coconut branch. Dressed only in a sarong, his rugged muscles shone in the light. The Girl ran, and ran, and ran. Sand scattered from beneath her feet. Among the many people, she had eyes for only one man.

'Bapak! Bapak! she cried as she fell to embrace his feet.

He caressed her hair as she kissed his instep. 'Are you well, nak?'

Their torches lowered, the villagers stood in a circle around the father and daughter, watching.

'*Pangestu*. May you be blessed, bapak'.

No one spoke. The villagers stood still and unmoving, like a group of statues.

'Stand up, nak'.

The Girl stood and looked at the faces around her. Each time she looked at someone, that person nervously bowed his head. The Girl shrank back into herself. They had changed. She had never been treated like this before. Never, they had changed, she repeated. She felt strange and lonely, as if she was a monkey in a cage. Using her father's strong hand, the Girl rose to her feet.

'Let's go home. Your mother is waiting for you.'

She looked at her father and he cautiously avoided her gaze. Bapak? Even my father won't look at me. Why? His own child. The earth beneath her feet shook. Her last remaining shelter had vanished.

(8) Indonesia: Amok

Anon, *Hikayat Hang Tuah*

Taming Sari has run amok in the audience-hall, slaughtering lords, princes and warriors. Tun Tuah is the only one brave enough to confront him. The story raises not only the issue of the unquestioned loyalty of Tun Tuah who risks his life for his ruler but also that of the relationship of Malacca and Majapahit, the two most powerful empires of their times and, by implication, that of Malays and Javanese. Needless to say, in this text it is the bravery, wit and cunning of the Malays which gain the upper hand over the cowardice and brutish force of the Javanese. From Hasnah Haji Ibrahim's translation (see Booklist).

When Taming Sari saw a Malay warrior standing in the middle of the audience-hall with a drawn creese, he ran forward and tried to stab Tun Tuah, saying, 'Who are you who stands in my path?' Tun Tuah leapt aside, and answered, 'I am the knight of the Raja of Melaka. They call me the Laksamana, knight of the land of the Malays, and who may you be?' The other replied, 'I am the old warrior of the land of Majapahit'. Tun Tuah then leapt up and sliced with his long creese. It touched the old man and sent him sprawling, but left no mark whatsoever; Taming Sari jumped up and executed a jig before making rapid lunges at Tun Tuah's chest. Tun Tuah had to keep jumping to left and right to evade Taming Sari.

The spectators watched the duel excitedly. Then the thought crossed Tuah's mind, 'What, I wonder, makes him invincible? I think it is his creese. What can he be after? Anyway, I better try to get his creese'.

When Tun Tuah had decided on this course of action, he said, 'Hey Taming Sari, what is it that your heart desires? You are on your own; Betara Majapahit is a mighty ruler; he can easily use guile to lead you to your death. If you want to stay alive, let us unite against the Betara of Majapahit, and kill Pateh Gajah Mada and the nobles. Then we spruce up the fighting ranks and you can be ruler and I your Pateh Gajah Mada; who can take the both of us? Now your creese looks fragile to me; take my second creese and together we will swamp the palace'. When Taming Sari heard Tun Tuah's words – he felt there may be truth in them – so he said, 'If what you say is true, then let me take a look at your creese, so I'll be convinced'. Tun Tuah immediately drew his second creese and handled it to Taming Sari. He accepted the creese, drew it from its sheath and said, 'It truly is magnificent, strong and sharp'. Then Tun Tuah said, 'My creese has recently taken a warrior right in front of Betara Majapahit and Pateh Gajah Mada'. Said Taming Sari, 'It is as the Laksamana says. If your lordship wants my creese, then you shall have it; I will give it to no other', and so saying, he sheathed his creese and handed it to Tun Tuah. With Taming Sari's creese safely in his hands, Tun Tuah then drew his own creese and said to Taming Sari, 'And now I shall kill you!'

(9) Indonesia: The Individual

Chairil Anwar, '*Spirit*'

In many ways Chairil Anwar represents the new city dweller, highly individual and largely on his own. The sentiments expressed here could be those of many a person in any of the large urban centres of Indonesia which only began to develop and grow over the last one hundred years. The poem was written in March 1943. Translated by E. Ulrich Kratz.

When my time has come
I know, nobody will grieve
not even you

There is no need for all this sobbing!

I'm a wild animal
expelled from the pack

Let bullets pierce my skin
I shall rage and charge

Wounds and poison I carry running
running

until bitterness and pain are gone.

And I shall care even less
I want to live another thousand years.

(10) Indonesia: The King's Son

Satyagraha Hurip, *Bisma: Warrior Priest of the Mahabharata*

The ancient Mahabharata story not only provides the script for the traditional Javanese shadow-play and all others forms of wayang, but also the inspiration for contemporary writers who share with their readers an understanding of the pertinence of the drama's symbolism to present days.

Beside the pool of his Palace, Santanu slowly returned to consciousness, from those happy memories to the sad present. He drew in a deep breath that betrayed the sorrow of his spirit. He felt weak. A stern, poignant sadness clouded his face. 'Why?' he asked himself.

Seven times had he got his beloved *Prameswari* with child. Each time had his hopes risen, for himself and for his people of Hastinapura. Seven times had handsome healthy babies been born. But then, seven times had his Queen immediately thrown her newborn babies into the River Jamuna. She had done it so calmly, as if it were no crime at all.

It was strange, too, that as soon as she had done this terrible deed, she would return to her duties as if nothing unusual had happened. Despite his revulsion at her indecent actions, despite his anguish for the souls of those lost princes of Hastinapura and despite his deep-seated respect for human life, Santanu had wisely kept his own counsel. He continued to idolise his *Prameswari*, in spite of her outrageous behaviour on those seven occasions.

Oblivious to the passing of time, King Santanu spent the entire night beside the lotus pool. Then the eastern skies began to glow faintly, as if the sun had been cunningly hiding from the earth and was at last preparing to show itself. The lotus flowers were about to blossom, the birds began their morning songs or soared up to the clouds. Roosters crowed in reply. Sadly the King arose and went with heavy steps and a heavier heart towards the royal bedchamber, back to the Queen he had left sleeping so peacefully.

He was alarmed to see *Sri Prameswari* was already awake and walking towards him down one of the palace hallways. She carried a new-born babe in her arms. How strong and healthy the infant was. Such a child could only have been born of the womb of a beautiful princess who had been blessed by the seed of a great and handsome king. This was surely Santanu's son.

The Queen was more beautiful than ever. Here eyes reflected the joy in her heart. She walked slowly, as women do who have just given birth. Her face was shining and a smile sucked in her sweet cheeks.

'Wife, stop for a moment!' Santanu implored her. 'Must it always be like this, my beloved? Let us speak of this matter. Little sister, do as I ask, I beg you'.

Sri Prameswari knelt and held out the baby for the King to see. Santanu was filled with sombre emotion.

'Oh wife of mine,' he stammered hoarsely, 'You know that my people have long been looking forward to the birth of an heir to the throne, an heir of my own flesh and blood, of my own seed. Seven times now have our hearts throbbed and seven times have we sung our praises and thanks to the Gods in Heaven. But each time we have been disappointed because you have immediately thrown the new-born infant into the River Jamuna'.

The King lost control and shouted at his wife, 'What a great crime you have commited! You murderer of babies!'

(11) Indonesia: Leaving Old Certainties

Soetan Takdir Alisjahbana, '*To Sea, The New Generation*'

The imagery of this poem which evokes a generational change is of course one all Indonesians are familiar with given that most live close to the sea, which is their friend and foe alike, offering food and the means of communication on the one hand, threatening and destroying on the other. Translated by E. Ulrich Kratz.

We have left you,
the calm lagoon without a ripple,
sheltered by a leafy mountain
from wind and storm.
For once we have woken up
from a pleasant dream:

'Joyful waves chase each other
in the blue arena rimmed by the sky.
The flat sands kissed over and over,
the steep banks challenged and attacked,
jesting with the wind,
racing with the clouds'.

Ever since, the soul has become restless,
always struggling, never quieting down,
the old tranquility feels rigid,
the sheltering mountain an obstacle.
The heart revolts wishing to be free,
attacking everything in its way.
Thunder roars, we fall,
lashed incessantly by the clittering pearls,
tumultuous the roaring sound,
horrifying the echo of the victorious sound.
sighs and laughter taking turns
yells and screams greeting each other.

But no matter how difficult the journey
the body lashed, the head beaten,
the heart broken, the thoughts confused,
still, to return there is no wish,
the old tranquility is not bemoaned.

We have left you,
the calm lagoon without a ripple,
sheltered by a leafy mountain
from wind and storm.
For once we have woken up
from a pleasant dream.

(12) Indonesia: The Park

Danarto, '*Love Charm*'

A typically disturbing scene from a short story by Danarto, taken from the collection Abracadabra.

It was a beautiful park. Many people visited it. Old men and women, young people in couples or alone, children playing chasings, folk sitting on the benches. Pensioners, civil servants, labourers, farmers who had finished their visit to town and were ready to return to their villages, professors and intellectuals, students, weary artists, merchants, medicine vendors, blackmarketeers, trishaw drivers, ragged, hungry and dirty tramps and beggars. You decided what to do in the park once you arrived, the important thing was that you came. Talk? Think? Enjoy the flowers? Look at everyone else looking at everyone else? Rest your eyes (dirty old man!)? Find a girl-friend? Get divorced? Fight? Plan something? Count your profits? Reach a conclusion? Search for inspiration? Tell dirty jokes? Try to find God, wherever He might be? People did all of those things. The pregnant woman was in a familiar part of the park. She came there every day. And ate the flowers. She was a wretched tramp. The other beggars were cleverer than she was, and she always lost when they fought over food in the rubbish tins. She never found a thing. So she had decided to eat the flowers. She ate them every day. At first she couldn't stand them. Gradually she got used to them. She ate flowers daily. There were Roses, Jasmine, Tuberose, Orchids, and such like.

'Good afternoon, pregnant lady,' the flowers greeted her in chorus, like school-children addressing their teacher.

'Good afternoon, my darlings', the pregnant woman replied as she approached them. She walked around the flowers and smiled.

'Your belly seems bigger', said the Rose.

'Watch out you don't topple over', said the Jasmine.

'You look like you're going to explode, lovely lady!' added the Tuberose.

The woman giggled so hard that her breasts flapped and her stomach shook like an earth-quake. The various buds of flowers laughed with her.

(13) Indonesia: The Teacher

Mochtar Lubis, *A Road with No End*

Isa, the Jakarta teacher, is caught in the turmoil and misery of the early days of independence.

As the old dusty wall-clock struck eleven, Isa raised his head and laid his pen and pencil on the table. He had finished marking his pupils' exercises. He put the exercise books together and placed them carefully back into his desk drawer. As he did so he caught sight of four packages of new ones – fifty in each bundle, still unopened.

Isa listened carefully. The school was silent. The other teachers had gone home. His head was aching. Some had taken their work to finish at home. Exercise books were expensive on the open market. At home there was no money. If he took a bundle, he thought no one would know – and with the money he could buy rice. A feeling of embarrassment stole through him as this thought entered his mind.

That the desire to steal should ever enter my mind! he thought, ashamed of himself. He swiftly closed the desk drawer and locked it, as though afraid of being tempted if he looked at them for too long. For a few moments he sat resting his chin on his hand. Then he took a glass standing upside down on his desk. It was grimy as though rarely washed with soap. Isa stood up and went outside to the tap next to the back wall of the class. His stomach rumbled because he had had nothing to eat. He filled the glass, raised it high as though proposing a toast in wine, and he drank the water in large gulps. His Adam's apple rose and fell visibly with every gulp. He filled the glass again and drank it down, then half-filled it, dipped his finger in it and twisted it around the length of the glass, shook the water about vigorously and emptied it onto the grass. He held the glass up to the light – it's clean, he thought to himself. He walked back towards the classroom, his left hand patting his stomach: 'You're full now. No more playing up', said the hand to his empty stomach – he'd taken nothing since early morning, and his stomach fell silent. He felt a slight return of energy to his listless body and realised his headache had gone. Just hunger, perhaps, he thought, fortunately not illness. The thought heartened him. His step was firmer as he went into the classroom.

(14) Indonesia: Train Journey

Amal Hamzah, '*Spy-glass*'

A train journey through the past.

I leaned very comfortably against the back of the seat, my eyes partially closed, but open sufficiently to spy on the actions of fellow-travelers through my eyelashes. The coach was filled with the reverberation of the voices of the people who were chatting. There were high voices, low voices, and also hoarse voices which sounded like the striking of an empty pail. Actually, I was happy to be among so many passengers. There were all sorts of conversations, but the majority of them revolved around the issue of rice. Rice, rice, from the city this four-letter word which here means existence, life or death, had been with me.

Through the window I could see the paddy fields filled with green rice plants. In two more months at the most they would be ready for harvest. Thank God, let them be wealthy again with the paddy which they reap.

In the meantime, the train arrived in Parungpandjang. I stood up and stuck my head out of the window to look for a woman selling food.

Parungpandjang was filled with people selling things. The train stopped here for some time in order to wait for the other train coming from Rangkas, and thus provided the passengers with an opportunity to fill their stomachs with all kinds of sweets, cooked rice, roasted chicken, eggs, and ice water mixed with red colored syrup, stagnant in glasses smeared with dirt.

My eyes searched and searched, but I couldn't find her. Long ago there was a woman here, a vendor of salted eggs. Often when I and my friend (ah, how many years ago it must have been, I was still in school at that time) went to Pasirleundjang, we bought up all the salted eggs. We paid one or two guilders, not minding how many eggs there were. The village girl was beautiful, so we were quickly attracted by her and from the time we first met her, it had become an unwritten rule that we had to buy all her eggs, at a price that was much too high! Well, what's the use of money if not to bring happiness.

My eyes searched the platform, among the many vendors, but she was not to be seen.

(15) Indonesia: Wayang Kulit

Amir Hamzah, '*Because of You*'

Quite apart from its intrinsic merits as an accomplished expression of man's argument about his relationship with God, this poem is one of the first instances when a writer originating from one ethnic group would take his imagery from another. Amir Hamzah was a Malay nobleman, yet the shadowplay (wayang) and puppeter (dalang) are concepts which are considered intrinsic to Javanese cultural life. Translated by E. Ulrich Kratz.

Given life because of you
all flowers shed their petals
bringing to flower love in my soul
giving fragrance to my heart

life is like a dream
like a play on the unfurled screen
I am the dreamer and the dancer
the conscious and unconscious taking turns

Thus taking form on the flat screen
shadows and colours offering emotion
cordial longing joins in
two souls become one – intimately –

I am a puppet you are a puppet
amusing the *dalang* who sets the tune
on the open screen exchanging glances
for one melody only, the length of a song

the glittering puppets he exchanges again
I and you are put into the chest
I am a puppet you are a puppet
pleasing the *dalang* accompanying the verse

(16) Lake Toba

Sitor Situmorang, '*The Lost Child*'

Sitor Situmorang is a Batak who originates from the shores of Lake Toba in North Sumatra where the poem with its autobiographical undercurrents presumably is set. The island in the poem might well be that of Samosir in the middle of the lake. Sitor Situmorang had spent several years in Europe before writing this poem. Translated by E. Ulrich Kratz.

In the midday heat
the speck of a boat emerges on the lake
mother is anxious, to the beach she runs
to welcome the long-awaited child

The dot of a boat becomes real
looking at it the tears flow
the child has arrived from his wanderings
as soon as he steps off mother embraces him

Father sits in the centre of the house
as if he hadn't bothered waiting
the child feels dejected at mother's side
– men properly restrain their feelings –

The child sits down, is told to talk
a chicken is slaughtered, rice is cooking
The whole village keeps asking
are you married, any children?

The lost child is now back
not a single person he knows anymore
how many harvests have there been
whatever has happened?

The whole village keeps asking
any children, how many?
the lost child just keeps silent
he rather would want to ask the questions

After the meal at dusk
mother approaches him, wants to be talked to
the child looks, the mother asks
wanting to know if it is cold in Europe

The child keeps silent remembering things forgotten
the cold of Europe, the seasons of its cities
mother is quiet, has stopped talking
without resentment, only with joy

Night has come, mother has fallen asleep
father has been snoring long since
on the beach the waves swish
knowing, the child has not returned

(17) Lombok

Alfred Russel Wallace, *The Malay Archipelago*

Alfred Russel Wallace stands unjustly in the shadow of Darwin. He is remembered today by the Wallace line which runs past Bali and which demarcates the presence of Asian and Australian flora and fauna through the Archipelago. His seminal work, The Malay Archipelago (subtitled The Land of the Orangutan and the Bird of Paradise. A Narrative of Travel with Studies of Man and Nature) is still in print. The terraced paddy fields of Bali and Lombok fascinate visitors to this day.

Soon after passing Mataram the country began gradually to rise in gentle undulations, swelling occasionally into low hills towards the two mountainous tracts in the northern and southern parts of the island. It was now that I first obtained an adequate idea of one of the most wonderful systems of cultivation in the world, equalling all that is related of Chinese industry, and as far as I know surpassing in the labour that has been bestowed upon it any tract of equal extent in the most civilized countries of Europe. I rode through this strange garden utterly amazed, and hardly able to realize the fact, that in this remote and little known island, from which all Europeans except a few traders at the port are jealously excluded, many hundreds of square miles of irregularly undulating country have been so skilfully terraced and levelled, and so permeated by artificial channels, that every portion of it can be irrigated and dried at pleasure. According as the slope of the ground is more or less rapid, each terraced plot consists in some places of many acres, in others of a few square yards. We saw them in every state of cultivation; some in stubble, some being ploughed, some with rice-crops in various stages of growth. Here were luxuriant patches of tobacco; there, cucumbers, sweet potatoes, yams, beans or Indian-corn, varied the scene. In some places the ditches were dry, in others little streams crossed our road and were distributed over lands about to be sown or planted. The banks which bordered every terrace rose regularly in horizontal lines above each other; sometimes rounding an abrupt knoll and looking like a fortification, or sweeping round some deep hollow and forming on a gigantic scale the seats of an amphitheatre. Every brook and rivulet had been diverted from its bed, and instead of flowing along the lowest ground were to be found crossing our road half-way up an ascent, yet bordered by ancient trees and moss-grown stones so as to have all the appearance of a natural channel, and bearing testimony to the remote period at which the work had been done.

(18) Lake Maninjau: West Sumatra

Albert S. Bickmore, *Travels in the East Indian Archipelago*

We follow here the author on his way to Lake Maninjau near Bukittinggi (the Fort de Kock of Dutch times). The '44 bends' down to the lake are as famous today as they were arduous to surmount then.

From Matua our course changed to the west and lay through broad sawas filled with half-grown rice. It slowly ascended, until we found ourselves on the edge of a crater of most enormous dimensions. Thick rain-clouds gathered and began pouring down heavy showers, which obscured everything about us, and I could only see that we stood on the edge of a vast yawning gulf. Our way now rapidly descended first to the right and then to the left, and, as I looked down into the deep abyss which we were descending, such thick vapors enveloped us that every thing was hidden from our view at the distance of a hundred yards, and it seemed as if we must be going down into the Bottomless Pit. Down and down we went, until at last I became quite discouraged, and seriously began to think of explaining to my native guide that the wisest heads which lived in my land believe that the centre of the earth is nothing but a mass of molten rock, and to inquire of him whether he was sure we should stop short of such an uncomfortable place, when the thick mist which enshrouded us cleared away, and I beheld far, far beneath me a large lake, and above me the steep, overhanging crater-wall which I had descended; but I was only half-way down, yet I had the satisfaction of knowing there was an end to the way, and, besides, the road was not so steep, and consequently not so slippery as the half we had already come. So we slipped and plodded on, and early in the afternoon I came to the residence of the *controleur* of that region, at the village of Manindyu, on the east side of the lake.

The height of the edge of the crater where we began to descend is thirty-six hundred feet, and that of the lake fifteen hundred and forty above the sea. The perpendicular distance that we had come down, therefore, was over two hundred feet; but to come that distance, our road had zigzagged so continually to the right and left, that we had travelled five miles. Toward evening the rain ceased, and the *controleur* conducted me a short distance north of the kampong to a hot spring, where the natives have a square pool for bathing, and covered it with a small house, for they ascribe all sorts of healing virtues to this warm water. I found the water to be perfectly pure to the eye, and free from any sensible escape of gas. Its temperature was 102½° Fahrenheit, and an abundance of algae was seen on the rocks beneath its surface.

At sunset, the heavy clouds that had filled the crater during the day slowly rose upward, but not so high at first as to allow us to see the tops of the peaks in the serrated crest of the crater-wall opposite. The bright sunlight, therefore, shone in through the triangular openings between the lower surface of the level clouds, and the bottoms of the sharp valleys, and these oblique bands of golden light fell on the water at some distance from the opposite shore, and then came over the lake and illuminated the place where we sat watching this unique and magnificent view.

After the sunlight had faded, the clouds rose higher, and I could look round and behold all sides of the largest crater it has been my privilege to see, and indeed one of the largest in the world.

(19) Minangkabau

Hamka, *'A Deserted Child'*

The dilemma faced by Marjam is one found all over Indonesia and not only in the Minangkabau region of West Sumatra where this particular story is set.

Marjam was still young, under thirty, and she had only one child, so that it was not right that she remain unmarried forever. But because it is the custom nowadays for people to be disdainful of divorcees, especially those with children, no one had yet appeared to ask for her hand, and she herself, as we have seen, did not yet have any intention of replacing her son's father.

But poverty often changes the plans people have made for their lives. Money also frequently tempts the poor man to alter his views. How could Marjam be expected to go on enduring misery forever? The tuition had not been paid for three months, and she could scarcely clothe herself decently. Her mother, who up to now had been able to help her, was growing older all the time.

In this state of affairs, a proposal of marriage arrived from a merchant who was more than fifty years old. He did not live permanently in the village; he ran a small business in the city. He had ex-wives in every corner of the village, and he had a senior wife too. He told Marjam's mother that if Marjam would consent to become his wife he would divorce his senior wife, because she had not borne any children, although he had had two or three children by his ex-wives.

Marjam knew what a cruel man her prospective husband was; she realized that to marry someone like that meant putting herself into the tiger's mouth. She would therefore have preferred to remain single for the rest of her life. But her own mother kept coaxing her with a variety of arguments. In particular, she said that Marjam was old now, and she had a son who was getting bigger all the time, while his father had vanished without a trace, and had never sent her so much as half a cent, much less any clothing. But if Marjam had a husband, especially a rich one, her life would be easy. If she took care to keep in the good graces of her husband, he would certainly not allow Rahim to be neglected, even though he was merely his stepson. Especially when the merchant had expressly declared that he felt pity at the sight of the young divorcee's fate.

Marjam promised to consider the man's proposal for a week. Meanwhile another letter demanding payment arrived from the school teacher: if Rahim's tuition of Rp. 2.25, which had not been paid for three months, was not brought in by the coming Saturday, the boy would be expelled.

'Accept Baginda Saheh's proposal, Marjam, use the bridal payment he'll give to pay the debt at the school', said her mother.

'What will happen to Rahim?' she asked.

'If Baginda Saleh takes you to the city, let Rahim stay with me in the village. You can just send the money for his tuition every month. I can take very good care of him'.

'. . . Oh, my poor child!' sighed Marjam.

'Accept the proposal', her mother repeated.

'What else can I do? I accept it'.

(20) PREANGER: WEST JAVA

Laurens van der Post, *The Night of the New Moon*

Van der Post was a prisoner of war in Java. In this extract he describes the impact the Preanger landscape made on him when captivity had heightened his perceptions 'to an extra-sensory degree'.

In addition to the heightening of perception of which I have spoken, there was the stimulation of one's senses provided by the extraordinary beauty of the scene itself. For me there is no scene of greater beauty on earth than this high plateau on which our prison stood. Immediately behind us there was the great volcano of Tangkoeboehan-praauw, which is a Malay name meaning literally 'the ship turned upside down', because the shape of the mountain could with the help of a little poetic imagination be visualized as a legendary Malay ship turned upside down and petrified by time; so much so that I often thought of it at night as a symbol of our own state – for whose world could have been turned more upside down than ours? All around Tangkoeboehan-praauw, as far as one could see, stretched great terraces of rice descending to a plain full of the geometric shapes of more and more paddy fields.

On these terraces and in these paddy fields one would see the peasants of the island at work under their wide brimmed hats of golden rice-straw, in the slow, patient, timeless manner of souls dedicated to cultivating the earth, which always suggests that the greatest and longest and most terrible of wars and the most powerful of dynasties could come and go but only the cultivator would be there to go on for ever . . .

What made this moment of beauty most poignant of all, perhaps, was that for people who had been so long in prison as ourselves it was an unchanging kind of beauty. It had been like that every day since we had been incarcerated. It had been like that because there were no seasons in Java: the jewelled land, from end to end, was like a long emerald strung on a shining cord of the equator itself and the climate seemed forever the same.

(21) Preanger: West Java

Eliza Ruhamah Scidmore, *Java: The Garden of the East*

The landscape of the Preanger region of West Java viewed from the train at the end of the 19th century.

The train climbs very slowly from Bandong to Kalaidon Pass, and, after toiling with double engines up the steep grades, it rests at a level, and there bursts upon one the view of the plain of Leles – the fairest of all tropical landscapes, a vision of an ideal promised land, and such a dream of beauty that even the leaden blue clouds of a rainy afternoon could not dim its surpassing loveliness. The railway follows a long shelf hewn high on the mountain wall, that encircles an oval plain set with two conical mountains that rise more than two thousand feet above the level of this plain of Leles, itself two thousand feet above the level of the sea. The finely wrought surface of the plain – networked with the living green dikes and terraces of rice-fields, which, flooded, gleam and glitter in the fitful sun-rays, or, sown and harvested, glow with a mosaic of green and gold – is one exquisite symphony in color, an arrangement in greens that holds one breathless with delight. All the golden greens of rice seed-beds, the intense, vivid greens of young rice transplanted, the opaque and darker greens of advanced crops, and the rich tones of stubble are relieved by the clumps and masses of palms and fine-leaved trees, which, like islands or mere ornamental bits of shrubbery, are disposed with the most admirable effect to be attained by landscape art. Each of these tufted clumps of trees, foregrounded with broad, translucent banana-leaves, declares the presence of toy villages, where the tillers of the plain, the landscape-farmers, and the artist-artisans have woven and set up their pretty basketry homes. A masterpiece, a central ornament or jewel, to which the valley is but the fretted and appropriate setting, a very altar of agriculture, a colossal symbol and emblem of abundance, is the conical Goenong-Kalaidon, a mountain which rises three thousand feet from the level of the plain, and is terraced all the way from base to summit with narrow ribbons of rice-fields – the whole mountain mass etched with myriad fine green lines of verdure, wrinkled around and around with the curving parapets and tiny terraces that retain the flooded hanging gardens. . . .

The railway, dipping nearly to the level of the plain as it describes a great curve around the gloriously green Kalaidon, again ascends along the side of the mountain wall, loops itself around the Haroeman pyramid, and halts at the station of Leles. From that point one has a backward view over the enchanting picture (a line of white bridges and culverts marking the path of the railway along the mountain-side) and he looks directly across at the soft green slopes of Haroeman, which faces him – that vast green dome or pyramid, which is a little world in itself, with uncounted villages nestling under clumps of palm-trees that break the lines of singing terraces, and those peasants of the hanging gardens looking down upon the most pleasing prospect, the most beautiful landscape in all Java, which should be world-famous, and whose charm it is as impossible to exaggerate as to describe.

(22) Sumatra

Sanoesi Pane, '*Poem*'

When new poetry first began to emerge any reference to specific places and names was almost incidental since writers were most concerned to give air to individual emotions and feelings which may well have been sparked off by their experience and perception of their own country. Like many of the early writers Sanoesi Pane hailed from Sumatra. Translated by E. Ulrich Kratz.

Where lies the worth of a poetic composition
not in the purpose of its meaning,
its form, the beautiful word
chosen and weighed with discrimination

The first question comes from the heart
after the poem has been read to the end
how far that what is called sacred
composes itself in wisdom.

The feelings of the poet when he arranges
the words which come in droves
from within, and not those that are contrived,

must return within the reader
like the image in the mirror
and must shake his innermost self.

(23) Sumatran Forest

Mochtar Lubis, *Tiger!*

This is the opening of Mochtar Lubis's didactic novel, set in the ancient forests of Sumatra.

The great forest spread over the whole island, reaching from the sandy beaches, where ocean waves generated in the far Antarctic lashed the shore after their long journey, to the high mountain peaks perpetually blanketed in thick clouds. The face of the forest was ever-changing. Close to the shore a dense mangrove swamp formed a tangled barrier; moving inland and to higher ground the trees and shrubs varied continuously, until deep in the interior they grew large and tall, with ancient patterns of lacy moss etched along their branches.

Most of the ancient forest had never been penetrated by modern people and its inner reaches were rich with life. A myriad of wild creatures thrived in these depths, and there was a splendid array of plants with exotic orchids commonly crowning the towering trees.

In the forest canopy a host of birds, siamangs, monkeys, and other primates went about their lives while below, on the ground, *harimau*, elephants, and sun bears pursued their constant wary quest for food. The river banks and nearby meadows were the domain of tapirs, rhinoceroses, snakes, crocodiles, and deer. Insects swarmed everywhere.

Many parts of the forest were eerie, filled with bogs and unexplored murky hollows which had remained dark and wet for centuries. But there were also beautiful and inviting places, not unlike the enchanted forests of fairy tales. These open glades in the primeval forest were lushly carpeted with green grass and were peaceful and fresh. They were often ringed by graceful *cemara* trees, which filled the air with the heavy scent of their sap. In the midst of these exquisite meadows, there were inevitably small streams of cool crystal water winding and splashing, bubbling and whispering. One would be hard-pressed to resist the temptation to stop and rest there.

Within the forest one could find rattan, *damar*, and many kinds of valuable wood. Humans may have lived here in ancient times before moving to the cities and towns. Now they returned only sporadically to seek their livelihood by gathering the products of the forest.

(24) North Sumatra

Madelon H. Lulofs, *Rubber*

This description of a tropical forest about to be taken under plantation cultivation can hardly be bettered.

The stony, meandering path lay ahead. On both sides was the tropical forest, sombre, impenetrable, with gigantic trees twenty and thirty times as tall as a man, and creepers hanging densely between them. It seemed to be lifeless, because all life within it was secret. Sometimes a monkey jumped suddenly across the lower branches, glanced inquisitively at the passing car, grimaced, and screamed challengingly. Sometimes a great lizard darted swiftly across the path, which continued to get worse and worse. The car bumped and shook, and John held his hand tightly over his stomach so that he should not feel the shaking too much. He had removed the topee from his damp hair. Occasionally he closed his eyes. The blood boomed in his ears, his head thumped. There was no sound except the panting of the engine and the creaking of the body of the car. The native chauffeur remained unmoved. He drove on, cautious and passive. The last ten miles took an hour.

Everywhere spread the tropical forest, with its trees and its creepers and its tenacious weeds. Then, abruptly, the road came out into the new plantation, Tumbuk Tinggih. Here the mighty forest had been cut away, burnt, annihilated. Between two rows of low hills lay the flat strip of dull brown land, colourless, featureless, endless. Far away in the distance stretched the opaque green forest, an enemy at bay. And over all this endless solitude, this mournful monotony, glowed the hot shimmering sky, the blinding sunlight.

On this sad, inhospitable, repulsive land the coolies were setting out sticks to mark the places where the young rubber trees were to be planted. Hundreds of brown, half-naked bodies bent down for ten hours a day in the same regular, monotonous labour. Their backs were shiny with sweat. Their broad, naked feet sank into the loose earth. When one of them shouted to another, his voice resounded across the wide plain, and an echo came back from the distant forest.

(25) Sunda Straits

Willem Ysbrandtszoon Bontekoe, '*Description of the East-Indian voyage*'

Thrown off-course by violent storms and uncertain of their directions, the first European voyagers welcomed the sight of the Sunda Straits which, once negotiated, promised shelter and the first fresh provisions after many perilous months on sea.

When day broke we saw three islands ahead. We decided to make for them in hope that there were no people and that we might find something to eat. We reached them the same day. We immediately discovered fresh water, and found some reeds which grew as big as a man's leg. These are called bamboos. We broke through the joints with a stick, leaving the lowest intact, filled them with water, and inserted a plug at the top. In this way we were able to bring as much as two tons of water aboard. We also found some palms, the tips of which were as tender as the pith of rushes; we cut these down as well, and brought along those parts that were fit to eat. The men scoured the island looking for food, but discovered nothing else of worth.

I went off by myself and, seeing a hill (the highest point on the island), climbed up and looked around me. I was very troubled and sad of heart, for it was largely up to me, I thought, to find our way, whereas I had never been in the East Indies before and had no navigation instruments – in particular, as I have said, no compass. Hence, I thought it best to trust myself to the Lord, for I was truly at my wits' end, as so often before. I fell to my knees and prayed to the Lord, who had saved me and guided me under His merciful wings, who had rescued me from fire and water, from hunger and thirst, and from evil men. I besought Him in His fatherly goodness to preserve me still, and to open my eyes to the right way so that we might be restored to our nation and our friends. Indeed, with deep sighs I prayed, 'O Lord, show us the way and guide us. But if in Thy wisdom Thou thinkest best not to restore me to my home land, suffer then – if it be Thy divine will – some of our company to be saved so that men will know how it fared with us and our ship'. Having so spoken with God, I stood up to go back down the hill. Casting my eyes round about me as before, behold, I saw on my right hand that the clouds were dispersing away from the land so that the horizon was clearing. From my vantage point I observed two high, blue mountaintops. It immediately crossed my mind that I had heard Willem Cornelisz Schouten, who had been in the Indies two or three times, say – this was back in Hoorn – that there were two high, blue mountains at the tip of Java. We had now come along the coast of Sumatra, which lay to Java's left, while these peaks I saw were on the right, and in between there was a gap in which I saw no land at all. I knew the Sunda Strait ran between Java and Sumatra. Hence, I was persuaded that we were on the right course. I descended the hill in a cheerful frame of mind, and informed the merchant that I have seen the two mountains. As I spoke the clouds were covering them again so that they could not be seen. I also mentioned what I had heard from Willem Cornelisz Schouten and the conclusion I had drawn from this, namely, that we were just outside the Sunda Strait. 'Well, Captain', the merchant answered, 'if this is your conviction, let's call the men together and set out in that direction. In my opinion your reasoning and conclusion are well-founded'.

(26) Surabaya

Idrus, '*Surabaya*'

The Battle of Surabaya in East Java was fought largely between British forces and Indonesian irregulars. In the end, it turned Britain's attitude in favour of the Indonesian struggle for Independence.

As the fighting began to end in early December, people began to think of the old God again. Each night Revolutionary Radio broadcast from the *Koran*. '*Allahu akbar*. God is great. *Allahu akbar* . . .'. For some reason – perhaps He didn't have a radio, or perhaps He was bored with those who only remembered Him when they were in trouble – He didn't hear the melodious chanting. The Indonesians suffered defeat after defeat until they were, as the Allied radio station said, 'pacified'.

The cowboys had fought the baddies and lost. The wounds still festered, the people of Surabaya still suffered. There was always the possibility of being hit by a stray bullet, imprisoned or breathing one's last. But until such time, people would neither complain nor would they surrender. Like the Germans, they refused to bow in defeat as the Japanese had done. They were as proud as the Indonesian politicians imprisoned by the Dutch before the Second World War.

A religious leader went mad and died. He had been a good friend of the Japanese and trusted them completely. But when the Japanese behaved as the Dutch had before them, cruelly and breaking every promise made, he distrusted them as one distrusts the older brother they claimed to be: one does not beat him to death, one simply waits for circumstances to catch up with him instead. The priest improved a little with the declaration of independence, 17th August 1945, and rapturously joined everyone else in shouting 'Liberty! Liberty!' Unfortunately his recovery was only temporary. When the boys behaved like cowboys, kissing the girls and their revolvers in public, he became mad again. He could not praise their new God.

The young men no longer strutted around like cowboys. They lived together in long-huts. Each morning they ate a little stale bread and climbed onto the English trucks and went to work constructively: sweeping the streets, stacking bricks from ruined buildings, unloading ships in the harbour. This change in behaviour, gentle reader, was not voluntary. Each morning the Gurkhas screamed and shouted at them to wake up. The Gurkhas were a happy lot. The Indonesians smiled bitterly and hung their heads in shame as they drove along the streets.

They had no free-will. They were prisoners-of-war and worked without complaining. Their bitter smiles were iron, purified iron, as tough as liberty itself.

A young girl told everyone she met, Indonesian, English and Gurkha: 'I'm not a virgin anymore! See for yourself! Have a look, go on!' Then she slid her hands like a magician under her skirt, and pulled out a dirty yellow-stained rag. The Englishmen looked, then turned quickly away, smiling knowingly. The Gurkhas laughed and looked at her for minutes at a time, as though bewitched. Indonesians did not look at all. Their faces reddened with hatred and bitterness. They walked quickly on, thinking: 'Another victim of the Revolution!' And then, fiercely: "So am I. Everyone is, every Indonesian . . .'.

(27) Yogyakarta

Chairil Anwar, *'Diponegoro'*

The name of Pangeran Diponegoro (1785–1855), a member of the royal court of Yogyakarta, has been imbedded in the mind of every nationalist for his opposition towards the Dutch and those members of his family whom he perceived as siding with them against him. Prince Diponegoro's 'rebellion' was the cause of the Java War (1825–30) which in the end strengthened the control of the Dutch and led to Diponegoro's exile first in Menado and later in Macassar where he died. His grave can still be visited in present-day Ujung Pandang, South Sulawesi. Chairil Anwar too was born in North Sumatra but spent most of his short life in what was then Batavia, Indonesia's capital Jakarta. This poem was written during the Japanese occupation and was clearly intended as an allegorical call to resistance.

In these times of development
you Sir, live again

And the embers of admiration become a fire

At the very front you wait
Without trembling. Your opponents a hundredfold.

Sword on your left, dagger on your right
carrying an undying spirit as a sash.

FORWARD

These lines have neither drum nor beat
Trust is the sign of attack.

Meaningful once
and then death.

FORWARD

For your Country
providing the fire.

Destruction above serfdom
Extinction above oppression.

Although only in death it can be achieved
in life it has to be felt.

Forward.
Advance.
Attack.
Charge.

(28) Yogyakarta

Y.B. Mangunwijaya, *The Weaverbirds*

The boy Teto recounts the return of his father, a former officer in the Royal Dutch Indies Army from military detention and reveals his own sympathies for the Dutch.

It was after sunset when there came a knock at the door. When the door was opened, the figure of a man standing in the threshold startled us half to death. Mama screamed and threw herself into the man's arms. Without previous warning, my father had come home.

Papa had just been released from military detention after being confined for several months for his opposition to the Japanese war effort. Our bright and shining world had quickly come to ruin. The Japanese had arrived. The defeated Royal Dutch Indies Army had been decommissioned. Mama and I were forced to move from the base, taking lodging with family friends in Embang Menur, an elite residential area of the city. Our own home had been confiscated and was now occupied by the enemy. Even as early as the outbreak of hostilities, all civilians had been removed from the base.

Papa had aged quickly and was now even more taciturn and withdrawn than he had been in the past. When Prince Hendraningrat invited him to take refuge in the palace, he had politely refused. It seemed that his hopes had collapsed along with the Dutch Colonial Army. Instead of moving to the palace he chose the opposite course, taking quarters in a small house in Patrabangsan, a village on the city's edge. Only Mama continued to make trips to Surakarta, selling there what she could as a source of cash to see us through those difficult times. My old friends, the army brats, had long since scattered to the winds. Papa kept his lips fairly well sealed about his own feelings, but I knew that he was waiting for an Allied Forces victory and the return of the Dutch. The people in Plengkung, the hamlet in which we lived, knew that Papa had been an army captain, a high rank by the standards of those days. But because he so easily accustomed himself to the cooperative spirit of village life, our life in Plengkung seemed safe and secure. We seemed almost invisible, submerged as we were in village life.

Our little bungalow was almost completely hidden behind a large house that had once belonged to a Dutch Major but was now occupied by a Japanese officer. The Japanese officer lived there with his mistress, a woman we called Auntie Pauline. Auntie Pauline's husband had been a sergeant in the Colonial Army but was now a prisoner in Burma. Auntie Pauline had gone on to make ends meet by becoming the mistress of this Japanese officer. Though in truth Auntie Pauline was a sweet and kindhearted woman, it turned my stomach to look at her. I could never understand why Mama and Papa, who were otherwise so upright, could treat Auntie Pauline so kindly; to my taste, altogether too kindly.

Biographies and literary notes

ABDUL HADI, W(idji) M(uthari) (1946–). Born in **Sumenep**, Madura. One of Indonesia's foremost poets, his poetry is turning increasingly towards mysticism.

ABDUL MUIS, (1886–1959). Born in **Bukittinggi**, West Sumatra, died in Bandung, West Java. A member of the nationalist movement he wrote several novels, of which *Salah Asuhan*

(*Wrong Upbringing*, 1928) in which he condemns Western style education and Indonesian attempts at assimilation as misguided, is probably the most famous.

ABDULLAH (bin Abdul Kadir) MUNSYI (1796–1854). Born in Malacca, died while on the pilgrimage in Mecca. Abdullah was of Indian and Malay extraction. Versed in traditional Malay literature and steeped in Malay Islamic culture, for most of his life he was employed by Western missionaries and British officials as a teacher of Malay, hence the honorific title *munsyi*, as a scribe and a printer. Inspired by Raffles and others he took to writing himself and produced what is considered one of the first autobiographies, the *Hikayat Abdullah* of the region. His admiration for what he considered Western efficiency and its reward of achievement made him highly critical of contemporary society and endeared neither his work nor himself to several generations of Malays (◊ *Hikayat*).

ACHDIAT KARTA MIHARDJA (1911–). Born in **Cibatu** near **Garut** in West Java, he is most famous for his novel *Atheis* (*The Atheist*) in 1949 which analyses the spiritual torment of a young man coming from a strongly religious family who, in his love for a woman, is confronted with modern radical thinking.

Adab. Like *kitab* ◊, *adab* literature is related to Islam and its influence on the nature of state and society, and consists of mirrors of conduct for rulers and nobles. These texts are modelled on Middle Eastern originals, partly translated and partly interspersed with original passages relating to Malay history and society in an Islamic context. Their importance must have been considerable for the newly converted courts wishing to equip themselves with the right religious credentials.

AHMAD TOHARI (1948–). Born in Tinggarjaya, Jatilawang near **Banyumas** in Central Java, Ahmad Tohari is a popular novelist and short story writer whose work excels in compassionate descriptions of the life of the peasants and the poor who are the victims of fate and circumstance.

AJIP ROSIDI (1938–). Born in **Jatiwangi** in West Java, he now lives in Japan where he is a guest professor at the Osaka University of Foreign Studies. A committed Muslim, he has written (in part religious) poetry, short stories and novels and is interested in Sundanese folklore. As a critic and scholar he has written important books and articles on the nature and genesis of Indonesian literature, and as a publisher he has made an important contribution to the general knowledge of Indonesian literature by re-publishing important yet hitherto inaccessible texts. Ajip Rosidi is closely associated with the efforts of those writers who called for a clearer Indonesian cultural identity.

AMIR HAMZAH (1911–46). Born in **Binjai**, North Sumatra of an aristocratic family, he was killed 19 March 1946 in **Kuala Binjai** close to his birthplace in the course of the Social Revolution which swept North Sumatra early during the Independence struggle and was aimed against supposed sympathizers with the Dutch. Ironically, Amir Hamzah's life had been characterized by his support

Danarto

for the nationalist movement and, at the time of his murder, he was an official representative of the young Republic. He is one of the founders of the influential cultural and literary journal *Poedjangga Baroe* (*The New Poet*) and is considered one of Indonesia's most outstanding poets (Extract 15).

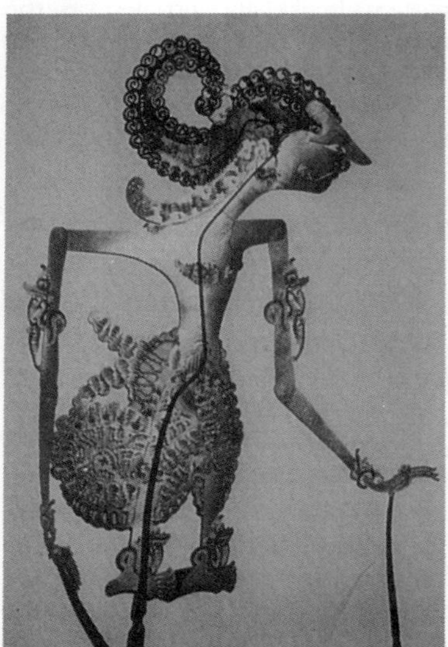

Wayang puppet

ARMIJN PANE (1908–70). Born in **Muara Sipinong**, South Tapanuli, North Sumatra and died in Jakarta. He worked for much of his life as a journalist and editor and is best known for his novel *Belenggu* (*Shackles*) published in 1938. He is one of the founders of the literary journal *Poedjangga Baroe* and has written penetrating essays on the early years of Indonesian literature.

BUDI DARMA (1937–). Born in Rembang, Central Java. A university professor in English literature, he brought his own style to Indonesian literature with his two novels *Olenka* and *Rafilus* and his collection of short stories *Orang-orang Bloomington* (*The People of Bloomington*).

CHAIRIL ANWAR (1922–49). Born in **Medan**, North Sumatra, died in Jakarta. He is widely seen as the most innovative and provocative Indonesian poet this century (Extracts 9 and 27). With seemingly little regard for accepted literary conventions and norms he created poems as buoyant and anarchic as his own lifestyle. His two slim collections *Kerikil Tajam* (*Sharp gravel*) and *Deru Campur Debu* (*Noise and Dust*) are at the heart of the Indonesian literary canon today.

DANARTO (1940–). Born in **Mojowetan**, Central Java, Danarto is a writer whose short stories are said to be inspired by Javanese and Islamic mysticism alike. The rich and often perturbing imagery of his work has been translated into English by H. Aveling (Extract 12).

EMHA AINUN NADJIB (1953–). Born in **Jombang**, East Java, he has a traditional Islamic educational background but is considered progressive and a modernist in religious terms. A very popular, irreverent essayist with a strong social commitment, he has also written some short stories and a large number of religiously inspired poems.

GERSON POYK (1931–). Born on the small island of **Roti**, off Flores in **East Nusa Tenggara**. A one-time teacher and a journalist Gerson has made it his task to relate the lives of the peoples of the eastern islands of Indonesia to an urban reading public. His short stories are full of local colour.

HAMKA (Haji Abdul Malik Abdullah) (1908–81). Born in **Sungaibatang**, Maninjau, West Sumatra, died in Jakarta. A trained and highly distinguished modernist *ulama* (theologian), Hamka endeavoured all his life to make literature as such acceptable to Muslim scholars (Extract 19). To this end he not only wrote poems, short stories and novels himself, but also acted as editor and publisher of religiously inspired literature which he wanted to be seen and judged in the context of Indonesian literature at large.

HAMZAH FANSURI. We know nothing of his life except that he was born in **Fansur**, the present-day **Barus** on the north-west coast of Sumatra where he also lived during the second half of the 16th century. He is considered the most important traditional Malay writer. An Islamic mystic in the tradition of Ibn al-'Arabi he is credited with the creation of the *syair* ◊ which was the most important poetic genre of Malay literature. As a literary device, it had a considerable impact on the development of Indonesian poetry.

Hikayat. Despite its Arabic name which means story, the *hikayat* as a prose genre is probably of pre-Islamic origins. Non-religious *hikayats* are imaginative stories related to a distant and unspecified past with a plot set in some equally unspecified kingdom beyond the seas, mountains, forests, clouds and rivers. The stories are full of romance, chivalry, mischievous demons and helpful gods and spirits. They are partly based on literary models like the Malay version of the Indian *Ramayana* which draws on Indian mythology and folklore but as frequently they are enriched with or largely consist of indigenous materials. This is the case with the *Panji* tales which narrate the ultimately successful heroic (and amorous) quest of Panji, a knight-errant said originally to hail from Eastern Java. In fact these *hikayat* possess all the elements generally attributed to traditional tales of folklore which are also referred to as *ceritera*. So far very few of these particular *hikayat* have been edited and studied in detail.

Another type is the religious Islamic *hikayat* which embraces the wealth of popular stories about the prophet, his family and famous defenders of the faith including for example Alexander the Great, whose life preceded that of the Prophet Muhammad by several centuries. Some of these stories are translations and adaptations, but there are also others which seem to originate from within the Malay cultural sphere.

The *hikayat* is not always correctly associated with chronicles and other texts of a historical nature. Yet there are texts called a *hikayat* which by their nature are quite different from the ones just described and with which we definitely leave the realm of fiction. Among the most famous texts of traditional Malay literature which have been called a *hikayat*, are the *Hikayat Hang Tuah* (Extract 8 see also Extract 9 in Malaysia) and the *Hikayat Abdullah*. The *Hikayat Hang Tuah* recalls the life of the most famous of all Malays, Hang Tuah, the admiral and loyal servant of the rulers of Malacca, who, if the manuscripts are to be believed, must have walked among the Malays for 150 years before disappearing upriver into the jungle where he still lives today. These superhuman feats notwithstanding, the background of the *Hikayat Hang Tuah* is clearly historical. This text is probably one of the most fascinating and detailed accounts of Malay values, norms, cultures and society prior to the arrival of the Europeans. It might even be regarded as the indigenous Malay equivalent to the princely mirrors of conduct brought in from abroad, illustrating the proper ways of conduct of the ordinary Malay even in the face of royal misdemeanour. The talent of its anonymous author(s) is demonstrated by the skill with which certain themes and topics such as the question of friendship and loyalty have been developed in the framework of the story. In its present form *Hikayat Hang Tuah* originates probably from the 17th century.

Hikayat Abdullah is much more recent and recounts the life of a Malay scribe and man of all trades, Abdullah ◊, who in the first half of the 19th century introduced generations of foreign missionaries and colonial officers to the Malay way of life. The *Hikayat Abdullah*, first published in 1849, has been hailed as the beginning of modern literature but despite all its linguistic and thematic innovations, the work is the exception rather than the rule, as it was created by a man who had come under the impact of European concepts and thoughts at a time when this was not yet common.

Kitab. A large part of the earliest manuscripts we know are theological treatises, many of which are translations of Middle Eastern sources, and it is this, largely translated, theological literature, which falls under the category of *kitab* literature. If one were to look for an explanation for the early predominance of theological literature one could argue that this was due to the tremendous preoccupation of the Malays of that time with the new religion. A further reason might be the theologian's need for reference and reliance on the written word which saved manuscripts from extinction and guaranteed their perpetuation in a largely oral and aural culture.

Besides translated *kitab* literature, which through its wide range of texts offers the reader useful insights into the intellectual process of Islamization and its spiritual sources, the existence of original theological and religious works written in Malay by Malays must be emphasized. In fact the best known Malay writer of traditional literature, Hamzah Fansuri, was an Islamic mystic of outstanding qualities. It might be added in this context that we have little detailed information about the active role Malay scholars played throughout the centuries as religious teachers and writers in their own right in the scholarly centres of Cairo and Mekka.

IDRUS (1921–79). Born in **Padang**, West Sumatra where he also died on 18 May 1979. Idrus, who introduced

New Realism to the Indonesian prose writing of the early days of the Revolution, is best known for his sketches on the Battle of Surabaya which he published under the name of this East Javanese city and which, on account of their lack of partisanship for the Indonesian cause earned him severe albeit misguided criticism (Extract 26).

IWAN SIMATUPANG (1928–70). Born in **Sibolga**, Central Tapanuli, North Sumatra, died 4 August 1970 in Jakarta. Considered a proper modern novelist, much of Iwan's work still awaits a fuller analysis. Lacking any obvious local colour, his work has been linked to existentialism and the nouveau roman. While the intellectual links of his writing reach deeper into European philosophical traditions than is suggested by these superficial links, Iwan is on record as having tried throughout his life to write the first truly Indonesian novel.

MAS MARCO KARTODIKROMO (1890–1932). Born in **Cepu**, Central Java, he died 18 March 1932 in internal exile in **Digul**, Irian Jaya. A journalist and political activist he wrote several novels in colloquial Malay to further the nationalist cause. Mas Marco is said to have been the model for Mienke in the famous tetralogy of Pramoedya Ananta Toer ◊ about the late colonial era and the Indonesian national awakening.

MOCHTAR LUBIS (1922–). Born in **Padang**, West Sumatra. Mochtar Lubis is one of Indonesia's foremost men of letters and intellectuals with a broadly humanist and liberal worldview. A literary author, journalist and publisher of repeatedly banned newspapers, Mochtar Lubis has always claimed the moral high ground in his writings. His didactic novels which deal with contemporary social and ethical issues repeatedly have earned him the wrath of the authorities. In consequence he was imprisoned and put under house arrest under the Old and the New Order. His novel *Twilight in Jakarta* was first published in an English translation before it became available seven years later in 1970 in Indonesian. However, it is the earlier *A Road with No End* (Extract 13) which was published in 1952 and the much later *Tiger!* (Extract 23) published in 1975 which, together with his penetrating and satirical short-stories, established his recognition as an artist.

NH DINI (1936–). Born in **Semarang**, Central Java where she continues to live today. A long established and highly regarded writer of short stories and novels Nurhajati Sri Hardini belongs to the small group of Indonesian women writers. Both her very Javanese upbringing and her extended residence overseas are reflected in Dini's work which hints at a very strong and independent character.

Mochtar Lubis

Pantun. According to one view a *pantun* consists of four lines, rhymed abab, the first two of which (called *sampiran*, 'peg, hook') are said to prepare lines three and four phonetically by means of a similar sound. Perhaps, it might be said that the successful *pantun* will meet all the criteria generally required from a good work of poetry and display harmony between form and content. Generally the *pantun* is of a proverbial nature although there exist other types as well.

PRAMOEDYA ANANTA TOER (1925–). Born in **Blora** on the border of Central and East Java. He is arguably the best known Indonesian author at home and abroad (Extracts 4 and 7). His work has been banned in Indonesia since 1965. While his early novels and short stories, much of them written in a Dutch prison, focus expressively and movingly on the human suffering brought about by the Revolution, his most recent and internationally acclaimed tetralogy of novels, first written during the 1970s in an Indonesian prison camp on the island of **Buru**, depict the state of colonial society and the beginnings of the nationalist movement early in the 20th century. Following a visit to the Netherlands early in the 1950s which made him very critical of liberal social and cultural postures and another one to China which impressed him strongly, Pramoedya became an outspoken supporter of the political Left. He was at the forefront of those who condemned and attacked most strongly intellectuals and artists (some of whom lost their livelihood in due course) who did not side with the socialist cause. Imprisoned after the events of 1965 for nearly 13 years without trial Pramoedya, whose movements remain restricted, continues to write and publish, only to see his works banned at home with monotonous regularity.

PUTU WIJAYA (1944–). Born in **Puri Anom**, Tabanan, Bali. I Gusti Ngurah Putu Wijaya is today best known for his absurdist plays and the human alienation articulated in his (mini-)novels.

RIVAI APIN (1927–). Born in **Padangpanjang**, West Sumatra. Rivai was first acclaimed for his poetry published (jointly with Chairil Anwar ◊ and Asrul Sani) in 1950 which reflected the ideals and spirit of the newly won independence of the country. Later an essayist and the editor of a cultural journal of the Left, after 1965 he was imprisoned and has not published since 1965.

ROSIHAN ANWAR (1922–). Born in **Kubang nan Dua**, Payakumbuh, Lima Puluh Kota, West Sumatra. A leading journalist, Rosihan has written poems and short stories.

S. RUKIAH (1927–). Born in **Purwakarta**, West Java, she wrote her most outstanding prose and poetry during the struggle of the Revolution in which she took part. She later became a member of Lekra.

SANOESI PANE (1905–68). Born in **Muara Sipongi**, South Tapanuli, North Sumatra he died 22 February 1968 in **Jakarta**. Next to Amir Hamzah ◊, his brother Armijn ◊ and Sutan Takdir Alisjahbana ◊, Sanoesi is one of the most outstanding writers of the pre-war period. His plays and his poetry show clearly how the author, while firmly adhering to 'Eastern' values, is seeking individual salvation and social renewal (Extract 22).

SAPARDI DJOKO DAMONO (1940–). Born in **Solo**, Central Java. Hailed as the second Amir Hamzah◊, his poetry shows great individuality and concern for the human condition. In his capacity as a university lecturer Sapardi is a critical observer of Indonesian literature.

SATYAGRAHA HURIP (1934–). Born in **Lamongan**, East Java. A journalist by profession, he has written and published several collections of short stories, as well as *Bisma: Warrior Priest of the Mahabharata* (Extract 10).

SITOR SITUMORANG (1924–). Born in **Harianboho**, North Tapanuli, North Sumatra. Sitor became first known for his existentialist poetry which seemed to reflect the modern Indonesian intellectual's alienation from his traditional surroundings, made more striking by the fact that stylistically it echoed the essence of traditional poetics (Extract 16).

SUBAGIO SASTROWARDOYO (1924–). Born in **Madiun**, East Java. A perceptive literary critic, Subagio is one of the most respected contemporary poets whose work reflects a highly philosophical attitude and deep emotions.

SOETAN TAKDIR ALISJAHBANA (1908–). Born in **Natal**, South Tapanuli, North Sumatra. Still busy as a writer and cultural activist today, Takdir Alisjahbana has been hailed as the pioneer of contemporary Indonesian language, which he championed throughout his life and for which he wrote an influential grammar. Involved in the arts since the days of *Poedjangga Baroe* which he co-founded, his literary work has pronounced didactic qualities (Extract 11).

Sitor Situmorang

SUTARDJI CALZOUM BACHRI (1941–). Born in **Rengat**, Indragiri Hulu, Riau Province, Sumatra. The self-styled president of all Indonesian poets first became famous for his interest in traditional Malay poetics. Of late this once highly extrovert poet has turned towards Islamic mysticism.

Syair. The term *syair* originates from Arabic, yet in its Malay form the *syair* cannot be compared directly with any Arabic or Persian poetical model. It is assumed that the Malay *syair* was established firmly as a literary form in Malay literature by the Sumatran mystic Hamzah Fansuri ◊ at the end of

Laurens van der Post

the 16th century. With its final rhyme scheme *aaaa* the *syair* can achieve epic length. The *syair* was not only used to express in a symbolic way the feelings of a mystic or a lover, but also to narrate historical and legendary events at considerable length; indeed, a closer look reveals that a certain type of *syair* covers the same ground as the *hikayat* and there are cases where the same topic has been treated in both poetry and prose. In contrast to the *hikayat* the *syair* appears to have been more ready to deal with contemporary events.

TAUFIQ ISMAIL (1937–). Born in **Bukittinggi**, West Sumatra. Taufiq who has published poetry since the mid 1950s came to public prominence in the aftermath of the events of 1965 when his poetry of protest supported the students demonstrating against Sukarno. Recently his poetry has acquired an Islamic colour.

UMAR KAYAM (1932–). Born in Ngawi, East Java. Most of Umar Kayam's short stories and his most recent novel, *The Priyayi* (1992), concern themselves with the moral and social values of Javanese, feudal society, and their challenge to the conscious individual.

Undang-undang. A group of prose texts, the *undang-undang* consist of legal digests and treatises. To them in a way the same rule applies as to theological texts, in that they had to be available for reference and thus were copied frequently and accurately. Very few of these texts are complete today and they are usually found in numerous fragments and hybrid copies prepared for Europeans.

UTUY TATANG SONTANI (1920–79). Born in **Cianjur**, West Java, died 17 September 1979 in Moscow, USSR. Basically an apolitical playwright, Utuy became drawn into the political conflict of the late 1950s and early 1960s. His banned work, which also includes a historical novel, is considered to be outstanding.

VAN DER POST, Laurens (1906–). South African writer imprisoned in Indonesia during the second world war. *The Seed and the Sower* (1963) and *The Night of the New Moon* (1970, Extract 20) describe his experiences.

Y.B. MANGUNWIJAYA (1929–). Born in **Ambarawa**, Central Java. A trained architect and Catholic priest, Mangunwijaya's essays and novels are considered landmarks in Indonesian literary history. His most well-known novel is *The Weaverbirds* (Extract 28).

YUDHISTIRA ARDHI NOEGRAHA (1954–). Born in Karanganyar, Subang, West Java, he became famous in the 1970s for his irreverent approach to recognized poets and poetry. He has since written several equally outrageous novels which break with established conventions.

The Philippines

Isagani R. Cruz

> 'The hustle and bustle everywhere, so many carriages and cabs at a dash, Europeans, Chinese, and natives, each dressed after their own fashion, fruit pedlars, messengers, porters stripped to the waist, foodshops, inns, restaurants, shops, carts pulled by philosophical carabaos, the noise, the incessant movement, the sun itself, a certain smell, the riot of colours – he had almost forgotten what Manila was like'.
> *Jose Rizal, Noli Me Tangere*

Geography may not be destiny, but it explains many characteristics of literary texts created by writers born or bred in the Philippines.

Lying north–south above the equator, at the north-eastern margin of South-east Asia, the Philippine archipelago was the first Asian landfall on the Pacific for seaborne imperialists from Spain in the 16th century and from the USA in the 20th century. Before the economic emergence of Japan, Hong Kong, Singapore, South Korea and Taiwan in the 20th century, the Philippines thus became the most Westernized country in Asia, particularly in literature, culture and religion. Even in the greatest days of the Srivijaya (683–1200), Majapahit (1293–1380) and Ming (1368–1644) empires to which it briefly nominally belonged, the archipelago remained marginal, assimilating little from these ancient cultures.

At the same time, being far from Europe and North America, the Philippines has not let 400 years of Western colonization alienate it completely from Asia. In blood and mind, Filipinos do not differ significantly from Malays and Chinese. Traditional Asian values may be seen at work even in modern-day Manila, where business and industry thrive in a unique mix of Spanish feudalism, American capitalism, Japanese technology, Chinese pragmatism and Malay piety, not to mention a dominant Roman Catholicism and an indigenized Islam. The major Philippine exports, such as copper, gold, sugar, coconut, copra, semiconductors and garments, share top billing in the economy with exports to numerous countries of overseas workers such as doctors, nurses, engineers, computer scientists, teachers, artists, singers, dancers, accountants, construction labourers, domestic helpers and entertainers. The major components of the Philippine value system – respect for others, self-respect, close family ties, a sense of humour, creativity, industriousness, faith and instinct for survival – combine the best traits of East and West. Literary texts display the fruits of this marginal geography and cosmopolitan history.

Physical Geography

Lying 800 kilometres off the coast of the Asian mainland to which it used to be connected by land bridges before Pleistocene times, the Philippines is now surrounded by water, the Pacific Ocean on the east, China Sea on the west and north and Celebes Sea on the south. It lies between latitude 40°40′ and 21°10′ N and longitude 116°40′ and 126°34′ E. Together, its 7 100 islands occupy a space 1 855 kilometres long and 1 108 kilometres wide, or roughly 300 000 square kilometres. The largest islands (in order) are Luzon in the north, Mindanao in the south, Samar, Negros, Palawan, Panay, Mindoro, Leyte, Cebu, Bohol and Masbate (the last nine and other smaller islands in the centre of the country being collectively called the Visayas). On the largest island can be found Manila, political, commercial and cultural centre of the country; on the ninth largest is Cebu City, a second centre of commerce and culture, which now also has an international airport. Culturally, the islands are both united and divided by water: neighbouring islands, trading with each other, tend to have similar cultures, but often have different languages, leading to distinct literary traditions.

---

[a] *Vigan's colonial architecture is celebrated in Extract 4.* [b] *Described in Extract 1.* [c] *Manila appears in numerous works of Philippine fiction, including probably the most famous Philippine novel of all time, Rizal's Noli Me Tangere; The 'University Belt' is described in Extract 13; Chinatown is depicted in Extract 11; the River Pasig which connects Manila with Southern Luzon is the scene of the denouement of Rizal's novel The Reign of Greed (Extract 16).* [d] *An active volcano, which features several times in Philippine literature – the massive 1928 eruption is evoked in Extract 14.* [e] *Contains many famous caves, among them the Manunggul Cave.* [f] *Arrival point for the 10 Malay 'datus', a major legend in Philippine literature.* [g] *Norman Mailer served in the island of Leyte in the second world war and the island is probably the model for the fictional island of 'Anapopei' in The Naked and the Dead.*

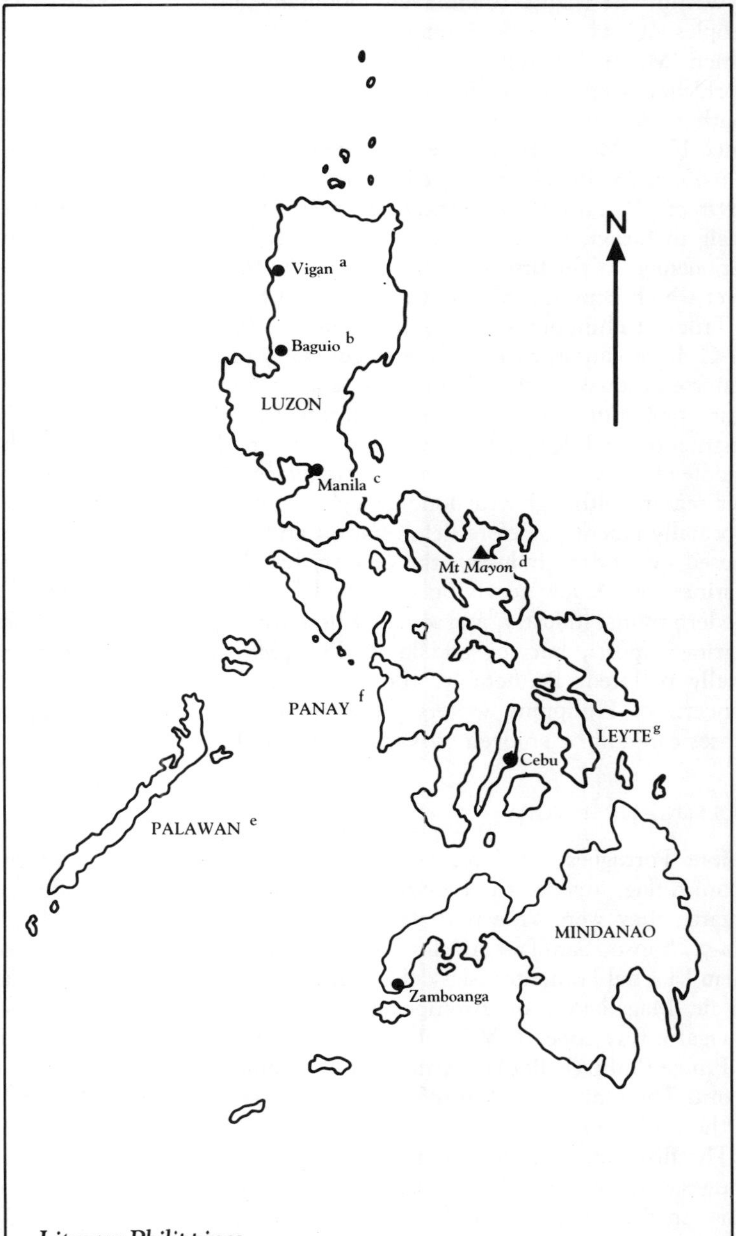

Literary Philippines

Within the islands themselves, mountain ranges and rivers divide peoples and subcultures. Around 200 mountains are volcanoes, one of which (**Mount Pinatubo**) erupted in 1991 and caused climate changes worldwide. Even the smallest volcano (**Mount Taal**), a tourist spot just south of Manila, is extraordinarily active, having erupted 22 times since 1572. **Mount Mayon**'s eruptions are well documented in literary texts, many writers having lived in southern Luzon, where it is located (Extract 14). Philippine rivers are likewise interesting. The large **River Pasig** in Luzon, for example, has important literary significance: the denouement of the first novel of Jose Rizal ◊ (1861–96) happens on this river which connects Manila with southern towns (Extract 16).

Tropical Philippines is generally humid and hot, averaging 20°C to 34°C. In mountain cities such as **Baguio City** (devastated in 1990 by a major earthquake), the temperature is a bit lower (Extract 1). Every year, typhoons come at irregular intervals, bringing rains, floods, destruction and death. Monsoon rains tend to cluster together in the middle of the year, around June to October, marking a kind of rainy or wet season, although year-long droughts have not been uncommon, especially recently. Before deforestation and other ecological damage caused by modern industry, the country had lush forests and vibrant marine life. A few surviving unspoiled beaches form the core of a modern tourist industry, and some offshore fishing sites are still used for marine exports, but, by and large, Philippine waters have become fatally polluted. Predictably, the environment forms an important concern of Philippine writers. Nevertheless, the famed Philippine sunset can still be enjoyed on various islands (Extract 6).

Political History

Before Portuguese explorer Ferdinand Magellan, sailing under the Spanish flag, invaded the islands in 1521 and called them Islas de San Lazaro, they were known to travellers as Ophir, Maniolas, Mo-yi, Ma-yi, Sansu, San-Tao and Lu-sung. Spaniards after Magellan called them Islas del Poniente, Islas del Oriente, Islas de Luzones, Archipelago de Magallanes, or Archipelago de Celebes. In 1573, Spanish navigator Ruy Lopez de Villalobos coined the name Filipinas in honour of Prince Philip (Felipe) of Asturias, who later became King Philip II of Spain. The United Nations refers to the country today as the Republic of the Philippines.

The first humanlike beings arrived in the country through five land bridges connecting different islands to different parts of continental Asia. In the middle of the Pleistocene period or 500 000 to 400 000 BC, homo erectus arrived in the islands, as evidenced in a 400 000-year-old archaeological find in Cagayan. Homo sapiens arrived 55 000 to 45 000 BC, apparently mostly settling in the vicinity of Palawan, where a major archaeological find – the 50 000-year-old Tabon cave – has given researchers clues to pre-historic lifestyles. The first identifiable tribe to arrive in the islands was the Negrito, around 30 000 to 25 000 BC. Also known as Aetas, Itas, Bataks, Agtas, Atis and Balugas, Negritos are used as symbols in literature for native, uncolonized Filipinos, although they were, of course, not the only nor even the first prehistoric peoples to arrive on the islands. They remain today relatively uncivilized. The name Aeta became a household word worldwide when hundreds of Aetas living on the slopes of Mount Pinatubo died during the great 1991 eruption. In the southern island of **Panay**, the Atis have inspired a local carnival frequented by tourists and recently immortalized in the novel *State of War* (1990) by Ninotchka Rosca (1946–).

Several overlapping waves of migration then occurred by sea. Among the first to arrive were neolithic Austronesians, including Indonesians, 4000 to 3000 BC. Another wave came from Indo-China and South China 13 000 to 500 years BC. A third wave came from the South 300 to 200 BC. Of major cultural importance was the coming of Indonesians in 1500 BC; they created one of the engineering marvels of the ancient world – multi-layered rice terraces built along the slopes of mountains in northern Luzon. Still used by some mountain people, the rice terraces have become a major tourist attraction at the town of **Banaue**. The Malays soon forced the Negritos and other earlier migrants out of the lowlands and into the mountains. This dispossession of roughly 10% of the population has become a major theme of writers, who use it to symbolize injustice and racism. In the late 20th century, it became fashionable, particularly for Christian lowlanders, to refer to these upland tribes as 'ethnic minorities'; sometimes, the term also (inaccurately) includes lowland believers in Islam.

Even more important to literature than the arrival of mountain engineers was a particular boat journey from Borneo of a group of ten Malay *datus* (chieftains) with their tribes. Although its historicity has been disputed, the event has been immortalized in a major legend, as well as modern poetic adaptations. Arriving in the southern island of **Panay**, the *datus* set up a complex civilization, the features of which still influence much of the present-day behaviour even of Christian Filipinos. For example, the vessel used by each tribe was called a *barangay*. The name was used eventually to signify the tribe itself and remains in the 20th century as an official name for political districts. The spirit of the *barangay* – a communality spiced with a shade of siege mentality – remains a major force in Philippine socio-psychology: in literature as in life, *barangays* and their equivalents (extended families or clans) often attract more loyalty than the nation itself.

The social structure at the time was class-based. In each *barangay* consisting roughly of a few hundred people, there was a ruling class or nobility which administered and eventually claimed private ownership of communal land; this class was headed by the *datu*. A sense of what life was like then for the privileged can be had from surviving epics (Extract 13). Remnants of this class structure can be seen even in 20th century urban society, where domestic helpers (who usually live in their masters' houses) work for slave wages. These domestic helpers became archetypal figures in an early 20th century dramatic form called *sarsuwela* and remain important character types in popular fiction and film.

Pre-colonial Philippines consisted mainly of separate tribes living in separated parts of islands or in different islands, having at most two common related root languages, but developing those languages in relative isolation. More than 80 different (ie mutually unintelligible) languages and hundreds of distinct dialects were formed by this fragmentation of the early migrants. Since literatures are indissolubly bound to the languages in which they are spoken or written, the literary traditions of the different tribes were bound to differ, but not so radically as to deny their common origins.

The earliest Filipinos spent their waking hours looking after their food needs, either by picking, hunting, or planting. Despite the relative lack of idle time, however, pre-historic Filipinos managed to fashion 'useless' things such as jewellery and pottery. The oldest jars found in archaeological digs in the islands date back to 1500 BC. One famous burial jar in **Manunggul Cave** in Palawan, for instance, praised as one of the most beautiful in ancient Southeast Asia, depicts a boat journey to the spirit world. In the ancient epic *Darangen*, souls are routinely transported into a next world where beings act exactly as they do on earth. The presence of such artefacts, artistic or literary, proves the existence of an intellectual culture still largely unappreciated.

Chinese history records trade with tribes living in the archipelago as early as 982 AD. By the late 12th century, Chinese–Philippine economic trade and cultural exchange were flourishing. An interesting story about how trade was then conducted persists to this very day. It is said that Chinese traders allowed Filipinos to come aboard their boats and to take whatever they wanted, without receipts or any sort of identification system. Several months later, when the traders would visit the islands again, the Filipinos would give them pearls, shell, nuts, cloth and other native products, in return for whatever they took the last time. This inherent honesty serves to explain why trickster tales were widely popular in pre-colonial times. The dishonesty of the trickster (variously called *Pusung*, *Pusong*, or *Pilandok*) was funny only because it was considered unusual conduct.

Ancient trade was not limited to China, of course. **Sulu** at the southern end of the Philippines was a major trading port from the 10th to the 13th centuries, attracting merchants from as far away as Brunei and Siam. With trade naturally came religion. Tradition holds that the Arabian scholar Mudum came to Sulu from Malacca around 1380 and started the Izlamicization of the archipelago. By the middle of the 15th century, a Sultanate (equivalent to a modern theocratic city) had been established in Sulu under Sharif ul-Hashim.

Only the coming of Catholic Spanish conquistadors and missionaries stopped the conversion of the entire archipelago to Islam. In a re-enactment of the European Crusades, Spanish soldiers, brandishing cross and sword, pushed back Islam to the southern end of **Mindanao**, which has remained Islamic to this day. Unable to cross formidable mountains, the Spaniards soon gave up serious attempts to convert the strongholds of the Sultanate and limited themselves to sporadic skirmishes with the Muslims (derogatorily called *Moros* in those days, after the Spanish Moors or Mussulmans). The geographic defences of the Sultanate were so impenetrable, in fact, that even American, Japanese and modern Philippine military forces were not able to force themselves on the Mindanao Muslims, leading to a protracted secessionist war in the latter half of the 20th century. Literature, following political events, mirrors this great divide in religion: Islamic literary texts are almost completely alien in tone and tenor to Christian texts written outside southern Mindanao. Christian traditional plays routinely depict *Moros* as enemies and even devils.

By 1572, the Spaniards had conquered the area around **Manila** and established it as the capital city of what was legally called El Nuevo Reyno de Castilla, a name everybody ignored in favour of the more common Filipinas. Huge walls were put up around the mouth of the Pasig river, everyone then living in the area was evicted, and only Spaniards were allowed to live within the walls (hence the name, **Intramuros**). The Spaniards who came from Spain were called *Peninsulars* (ie from the Spanish peninsula); pure-blooded Spaniards who were born in the islands were derogatorily called Filipinos. Hence, the first Filipinos, strictly speaking, were not native at all, but were first-generation immigrants. Eventually, people not born in Spain or born to Spanish parents but who were products of intermarriage were allowed inside the walls and were known as *mestizos*. Curiously, these *mestizos* did not suffer from the stigma of being half-breeds; on the contrary, they were accorded high social status even by natives themselves, then called *indios* (from a mistaken notion that the islands were part of the fabled Indies). Only in the period of Rizal's ◊ novels was the name Filipino appropriated by native nationalists. The word *mestizo*, already commonly used also to refer to natives with mixed Chinese blood, eventually extended its meaning to refer to all natives with skin whiter or less brown than usual.

By and large, the coming of the Spaniards had no immediate effect on literature. Epics continued to be created and recited, particularly in mountain towns where no Spaniard had set foot. Myths and legends continued to be fashioned, although they now had to explain who the Spaniards were. One Tinguian legend describes Spaniards as long-lost brothers who went away and have now returned; this legend sheds some light on the puzzling ease with which the obviously outnumbered Spaniards were able to disarm native warlords, who were famous for being ferocious and unforgiving in battle. Magellan himself lost his life fighting a small tribe in **Mactan** island, led by a chieftain named Lapu-Lapu, now nationally venerated as the first anti-colonial fighter. Yet, though they were never more than 5 000 before 1896 in the islands, the Spaniards were able to subdue a warrior people who were already at least 1 million in 1565 and almost 7 million by 1898. Perhaps, as the legend says, the natives did not realize until too late that the Spaniards were not long-lost blood brothers but aliens without Philippine interests at heart.

By all accounts, sometimes even by Spanish authorities themselves, Spanish colonization was a disaster. Particularly ill-advised was a land grant system initiated almost immediately upon arrival by the Spaniards. The system took over many of the features of pre-colonial society, particularly its class structure. The landholding class of *indio* nobility was expanded to include Spanish colonial officials and Catholic friars. The rest of the *indios* became slaves for all practical purposes, paying tribute and working the fields for the landlords. The result was a totally feudal society which had no place for vertical mobility or personal merit. Massive dissatisfaction with the class structure was inherently engendered, with race being added to the equation. The roots of the class conflict that became the major theme of post-war literature (Extract 7) and led to an actual people's revolution in the 20th century can thus be traced to the 16th century. Social structure is as much a Spanish heritage as the old colonial houses in **Vigan** (Extract 4).

By the beginning of the 18th century, Spain had to acknowledge that the islands had lost the wealth they had before the conquistadors arrived. Part of the colonization problem was obviously geographic: to reach the islands, all communications had to go the long way through Mexico, a series of boat journeys that took several months. It was not unusual for an order from Spain, for instance, to be implemented in the islands only after five years. The core of the problem, however, was systemic: Spain's allocation of lands and peoples as rewards to Spaniards already in the islands legalized slavery and land expropriation.

One symptom of the problem has become immortalized in literature – the Spanish friar, often the only Spaniard natives encountered in their whole lives. Human beings that they were, friars often became abusive not only of their spiritual, but more importantly of their temporal authority; there was usually no shortage of illegitimate *mestizos* whenever a friar was around.

There were more than 200 unsuccessful attempts to mount armed rebellions against the colonial authorities. Among those particularly relevant to literature were one led by Sulayman in 1564 and one in 1762–63 led by a woman, Gabriela Silang, whose rebel husband had been killed by Spanish soldiers. Women taking up their spouse's or father's causes are not limited to the Philippines, but Silang takes on added meaning in Corazon Aquino's successful use of people power in 1986 to vanquish Ferdinand and Imelda Marcos.

Silang's eventually futile stand was made during the two-year period of British conquest of the islands during the Seven Years' War (1756–63). Although temporary, the British victory had one crucial psychological consequence. Before the fall of the city, the *indios* had considered the Spanish military to be invulnerable; the coming of the British served as an eye-opener to nationalists – the Spaniards were mere mortals and could be defeated.

The critical mass finally coalesced and the time for revolution finally came in the second half of the 19th century, when Spanish oppression became completely intolerable even for the privileged native nobility. The catalyst for the nationwide uprising was novelist and poet Rizal, ironically a pacifist intellectual educated in Spain who cautioned against armed struggle; his execution in 1896 by Spanish authorities on transparently false charges of treason led to public indignation, which was quickly exploited by a then-existing revolutionary organization led by Andres Bonifacio (1863–97), himself a poet, sometime intellectual disciple of Rizal and admirer of the French Revolution. Despite several false military starts and the arrival of Spanish reinforcements, the organization (known as the Katipunan) quickly gained the upper hand through sheer numbers and passion. Bonifacio himself did not live to see the end of the Philippine Revolution of 1896; he was killed in 1897 in a petty dispute with fellow general Emilio Aguinaldo, a non-writer who eventually became President of the First Philippine Republic.

Although Aguinaldo succeeded in liberating most of the islands, including Luzon with the exception of **Intramuros** and a major port in **Cavite** just south of Manila, the first Republic was short-lived. Even while independence was being proclaimed in Kawit, Cavite, on 12 June 1898, a Constitution was being written in Malolos, Bulacan, and Philippine diplomatic representatives were already hard at work in Australia, Hong Kong, England, France, Japan and the USA, American President William McKinley and Assistant Secretary of the Navy Theodore Roosevelt were formulating the doctrines of Manifest Destiny and Benevolent Assimilation. McKinley totally ignored the anti-imperialist sentiments of most major American writers of the day, including Mark Twain (Extract 18), and set out to conquer the Philippines, then derogatorily renamed The Philippine Islands.

In April 1898, while Filipino soldiers were implementing a strategy of siege against 13 000 surviving Spanish soldiers inside Intramuros, Commodore George Dewey and the Spanish commander struck a deal to stage a mock battle on 13 August, a particularly rainy day that has become an important symbol in Philippine poetry. After a few token cannon blasts from Dewey's ships, the white flag of surrender immediately went up over the walls. American troops entered the city and barred the Filipinos from entering. The Philippine–American war began the following year (Extract 17); close to 127 000 American soldiers were sent to the Philippines, only 4 000 of whom were killed. The Philippine side counted at least 200 000 dead; one American general estimated a high of 600 000 Filipinos dead, an astonishing proportion of the 7 million population then. Although Aguinaldo was finally captured in 1901, the last Philippine general was not captured until 1906, and the last major battle in the south was not fought until 1912. By then, however, the Americans had established a colonial government in Manila, and most of the landed nobility that had prospered under Spain had pledged allegiance to the American flag.

The American occupation of the Philippines was short but traumatic for Filipinos. In 1903 William Howard Taft seized friar lands owned by the Philippine Republic and illegally sold them to willing members of the Philippine elite. A wedge that would last the whole of the 20th century was thus placed between the vast majority of Filipinos who were still waging war against the new colonizers and a tiny minority of wealthy Filipinos who had decided to collaborate with the enemy; the masses would not own any land and the elite would own all the land that was not government property.

American authorities, realizing that Filipinos would be impossible to govern as long as American treachery was remembered, set out to erase national memory and to rewrite Philippine history from an American point of view.

Another key strategy was the suppression of local languages and the implantation of English. Among writers, the language question soon became the major issue of the 20th century. Those who wrote in English continually apologized for writing in the language of the conquerors, while those who continued to write in Philippine languages accused them of irrelevance, if not outright treason.

Thankfully, the American occupation did not last long. The

Norman Mailer

American people themselves, speaking through their Congress, gave notice to the White House that imperialism was not among American ideals, particularly since it was not democracy that was being introduced to the Philippines but a kind of commercial aristocracy. In fact, the commonwealth government that the US colonial authorities eventually established was a mere continuation of the pre-Spanish class-based *barangay* system, with landed families inheriting political and economic fortunes. The US government, after intensive lobbying by Filipinos who had learned enough English to move around Capitol

Hill, finally promised to recognize Philippine independence by 1946, but before a peaceful transition from colony to a second independent republic could be planned, the Japanese and the USA had entered the second world war. Four hours after bombing Pearl Harbor on 7 December 1941, Japanese aircraft completely destroyed American planes stationed at Clark Air Base and made inevitable the eventual victory of Japanese troops who landed on the islands only hours later. When the Americans returned to the Philippines, their soldiers included a young Norman Mailer, who worked his wartime experiences into the novel *The Naked and the Dead* (Extract 6).

In January 1942, General Masaharu Homma started establishing commissions in preparation for what was to become the Second Philippine Republic, with the express intention of removing American influence from culture and education. Tagalog, used as the main language of communication during the Philippine Revolution of 1896 and the official national language according to the Constitution of the first Revolutionary Government, became the official and national language of the Philippines. Among the subjects taught in numerous schools opened almost immediately upon occupation were the Tagalog language, Philippine history and character education. Foreigners were not allowed to teach Philippine history and ironically, under still another imperialist master, Filipinos started to think of their history in their own terms.

Not all Filipinos, however, took the Japanese invasion as a blessing in disguise. The Communist Party of the Philippines, established earlier in 1930 in obvious admiration of intellectual and political currents in the USSR and in the USA, became the only organized force capable of mounting active resistance to the new colonizers. Meeting in February 1942, in Central Luzon, the Party created an Anti-Japanese People's Army or *Hukbo ng Bayan Laban sa Hapon* (*Hukbalahap* for short, or even shorter, *Huk*). Members were recruited from Communists and non-Communists alike and the *Huks* soon became a significant guerrilla force throughout the country. American soldiers worked with the *Huks* to gather intelligence about Japanese troop movements, in preparation for anticipated liberation. Long before atomic bombs were used by the USA in 1944, the Chinese Communist Party under Mao Tse-Tung was inflicting major defeats on an overextended Japanese army on the Chinese mainland, thus forcing Japan to cut back on her military strengths in the Philippines. Such help was received with gratitude by the *Huks* and that gratitude became a crucial factor in the literary revolution of the 1960s.

Once Japan surrendered, the USA found itself honour-bound to recognize Philippine political independence. But before leaving the islands, the US authorities extracted a major concession, which became the theme of countless literary works. This was a network of several military bases throughout the country, the largest of which – **Subic Naval Base** and **Clark Air Base** – were stark reminders that the Americans had not yet left the islands. Only in 1987 did a new Philippine Constitution forbid the presence of foreign military troops on the islands, and only in 1991 did the Philippine Senate manage to vote against the continuance of the bases.

The third Philippine Republic established on 4 July 1946 was not very different from the first two, particularly in terms of personalities. The elite continued its hold on political power and the uneducated masses continued to lack access to government. Since the elite was widely and correctly perceived to have collaborated not only with the Americans but also with the Japanese, Communist *Huks* refused to disband the footholds they had established during the Japanese war. By 1950, the Communists were confident enough to attempt a major invasion of Manila, but the government, helped by US military advisers, defeated them and captured their leaders.

Communism is extremely important in Philippine literary history because the Communist Party of the Philippines was re-established in 1968 by a poet writing in English, Jose Ma. Sison (1939–), who was inspired by Mao's writings and wrote voluminously on the Chinese example. Philippine writers religiously read Mao's talks at Yenan, as well as an essay by Sison explaining how to apply Maoism to Philippine literature. In 1972, President Ferdinand Marcos, himself an amateur poet, declared martial law ostensibly to rid the country of Communists, arrested or forced into exile numerous writers and re-established literary censorship. Although literature had always played a major role in Philippine politics, it was only during martial law that it was acknowledged as a major player in the battle for the minds and hearts of Filipinos. Soon enough, Marcos realized that keeping writers silent was impossible, since surreptitious literary publications and dramatic productions multiplied anyway; he eventually established his own centre for writers and funded the publication of creative works, even Marxist ones, as long as they did not personally mention him or his family.

During what Marcos called the Fourth Philippine Republic, simply referred to by writers as 'martial law', the opposition was led by poet and journalist Benigno Aquino, Jr. His assassination upon his return to Manila in 1983 turned the tide against Malacanang Palace. Led by his widow Corazon Cojuangco Aquino (who belonged to the elite family of the Cojuangcos of Central Luzon), the elite came out in force to defend two of their own, then Defense Secretary Juan Ponce Enrile and then Vice-Chief of Staff General Fidel Ramos, who had taken a last stand in a military camp against the dictator. The coup d'état worked, and Aquino was established as President of the Revolutionary Government and later, when a new Constitution was ratified in 1987, of a new Republic. Soon enough, the Fifth Republic was unsuccessfully attacked from within by coups launched by the newly-politicized military and from without by an enormous foreign debt entered into by the Marcos regime. In 1992 Ramos succeeded Aquino as President in disputed elections.

Languages

There are around 85 different languages and hundreds of dialects of these languages spoken and sometimes written in the islands. The great diversity of languages and dialects has led to the formation of an estimated 111 cultural or subcultural groups in a rapidly growing population of more than 65 million. Except for imported languages (Hokkien Chinese, Mandarin Chinese, English, Spanish, Arabic, Japanese) however, all languages spoken in the Philippines belong to the Hesperonesian or Western Austronesian branch of the Austronesian or Malayo-Polynesian family.

The nine major Philippine languages are (in order of number of speakers): Tagalog, Cebuano (sometimes called Bisayan or Sugbuanon), Ilokano, Hiligaynon, Bikol, Samar-Leyte (also called Waray), Kapampangan, Pangasinan and Maranao-Maguindanao. The principal dialects of Tagalog are Manila Tagalog, Bulacan Tagalog, Nueva Ecija Tagalog, Tayabas Tagalog, Batangas Tagalog and Marinduque Tagalog. The main dialects of Cebuano are Cebu Cebuano, Negros Cebuano, Bohol Cebuano and Davao Cebuano. The main dialects of Hiligaynon are Ilonggo, Kiniray-a, Aklanon, Cuyonon and Palawanon. When two persons whose native languages are different from each other meet, they generally communicate in Filipino, which is widely and legally recognized as the national lingua franca. When the two persons live in adjoining geographic areas, however, they are more likely to use a regional lingua franca, such as Ilocano (used in northern Luzon and northern islands), Tagalog (used in central and southern Luzon), Cebuano (used in most parts of the Visayas and most of Mindanao) and Hiligaynon (used in some parts of the Visayas and Mindanao).

Tagalog was the lingua franca of the Philippine Revolution of 1896 and, as a result, the 1897 provisional constitution of the First Philippine Republic established Tagalog as the official language of the new nation. In 1959, the Tagalog-based official language which then still had no name was finally christened Pilipino by the Department of Education. Because of regional resentment against the Tagalogs, however, the national language was again renamed in 1973 as Filipino, its present name. Filipino was defined as the official language based on

Pilipino (itself based on Tagalog), but no steps were actually taken to distinguish this new language from the Tagalog actually spoken in central Luzon. It remained for the 1987 Constitution to define Filipino as the lingua franca actually already existing in the entire islands.

An interesting linguistic phenomenon is Taglish, sometimes regarded as code-switching between Tagalog and English and sometimes as modern Tagalog with a lot of lexical borrowings from English. Taglish has been used with some success in modern romance fiction. Near Taglish on a linguistic cline is Philippine English, itself sometimes characterized as a major variety of international English and sometimes as pidgin. Philippine English is the standard English used by Filipinos writing in English.

Not all the Philippine languages are important for literary history. There are significant numbers of literary texts (such as poems, plays, novels and short stories) in the eight major languages, as well as in Gaddang, Ibanag, Ifugao, Ilongot, Isinay, Ivatan, Mandaya, Mansaka, Maranao, Palaweno, Sambal, Subanon, Tausug and some others. There are also enough literary works written in the imported languages of Chinese (Extract 11), English and Spanish to consider them major strains in literature.

Literary Periods

Viewed diachronically, Philippine literature may be said to be characterized by a gradual, unbroken development of indigenous literary genres which changed primarily to adapt to new social and political conditions or to adopt foreign literary influences. In the Philippine narrative tradition in poetry started by pre-Islamic folk epics, for example, Christian influences were absorbed by Spanish-period quasi-folk epic poems, and American modernist poetic strategies were adopted by modern literary epics.

Most histories of Philippine literature identify four literary periods pegged to colonization: Pre-Colonial (also called Pre-Spanish, before 1521), Spanish Colonial (1521–1898), American Colonial (1898–1946) and Post-Colonial (also called Post-war, Modern, or Contemporary, 1946–the present). Like most periodizations based on politics, this periodization meets with only limited success, although it is more useful than a classification according to more literary standards (such as language, genre, or medium).

Pre-colonial Literature

Poets were crucial to pre-colonial tribal societies, being guardians of collective memory as well as the only skilled entertainers around. Until the coming of an entertainment industry in the 20th century, poets were to keep this centrality in society, particularly in terms of being a kind of political conscience to undermine the authority of *datus*, friars, governors and ruling classes. Anonymous and trained since childhood by parents or other older persons, pre-colonial poets memorized extraodinarily long verse narratives recognized today either as individual epics or songs belonging to epic cycles. There were also a few anonymous proto-playwrights, who fashioned narratives to unify religious rituals and practices. Some of these indigenous dramatic rituals may still be seen in remote villages even today; examples are the elaborate Maranao *kashawing* (Pact with the Gods), the Zambales Negrito honey dance, the Tausug butterfly love dance and the Mansaka *Gasarod na Sayaw* (war dance). Anthropologists mention the Ifugaw *ch'along*, the Bagobo *pag-huaga* and theTagbanwa *pagdiwata* as major dramatic genres during the period.

Poets put into memorizable regular verses the most important events – real or apocryphal – in the histories of their communities. Taking images from everyday life, such as fishing, farming, hunting, weaving, trade, play and courtship, poets created a world extremely similar to the one their audiences lived in, yet sprinkled with enough supernatural fancies and generational wisdom to be more interesting than everyday reality. Poems were recited in public, during communal gatherings attended by most of the tribe members under the watchful eyes of the tribal elite. Because of elite patronage, poets tended to make their epic heroes members of the elite, with villains taken from folklore or, if human, from other tribes. Nevertheless, although expected to pass on received wisdom, poets often succeeded in subverting social norms by eschewing realism and exaggerating fantasy. In what would be recognized much later in the 20th century as the clever use of fantasy to avoid censorship, poets instinctively deconstructed their own recitings through various defamiliarizing techniques.

In less public gatherings, such as family meals, the non-nobility had more fun with imaginative literature. Trickster tales circulated which invariably portrayed rulers as mentally retarded and fair game for intelligent and irreverent slaves. Legends or folk tales portrayed the *datus* as cuckolds. One famous folk story loosely based on the historical boat journey of datus to Panay island had *Datu* Sumakwel's wife having an affair with an ordinary soldier right under the *Datu*'s nose – an early attempt at Shakespeare-style subversion.

Poets were thus not separated from the political and social lives of their communities. They recited epics not merely from a sense of duty to the past, but also because they had something personal to deliver – often didactic messages subtly condemning the excesses of the nobility.

At the same time, the world of the nobility as portrayed in the epics was, at least on the surface, an ideal world of beauty, youth, strength, courage and intelligence. Some beliefs about marriage and property seem to have been ideals, because they do not fit what we know of pre-colonial society. Many of the proverbs share this idealization: everyday conduct was almost certainly not as rational or ethical as the proverbs would make it appear.

Surviving poems of the period place a lot of value on respect – for others, for elders, for nobles. Although pre-colonial Philippines, like most other tribal societies, was patriarchal, women occasionally appeared as epic heroes or as equal to men in lyric love poems. Most of the early poets, in fact, were women; even the pagan priests tended to be female.

There were basically two types of literature before colonization: written and oral. Spanish chroniclers thought that there was universal literacy among Filipinos before the 16th century, but more recent evidence points to a less impressive pre-colonial society: if there was high literacy, it was probably only due to the literacy campaigns of Islamic missionaries and, therefore, was confined mainly to the older southern towns. There was indeed a syllabary at the time, and most scholars believe that monorhyming poems in stanzas of varying length (called *ambahan*) started before Christianity and probably even before Islam. These poems were carved into the barks of trees, on leaves and on bamboo tubes; even today, some Mangyans in Mindoro continue to write such poems on bamboo. Practically all of such pre-colonial writings disappeared for three reasons: the first was the inherent short life of the writing materials, the second was the deliberate neglect of these materials by Spanish authorities and the third was the active campaign of the friars to destroy these 'works of the devil'.

The friars also tried to eradicate oral literature, considered pagan and unworthy of Christian society. Since the friars were able to control only the lowlands, however, epics and folk tales in the uplands remained unsuppressed; some of these upland epics survived up to the 20th century when researchers managed to get them down on audiotape for transcription and translation. Only two lowland epics were able to withstand the Spanish onslaught: *Biag ni Lam-ang* in Ilokano and *Ibalon* in Bikol. There was apparently a Tagalog epic that has now been totally lost.

There were two types of oral literature: narrative and non-narrative. Among narratives, the epic was the major form. From epics derived most prose narratives such as myths and legends.

Poetry was dominated by the *tulang-bayan*, but shorter forms, often in rhyming couplets, were also popular as *bugtong* (riddle) or *sawikain* (proverbs or sayings). Intellectual in appeal, such couplets reveal a society able to appreciate irony and metaphor. Folk musical verse (*awiting-bayan*) were popular particularly among certain tribes; extant examples are the *ambahan* among Mangyans, *laji* among Ivatans, *hadis* among Tausugs and *tigsik* among Bikolanos. Always highly conventional in rhyme schemes and metrical patterns, these local forms prove the existence of a highly literate society, if not in terms of reading, at least in terms of listening.

Spanish Colonial Literature

Literature did not suddenly change with the coming of Spanish imperialists to the islands. In fact, the earliest books printed under Spanish auspices contained literary texts which were indistinguishable from pre-colonial texts in terms of forms and techniques. Many of the oral genres, such as the proverb, the riddle and even the long epic, continued to be composed, particularly in the first century of colonization. In most areas of the country still not visited by Spanish colonizers, literature continued to be created and appreciated within a pre-colonial context. Some scholars argue that even drama did not feel Spanish influence until late in the colonial period; popular forms during the period, such as *duplo* (verse joust), *karagatan* (verse joust) and *karilyo* (shadow play), may feasibly be said to be pre-colonial.

Nevertheless, Spanish influences started to make themselves felt soon enough in oral literature. Interesting hybrid epics, such as a revised *Lam-ang*, have pre-colonial characters getting married in church after fighting pre-historic monsters; sometimes, the monsters would be Spaniards. Other narrative forms, such as myths and legends, started to be composed independently of the folk epics. Some legends told of the origins of Catholic icons such as the Santo Nino image (or Child Jesus), still omnipresent in 20th century Philippine society. Satan started to appear as a character in folk tales. Even proverbs and riddles started to refer to Christian practices and doctrines. For the vast majority of natives, oral literature remained the only form of literature, because the number of printing presses in the country was relatively small throughout the whole course of Spanish colonization.

Spanish emphasis on European Catholicism, however, soon changed the face of written and even dramatic literature. Owned and supervised by Spanish friars, the printing presses ensured that only doctrinally harmless texts reached the reading public. The lives of the saints became a favourite source of plots and allusions. Poems started to be written bilingually, with lines alternately in vernaculars and in Spanish. More important for literary history, for the first time since Philippine literature started, authors started to put their names down on paper. The bilingual poems, for example, led to the identification and subsequent fame of their writers, called ladino poets.

The major epic poem of the period was a recreation of the passion (*pasyon*) of Jesus of Nazareth. In several versions, the *pasyon* moved quickly from the printed page to household level; even today, the *pasyon* is still recited in many street corners or homes (particularly in non-urban places) every Holy Week. Using what today would be called theatre workshop techniques, a theatrical adaptation of the *pasyon* (*sinakulo* or passion play) was soon conceived and mounted by numerous communities on their own; it lost popularity only in the early 20th century with the emergence of legitimate theatre and film, but can still be caught during Holy Week in revivals in urban centres or in original improvisational form in outlying towns.

Metrical romances (alternatively labeled *awit* or *korido* according to metrical scheme) were extremely popular among the literate. These romances tended to borrow their themes, characters and even lines from European originals, translations of which had become widely available on the streets. Examples of popular Tagalog romances were *Ibong Adarna*, *Bernardo Carpio* and *Don Juan Tinoso*. These romances eventually metamorphosed into a theatrical form called *komedya*, a kind of Romeo-and-Juliet stylized dance-drama, with a Christian prince in love with a Muslim princess (or Muslim prince with a Christian princess), and leading their respective religious groups to war, with Christians predictably winning at the end. Considered outstanding writers of the *komedya* were Jose de la Cruz (1746–1829) and Balagtas (1788–1862) ◊.

Ironically, the catechetical *pasyon* became instrumental in keeping alive the desire for liberty of many Filipinos. The political implications of images of Jesus and his disciples defying established religious authority were not lost on *indios* who quickly identified the Jerusalem villains with familiar Spanish friars. Even more transparent was a metrical romance, Balagtas's *Pinagdaanang Buhay ni Florante at ni Laura sa Cahariang Albania* (*Florante and Laura* ◊, 1838), which provided an allegory of the Spanish Philippines as a desperate wasteland of traitors (Extract 8). On one of his transoceanic voyages, the novelist Rizal had only one book with him and it was *Florante and Laura*, which radicalized his political position.

Balagtas ◊ and Rizal ◊ are generally considered the two major writers of the Spanish colonial period. Balagtas wrote primarily in Tagalog; he was prolific, but only *Florante and Laura* and a *komedya* entitled *Orosman and Zafira* (c 1857) have survived time and criticism. Rizal wrote in several languages, but his two best known and nationally-loved novels are in Spanish, though read nowadays mostly in translation (Extract 16). Convinced that the only way to fight Spanish oppression was to expose it in literature, Rizal wrote voluminously and effectively, serving quickly as a model of intellectual and honest resistance to the Spanish regime. Heavily influenced by Balagtas, Rizal in turn influenced every writer who came after him, all the way to the late 20th century, when novelists as diverse as F. Sionil Jose (1924–) ◊ and Rosca continued to follow the picaresque narrative structure he established in his novels (Extract 12). His two most famous novels are *Noli me Tangere* (*Do not Touch Me*) (1887) ◊ and *El Filibusterismo* (*Subversive*) (1891) ◊.

Rizal's use of European realism within the context of conventional romanticism was a first in Philippine literary history. His contemporaries, who were more actively involved in political and often armed struggle, restricted themselves to poetry and shorter prose essays. Bonifacio and del Pilar both showed tremendous poetic skills in their verse calls to revolt. To show how potent literature was felt to be, it is interesting to recall that Bonifacio, in the middle of the Philippine Revolution, took time off to translate Rizal's long poem *Mi Ultimo Adios* (1896) into Tagalog.

By the end of the Spanish colonial period, Philippine literature had defined its role vis-à-vis society: it was going to be in the vanguard – in writing as well as actual action – of political change. The poets and novelists at the helm of the Philippine Revolution anticipated the poet Mao's own leadership of the Chinese Revolution and even sometime literary writers Marx and Engels's leadership of European communism.

American Colonial Period

The American period started with playwrights being imprisoned for staging anti-imperialist (then called 'seditious') plays in many theatres throughout the country. Particularly useful as a vehicle for political propaganda was the genre of the *sarsuwela*, a musical form where servants (the modern equivalent of pre-colonial slaves) were allowed because of their supposed illiteracy to poke fun at colonial officials. Allegorical, sometimes direct, satire ruled the stage, but US military authorities, sometimes staging riots inside theatres, soon forced playwrights to restrict themselves to harmless love stories involving poor country Romeos falling in love with wealthy urban Juliets. The wild anger of such playwrights as Aurelio Tolentino (1868–1915), Juan Abad (1872–1932) and Severino Reyes (1861–1942) thus soon melted into the cautious, even if still seething, indirectness of Patricio Mariano (1877–1935), Claro M. Recto (1890–1960) and Wilfrido Ma. Guerrero (1917–). The tradition of politically radical theatre, however, never died down. At the end of the period, when the Japanese imperialists controlled Manila, playwrights once again rose to the occasion and used the theatre as the propaganda arm of guerrillas.

The deliberate campaign of US colonial authorities to Americanize Philippine culture succeeded in marginalizing pre-colonial forms such as the epic and Spanish colonial forms such as the *komedya*. Lyric poetry in the vernaculars, however, continued to be written in the traditional manner, but American poetic modernism, backed up by New Critical theory and practice as learned by Filipino scholars sent to study in the USA, soon fomented a major revolution in poetics. Nevertheless, new texts belonging to oral forms such as the riddle and the proverb continued to be produced, this time influenced by American literary and non-literary sources.

Printed literature consolidated its dominance during the American colonial period, due to several factors. One was the lifting of official government censorship of publishing houses, the Spanish period *Comision de Censura* (Commission on Censorship). Second was the proliferation of small publishing houses, many of which published poems, serialized novels, essays and even folk tales. Third was the general increase in capital that could be channeled to printing. Fourth was the establishment in 1922 of *Liwayway*, a magazine that soon became the principal outlet of Tagalog fiction; the sister publications of *Liwayway* in Cebuano, *Hiligaynon* and *Iloko* played similar roles in the provinces. Fifth was the increase in the number of weekly magazines, which usually featured literary pieces. Finally, there was the general increase in literacy, helped by the Americans' general education campaign.

Themes, types and techniques from oral literature, however, found themselves reborn within the more robust forms of written literature. Novels, for instance, continued the epic tradition. The romantic and allegorical tradition that had realistic force, which first saw the light in pre-colonial oral folk tales, continued albeit transformed in short stories. Interestingly enough, some of the settings of short stories then can still be seen in today's countryside (Extracts 3 and 5). Among the major short story writers born in this period were Jesus Balmori (1886–1948), Arturo B. Rotor (1907–1990), Manuel E. Arguilla (1910–1944) ◊, Deogracias A. Rosario (1894–1936), Jesus A. Arceo (1915–), Francisco Arcellana (1916–) ◊, Macario Pineda (1912–1950), N.V.M. Gonzalez (1915–), Nick Joaquin (1917–) ◊, Kerima Polotan Tuvera (1925–) and Genoveva Edroza Matute (1915–) ◊.

Lyric poetry derived many of its characteristics from pre-colonial folk poetry, and drama often made explicit use of styles first seen in the *duplo* and the *komedya*. A case in point is the American period Tagalog *balagtasan* (similar to the Iluko *bukanegan*, the Kapampangan *crissotan* and the Spanish *polemica poetica*), a poetic joust continuing the *duplo* and using techniques from folk poetry. Even in what was then considered modern poetry (Extract 9), traditional themes were still used by poets such as Fernando Ma. Guerrero (1873–1929), Cecilio Apostol (1877–1936), Jose Garcia Villa (1906–) ◊, Lope K. Santos (1879–1965), Jose Corazon de Jesus (1896–1932), Amado V. Hernandez (1903–1970) ◊, Alejandro G. Abadilla (1904–1969) and Angela Manalang Gloria (1907–).

The most important literary effects of the American occupation were felt in two fields: language and fiction. Writing in the English language was privileged through government-sponsored publications, thus attracting younger writers to the language and decimating the ranks of vernacular writers. The genre of the short story was introduced via schools, and both English writing and vernacular writing soon focused on this form, with energies being distracted from the creation of longer works. Despite the logistical support given to English, however, the vernacular novel continued its healthy growth in the hands of writers who were unimpressed by American achievements in literature. Similarly, even in towns close to American military bases, old Philippine traditions remained intact (Extract 15).

The politically radical tradition of the late 19th century continued to hold sway among writers, even those writing in the new imported language. Realism as interpreted by Rizal continued to be the dominant mode, although educational emphasis on the American mandarin group of Henry Wadsworth Longfellow soon led to a diminution of political consciousness and a new focus on nature imagery among writers in English. Writers in various vernacular languages nevertheless continued to use literature as a vehicle for political reform. Together with the subversive playwrights early in the period, poets such as Lope K. Santos (in Tagalog), Fernando Ma. Guerrero (in Spanish) and Jesus Balmori (in Spanish) attacked American colonization explicitly and fearlessly. Even late into the period, poetry served as the principal outlet for writers outraged by US rule. Still recited orally at town feasts, even if already in the process of being transformed by printing, US colonial period poems were often identified with highly visible and popular poets, such as Corazon de Jesus, Amado V. Hernandez and Iluminado Lucente (1885?–1960).

Although historically a separate colonial period, the Japanese occupation (1941–1945) is not usually considered long enough to have spawned a separate literary entity. The emphasis placed by the Japanese on Tagalog forced writers in English to shift to the vernacular languge, thus introducing to Tagalog literature all the modernist trends previously available only in English. The *Liwayway* chain did not cease publication, giving writers in the vernaculars ample space to exercise their artistic muscles. Because of strict censorship, of course, politically radical texts were not printed, and political activism had to shift to the non-printed scripts of theatre performances. Among the courageous stage directors then was Lamberto V. Avellana (1915–91), who later directed films, among which was a film version of Joaquin's *Portrait of the Artist as Filipino* (1952).

Post-colonial Period

At the beginning of the post-colonial period, authors still held the central roles in society that they had held since pre-colonial times. In other words, poets still tended to be looked up to for collective memory, received wisdom, new ideas, nationalist aspirations and sometimes even political leadership. Soon after the granting of political independence in 1946, however, the bulk of government power shifted to English-speaking politicians who had no background or even interest in writing, and writers were effectively marginalized. The increasing use of English as a literary language helped in this marginalization; the vast majority of Filipino readers were illiterate in English, though they were highly literate in their native languages and could appreciate the numerous novels being serialized in *Liwayway* and similar magazines. Among the writers who refused to write in English and therefore still maintained their enormous reputation among readers were Godofredo M. Roperos (1930–) and Marcel Navarra (1914–84) ◊ in Cebuano, and Fausto J. Galauran (1904–71), Hernandez, Liwayway Arceo (1924–), Lazaro Francisco (1898–1980) and Matute in Tagalog. Among the first casualties of the return to English after the Pacific War was the theatre, which virtually disappeared in the 1950s and early 1960s, primarily because the English language was blatantly incongruous on stage; nevertheless, Guerrero and Alberto S. Florentino (1931–) were able to write a number of memorable plays by forcing the English language to approximate the rhythms of native speech.

The alienation from society that started in the middle of the American colonial period reached alarming proportions by the end of the 1950s, leading to political soul-searching among writers in the 1960s. Led by American modernism to a concept of an aesthetic realm which was neither dependent on nor responsible for society, writers had relinquished their traditional role as leaders of revolutions or governments. Writers in the 1960s, mainly under the influence of a revived Communist Party, started to ask fundamental questions about the ethical and political roles of literature. The social unrest of the period, which climaxed in the imposition of martial law in 1972, itself gave writers plenty of raw material for their protest plays, poems and stories. Particularly active were playwrights, who translated political events almost immediately into theatrical performances either on legitimate stages or in street demonstrations; the tradition of the stage as a 'living newspaper', which first saw light in the early American colonial period, was thus revived.

Poetry underwent a conscious revolution led by young writers who hesitated between turning their backs on American influence and turning American influence to advantage. Rolando Tinio (1937–)

and Jose Lacaba (1945–) led the *Bagay* (Thing) Poets in using Anglo–American imagist techniques to attack what they perceived as harmful Americanization of Philippine culture. Virgilio S. Almario (1944–) ◊, Rogelio Mangahas (1939–) and Lamberto Antonio (1946–) led another group which deliberately followed Alejandro G. Abadilla (1904–69) in challenging the stylistic conventions of Tagalog poetry while continuing its radical political stance. Almario's group published the poetry anthology *Manlilikha* (Creator), which was heavily influenced by Walt Whitman and T.S. Eliot.

The poets were soon joined by an organized group of young writers who saw the need to get away from the formulas then becoming petrified in the *Liwayway* chain of magazines. Using modernist and realist techniques in their short story anthology *Mga Agos sa Disyerto* (Desert Currents) in 1964 and in their individual novels, writers such as Efren R. Abueg (1937–) ◊, Edgardo Reyes (1938–) and Rogelio Sicat (1940–) became household names in their pursuit of fiction that dealt with the lives of the poor. Elsewhere in the country, Cebuano, Waray and Iloko writing continued, although with proportionately fewer readers, since Tagalog and English were rapidly becoming second languages in the non-Tagalog regions.

In 1970, the Bagay, Manlilikha and Agos writers joined a large association of progressive young writers named *Panulat sa Kaunlaran ng Sambayanan* or PAKSA (Writing for the Country's Progress), but the growth of this umbrella organization was aborted by the declaration of martial law in 1972. PAKSA published an anthology *Sigwa* (Storm) in 1972, considered a landmark in contemporary writing. The dictatorship saw the imprisonment of numerous writers, particularly members of PAKSA, who nevertheless did not stop writing politically radical works. Because of strict censorship, however, direct didacticism was abandoned in favour of more subtle allegory. Political content thus soon became an undertone rather than the apparent subject of many works of fiction and poetry. Experts at such indirect writing were members of a young writers' group called *Galian sa Arte at Tula* (Art and Poetry Guild), such as Teo Antonio (1946–). As always, drama remained relatively unafraid to challenge directly political oppressors. A number of major playwrights, such as Tony S. Perez (1951–) and Rene O. Villanueva (1954–), produced play after play attacking various aspects of the dictatorship, sometimes with devastating effect on young students who formed the bulk of theatre audiences. Generally considered major plays of the period were *Bayan-Bayanan* (*Ersatz Country*, 1977) by Bienvenido Noriega (1952–) and *Juan Tamban* (1979) by Marilou Jacob (1948–).

The traumatic shock of Aquino's assassination in 1983 and the subsequent restoration of elite democracy in 1986 became signals for a sudden outburst of literary energies. Newspapers and magazines were filled with protest (and later, exuberant) poems. Among the noteworthy products of the time was a collection of protest poems by a group of English-language poets called Philippine Literary Arts Council (PLAC), which included Gemino H. Abad (1939–), Cirilo F. Bautista (1941–) ◊, Alfrredo Navarro Salanga (1948–88), Ricardo M. de Ungria (1951–) and Alfred A. Yuson (1945–). Most major writers, however, did not consider Corazon Aquino to be any different from Ferdinand Marcos in terms of commitment to truth and beauty, and literature does not show any major shift in conventions or themes before and after 1986 (Extracts 2 and 10). Only the relative freedom of underground or rebel writers to publish their works in book form may be considered a change, although most school courses in literature continued to ignore alternative writing. Among major committed writers who caught the attention of mainstream critics were Mila D. Aguilar (1949–) and Sison.

Literary criticism, which soon became literary theory in solidarity with theorists around the globe, particularly in other formerly colonized countries, achieved full bloom in the post-colonial period, with the emergence of Bienvenido Lumbera (1933–), Epifanio San Juan, Jr (1938–), Soledad Reyes (1946–), Almario and several other critics. The increase in universities offering postgraduate courses in literature led to much historical research, not only in mainstream literary movements, but in regional literatures.

Finally, an account of post-colonial and even American colonial period writing would not be complete without mention of financially generous literary awards, which often served as inspiration for writers to produce new and exciting works. Locally the most prestigious is the Carlos Palanca Memorial Awards in Literature (1950–); regionally, the most desired international award is the South East Asian Writers (SEAWRITE) Award given in Thailand (1979–). Also important are other local awards such as Premio Zobel (1922–), the Cultural Centre of the Philippines Literary Contests (1987–), the *Talaang Ginto* (Golden Roll) of the National Language Institute (1963–) and the National Book Awards (1981–) of the Manila Critics Circle, all of which often succeed in identifying promising writers and giving much-needed cash or added prestige to established ones.

BOOKLIST

What follows is intended as a representative rather than comprehensive list of books about the Philippines. Where several editions exist, in general the latest and most readily available edition has been listed. For most of the extracted works, information on the original English language publisher can be found in 'Acknowledgements and Citations' at the end of the volume, as can the exact location of the extracts and the editions from which they are taken. Extract numbers are highlighted in bold.

Abad, Gemino H., and Edna Z. Manlapaz, eds, *Man of Earth: An Anthology of Filipino Poetry and Verse from English, 1905 to the Mid-50s*, Ateneo de Manila University Press, Quezon City, 1989.

Agoncillo, Teodoro A., *A Short History of the Philippines*, Mentor Books, New English Library, London, 1969.

Alma, Rio (Virgilio S. Almario) (Marne L. Kilates, trans), 'Vigan' in Alfrredo Navarro Salanga, Marne L. Kilates and Mike L. Bigornia, eds, *Selected Poems, 1968–1985*, Maya Books, Quezon City, 1987. **Extract 4.**

Arguilla, Manuel E., 'Midsummer' in *How my Brother Leon Brought Home a Wife and Other Stories*, Philippine Book Guild, Manila, 1940. **Extract 5.**

Baquiran, Romulo P. Jr, Fidelito C. Cortes, Rafael Ma. Guerrero, and V.E. Carmelo D. Nadera, Jr, eds, *UMPIL (Unyon ng mga Manunulat sa Pilipinas), Directory of Filipino Writers*, Unyon ng mga Manunulat sa Pilipinas, Manila, 1991.

Balagtas, Francisco (Tarrosa Subido, trans, Patricia Melendrez Cruz, ed), *Florante and Laura (Pinagdaanang Buhay ni Florante at Laura sa Cahariang Albania)*, in Jovita Ventura Castro *et al*, *Anthology of ASEAN Literatures: Philippine Metrical Romances*, Nalandangan, Manila, 1985. **Extract 8.**

Casper, Leonard, ed, *Modern Philippine Short Stories*, The University of New Mexico Press, Albuquerque, 1962.

Coates, Austin, *Rizal: Philippine Nationalist and Martyr*, Oxford University Press, London, 1968.

Coronel, Ma Delia, trans, *Darangen*, Mindanao State University, Marawi City, 1986. **Extract 13.**

Corpuz, Onofre D. *The Roots of the Filipino Nation*, 2 vols, Aklahi Foundation, Quezon City, 1989.

Cruz, Isagani R., *Beyond Futility: The Filipino as Critic*, New Day Publishers, Quezon City, 1984.

Dimalanta, Ophelia Alcantara, *Montage*, University of Santo Tomas Publications, Manila, 1974. **Extract 1.**

Evasco, Marjorie E., 'Birthing Poems', *Dreamweavers: Selected Poems 1976–86*, Editsource, Manila, 1987. **Extract 2.**

Guerrero, Amado (Jose Ma. Sison), *Philippine Society and Revolution*, International Association of Filipino Patriots, Oakland, 1979.

Hagedorn, Jessica, *Dogeaters*, Penguin Books, London, 1990.

Hernandez, Amado V. (E. San Juan, trans), 'Irony', in *Introduction to Modern Pilipino Literature*, Twayne, New York, 1974. **Extract 7.**

Hsieh Hsing, Grace (John Shih, trans), 'Ongpin Street', *To the Flowers a Collection of Poems*, Manila, 1991. **Extract 11.**

Joaquin, Nick, *Tropical Gothic*, University of Queensland Press, St. Lucia, Queensland, 1972.

Jose, F. Sionil, *Mass*, Allen and Unwin, London, 1984; Solidaridad Publishing House, Manila, 1983. **Extract 12.**

Lumbera, Bienvenido, and Cynthia Nograles Lumbera, ed, *Philippine Literature: A History and Anthology*, National Book Store, Manila, 1982.

Mabanglo, Ruth Elynia (B.S. Medina, Jr trans), 'After the Revolution', translation not previously published. **Extract 10.**

Mailer, Norman, *The Naked and the Dead*, Signet, New American Library, New York, 1948/Paladin, London, 1991. **Extract 6.**

Navarra, Marcel M. (Teresita G. Maceda, trans), 'The awakening' in *Mga Piling Kuwentong Sebuwano*, University of the Philippines Press, Quezon City, 1986. **Extract 3.**

Rizal, Jose (Charles E. Derbyshire, trans), *The Reign of Greed*, Philippine Education Co, 1927. **Extract 16.**

Rizal, Jose (Leon Ma. Guerrero, trans), *Noli Me Tangere*, Longman, London, 1961.

Rizal, Jose (Leon Ma. Guerrero, trans), *El Filibusterismo (Subversive)*, Longman, London, 1965.

Rosca, Ninotchka, *State of War*, Norton, New York, 1988.

San Juan, E., Jr, ed, *Introduction to Modern Pilipino Literature*, Twayne Publishers, New York, 1974.

Santayana, George, 'Young Sammy's First Wild Oats', in Roger J. Bresnahan, ed, *In Time of Hesitation: American Anti Imperialists and the Philippine American War*, New Day Publishers, Quezon City, 1981; also Douglas L. Wilson, ed, *Nine Essays by George Santayana*, Harvard University Press, Cambridge, MA, 1967. **Extract 17.**

Santos, Bienvenido N., *Scent of Apples: A Collection of Stories*, University of Washington Press, London, 1979.

Santos, Bienvenido, *The Volcano*, New Day Publishers, Quezon City, 1986. **Extract 14.**

Soto, Juan Crisotomo, *Lidia*, in Edna Zapanta Manlapaz, ed, *Kapampangan Literature: A Historical Survey and Anthology*, Ateneo de Manila University Press, Quezon City, 1981. **Extract 15.**

Twain, Mark, 'Summary of the Philippine "Incident": "The Philippine incident is now closed – substantially" ', in Roger J. Bresnaham, ed *In Time of Hesitation: American Anti Imperialists and the Philippine American War*, New Day Publishers, Quezon City, 1981; also Philip S. Foner, *Mark Twain Social Critic*, International, New York, 1958. **Extract 18.**

Valeros-Gruenberg, Estrellita and Florentino B. Valeros, *Filipino Writers in English: A Biographical and Bibliographical Dictionary*, New Day Publishers, Quezon City, 1987.

Villa, Jose Garcia, 'First a poem must be magical', *Have Come Am Here*, Viking Press, New York, 1942. **Extract 9.**

Extracts

(1) Baguio City

Ophelia Alcantara Dimalanta, *Pale Thoughts upon a Pale City*

Billed as the 'Summer Capital of the Philippines', Baguio City was devastated by a strong earthquake in 1990. Dimalanta describes how it appears to a lowland resident visiting during Manila's long, hot summer months.

City of vaguely fashioned needs
Suspended upon quaint disenchanted clouds,
Invalid, morning would find it as
Comatose as this part of me
Unreal and misty down Session Road,[1]
Hanging by a flimsy string,
Giddy for warmth, in the cool,
Fog-bated breath.

[1]Baguio City's main throughfare.

(2) Bohol

Marjorie E. Evasco, *'Birthing Poems'*

The country's leading feminist poet talks of being a woman in the southern part of the Philippines, where women carry the double burden of working in rice fields and keeping house.

It is marking time: my heart-
skin, the color of moon
rising in women, ripens to the double-
edged blade mother used to crop
the first locks off my head
to make me speak, or glean
the first offering of rice
goldened under the solstice sun.
When it cuts doubly deep, I hear
rivers rising, women howling
lunar canticles of longing.
Now I must learn my mother's tongue,
know how it cuts against the grain.

(3) Cebu

Marcel M. Navarra, *The Awakening*

Competing with Manila as the country's premier city is the southern city of Cebu, which now combines unspoiled beaches with modern commercial districts. In this portion of a short story told from the point of view of a young boy, Navarra describes life in rural Cebu in the first half of the 20th century.

We followed a narrow trail that ended on the doorstep of Gavino's hut. From afar, Gavino's hut looked like a pile of dried coconut leaves. Actually, the dried leaves were made to lean on a bamboo pole both ends of which were tied to two coconut trees – this was what Gavino's hut was made of. Here he spent the whole day, here he cooked his meals, here he rested during midday after gathering tuba from three coconut trees. Only in the evening did Gavino leave the hut to sleep in the house of a niece who had gotten married to a tuba trader.[1]

We slowly opened the matted coconut leaves which served as a door. Piled up inside the hut were bamboo tubes used as tuba containers. On top of a legless bamboo bed were a chipped cooking pot and a plate on which some malunggay[2] leaves had stuck. Just as Diyak Arsenio had suspected, Gavino was not in his hut.

Leaving Gavino's hut, we slowly inched our way through two rows of maguey plants that had not yet been cut though the time was right for cutting. We carefully parted the thorny thick leaves that obstructed the way. Near the edge of the cliff stood the sineguelas[3] tree protected by the branches of a large balete[4] tree.

[1]Local wine. [2]A kind of herb. [3]Fruit. [4]Folkloric fig tree.

(4) Ilocos Sur: Vigan

Rio Alma (Virgilio S. Almario), *'Vigan'*

The Ilocano city of Vigan in northern Luzon island has preserved most of its Spanish-type colonial architecture. A leading Tagalog poet describes the experience of going north in space or, in effect, going back to the 19th century in time.

A return to the past, this journey
Of the eyes among ancient adobe, tile roof, narra
Spared by storm, temblor, fire and war.
Each corner is archive, each chip of stone
A page of history.
. . .

These are the wind's memoirs, tales the white ant brings with its gnawing,
At the capiz-shell window, the rotting carriage, antique closet,
Threadbare curtains and cushions, yellowed manuscripts.

(5) La Union: Nagrebcan

Manuel E. Arguilla, *Midsummer*

Much of the Philippine countryside remains the way it was on northern Luzon island in the first half of the 20th century, as Arguilla describes it at the beginning of one of his best short stories.

He pulled down his hat until the wide brim touched his shoulders. He crouched lower under the cover of his cart and peered ahead. The road seemed to writhe under the lash of the noon-day heat; it swung from side to side, humped and bent itself like a fleeing serpent, and disappeared behind the spur of a low hill on which grew a scrawny thicket of bamboo.

There was not a house in sight. Along the left side of the road ran the deep, dry gorge of a stream, the banks sparsely covered by sun-burned *cogon* grass. In places, the rocky, waterless bed showed aridly. Farther, beyond the shimmer of quivering heat waves rose ancient hills not less blue than the cloud-palisaded sky. On the right stretched a sandy waste of low rolling dunes. Scattered clumps of hardy *ledda*[1] relieved the otherwise barren monotony of the landscape. Far away he could discern a thin indigo line that was the sea.

The grating of the cartwheels on the pebbles of the road and the almost soundless shuffle of the weary bull but emphasized the stillness. Now and then came the dry rustling of falling earth as slumps from the cracked sides of the gorge rolled down to the bottom.

[1]Kind of grass.

(6) Leyte

Norman Mailer, *The Naked and the Dead*

The fictional island Anopopei looks very much like Leyte in central Philippines, where Mailer served with the US army during the second world war. In this extract from the bestselling war novel, he describes the Philippine sunset, famed for its exceptional beauty.

The sunset was magnificent with the intensity and brilliance that can be found only in the tropics. The entire sky was black with the impending rain except for a narrow ribbon along the horizon. The sun had already disappeared, but its reflection was compressed, channeled into a band of color where the sky met the water. The sunset made an arc along the water like the cove of a harbor, but a strange and illusory harbor, washed in a vivid spectrum of crimson and golden yellows and canary greens. There was a string of tiny clouds shaped like miniature plump sausages and they had become a royal stippled purple. After a time, the men had the impression they were staring at a fabulous island which could have existed only in their imagination. Each detail glowed, became quiveringly real. There was a beach whose sands were polished and golden, and on the false shore a grove of trees had turned a magnificent lavender-blue in the dusk. The beach was separate from everything they had ever known; it possessed every outcropping of rock, every curve of sand dune on a barren and gelid shore, but this beach was alive and quivering with warmth. Above the purple foliage the land rose in pink and violet dales, shading finally into the overcast above the harbor. The water before them, illumined by the sunset, had become the deep clear blue of the sky on a summer evening.

(7) Luzon

Amado V. Hernandez, *Irony*

The poet describes two of several socio-economic contradictions that can still be found in the Philippines.

The impoverished hut shivers with cold –
under its roof not a bit of coal:
the father, though a miner, has lost what he found
when he mined abundant carbon in the earth.

Hungry is the whole family without rice,
their enormous debt still piles up for weeks:
the farmer twists in hunger
though the harvest fills the overflowing granary.

(8) Manila

Francisco Balagtas, *Florante and Laura*

In a classic Tagalog metrical romance that inspired imitators as late as the middle of the 20th century, Balagtas attacks Spanish colonial authorities, charging them with destroying the moral fibre of his people.

There, hapless state, and even 'yond
Treason has flung his tyrant-bond,
Virtue the while lies moribund,
Stifled in sloughs of deep despond.

All noble deeds are hurled amain
Amidst indignity and disdain,
The wise when to the gravehole ta'en,
Must coffinless therein remain.

Whereas the wicked and the mean
On thrones of honor sit serene
And before those of bestial mien
Incense is burnt sweet-scented, clean.

(9) Manila

Jose Garcia Villa, *'First, a Poem must be Magical'*

The foremost Filipino poet writing in English before the Pacific War defines poetry in images that transcend Philippine geographical boundaries.

First, a poem must be magical,
Then musical as a sea-gull.
It must be a brightness moving
And hold secret a bird's flowering.
It must be slender as a bell,
And it must hold fire as well.
It must have the wisdom of bows
And it must kneel like a rose.
It must be able to hear
The luminance of dove and deer.
It must be able to hide
What it seeks, like a bride.
And over all I would like to hover
God, smiling from the poem's cover.

(10) Manila: Edsa

Ruth Elynia S. Mabanglo, *'After the Revolution'*

After the People Power Revolution in 1986 on Epifanio de los Santos Avenue (EDSA), nothing really changed in the Philippines, claims feminist poet Mabanglo, who describes a typical post-revolution street scene near the famous avenue.

Nothing has changed, nothing has become different yet,
In the people's aims and actions.
You will still find at the corner of Santol
The sampaguita[1] child vendor
Peddling honor and childhood that have
Grown old.
Grimy still is the newsboy
Who is death riding the footboards.[2]

[1]Ubiquitous flower sold on streets. [2]Back exits of public transport vehicles.

(11) Manila: Ongpin

Grace Hsieh Hsing, *Ongpin Street*

A leading Chinese–Filipino poet describes how she feels towards Ongpin Street in Manila's Chinatown. Despite being Filipino in every way, she remains tied to her roots in China.

I visit Ongpin Street to read disorderly Chinese signs
I visit Ongpin Street to view unfamiliar Chinese faces
I visit Ongpin Street to hear licentious Chinese songs
I visit Ongpin Street to step upon dirty Chinese roads

Whenever I think of China
I visit Ongpin Street
Ongpin Street is in Chinatown

Chinatown is not in China
Chinatown is not China

(12) Manila: Recto

F. Sionil Jose, *Mass*

C.M. Recto Avenue (across Mendiola Bridge from Malacanang Palace, seat of the Philippine government) is also known as University Belt, becausae of many universities in the area. One of the country's best-known novelists in English follows the thoughts of a student going to university for the first time.

Recto!

The jeepney[1] drivers shout it, this name that circumscribes, describes youth, the urban malady and pollution, *bakya*[2] supermarket at one end which is Divisoria, and vision and corruption – whichever you want to append – at the other . . . Malacañang. It is this other end, the vision-corruption part which would be familiar grounds to me for four years.

Recto! Rectum of Manila! Here are the odors of the posterior, particularly when the sun is warm and there would be a busted sewer gushing yellowish froth, and flies as big as bottle caps on the garbage piles; but we are young and if we see them, we look away. They will all be swept clean when the revolution comes and this Recto, this will be the boulevard of great erudition; it will be the avenue of hope. It already is to thousands upon thousands like me, for it is here where I go to school. Recto has these piles, these diploma mills, about half a dozen of them, and at dusk they clog the street and the narrow, smelly sidewalks . . . the students pouring in and out of the airless schoolrooms, their young voices mingling with the noxious bedlam of a thousand jeepneys. Coming out of one of the Kung Fu movies on any afternoon, the faces I see have a certain pallid gloss to them – a trick of sunlight maybe, but it may just as well be the kind of funereal patina that should cover everyone, for in this mess of mass, these young people, like me, are the great unwashed hoping to be scrubbed clean, hoping to be somebody other than our anonymous selves.

[1]Public transport vehicle. [2]Lower-class.

(13) MINDANAO: LAKE LANAO

Darangen

In their tribal epic, the Maranaos of southern Philippines tell the story of their ancestors who lived before the coming of Islam to the Philippines. Here, a ritual of dressing is described. Translation by Ma Delia Coronel. (See Booklist).

The prince continued dressing up.
He put on the shirt that was used
To cover the breast and stomach,
A special work of the ladies.
He put on the embroidered coat –
It was beautiful and well made.
He then carefully fixed it up
On top of his clothes and made sure
Each part had fitted well, pulling
The sleeves over his sturdy arms!
He moved slowly and as he shrugged,
His clothes fell properly in place.
He looked so well in them, shining
As bright as a star in the sky
The biggest and the brightest one,
A magnificent, dazzling sight
For our handsome smart young datu[1]
Wore his clothes well, they fitted
Him perfectly, being the kind
Of clothes that were usually made
In deep secret as the weaver
Kept her art exclusively hers.
The clothes were so fine they rippled
When the wind blew, the craftsmanship
Seen in the way it was woven
From thread spun from the finest gold
Mixed with the smoothest of silk threads!

[1]Tribal or community leader.

(14) Mount Mayon

Bienvenido N. Santos, *The Volcano*

The Philippines is full of active volcanoes. Among the most destructive is Mount Mayon, in southern Luzon island. Santos describes its 1928 eruption, very much like the 1991 eruption of Mount Pinatubo.

All night the volcano continued erupting at increasingly longer intervals, but the violence of every blast showed no abating. On the other hand, every last eruption seemed the strongest, as though each added hour between every eruption increased the churning fury of the flames in the clogged crater and would any moment explode the whole mountain.

By morning, it looked as if the sun was late in rising though it was there. A spray of lava dust floated in the air, darkening the morning like twilight, covering the streets and the grass, the rooftops, and the bare heads of those who stayed outside waiting for the worst, so that all walked about with a touch of gray on their hair, including the little ones. A sudden, general aging had come upon all, it seemed, like a promise of death.

Night came quickly there before the sun went down, as if it had not left at all and morning had never come. Now that true darkness had settled down around the burning mountain, the crater shone bright red, and the smoke, too, was spangled with glow-stones that shot up in the air like giant fireworks. Meanwhile the lava streams seemed wider and deeper now, endangering the towns at the base of the volcano towards which they were flowing.

(15) Pampanga: Angeles

Juan Crisostomo Soto, *Lidia*

In the most famous Kapampangan novel of all time, one of Pampanga's major writers describes a typical Philippine town feast. Culiat was the former name of Angeles, Pampanga, once the site of one of the largest American airbases, before the entire area was devastated by Mount Pinatubo's 1991 eruption.

As was the custom: lights, music, flowers, silk, gauze, ornaments, gaiety, joy, and color, harmoniously coming together in the happy feast of the La Naval at Culiat. In the town of the Angelos, Hensons, Mesinas, and other families whose names gave it prestige, were gathered all the goodness, beauty and distinction of this fiesta. On that day, Culiat – the industry of whose people brought it prosperity – was like a golden cup into which had been poured a thousand rays of light and color, of beauty and distinction; in her wide streets, clean and straight, flowed the brilliance of beauty and untold wealth.

Starting on the eve of the feast, not a small number of visitors came; crowds of people filled the streets: girls and boys, young women and young men, the happy youth who always brighten up every festivity, made their presence felt there. The young Filipina with brown cheeks, the model of refinement, clothed in a piña[1] dress decorated with multi-colored sequins, stood out in the streets, especially when the sunlight shone on her, making the sleeves of her dress seem like the translucent wings of a butterfly when it has just emerged from its cocoon and put on its garb of shimmering velvet.

The streets, houses – crystal palaces of the brown nymphs – are all aglow with light; from every side you hear music coming from the keys of a piano, or from the strings of a thousand harps, guitars, and *bandurrias*,[2] or from the sweet and tender sounds of an orchestra welcoming visitors. In the midst of that music, there suddenly rises the high soprano voice, sweet and tender, of a young woman with a swan-like neck; her voice trembles either from anxiety over the ascending scale of notes or from embarrassment caused by a young man's fixed gaze on her. Everything is in motion, as if to keep pace with the lively tempo of the fiesta.

[1]Pineapple fibre. [2]Native guitars.

(16) Pasig River: Laguna De Bay

Jose Rizal, *The Reign of Greed*

Using a steamship plowing the once-magnificent Pasig River, which connects southern Luzon with Manila, national hero Jose Rizal creates a metaphor for Philippine society.

One morning in December the steamer *Tabo* was laboriously ascending the tortuous course of the Pasig, carrying a large crowd of passengers toward the province of La Laguna. She was a heavily built steamer, almost round, like the *tabu*[1] from which she derived her name, quite dirty in spite of her pretensions to whiteness, majestic and grave from her leisurely motion. Altogether, she was held in great affection in that region, perhaps from her Tagalog name, or from the fact that she wore the characteristic impress of things in the country, representing something like a triumph over progress, a steamer that was not a steamer at all, an organism, stolid, imperfect yet unimpeachable, which, when it wished to pose as being rankly progressive, proudly contented itself with putting on a fresh coat of paint. Indeed, the happy steamer was genuinely Filipino! If a person were only reasonably considerate, she might even have been taken for the Ship of State, constructed, as she had been, under the inspection of *Reverendos* and *Ilustrisimos*.

Bathed in the sunlight of a morning that made the waters of the river sparkle and the breezes rustle in the bending bamboo on its banks, there she goes with her white silhouette throwing out great clouds of smoke – the Ship of State, so the joke runs, also has the vice of smoking! The whistle shrieks at every moment, hoarse and commanding like a tyrant who would rule by shouting, so that no one on board can hear his own thoughts. She menaces everything she meets: now she looks as though she would grind to bits the *salambaw*, insecure fishing apparatus which in their movements resemble skeletons of giants saluting an antediluvian tortoise; now she speeds straight toward the clumps of bamboo or against the amphibian structures, *karihan*, or wayside lunch-stands, which, amid *gumamelas* and other flowers, look like indecisive bathers who with their feet already in the water cannot bring themselves to make the final plunge; at times, following a sort of channel marked out in the river by tree-trunks, she moves along with a satisfied air, except when a sudden shock disturbs the passengers and throws them off their balance, all the result of a collision with a sand-bar which no one dreamt was there.

Moreover, if the comparison with the Ship of State is not yet complete, note the arrangement of the passengers. On the lower deck appear brown faces and black heads, types of Indians,[2] Chinese, mestizos,[3] wedged in between bales of merchandise and boxes, while there on the upper deck, beneath an awning that protects them from the sun, are seated in comfortable chairs a few passengers dressed in the fashion of Europeans, friars, and government clerks, each with his *puro* cigar, and gazing at the landscape apparently without heeding the efforts of the captain and the sailors to overcome the obstacles in the river.

[1]Water dipper. [2]Natives. [3]Persons of mixed descent, usually Chinese and native.

(17) Philippines: American Period

George Santayana, *Young Sammy's First Wild Oats*

In a long, comic fable, Spanish philosopher Santayana – who was then teaching at Harvard – deplores the racism at the root of the American colonization of the Philippines. In this portion, Sam – son of Uncle Sam – celebrates his victory over Spain by raping a young Filipino woman.

But with that poor Filipina,
when she shrank from his caress,
His contemptible demeanor
isn't easy to express.

First he bought her, then he kicked her;
but the truth is, he was drunk,
For that day had crowned him victor,
and a Spanish fleet was sunk.

You perceive I do not spare him,
nor am blinded to his motes
By the Christian love I bear him;
yes: he's sowing his wild oats.

But you can't deny him talent;
once his instinct is awake,
He can play the part of gallant
and of soldier and of rake.

(18) Philippines: American Period

Mark Twain, *Summary of the Philippine 'Incident': 'The Philippine incident is closed – substantially'*

Many American writers were appalled by the US government's decision to wage war on Filipinos at the turn of the century. In his familiar satirical style, Twain summarizes the 'gains' made by American soldiers led by Lt Gen Arthur MacArthur, to whom is attributed the quote in the title.

We may now take an account of stock and find out how much we have made by the speculation – or lost. The Government went into the speculation on certain definite grounds which it believed from the viewpoint of statesmanship, to be good and sufficient. To wit: 1, for the sake of the money supposed to be in it; 2, in order to become a World Power and get a back seat in the Family of Nations.

We have scored on number 2. We have secured a back seat in the Family of Nations. We have scored it and [are] trying to enjoy the tacks that are in it. We are a World power, no one can deny it, a brass-gilt one, a tuppence, ha'penny one, but a World Power just the same. We have bought some islands from a party that did not own them; with real smartness and a good counterfeit of disinterested friendliness, we coaxed a weak nation into a trap, and closed it upon them; we went back on our honored guest of the stars and stripes when we had no further use for him, and chased him into the mountains; we are as indisputably in possession of a wide-spreading archipelago as if it were our own property; we have pacified some thousands of islanders and buried them; destroyed their fields; burned their villages and turned their widows and orphans out of doors; furnished their heart-breaking exile to dozens of disagreeable patriots and subjugated the remaining millions by Benevolent Assimilation which is the pious new name of the musket; we have acquired property in the three hundred concubines and other slaves of our business partner, the Sultan of Sulu, and hoisted our protecting flag over that swag.

Biographies and literary notes

Virgilio Almario

ABUEG, Efren R(eyes) (1937–). Philippine novelist writing in Tagalog; born in **Cavite**; educated at De La Salle University; winner of national awards; member of influential *Agos sa Disyerto (Currents in the Desert)* group which revolutionized Tagalog short story writing in the 1960s. His seven major novels include *Habagat sa Lupa* (*Storms on Earth*, 1963), and *Dilim sa Umaga* (*Darkness in the Morning*, 1967). Some of his short stories have been translated into English, Chinese, Ukranian, and Russian. He has also edited several books.

ALMARIO, Virgilio S. (pseudonym Rio Alma) (1944–). Philippine poet and critic writing in Filipino; born in **Bulacan**; educated at University of the Philippines; winner of South-east Asia Writers Award (SEAWRITE), 1989, and national awards; member of the Manila Critics Circle. His poems are collected in *Makinasyon at Ibang Tula* (*Mechanisation and Other Poems*, 1968), *Doktrinang Anak Pawis* (*Proletarianism*, 1979), *Mga Retrato at Rekwerdo* (*Portraits and Memories*, 1984), *Palipad-Hangin* (*Balloon*, 1985), *(A)lamat at (H)istorya* (*Myth and History*, 1986), *Katon Para sa Limang Pandama* (*Primer for Five Senses*, 1987), *Selected Poems, 1968–1985* (1987), *Mga Retaso ng Liwanag* (*Pieces of Light*, 1990). His books of criticism include *Ang Makata sa Panahon ng Makina* (*The Poet in the Machine Age*, 1972), *Balagtasismo versus Modernismo* (*The Balagtas Syndrome versus Modernism*, 1984), *Taludtod at Talinghaga* (*Verse and Metaphor*, 1985), *Kung Sino ang Kumatha kina Bagongbanta, Ossorio, Herrera, Aquino de Belen, Balagtas: Mga Imbestigasyon sa Panitikan ng Kolonyalismo* (*Who Authored Bagongbanta, Ossorio, Herrera, Aquino de Belen, Balagtas, and others: Investigations into the Literature of Colonialism*, 1992) and *Panitikan ng Rebolusyon* (*Literature of the Revolution*). Extract 4 is his description of the Ilocano city of **Vigan**.

Ang Bantay Sang Patyo (*The Guardian of the Cemetery*, 1925). Philippine novel in Hiligaynon by Magdalena Jalandoni. An apparently autobiographical love story set in **Iloilo** at the end of the 19th century, which turns tragic when misunderstandings, parents, and wealthy rivals intervene.

ARCELLANA, Francisco A. (1916–). Philippine short story writer writing in English, Philippine National Artist for Literature; born in **Manila**; helped organize Veronicans, a pre-Pacific War group which greatly influenced writing in English; founded post-war University of the Philippines Creative Writing Center. Arcellana's best pieces are collected in *The Francisco Arcellana Sampler* (1990).

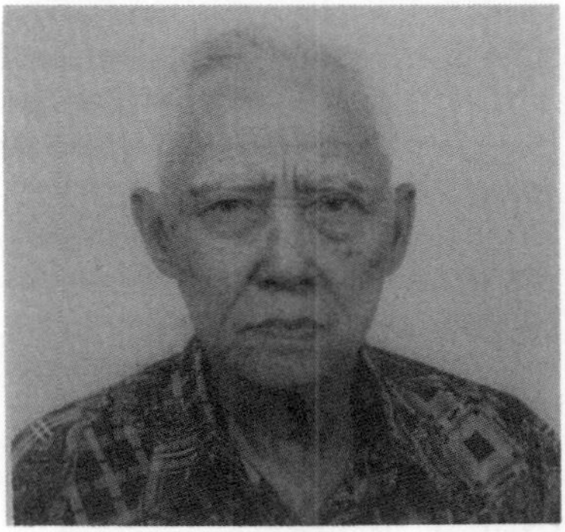

Francisco Arcellana

ARGUILLA, Manuel E. (1910–44). Philippine short story writer writing in English. Born in **La Union**; executed by the Japanese during the Pacific War for guerrilla activities. His 150 stories remain unexcelled for craft. His 'Midsummer' was included in Edward O'Brien's 1936 *Yearbook of the American Short Story*. His best stories are collected in *How My Brother Leon Brought Home a Wife and Other Stories* (1940) – Extract 5.

BALAGTAS, also known as Francisco Baltazar (1788–1862). Philippine poet and playwright writing in Tagalog. Born in **Bulacan**; considered one of two major writers of the 19th century (the other being Jose Rizal ◊); imprisoned on false charges; his met-

Cirilo F. Bautista

rical romance *Pinagdaanang Buhay ni Florante at Laura sa Cahariang Albania* (1838), popularly known as *Florante at Laura* ◊, used allegory to attack Spanish colonialism (Extract 8); his major play *Orosman at Zafira* (1857) dwelt on political power and personal passion.

BAUTISTA, Cirilo F(rancisco) (1941–). Filipino poet and critic writing in English and Tagalog; born in **Manila**; educated at De la Salle University; winner of national awards. His poetry books include *The Cave and Other Poems* (1968), *The Archipelago* (1970), *Charts* (1973), *Telex Moon* (1975), *Sugat ng Salita* (*Wounding Words*, 1985) and *Boneyard Breaking* (1992); his short fiction is collected in *Stories* (1990) and his critical essays in *Breaking Signs: Lectures on Literature and Semiotics* (1990). His works have been published elsewhere in Asia, as well as in Romania, Japan, Holland, Germany, and the USA.

CRUZ, Isagani R. (1945–). Philippine playwright and critic writing in Filipino and English. Born in **Manila**; educated at University of Maryland; winner of Southeast Asia Writers Award (SEAWRITE), 1991, and national awards; founding chair of Manila Critics Circle. His best plays are collected in *Josephine at iba pang Dula* (*Josephine and Other Plays*, 1984). His other books include *Beyond Futility: The Filipino as Critic* (1984). He has been published in Hong Kong, Malaysia, Singapore, the UK, and the USA. He was a Visiting Fellow at St Antony's College, Oxford, in 1988.

DIMALANTA, Ophelia Alcantara (1934–). Philippine poet and critic writing in English; born in **Metro Manila**; educated at the University of Santo Tomas; winner of national awards; member of the Manila Critics Circle. Her poems are collected in *Montage* (Extract 1, 1969), *The Time Factor and Other Poems* (1982), *Flowing On* (1988) and *Lady Polyester* (1993). Her book of critical essays *The Philippine Poetic* (1976) studies award-winning poetry collections.

EVASCO, Marjorie M(arie), also known as Marjorie Pernia (her estranged husband's name) (1953–). Philippine poet writing in English. Born in **Bohol**; educated at Silliman University. Her first book of poems, *Dreamweavers* (Extract 2, 1987), won a Manila Critics Circle National Book Award; anthologized in India, Malaysia, Japan, the USA, Canada, France and Germany.

El Filibusterismo (*Subversive*, 1891). Philippine novel in Spanish by Jose Rizal. Published in Berlin; sequel to *Noli Me Tangere* ◊. Disguised as political power-broker Simoun, Ibarra returns to Manila to provoke armed revolution against Spanish friars, but a naive student frustrates his grand plan to assassinate all the villains in one fell swoop.

Florante at Laura (*Florante and Laura*, 1838). Philippine metrical romance in Tagalog by Balagtas ◊, which determined directions of Tagalog writing for more than a century; 1 708 lines in 4-line stanzas. Complete title: *Pinagdaanang Buhay ni Florante at ni Laura sa Cahariang Albania* (*Lives of Florante and Laura in the Kingdom of Albania*). The Albania of the title has nothing to do with the real Albania; it is really a mythical place (suspiciously like Spanish period Philippines) where injustice reigns. Laura's love Florante is outmanoeuvred politically by the villain, who throws him into a forest where he is given up for dead. With the help of a Muslim prince and the latter's female friend (male and female both being warriors at the time), Florante escapes and regains his throne (Extract 8).

HERNANDEZ, Amado V. (1903–70). Philippine poet and novelist writing in Tagalog. Named Philippine National Artist for Literature after his death; alive, he was imprisoned for anti-government activities. Championed art committed to labour. His major novel *Mga Ibong Mandaragit* (*Birds of Prey*, 1959) continues the story of Jose Rizal's *El Filibusterismo* ◊. His prison poems are collected in *Isang Dipang Langit* (*Rice Grains*, 1961). Other publications include an epic poem *Bayang Malaya* (*Free Country*, 1955) and the novel *Luha ng Buwaya* (*Crocodile Tears*, 1972). 'Irony' (Extract 7) describes the socio-economic contradictions of poverty.

HSIEH HSING, Grace (1938–). Philippine poet writing in Chinese; born in Shanghai; grew up in Taiwan and studied at Taipei National College of Fine Arts; emigrated to the Philippines in 1964. Her poems have appeared in Taiwan, China, Hong Kong, Singapore, and Malaysia. She has two collections of poetry: *The Persian Cat* (1990) and *To the Flowers* (Extract 11, 1990).

JALANDONI, Magdalena G. (1893–1978). Philippine novelist, poet, and playwright in Hiligaynon; born in **Jaro, Iloilo**; wrote more than 50 novels, some in verse. Among her best-known novels are *Ang Bantay sang Patyo* (*The Guardian of the Cemetery*, 1925), *Ang mga Tunok sang Isa ka Bulak* (1909), *Lucia* (1919), *Ang Panaad nga Natuman* (1932), and *Ang Dalaga sa Tindahan* (1935). She continued the metrical romance tradition in prose.

JOAQUIN, Nick M. (pseudonym Quijano de Manila) (1917–). Philippine novelist and poet writing in English; born in **Manila**; Philippine National Artist for Literature; winner of Southeast Asia Writers Award

Isagani Cruz

(SEAWRITE), 1980; educated in Hong Kong. He has written dozens of books; among the best are *Prose and Poems* (1952), the novel *The Woman Who Had Two Navels* (1961), and the play *Portrait of the Artist as Filipino* (1966).

JOSE, F. Sionil (1924–). Philippine novelist writing in English; born in **Pangasinan**; winner of Ramon Magsaysay Award (1980); publisher and editor of *Solidarity* journal since 1965; national secretary of the Philippine Centre of International PEN. His novels include *The Pretenders* (1962), *Tree* (1978), *My Brother, My Executioner* (1979), *Mass* (Extract 12, 1982), *Po-on* (1984), *Ermita* (1991), *Gagamba* (1991) and *Viajero* (1993). His short stories are collected in *The God Stealer* (1968), *Waywaya* (1980), *Platinum* (1983), *Olvidon* (1988), and *Selected Short Stories* (1991). He has a book of poems, *Questions* (1988). He has been translated into several languages.

Lidia (1907). Philippine novel in Kapampangan by Juan Crisostomo Soto. A romance starring the rich and famous of rural **Pampanga**, north of Manila. Unable to extricate himself from a classic love triangle, a desperate young man kisses a hesitant young woman in public, causing grave public scandal. The man is later found dead, but love conquers all, even death (Extract 15).

MABANGLO, Ruth Elynia S. (1949–). Philippine poet writing in Tagalog; born in **Manila**; educated at Manuel L. Quezon University. Winner of national awards; her books include *Supling* (*Child*, 1970) and *Mga Liham ng Pinay* (*Letters from Filipinas*, 1990) and *Kung Di Man: Mga Tula ng Pag-ibig 1970–92* (*If Not: Love Poems, 1970–92*). 'After the revolution' (Extract 10) describes post People's Power Manila.

MAILER, Norman (1923–). American novelist and journalist, born in New Jersey and raised in Brooklyn. A pioneer of 'new journalism', Mailer's first novel *The Naked and the Dead* (1948, Extract 6) is an uncompromising war novel based on his service in the Philippines in the second world war.

MATUTE, Genoveva Edroza (1915–). Philippine short story writer writing in Tagalog; born in **Manila**; educated at University of Santo Tomas. She is the winner of national awards; her 43 books include *Ako'y Isang Tinig* (*I Am A Voice*, 1952) and *Piling Maiikling Kuwento, 1939–1992* (*Selected Short Stories, 1939–1992*, 1992). She has also edited several books.

MEDINA, B(uenaventura) S(alvador), Jr (1929–). Filipino novelist and critic writing in Tagalog and English; born in **Manila**; educated at Centro Escolar University. His poetic fiction includes the novels *Moog* (*Fort*, 1991) and *Alaga* (*Ward*, 1993). His other works include an edition of *Orosman at Zafira ni Balagtas* (*Orosman and Zafira by Balagtas*, 1990), a collection of essays *Pintig* (*Pulsebeat*, 1966), a collection of short fiction *Gantimpala* (*Prize*, 1972), and a literary history *The Primal Passion* (1976).

NAVARRA, Marcel M. (1914–84). Philippine short story writer writing in Cebuano; born in **Carcar**; called the 'Father of the modern Cebuano short story'. His best stories are collected in *Mga Piling Kuwentong Sebuwano* (*Selected Cebuano Stories*, 1986), including the influential 'Ug Gianod Ako (And I Was Carried Away)', (1937). Part of 'The awakening' from the same collection is included in Extract 3.

Noli me Tangere (*Do Not Touch Me*, 1887). Philippine novel in Spanish by Jose Rizal. Published in Berlin. Fresh from studies in Europe, Ibarra returns home to promote political reform through education, but faces two forces – Spanish friars who do not want to give up political power and native revolutionaries who want more radical change. At the end of the novel, Ibarra flees for his life, pursued by Spanish soldiers and helped by the revolutionary Elias. Generally considered the greatest Philippine novel of all time.

RIZAL, Jose (1861–96). Philippine novelist and poet writing in Spanish and Tagalog; executed by Spanish colonial authorities for his anti-government writings, particularly the novels *Noli Me Tangere* (*Do Not Touch Me*, 1887) ◊ and *El Filibusterismo* (*Subversive*, 1891) ◊; one of two major Philippine writers of the 19th century (the other being Balagtas ◊); a medical doctor by profession, he was widely-travelled and made significant contributions to scholarship in literary history, linguistics, and science; his patriotic poem *Mi Ultimo Adios* (*My Last Farewell*, 1896), completed the night before his execution, has been translated into more than 47 foreign and 34 Philippine languages. *The Reign of Greed* (Extract 16, 1891) describes the **Pasig River** which connects Southern Luzon to Manila.

B.S. Medina, Jr

Rosales Saga. Five novels by Philippine writer F. Sionil Jose, dealing with characters associated with the semi-fictional town of Rosales in northern Philippines: *Po-on* (1984), *Tree* (1978), *My Brother, My Executioner* (1979), *The Pretenders* (1962), *Mass* (1982). Widely-acclaimed as a microcosm of Philippine history and society; starts with the last years of the Spanish empire and brings the story of one family down to the radical student movement during the Marcos dictatorship.

SANTAYANA, George (1863–1952). Spanish American philosopher. Born in Madrid and taken to the USA by his family in 1871. Professor of Philosophy at Harvard (1889–1912). His major philosophical work is *The Life of Reason*, a five volume study. *The Last Puritan* is his only novel, published in 1935. Santayana was a forthright critic of American imperialism (Extract 17).

SANTOS, Bienvenido N. (1911–). Philippine–American novelist and poet writing in English; born in **Manila**, now a citizen of USA; educated at University of Illinois; academic administrator and professor at several universities; winner of numerous awards, including American Book Award and Manila Critics Circle National Book Award. His novels include *Villa Magdalena* (1965), *The Volcano* (Extract 14, 1965), *The Praying Man* (1982), *The Man Who (Thought He) Looked Like Robert Taylor* (1983), and *What the Hell For You Left Your Heart in San Francisco* (1987). His short stories are collected in *You Lovely People* (1955), *Brother My Brother* (1960), *The Day the Dancers Came* (1967), *Scent of Apples* (1979), and *Dwell in the Wilderness* (1985). He has two books of poems: *The Wounded Stag* (1956) and *Distances in Time* (1983). He has an autobiography, *Memory's Fictions* (1993).

SOTO, Juan Crisostomo (1867–1918), Philippine poet, playwright, and novelist writing in Kapampangan; his major play *Alang Dios* (*There Is No God*, 1902) in the *sarswela* (musical) mode was very popular; although his short stories usually involve tragic loves, his 'Y Miss Phathupats' (1907) is a comic masterpiece. His novel *Lidia* (1907) ◊ is the most popular Kapampangan novel of all time (Extract 15). Like most poets of his time, he wrote patriotic poems.

TWAIN, Mark (Samuel Langhorne Clemens) (1835–1910). American novelist, short-story writer, humorist and social critic (Extract 18). Twain left school at 12 and travelled widely, both in the USA and internationally. His most famous works are *The Adventures of Tom Sawyer* (1876) and *Adventures of Huckleberry Finn* (1884).

VILLA, Jose Garcia (1912–). Philippine poet writing in English; Philippine National Artist for Literature; as literary godfather before the Pacific War, he upheld the primacy of craft over content; he has spent most of his postwar life in New York. Among his books are *Footnote to Youth* (1933), *Poems by Doveglion* (1941), *Have Come, Am Here* (Extract 9, 1942), and *Selected Poems and New* (1958).

Hong Kong

Mimi Chan

> 'It has a glorious bay, the movement of ships on the ocean is beyond anything I have seen in pictures, excellent roads, trolleys, a railway to the mountains, museums, botanical gardens . . .'
> *Anton Chekhov, Selected Letters*

Hong Kong is situated on the south-east coast of China. It comprises **Hong Kong island**, the small district of **Kowloon** on the mainland just opposite, and a larger area of the mainland, called the **New Territories**. The New Territories covers an area of 919 square kilometres. It is in the form of a peninsula with its northern boundary roughly along the Shum Chun River from Deep Bay to the northern shore of Mirs Bay. The New Territories include 235 islands, the biggest being Lantau, Lamma and Cheung Chau. The island of Hong Kong, which has given the territory its name, is less than one-tenth of the size of the New Territories and has an area of 82 square kilometres. Kowloon has an areas of only nine square kilometres, again only a tenth of the size of the island.

Hong Kong became a British colony in the 19th century. Britain concluded three treaties with the then Chinese government relating to Hong Kong: the Treaty of Nanking, signed in 1842 and ratified in 1843 under which Hong Kong island was ceded in perpetuity; the Convention of Peking in 1860 under which the southern part of the Kowloon peninsula and Stonecutters Island were ceded in perpetuity; the convention of 1898 under which the New Territories were leased to Britain for 99 years.

Under the terms of the Sino-British Joint Declaration signed in December 1984, British administration and jurisdiction over Hong Kong will continue until 30 June 1997 and from 1 July 1997 Hong Kong will become a Special Administrative Region (SAR) of the

People's Republic of China. The Joint Declaration provides that for 50 years after 1997 Hong Kong's lifestyle will remain unchanged, and China's socialist system and policies will not be practised in the SAR. From midnight, then, on 30 June 1997 over 140 years of British rule will come to an end.

Hong Kong Literary Culture

For the vast majority of the local population the end of British rule in Hong Kong is a source of apprehension not because of any cultural ties or feelings of affinity with the British, but rather because of a perceived threat to prosperity, stability, civil and other liberties. The British 'way of life', its literature and its culture, have never been assimilated by the majority of the local population. As for the English language, the utility of knowing the language has long been established, but, with the exception of a small minority of Western-educated returned students and remnants of more anglophile times, there is no particular 'love' of the language for its own sake. From the earliest times the local population and the British developed separately. They literally lived apart, with special zones off bounds to the Chinese, such as the **Peak** and a part of **Tsimshatsui** in Kowloon, for 'sanitary reasons'. The illicit lovers in Somerset Maugham's *The Painted Veil* (Extract 4) use a 'filthy little house' in **Victoria Road** in the Chinese part of the city for their assignations. The European community developed a strong social life, centring around amateur theatricals, the **Hong Kong Club** (which came into existence in 1846) and various sporting activities. In education, throughout the 19th century the Chinese continued to support their own vernacular schools in Chinese and Chinese education could be given without government grant or inspection. In the government-funded schools, only a very small number received what was known as a 'European education in a European language'. Some wealthy local Chinese sent their children to be educated in Britain, but until the 1960s the **University of Hong Kong**, the only tertiary institution in the territory, provided Hong Kong with the vast majority of its bilingual civil servants as well as educators, physicians, engineers and other professionals. The English language and Western culture were made available to those educated in the missionary schools, run by various religious denominations in the colony.

Thus, notwithstanding the years of British rule, Hong Kong has remained essentially a Chinese city. Its situation is very different from that of a South-east Asian community like Singapore, where English serves as the *lingua franca* for the various ethnic and linguistic communities. Thus, although the aim of this chapter is to include a blend of local Hong Kong writers and Western writers, the mix is, I am afraid, very uneven as almost all the writers in English of any repute tend to be at least half Western. There is no dearth of 'Hong Kong literature' written in Chinese, but, little of it has been translated for an international market.

There are at least three possible obstacles to the development of Hong Kong English writing. In an interview for the now defunct *All Asia Review of Books* in 1989, Timothy Mo focuses on the linguistic obstacle, and advances a simplistic reason for the dearth of Hong Kong English writers:

> . . . there's the language problem, Indians have no problem writing good English but no Cantonese or Chinese has that expertise.

The second obstacle is psychological. The links with China run deeper than just the sharing of a written language. In spite of the popularly held view that Hong Kong people spurn literary and artistic pursuits because of their preoccupation with making money, it is considered a mark of cultivation among the older members of the upper levels of society to be able to write poetry in Chinese, to paint a little and produce good calligraphy. However, there is certainly no particular general urge to try writing English poems, nor any particular prestige attached to the ability to do so. Perhaps unfairly, many educated Chinese find Pearl Buck, Lin Yutang and Maxine Hong Kingston exploitative and the 'quaintness' of their material patronising. The third possible obstacle to the development of a Hong Kong literature is lack of creativity. I need not labour the point that linguistic competence is not necessarily coupled with creative talent. Even those in whom creativity and linguistic facility meet may have no inclination whatsoever to write in a 'borrowed tongue'.

Early Literary History

Virtually nothing in the way of a distinctive literature from or about Hong Kong was written in the 19th century. Hong Kong was still essentially a trading post and had not yet developed an identity of its own. The gutsy times of those early years are reflected in later literature, after Hong Kong had won recognition for being an 'exciting' place.

Two very well-known 20th century works deal with the early years of settlement. One in particular has reached a very wide public from its film version; this is James Clavell's *Taipan*, which deals with the fortunes of a British trading company, the princely *hong*. Clavell ◊ cautiously includes a prefactory note: 'Of course, this is not a history but a novel. It is peopled with men and women created out of the author's imagination, and no reference to anyone, or to any company, that was – or is part – of Hong Kong is intended'. Nevertheless, most familiar with Hong Kong have made the inevitable connections. The Scottish adventurer and founder of the princely *hong*, the Noble House, is one Dirk Struan. He became the ruler or *taipan* of the most powerful trading company in the Far East. He was also a pirate and an opium smuggler. The film of *Taipan* brought fame to Chinese actress Joan Chen, although it was generally panned, especially in Hong Kong; not the least because of its 'lack of authenticity' and the chauvinistic and racist portrayal of May-May, Struan's mistress, which came in for considerable criticism. The geographical locales and the names referred to in *Taipan* are still familiar, but very much changed from what is described in the novel as 'thirty square miles of mountainous stone on the north tip of the huge Pearl River in south China'. The **harbour**, which plays such a part in Struan's legal and illegal trading activities is described time and time again. **Happy Valley**, where Struan and May-May had their home and where they die in the typhoon that closes the novel, covered a larger district than the present Happy Valley, site for one of Hong Kong's two racecourses, and stretched over present-day **Wanchai** to the sea, described in all its destructiveness in the novel. Happy Valley racecourse also features in *Noble House*, another Clavell novel set in Hong Kong (Extract 5).

Another novel which deals with the founding of Hong Kong is Timothy Mo's ◊ critically acclaimed *An Insular Possession* (1986). Set in the period of the first Opium War, *An Insular Possession* deals with the adventures of two young Americans and conveys the tone and ethos of the period through the use of newspaper extracts, letters and diaries. The **South China coast** and **Hong Kong harbour**, as in *Taipan*, play an important part in the story, and so does **Macau**, the Portuguese

---

[a] Pokfulam is the university area. George Bernard Shaw delivered a controversial address at the university's Great Hall in 1933; the British poet Edmund Blunden was Head of the English Department from 1953 to 1965. [b] Hong Kong's famous Foreign Correspondents' Club is featured in The Honourable Schoolboy by John le Carré as well as in other novels set in Hong Kong. [c] The Aberdeen Tunnel leads to Aberdeen (described in Extract 1) and the port of Stanley, where many Hong Kong residents were interned during the second world war. [d] The Happy Valley race course appears in James Clavell's Taipan and Noble House (Extract 5). [e] Former red light district which features in numerous novels about Hong Kong, including Taipan by James Clavell and The World According to Suzie Wong by Richard Mason. See especially the Luk Kwok hotel, reputed to have been the prototype for the hotel in Mason's novel. [f] The 1 o'clock gun featured in Noel Coward's poem 'Mad Dogs and Englishmen' is fired daily from Causeway Bay. [g] The scene of Kitty and Charlie's afternoon assignations in Somerset Maugham's The Painted Veil.

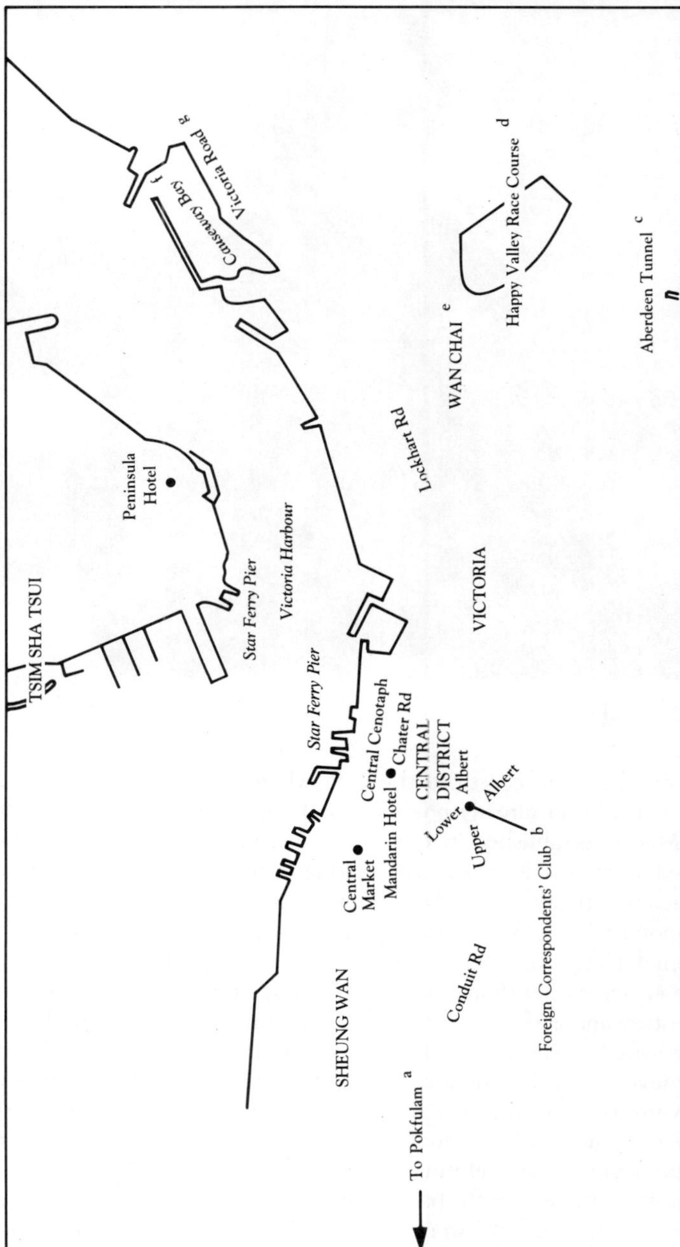

Central District and Victoria

James Clavell

colony on the same coast. In the days when Hong Kong was still a barren rock Macau already boasted a fashionable social life. The old city of Macau, established in 1557 and a fascinating place to visit, has remained much less developed than Hong Kong in its over 400 years as a Portuguese enclave. It is best known for its gambling, and many contemporary 'Hong Kong novels' include Macau for 'local colour'.

Colonial Hong Kong began to draw the attention of writers who were observers, rather than part of Hong Kong life. The last years of the 19th century and early years of the 20th century saw a growth in 'Hong Kong writing by visitors'. By the close of the 19th century Hong Kong had achieved steady economic growth. Following John Pope Hennessy's governorship (1877–82) the status of the Chinese community steadily rose, helped by permanent representation on the Legislative Council. An important reform came in 1897 when the system of night passes for Chinese which had been in existence since 1843 was abolished. While efforts were made to defer to Chinese feelings, complaints were heard that the Chinese were not so subservient as they had been. The period from the close of the 19th century to 1918 was one of steady economic and administrative development, interrupted only by the first world war.

This was the Hong Kong Anton Chekhov ◊ encountered when he passed through Hong Kong on his way home from a stay in the penal Colony of Sakhalin. He described the port in a letter written in Moscow to Alexei Suvorin dated 9 December 1890 (the letter appears in *The Selected Letters of Anton Chekhov*, see Booklist):

> The first foreign port on my journey was Hong Kong. It has a glorious bay, the movement of ships on the ocean is beyond anything I have seen even in pictures, excellent roads, trolleys, a railway to the mountains, museums, botanical gardens; wherever you turn you will note evidences of the most tender solicitude on the part of the English for men in their service; there is even a sailors' club. I drove around in a rickshaw, i.e., was borne by humans, bought all sorts of rubbish from the Chinese and got indignant listening to my Russian traveling companions abusing the English for exploiting the natives. Thought I to myself, yes, the English exploit the Chinese, the Sepoys and the Hindus, but they do give them roads, plumbing and Christianity; you exploit them too, but what do you give them?

Rudyard Kipling ◊, that great exponent of British values, saw much to admire in the British contributions in Hong Kong. He came in 1889 on his way from India to England and sent dispatches about his travels to the Allahabad *Pioneer*, which were subsequently collected in the volume *From Sea to Sea* (1889). Kipling saw Hong Kong as a miniature of the empire, fortified by a British garrison, commercially successful, and efficiently administered. He claimed there was much about Hong Kong that reminded him of British India, and so impressed was he by the industry of the workers in Hong Kong that he jestingly told his Anglo-Indian readers that they had conquered the wrong country. But a trip to Canton changed his opinions of the Chinese. He was repelled by the 'yellow devils' and hurried back to Hong Kong, and its reassuring colonial lifestyle. One facet of Hong Kong life appalled Kipling, and that was its vice. What really revolted him was that there were actually *white* prostitutes in the city.

'Visitor Literature' continued to appear in the first decades of the 20th century. W. Somerset Maugham ◊ made a contribution to this genre. A long journey to China resulted in his vignettes of China and China coast life and characters in *On a Chinese Screen* (1922). The combination of Hong Kong and Mainland China provided interesting contrasts in his novel, *The Painted Veil* (Extract 4) which describes a 'high colonial' life style. Because of a threatened libel suit Maugham changed Hong Kong to an imaginary colony of 'Tching-Yen'. In his preface Maugham describes the genesis of his novel. He saw China and Hong Kong as the ideal setting for a story which has the force of a morality play: the heroine becomes a better woman through suffering. Maugham saw through the sham and complacency of colonial life. The Chinese characters in his work are mainly servants or tradesmen and the lives of the colonizers and colonized are quite separate. To a great extent this remains true today, although the power structure is entirely different. Through his heroine, Kitty, Maugham portrays the general feelings of the British about the Chinese prevalent at the time: confronted by a beautifully made up Manchu lady in full costume; she is made to feel 'all thumbs' despite the fact that 'Kitty had never paid anything but passing and somewhat contemptuous attention to the China in which fate had thrown her' and 'Kitty had never heard the Chinese spoken of as anything but decadent, dirty and unspeakable'. In the opening chapters, from which Extract 4 comes, the contempt in which Chinese servants in particular and the Chinese in general were held is evident. They even turned knobs in a contemptibly sneaky fashion: 'Only a Chinese would turn a handle in that way'. In many cases, the contempt was mutual – not that the British noticed nor cared. The cheating wife, Kitty, reassures herself: 'It must have been one of the servants and after all they didn't matter. Chinese servants knew everything anyway. But they held their tongues'.

The contempt in which many Hong Kong Chinese hold Westerners is reflected in the terms they use to describe them. *Gweilo* (literally 'ghost' or 'devil man') is used almost non-connotatively today by locals and expatriates alike. But, like the earlier *fanqui* or *fankwei* (literally 'barbarian devil'), it gives a good indication of the attitude of local people to the Western intruders. Mutual misjudgement and oversimplification have characterized relations between the races, in literature as in real life. In James Clavell's *Noble House* (1963), an attempt is made to portray the raunchy, earthy Cantonese servants in a hotel given the pseudonym 'Victoria and Albert', but which is probably the **Mandarin Oriental** from the description of its location on Connaught Road and its decor. Clavell tries to capture the contempt for Westerners which he is aware exists, but reading the coarse comments on the sexual desirability of the American heroine and the vileness of 'barbarian sin' of physically repulsive and foul-mouthed 'Daytime Chang' and 'Third Toiletmaid Fung' the average Western reader is encouraged to be contemptuous of the Chinese. To add insult to injury Clavell makes 'Daytime Chang' full of grudging admiration – indeed desire – for the blonde barbarian heroine.

Returning to Hong Kong's literary visitors, Bernard Shaw ◊ caused a big stir in educated circles when he descended upon Hong Kong on Saturday, 11 February 1933. His visit was given extensive coverage by

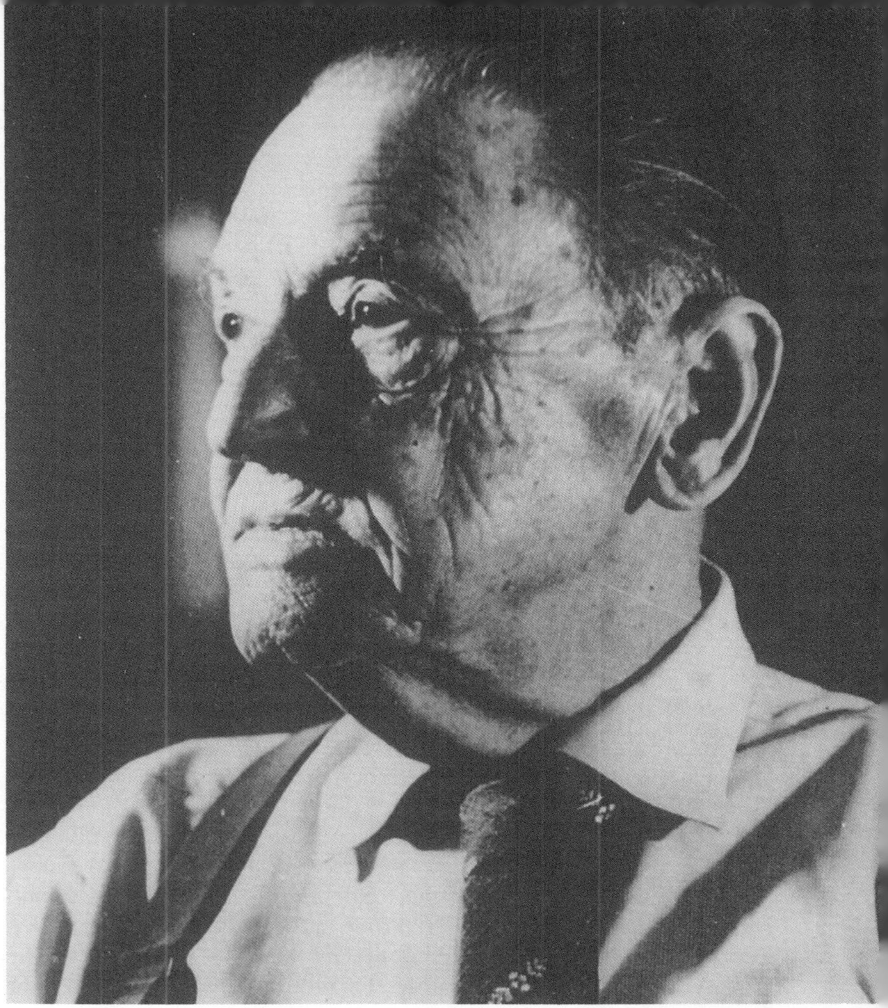

W. Somerset Maugham

the local press and the British community was quite prepared to lionize him. Even after the Rotarians had been snubbed by him, the Rotarians' Vice-President stated to a meeting of his fellow Rotarians, 'I am a great admirer of Mr Shaw and have benefitted intellectually from reading his works'. The press followed Shaw's every move. In the **Great Hall of the University** in Pokfulam Road he delivered a stirring speech to a packed audience made up of students and distinguished guests. The speech was deliberately provocative in typical Shavian manner. A short extract reproduced in the contemporary *South China Morning Post* will suffice to illustrate this:

> If you read, read real books and steep yourself in revolutionary books. Go up to your neck in Communism, because if you are not a red revolutionist at 20, you will be at 50 a most impossible fossil. If you are a red revolutionist at 20, you have some chance of being up-to-date at 40.

The speech aroused a great deal of controversy in Hong Kong but always, underneath the comments and criticisms from the expatriate community lurked the sentiment that Hong Kong, so much on the periphery of what they considered to be the civilized world, had been lucky to have been visited by the literary lion at all. As one editorial in the *South China Morning Post* put it:

> There is only one Shaw, and that he should grace Hong Kong but once in his lifetime is an historical event, to be appreciated in all humility. In comparison, what matters? If in fact the Shavianism has been overdone, having acquitted Shaw of blame it can only be pleased that seldom does a fish worth baiting come this way. As we are, Shaw has come and Shaw has gone; and so back into our narrow beds creep and let no more be said.

The British felt exiled from their own culture. The quotations in this section are reproduced with a description of Shaw's journey in P. Gray's *Shaw in China* (see Booklist).

The day before he delivered his lecture at Hong Kong University Shaw had taken 'tiffin' at the residence of Sir Robert Ho Tung, certainly one of Hong Kong's most colourful figures. A Eurasian who had risen from rags to riches at the time of Shaw's visit, Sir Robert was associated with virtually every important business enterprise in the Colony and was almost certainly the prototype for the flamboyant Eurasian, Sir Jonathan Sekloong, in Robert Elegant's *Dynasty* ◊ (Extract 11). Sir Robert had a number of residences in Hong Kong as well as abroad, but 'Idlewild', to which Shaw was invited, must have held a special place in his heart. 'Idlewild' was located in the present mid-levels, **Seymour Road**, and according to the description of Sir Robert's daughter, Irene Cheng, 'was a large, well-known house, with an excellent view of the harbour and with gardens on several levels linked to each other by flights of steps and pathways . . .'. Unfortunately, it has been demolished and replaced by an architecturally uninteresting highrise block of flats called 'Hong Kong Gardens'.

An interesting characteristic of Sir Robert Ho Tung pointed out by C.H.J. Lethbridge was that, in spite of his European appearance, he 'adopted the manners, deportment, and costume of a Chinese gentleman, and did not seek to pass as a European nor to enter European society'. The 'Chineseness' of 'Idlewild's' interior left a very strong impression on Shaw. He subsequently used the private temple inside 'Idlewild' as a setting for Act III of *Buoyant Billions* and related his experience there in an article on 'Aesthetic Science':

> When I was in Hong Kong, I was entertained very agreeably indeed by Sir Robert Ho Tung. We were both of the age at which one likes a rest after lunch. He took me upstairs into what in England would have been a drawing room. It was a radiant miniature temple with an altar of Chinese vermilion and gold, and cushioned divan seats round the walls for the worshippers. Everything was in such perfect Chinese taste that to sit there and look was a quiet delight. A robed priest and his acolyte stole in and went through a service. When it was over I told Sir Robert that I had found it extraordinarily soothing and happy though I had not understood a word of it. 'Neither have I', he said, 'but it soothes me too'.

Hong Kong's next important literary visitors were W.H. Auden ◊ and Christopher Isherwood ◊ who passed through Hong Kong in 1938 on their way to China to write about the Sino-Japanese War. Their voyage seemed unreal and is described in their jointly authored book, *Journey to a War*. They had hoped to find reality on arrival in Hong Kong. Instead the sense of unreality persisted:

> At Hong Kong, we had said to each other, we shall wake up, everything will come true. But we hadn't woken; only the dream had changed. The new dream was more confused than the old, less soothing, even slightly apprehensive. It was all about dinner – parties at very long tables, and meetings with grotesquely famous newspaper-characters – the British Ambassador, the Governor, Sir Victor Sassoon. We seemed to be in a perpetual hurry, struggling into our dinner-jackets, racing off in taxis to keep appointments for which we were already hopelessly late . . . There were warnings, too; some of them as fantastic as any nightmare: 'Never mix with a Chinese crowd, or you'll get typhus'. 'Never go for a walk alone, or they may shoot you as a spy'.

They hoped they would wake up from the dream when they arrived in 'dangerous, unpredictable war-time China' – the real world. Auden's sonnet 'Hong Kong' attempts to capture this unreal quality (Extract 9). The Hong Kong expatriates continue to play their parts in a domestic comedy when 'off-stage' a war is raging.

A new stage was reached in 'Hong Kong literature' with the war. Emily Hahn's ◊ *China to Me* (1944) is a fascinating account of life in China and Hong Kong before and during the second world war. In

1940, China was embroiled in chaos, while expatriates in Hong Kong continued to slumber in total oblivion of the war in Asia.

> One of the irritating things about the British point of view which you noticed in the Hong Kong residents was their stubborn refusal to consider the Far East situation. The war meant to them the war in Europe. That they took very seriously. The women . . . learned how to do nursing so that they could stay in the Colony, the young men all joined up and wore uniforms, and there were bazaars and benefit balls one after another, to collect funds for airplanes. The airplanes, however, were all to be sent to Europe and used against Hitler; that was the theme of all the propaganda we were given.

The expatriate community was rudely awakened from its dream when the Japanese invaded the Colony in 1942. Emily Hahn is one of a number of writers who have given accounts of the mass internment of Europeans by the Japanese occupation forces. The experience of internment of British, American, Dutch and Belgian residents, among them a good number of Eurasians, in picturesque **Stanley** produced a number of reminiscences, one of which was by Jean Gittins, who wrote *Eastern Windows, Western Skies*. Today Stanley is still the site of a prison, but it is also a great tourist attraction, with lowrise apartments and bungalows, a beach and a popular tourist market.

Emily Hahn offered a different perspective from that of the 'visitors'. Maugham, Shaw, Auden and Isherwood all saw the marginality and the ludicrous pretensions of the white community in Hong Kong, but they were merely visitors who did not really know the Chinese. Emily Hahn had spent five years in Shanghai before coming to Hong Kong and lived in Hong Kong from 1940 to 1944. She was married to a Chinese man in Shanghai. Although she is not universally she admired among sinologists and her judgements are not always considered sound, she wrote not as a mere 'visitor'. Her Hong Kong Chinese characters have distinguishing qualities and speaking parts.

Hong Kong emerged from the second world war in a more sombre mood. A good number of residents had died in internment, including Professor R.K.M. Simpson, the man who had accompanied Shaw on his drive around the island. The next great impetus to the development of 'Hong Kong literature' came with the Communist takeover of China in 1949.

Post-war 'Indigenous' Writers

Until the mid-1950s some graduates from Hong Kong secondary schools, indeed some of the wealthiest ones, went to universities on the

Hong Kong hotels

Hong Kong's five star hotels play a central role in the commercial and social life of the colony. To a far greater extent than in Europe or America, they serve residents as well as visitors. Audrey Chen and Ian Davidson in Running Dog, *for example, meet at a reception at the Hilton (Extract 6) and the cocktail party in David Wong's story of that name would almost certainly have taken place in a reception room at one of the hotels in Central (Extract 3).*

Moreover, if there really is such a thing as an international jet set, the guest lists at the Peninsula, the Mandarin and the Hilton testify that it touches down in Hong Kong. For royalty, the Mandarin shades it over the Peninsula (24 listed guests as against 21), but for film stars the Peninsula (58 including Marlon Brando, Charlie Chaplin, Bob Hope and Elizabeth Taylor) is clearly the favourite over the Mandarin (37, including Roger Moore, Charlotte Rampling and Gina Lollobrigida) or the Hilton (which has played host to George Bush, but to few artists).

As for literary guests, the lists are disappointingly low-brow, but the Peninsula again seems the favourite:

> Mandarin: *Arthur Hailey, Barbara Cartland, James Mitchener, Robert Elegant, Jan Morris, Gavin Young.*
>
> Pensinula: *Arthur Clarke, James Clavell, Noel Coward, Allen Drury, Frederick Forsythe, Milton Friedman, Joseph Heller, Arthur Miller, Tennessee Williams.*

Chinese mainland. Hong Kong was considered very provincial and backward. The centres of Chinese culture were, after all, in China itself. In *China to Me* Emily Hahn, who was familiar with the Chinese mainland, wrote:

> I found an entirely new (to me) kind of Chinese living in Hong Kong. The Cantonese who make up the bulk of the population have stubbornly resisted change, and in Hong Kong you will find many old customs and traditions flourishing in a lively manner which you can't find anywhere else in China. Perhaps this is because the rest of China has been exposed to the progressive influence of the Chiangs and their sort; I don't know. The streets of the city were always full of long funeral processions, gay with costumes and discordant with brass bands. There were still brides carried about in Sedan chairs, their faces hidden. Now and then I even saw a naked baby with a little lock of hair braided into a queue on the top of his head.

This changed after 1949. Children growing up in Hong Kong, many of them refugees from the mainland, began to see their future as lying in British Hong Kong or in Western countries like the USA, Canada or Australia. The temporary severing of spiritual links with China was particularly marked after 1957 with all the upheavals on the mainland – including the Great Leap Forward and the Cultural Revolution. It was not until the very late 1970s that Hong Kong people began to go in great numbers to China again. Thus the 1950s and 1960s saw the brightest students in Hong Kong attending Hong Kong University. This period coincides with what one might call 'the golden age of Hong Kong English writing'. A great deal of such writing from local Chinese writers was produced, or at least appeared in print, after the 1960s, and indeed is still appearing sporadically now, but, with some exceptions, the proponents of the art are essentially products of the 1950s and 1960s.

Running Dog was an ambitious effort published in 1981 (Extract 6). This novel is almost a literary curiosity today because of its rarity value. Lee Ding Fai ◊ is the masculine-sounding pseudonym of a local woman who received a Western-style education. Her novel is not only sociologically interesting, in that it gives a knowledgeable Chinese eye view of Hong Kong, but is also a good read. Unfortunately it failed to attract the attention it deserved.

In prose, the local writer to have received perhaps the most attention is David T.K. Wong ◊, an ex-civil servant. In the autumn of 1990 the local English literary community – what there is of it – was agog over the publication of the 62-year old David Wong's collection of short stories (Extract 3). At last a Hong Kong 'voice' in English. Although the collection did not appear until 1990 Mr Wong – now resident in the UK – had been dabbling in creative writing for a long time. His collection is unique in that, while local writers do occasionally enter short stories competitions sponsored by local businesses or institutions, none had before been published in a blaze of at least local publicity.

Although the eminent poet Edmund Blunden ◊ was head of the English department at **Hong Kong University** from 1953–65 (see below), none of his students has achieved an international reputation as a creative writer in English although there are a few published translators. A poet who has won a slight measure of recognition beyond Hong Kong is Louise Ho, an academic who teaches English literature at the Chinese University of Hong Kong (Extract 8). Her poems have been published in a slim volume by the Hong Kong Arts Centre and more recently in a publication entitled *Poetry Canada*. *Hong Kong: Images on Shifting Waters* is an interesting volume of poems which appeared in 1977, edited by T.C. Lai and Joyce Hsia (Extracts 8, 10 and 12), with contributions from R.K.M. Simpson and Edmund Blunden, and also, more significantly, from 'indigenous' poets who received their academic training in the English Department of Hong Kong University in the 1950s and 1960s. By the time the book was published 'indigenous' practitioners had all but faded away, with the opening up of China and the re-forging of close bonds with the People's Republic.

Han Suyin

Post-war 'International' Writers

With the great influx of refugees from the Chinese mainland into Hong Kong since 1949, many of them entrepreneurs with both capital and skills, Hong Kong grew from a provincial outpost to a cosmopolitan metropolis, a financial, commercial and industrial centre which attracted international interest. One writer who capitalized on the exotic blend of the mid-20th century and the Victorian pomp and circumstance of a colonial civil service post was Austin Coates ◊, who was able to win himself an international readership with tales of his Hong Kong and other Asian experiences. He is best known for *City of Broken Promises* (1966), a story of a Macanese woman's rise from poverty to wealth and power which was adapted into a musical. *Myself A Mandarin* (1968) relates Coates's experiences as a civil servant in Hong Kong, where he served for seven years. He arrives in Hong Kong in early 1949, on the eve of the Communist takeover. Coates had been informed by a printed notification before arrival to equip himself with a sword. He explains:

> It . . . began to appear that the sword and the Chinese civil war were not connected. This, so far as it went, was reassuring. But it also showed that in some curious way two separate centuries had become entangled. The Chinese civil war was taking place in the twentieth century, while the Hong Kong Government, who required me to arrive with a sword, was apparently living in the Victorian era.

The quaint anachronisms of colonial rule gained Coates's work some reputation and a British television series was based on the adventures of Coates as a magistrate.

It was the combination of a giant Communist neighbour and its own development into an international business centre that catapulted Hong Kong into the limelight and drew the attention of an international reading public. The contrasts of a territory in which the world saw – rightly or wrongly – the home of capitalism run wild separated by just a border from China gave international writers a good backdrop, as did the cloak-and-dagger potential of spying, agents and intrigue on both sides of the order. Apart from the high-level dynamics created by economics and politics there was the age-old theme of East–West contrast on a more human level. Love stories, meant for an international audience, almost always involve Western Man and Chinese Woman. Possibly the earliest 'international' Hong Kong novel is Han Suyin's ◊ *Many Splendoured Thing* (1952), which takes the East–West liaison and sets it against the backdrop of a Hong Kong filled with refugees pouring out from China (Extract 1). It was made into a very successful film starring William Holden and Jennifer Jones. Some of the most memorable scenes were shot in the former **Foreign Correspondents' Club** on **Conduit Road** in the mid-levels, now the site of anonymous apartment blocks. Han Suyin worked for some time as a medical doctor in Hong Kong University's teaching hospital, **Queen Mary**.

Many first-time visitors in the 1960s and 1970s associated Hong Kong with Richard Mason's *The World of Suzie Wong* (1959) – Extract 13. Suzie's world has undergone radical changes. The **Wanchai** bars which proliferated during the years of the Vietnam War have all but disappeared, giving way to office buildings, restaurants and discos. However, visitors to Wanchai will still be able to see the **Luk Kwok Hotel**, which was supposed to be the original for Mason's Nam Kwok Hotel. The basis of *The World of Suzie Wong*'s enormous commercial success as a book and film lay in Mason's reworking of a number of clichés into a romantic potboiler.

For the elite of the 1950s and 1960s English was the preferred language, and a centre of the English language was the University of Hong Kong. Edmund Blunden ◊, the eminent poet, later holder of the Oxford Chair of Poetry (1966–1968), was Head of the **English Department** at the **University of Hong Kong** from 1953 to 1965. The 'Blunden era' produced some of the leading figures in Hong Kong today in the civil service, commerce and the law. Blunden also presided over a group of devoteés, some of whom went on to further their literary studies abroad, notably in Britain.

Blunden lived in Hong Kong for over a decade, and he was a prolific writer. He would write poetry much as one would dash off a note – to congratulate, to condole, to thank, to recollect a particular shared experience. A good number of the poems he wrote while in Hong Kong relate to Hong Kong sights and experiences (Extract 12). His office is at the corner of the **second floor of the Main Building**, just under the clock tower. The office is unofficially called 'the Blunden Room', and when I was its occupant at least two literary pilgrims came to pay homage – to the room, that is.

The view from that side of the building is now spoilt by a number of block-like highrises, but there was a gentler time in 'the Blunden era' when the office boasted a magnificent sea view, made the more interesting by the bustling activity of boats. Blunden's 'View from the University of Hong Kong' sees the ships as being '. . . like a large cheerful family'. Blunden lived in a Victorian brick house on **University Drive**, on the hill behind the Main Building. Today, the houses, and their idyllic rustic setting, complete with a lily pond, have made way for the construction of concrete structures associated with a 'modern' campus.

Robert Elegant turned his expertise in Chinese history and Chinese affairs to great advantage in *Dynasty* (1977) where he played up the contrasts between East and West (Extract 11). One of his themes is power: political as well as economic. James Clavell, less informed about things Chinese, is also concerned with power in his novels about Hong Kong, *Taipan* and *Noble House* (Extract 5).

Others joined the Hong Kong bandwagon, with varying degrees of success. John Gordon Davis ◊ had the advantage of working experience in the Hong Kong civil service when he wrote his story of love and intrigue, *The Years of the Hungry Tiger* (1983). Christopher New ◊, a full-time academic at the University of Hong Kong, tried his hand in *The Chinese Box* (1975) and *Goodbye Chairman Mao* (1979). The same essential ingredients were included: the Chinese woman love interest, intrigue relating to communist China, the exotic background of Hong Kong, the essentially empty existence of members of the expatriate community, but neither Davis nor New created a great deal of impact with their 'Hong Kong novels'. Other, less successful novels, included *The Sanctuary* (1984) by Anthony Cooper, a civil servant, and *Miller* by Geoffrey Thursby. Anthony Cooper includes the topical issue of Vietnamese refugees in his work.

Hong Kong's reputation as an exciting international city is attested to by a writer as well-known as John le Carré using the **Foreign Correspondents' Club** as a setting to add a bit of exotic colour to *The Honourable Schoolboy*. The *Hong Kong Foreign Correspondents' Club* (1990) is the title of a recent work by Anthony Spaeth. Interest in the club is not surprising in view of the tendency of correspondents to try their hand at fiction. The title reflects the fact that the characters in the book always gravitate back to the club in Hong Kong, wherever their missions take them.

A writer who now enjoys an international reputation but who ethnically is half-Chinese, being the son of a Hong Kong solicitor, is Timothy Mo ◊. His first novel, *The Monkey King* (1977) is set in Hong Kong, with a set of local and Macanese characters (Extract 7). *Sour Sweet* is about Hong Kong people transplanted to the UK. In an interview in the *All Asia Review of Books* Timothy Mo claimed to be 'the greatest writer to have come out of Hong Kong in 140 years' although he can no longer be considered to be of Hong Kong since he has lived in the UK since the age of ten.

Towards the Post-Colonial Era

With 1997 drawing nearer, Hong Kong is entering its last phase of colonialism and a number of Western writers have found potential in the impending handover. Douglas Hurd, Britain's Foreign Secretary, has written imaginatively about the handover in his novel *The Smile on the Face of the Tiger*. In *Change of Flag* Christopher New tries to convey the poignancy of the end of an era through the lives of a Eurasian family, the fortunes of whose forebears are the subject of his commercially more successful *Shanghai* (1985).

It seems probable that Hong Kong's role as a picturesque and exotic backdrop to many Western novels will continue and may even flourish. The future for indigenous writing is less clear. Employers and educators complain about falling English standards and it seems unlikely that Hong Kong will produce writers in English who can measure up to international or even regional standards. Nevertheless, 1997 has provided local writers with new subject areas. Recent writing has gone beyond general speculations about identity and the generation gap, instead concentrating on more focused analyses of nationalism, freedom, love of country and divided loyalties. It is with such themes that the post-colonial literature is likely to be involved.

BOOKLIST

What follows is intended as a representative rather than comprehensive list of books about Hong Kong. Where several editions exist, in general the latest and most readily available edition has been listed. For most of the extracted works, information on the original English language publisher can be found in the 'Acknowledgements and Citations' section at the end of the volume, as can the exact location of the extracts and the editions from which they are taken. Extract numbers are highlighted in bold.

Auden, W.H., and Christopher Isherwood, *Journey to a War*, Faber, London, 1973. **Extract 9**.

Blunden, Edmund, 'A Hong Kong house', in Joyce Hsia and T.C. Lai, eds, *Hong Kong: Images on Shifting Waters*, Kelly and Walsh, Hong Kong, 1977. **Extract 12**.

Chekhov, Anton, *A Journey to Sakhalin*, Ian Faulkner, Cambridge, 1993.

Chekhov, Anton (Lillian Hellman, ed), *The Selected Letters of Anton Chekhov*, Pan, 1989.

Cheng, Irene, *Clara Ho Tung: A Hong Kong Lady, Her Family and Her Times*, Chinese University Press, Hong Kong, 1976.

Clavell, James, *Noble House*, Hodder and Stoughton, 1981. **Extract 5**.

Clavell, James, *Taipan*, Hodder and Stoughton, 1984.

Coates, Austin, *City of Broken Promises*, Heinemann, Singapore, 1966.

Coates, Austin, *Myself a Mandarin*, Heinemann, Singapore, 1968.

Cooper, Anthony, *The Sanctuary*, Communication Management, Hong Kong, 1984.

Coward, Noel, 'Mad Dogs and Englishmen' in *The New Oxford Book of Light Verse*, Oxford University Press, Oxford, UK, 1978. **Extract 2**.

Davis, John Gordon, *The Years of the Hungry Tiger*, Corgi, London, 1983.

Elegant, Robert, *Dynasty*, McGraw-Hill, New York, 1977. **Extract 11**.

Endacott, G.B., *A History of Hong Kong*, Oxford University Press, Hong Kong, 1973.

Gittins, Jean, *Eastern Windows, Western Skies*, South China Morning Post, Hong Kong, 1969.

Gray, P., 'Hong Kong, Shanghai, The Great Wall: Bernard Shaw in China', *Shaw in China*, Pennsylvania State University Press, 1985.

Hahn, Emily, *China to Me*, Virago, London, 1987.

Han Suyin, *Many Splendoured Thing*, Triad, Arrow, 1992. **Extract 1**.

Ho, Louise, 'Sheung-shui Pastoral' in Joyce Hsia and T.C. Lai, eds, *Hong Kong: Images on Shifting Waters*, Kelly and Walsh, Hong Kong, 1977. **Extract 8**.

Hsia, Joyce, 'A matter of time', in Joyce Hsia and T.C. Lai, eds, *Hong Kong: Images on Shifting Waters*, Kelly and Walsh, Hong Kong, 1977. **Extract 10**.

Hurd, Douglas, and Andrew Osmond, *The Smile on the Face of the Tiger*, Collins, London, 1969.

Kipling, Rudyard, *The Seven Seas*, Methuen, 1896.

le Carré, John, *The Honourable Schoolboy*, Knopf, New York, 1977.

Lee Ding Fai, *Running Dog*, Heinemann, Singapore, 1980. **Extract 6**.

Letherbridge, C.H.J., *Hong Kong: Stability and Change*, Oxford University Press, Hong Kong, 1978.

Mason, Richard, *The World of Suzie Wong*, Fontana, London, 1969. **Extract 13**.

Maugham, W. Somerset, *On a Chinese Screen*, Mandarin, London, 1991.

Maugham, W. Somerset, *The Painted Veil*, Mandarin, London, 1991. **Extract 4**.

Mo, Timothy, *An Insular Possession*, Chatto and Windus, London, 1986.

Mo, Timothy, *The Monkey King*, André Deutsch, London, 1977. **Extract 7**.

Mo, Timothy, *Sour Sweet*, André Deutsch, London, 1982.

New, Christopher, *Change of Flag*, Futura Publications, London and Sydney, 1985.

New, Christopher, *The Chinese Box*, W.H. Allen, London, UK, 1975.

New, Christopher, *Goodbye Chairman Mao*, Coward, McCann & Geoghegan, 1979.

Shaw, George Bernard, 'Aesthetic Science', *Design 46*, The British Council for Industrial Design, 1946.

Spaeth, Anthony, *The Hong Kong Foreign Correspondents Club*, Secker & Warburg, 1990.

Thursby, Geoffrey, *Miller*, Communications Management, Hong Kong, 1983.

Wong, David T.K., *Lost River and Other Stories*, Asia 2000, Hong Kong, 1990. **Extract 3**.

Extracts

(1) Aberdeen

Han Suyin, *A Many Splendoured Thing*

Some of the most colourful aspects of Hong Kong life are introduced in this extract from Han Suyin's famous novel, which tells of the lovers' outing to Aberdeen on the Moon Feast. Aberdeen's floating restaurant is still popular, although the port is much more built up than at the time described here.

Now the moon feast was come, the fifteenth day of the eighth month, the Harvest Festival which was also my birthday in the Chinese calendar style. 'Let us celebrate the moon and you', said Mark. 'We shall drink the Maotai wine in stone bottles which you brought back from China, and I can look at you, and as always, become unlucid, and delightfully muddled'.

And so with friends we went to look at the moon on the water at the fishing village so prosaically called Aberdeen by the English. There on an arm of sea resting between the island of Hongkong and a tiny islet called Aplichau, Duck's Tongue, strung along the main motor road circling the island, is a fast growing townlet where live the fishing people. Along the coast of the island, and the New Territories and Kowloon on the mainland opposite, are dotted the villages, temples and fleets of the sea-peasant, separate from the land-bound toiler by customs and religious rites exclusive of his profession. It is a beautiful sight from the hills, the deep blue, narrow bay at Aberdeen compact with close-huddled junks at rest. The boat-women are strong and dauntless, and among the careless children who get run over by the drivers of Hongkong, the Aberdeen fishermen's children are many. Unused to the dangerous land, they play among the motor road's intermittent stream of cars as they would on the safe planks of their family junks.

There in a row in the middle of the small bay are strung the houseboat restaurants, expensive and popular, where the tourist and the rich spend on one meal enough to feed many an extensive boat family for a month.

(2) Causeway Bay

Noel Coward, '*Mad Dogs and Englishmen*'

Hong Kong's noonday gun is mounted opposite the Excelsior Hotel in Causeway Bay and fired by a Jardine and Matheson employee hired specifically for that purpose. The gun features in the last stanza of Noel Coward's famous satirical poem about the British colonisers' stodginess and unwillingness to adapt to local customs.

Mad dogs and Englishmen
Go out in the midday sun.
The smallest Malay rabbit
Deplores this foolish habit.
In Hong Kong
They strike a gong
And fire off a noonday gun,
To reprimand each inmate
Who's in late.
In the mangrove swamps
Where the python romps
There is peace from twelve to two.

Noel Coward firing the Noonday Gun

Even caribous
Lie around and snooze,
For there's nothing else to do.
In Bengal
To move at all
Is seldom, if ever done,
But mad dogs and Englishmen
Go out in the midday sun.

(3) Central

David T.K. Wong, '*The Cocktail Party*'

K.B. Woo is described as Hong Kong's 'most famous tycoon' so his office would almost certainly be towards the top of one of Central's spectacular skyscrapers. David Wong skilfully sets the scene for an ironic tale of betrayal in a materialistic and cosmopolitan society (included in the collection Lost River and Other Stories).

The cocktail party is an all-purpose rite in darkest Hong Kong. It can be used to celebrate a betrothal, an anniversary or a national day, to gain face or to give face, to launch a business, to seal a contract or to reassure a creditor. It can be employed just as easily to turn a heart, to slight an enemy or to forestall a social death. Chinese Communist cadres adapt to it in no time at all. Sometimes even the underworld flouts the success of its criminal undertakings with such parties.

No one is more familiar with the multifarious uses of the cocktail party than K.B. Woo, that billionaire entrepreneur known to admirers and foes alike simply as 'K.B.'. As the most famous tycoon in a city replete with taipans and captains of industry, he is the darling of the cocktail cult. His name figures in the invitation lists of virtually everybody pretending to the upper crust. It is not unusual, therefore, for him to attend three or four cocktail parties on a single day. He attends them grudgingly, however, as a concession to his shareholders, his financial backers and the legion of photographers, financial journalists and social reporters who keep his name in the public eye. He knows that an unexplained absence will only provide grist for the rumour mills.

In truth, K.B. finds cocktail parties an interminable bore. He had thought otherwise when he was just the impecunious son of a roadside hawker of fish balls and noodles. Then he had hankered after the untasted glamour of such occasions. But now, as chairman of Trans Universal Enterprises, that famous international conglomerate he had built up from scratch, such parties have become an imposition, deflecting him from the serious business of exploiting the greed of others.

Indeed, he wishes nothing better than to be relieved of the rituals of the cocktail cult. He resents their artificiality and their pretences. Mixing with mediocrities is bad enough, but the charade of smiling at dowagers with vanities as outrageous as their overrouged faces, of humouring commercial parasites weedling for crumbs of insider information or of posing for photographs with treacherous rivals coveting various bits of his empire seems beneath a person who has already paid his way to the top.

Such are K.B.'s thoughts as he prepares to leave for Lulu's cocktail party to launch the high fashion boutique he has agreed to finance. As he tidies his papers he feels a vague distress and being in the privacy of his office he gives rein to his discomfort. He allows his penetrating brown eyes to mist over behind his gold-rimmed glasses and his high intelligent forehead to knit into a frown. He compresses his mouth into a severe line and in the process his jowl quivers with unfamiliar tension. All of a sudden a certain crudity or want of refinement returns to his features, so that neither his immaculate Savile Row suit nor his expensive accoutrements prove sufficient disguise to hide his humble origins.

He knows deep down he is going to lose Lulu, no matter what he does. She has told him as much. But he still refuses to reconcile himself to that prospect. She remains the only pleasant thing that has happened to him through a cocktail party. That was more than five years back, when he was foty-five, and nothing quite as pleasant has happened to him since.

The remembered thrill of that meeting still quickens his blood. He had just acquired his first bank and had hosted a small cocktail reception at a leading hotel for the lawyers, accountants, merchant bankers and others involved in the deal. At the end of the function Lulu had come up to him with a leather folio containing the bill.

Perhaps he had been unduly elated by his acquisition or perhaps he had a few too many to drink, but the sight of Lulu simply stopped him in his tracks. She must have been fresh out of school for she could have been no more than twenty. Her face, then as now, had been at once childlike in its innocence and mysterious with Oriental complexities. Her eyes had a bright, trusting quality, her nose was dainty and her mouth, pleasingly large against the other features of her face, hinted at unawakened passion. Her long silky hair, black as a raven's sheen, swung sensually against her crimson Chinese long gown. Although the gown was no more than a uniform for hotel staff, on her it had looked provocative, for it hugged the agreeable contours of her body and revealed two tantalizing slivers of thigh between its tall side slits. She had looked so unspoilt, so vulnerable, so in need of protection, that his bowels had churned and he felt a surge of libido inappropriate for his years.

'Hope everything has been satisfactory, Sir', Luly had said in a cheerful voice, as a prelude to presenting the bill. At the same time she had flashed a smile which melted into dimples on her cheeks.

He had peered at the identification tag pinned on her gown, noting that it read: 'Lulu. Trainee. Customer Relations'. He had never felt so powerful and irresistable as he did then. So, waving aside the proffered folio, he had declared: 'Lulu, you're being wasted. Have dinner with me in Paris next Saturday and I'll give you the world'.

(4) Happy Valley

W. Somerset Maugham, *The Painted Veil*

The opening of Somerset Maugham's novel about a shallow expatriate wife who cheats on her husband with an equally shallow colonial administrator. The novel reflects the social stratification of the expatriate community in the early 20th century and its general attitude to the Chinese. Happy Valley is today an upper middle class suburb favoured by fairly affluent Chinese. It is also the site of the famous Happy Valley racecourse.

She went out on to the verandah and watched him leave the house. He waved his hand to her. It gave her a little thrill as she looked at him; he was forty-one, but he had the lithe figure and the springing step of a boy.

The verandah was in shadow; and lazily, her heart at ease with satisfied love, she lingered. Their house stood in the Happy Valley, on the side of the hill, for they could not afford to live on the more eligible but expensive Peak. But her abstracted gaze scarcely noticed the blue sea and the crowded shipping in the harbour. She could think only of her lover.

Of course it was stupid to behave as they had done that afternoon, but if he wanted her how could she be prudent? He had come two or three times after tiffin, when in the heart of the day no one thought of stirring out, and not even the boys had seen him come and go. It was very difficult at Hong Kong. She hated the Chinese city and it made her nervous to go into the filthy little house off the Victoria Road in which they were in the habit of meeting. It was a curio dealer's; and the Chinese who were sitting about stared at her unpleasantly; she hated the ingratiating smile of the old man who took her to the back of the shop and then up a dark flight of stairs. The room into which he had led her was frowsy and the large wooden bed against the wall made her shudder.

'This is dreadfully sordid, isn't it?' she said to Charlie the first time she met him there.

'It was till you came in', he answered.

Of course the moment he took her in his arms she forgot everything.

(5) Happy Valley Racecourse

James Clavell, *Noble House*

James Clavell gives a vivid account of the excitement of the race, introducing the elements of intrigue that tend to be associated with the sport, and linking this with the power politics of the business world. The extract opens with the Taipan, Ian Dunross, announcing the result of a disputed race.

'May I use the mike?'

'Oh of course'. The man hastily moved and Dunross sat in his place. He clicked on the switch. 'This is Ian Dunross, the stewards have asked me to make two announcements . . .'.

The silence was vast as his words echoed and re-echoed over the stadium. The fifty thousand held their breaths, careless of the rain, in the stands and on every soaring level. 'First, the result of the fifth race'. Dead silence but for the sound of the rain. Dunross took a deep breath. 'Pilot Fish by a nose from Noble Star by a whisker from Butterscotch Lass . . . ' but the last was drowned by the cheers and counter cheers, happiness and disgust, and everyone throughout the stadium was shouting, arguing, cheering, cursing and down in the paddock, Gornt was astonished, having been convinced that his jockey had been seen as he had seen him, had been caught and carpeted and the result would be set aside. In the pandemonium the winning numbers flashed on to the tote: one, seven, eight.

Dunross waited a moment and breezily repeated the result in Cantonese, the crowd more docile, their pent-up anxieties allayed, for the stewards' decision was final. 'Second, the stewards have decided, due to the weather and bad conditions, to cancel the rest of the meet . . .' A vast groan went over the crowd. '. . . actually to postpone until next Saturday for another special meet'. A sudden great roar and excitement picked up. 'We will have a meet of eight race and the fifth will be the same as today, with the same runners, Pilot Fish, Butterscotch Lass, Winning Billy, Street Vendor, Golden Lady,

Lochinvar and Noble Star. A special return challenge with double stakes, 30,000 added . . .'.

(6) Hilton Hotel

Lee Ding Fai, *Running Dog*

A rare local Chinese view of the pretentious and patronizing attitude of expatriate men very common until recently. What the extract lacks in subtlety it makes up for with a degree of genuine feeling. Audrey and Ian Davidson meet at a cocktail party at the Hilton.

It was ludicrous that her father should have thought it necessary to help her find suitors, not that she could be moved by the charms of any of her present admirers to the point of wishing marriage, or that they could have such serious intent either. For instance, there was Ian Davidson, one of the assistant managers at Jardine Matheson whose impression of the Orient was first gleaned from his reading of the history of the East India Company and the stories of W. Somerset Maugham. Blond, lean, and very Anglo-Saxon looking, his blatant arrogance sometimes irritated her to the point of fury. He was introduced to her at a cocktail party, hosted by an airline company which was expanding its air freight department.

'You went to school in America, didn't you?' he commented blandly. 'A lot of Chinese students want to go there, I understand. It's easier, I suppose. Of course, their college is really a school to us'.

She sipped her drink, and returned a shrug and a slight smile.

'I wouldn't mind going there to have a look myself, though there are other places that one would rather go first'. He stopped a waiter, picked up a small square of salmon sandwich with his fingers, and, before popping it into his mouth, asked with marvellous casualness in his perfect Queen's English: 'So where exactly were you when you were there?'

'In a school called Smith somewhere in the wilds of Massachusetts', she replied.

'Really, how interesting'.

His obnoxiousness fascinated rather than offended her. He was like a kid turning up his nose at another boy's possessions. And he talked about his work and his company as if without it Hong Kong's trade and commercial interest would come tumbling down to the ground.

'It's a good thing for us you've decided to come here'. Audrey said, flashing him an innocent smile.

'Well, one likes to think one can be of some help, you know.'

'Yes, I know'.

(7) Hong Kong: Chinese New Year

Timothy Mo, *The Monkey King*

A dilapidated flat in an old building. Very few such large ramshackle flats exist today. The low-rises have given way to apartment blocks with matchbox-like units. Timothy Mo gives a down-to-earth description of the antics of Mr Poon and his extended family on Chinese New Year's Day, the most important Chinese Festival. The household includes the Macanese hero, Wallace, who has married into the family for survival. The author uses a strange China Coast pidgin in the dialogue.

The family rose in a group, somewhat earlier than normal for the sisters, on New Year's Day. This was a gesture of solidarity that also spared Wallace Eldest Sister's usual agonised performance in the bathroom. The normal routines of the day were abridged. No one washed. The women dressed themselves in their finest clothes and made their way to the kitchen where they ate a monster breakfast.

Wallace sent May Ling ahead while he rubbed Vaseline into his hair and raked it into a glossy skull-cap. Then he wiped his fingers on his trousers and brushed through the bead curtain into the kitchen. He was last. Mrs Poon presided over a steaming pot of congee. The sisters were in long, glowing cheongsams, daringly slashed to the knee at the sides. Eldest Sister's was orange, Second Sister's primrose. Their necks looked unnaturally elongated in the stiff, orthopaedic-style stock collars. Despite their brocade jackets, they shivered guardedly, rippling the clinging silk of the dresses. The hems of the cheongsams rose, revealing the toes of frayed slippers. May Ling was wearing an obsolescent, now matt, version of the sisters' costumes, a hand-down from their wardrobes. The sisters themselves were thin but the dress hung on May Ling. Fong wore a still shabbier cheongsam. She watched the amahs hand steaming bowls to her sons.

Wallace honked with satisfaction over the congee which had been specially enriched with meat. He helped himself to another dough-stick. Ah King scowled. This was the first breakfast Wallace had ever taken in the kitchen. He grabbed another stick and ate them together from his fist.

(8) Hong Kong: Chinese Peasants

Louise Ho, '*Sheung-shui Pastoral*'

Hong Kong still has a small farming community, which can be seen on Lantau and in other outlying areas. Sheung-shui is in the New Territories of Hong Kong.

Three fingers,
One man and two women,
Appeared,
With white hats on their backs.
Three black figures,
Etched against a tawny sunset,
By a country road.
Peasants, no doubt,
With plastic slippers on.
Their new hats in
Tightly woven straw,
Milky white against their black peasant suits.
Clean and inhuman
They pressed forward
With methodical tread
Into the sunset
Like figures splashed on some bill board
Advertising acrylic colours.
Paints that do not mix or blend,
That cannot hide the crudity of flat monochromes.
(One must not puke at cheap adverts
Seeing how well they can mirror life!)
One woman held the man's wrist
For support. She seemed to limp
A little: the register of a limp
Not its helplessness. She showed
That self-reliance
Old peasant women sometimes have,
On they went
Their measured way
From nowhere to nowhere.
What secret is yours,
You dark people who follow the sun?

(9) Hong Kong: Expatriate Community

W.H. Auden, *'Hong Kong 1938'*

Auden's view of the expatriate community at the time of the Sino-Japanese War. The expatriates play roles in a domestic comedy while war rages in the real world.

Its leading characters are wise and witty;
Substantial men of birth and education
With wide experience of administration,
They know the manners of a modern city.

Only the servants enter unexpected;
Their silence has a fresh dramatic use:
Here in the East the bankers have erected
A worthy temple to the Comic Muse.

Ten thousand miles from home and
  What's-her-name,
The bugle on the Late Victorian Hill
Puts out the soldier's light; off-stage, a war

Thuds like the slamming of a distant door:
We cannot postulate a General Will;
For what we are, we have ourselves to
  blame.

(10) Hong Kong: The Vanishing House

Joyce Hsia, *'A Matter of Time'*

Joyce Hsia laments the passing of Hong Kong houses and their replacement by high-rises. Visitors interested in seeing examples of Hong Kong's few remaining houses can find a few old-style villas on the road to Stanley.

Hong Kong House: a soon-to-be relic
of a passing era of leisure and space
where sun pierces verandah windows
splaying a red carpet and acquiescent piano;
hibiscus bloom in an untended garden and
a vine's tendrils straddle a king palm.

Ceilings soar with lazy fans pertinent
in long summer days heavy with heat
A high-voltage air conditioner alternates
but kills the solace of French doors
swinging open to the wild camelia's bloom
and the call of cockatoos in their white
armour and sulfer crowns, replete with
raucous call from mates or contenders
in their luxuriant green enclosure.

Insects run rampant, but so do lizards
whose work is clean and knife thrusts quick
The mother cat hides her brood deviously but
with ease and need not readily capitulate
Children are free to spread inexhaustible wings
as elders expand on alien themes without
partitions reverberating on either side . . .

. . .

The house stands as a memorial
to an easier breathing space –
a luxury Hong Kong can no longer afford.
As the bulldozer moves it must go to
allow for the utilitarian skyscraper
but where will the wilderness of birds
find retreat and who can resurrect this
oasis of green where the azalea hailed
its profound profusion –

In an eclipsing cage of glass and steel.

(11) The Peak

Robert Elegant, *Dynasty*

The Peak is the location of some of the most expensive homes in the territory. A peak address tends to have great snob value and for many years the Chinese were not allowed to live on the Peak. Robert Elegant sets the tone for his story of wealth of power with his description of the splendours of Sekloong Manor and the general opulence on display on the occasion of the dowager Lady Mary Sekloong's 90th birthday.

On The Peak itself, the leaden fog blotted out all the works of man and nature. The gross gray mass flowed over villas and mansions, over broad roads and narrow byways, over trees, flowers, and rocks. In the feeble orange glow of sodium streetlights, motorcars crawled along Magazine Gap Road into Peak Road. Drivers craned their heads through the windows, searching for the white centerline to avoid the precipice on the left. Only the diffuse loom of lights warned of oncoming traffic. Automobiles appeared like gleaming spirit cars, to be ingested again by the blackness.

Turning sharply right, a stately Rolls-Royce Phantom IV shone its locomotive headlights on the leering tortoise gargoyles astride the arch guarding the private road to Sekloong Manor. Greasy tentacles of fog coiled around the upturned eaves of the twenty-five-foot-high gate, and its canary-yellow tiles gleamed insubstantial when the mist momentarily parted. On the broad crossbeam, illuminated by the Phantom's uptilted lights, a golden dragon writhed in high relief. The supreme beast's black claws clutched white clouds, and its out-spread wings shaded from pale azure roots to the broad, bright carnelian tips. Its crimson eyes fixed on the pearl shimmering before its open jaws; the great reptile appeared in the shifting light to lunge toward the unattainable gem.

Each of the beast's feet had four claws, since only the Emperor's dragon might display five claws. But its hue was indistinguishable from the Imperial yellow, and the carving was as fine as any outside the Imperial City in Peking. The dragon represented the Emperor's temporal and spiritual power, for he was Tien-tze, the Son of Heaven.

Jonathan, founder of the House of Sekloong, had taken the winged dragon as his own symbol almost a century earlier, when the Emperor still reigned. The gesture was then not merely presumptuous; it verged upon blasphemy. But Jonathan Sekloong spurned his contemporaries' shocked remonstrances. He had, he said, been born in Sekloong, which means Stone Dragon, and had taken both the town's name and its symbol as its own. His Chinese mother could not give him a name, and his Irish father would not.

During the ensuing years, the ultimate symbol of grandeur had come to seem no more than Jonathan's due. The Emperor had been dethroned, and the Ta Ching Chao, the Great Pure Dynasty, had been overthrown. But Jonathan Sekloong had flourished, building a great commercial empire and founding a dynasty that endured. His achievements recognized by two British knighthoods and, subsequently, by a baronetcy, he had died Sir Jonathan at the age of ninety-seven, in 1950.

(12) Pokfulam

Edmund Blunden, '*A Hong Kong House*'

Presumably this poem describes Blunden's house where he lived until 1965 in Pokfulam, in the hills behind the University of Hong Kong, the house being part of the university estate. It is an observant description of nature around a colonial residence before such homes were replaced by anonymous high-rises.

'And now a dove and now a dragon-fly
Came to the garden; sometimes as we sat
Outdoors in twilight noiseless owl and bat
Flew shadowily by.
It was no garden, – so adust, red-dry
The rock-drift soil was, no kind root or sweet
Scent-subtle flower would house there, but I own
At certain seasons, burning bright,
Full-blown,
Some trumpet-purple blooms blazed at the sun's huge light'.

And then? tell more.
'The handy lizard and quite nimble toad
Had courage often to explore
Our large abode.
The infant lizard whipped across the wall
To his own objects; how to slide like him
Along the upright plane and never fall,
Ascribe to Eastern whim.
The winged ants flocked to our lamp, and shed
Their petally wings, and walked and crept instead.

'The palm-tree-top soared into the golden blue
And soaring skyward drew
Its straight stem etched with many rings,

And one broad holm-like tree whose name I never knew
Was decked through all its branches with broidering leaves
Of pattern-loving creepers; fine warblings
And gong-notes thence were sounded at our eaves
By clever birds one very seldom spied,
Except when they, of one tree tired,
Into another new-desired,
Over the lawn and playthings chose to glide'.

(13) Wanchai Ferry

Richard Mason, *The World of Suzie Wong*

The novel begins on the Kowloon Yaumatei ferry pier and then on the ferry itself, headed for Wanchai on the Hong Kong side. In this passage Mason rather aggressively packs in a great deal of 'local colour' typical of the 1950s and 1960s as a background for the meeting between the naive Western man and the Chinese girl who strikes the reader as one literary Chinese stereotype who describes herself in terms of another.

The ferryboat came churning alongside and the crowd moved forward. We jostled together up the gangplant and chose one of the slatted bench-seats on the covered top deck. The ferries were Chinese owned and run, and very efficient, and we had hardly sat down before the water was churning again, the engines rumbling, the boat palpitating – and we were moving off busily past the Kowloon wharves, past anchored merchant-ships, past great clusters of junks. Ahead, on the island across the channel, was Hong Kong, squeezed into a coastal strip a few hundred yards wide, with the miniature skyscrapers in the centre and on either side the long waterfront, stretching for miles, wedged with sampans and junks; and behind rose the steep escarpment of the Peak, shedding the town and the lower social orders as it climbed, until at the higher altitudes there remained only a sprinkling of white bungalows and luxury flats inhabited by the élite.

We rounded the tip of the Kowloon peninsula, heading slantwise across the channel for Wanchai, the most populous district of Hong Kong's eastern flank. I turned to look at the girl beside me. Her face was round and smooth, her eyes long black ellipses, and her eyebrows so perfectly arched that they looked down – but in fact they had only been helped out with pencil at their tips. Her cheekbones were broad, with hints of Mongolia.

'Aren't you a northerner?' I said.

'Yes, Shanghai.'

'But now you live in Hong Kong?'

'North Point'.

'That's a good district'. And it accounted for her being on this ferry, since North Point lay beyond Wanchai – the expensive suburb beyond the slums – and the Wanchai pier was the nearest ferry-point.

'Yes, only I like Repulse Bay better. Nicer house'.

'You mean you've got two houses?'

'Four'.

'*Four?*' I knew that Chinese taipans, who made the richest Europeans seem like paupers, often owned two or three houses, but four was surely a record. 'You mean all in Hong Kong?'

'Yes, Hong Kong. My father is very rich, you know'. She looked pleased with herself, boasting with the naïveté of a child.

'Well, so I gather. And where are the other two houses?'

She counted off the first on her fingers and went on. 'Number three, Conduit road, Number four, Peak. Number five – '

'Not *five*!'

'Yes, I forgot – number five, Happy Valley. But that's just small, you know – only ten rooms'.

Biographies and literary notes

AUDEN, W.H. (1907–1973). Brought up in Birmingham, Auden began to be taken seriously as a poet while still at Christ Church, Oxford. After Oxford he established his reputation as the most talented voice of his generation. With his friend Christopher Isherwood he wrote *Journey to a War* (1939) which records a journey to China (Extract 9). They passed Hong Kong on their way to war-torn China in 1938. It was their first journey to any place east of Suez. They spoke no Chinese and had no special knowledge of Far Eastern affairs.

BLUNDEN, Edmund (1896–1974). Educated at Christ's Hospital and Queen's College, Oxford, Blunden served in the first world war and wrote of his experiences in *Undertones of War* (1928). From 1953 to 1965 he was Professor of English at **Hong Kong University**, following which was appointed professor of poetry at Oxford. Throughout his working life as a teacher, poet and scholar he produced a wide variety of critical and editorial work, with emphasis on John Clare and the Romantics and his fellow war poets. Blunden wrote numerous poems about his years in Japan and Hong Kong (Extract 12).

CHEKHOV, Anton (1860–1904). Born in Taganrog in the south of Russia. Playwright and short story

Edmund Blunden

writer. In 1890, he made a trip to the prison island of Sakhalin in the Far East, his account of the journey is available in translation as *Journey to Sakhalin*. He stayed in Hong Kong on his way home.

CLAVELL, James (1924–). A half-Irish Englishman, born in Australia and now living mostly in Canada and the USA, Clavell was brought up in the UK and served as a captain in the Royal Artillery during the war. In 1942 he was captured by the Japanese and sent to Changi jail in Singapore. His first best-selling novel, *King Rat*, is based upon his experiences there. After the war Clavell went into the film business and has written, produced and directed some highly successful films, for example *To Sir with Love* and *The Last Valley*. *King Rat* was followed by *Taipan*, the second in his Asian saga, then by *Shogun*, set in 17th century Japan. *Noble House* is also set in Hong Kong (Extract 5).

COATES, Austin (1922–). The son of Eric Coates, composer of *Sleepy Lagoon*, the *Knightsbridge March* and other famous pieces of music, Austin Coates was brought to India by war service in 1944. He has lived in Asia almost since that date. For seven years he was Assistant Colonial Secretary and Magistrate in Hong Kong, later becoming Chinese Affairs Officer. Among his best-known works are *City of Broken Promises* (1967) set in Macau and *Myself a Mandarin* (1968) based on his experiences as a Hong Kong magistrate.

COWARD, Noel (1899–1973). The famous actor, dramatist and composer was born in Middlesex, England. As a dramatist he is best remembered for his smart sophistication and defiance of convention as well as his technical accomplishment. His humorous poem mocking British colonials 'Mad Dogs and Englishmen' is well-known (Extract 2). A famous Hong Kong pub, 'Mad Dogs', took its name from the poem.

DAVIS, John Gordon. A barrister who spent many years as Crown Counsel in Rhodesia and then Hong Kong, Davis has written a number of novels about Rhodesia. *The Years of the Hungry Tiger* is a novel about the love between a Chinese woman and British policeman and is set in Hong Kong.

Dynasty. Robert Elegant's ◊ epic novel gives an account of generations of a dynamic Eurasian family. Sir Jonathan Sekloong, son of a Chinese mother and Irish father, built a legendary trade empire in Hong Kong, and his descendants include figures powerful in international trade, politics and society. We are given a broad sweep of Hong Kong history from the decline of the Ch'ing Dynasty until 1970 (Extract 11).

ELEGANT, Robert S. (1928–). A graduate from the University of Pennsylvania, Yale's Institute for Far Eastern Languages, Elegant also holds two Master's Degrees from Columbia University – one in journalism and the other in Chinese and Japanese studies. He is well-known for his knowledge and understanding of Chinese history and attitudes. From 1956 to 1962 he was in India and Hong Kong for *Newsweek*. Later he headed the news bureau of the *Los Angeles Times* in Hong Kong until 1970. In 1976 he left daily journalism and devoted himself to his own writing. He has written non-fiction works on China as well as best-selling novels, one of the best known of which is *Dynasty*, which deals with the fortunes of a Hong Kong family.

HAHN, Emily (1905–). Born in St Louis, Missouri, Hahn was the first woman to take a degree in mining from the University of Wisconsin's College of Engineering. She later studied minerology at Columbia University and anthropology at Oxford University. In 1935 she set off on a world tour which took her to the Far East for nine years. *China to Me* (1944) is her story of those years, five of them spent in Shanghai and the rest in Hong Kong. The book is an account of life in the China Mainland and Hong Kong before and during the second world war.

HAN Suyin (1917–). The daughter of a Belgian mother and a Chinese father, in 1938 she married an ex-Sandhurst Chinese officer, who later became a general in Chiang Kai-shek's army, and practised midwifery in the interior during the Sino–Japanese War. From this experience she wrote her first book, *Destination Chungking*, in 1940. She later qualified as a medical doctor in London. After her husband was killed in 1947, she spent a year as house surgeon at the Royal Free Hospital before accepting a doctor's post in Hong Kong. It was in Hong Kong that she wrote the Eurasian love story, *A Many-Splendoured Thing*, which won her international fame as a writer (Extract 1). It was made into a very successful film starring William Holden and Jennifer Jones. Since that time Han Suyin has written numerous books, both novels and non-fiction.

ISHERWOOD, Christopher (1904–80). Born in Cheshire and died in California. Isherwood travelled a great deal and his works reflect his itinerant life: eg *Goodbye to Berlin*, *The Condor and the Cows* (set in South and Central America) and, towards the end of his life, translations of Indian philosophy and religion. He met W.H. Auden ◊ at preparatory school. They collaborated together on three plays as well as *Journey to a War*, part of which describes their stay in 1930s Hong Kong (Extract 9).

KIPLING, Rudyard (1865–1936). Born in Bombay, Kipling travelled throughout Asia. Although he wrote far more on India than anywhere else, *From Sea to Sea* and *The Seven Seas* recount his travels to Hong Kong and Japan.

LEE Ding Fai. This is the pen name of a Hong Kong Chinese woman whose husband was on the staff of the

Rudyard Kipling

Chinese University of Hong Kong. She has so far published one novel, *Running Dog*, which tells the rags-to-riches story of a young Chinese refugee who escapes to Hong Kong from China, and his subsequent adventures in capitalist Hong Kong (Extract 6).

MASON, Richard (1919–). Born near Manchester, Mason worked first on a film magazine and later for the British Council. His interest in the East dates from the second world war. He draws on his knowledge of Hong Kong, where he has lived, in *The World of Suzie Wong* (Extract 13).

MAUGHAM, W(illiam) Somerset (1874–1965). Maugham was born in Paris, the son of a solicitor to the British Embassy. After completing his medical studies he decided not to practise medicine and went to Seville to write. He was a very successful writer of fiction, travel books and plays. In 1919 he went on his first visit to China. The following year he journeyed to Malaya, Indo-China and again to China. Travel provided Maugham with numerous plots and themes for his short stories, although the stories he wrote about South-east Asia and its expatriate communities angered many residents. *The Painted Veil* ◊ set in Hong Kong and the Chinese Mainland provoked a libel suit (Extract 4). Maugham travelled to China again in 1921 and this second visit inspired him to write *On a Chinese Screen*, a potpourri of sketches and vignettes of Chinese and expatriates. See ◊ Thailand and ◊ Singapore.

MO, Timothy (1950–). Born in Hong Kong to a Cantonese father and English mother, Mo received his early schooling in Hong Kong but continued his education in England, completing his university studies at Oxford. His first novel was *The Monkey King* ◊ (Extract 7). Set in Hong Kong and peopled by a group of Chinese and Eurasian characters, it won the Geoffrey Faber Memorial Prize in 1978. This was followed by *Sour Sweet* (1982) which explores a society hitherto not dealt with in fiction in English – the Chinese in Britain. *Sour Sweet* was made into a film, with Hong Kong and Chinese actors and actresses taking leading roles. *An Insular Possession* (1986) is set on the South China coast during the time of the first Opium War.

The Monkey King. Timothy Mo's first novel centres around the antics of a part-Portuguese youth, Wallace Nolasco, who leaves Macau for Hong Kong to marry May Ling, youngest daughter of a parsimonious Cantonese-business man, Mr Poon. Wallace marries in order to avoid starvation, but he finds strange goings-on in the Poon household. The book is filled with a host of eccentric characters, and there are some very comic moments, but the farcical has tragic undertones (Extract 7).

NEW, Christopher (1932–). New is Senior Lecturer in Philosophy in the University of Hong Kong, where he has taught for many years. His novels about Hong Kong are *The Chinese Box* (1975), *Goodbye Chairman Mao* (1979) and *Change of Flag* (1990).

The Painted Veil. Maugham's novel tells the story of the weak and self-centred wife of Walter Fane, a British bacteriologist stationed in Hong Kong. After Walter discovers her affair with the Assistant Colonial Secretary, he decides on a strange revenge: he compels her to go with him to an ancient Chinese city, Mei-tan-fu, which is being ravaged by a cholera epidemic. Ironically it is Walter who dies and Kitty who survives, a much better human being as a result of her suffering (Extract 4).

SHAW, George Bernard (1856–1950). Shaw was born in Dublin and was well known as a journalist and public speaker when his first play appeared. He wrote over 50 plays. Shaw visited China in 1933, passing through Hong Kong on his way. He caused a furore with a controversial speech delivered in the Great Hall of the University urging students to steep themselves in communism.

David Wong

WONG, David T.K. (1928–). Wong worked in the Hong Kong civil service for many years before joining the private sector as a businessman. He has lived in Australia and the USA and now lives in the UK. He has been writing for many years; his short stories have appeared in local English language magazines. *Lost River and Other Stories* is his first published collection of short stories (Extract 3).

Acknowledgments and Citations

The author and publisher are very grateful to the many literary agents, publishers, translators, authors and other individuals who have given their permission for the use of extracts and photographs, supplied photographs or helped in the location of copyright holders. Every effort has been made to identify and contact the appropriate copyright holders or their representatives. The publisher would welcome any further information.

EXTRACTS

BURMA: (1) Nu Yin, 'Two Strings of Beads' in Keith Bosley, ed, *The Elek Book of Oriental Verse*, Paul Elek, London, 1979, pp 122–123. By permission of John Okell and Keith Bosley. (2) MiMi Khaing, *Burmese Family*, Longman India, 1946, pp 37–38. By permission of Orient Longman. (3) H. Fielding-Hall, *The Soul of a People*, Macmillan, London, 1898, pp 185–186. (4) MaMa Lay, *Not Out of Hate*, Ohio University Press, 1991. By permission of Ohio University Press. (5) Trans A. J. Allott. (6) MiMi Khaing, *Burmese Family*, Longman India, 1946, pp 39–40. By permission of Orient Longman. (7) George Orwell, *Burmese Days*, Penguin Harmondsworth. By permission of the late Sonia Brownell Orwell and Martin Secker and Warburg. © 1934 by George Orwell and renewed 1962 by Sonia Pitt-Rivers, reprinted by permission of Harcourt Brace & Company. (8) Seindakaw-thu, 'A Soldier's Letter' in Keith Bosley, ed, *The Elek Book of Oriental Verse*, Paul Elek, London, 1979, pp 121–122. By permission of John Okell and Keith Bosley. (9) Maung Htin, *NgaBa (The Peasant)*. Trans A.J. Allott. (10) Maung Maung, *To a Soldier Son*, Sarpay Beikman, Rangoon. (11) U Lat, *Shwe-pyi-so*. Trans A.J. Allott. (12) Maurice Collis, *She was a Queen*, New Directions, New York, 1992, pp 67–71. By permission of New Directions Publishing Corp. (13) Maurice Collis, *Trials in Burma*, Faber and Faber, London, 1938, pp 38–41. By permission of Louise Collis. (14) U Sein Tin, *War Diary*. By permission of Colleen Beresford. (15) Minister Pade-tha-ya-za, *The Farmer's Family*, in Keith Bosley, ed, *The Elek Book of Oriental Verse*, Paul Elek, London, 1979, pp 120–121. By permission of John Okell and Keith Bosley. (16) Lt Col J.H. Williams, *Elephant Bill*, Rupert Hart-Davis, London, 1965, pp 68–70. By permission of HarperCollins Publishers Ltd. **THAILAND:** (1) Malcolm Smith, *A Physician at the Court of Siam*, Oxford in Asia Paperbacks, OUP, Singapore, 1982, pp 13–16. (2) Botan, *Letters from Thailand*, Editions Duang Kamol, Bangkok, 1982, pp 19–20. (3) Kukrit Pramoj, *Four Reigns*, Editions Duang Kamol, Bangkok, 1981, pp 1–3. (4) Kon Krailat, 'In the Mirror' in Benedict R. O'G. Anderson and Ruchira Mendiones, ed, *In the Mirror: Literature and Politics in the American Era*, Editions Duang Kamol, Bangkok, 1985, pp 213–214. By permission of Benedict R. O'G. Anderson. (5) Jason Schoonover, *Thai Gold*, Bantam, New York, 1989, pp 59–60. By permission of Jack McClelland. (6) Naowarat Pongpaiboon, 'The Day that Killed the Dove' in Naowarat Pongpaiboon, Robert Cumming, Deborah Cumming, Michael Wright and Poornpan Sodsie, *Mere Movement*, Kao Kai Publishing, Bangkok, 1984. By permission of Kao Kai Publishing. (7) Yukio Mishima, *The Temple of Dawn*, Pocket Books, New York, 1975, pp 11–12. E. Dale Saunders, trans. Copyright © 1973 by Alfred A. Knopf Inc. Reprinted by permission of the publisher. Also by permission of Reed Consumer Books on behalf of Secker and Warburg and Charles E. Tuttle Co Inc. (8) Somerset Maugham, *The Gentleman in the Parlour*, Paragon, New York, 1989, p 168. By permission of William Heinemann Ltd. By permission of A.P. Watt on behalf of the Royal Literary Fund. (9) Joseph Conrad, *The Secret Sharer* in *Twixt Land and Sea: Tales, Joseph Conrad Complete Works*, Vol XIX, Canterbury Edition, Doubleday, Page & Com, Garden City, NY, 1924, pp 91–92. (10) Reginald Campbell, *Teak Wallah: Adventures of a Young Englishman in Thailand in the mid–1920s*, Oxford University Press, 1986, pp 134–136. By permission of Guy Arnold for the Reginald Campbell Estate. (11) Khamsing Srinawk, 'Breeding Stock' in *The Politician and Other Stories*, Oxford in Asia Modern Authors, Oxford University Press, Kuala Lumpur, 1975. By permission of Oxford University Press. (12) M. Henri Mouhot, *Travels in Indo-China*, White Lotus, Bangkok, 1986, pp 126–127. (13) Phra Mahanak, *Bunnowat Kham Chan*. Trans Thomas J. Hudak. (14) Si Dao Ruang, 'Mother of waters, Thaokae Bak and a Dog' in Benedict R. O'G. Anderson and Ruchira Mendiones, ed, *In the Mirror: Literature and Politics in the American Era*, Editions Duang Kamol, Bangkok, 1985, pp 176–177. By permission of Benedict R. O'G. Anderson. (15) Angkarn Kalayaanaphong, 'Grandma' in Herbert P. Phillips, ed, *Modern Thai Literature With an Ethnographic Interpretation*, University of Hawaii Press, Honolulu, HI, 1987. By permission of University of Hawaii Press. (16) Sujit Wongthet, 'Second Nature' in Benedict R. O'G. Anderson and Ruchira Mendiones, ed, *In the Mirror: Literature and Politics in the American Era*, Editions Duang Kamol, Bangkok, 1985, pp 98–99. By permission of Benedict R. O'G. Anderson. (17) Rama I, *Ramakian* in Theodora Bofman, *The Poetics of the Ramakian*, Special Report No 21, Center for Southeast Asian Studies, Northern Illinois University, 1984, pp 118–119. By permission of Center for Southeast Asian Studies, Northern Illinois University. (18) Niwet Kanthairat, '12.00 Noon' in Benedict R. O'G. Anderson and Ruchira Mendiones, ed, *In the Mirror: Literature and Politics in the American Era*, Editions Duang Kamol, Bangkok, 1985, pp 235–237. By permission of Benedict R. O'G. Anderson. (19) Khammaan Khonkhai, *The Teachers of Mad Dog Swamp*, University of Queensland Press, St Lucia, Queensland, Australia, 1982, pp 40–42. By permission of Gehan Wijeyewardene. **LAOS:** (1) Outhine Bounyavong, *Just a Pair of Birds*. By permission of Outhine Bounyavong. (2)–(8) Trans Peter Koret. (9) Harry A. Franck, *East of Siam*, T. Fisher Unwin, London, 1926. (10) Henri Mouhot, *Travels in Indo-China*, White Lotus, Bangkok, 1986. (11) Trans Peter Koret. (12) Louis de Carne, *Travels in Indo-China and the Chinese Empire*, Chapman Hall, London, 1872. **CAMBODIA:** (1) Margaret Drabble, *The Gates of Ivory*, Penguin, London, 1992, pp 238–240. © Margaret Drabble, 1991. By permission of Penguin and Peters Fraser & Dunlop. (2) Pang, *The Story of Ankor Vat* in E. Aymonier, *Textes Khmers*, Saigon, Vietnam, 1878. By permission of Judith Jacob. (3) Judith M. Jacob and Edwin Morgan, 'Extracts from The Reamker' in Keith Bosley, ed, *The Elek Book of Oriental Verse*, Paul Elek, London, 1979, pp 94–95. By permission of Judith Jacob. (4) Judith M. Jacob and Kuoch Haksrea, trans, *The Reamker (Ramakerti). The Cambodian Version of the Ramayana*, Royal Asiatic Society, London, 1986. (5) King Sri Dhammaraja, 'Last poem to a loved one', Kambujasuriya, 1939. (6) 'The Tryst' from Dhingra, Baldoon, *Asia Through Asian Eyes*, Thames and Hudson, London, 1959. By permission of Thames and Hudson. (7) Judith Jacob and Edwin Morgan, trans, 'The Code of Behaviour for the Young' in Keith Bosley, ed, *The Elek Book of Oriental Verse*, Paul Elek, London, 1979, pp 95–96. By permission of Judith Jacob. (8) *Sang Sel Chey* in E. Powys Mathers, *The Eastern Anthology. Vol IV. Eastern Love Tales of Cambodia and Songs of the Love Nights of Lao, Vol 10*, John Rodker, London, 1929. (9) Keng Vannsak, 'Prison de la Passion', Phnom Penh, Cambodia, 1956. By permission of Judith Jacob. (10) Molyda Szymusiak (Linda Coverdale, trans), *The Stones Cry Out*, Jonathan Cape, London, 1986. By permission of Random Century Ltd. Translation © 1986 by Farrar, Strauss & Giroux, Inc. Reprinted by permission of Hill and Wang, a division of Farrar, Strauss & Giroux, Inc. **VIETNAM:** (1) Bao Ninh, *The Sorrow of War*, Secker and Warburg, London, 1993, pp 2–3. By permission of Secker and Warburg. (2) Rhodes of Vietnam, *The Travels and Missions of Father Alexandre de Rhodes in China and other Kingdoms of the Orient*, Newman Press, Westminster, MD, USA, 1966. (3) Nguyen Thi Hinh, *Reminiscences of Old Thang Long City*, Vietnamese Studies, Hanoi, 1977, p 166. (4) Jean Larteguy, *Yellow Fever*, London, 1965. (5) Truong Vinh Ky, *Voyage to Tonking in the Year AT-HOI*, SOAS, London, 1982, pp 103–104. By permission of SOAS. (6) Michael Herr, *Dispatches*, Picador, London, 1977, p 38. By permission of Random House, Inc. (7) Marguerite Duras, *The Lover*, Flamingo, London, 1986, pp 50–52. © 1985 by Random House, Inc and William Collins Sons & Co Ltd. Reprinted by permission of Pantheon Books, a division of Random House, Inc and HarperCollins Publishers Limited. (8) Graham Greene, *The Quiet American*, Heinemann, London, 1979, pp 84–85. By permission of David Higham Associates. (9) Nguyen Cong Hoan, *The Carrion Eaters*, in *Vietnamese Literature*, Foreign Languages Publishing House, Hanoi, 1982, p

556. By permission of Nha Xuat Ban The Gioi. (10) Nguyen Du, *The Tale of Kieu*, in *Vietnamese Literature*, Foreign Languages Publishing House, Hanoi, 1982, pp 339–340. By permission of Nha Xuat Ban The Gioi. (11) Ho Xuan Huong, 'Complaint of the No 2 Wife' in *All She Wants*, Tuba Press, London, 1987. (12) Ho Chi Minh, *Prison Diary*, Foreign Languages Publishing House, Hanoi, pp 20 and 45. By permission of Nha Xuat Ban The Gioi. (13) Doan Thi Diem, *The Lament of a Warrior's Wife* in *A Thousand Years of Vietnamese Poetry*, New York, 1975. (14) Gabrielle M. Vassal, *On and Off Duty in Annam*, Heinemann, 1910, pp 156–157. (15) Nguyen Huy Thiep, *The General Retires and Other Stories*, Oxford University Press, Singapore, 1992, pp 164–165. By permission of Oxford University Press. (16) David Halberstam, *One Very Hot Day*, The Bodley Head, London, 1964. **MALAYSIA:** (1) Muhammad Haji Salleh, 'Three Beserah Fishermen' in *Time and its People*, Heinemann, Singapore, 1978, pp 3–4. By permission of Muhammad Haji Salleh. (2) Paul Theroux, 'Reggie Woo', in *The Consul's File*, Penguin, 1979. By permission of Aitken, Stone and Wylie Ltd. (3) Shahnon Ahmad, *No Harvest but a Thorn*, Oxford University Press, Kuala Lumpur, 1972, pp 7–8. By permission of Shahnon Ahmad. (4) W. Somerset Maugham, 'A Casual Affair', *Maugham's Malaysian Short Stories*, Heinemann, London, 1969, pp 166–167. By permission of William Heinemann Ltd. By permission of A.P. Watt on behalf of the Royal Literary Fund. (5) Sir Hugh Clifford, *Stories By Sir Hugh Clifford*, Oxford University Press, Kuala Lumpur, 1966, pp 157–159. (6) Wong Phui Nam, 'Poem for a Birthday' in Edwin Thumboo, ed, *The Second Tongue: An Anthology of Poetry from Malaysia and Singapore*, Heinemann, Singapore, 1976, p 163. By permission of Wong Phui Nam. (7) Anthony Burgess, *Time for a Tiger*, Penguin, Harmondsworth, UK, 1987, p 33. By permission of Artellus Ltd. (8) Ee Tiang Hong, 'Heeren Street, Malacca' in Edwin Thumboo, ed, *The Second Tongue: An Anthology of Poetry from Malaysia and Singapore*, Heinemann, Singapore, 1976, pp 104–105. (9) Usman Awang, *Death of a Warrior (Jebat)*, Dewan Bahasa dan Pustaka, Kuala Lumpur, 1992, pp 84–85. Extracts with the permission of the Director General of Dewan Bahasa dan Pustaka. (10) C.C. Brown, trans, *The Malay Annals*, Oxford University Press, Kuala Lumpur, 1970, pp 130–132. By permission of Oxford University Press. (11) Isabella Bird, *The Golden Chersonese and the Way Thither*, Oxford University Press, Kuala Lumpur, 1967. (12) Joseph Conrad, *Lord Jim*, Penguin, Harmondsworth, UK, 1964. (13) Frank Swettenham, *Malay Sketches*, Graham Brash, Singapore, 1984. (14) Baha Zain, 'Toilet Paper City' in Muhammad Haji Salleh, ed, *The Puppeteer's Wayang: A Selection of Modern Malaysian Poetry*, In Print and Dewan Bahasa dan Pustaka, Brighton, UK, 1992, pp 20–21. By permission of In Print Publishing Ltd and the Director General of Dewan Bahasa dan Pustaka. (15) Usman Awang, 'Chinese Neighbour's Child' in *Salam Benua: Greetings to the New Continent*, Dewan Bahasa dan Pustaka, Kuala Lumpur, 1982, p 43. Extracts with the permission of the Director General of Dewan Bahasa dan Pustaka. (16) Henri Fauconnier, *The Soul of Malaya*, Oxford University Press, Kuala Lumpur, 1990, pp 122–124. By permission of Unwin Hyman, an imprint of HarperCollins Publishers Ltd. (17) Lee Kok Liang, *Flowers in the Sky*, Heinemann, Singapore, 1981, pp 112–113. By permission of Mrs Lee Kok Liang. (18) K.S. Maniam, *The Return*, Skoob Books, London, 1993, p 1. (19) W. Somerset Maugham, 'The Yellow Streak' *Maugham's Malaysian Short Stories*, Heinemann, London, 1969, pp 151–152. By permission of William Heinemann Ltd. By permission of A.P. Watt on behalf of the Royal Literary Fund. **SINGAPORE:** (1) Arthur Yap, 'Old House at Ang Siang Hill' in Edwin Thumboo, ed, *The Poetry of Singapore*, ASEAN Committee on Culture & Information, Singapore, 1988, p 495. By permission of Arthur Yap. (2) Patrick Anderson, *Snakewine*, Chatto and Windus, London, 1955, pp 37–38. (3) Lee Tzu Pheng, 'Bridal Party at the Botanics'. By permission of Lee Tzu Pheng. (4) Boey Kim Cheng, 'Jungle Trek' in *Somewhere Bound*, Times Books International, Singapore, 1989, p 30. (5) Catherine Lim, 'The Chosen One' in *Little Ironies*, Heinemann, Singapore, p 68. By permission of Heinemann Asia. (6) Ronald Alcantra, *An Eclipse Leaves No Shadows* in Robert Yeo, ed, *Prize Winning Plays I*, Federal, Singapore, 1980, pp 109–110. By permission of Ronald Alcantra. (7) Wong May, 'Kampong Bahru 1975' in Edwin Thumboo, ed, *The Poetry of Singapore*, ASEAN Committee on Culture and Information, Singapore, 1984, pp 506. (8) Edwin Thumboo, *Ulysses by the Merlion*, Heinemann Asia, Singapore, 1977, pp 18–19. By permission of Edwin Thumboo. (9) Joseph Conrad, *Youth, Heart of Darkness and The End of the Tether*, J. M. Dent, London, 1974. (10) J.G. Farrell, *The Singapore Grip*, Fontana, London, 1979, pp 185–186. By permission of Weidenfeld and Nicholson. (11) Rex Shelley, *The Shrimp People*, Times Books International, Singapore, 1991. (12) Wong Yoon Wah, 'Fort Silosa' in *Beyond Symbols*, Singapore association of Writers, Singapore, 1984, pp 27–28. By permission of Wong Yoon Wah. (13) Paul

Theroux, *Saint Jack*, Penguin, Harmondsworth, UK, 1976, pp 155–156. By permission of Aitken, Stone and Wylie. (14) D.J. Enright, 'Small Hotel', *The Collected Poems of D.J. Enright*, Oxford University Press, 1990. By permission of Watson, Little Limited. (15) D.J. Enright, 'The Mysterious Incident at the Admiral's Party', *The Collected Poems of D.J. Enright*, Oxford University Press, 1990. By permission of Watson, Little Limited. (16) Robert Yeo, *One Year Back Home*, Solidaridad, Manila, 1990. **INDONESIA:** (1) Colin McPhee, *A House in Bali*, Victor Gollancz, London, 1947, pp 40–41. By permission of Aitken, Stone & Wylie. (2) Anna Forbes, *Insulde, Experiences of a Naturalist's Wife in the Eastern Archipelago*, Blackwood, Edinburgh, UK, 1887, pp 57–59. (3) Johan Splinter Stavorinus, *Voyages to the East Indies*, in Cornelia Niekus Moore, *Insulinde: Selected Translations from Dutch Writers of Three Centuries on the Indonesian Archipelago*, The University of Hawaii Press, 1978, pp 20–21. By permission of University of Hawaii Press. (4) Pramoedya Ananta Toer, *Vanished Childhood*, in John M. Echolls, ed, *Indonesian Writing in Translation*, Modern Indonesia Project, Publication No 3, Cornell University, 1956, pp 153–154. By permission of the Modern Indonesia Project. (5) M. McMillan, *A Journey to Java*, Holden and Hardingham, London, 1914, pp 256–259. (6) Raden Adjeng Kartini (Agnes Louise Symmers, trans), *Letters of a Javanese Princess*, Duckworth, London, 1921, pp 4–5. (7) Pramoedya Ananta Toer, *The Girl from the Coast*, Select Books, Singapore, pp 108–110. By permission of Harry Aveling. (8) Hasnah Haji Ibrahim, ed, *Hikayat Hang Tuah*, in *Malaysia Indigenous Traditions*, Ministry of Education, Kuala Lumpur, Malaysia, 1985 (Anthology of Malaysian Literatures, Vol 1), pp 397–401. (9) Chairil Anwar, 'Spirit'. Trans E. Ulrich Kratz. (10) Satyagraha Hurip (David Irvine, trans), *Bisma: Warrior Priest of the Mahabharata*, Pustaka Sinar Harapan, Jakarta, 1990, pp 5–6. By permission of Pustaka Sinar Harapan. (11) Soetan Takdir Alisjahbana, 'To Sea, The New Generation'. Trans E. Ulrich Kratz. (12) Danarto, 'Love charm' in *Abracadabra*, Heinemann Educational Books Ltd, 1978, pp 51–52. By permission of Harry Aveling. (13) Mochtar Lubis, *A Road with no End*, Hutchinson, 1968, pp 1–2. By permission of Mochtar Lubis. (14) Amal Hamzah, 'Spy-glass' in John M. Echolls, ed, *Indonesian Writing in Translation*, Modern Indonesia Project, Publication No 3, Cornell University, 1956, pp 87–88. By permission of the Modern Indonesia Project. (15) Amir Hamzah, 'Because of you'. Trans E. Ulrich Kratz. (16) Sitor Situmorang, 'The Lost Child'. Trans E. Ulrich Kratz. (17) Alfred Russel Wallace, *The Malay Archipelago*, Dover Publications, New York, 1962, pp 125–126. (18) Albert S. Bickmore, *Travels in the East Indian Archipelago*, Oxford University Press, Singapore, 1991, pp 398–400. (19) Hamka, 'A Deserted Child' in Rufus S. Hendon, ed, *Six Indonesian Short Stories*, Yale University Southeast Asian Studies, Translations Series No 7, 1968, pp 5–7. (20) Laurens van der Post, *The Night of the New Moon*, Penguin, Harmondsworth, 1977, pp 60–63. By permission of Chatto and Windus. (21) Eliza Ruhamah Scidmore, *Java: The Garden of the East*, Oxford University Press, 1984. (22) Sanoesi Pane, 'Poem'. Trans E. Ulrich Kratz. (23) Mochtar Lubis, *Tiger!*, Select Books, Singapore, 1991, pp 1–2. By permission of Mochtar Lubis and Select Books. (24) Madelon H. Lulofs, *Rubber*, Oxford University Press, Singapore, 1989, pp 6–7. (25) Willem Ysbrandtszoon Bontekoe, 'Description of the East-Indian Voyage' in Cornelia Niekus Moore, *Insulinde: Selected Translations from Dutch Writers of Three Centuries on the Indonesian Archipelago*, The University of Hawaii Press, 1978, pp 14–15. By permission of University of Hawaii Press. (26) Idrus, 'Surabaya' in Harry Aveling, ed and trans, *From Surabaya to Armageddon*, Heinemann, Singapore, 1976, pp 18–21. By permission of Harry Aveling. (27) Chairil Anwar, 'Diponegro'. Trans E. Ulrich Kratz. (28) Y.B. Mangunwijaya (Thomas M. Hunter, trans), *The Weaverbirds*, Lontar Foundation, Jakarta, 1991, pp 37–38. By permission of the Lontar Foundation (original title, *Burung-Burung Manyar*, published by Penerbit Djambatan). **THE PHILIPPINES:** (1) Ophelia Alcantra Dimalanta, 'Pale Thoughts upon a Pale City' in *Montage*, University of Santo Tomas Publications, Manila, 1974. By permission of Ophelia Alcantra Dimalanta. (2) Marjorie E. Evasco, 'Birthing Poems' in *Dreamweavers: Selected Poems 1976–86*, Editsource, Manila, 1987. By permission of Editsource. (3) Marcel M. Navarra, 'The Awakening' in *Mga Piling Kuwentong Sebuwano*, University of the Philippines Press, Quezon City, 1986, p 220. By permission of Sentro ng Wikang Filipino. (4) Rio Alma (Virgilio S. Almario), 'Vigan' in Alfrredo Navarro Salanga, Marne L. Kilates and Mike L. Bigornia, eds, *Selected Poems, 1968–1985*, Maya Books, Quezon City, 1987. By permission p 49. By permission of Virgilio S. Almario and Marne L. Kilates. (5) Manuel E. Arguilla, 'Midsummer' in *How my Brother Leon Brought Home a Wife and Other Stories*, Philippine Book Guild, Manila, 1940, p 15. (6) Norman Mailer, *The Naked and the Dead*, Signet, New American Library, New York, 1948, p 355. Copyright © 1948, renewed 1978, by Norman Mailer, reprinted with the permission of Wylie, Aitken & Stone, Inc. (7) Amado V. Hernandez, 'Irony' in Epifanio San Juan, Jr, ed, *Introduction to Modern Pilipino Literature*, Twayne, New York, 1974. Reprinted with permission of Twayne Publishers, an imprint of Macmillan Publishing Company. Copyright © 1974 by Twayne Publishers, Inc. (8) Francisco Balagtas, *Florante and Laura* in Jovita Ventura Castro et al, *Anthology of ASEAN Literatures: Philippine Metrical Romances*, Nalandangan, Manila, 1985, pp 340–341. By permission of the literary estate of Trinidad Tarrosa Subido. (9) Jose Garcia Villa, 'First, A Poem Must be Magical' in *Have Come, Am Here*, Viking, New York, 1942. By permission of Alberto Florentino. (10) Ruth Elynia S. Mabanglo, 'After the revolution'. By permission of B.S. Medina. (11) Grace Hsieh Hsing, 'Ongpin Street' in *To the Flowers a Collection of Poems*, Manila, 1991, pp 24–25. By permission of Grace Hsieh Hsing and John Shih. (12) F. Sionil Jose, *Mass*, Solidaridad, Manila, 1983, p 228. By permission of F. Sionil Jose. (13) Ma Delia Coronel, trans, *Darangen*, Mindanao State University Press, Marawi, The Philippines, 1986, p 105. By permission of Sr Ma Delia Coronel. (14) Bienvenido N. Santos, *The Volcano*, New Day Publishers, Quezon City, 1986, p 25. By permission of Bienvenido N. Santos. (15) Juan Crisotomo Soto, *Lidia*, in Edna Zapanta Manlapaz, ed, *Kapampangan Literature: A Historical Survey and Anthology*, Ateneo de Manila University Press, Quezon City, 1981. By permission of Ateneo de Manila University Press. (16) Jose Rizal, *The Reign of Greed*, Philippine Education Co, 1927, pp 1–2. (17) George Santayana, *Young Sammy's First Wild Oats*, in Douglas L. Wilson, ed, *Nine Essays by George Santayana*, Harvard University Press, Cambridge, MA, 1967. By permission of Harvard University Press. (18) Mark Twain, *Summary of the Philippine 'Incident': 'The Philippine Incident is Closed – Substantially'* in Roger J. Bresnahan, ed, *In Time of Hesitation: American Anti-Imperialists and the Philippine American War*, New Day Publishers, Quezon City, 1981. **HONG KONG:** (1) Han Suyin, *A Many Splendoured Thing*, Triad, Arrow, 1992, p 160. By permission of Han Suyin. (2) Noel Coward, 'Mad dogs and Englishmen' in *The New Oxford Book of Light Verse*, Oxford University Press, Oxford, 1978, p 237. © 1932 by Noel Coward. By arrangement with Michael Imeson Playwrights Ltd, 28 Almeida Street, London N1 1TD. (3) David T.K. Wong, 'The Cocktail Party' in *Lost River and Other Stories*, Asia 2000, Hong Kong, 1990, pp 75–77. By permission of David Wong and Asia 2000. (4) W. Somerset Maugham , *The Painted Veil*, Mandarin, London, 1991, pp 16–17. By permission of William Heinemann Ltd. By permission of A.P. Watt on behalf of the Royal Literary Fund. (5) James Clavell, *Noble House*, Hodder and Stoughton, 1981, p 909. By permission of Hodder and Stoughton and Leopard Publishing. (6) Lee Ding Fai, *Running Dog*, Heinemann, Singapore, 1980, pp 146–147. By permission of Heinemann Asia. (7) Timothy Mo, *The Monkey King*, Andre Deutsch, London, 1982, pp 35–36. (8) Louise Ho, 'Shang-shui Pastoral' in Joyce Hsia and T.C. Lai, eds, *Hong Kong: Images on the Shifting Waters*, Kelly and Walsh, Hong Kong, 1977, p 98. By permission of Kelly and Walsh. (9) W.H. Auden, 'Hong Kong 1938' W.H. Auden and Christopher Isherwood, *Journey to a War*, Faber, London, 1973. © 1945 by W.H. Auden. By permission of Faber and Faber and Random House Inc. (10) Joyce Hsia, 'A Matter of Time' in Joyce Hsia and T.C. Lai, eds, *Hong Kong: Images on the Shifting Waters*, Kelly and Walsh, Hong Kong, 1977, pp 107–108. By permission of Kelly and Walsh. (11) Robert Elegant, *Dynasty*, McGraw-Hill, New York, 1977, pp 20–21. (12) Edmund Blunden, 'A Hong Kong House' in Joyce Hsia and T.C. Lai, eds, *Hong Kong: Images on the Shifting Waters*, Kelly and Walsh, Hong Kong, 1977, pp 37–37. By permission of Claire Blunden. (13) Richard Mason, *The World of Suzie Wong*, Fontana, London, 1969, pp 5–7. By permission of A.M. Heath & Co Ltd.

PICTURES

Front cover and spine – courtesy of Heather Swabey. Back cover – courtesy of Raffles Hotel. p 16 – courtesy of George Orwell Archive, University College London. p 19 – courtesy of Louise Collis. p 20 – courtesy of British Council. pp 59, 73, 74, 107, 110, 112, 113, 115, 116 – courtesy of External Culture Relations Division, Bangkok. p 112 – courtesy of Penguin Books. pp 125, 126 – courtesy of Peter Koret. pp 155, 158 – courtesy of Judith Jacob. p 161 – courtesy of Penguin Books. p 178 – by William Karel. p 200 – courtesy of HarperCollins. pp 210, 215, 247, 250 – courtesy of Dewan Bahasa dan Pustaka. pp 218, 221 – courtesy of Raffles Hotel, Singapore. p 248 – courtesy of Mrs Lee Kok Liang. p 249 – courtesy of K.S. Maniam. p 254 – courtesy of Edwin Thumboo. p 263 – courtesy of Raffles Hotel Singapore. p 266 – courtesy of D.J. Enright. p 292 – courtesy of Wong Yoon Wah. pp 306, 314, 352, 357 (top) – courtesy of Tempo Majalah Berita Mingguan. p 309 – courtesy of Mary Fennessy. p 352 (bottom) – Heather Swabey. p 355 – courtesy of Mochtar

Lubis. p 358 – courtesy of Penguin Books. p 369 – courtesy of HarperCollins. p 398 – courtesy of Virgilio Almario. p 399 – courtesy of Francisco Arcellana. p 400 – courtesy of Cirilo F. Bautista. p 401 courtesy of Isagani Cruz. p 403 – courtesy of B.S. Medina, Jr. p 410 – photograph by Annie Liebovitz, courtesy of Hodder and Stoughton. p 413 – courtesy of William Heinemann. p 417 – courtesy of Heather Swabey. p 419 – photograph by Catherine Borgeaud. p 426 – courtesy of The Noel Coward Estate. p 440 – courtesy of Claire Blunden. p 442 – courtesy of Raffles Hotel, Singapore. p 443 – courtesy of David Wong.

GENERAL

Only the contributors know how long this book has been in gestation. Thanks are due to them for their patience and understanding and the excellence of their contributions. In addition we are grateful to the following for help in finding authors and tracking down copyright holders: Edwin Thumboo, Margaret Lim, Irene Khng, Peter Wesley-Smith, Robert Yeo, Roger Bresnahan, Muhammad Haji Salleh, Abdul Majid b Nabi Baksh, David Smyth and Manas Chitakasam.

INDEX

This is an index to authors. (E) = extract. Bold type = biographical entry.

TRAVELLER'S LITERARY COMPANIONS

Traveller's Literary Companion to Africa *by Oona Strathern*. The literary heritage of Africa is almost as vast and multi-faceted as the continent itself. The work of writers such as Chinua Achebe and Nobel Prize winners Wole Soyinka and Naguib Mahfouz has become well known in the West, but this literary companion is a treasure trove of less familiar writers such as Sembene Ousmane, Cyprian Ekwensi and Dennis Brutus. Africa has inspired many Western writers, and Conrad, Blixen, Boyd, Greene, Shakespeare, Rimbaud and Albert Camus all make their mark on this literary odyssey.

Traveller's Literary Companion to Japan *by Harry Guest*. Japan has one of the world's richest literary heritages. This literary companion ranges from Murasaki Shikibu's *The Tale of Genji* through to Novel Prize winner Yasunari Kawabata and contemporary writers such as Haruki Murakami. The book skilfully relates many of the passages in the literature to sites in Japan (including the Golden Pavilion in Kyoto, Lake Biwa and Awaji and Shodo islands), making this an ideal book for the visitor or resident. Western writers who used Japan as a locale, such as Clavell and Kipling, are covered, as are such major Japanese figures as Mishima, Basho, Tanizaki, Soseki, and many others.

Traveller's Literary Companion to South & Central America *by Jason Wilson*. The countries of South and Central America have long provided American and European writers with compelling settings. There has also been a stunning explosion of new writing from Latin American authors, adding to established names like Borges and García Márquez. This book embraces a vast array of authors, in over 250 extracts, including Voltaire, Carlos Fuentes, Manuel Puig, Len Deighton, Joan Didion, Mario Vargas Llosa, Gabriel García Márquez, Graham Greene, William Burroughs, Charles Darwin, Malcolm Lowry, Octavio Paz, and Isabel Allende. 21 countries covered.

Forthcoming
The Indian subcontinent
Eastern and Central Europe
France
The Caribbean